The Refinement of Econometric Estimation and Test Procedures

T0300553

The small sample properties of estimators and tests are frequently too complex to be useful or are unknown. Much econometric theory is therefore developed for very large or asymptotic samples where it is assumed that the behaviour of estimators and tests will adequately represent their properties in small samples. Refined asymptotic methods adopt an intermediate position by providing improved approximations to small sample behaviour using asymptotic expansions. Dedicated to the memory of Michael Magdalinos, whose work is a major contribution to this area, this book contains chapters directly concerned with refined asymptotic methods. In addition, there are chapters focussing on new asymptotic results; the exploration through simulation of the small sample behaviour of estimators and tests in panel data models; and improvements in methodology. With contributions from leading econometricians, this collection will be essential reading for researchers and graduate students concerned with the use of asymptotic methods in econometric analysis.

Garry D. A. Phillips is Professor of Econometrics and Distinguished Senior Research Fellow in the Economics section of Cardiff Business School, Cardiff University.

Elias Tzavalis is Professor of Financial Econometrics in the Department of Economics, Athens University of Economics and Business.

The Refinement of Econometric Estimation and Test Procedures: Finite Sample and Asymptotic Analysis

Edited by

Garry D. A. Phillips and Elias Tzavalis

CAMBRIDGE
UNIVERSITY PRESS

CAMBRIDGE UNIVERSITY PRESS
Cambridge, New York, Melbourne, Madrid, Cape Town,
Singapore, São Paulo, Delhi, Mexico City

Cambridge University Press
The Edinburgh Building, Cambridge CB2 8RU, UK

Published in the United States of America by Cambridge University Press, New York

www.cambridge.org
Information on this title: www.cambridge.org/9781107406247

First published 2007
First paperback edition 2012

A catalogue record for this publication is available from the British Library

Library of Congress Cataloguing in Publication data
The Refinement of econometric estimation and test procedures: finite sample
and asymptotic analysis/editors: Garry D. A. Phillips and Elias Tzavalis.
p. cm.
Includes bibliographical references and index.
ISBN 0-521-87053-4 (hbk)
1. Econometrics. 2. Estimation theory. I. Philips, G. D. A. II. Tzavalis, Elias.
III. Title
HB139.R44 2007
330.01′519287 – dc22
2006037806

ISBN 978-0-521-87053-5 Hardback
ISBN 978-1-107-40624-7 Paperback

To Mary Magdalinos

Contents

List of figures

List of tables

List of contributors

KARIM ABADIR is Professor of Econometrics at the Departments of Economics and Mathematics at the University of York.

CHRISTOPHER L. CAVANAGH works for CRA International.

PHOEBUS J. DHRYMES is the Edwin W. Rickert Professor of Economics at the Department of Economics, Columbia University.

GRANT HILLIER is Professor of Econometrics at the Department of Economics, University of Southampton.

HELEN KANDILOROU is Assistant Professor at the Department of Statistics, Athens University of Economics and Business.

GEORGE KAPETANIOS is Professor of Economics at the Department of Economics, Queen Mary University of London.

JAN F. KIVIET is Professor of Econometrics and Fellow of the Tinbergen Institute at the Faculty of Economics and Econometrics, University of Amsterdam.

QI LI is Professor of Economics at the Department of Economics, University of Texas A&M.

TASSOS MAGDALINOS is a Lecturer at the Department of Mathematics, University of York.

JAN MAGNUS is Professor of Econometrics at the Department of Econometrics and Operations Research, Tilburg University.

GEORGE P. MITSOPOULOS is a researcher at the Department of Economics, Athens University of Economics and Business.

GRAYHAM MIZON is Professor of Econometrics and Head of the School of Social Sciences, Southampton University.

HASHEM PESARAN is a Fellow of Trinity College and Professor of Econometrics at the Department of Applied Economics, Cambridge.

GARRY D.A. PHILLIPS is Professor of Econometrics and a Distinguished Senior Research Fellow in the Economics Section of Cardiff Business School.

PETER C.B. PHILLIPS is Professor of Econometrics at the Cowles Foundation, Yale University.

THOMAS J. ROTHENBERG is Professor of Economics at the University of California at Berkeley.

RICHARD J. SMITH is Professor of Econometrics at the Department of Applied Economics at the University of Cambridge.

ARIS SPANOS is the Wilson Schmidt Professor of Economics at the Department of Economics, 3016, Virginia Polytechnic Institute and State University.

ANNA STASZEWSKA is at the Warsaw School of Economics, Warsaw, Poland and is also Chair of Econometric Models and Forecasts at the University of Lodz, Poland.

THANASIS STENGOS is Professor of Economics at the Department of Economics, University of Guelph.

SPYROS SYMEONIDIS is Assistant Professor of Econometrics at the Department of Economics, University of Ioannina, Greece.

ELIAS TZAVALIS is Professor of Economics at the Department of Economics, Athens University of Economics and Business.

Preface

This book is dedicated to the memory of Michael Magdalinos, formerly Professor of Econometrics at the Athens University of Economics and Business, who died in August 2002 at the age of 52.

Professor Magdalinos was, in the opinion of many, the leading econometric theorist in Greece for a substantial number of years. In 1998 he was ranked among the top few econometricians in Europe, and compared favourably with the world's best, in the *Journal of Econometric Theory* rankings. In 1999 his achievements were recognised when he was appointed to a Personal Chair in Theoretical Econometrics. He had a considerable international reputation and his untimely death at the peak of his academic powers deprived not only Greece but the academic world as a whole of an outstanding scholar. However, as well as being a fine scholar he was a warm and friendly person and an inspiration to others. He was a great personality and enormous fun to be with, he was an altogether delightful man.

In November 2003 the Department of Economics of the Athens University of Economics and Business promoted a one-day conference to honour the memory and achievements of Michael Magdalinos. A distinguished group of international scholars were invited to participate in the programme. Some of them had been his co-authors and some, such as Elias Tzavalis, were former students. Others had known him for a long time and shared his academic interests while others were scholars who may not have known him well but whose work he was known to admire. Inevitably the restriction on numbers meant that many more who would have gladly participated were unable to do so. Hence those of us who presented our own tributes to his memory were conscious that we spoke not only for ourselves but also for many colleagues throughout the world.

The current book is essentially based on the papers that were presented at the conference. It does however have a few unusual features. It includes, for example, Michael's last paper, not previously published, which was written jointly with his last PhD student George Mitsopoulos. In addition there is a chapter by Michael's son, Tassos, himself a theoretical econometrician, written jointly with Peter Phillips.

We believe that this book will be a significant contribution to the econometric literature while, at the same time, providing a fitting tribute to the memory of our great friend. It is something that his family can treasure for all time.

GARRY D. A. PHILLIPS
ELIAS TZAVALIS

Acknowledgements

The editors would like to thank the Rector of the Athens University of Economics and Business, Professor George Venieris, for supporting the conference "Contributions to Econometric Theory: In Memory of Michael Magdalinos" hosted by the Department of Economics in November 2003. In addition we should like to thank the other members of the Scientific Committee, particularly Professor Georgios K. Christou, who chaired the committee, and his colleagues Professor Konstantine Gatsios, Professor Tryphon Kolintzas and Professor Helen Louri who gave valuable assistance. Maria Zanti provided excellent secretarial support.

The editors would also like to acknowledge most helpful assistance by Chris Harrison, Editor, Economics and Business, Cambridge University Press, for the positive way he dealt with the initial submission, and his Assistant Editor, Dr Lynn Dunlop, for help in preparing the final manuscript. Finally, Carlos Belando Ronda of the Departmento Fundamentos Del Analisis Economico at the University of Alicante, and Emma Iglesias of the Department of Economics, Michigan State University, provided invaluable help in dealing with many of the technical problems that arose.

Michael Magdalinos 1949–2002

Michael Magdalinos obtained his PhD at the University of Southampton in 1983. His supervisor was Grayham Mizon while Garry Phillips was the external examiner. The thesis title was 'Applications of Refined Asymptotic Theory in Econometrics' and this work provided the foundation for much of his subsequent research. Indeed the title of this book *The Refinement of Econometric Estimation and Test Procedures: Finite Sample and Asymptotic Analysis*, while being chosen as an appropriate general description of the book's contents, is also indicative of the general thrust of his academic research.

Refined asymptotic methods use asymptotic expansions rather than first-order normal approximations and lead to a general estimation theory which, though more complicated than the theory based on first-order normal approximations, is still simple enough to render general insights and provide comparisons sufficiently simple to be of practical use. The analytical results obtained so far in this area can be used to compare the relative merits of alternative estimators, especially those of ordinary least squares (OLS), two-stage least squares (2SLS), instrumental variables (IV), maximum likelihood (ML) and limited information maximum likelihood (LIML), as well as of alternative testing procedures based on them. This volume is dedicated to the memory of Michael Magdalinos whose work constitutes a major contribution to this area of econometrics. Some of his more important publications, which are particularly illustrative of his work, are summarized as follows.

In his first major paper, published in the *Review of Economic Studies* (1985), he considered the problem of selecting the 'best' estimator among a wider class of IV estimators for simultaneous equation systems. Concentration comparisons, based on the Edgeworth approximation to the distribution of these estimators, lead to selection rules of sufficient simplicity to be useful in applied econometric work. These depend on the sample size, the number of regressors and the degree of overidentification. The rules suggest that when the sample and *a priori* information are weak, that is, the sample size and the order of overidentification are both small, then the available sample information is not adequate to support estimation techniques more sophisticated than OLS. When the sample information is adequate but the *a priori* information is weak, then the 2SLS estimator is preferable, since it is more concentrated than the LIML estimator. Finally, when both the sample and the *a priori* information are strong, then we should prefer the LIML since it is median unbiased. The paper gave precise criteria for practical implementation of these rules.

In the *Journal of Econometrics* (1990), he compared the finite-sample performance of the three alternative classical testing principles: the Wald, likelihood ratio (LR) and Lagrange multiplier (LM) principles, as well as their instrumental variables generalizations, applied to testing a set of linear restrictions in a structural equation with stochastic regressors. By deriving the third-order local power function of these tests, he showed that the classical tests are locally biased for a subset of the parameter space in small samples. The problem is more severe for the Wald test that is calculated from the TSLS estimator. The comparison of the local power of the size-corrected tests shows that, under certain conditions, the LR test is preferred among the others since it is minimax and it is more powerful than the LM test.

In two papers in the *International Economic Review* (1988) and *Journal of Econometrics* (1996, with Symeonids) he re-examined the interpretation and the third-order power of the Anderson–Rubin–Sargan–Basmann (ARSB) tests of the validity of overidentifying structural restrictions in a classical simultaneous equation system. This work showed that a more illuminating interpretation of these tests is one of testing the orthogonality conditions only for the instruments that overidentify the equation, a characteristic that was also realized by Sargan (1958). To second-order accuracy, it was shown that the ARSB tests are unbiased against the alternative of false orthogonality conditions, whereas there is a subset of the parameter space where the tests are biased under the alternative of false structural restrictions. Building on the above work, his *Econometrica* (1994) paper proposed a ML approach for testing the admissibility of a subset of (overidentifying) stochastic instruments. Based on third-order asymptotic theory, he shows that a simple linearization of the LR test which is equal to the difference of two of Sargan's (1958) mispecification statistics (see also Hansen, 1982) based on the LIML estimator, provides a test statistic which is independent of the correlation between the regressors and the errors and performs better than other admissibility tests. As testing for orthogonality conditions involved running auxiliary regressions, respecifying the structural equations and testing again for orthogonality until the correct set of instruments is chosen, a less cumbersome approach was to be welcomed and this was provided in the *Journal of Economics and Statistics* (2001), with Helen Kandilorou, where he suggested a new and much simpler procedure. This approach encompassed the dual problems of testing structural restrictions and orthogonality conditions and placed them in a single equation framework where, after appropriate transformations, the familiar regression techniques could be applied.

In his *Journal of Econometric Theory* (1985) and *Journal of Econometrics* (1995, with Symeonides) papers, he suggested size corrections for the Wald-test statistic in the linear regression model and for the F and t-test statistics in the linear regression model with AR(1) errors respectively, employing Cornish–Fisher expansions. The aim of these corrections was to adjust the nominal size of these tests to their true size. Apart from testing, these corrections are necessary for power comparisons (see also his *Journal of Econometrics*, 1990 paper). Whereas the Edgeworth expansion can be used to correct the critical values of the asymptotic distribution, the Cornish–Fisher expansion enables a correction of the test statistics themselves. The two types of expansion are asymptotically equivalent, but the Cornish–Fisher expansion avoids the problem of assigning negative probabilities in the tails of the distribution. To derive approximations to the distributions of the test statistics, he employed stochastic expansions of them which can significantly facilitate the derivations and the interpretation of the adjusted tests. The relationship between the stochastic expansion of a test statistic and the asymptotic approximation of its distribution is given in his comprehensive study of stochastic expansions and asymptotic approximations in his *Journal of Econometric Theory* (1992) paper. As shown in this paper, the combination of stochastic expansions and formal Edgeworth approximations, apart from being an analytically efficient method, typically leads to simple interpretable formulas that are most suitable for work in finite sample econometrics.

A characteristic of his work is its profound nature, the high standard of scholarship and the demonstration of an outstanding grasp of a relatively complex area of statistical econometrics. He was, indeed, a major figure in the field of theoretical econometrics.

Introduction

Twenty-two authors have contributed to this book which comprises 14 chapters. Chapters 1–5 are primarily concerned with econometric estimation and examine the properties of estimators in finite and asymptotic samples. The first of these, by Michael Magdalinos and Mitsopoulos, derives a partial solution for the maximum likelihood normal equations in models with autoregressive conditionally heteroscedastic errors under the assumption that the errors belong to the Pearson family of distributions. It is shown through Monte Carlo simulations that there may be significant efficiency gains for maximum likelihood estimation compared to quasi maximum likelihood estimation. This is followed in Chapter 2 by Spanos who revisits the statistical foundations of instrumental variable (IV) estimation to ascertain the reliability and precision of instrumental variable-based inference. The paper stresses that the choice of instruments and the optimality of the resulting IV estimator entails both theoretical as well as statistical considerations. Chapter 3 is by Garry Phillips and takes another look at the problem of deriving moment approximations for two-stage least squares in the classical simultaneous equation model. In particular, approximations for the first and second moments are found in a simultaneous equation model in which the disturbances follow a system autoregressive scheme. The results are compared to Nagar's original approximations for serially independent disturbances. In Chapter 4, Smith is concerned to adapt the general empirical likelihood (GEL) unconditional moment methods developed earlier, to the conditional moment context. In particular, GEL estimators are developed which achieve the semi-parametric efficiency lower bound. The requisite GEL criteria are constructed by local smoothing. The paper also provides a local GEL criterion function test statistic for parametric restrictions. Chapter 5, the final chapter of this group, by Peter Phillips and Tassos Magdalinos, focuses on an asymptotic theory for autoregressive time series with weakly dependent innovations and a root of the form $\rho_n = 1 + c/n^{\alpha}$, involving moderate deviations from unity where $\alpha \in (0, 1)$, and follows on to their earlier work with independent errors. In the explosive case where $c > 1$ the limit theory for the serial correlation coefficient is Cauchy while for $c < 0$ and $\alpha \in (1/2, 1)$ the limiting distribution is normal and the convergence rate lies between the stationary and local to unity cases. It is also shown that weakly dependent errors induce a bias in the limiting distribution analogous to that of the local to unity case.

Chapters 6–9 fall under the general heading of issues and methods of econometric testing, commencing with a paper by Cavanagh and Rothenberg. This examines the use of higher-order approximations in distinguishing between asymptotically equivalent general likelihood-based hypothesis tests. Criteria are presented for the admissibility or otherwise of commonly used test procedures. Chapter 7 by Symeonides, Kandilorou and Tzavalis examines how in the classical regression framework with heteroscedastic errors, the standard t and F statistics can be size-corrected using Cornish–Fisher expansions. Unlike test statistics which are adjusted based upon the Edgeworth approximation, the Cornish–Fisher corrected test statistics do not have the drawback of assigning negative tail probabilities. The performance of the size-corrected tests in improving the test size is then examined in a set of simulation experiments. Chapter 8 by Li and Stengos proposes a non-nested testing procedure for discriminating between alternative sets of regressors in a non-parametric context which involves double kernel estimation. The small sample performance of the test is examined through Monte Carlo simulations and found to have good size and power properties. Chapter 9, the last in this group, is by Dhrymes and deals with the problem of testing for the presence of autocorrelation in a system of general linear models when the model is formulated as a vector autoregression with exogenous variables. The solution to the problem is presented as a generalization of Durbin's h-statistic; however, it is a feature of the paper that derivations are from first principles and do not use Durbin's original arguments.

In Chapters 10 and 11, dynamic panel data models are the focus of interest. First, in Chapter 10, Kapetanios and Pesaran consider the analysis of large panel data models in the presence of error cross-section dependence and compare two alternative methods for estimation and inference in panels with a multifactor error structure. The two approaches based, respectively, on proxying unobserved factors with cross-sectional averages and augmenting panel regressions with factor estimates based on principal components, are compared in extensive Monte Carlo experiments. In Chapter 11, Kiviet notes that in dynamic panel data models with individual specific effects, a large number of alternative estimation techniques have been proposed and extensive Monte Carlo simulations have examined their performance in small samples. It is argued that such studies have generally been too narrowly focused to enable fair and informative conclusions to be reached when comparing alternative inference techniques. Improvements in designing Monte Carlo contests are required and a way forward is illustrated in the context of GMM estimation of a stable first-order autoregressive panel relationship with an unknown intercept, random unobserved individual effects and i.i.d disturbances.

Chapters 12–14 do not fall into a distinct category. In Chapter 12, Abadir and Magnus note that the well-known transformation theorem is one of the very few major statistical theorems for which there is no proof in the statistical literature since it requires advanced results from real analysis. They present a simple proof which uses the idea of conditioning for continuous random variables. The approach used illustrates how conditioning can provide some short-cuts to proofs by reducing the dimensionality of statistical problems. Chapter 13 by Hillier is concerned with the derivation of the joint density of the sum and sum of squares of nonnegative random variables especially in the context of minimally sufficient statistics. A closed form expression is not so far available and Hillier uses a differential-geometric approach to derive this joint density for the class of exponential models in which either or both statistics are minimally sufficient. An application to the censored normal model is also considered. Finally, in Chapter 14 Mizon and Staszewska examine the efficacy of alternative methods of response analysis in economic policy investigations. Different types of response analysis are illustrated graphically and the non-stationary case is examined using the vector equilibrium correction model. The importance of distinguishing between responses to shocks and to policy changes is stressed as is the appropriate choice of conditioning variables and it is argued that a careful selection of the latter is preferable to arbitrary orthogonalization.

1 Conditional Heteroskedasticity Models with Pearson Family Disturbances

*Michael A. Magdalinos and George P. Mitsopoulos**

1 Introduction

The Autoregressive Conditional Heteroskedasticity (ARCH) model was introduced by Engle (1982). In this model the conditional variance of the errors is assumed to be a function of the squared past errors. Engle derives the Maximum Likelihood (ML) estimator for the ARCH model under the assumption that the conditional density of the error term is normal. Bollerslev (1986), suggested the Generalized Autoregressive Conditional Heteroskedasticity model (GARCH) in which the conditional variance of the errors is assumed to be a function of its lagged values and the squared past errors. Bollerslev derives the Maximum Likelihood (ML) estimator for the GARCH model under the assumption that the conditional density of the error term is normal. The ARCH and GARCH models are useful in modelling economic phenomena, mainly in the theory of finance (see e.g., Bollerslev *et al.* 1992 and Engle, 2002). In the above models the conditional density of the error term is assumed to be normal but in the applications with actual data, distributions other than the normal have been observed with fatter tails or with skewness significantly different from zero. For this reason, in particular applications with real data, other distributions have been used. Bollerslev (1987) used the Student's t distribution to model the monthly returns composite index. Baillie and Bollerslev (1989) also used the Student's t distribution while Hsieh (1989) chose the mixture Normal–Lognormal to model daily foreign-exchange rates. Jorion (1988) employed a mixture distribution of Normal–Poisson to model the foreign exchange and stockmarkets. Hansen (1993) used the skewed Student's t with a shape parameter, which may vary over time, to model exchange rates. Peruga (1988)

* In memory of my coauthor Professor Michael Magdalinos. The author G. Mitsopoulos is grateful to G. Phillips, E. Tzavalis and S. Symeonides for helpful comments on the first draft of the paper.

found empirical evidence of high skewness and kurtosis in exchange rates, and so on.

As an alternative approach, instead of using a specific distribution for the error term structure, non-parametric and semi-parametric techniques have been used to approximate the true error density. A Gaussian kernel was used in Pagan and Hong (1991) to model the risk premium. Pagan and Schwert (1990) again use a Gaussian kernel and include in the variance specification a Fourier transformation to model the stockmarket volatility. A Gaussian kernel was used in Sentana and Wadhwani (1991) to model stockmarket returns. Engle and Gonzalez-Rivera (1991) use a semi-parametric technique developed by Tapia and Thompson (1978) to model the exchange rate between the British pound and the US dollar. Tzavalis and Wickens (1995) use Cram–Charlier polynomials in order to incorporate in the model additional information for skewness and kurtosis, and so on. For a review of the Autoregressive Conditional Heteroskedasticity models, theory and applications, see Bollerslev *et al.* (1992), Bollerslev *et al.* (1994), Engle (2002).

Moreover, Magdalinos and Mitsopoulos (2003) use the Pearson System of Distributions (PSD) (see Eldetron and Johnson, 1969; Kendall and Stuart, 1977 and Johnson and Kotz, 1970) in order to approximate the error density in the case of the linear regression model. Here, we extend the use of the PSD for the case of the ARCH and GARCH models. The PSD includes a wide range of distributional shapes (such as Normal, Beta, Gamma, etc.), and is parsimoniously parameterized in terms of its first four cummulants. This is very convenient, as in practical cases it is unlikely to obtain reliable sample information for the higher-order cummulants. The definition of PSD is given in terms of the derivative of the log-density function. This implies that the score vector corresponding to the ARCH or GARCH models can be derived without the explicit identification of the error distribution.

The rest of the chapter is organized as follows. In section 2 we assume that the true error density belongs to the PSD and derive the one-step scoring estimator for the unknown parameters of the GARCH model. In section 3 we present an experimental study of the properties of the proposed estimator, while remarks and conclusions are presented in the concluding section 4.

2 GARCH with Pearson Family Disturbances

Let y_t, $(t = 1, \ldots, T)$ be an observable random variable, $x_t' = (1, x_{1t}, \ldots, x_{nt})$, $(t = 1, \ldots, T)$, be a vector of the regressors and b be the $n \times 1$ vector of unknown parameters. Also, let D_t be the information set available at time t and $\sigma(x_t)$ be the information set containing the information for the contemporaneous regressors. Using these information sets, define $\Delta_t = \sigma\{\sigma(x_t) \cup D_{t-1}\}$ as the information set containing the information from the contemporaneous regressors and all the past information. Moreover, let h_t be the conditional variance of the error term, which is a stochastic process and $\varphi(\cdot)$ the conditional density of y_t on Δ_t.

The above model may be written as

$$y_t \mid \Delta_t \sim \varphi(x_t' b, h_t). \tag{1}$$

Given the model (1), we assume that the conditional variance h_t is a stationary process. Then the Wold Decomposition Theorem (see e.g., Priestley, 1981, p. 756) implies that h_t can be expressed as a summable $MA(\infty)$ process, that is, in the form

$$h_t = \alpha_0 + \sum_{i=1}^{\infty} \alpha_i \varepsilon_{t-i}^2, \ \sum_{i=1}^{\infty} \alpha_i^2 < \infty \tag{2}$$

where ε_t is a white-noise process. This can be seen as a direct extension of the fact that an element of a linear space can be expressed in terms of an orthogonal basis. The choice of the basis, however, is arbitrary. Here we choose a positive basis to emphasize the fact that the conditional variance h_t is non-negative.

If we impose in (2) the following restrictions

$$\alpha_{p+1} = \alpha_{p+2} = \alpha_{p+3} = \cdots = 0 \tag{3}$$

then the representation (2) provides the theoretical foundation for the ARCH(p) model. Assumption (3) means that the conditional variance h_t is independent of the information $p+i$, ($i = 1, 2, \ldots$), periods in the past.

If assumption (3) cannot be made, or if p is relatively large, then a more parsimonious parameterization can be obtained as follows. The representation (2) can be written as

$$h_t = A(L)\varepsilon_t^2, \ A(L) = \sum_{i=0}^{\infty} \alpha_i L^i \tag{4}$$

where L is the lag operator. Dhrymes (1971) shows that the linear space of the lag operators of the form

$$A(L) = \sum_{i=0}^{\infty} \alpha_i L^i, \ \sum_{i=0}^{\infty} \alpha_i^2 < \infty \tag{5}$$

is isomorphic to the space of real polynomials

$$A(x) = \sum_{i=0}^{\infty} \alpha_i x^i, \; x \in \mathbb{R}, \; \sum_{i=0}^{\infty} \alpha_i^2 < \infty. \tag{6}$$

This means that the properties of the two spaces are the same, so that a theorem that holds in one space is also valid in the other. It is well-known (see e.g., Bultheel, 1987, p. 36) that the polynomial (6) is approximated equally well by a Pade approximation of the form

$$R(x) = \frac{A_p(x)}{1 - B_q(x)}, \; A_{\mathrm{p}}(x) = \sum_{i=1}^{p} \alpha_i x^i, \; B_{\mathrm{q}}(x) = \sum_{j=1}^{q} \beta_j x^j \tag{7}$$

for finite values of p and q.

Hence we can approximate (2) by

$$h_t = \delta + R(L)\varepsilon_t^2 = \delta + \frac{A_p(L)}{1 - B_q(L)}\varepsilon_t^2$$

or

$$\left[1 - B_q(L)\right] h_t = \delta \left[1 - B_q(L)\right] + A_p(L)\varepsilon_t^2 \tag{8}$$

that is, the GARCH(p, q) representation

$$h_t = \alpha_0 + \sum_{i=1}^{p} \alpha_i \varepsilon_{t-i}^2 + \sum_{j=1}^{q} \beta_j h_{t-j} \tag{9}$$

where $\alpha_0 = \delta\left[1 - B_q(L)\right] = \delta(1 - \beta_1 - \beta_2 - \cdots - \beta_q)$.

Now consider the GARCH(p, q) model that is defined by (1) and (9). The error term of this model is

$$\varepsilon_t = y_t - x_t' b \tag{10}$$

where it is assumed that the density of ε_t is $g(\varepsilon_t)$.

It is more convenient to work with the standardized residuals

$$u_t = h_t^{-1/2} \varepsilon_t \tag{11}$$

and assume that the density of u_t is $f(u_t)$.

The conditional variance h_t that is defined in (9) may be written as

$$h_t = \alpha_0 + \alpha_1 \varepsilon_{t-1}^2 + \cdots + \alpha_p \varepsilon_{t-p}^2 + \beta_1 h_{t-1} + \cdots + \beta_q h_{t-q} = \xi_t' \omega \quad (12)$$

where

$$\xi_t' = \left(1, \varepsilon_{t-1}^2, \ldots, \varepsilon_{t-p}^2, h_{t-1}, \ldots, h_{t-q}\right)$$

$$\omega' = \left(\alpha_0, \alpha_1, \ldots, \alpha_p, \beta_1, \ldots, \beta_q\right) = \left(\alpha', \beta'\right).$$

Moreover let the shape (nuisance) parameters of the density $f(u)$ of u_t be $\gamma' = (\gamma_1, \gamma_2)$ where γ_1 and γ_2 are the skewness and kurtosis coefficients respectively.

We assume that the unknown density $f(u_t)$, of the disturbances u_t, belongs to the PSD. Since u_t are standardized, the equation defining the PSD can be written as

$$\frac{d \log f(u)}{du} = \frac{u - c_1}{c_1 u + c_2(u^2 - 3) - 1} \equiv \eta(u) \quad (13)$$

where

$$c_1 = -\gamma_1(\gamma_2 + 6)/A, \quad c_2 = -\left(2\gamma_2 - 3\gamma_1^2\right)/A, \quad A = 10\gamma_2 - 12\gamma_1^2 + 12.$$

Substituting in (13) for c_1, c_2 we find

$$\eta(u) = \frac{\gamma_1(\gamma_2 + 6) + 2(5\gamma_2 + 6\gamma_1^2 + 6)u}{3\gamma_1^2 - 4(\gamma_2 + 3) - \gamma_1(\gamma_2 + 6)u - (2\gamma_2 - 3\gamma_1^2)u^2}. \quad (14)$$

For the GARCH(p, q) model (1), (9), (11), the conditional density of y_t is defined as

$$\varphi(y_t \mid \Delta_t) = \frac{1}{h_t^{1/2}} f(u_t) \quad (15)$$

and the log-likelihood function for the tth observation is

$$\ell_t(\theta) = -\frac{1}{2} \log h_t + \log f(u_t) \quad (16)$$

where $\theta' = (b', \omega') = (b', \alpha', \beta')$ the set of the unknown parameters.

So that the conditional log-likelihood function for all observation is

$$L(\theta) = \sum_{t=1}^{T} \left(-\frac{1}{2} \log (h_t) + \log f(u_t) \right). \tag{17}$$

The log-likelihood function (16) depends on the functional form of the density $f(u)$ which includes the unknown shape parameters γ. However, if we assume that the shape parameters γ are known, then using (16) we can define the score vector, corresponding to the mean and variance parameters, for the tth observation, $s_t(\theta)$, as

$$\begin{aligned} s_t(\theta) &= \frac{\partial \ell_t(\theta)}{\partial \theta} = -\frac{1}{2h_t}\frac{\partial h_t}{\partial \theta} + \frac{\partial \log f(u_t)}{\partial u_t}\frac{\partial u_t}{\partial \theta} \\ &= -\frac{1}{2h_t}\frac{\partial h_t}{\partial \theta} + \eta(u_t)\frac{\partial u_t}{\partial \theta}. \end{aligned} \tag{18}$$

Since $\theta' = (b', \omega')$ we obtain from (18)

$$s_t(b) = \frac{\partial \ell_t(\theta)}{\partial b} = -\frac{1}{2h_t}\frac{\partial h_t}{\partial b} + \eta(u_t)\frac{\partial u_t}{\partial b} \tag{19}$$

$$s_t(\omega) = \frac{\partial \ell_t(\theta)}{\partial \omega} = -\frac{1}{2h_t}\frac{\partial h_t}{\partial \omega} + \eta(u_t)\frac{\partial u_t}{\partial \omega} \tag{20}$$

where the derivatives of u_t with respect to b and ω are

$$\frac{\partial u_t}{\partial b} = -\frac{1}{h_t^{1/2}}x_t - \frac{u_t}{2h_t}\frac{\partial h_t}{\partial b} \tag{21}$$

$$\frac{\partial u_t}{\partial \omega} = -\frac{u_t}{2h_t}\frac{\partial h_t}{\partial \omega}. \tag{22}$$

Substituting (21) in (19) and (22) in (20) we obtain for the score vector

$$s_t(b) = -\frac{\eta(u_t)}{2h_t}x_t - \frac{1}{2h_t}(\eta(u_t)u_t + 1)\frac{\partial h_t}{\partial b} \tag{23}$$

$$s_t(\omega) = -\frac{1}{2h_t}(\eta(u_t)u_t + 1)\frac{\partial h_t}{\partial \omega} \tag{24}$$

where

$$\frac{\partial h_t}{\partial b} = -\sum_{i=1}^{p} \alpha_i \varepsilon_{t-i} x_{t-i} + \sum_{i=1}^{q} \beta_i \frac{\partial h_{t-i}}{\partial b} \tag{25}$$

$$\frac{\partial h_t}{\partial \omega} = z_t + \sum_{i=1}^{q} \beta_i \frac{\partial h_{t-i}}{\partial \omega}. \tag{26}$$

The Full Information Maximum Likelihood estimation of all the unknown parameters θ and γ is impossible, since the exact functional form of the density $f(u)$ is unknown. For this reason the following estimation procedure is used.

Assume some initial consistent estimates $\hat{\theta}$ for the set of the unknown parameters θ; these estimates may come from the application of the QML as defined in Bollerslev and Wooldridge (1992). Using these estimates we can estimate the residuals $\hat{\varepsilon}_t$, the variance $\hat{h}_t$ and the standardized residuals $\hat{u}_t = \hat{\varepsilon}_t / \hat{h}_t^{1/2}$. The shape parameters $\gamma' = (\gamma_1, \gamma_2)$ may be estimated consistently from the standardized residuals $\hat{u}_t$ as

$$\hat{\gamma}_1 = \frac{1}{T} \sum_{t=1}^{T} \hat{u}_t^3, \ \hat{\gamma}_2 = \frac{1}{T} \sum_{t=1}^{T} \hat{u}_t^4 - 3.$$

Lastly, by using $\hat{\theta}$, $\hat{\gamma}$, $\hat{\varepsilon}_t$, $\hat{u}_t$, $\hat{h}_t$ we can define the one-step scoring estimator for the unknown parameters θ as

$$\tilde{\theta} = \hat{\theta} + k\hat{c} \tag{27}$$

where

$$\hat{c} = \left(\sum_{t=1}^{T} s_t(\hat{\theta}) s_t(\hat{\theta})' \right)^{-1} \sum_{t=1}^{T} s_t(\hat{\theta}) \tag{28}$$

is the correction vector and the constant $k \in (0, 1)$.

The correction vector (28) may be easily calculated from the regression of a vector m with all elements equal to one on a matrix Z with rows

$$z_t = \left(s_t(\hat{b}), s_t(\hat{\alpha}), s_t(\hat{\beta}) \right)$$

so will be

$$\hat{c} = (Z'Z)^{-1}Z'm. \tag{29}$$

We shall refer to $\tilde{\theta}$ as the Pearson Improved (PI) estimator for the case of the GARCH(p, q) model (1), (12). If $q = 0$ then the GARCH(p, q) model reduces to the ARCH(p) model and the estimator (27) will be the Pearson Improved (PI) estimator for the ARCH(p) model.

The use of $\hat{\gamma}$ in the estimation procedure can affect the efficiency of the estimator. The PI estimator would be fully efficient only in the special case of full adaptation. In the case considered here the PI estimator is not fully adaptive, since the conditions for adaptivity as they are cited in Bickel (1982) and Manski (1984) are not valid. On the other hand the proposed estimator is adaptive in the case of the simple GARCH model introduced by Gonzalez-Rivera and Racine (1995), since the conditions for successful adaptation cited therein are valid for our case.

3 Sampling Experiments

To examine the relative efficiency of the proposed estimator Monte Carlo experiments were carried out. To generate the data we used the same model as in Engle and Gonzalez-Rivera (1991), that is

$$\begin{aligned} y_t &= b_1 y_{t-1} + b_2 y_{t-2} + e_t, \\ e_t &= h_t^{1/2} u_t, \\ h_t &= \alpha_0 + \alpha_1 e_{t-1}^2 + \alpha_2 e_{t-2}^2 + \beta_1 h_{t-1}, \\ b_1 &= 0.5, b_2 = 0.15, \\ \alpha_0 &= 0.1, \alpha_1 = 0.1, \alpha_2 = 0.2, \beta_1 = 0.6. \end{aligned} \tag{30}$$

The disturbance term u_t was generated from one of the distributions that are given in Tables 1.1 and 1.2.

First, we generate an independent sample of random numbers, say v_t, for each of the distributions in Tables 1.1 and 1.2. Second, we transform each random sample so that it has zero mean and variance one (where it is needed), that is

$$u_t = (v_t - \mu_d)/\sigma_d$$

where μ_d is the mean and σ_d is the standard deviation of each distribution in Tables 1.1 and 1.2.

Table 1.1. *Distributions that belong to the PSD, with finite γ's*

	Distribution	μ_d	σ_d	γ_1	γ_2
1. $N(0,1)$	Standard Normal	0.000	1.000	0.000	0.000
2. $t(5)$	Student t with $v = 5$ d.f.	0.000	1.291	0.000	6.000
3. $B(0.5,3)$	Beta with parameters $a = 0.5$, $b = 3$	0.143	0.165	1.575	2.224
4. $B(4,2)$	Beta with parameters $a = 4$, $b = 2$	0.667	0.178	−0.468	−0.375
5. $G(0.5,1)$	Gamma with parameters $a = 0.5$, $b = 1$	0.500	0.707	2.828	12.000
6. $G(5,2)$	X^2, Chi square with $v = 10$ d.f.	10.000	4.472	0.894	1.200
7. $F(2,9)$	Fisher F with $v_1 = 2$ and $v_2 = 9$ d.f.	1.286	1.725	5.466	146.444

Table 1.2. *Distributions that belong to the PSD, with no finite γ's or do not belong to the PSD*

	Distribution	μ_d	σ_d	γ_1	γ_2
1. $t(3)$	Student t with $v = 3$ d.f.	0.000	1.732	—	—
2. $LN(0,1)$	LogNormal, the distribution of $\exp(z)$, where z is distributed as $N(0, 1)$	1.649	2.161	6.185	110.936
3. $W(2,1)$	Weibull with parameters $a = 2$, $b = 1$	0.886	0.463	0.631	0.245
4. $W(8,2)$	Weibull with parameters $a = 8$, $b = 2$	1.027	0.152	−0.534	0.328
5. VCN	Variance Contaminated Normal $0.9N(0, 0.1) + 0.1N(0, 9)$	0.000	0.995	0.000	21.821
6. BSM	Bimodal Symmetric Mixture of two Normals, $0.5N(-3, 1) + 0.5N(3, 1)$	0.000	3.162	0.000	−1.620

Then using the model described by relations (30), we recursively generate the variable y_t. To avoid starting problems we generate for y_t 10 percent more observations than are required for each sample size and then reject the first 10 percent of the generated observations.

For each distribution consider samples of $T = 500, 1000, 2000$ which gives a total of 39 experiments. Each experiment consists of 5,000 replications and is executed by a double precision Fortran program. The pseudo-random numbers were generated by NAG/WKSTN subroutines and by (tested) subroutines written by the authors.

The estimation procedure is the following.

First, estimate the parameters $\theta' = (b_1, b_2, \alpha_0, \alpha_1, \alpha_2, \beta_1)$ by using the QML procedure, as it is described in Bollerslev and Wooldridge (1992).

That is, maximize the log-likelihood function (17) by using the iterative procedure based on the Berndt *et al.* (1974) (BHHH) algorithm. The convergence criterion used in the BHHH updating regression was $R^2 < 0.001$. Second, use the QML estimates for the parameters θ to calculate the residuals $\hat{\varepsilon}_t$, the variance $\hat{h}_t$, the standardized residuals $\hat{u}_t$ and the shape parameters $\hat{\gamma}_1$, $\hat{\gamma}_2$. Using these estimates construct the matrix Z and apply (29) to obtain the improvement vector $\hat{c}$. Third, as in Magdalinos and Mitsopoulos (2003), calculate the constant $k = (1/exp(\|c\|))^2$, where $\|c\|$ is the Euclidian norm of the improvement vector (29). Lastly, by applying (27), obtain the PI estimator for the parameters θ.

Moreover, as in Engle and Gonzalez-Rivera (1991), we transform the residuals $\hat{u}_t$ in order to have mean 0 and variance 1 (where it is needed) and following the above steps produce the PIs estimator.

For each distribution we produce Monte Carlo estimates of the Bias and the Standard Deviation (StDev) of the QML estimator and of the estimators PI and PIs. Moreover, the efficiency gains of the proposed estimators were calculated by using the following formula

$$Efficiency\ Gains = 1 - \frac{StDev_i}{StDev_{QML}}, \quad i = PI, PIs$$

The results for the parameter Bias, Standard Deviation and the estimates of the efficiency gains are presented in the Tables 1.3 through 1.8. Moreover, Figures 1.1 through 1.6 illustrate the estimates for the efficiency gains.

As expected, the variability of the estimators in terms of standard deviation decreases as the sample size increases from $T = 500$ to $T = 2000$. More analytically, the performance of the QML estimator varies across error distributions and seems to depend on the kurtosis coefficient of the error distribution. The highest standard deviation of the QML estimator is observed in the cases of the distributions $LN(0,1)$ and $F(2,9)$; these distributions also present the highest kurtosis (see Tables 1.1 and 1.2). In the case of the distributions VCN, $G(0.5,1)$ $t(5)$, $B(0.5,3)$ and $G(5,2)$, where $\gamma_2 > 1$, the QML estimator shows a higher standard deviation than in the case of the distributions $W(8,2)$, $W(2,1)$ and $B(4,2)$, where $\gamma_2 < 1$. The standard deviation of the last distributions varies around that of the $N(0,1)$ distribution which is the ideal case for the QML estimator. Moreover, the QML estimator performs well in the case of the $t(3)$ distribution which has no definite skewness and kurtosis and in the case of the BSM distribution which is bimodal.

Table 1.3. *Comparison of Pearson estimators (PI, PIs) to QML estimator for the parameter* $b_1 = 0.50$

Error distribution	T	QML Bias	QML Standard deviation	PI Bias	PI Standard deviation	PIs Bias	PIs Standard deviation	Efficiency gains PI	Efficiency gains PIs
$N(0,1)$	500	−0.0013	0.046	−0.0013	0.047	−0.0032	0.047	−0.02	−0.02
	1000	−0.0007	0.032	−0.0004	0.033	−0.0018	0.032	−0.03	0.00
	2000	0.0003	0.022	0.0002	0.023	−0.0004	0.022	−0.05	0.00
$t(5)$	500	−0.0008	0.050	0.0000	0.046	−0.0024	0.045	0.08	0.10
	1000	0.0001	0.036	0.0002	0.032	0.0009	0.032	0.11	0.11
	2000	−0.0001	0.027	−0.0002	0.022	−0.0009	0.022	0.19	0.19
$B(0.5,3)$	500	−0.0038	0.050	−0.0221	0.041	−0.0017	0.034	0.17	0.32
	1000	−0.0014	0.037	−0.0205	0.031	−0.0003	0.027	0.17	0.27
	2000	−0.0001	0.027	−0.0175	0.024	−0.0001	0.021	0.10	0.22
$B(4,2)$	500	0.0001	0.045	0.0007	0.042	0.0008	0.039	0.07	0.13
	1000	0.0000	0.031	0.0005	0.030	0.0017	0.026	0.03	0.16
	2000	0.0002	0.022	0.0004	0.021	0.0011	0.018	0.05	0.18
$G(0.5,1)$	500	−0.0053	0.062	−0.0148	0.052	−0.0038	0.053	0.16	0.14
	1000	−0.0034	0.045	−0.0118	0.039	−0.0031	0.040	0.12	0.11
	2000	−0.0004	0.033	−0.0090	0.032	−0.0010	0.030	0.04	0.09
$G(5,2)$	500	−0.0010	0.048	0.0006	0.043	0.0003	0.042	0.10	0.12
	1000	−0.0008	0.034	0.0008	0.030	0.0004	0.029	0.12	0.15
	2000	−0.0010	0.025	0.0005	0.022	0.0003	0.020	0.12	0.20
$F(2,9)$	500	−0.0090	0.083	−0.0116	0.076	−0.0080	0.080	0.08	0.04
	1000	−0.0063	0.060	−0.0076	0.057	−0.0059	0.059	0.04	0.02
	2000	−0.0014	0.042	−0.0017	0.041	−0.0013	0.042	0.02	0.00

Table 1.3. *(cont.)*

		QML		PI		PIs		Efficiency gains	
Error distribution	T	Bias	Standard deviation	Bias	Standard deviation	Bias	Standard deviation	PI	PIs
$t(3)$	500	−0.0015	0.069	−0.0009	0.058	−0.0027	0.059	0.16	0.15
	1000	−0.0002	0.047	0.0002	0.039	−0.0008	0.039	0.17	0.17
	2000	−0.0001	0.037	0.0001	0.031	−0.0004	0.031	0.16	0.16
$LN(0,1)$	500	−0.0099	0.083	−0.0104	0.078	−0.0090	0.080	0.06	0.03
	1000	0.0095	0.064	−0.0094	0.063	−0.0093	0.064	0.02	0.00
	2000	−0.0030	0.048	−0.0029	0.047	−0.0029	0.048	0.02	0.00
$W(2,1)$	500	−0.0026	0.046	−0.0014	0.044	−0.0015	0.039	0.04	0.15
	1000	−0.0005	0.033	0.0003	0.031	0.0002	0.026	0.06	0.21
	2000	0.0003	0.023	0.0006	0.022	0.0002	0.018	0.04	0.22
$W(8,2)$	500	−0.0026	0.046	−0.0014	0.045	−0.0015	0.043	0.02	0.06
	1000	−0.0005	0.033	0.0003	0.032	0.0002	0.030	0.03	0.09
	2000	0.0003	0.023	0.0006	0.022	0.0002	0.021	0.04	0.09
VCN	500	−0.0003	0.079	0.0006	0.061	−0.0012	0.051	0.23	0.35
	1000	−0.0023	0.053	0.0000	0.040	−0.0015	0.031	0.24	0.42
	2000	−0.0009	0.040	0.0005	0.029	−0.0005	0.022	0.27	0.45
BSM	500	−0.0001	0.044	0.0013	0.044	0.0003	0.042	0.00	0.05
	1000	−0.0008	0.034	0.0003	0.037	−0.0007	0.033	−0.09	0.03
	2000	−0.0004	0.026	0.0002	0.029	−0.0004	0.025	−0.12	0.04

Table 1.4. *Comparison of Pearson estimators (PI, PIs) to QML estimator for the parameter* $b_2 = 0.15$

		QML		PI		PIs		Efficiency gains	
Error distribution	T	Bias	Standard deviation	Bias	Standard deviation	Bias	Standard deviation	PI	PIs
$N(0,1)$	500	−0.0021	0.046	−0.0021	0.047	−0.0043	0.047	−0.02	−0.02
	1000	−0.0001	0.033	−0.0005	0.034	−0.0015	0.033	−0.03	0.00
	2000	−0.0007	0.023	−0.0009	0.024	−0.0014	0.023	−0.04	0.00
$t(5)$	500	−0.0022	0.052	−0.0021	0.047	−0.0046	0.047	0.10	0.10
	1000	−0.0013	0.038	−0.0015	0.033	−0.0030	0.033	0.13	0.13
	2000	−0.0001	0.028	−0.0001	0.024	−0.0009	0.024	0.14	0.14
$B(0.5,3)$	500	0.0012	0.053	−0.0306	0.044	0.0021	0.037	0.16	0.30
	1000	0.0025	0.038	−0.0353	0.037	0.0028	0.028	0.03	0.27
	2000	0.0027	0.027	−0.0337	0.030	0.0027	0.022	−0.11	0.19
$B(4,2)$	500	−0.0031	0.046	−0.0035	0.043	−0.0010	0.040	0.07	0.13
	1000	−0.0006	0.032	−0.0013	0.031	−0.0001	0.027	0.03	0.16
	2000	−0.0002	0.023	−0.0001	0.022	0.0006	0.018	0.04	0.22
$G(0.5,1)$	500	−0.0001	0.067	−0.0141	0.055	0.0001	0.058	0.18	0.13
	1000	0.0028	0.048	−0.0096	0.042	0.0026	0.043	0.13	0.10
	2000	0.0019	0.034	−0.0080	0.033	0.0018	0.031	0.03	0.09
$G(5,2)$	500	−0.0014	0.048	−0.0017	0.043	−0.0025	0.042	0.10	0.13
	1000	−0.0003	0.035	−0.0001	0.031	−0.0007	0.029	0.11	0.17
	2000	0.0000	0.025	0.0007	0.022	−0.0002	0.020	0.12	0.20
$F(2,9)$	500	0.0001	0.097	−0.0070	0.089	0.0005	0.093	0.09	0.04
	1000	0.0039	0.064	0.0005	0.060	0.0040	0.063	0.06	0.02
	2000	0.0022	0.045	0.0014	0.045	0.0022	0.045	0.00	0.00

Table 1.4. *(cont.)*

		QML		PI		PIs		Efficiency gains	
Error distribution	T	Bias	Standard deviation	Bias	Standard deviation	Bias	Standard deviation	PI	PIs
t(3)	500	−0.0039	0.070	−0.0034	0.058	−0.0060	0.059	0.17	0.16
	1000	−0.0012	0.054	−0.0009	0.044	−0.0026	0.045	0.19	0.17
	2000	−0.0012	0.037	−0.0008	0.029	−0.0015	0.029	0.22	0.22
LN(0,1)	500	−0.0021	0.094	−0.0063	0.089	−0.0018	0.092	0.06	0.02
	1000	0.0057	0.072	0.0043	0.070	0.0058	0.072	0.03	0.00
	2000	0.0025	0.055	0.0024	0.054	0.0025	0.055	0.02	0.00
W(2,1)	500	−0.0005	0.047	−0.0012	0.045	−0.0021	0.040	0.04	0.15
	1000	−0.0003	0.033	−0.0002	0.031	−0.0008	0.026	0.06	0.21
	2000	0.0000	0.024	0.0004	0.023	−0.0004	0.018	0.04	0.25
W(8,2)	500	−0.0009	0.048	−0.0011	0.047	−0.0028	0.045	0.02	0.06
	1000	−0.0004	0.034	−0.0004	0.032	−0.0013	0.031	0.06	0.09
	2000	0.0002	0.024	0.0003	0.023	−0.0005	0.022	0.04	0.08
VCN	500	−0.0065	0.094	−0.0020	0.072	−0.0056	0.058	0.23	0.38
	1000	−0.0011	0.065	0.0003	0.048	−0.0024	0.036	0.26	0.45
	2000	−0.0016	0.045	−0.0003	0.033	−0.0020	0.024	0.27	0.47
BSM	500	−0.0026	0.044	0.0012	0.044	−0.0018	0.042	0.00	0.04
	1000	−0.0011	0.033	0.0021	0.036	−0.0007	0.033	−0.09	0.00
	2000	−0.0012	0.026	0.0017	0.030	−0.0010	0.025	−0.15	0.04

Table 1.5. *Comparison of Pearson estimators (PI, PIs) to QML estimator for the parameter* $\alpha_0 = 0.10$

Error distribution	T	QML Bias	QML Standard deviation	PI Bias	PI Standard deviation	PIs Bias	PIs Standard deviation	Efficiency gains PI	Efficiency gains PIs
N(0,1)	500	0.0149	0.046	0.0245	0.051	0.0138	0.047	−0.13	−0.03
	1000	0.0067	0.028	0.0174	0.033	0.0051	0.029	−0.16	−0.01
	2000	0.0045	0.019	0.0163	0.023	0.0023	0.020	−0.17	−0.02
t(5)	500	0.0134	0.054	0.0139	0.051	0.0076	0.049	0.06	0.09
	1000	0.0068	0.035	0.0080	0.033	0.0006	0.031	0.07	0.12
	2000	0.0026	0.023	0.0061	0.022	−0.0023	0.020	0.03	0.13
B(0.5,3)	500	0.0168	0.054	−0.0346	0.043	0.0039	0.042	0.22	0.23
	1000	0.0085	0.034	−0.0473	0.028	0.0010	0.028	0.17	0.18
	2000	0.0058	0.021	−0.0517	0.022	0.0013	0.019	−0.01	0.11
B(4,2)	500	0.0146	0.046	0.0120	0.042	0.0039	0.040	0.07	0.13
	1000	0.0068	0.029	0.0093	0.029	0.0001	0.024	0.02	0.18
	2000	0.0031	0.021	0.0106	0.020	−0.0001	0.016	0.02	0.23
G(0.5,1)	500	0.0166	0.069	−0.0073	0.062	0.0098	0.060	0.11	0.13
	1000	0.0076	0.044	−0.0141	0.043	0.0032	0.040	0.04	0.10
	2000	0.0019	0.026	−0.0170	0.032	−0.0017	0.026	−0.22	0.00
G(5,2)	500	0.0148	0.051	0.0123	0.044	0.0084	0.043	0.13	0.15
	1000	0.0075	0.032	0.0096	0.028	0.0038	0.026	0.12	0.20
	2000	0.0045	0.022	0.0090	0.020	0.0017	0.018	0.07	0.17
F(2,9)	500	0.0125	0.080	0.0034	0.079	0.0113	0.079	0.01	0.01
	1000	0.0032	0.054	−0.0010	0.055	0.0027	0.054	−0.02	0.00
	2000	−0.0076	0.030	−0.0090	0.031	−0.0077	0.029	−0.02	0.04

Table 1.5. *(cont.)*

		QML		PI		PIs		Efficiency gains	
Error distribution	T	Bias	Standard deviation	Bias	Standard deviation	Bias	Standard deviation	PI	PIs
$t(3)$	500	0.0080	0.070	−0.0035	0.060	−0.0065	0.060	0.14	0.14
	1000	−0.0022	0.048	−0.0114	0.041	−0.0166	0.041	0.14	0.15
	2000	−0.0086	0.029	−0.0166	0.026	−0.0234	0.026	0.09	0.09
$LN(0,1)$	500	0.0128	0.087	0.0090	0.087	0.0122	0.086	0.01	0.01
	1000	0.0015	0.058	0.0004	0.059	0.0014	0.059	−0.02	−0.02
	2000	−0.0079	0.033	−0.0080	0.033	−0.0079	0.033	0.00	0.00
$W(2,1)$	500	0.0128	0.045	0.0137	0.043	0.0038	0.037	0.05	0.19
	1000	0.0071	0.030	0.0115	0.029	−0.0001	0.023	0.05	0.24
	2000	0.0040	0.021	0.0117	0.021	−0.0028	0.015	−0.02	0.29
$W(8,2)$	500	0.0125	0.045	0.0169	0.046	0.0092	0.042	−0.02	0.07
	1000	0.0073	0.029	0.0137	0.030	0.0049	0.027	−0.03	0.09
	2000	0.0043	0.020	0.0133	0.022	0.0025	0.018	−0.14	0.09
VCN	500	0.0130	0.074	−0.0147	0.065	−0.0282	0.057	0.12	0.22
	1000	0.0040	0.049	−0.0269	0.045	−0.0421	0.035	0.09	0.28
	2000	−0.0020	0.029	−0.0337	0.031	−0.0506	0.022	−0.08	0.25
BSM	500	0.0139	0.043	0.0057	0.055	0.0121	0.044	−0.28	−0.04
	1000	0.0055	0.026	−0.0008	0.041	0.0047	0.027	−0.55	−0.01
	2000	0.0025	0.018	−0.0016	0.032	0.0022	0.019	−0.79	−0.06

Table 1.6. *Comparison of Pearson estimators (PI, PIs) to QML estimator for the parameter* $\alpha_1 = 0.10$

		QML		PI		PIs		Efficiency gains	
Error distribution	T	Bias	Standard deviation	Bias	Standard deviation	Bias	Standard deviation	PI	PIs
$N(0,1)$	500	−0.0055	0.056	0.0020	0.067	−0.0080	0.060	−0.20	−0.09
	1000	−0.0051	0.041	0.0073	0.048	−0.0044	0.041	−0.19	0.00
	2000	−0.0030	0.029	0.0105	0.035	−0.0029	0.029	−0.23	0.00
$t(5)$	500	−0.0085	0.069	−0.0050	0.069	−0.0091	0.066	0.01	0.04
	1000	−0.0072	0.051	−0.0011	0.050	−0.0067	0.047	0.03	0.10
	2000	−0.0071	0.036	0.0000	0.035	−0.0070	0.032	0.04	0.11
$B(0.5,3)$	500	−0.0037	0.069	−0.0413	0.049	−0.0206	0.053	0.29	0.23
	1000	−0.0032	0.049	−0.0468	0.036	−0.0147	0.040	0.27	0.17
	2000	−0.0015	0.035	−0.0475	0.030	−0.0097	0.032	0.15	0.10
$B(4,2)$	500	−0.0038	0.054	−0.0040	0.057	−0.0204	0.049	−0.06	0.09
	1000	−0.0030	0.040	0.0020	0.042	−0.0148	0.034	−0.05	0.15
	2000	−0.0022	0.029	0.0070	0.032	−0.0102	0.024	−0.12	0.17
$G(0.5,1)$	500	−0.0105	0.090	−0.0313	0.078	−0.0214	0.079	0.14	0.12
	1000	−0.0101	0.066	−0.0298	0.060	−0.0185	0.059	0.09	0.11
	2000	−0.0088	0.048	−0.0269	0.049	−0.0155	0.044	−0.02	0.08
$G(5,2)$	500	−0.0063	0.064	−0.0052	0.061	−0.0178	0.055	0.05	0.13
	1000	−0.0046	0.046	0.0014	0.044	−0.0115	0.038	0.04	0.16
	2000	−0.0037	0.034	0.0040	0.032	−0.0085	0.027	0.06	0.21
$F(2,9)$	500	−0.0142	0.110	−0.0277	0.104	−0.0240	0.104	0.05	0.05
	1000	−0.0178	0.081	−0.0248	0.081	−0.0217	0.079	0.00	0.02
	2000	−0.0205	0.056	−0.0235	0.057	−0.0217	0.056	−0.02	0.01

Table 1.6. *(cont.)*

		QML		PI		PIs		Efficiency gains	
Error distribution	T	Bias	Standard deviation	Bias	Standard deviation	Bias	Standard deviation	PI	PIs
$t(3)$	500	−0.0128	0.093	−0.0194	0.082	−0.0210	0.080	0.12	0.14
	1000	−0.0155	0.070	−0.0204	0.060	−0.0244	0.057	0.15	0.19
	2000	−0.0180	0.048	−0.0222	0.040	−0.0271	0.038	0.16	0.20
$LN(0.1)$	500	−0.0195	0.114	−0.0286	0.110	−0.0263	0.109	0.03	0.05
	1000	−0.0216	0.085	−0.0246	0.084	−0.0239	0.084	0.01	0.02
	2000	−0.0241	0.059	−0.0245	0.059	−0.0247	0.059	0.00	0.00
$W(2,1)$	500	−0.0048	0.058	−0.0025	0.061	−0.0174	0.049	−0.05	0.15
	1000	−0.0045	0.044	0.0037	0.045	−0.0124	0.033	−0.02	0.25
	2000	−0.0036	0.030	0.0083	0.033	−0.0093	0.022	−0.11	0.26
$W(8,2)$	500	−0.0053	0.059	0.0001	0.064	−0.0113	0.056	−0.09	0.05
	1000	−0.0042	0.043	0.0052	0.047	−0.0072	0.039	−0.09	0.08
	2000	−0.0033	0.030	0.0085	0.033	−0.0049	0.028	−0.10	0.08
VCN	500	−0.0200	0.098	−0.0377	0.092	−0.0343	0.090	0.07	0.08
	1000	−0.0190	0.075	−0.0406	0.065	−0.0438	0.062	0.12	0.17
	2000	−0.0160	0.054	−0.0403	0.048	−0.0500	0.042	0.10	0.23
BSM	500	−0.0041	0.047	−0.0210	0.064	−0.0078	0.049	−0.36	−0.05
	1000	−0.0029	0.034	−0.0171	0.051	−0.0049	0.035	−0.51	−0.02
	2000	−0.0016	0.024	−0.0121	0.042	−0.0026	0.024	−0.77	0.00

Table 1.7. *Comparison of Pearson estimators (PI, PIs) to QML estimator for the parameter* $\alpha_2 = 0.20$

		QML		PI		PIs		Efficiency gains	
Error distribution	T	Bias	Standard deviation	Bias	Standard deviation	Bias	Standard deviation	PI	PIs
$N(0,1)$	500	0.0076	0.082	0.0223	0.096	0.0075	0.086	−0.18	−0.05
	1000	0.0038	0.058	0.0234	0.071	0.0021	0.059	−0.23	−0.02
	2000	0.0020	0.040	0.0253	0.050	−0.0005	0.040	−0.25	0.00
$t(5)$	500	0.0074	0.111	0.0068	0.108	−0.0019	0.103	0.03	0.07
	1000	0.0004	0.080	0.0039	0.077	−0.0087	0.071	0.04	0.11
	2000	−0.0007	0.056	0.0067	0.055	−0.0084	0.050	0.03	0.10
$B(0.5,3)$	500	0.0133	0.114	−0.0679	0.094	−0.0012	0.086	0.18	0.25
	1000	0.0050	0.080	−0.0895	0.069	−0.0033	0.063	0.14	0.21
	2000	0.0058	0.055	−0.0951	0.055	0.0012	0.047	−0.01	0.14
$B(4,2)$	500	0.0049	0.079	0.0049	0.082	−0.0046	0.068	−0.04	0.14
	1000	0.0027	0.056	0.0108	0.062	−0.0028	0.046	−0.11	0.18
	2000	0.0005	0.041	0.0162	0.047	−0.0020	0.032	−0.15	0.22
$G(0.5,1)$	500	0.0192	0.163	−0.0139	0.150	0.0099	0.145	0.08	0.11
	1000	0.0086	0.119	−0.0218	0.115	0.0020	0.107	0.03	0.10
	2000	−0.0010	0.080	−0.0300	0.087	−0.0059	0.074	−0.09	0.08
$G(5,2)$	500	0.0060	0.095	0.0076	0.089	−0.0006	0.080	0.06	0.16
	1000	0.0044	0.068	0.0122	0.065	−0.0002	0.055	0.04	0.19
	2000	0.0037	0.049	0.0161	0.048	0.0006	0.038	0.01	0.22
$F(2,9)$	500	0.0244	0.203	0.0086	0.196	0.0184	0.191	0.03	0.06
	1000	0.0032	0.148	−0.0027	0.146	0.0017	0.144	0.01	0.03
	2000	−0.0156	0.097	−0.0168	0.098	−0.0156	0.097	−0.01	0.00

Table 1.7. *(cont.)*

		QML		PI		PIs		Efficiency gains	
Error distribution	T	Bias	Standard deviation	Bias	Standard deviation	Bias	Standard deviation	PI	PIs
$t(3)$	500	−0.0007	0.154	−0.0201	0.137	−0.0266	0.131	0.11	0.15
	1000	−0.0111	0.112	−0.0275	0.095	−0.0374	0.092	0.15	0.18
	2000	−0.0182	0.078	−0.0326	0.065	−0.0457	0.062	0.16	0.20
$LN(0.1)$	500	0.0303	0.215	0.0223	0.209	0.0255	0.206	0.03	0.04
	1000	0.0069	0.161	0.0055	0.160	0.0061	0.158	0.01	0.02
	2000	−0.0153	0.107	−0.0151	0.108	−0.0154	0.107	−0.01	0.00
$W(2.1)$	500	0.0055	0.086	0.0112	0.088	−0.0029	0.070	−0.03	0.19
	1000	0.0032	0.062	0.0146	0.065	−0.0047	0.047	−0.06	0.24
	2000	0.0031	0.043	0.0203	0.049	−0.0062	0.031	−0.14	0.27
$W(8.2)$	500	0.0049	0.087	0.0133	0.094	0.0023	0.082	−0.08	0.06
	1000	0.0031	0.063	0.0166	0.069	0.0017	0.057	−0.10	0.09
	2000	0.0028	0.044	0.0221	0.050	0.0019	0.040	−0.15	0.09
VCN	500	0.0463	0.200	−0.0127	0.193	−0.0304	0.181	0.04	0.09
	1000	0.0223	0.146	−0.0401	0.138	−0.0682	0.121	0.05	0.17
	2000	0.0047	0.098	−0.0594	0.098	−0.0931	0.077	−0.01	0.21
BSM	500	−0.0045	0.064	−0.0130	0.080	−0.0052	0.066	−0.25	−0.03
	1000	−0.0041	0.044	−0.0123	0.065	−0.0045	0.045	−0.48	−0.02
	2000	−0.0029	0.031	−0.0086	0.052	−0.0031	0.032	−0.69	−0.03

Table 1.8. *Comparison of Pearson estimators (PI, PIs) to QML estimator for the parameter* $\beta_1 = 0.60$

Error distribution	T	QML Bias	QML Standard deviation	PI Bias	PI Standard deviation	PIs Bias	PIs Standard deviation	Efficiency gains PI	Efficiency gains PIs
$N(0,1)$	500	−0.0261	0.099	−0.0222	0.105	−0.0243	0.103	−0.06	−0.05
	1000	−0.0130	0.065	−0.0088	0.069	−0.0105	0.066	−0.07	−0.02
	2000	−0.0097	0.045	−0.0045	0.048	−0.0052	0.045	−0.06	0.01
$t(5)$	500	−0.0338	0.132	−0.0258	0.124	−0.0275	0.125	0.06	0.05
	1000	−0.0188	0.088	−0.0119	0.081	−0.0126	0.081	0.08	0.08
	2000	−0.0106	0.060	−0.0060	0.054	−0.0065	0.055	0.11	0.09
$B(0.5,3)$	500	−0.0403	0.136	−0.0224	0.121	−0.0282	0.107	0.11	0.21
	1000	−0.0229	0.089	−0.0046	0.080	−0.0157	0.070	0.10	0.21
	2000	−0.0189	0.058	0.0001	0.052	−0.0138	0.049	0.10	0.15
$B(4,2)$	500	−0.0220	0.095	−0.0130	0.090	−0.0161	0.088	0.06	0.08
	1000	−0.0102	0.065	−0.0056	0.060	−0.0080	0.054	0.08	0.17
	2000	−0.0041	0.046	−0.0037	0.041	−0.0056	0.037	0.11	0.20
$G(0.5,1)$	500	−0.0596	0.194	−0.0428	0.179	−0.0506	0.177	0.08	0.09
	1000	−0.0375	0.135	−0.0222	0.120	−0.0313	0.123	0.11	0.09
	2000	−0.0215	0.082	−0.0084	0.074	−0.0181	0.075	0.11	0.09
$G(5,2)$	500	−0.0293	0.114	−0.0187	0.100	−0.0214	0.101	0.12	0.12
	1000	−0.0170	0.076	−0.0092	0.064	−0.0116	0.064	0.15	0.16
	2000	−0.0107	0.053	−0.0039	0.044	−0.0060	0.042	0.17	0.21
$F(2,9)$	500	−0.0825	0.231	−0.0742	0.226	−0.0808	0.229	0.02	0.01
	1000	−0.0527	0.173	−0.0487	0.170	−0.0519	0.171	0.02	0.01
	2000	−0.0225	0.106	−0.0214	0.105	−0.0226	0.105	0.01	0.01

Table 1.8. *(cont.)*

		QML		PI		PIs		Efficiency gains	
Error distribution	T	Bias	Standard deviation	Bias	Standard deviation	Bias	Standard deviation	PI	PIs
$t(3)$	500	−0.0605	0.190	−0.0483	0.175	−0.0482	0.176	0.07	0.07
	1000	−0.0332	0.135	−0.0248	0.117	−0.0250	0.117	0.13	0.13
	2000	−0.0149	0.088	−0.0090	0.073	−0.0088	0.074	0.16	0.15
$LN(0.1)$	500	−0.0918	0.249	−0.0886	0.248	−0.0902	0.247	0.00	0.01
	1000	−0.0567	0.187	−0.0556	0.187	−0.0566	0.187	0.00	0.00
	2000	−0.0301	0.120	−0.0300	0.121	−0.0299	0.120	−0.01	0.00
$W(2.1)$	500	−0.0231	0.100	−0.0136	0.093	−0.0144	0.086	0.07	0.15
	1000	−0.0140	0.069	−0.0062	0.062	−0.0077	0.054	0.10	0.21
	2000	−0.0098	0.048	−0.0026	0.044	−0.0026	0.035	0.09	0.27
$W(8.2)$	500	−0.0229	0.101	−0.0152	0.100	−0.0181	0.096	0.02	0.05
	1000	−0.0145	0.067	−0.0076	0.067	−0.0103	0.063	0.01	0.06
	2000	−0.0094	0.047	−0.0042	0.047	−0.0054	0.043	0.01	0.09
VCN	500	−0.0762	0.232	−0.0732	0.239	−0.0738	0.236	−0.03	−0.02
	1000	−0.0431	0.161	−0.0421	0.166	−0.0430	0.167	−0.03	−0.03
	2000	−0.0250	0.099	−0.0239	0.105	−0.0249	0.107	−0.07	−0.08
BSM	500	−0.0082	0.082	−0.0152	0.103	−0.0092	0.085	−0.26	−0.04
	1000	−0.0008	0.054	−0.0057	0.078	−0.0013	0.055	−0.44	−0.02
	2000	−0.0004	0.037	−0.0042	0.061	−0.0008	0.038	−0.64	−0.03

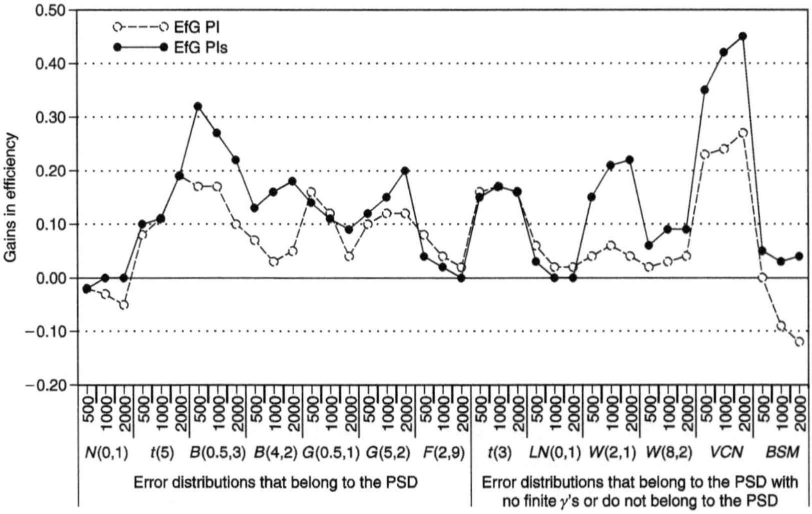

Figure 1.1 *Efficiency gains of the estimators PI and PIs with respect to the QML estimator for the parameter* $b_1 = 0.50$

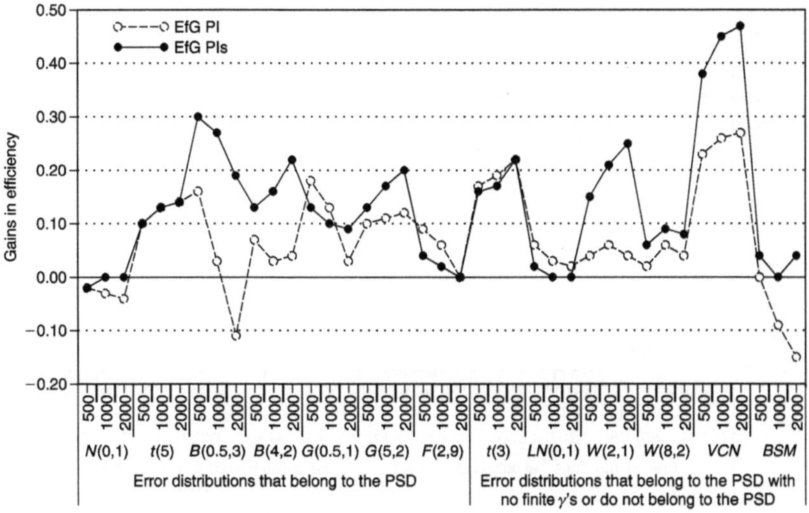

Figure 1.2 *Efficiency gains of the estimators PI and PIs with respect to the QML estimator for the parameter* $b_2 = 0.15$

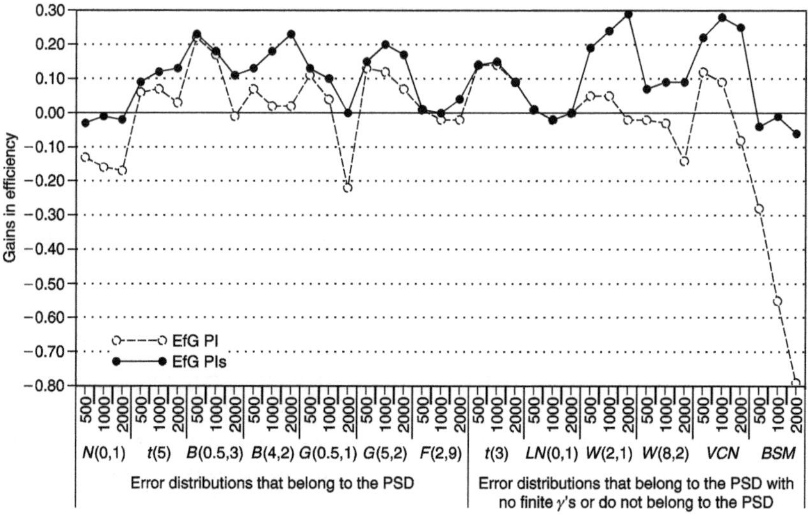

Figure 1.3 *Efficiency gains of the estimators PI and PIs with respect to the QML estimator for the parameter* $\alpha_0 = 0.10$

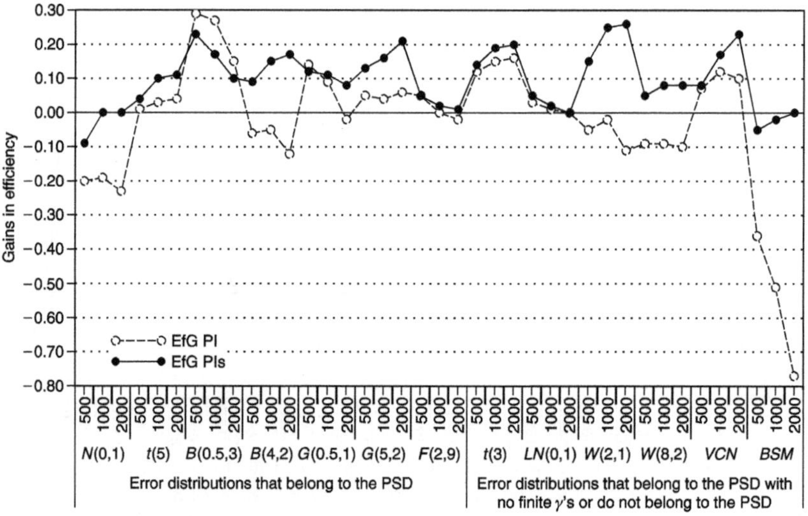

Figure 1.4 *Efficiency gains of the estimators PI and PIs with respect to the QML estimator for the parameter* $\alpha_1 = 0.10$

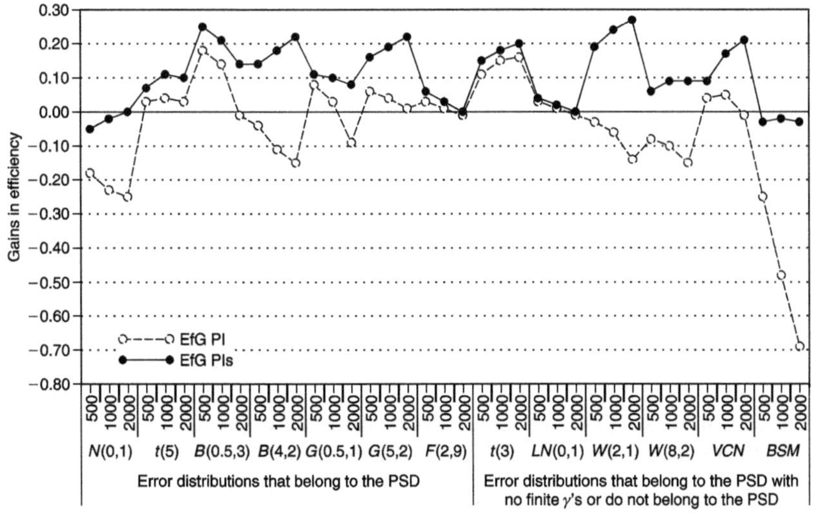

Figure 1.5 *Efficiency gains of the estimators PI and PIs with respect to the QML estimator for the parameter* $\alpha_2 = 0.20$

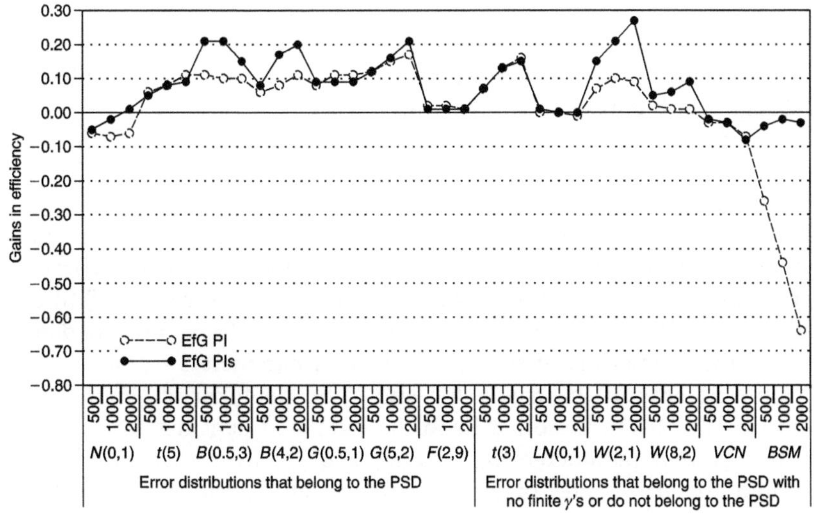

Figure 1.6 *Efficiency gains of the estimators PI and PIs with respect to the QML estimator for the parameter* $\beta_1 = 0.60$

The performance of the QML estimator increases with respect to the shape of each specific distribution since $t(5)$, $G(5,2)$ and $B(4,2)$ are "closer" to normality with respect to the $t(3)$, $G(0.5,1)$ and $B(0.5,3)$.

The performance of the PIs estimator with respect to the QML estimator in the $N(0,1)$ case is about the same in the sample size $T = 2000$, but in the smaller samples, that are considered, the PIs estimator fails to improve the performance of the QML. In all the other error distributions that are considered, the PIs estimator gives efficiency gains compared with the QML. This is true for all distributions considered (either belonging to the PSD or not), except in the case of the BSM distribution for the parameters of the variance equation (Tables 1.3 through 1.8; Figures 1.1 through 1.6). The results for the BSM are not surprising since this distribution is bimodal, while the PSD only includes unimodal distributions. Moreover, the efficiency gains of the PIs estimator vary across error distributions. In the case of the mean equation parameters b_1 and b_2 the efficiency gains vary from 10 percent to 47 percent for the $t(5)$, $B(0.5,3)$, $B(4,2)$, $G(0.5,1)$, $G(5,2)$, $t(3)$, $W(2,1)$ and VCN error distributions, while in other distributions they are below 10 percent, (Tables 1.3, 1.4; Figures 1.1, 1.2). For the variance parameters $\alpha_0, \alpha_1, \alpha_2$ and β_1, the efficiency gains of the PIs estimator are from 10 percent to 29 percent in the case of the error distributions $t(5)$, $B(0.5,3)$, $B(4,2)$, $G(5,2)$, $t(3)$, $W(2,1)$, VCN and samples $T \geq 1000$.

In some cases the PI estimator gives gains in efficiency but in other cases fails to improve the performance of the QML estimator (Tables 1.3 through 1.8; Figures 1.1 through 1.6).

In order to examine the other distributional aspects of the estimators, graphs were produced from the Monte Carlo estimates. Each density was estimated using the 5000 values of the corresponding estimator. For this purpose we used an Eapnechnikov kernel with optimum bandwidth obtained by least squares (Silverman, 1986, pp. 40–51). Here we give some of these graphs for the $t(5)$ and $W(2,1)$ error distributions at the sample size $T = 1000$. As we can see, the estimated densities of the estimators, of the mean equation parameters b_1 and b_2, are symmetric around the true value and rather leptokurtic (Figures 1.7 through 1.10). On the other hand the estimated densities for the variance equation parameters α_0, α_1, α_2 and β_1 are rather asymmetric around the true value of each parameter and positively skewed for the parameters α_0, α_1, α_2 and negatively skewed for the parameter β_1 (Figures 1.11 through 1.18).

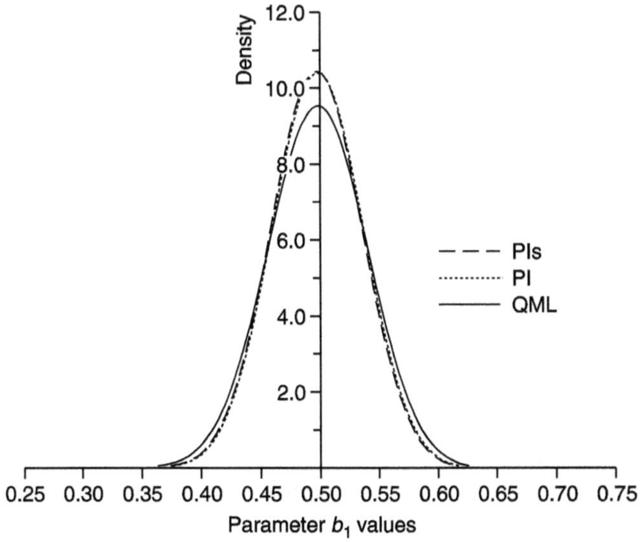

Figure 1.7 *Kernel estimates of the estimators densities for* $t(5)$ *disturbances, sample size* $T = 1000$

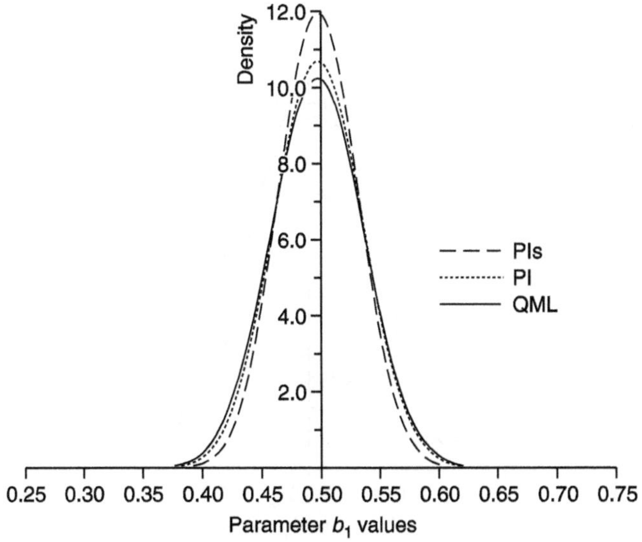

Figure 1.8 *Kernel estimates of the estimators densities for Weibull* (2,1) *disturbances, sample size* $T = 1000$

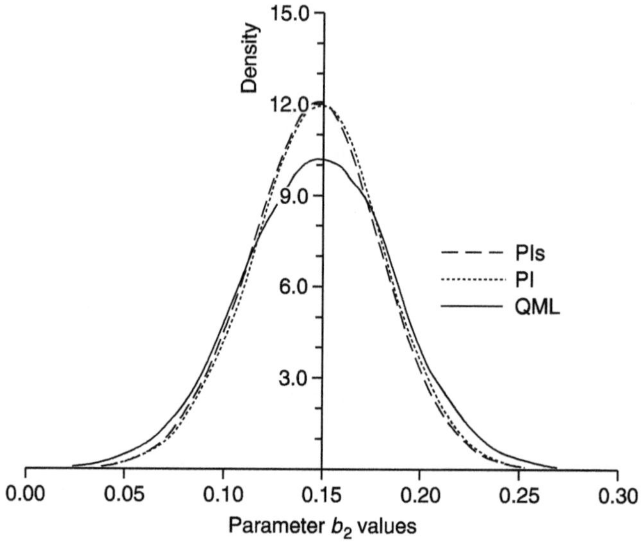

Figure 1.9 *Kernel estimates of the estimators densities for* $t(5)$ *disturbances, sample size* $T = 1000$

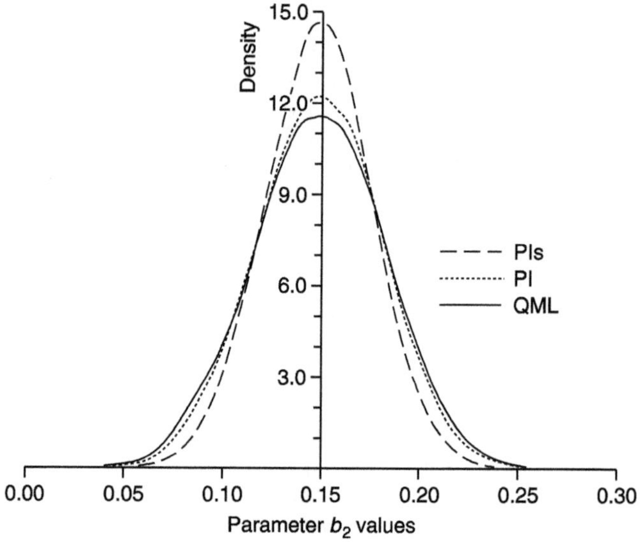

Figure 1.10 *Kernel estimates of the estimators densities for Weibull* (2,1) *disturbances, sample size* $T = 1000$

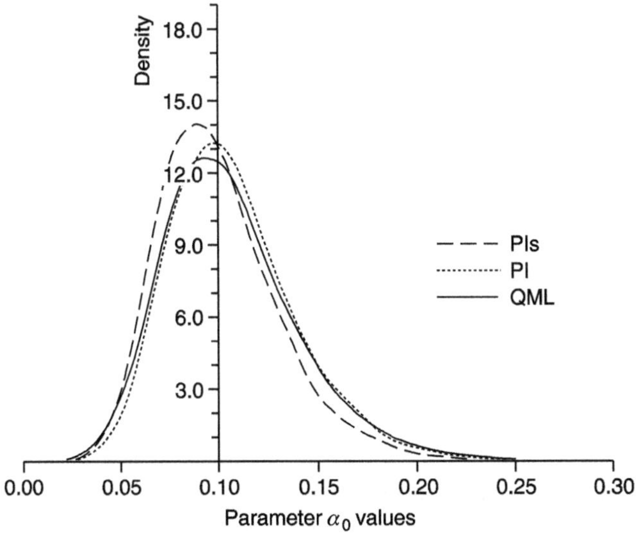

Figure 1.11 *Kernel estimates of the estimators densities for* $t(5)$ *disturbances, sample size* $T = 1000$

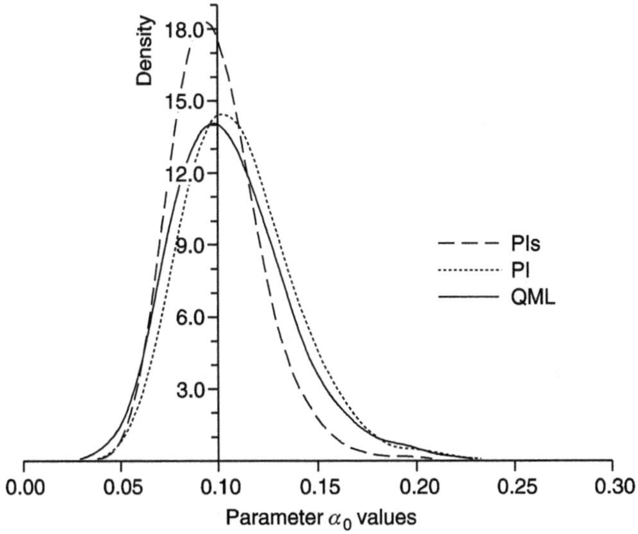

Figure 1.12 *Kernel estimates of the estimators densities for Weibull* (2,1) *disturbances, sample size* $T = 1000$

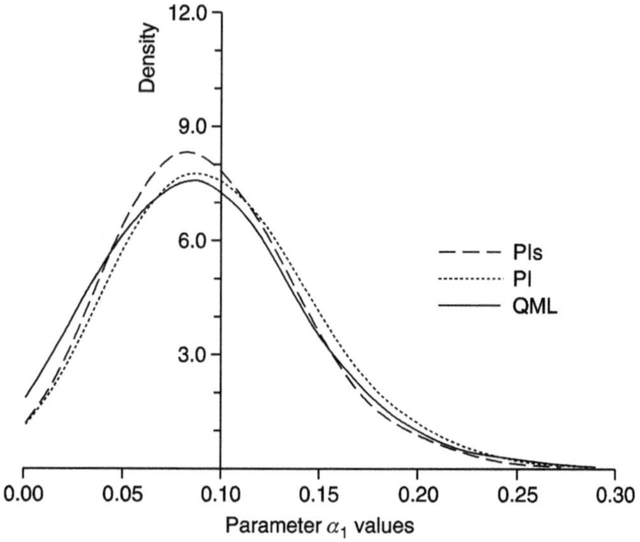

Figure 1.13 *Kernel estimates of the estimators densities for* $t(5)$ *disturbances, sample size* $T = 1000$

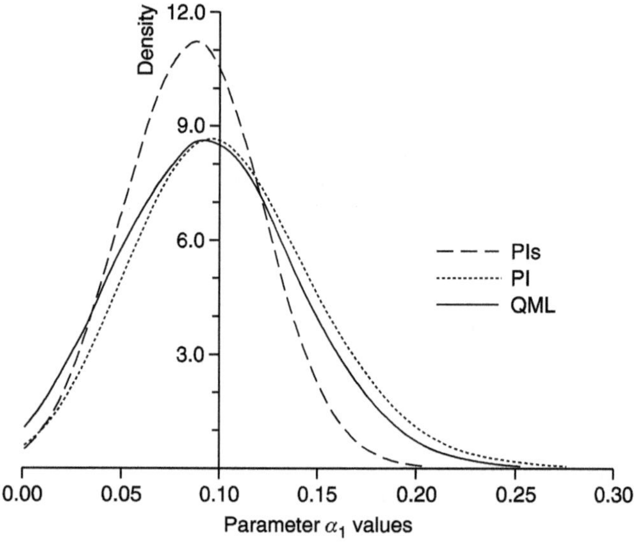

Figure 1.14 *Kernel estimates of the estimators densities for Weibull* (2,1) *disturbances, sample size* $T = 1000$

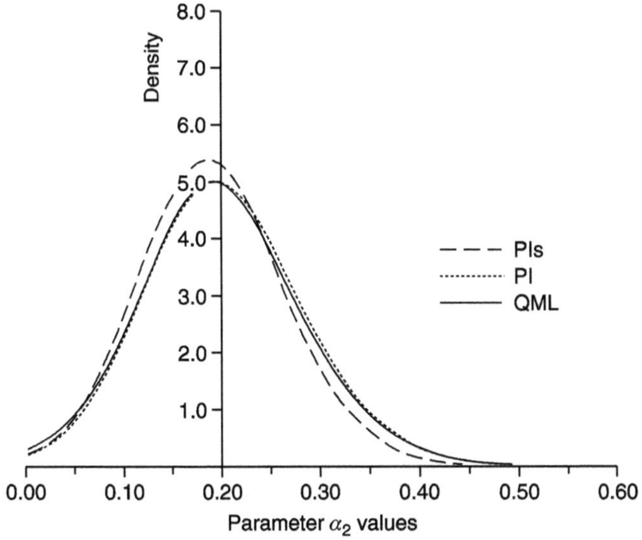

Figure 1.15 *Kernel estimates of the estimators densities for* $t(5)$ *disturbances, sample size* $T = 1000$

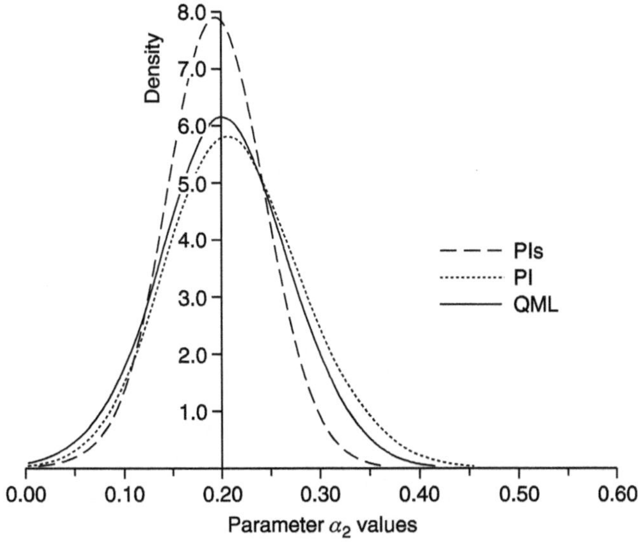

Figure 1.16 *Kernel estimates of the estimators densities for Weibull* (2,1) *disturbances, sample size* $T = 1000$

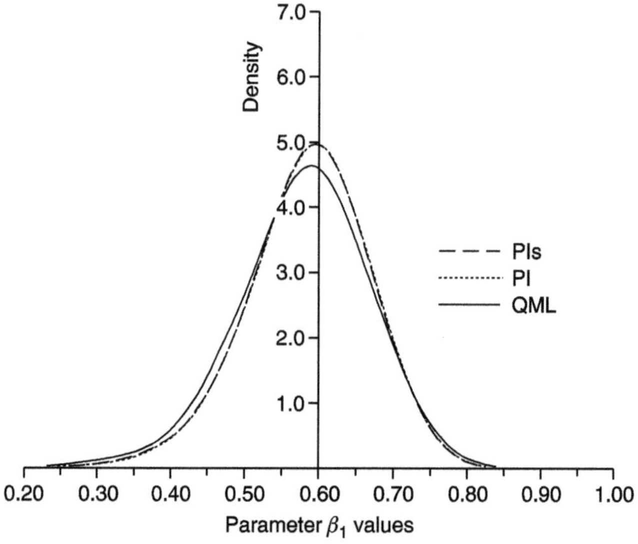

Figure 1.17 *Kernel estimates of the estimators densities for* $t(5)$ *disturbances, sample size* $T = 1000$

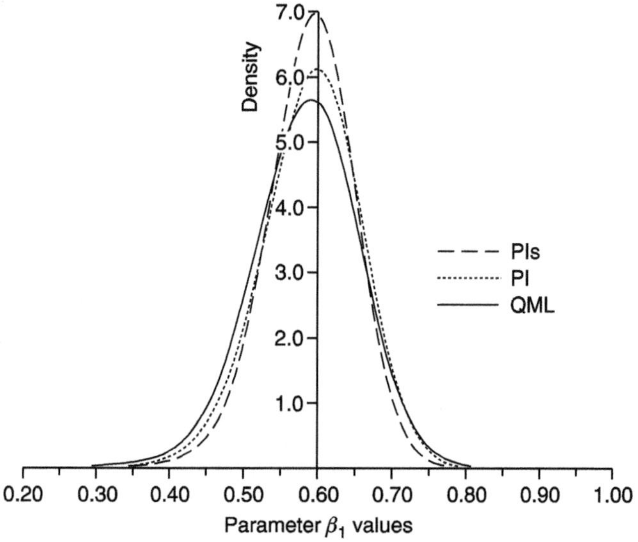

Figure 1.18 *Kernel estimates of the estimators densities for Weibull* (2,1) *disturbances, sample size* $T = 1000$

The figures show that for each parameter the distribution of the PIs estimator is more concentrated around the true value compared with the distribution of the other estimators.

Finally, according to the results for the Bias there is no systematic ranking of the estimators.

4 Concluding Remarks

In this chapter the use of the PIs estimator is proposed which employs additional information from the skewness and kurtosis of the error distribution to improve the QML estimator. Although this estimator is derived under the assumption that the error density belongs to the Pearson family of distributions, it performs equally well in all the cases of unimodal distributions. The proposed estimator gives efficiency gains, which in some cases are significant, but it does not seem to capture the total potential gain in efficiency. In that sense the estimator is not fully adaptive. In the applications with actual data, the PIs estimator has the advantage that we need not to assume a specific distribution for the error term. The computational requirements of the estimator are very modest, since the improvement vector (28) may be easily estimated by using (29). Moreover, the PIs estimator is computationally simpler than the non-parametric or semiparametric methods where additional smoothing parameters must be estimated.

Several generalizations of the proposed estimator are possible in the case of conditional heteroskedasticity models. The same estimation technique may be applied in the models: GARCH in Mean, Exponential GARCH, integrated GARCH and so on, but this work is beyond the scope of this paper and will be examined in a future work.

2 The Instrumental Variables Method Revisited: On the Nature and Choice of Optimal Instruments

*Aris Spanos**

1 Introduction

The method of Instrumental Variables (IV) was first formalized by Reiersol (1941) and Geary (1948, 1949) in the context of the errors-in-variables (confluence analysis) using time series data. The IV method was introduced as an alternative to least-squares in an attempt to deal with the inconsistency of the ordinary least-squares (OLS) estimator. Durbin (1954) systematized and extended the IV method to a general linear relationship where the explanatory variables are correlated with the error term. He also conjectured a direct relationship between the IV estimator and the limited information maximum likelihood (LIML) estimator in the context of the simultaneous equations model (SEM). This conjecture was formally confirmed by Sargan (1958) who extended the scope of the IV method by relating it to maximum likelihood methods, establishing the IV as a general estimation method in econometrics. Since then the IV method has been increasingly used both as a unifying concept in econometric estimation (see Hendry, 1976; Hausman, 1975; Bowden and Turkington, 1984; inter alia), as well as a computationally convenient method (see Brundy and Jorgenson, 1974; Hansen and Singleton, 1982). More recently, the IV method has been extended in a number of ways to unify estimation and testing procedures in a non-maximum likelihood framework (see White, 1982, 1984), misspecification testing (see Pagan, 1984), as well as unit-root testing (see Hall, 1989). Arguably, the most important extension has been the Generalized Method of Moments (GMM) proposed by Hansen (1982); see also Newey (1985). Despite the generality of the GMM, a case can be made that the method has largely retained the statistical underpinnings of the IV method; see Hall (1993) and Ogaki (1993).

* This chapter is dedicated to the memory of Michael Magdalinos, a real scholar and a wonderful friend.

1.1 *Where Do Valid Instruments Come From?*

In this chapter, it is argued that notwithstanding the extensive use and increasing importance of the instrumental variables (IVs) method, its foundations are statistically weak because they are deeply rooted in *non-verifiable* orthogonality conditions which involve unobservable *error terms*, and the choice of instruments appears to be a matter of "storytelling". Modellers often consider these non-verifiable conditions as the great strength of the method because it encourages the contemplation of *natural experiments* concerning the behaviour of economic agents, and economic theory – not statistics – guides the modelling; see Angrist and Krueger (1992), Card and Krueger (1992). It's not uncommon for economists to "vaunt" that the IV method frees them from "statistical shackles" because, with "suitable" choices of instruments, they can verify *any* theory or hypothesis!

Economic theory, via the specification of structural models, plays a crucial role in indicating variables that can be potentially used as instruments, but their appropriateness has an equally important statistical dimension. One aspect of the statistical dimension, the *weak instruments* problem, has been extensively discussed in the recent literature; see Nelson and Starz (1990a, b), Staiger and Stock (1997) and Wang and Zivot (1998). It turns out that weak instruments constitute one of several departures from the IV conditions that can give rise to *unreliable IV-based inference*, but very little attention has been paid to other forms of departures. The non-verifiability of some IV conditions renders the implementation of the IV method potentially unreliable because the nature, choice and optimality of instruments appear to depend almost exclusively on the modeller's *subjective beliefs* and his/her rhetorical skills. In particular, the probabilistic structure of the data appears to play no essential role. The only constraint seems to be that the instruments should be correlated with the endogenous variables, but even that is not a binding constraint because the modeller can change the instruments at will to achieve any correlational structure desirable. If we liken statistical inference to playing tennis, the above perspective on the IV method amounts to playing tennis with "the net down". The question is "whether there exists a net or not?"

The main objective of this chapter is to erect this "net" by arguing that, in addition to theory considerations, there are statistical binding constraints which render the IV method (inferentially) unreliable when ignored. The nature and choice of instruments is not as arbitrary as it appears at first sight if *reliability of inference* is a concern.

The primary thesis of the paper is that a structural model gains statistical "operational meaning" when embedded into a statistically adequate model specified exclusively in terms of the joint distribution of the observable random variables involved. That is, structural concepts gain statistical "operational meaning" only to the extent that they can be related to well-defined statistical concepts and procedures. The discussion emphasizes the implementation of the IV method with a view to enhancing the reliability and precision of IV-based inference. This re-casting attempts to systematize the statistical underpinnings of the IV method and shed some additional light on a number of issues including:

1 the nature and choice of instruments,
2 the endogeneity/exogeneity dichotomy,
3 the testing of overidentifying restrictions and exogeneity,
4 the problem of weak instruments, and
5 the issue of weak vs. strong probabilistic assumptions.

Section 2 summarizes the traditional IV argument as a prelude to proposing a statistical framework for IV-based inference in the form of the Implicit Reduced Form (IRF), discussed in section 3. The non-verifiable orthogonality conditions, on which the IV method is based, are given operational meaning in the context of the IRF in the form of the implicit statistical parameterizations for the structural parameters, and is used to elucidate the endogeneity/exogeneity issue. In section 4 the statistical adequacy of the IRF is shown to play a crucial role in the choice of instruments, the weak instruments problem, as well as the reliability of IV-based inference which is discussed further in section 5. The operationalization of the orthogonality and non-orthogonality conditions is utilized to elucidate testing overidentifying restrictions as well as exogeneity.

2 The Traditional IV Argument, a Summary

Let us summarize the traditional textbook argument concerning the instrumental variables (IVs) method in the case of the **linear structural model**:

$$y_t = \boldsymbol{\alpha}^\top \mathbf{X}_t + \varepsilon_t,\ \varepsilon_t \sim \mathrm{N}(0, \sigma^2),\ t \in \mathbb{T} := \{1, 2, \ldots, T, \ldots\} \tag{1}$$

where $\mathbf{X}_t$ is a $m \times 1$ vector of stochastic explanatory variables such that:

$$\text{(i)}\ \ E(\mathbf{X}_t \varepsilon_t) = \mathbf{d} \neq 0 \ \text{ or } \ \text{(i)}_\alpha \left(\frac{1}{T}\mathbf{X}^\top \boldsymbol{\varepsilon}\right) \xrightarrow{\mathbb{P}} \mathbf{d} \neq 0 \tag{2}$$

$\mathbf{X} = (\mathbf{X}_1, \mathbf{X}_2, \ldots, \mathbf{X}_T)^\top$ and $\boldsymbol{\varepsilon} = (\varepsilon_1, \varepsilon_2, \ldots, \varepsilon_T)^\top$. It is well-known that because of (2) the OLS estimators of $(\boldsymbol{\alpha}, \sigma^2)$, defined by:

$$\widehat{\alpha} = (\mathbf{X}^\top\mathbf{X})^{-1}\mathbf{X}^\top\mathbf{y}, \;\; s^2 = \frac{1}{T-m}(\mathbf{y} - \mathbf{X}\widehat{\alpha})^\top(\mathbf{y} - \mathbf{X}\widehat{\alpha}) \tag{3}$$

are *biased* and *inconsistent*. To see this consider:

$$\widehat{\alpha} = (\mathbf{X}^\top\mathbf{X})^{-1}\mathbf{X}^\top\mathbf{y} = \boldsymbol{\alpha} - (\mathbf{X}^\top\mathbf{X})^{-1}\mathbf{X}^\top\boldsymbol{\varepsilon} \Rightarrow E(\widehat{\alpha} - \boldsymbol{\alpha})$$
$$= E\left[(\mathbf{X}^\top\mathbf{X})^{-1}\mathbf{X}^\top\boldsymbol{\varepsilon}\right] \neq 0$$

since, $E(\mathbf{X}_t\varepsilon_t) \neq 0 \Rightarrow E(\varepsilon_t \mid \mathbf{X}_t) \neq 0$, and thus $\widehat{\alpha}$ is biased:

$$E(\widehat{\alpha} - \boldsymbol{\alpha}) = E\left[E(\widehat{\alpha} - \boldsymbol{\alpha}) \mid \mathbf{X}\right] = E\left[(\mathbf{X}^\top\mathbf{X})^{-1}\mathbf{X}^\top E(\boldsymbol{\varepsilon} \mid X)\right] \neq 0$$

and inconsistent ($\widehat{\alpha} \overset{\mathbb{P}}{\nrightarrow} \boldsymbol{\alpha}$, where "$\overset{\mathbb{P}}{\nrightarrow}$" reads "does not converge in probability"):

$$(\mathbb{P})\lim_{T\to\infty} \widehat{\alpha} = \boldsymbol{\alpha} + \mathbf{Q}_X^{-1}\mathbf{d} \neq \boldsymbol{\alpha},$$

where $\mathbf{Q}_X = (\mathbb{P})\lim_{T\to\infty}(\frac{1}{T}\mathbf{X}^\top\mathbf{X})$. Similarly, $E(s^2) \neq \sigma^2$, and $s^2 \overset{\mathbb{P}}{\nrightarrow} \sigma^2$:

$$(\mathbb{P})\lim_{T\to\infty}(s^2) = \sigma^2 - \mathbf{d}\mathbf{Q}_{\mathbf{X}}^{-1}\mathbf{d}^\top < \sigma^2$$

see Davidson and McKinnon (1993).

The IV method "tackles" these inference problems by introducing a $p \times 1$ $(p \geq m)$ vector of **instrumental variables $\mathbf{Z}_t$**, such that:

$$\begin{array}{llll}
\text{(ii)} & E(\mathbf{Z}_t\varepsilon_t) = 0 & \text{or} & \text{(ii)}_\alpha \;\; (\frac{1}{T}\mathbf{Z}^\top\boldsymbol{\varepsilon}) \overset{\mathbb{P}}{\to} 0 \\
\text{(iii)} & E(\mathbf{X}_t\mathbf{Z}_t^\top) = \boldsymbol{\Sigma}_{23} & \text{or} & \text{(iii)}_\alpha \;\; (\frac{1}{T}\mathbf{X}^\top\mathbf{Z}) \overset{\mathbb{P}}{\to} \boldsymbol{\Sigma}_{23} \neq 0 \\
\text{(iv)} & E(\mathbf{Z}_t\mathbf{Z}_t^\top) = \boldsymbol{\Sigma}_{33} & \text{or} & \text{(iv)}_\alpha \;\; (\frac{1}{T}\mathbf{Z}^\top\mathbf{Z}) \overset{\mathbb{P}}{\to} \boldsymbol{\Sigma}_{33} > 0
\end{array}$$

Note that (a) "$\overset{\mathbb{P}}{\to}$" reads "converges in probability" and (b) for simplicity we assume zero means for all the observable random variables in $\mathbf{W}_t := (y_t, \mathbf{X}_t^\top, \mathbf{Z}_t^\top)^\top$, without any loss of generality. The original IV formulation (see Sargan, 1958) and most subsequent discussions, emphasize the asymptotic conditions (ii)$_\alpha$–(iv)$_\alpha$, but we will focus more on the finite sample conditions (i)–(iv).

Assuming that $p \geq m$ (there are more instruments than explanatory variables), Sargan (1958) proposed the *generalized instrumental variable estimator* (GIVE):

$$\widehat{\alpha}_{IV} = (\mathbf{X}^\top \mathbf{P}_Z \mathbf{X})^{-1} \mathbf{X}^\top \mathbf{P}_Z \mathbf{y} \tag{4}$$

where $\mathbf{P}_Z = \mathbf{Z}(\mathbf{Z}^\top \mathbf{Z})^{-1}\mathbf{Z}^\top$. This estimator was derived by Sargan using asymptotic efficiency arguments in addition to consistency. His derivation amounted to choosing an "optimal" set of instruments as *linear* combinations of $\mathbf{Z}$, say $\mathbf{Z}^* = \mathbf{ZH}$, where $\mathbf{H}$ is a $p \times m$ matrix with $\mathsf{rank}(\mathbf{H}) = m$, in order to minimize the asymptotic covariance of (4). The minimization yields $\mathbf{Z}^* = \mathbf{ZH} = \mathbf{Z}(\mathbf{Z}^\top\mathbf{Z})^{-1}\mathbf{Z}^\top\mathbf{X}$, and the asymptotic distribution of (4), under certain regularity conditions on $\mathbf{Z}_t$ (see White, 1984), takes the form:

$$\sqrt{T}(\widehat{\alpha}_{IV} - \alpha) \,\widehat{\alpha}\, \mathsf{N}(0, \sigma^2 (\mathbf{\Sigma}_{23}\mathbf{\Sigma}_{33}^{-1}\mathbf{\Sigma}_{32})^{-1}).$$

$\widehat{\alpha}_{IV}$ is both consistent ($\widehat{\alpha}_{IV} \overset{\mathbb{P}}{\to} \alpha = (\mathbf{\Sigma}_{23}\mathbf{\Sigma}_{33}^{-1}\mathbf{\Sigma}_{23})^{-1}\mathbf{\Sigma}_{23}\mathbf{\Sigma}_{33}^{-1}\mathbf{\Sigma}_{31}$) and *asymptotically efficient* within the class of linear IV estimators; see Phillips (1980) on the finite sample properties of $\widehat{\alpha}_{IV}$. The probability limit of $\widehat{\alpha}_{IV}$ suggests that, in addition to conditions (i)–(iv), one implicitly assumes:

$$\text{(v)} \quad E(\mathbf{Z}_t y_t) = \sigma_{31} \neq 0, \quad \text{or} \quad \text{(v)}_\alpha \; \left(\tfrac{1}{T}\mathbf{Z}^\top \mathbf{y}\right) \overset{\mathbb{P}}{\to} \sigma_{31} \neq 0$$

in order to avoid the case $\widehat{\alpha}_{IV} \overset{\mathbb{P}}{\to} 0$.

The choice of instruments as envisaged by the above discussion is based on finding variables $\mathbf{Z}_t$ which are highly correlated with $\mathbf{X}_t$ but uncorrelated with the error ε_t. Given that the error ε_t is unobservable the instrument "exogeneity" condition $E(\mathbf{Z}_t\varepsilon_t) = 0$ is *not verifiable* and begs the very question it purports to answer: "on what basis does one decide that $E(\mathbf{X}_t\varepsilon_t) \neq 0$, in the first place and then that $E(\mathbf{Z}_t\varepsilon_t) = 0$?" The answer "economic theory decides" is clearly unsatisfactory because (i)–(v) are probabilistic conditions relating to the structure of the vector stochastic process $\{\mathbf{W}_t,\ t = 1, 2, \ldots, T\}$, which must have an important bearing upon the validity of these conditions.

3 A Statistical Framework for the IVs Method

The primary thesis of this chapter is that theory-based concepts like structural parameters, structural errors, orthogonality and non-orthogonality conditions, gain statistical "operational meaning" when embedded into a statistical model specified exclusively in terms of the joint distribution of the *observable* random variables involved, say $D(\mathbf{W}_1, \mathbf{W}_2, \ldots, \mathbf{W}_T; \boldsymbol{\phi})$. Statistical models are specified as reductions from $D(\mathbf{W}_1, \mathbf{W}_2, \ldots, \mathbf{W}_T; \boldsymbol{\phi})$ by imposing probabilistic assumptions from three basic categories: Distribution, Dependence and Heterogeneity; see Spanos (1986, 1989), Spanos and McGuirk (2001) for the details.

3.1 A Statistical Model

Assuming that $\boldsymbol{\zeta}_t$ is an observable square integrable random vector defined on a probability space $(S, \mathcal{F}, \mathbb{P}(.))$, we can think of a *statistical generating mechanism* as an orthogonal decomposition of the form:

$$\boldsymbol{\zeta}_t = E(\boldsymbol{\zeta}_t \mid \mathcal{D}_t) + \mathbf{u}_t, \mathcal{D}_t \subset \mathcal{F}, \ t \in \mathbb{T} \tag{5}$$

where $\mathbf{m}_t = E(\boldsymbol{\zeta}_t \mid \mathcal{D}_t)$ and $\mathbf{u}_t = \boldsymbol{\zeta}_t - E(\boldsymbol{\zeta}_t \mid \mathcal{D}_t)$ define the systematic and non-systematic components. By construction:

$$\left.\begin{array}{ll} \text{(a)} & E(\mathbf{u}_t \mid \mathcal{D}_t) = 0 \\ \text{(b)} & Cov(\mathbf{u}_t \mid \mathcal{D}_t) = Cov(\boldsymbol{\zeta}_t \mid \mathcal{D}_t) \\ \text{(c)} & E(\mathbf{m}_t^\top \mathbf{u}_t \mid \mathcal{D}_t) = 0 \end{array}\right\} \ t \in \mathbb{T} \tag{6}$$

It is usually the case that the sub-sigma-field $\mathcal{D}_t$ is generated by an observable random vector $\boldsymbol{\xi}_t$, also defined on $(S, \mathcal{F}, \mathbb{P}(.))$, that is $\mathcal{D}_t = \sigma(\boldsymbol{\xi}_t)$. This enables the modeller to specify a statistical model exclusively in terms of the underlying joint distribution of the observables $\mathbf{W}_t = (\boldsymbol{\zeta}_t, \boldsymbol{\xi}_t)$ and provide a complete probabilistic interpretation to all the components of the model.

The basic idea is that when a structural model is embedded into a statistical model of the above general form, we can bestow operational meaning to the structural concepts by relating them to a well-defined framework that provides the foundations and the overarching framework for statistical inference.

Let us see how such a statistical framework can be specified to embed the structural model:

$$y_t = \boldsymbol{\alpha}^\top \mathbf{X}_t + \varepsilon_t, \ \varepsilon_t \sim \mathsf{N}(0, \sigma^2), \ t \in \mathbb{T}, \tag{7}$$

subject to the IV conditions (all r.v's are in mean deviation form) listed in Table 2.1.

Table 2.1. *Conditions for instrumental variables*

(i)	Non-orthogonality:	$E(\mathbf{X}_t\varepsilon_t) \neq 0$
(ii)	Instrument exogeneity:	$E(\mathbf{Z}_t\varepsilon_t) = 0$
(iii)	Instrument relevance:	$E(\mathbf{X}_t\mathbf{Z}_t^\top) = \mathbf{\Sigma}_{23} \neq 0$
(iv)	Instrument non-collinearity:	$E(\mathbf{Z}_t\mathbf{Z}_t^\top) = \mathbf{\Sigma}_{33} > 0$
(v)	Instrument relevance:	$E(y_t\mathbf{Z}_t^\top) = \sigma_{13} \neq 0$

Looking at the moments conditions of Table 2.1, it becomes apparent that the underlying distribution, in terms of which these conditions can be formally defined, is the joint distribution of the observable random variables $\mathbf{W}_t := (y_t, \mathbf{X}_t, \mathbf{Z}_t)$:

$$\mathbf{W}_t \backsim \mathsf{D}(0, \mathbf{\Sigma}),\ \mathbf{\Sigma} > 0,\ t \in \mathbb{T}$$

For simplicity we will assume that $f(y_t, \mathbf{x}_t, \mathbf{z}_t; \boldsymbol{\phi})$ is multivariate Normal (see Spanos, 1995, on the role of normality in the case of linear/homoskedastic models):

$$\begin{pmatrix} y_t \\ \mathbf{X}_t \\ \mathbf{Z}_t \end{pmatrix} \backsim \mathsf{N}\left(\begin{pmatrix} 0 \\ 0 \\ 0 \end{pmatrix}, \begin{pmatrix} \sigma_{11} & \sigma_{21} & \sigma_{31} \\ \sigma_{12} & \mathbf{\Sigma}_{22} & \mathbf{\Sigma}_{32} \\ \sigma_{13} & \mathbf{\Sigma}_{23} & \mathbf{\Sigma}_{33} \end{pmatrix} \right), \quad t \in \mathbb{T} \tag{8}$$

The first issue we need to address is the **statistical model** based on $f(y_t, \mathbf{x}_t, \mathbf{z}_t; \boldsymbol{\psi})$ which will *embed* the **structural model** (7) together with conditions (i)–(v), in its context.

3.2 *Embedding a Structural into a Statistical Model*

An educated guess as to the statistical model that can accommodate conditions (iii)–(v) is $f(y_t, \mathbf{x}_t \mid \mathbf{z}_t; \boldsymbol{\psi}_2)$:

$$\begin{pmatrix} y_t \\ \mathbf{X}_t \end{pmatrix} \mid \mathbf{Z}_t \Bigg) \sim \mathsf{N}\left(\begin{pmatrix} \boldsymbol{\beta}_1^\top \mathbf{Z}_t \\ \mathbf{B}_2^\top \mathbf{Z}_t \end{pmatrix}, \begin{pmatrix} \omega_{11} & \omega_{12} \\ \omega_{21} & \mathbf{\Omega}_{22} \end{pmatrix} \right).$$

This conditional distribution is related to the joint distribution via:

$$f(y_t, \mathbf{x}_t, \mathbf{z}_t; \boldsymbol{\psi}) = f(y_t, \mathbf{x}_t \mid \mathbf{z}_t; \boldsymbol{\psi}_2) \cdot f(\mathbf{z}_t; \boldsymbol{\psi}_1),\ \forall (y_t, \mathbf{x}_t, \mathbf{z}_t) \in \mathbb{R}_W$$

where $\mathbb{R}_W := (\mathbb{R} \times \mathbb{R}^m \times \mathbb{R}^p)$, and the statistical model is based on the orthogonal decomposition:

$$\mathbf{y}_t = E(\mathbf{y}_t \mid \mathbf{Z}_t) + \mathbf{u}_t = \mathbf{B}^\top \mathbf{Z}_t + \mathbf{u}_t, \quad t \in \mathbb{T} \tag{9}$$

where $\mathbf{y}_t^\top := (y_t : \mathbf{X}_t^\top)$, $\mathbf{B}^\top := (\boldsymbol{\beta}_1^\top : \mathbf{B}_2^\top)$, $\mathbf{u}_t^\top := (u_{1t} : \mathbf{u}_{2t}^\top)$. Hence, the appropriate statistical model appears to be the **multivariate linear regression** (viewed as the implicit reduced form (IRF)):

$$\boxed{\begin{array}{c} y_t = \boldsymbol{\beta}_1^\top \mathbf{Z}_t + u_{1t}, \qquad \mathbf{X}_t = \mathbf{B}_2^\top \mathbf{Z}_t + \mathbf{u}_{2t} \\ \begin{pmatrix} u_{1t} \\ \mathbf{u}_{2t} \end{pmatrix} \sim \mathsf{N}\left(\begin{pmatrix} 0 \\ 0 \end{pmatrix}, \begin{pmatrix} \omega_{11} & \boldsymbol{\omega}_{12} \\ \boldsymbol{\omega}_{21} & \boldsymbol{\Omega}_{22} \end{pmatrix} \right) \end{array}} \tag{10}$$

where the underlying parameterization $\boldsymbol{\psi}_2 := (\boldsymbol{\beta}_1, \mathbf{B}_2, \omega_{11}, \boldsymbol{\omega}_{12}, \boldsymbol{\Omega}_{22})$ is:

$$\boldsymbol{\beta}_1 = \boldsymbol{\Sigma}_{33}^{-1}\boldsymbol{\sigma}_{31}, \ \mathbf{B}_2 = \boldsymbol{\Sigma}_{33}^{-1}\boldsymbol{\Sigma}_{32}, \qquad \omega_{11} = \sigma_{11} - \boldsymbol{\sigma}_{13}\boldsymbol{\Sigma}_{33}^{-1}\boldsymbol{\sigma}_{31}$$

$$\boldsymbol{\omega}_{12} = \sigma_{12} - \sigma_{13}\boldsymbol{\Sigma}_{33}^{-1}\Sigma_{32} = \boldsymbol{\omega}_{21}^\top, \qquad \boldsymbol{\Omega}_{22} = \Sigma_{22} - \Sigma_{23}\boldsymbol{\Sigma}_{33}^{-1}\Sigma_{32}$$

It is important to note that the statistical parameterization in $\boldsymbol{\psi}_2$ is inextricably bound up with the orthogonal decomposition (9) satisfying:

$$\begin{array}{ll} \text{(a)} & E(\mathbf{u}_t \mid \mathbf{Z}_t) = 0 \\ \text{(b)} & Cov(\mathbf{u}_t \mid \mathbf{Z}_t) = Cov(\mathbf{y}_t \mid \mathbf{Z}_t) \\ \text{(c)} & E(\mathbf{m}_t^\top \mathbf{u}_t \mid \mathbf{Z}_t) = 0, \text{ where } \mathbf{m}_t = E(\mathbf{y}_t \mid \mathbf{Z}_t) \end{array} \tag{11}$$

in so far as conditions (a)–(c) imply the parameterization in $\boldsymbol{\psi}_2$ and vice versa; see Spanos (1995) for the details.

The MLR model enables one to evaluate the validity of the IV conditions (iii)–(v) (Table 2.1), since condition (iv) is necessary for the existence of all these parameters (see Spanos and McGuirk, 2002), and (iii) and (v) can be assessed via the hypotheses:

(I) $\mathbf{B}_2 \neq 0, \ \boldsymbol{\beta}_1 \neq 0$

respectively. Moreover, (i) implies that:

(II) $E(\mathbf{Z}_t u_{1t}) = 0, \qquad E(\mathbf{Z}_t \mathbf{u}_{2t}^\top) = 0$

(III) $E(\mathbf{X}_t u_{1t}) = \boldsymbol{\omega}_{21} \neq 0, \quad E(\mathbf{X}_t \mathbf{u}_{2t}^\top) = \boldsymbol{\Omega}_{22} > 0$

3.3 *The Linking-up Model*

How does the structural error in (7) relate to the statistical errors $(u_{1t}, \mathbf{u}_{2t})$?

In order to make this connection more apparent let us proceed to reparameterize $f(y_t, \mathbf{x}_t \mid \mathbf{z}_t; \psi_2)$ using a further reduction of the form:

$$f(y_t, \mathbf{x}_t \mid \mathbf{z}_t; \psi_2) = f(y_t \mid \mathbf{x}_t, \mathbf{z}_t; \varphi_3) \cdot f(\mathbf{x}_t \mid \mathbf{z}_t; \varphi_2), \ \forall (y_t, \mathbf{x}_t, \mathbf{z}_t) \in \mathbb{R}_W. \tag{12}$$

This amounts to multiplying $(y_t, \mathbf{X}_t)$ by a non-singular matrix: $\mathcal{D} = \begin{pmatrix} 1 & -\omega_{12}\Omega_{22}^{-1} \\ 0 & \mathbb{I} \end{pmatrix}$:

$$\begin{pmatrix} y_t - \omega_{12}\Omega_{22}^{-1}\mathbf{X}_t \\ \mathbf{X}_t \end{pmatrix} \sim \mathsf{N}\left(\begin{pmatrix} [\beta_1^\top - \omega_{12}\boldsymbol{\Omega}_{22}^{-1}\mathbf{B}_2^\top]\mathbf{Z}_t \\ \mathbf{B}_2^\top\mathbf{Z}_t \end{pmatrix} \begin{pmatrix} \omega_{11} - \omega_{12}\boldsymbol{\Omega}_{22}^{-1}\omega_{21} & 0 \\ 0 & \boldsymbol{\Omega}_{22} \end{pmatrix}\right).$$

The resulting *reparameterized* statistical model is:

$$\boxed{\begin{array}{c} y_t = \boldsymbol{\alpha}_0^\top \mathbf{X}_t + \boldsymbol{\gamma}_0^\top \mathbf{Z}_t + \varepsilon_{0t}, \qquad \mathbf{X}_t = \mathbf{B}_2^\top \mathbf{Z}_t + \mathbf{u}_{2t} \\ \begin{pmatrix} \varepsilon_{0t} \\ \mathbf{u}_{2t} \end{pmatrix} \sim \mathsf{N}\left(\begin{pmatrix} 0 \\ 0 \end{pmatrix}, \begin{pmatrix} \sigma_0^2 & 0 \\ 0 & \boldsymbol{\Omega}_{22} \end{pmatrix}\right), \ t \in \mathbb{T} \end{array}} \tag{13}$$

where $\varphi_3 := (\boldsymbol{\alpha}_0, \boldsymbol{\gamma}_0, \sigma_0^2)$, $\varphi_2 := (\mathbf{B}_2, \boldsymbol{\Omega}_{22})$:

$$\boldsymbol{\alpha}_0 = \boldsymbol{\Omega}_{22}^{-1}\omega_{21}, \ \boldsymbol{\gamma}_0 = \boldsymbol{\beta}_1 - \mathbf{B}_2\boldsymbol{\alpha}_0, \quad \sigma_0^2 = \omega_{11} - \omega_{12}\boldsymbol{\Omega}_{22}^{-1}\omega_{21}$$

and the new statistical error is: $\varepsilon_{0t} = u_{1t} - \mathbf{u}_{2t}^\top\boldsymbol{\alpha}_0$.

A moment's reflection suggests that the number of unknown parameters of the original IRF ($\psi_2 = (\boldsymbol{\beta}_1, \mathbf{B}_2, \omega_{11}, \omega_{12}, \boldsymbol{\Omega}_{22})$) and the above reparameterized form in terms of (φ_2, φ_3) remains the same. Given that the statistical error term is defined by:

$$\varepsilon_{0t} = y_t - E(y_t \mid \mathbf{X}_t, \mathbf{Z}_t) \ \Rightarrow \ E(\mathbf{Z}_t\varepsilon_{0t}) = 0, \ E(\mathbf{X}_t\varepsilon_{0t}) = 0$$

in contrast to: $E(\mathbf{X}_t\varepsilon_t) \neq 0$. The advantage of this approach is that we will be able to give operational meaning to $E(\mathbf{X}_t\varepsilon_t) \neq 0$ in terms of transformations of the underlying statistical parameterizations.

3.4 *Reparameterization/Restriction*

A comparison between the first equation of the statistical (13) and the structural (7) models reveals that the link between the two specifications is provided by the restrictions $\boldsymbol{\gamma}_0 = 0$. If we were to impose the restrictions $\boldsymbol{\gamma}_0 = 0$, *in conjunction with* $\mathbf{B}_2 \neq 0$, $\boldsymbol{\beta}_1 \neq 0$, on the statistical (13), it will induce a reparameterization of $(\boldsymbol{\alpha}_0, \sigma_0^2)$, $\boldsymbol{\alpha}_0 \to \boldsymbol{\alpha}, \sigma_0^2 \to \sigma^2$, arising from imposing the restrictions: $\boldsymbol{\beta}_1 - \mathbf{B}_2\boldsymbol{\alpha} = 0$, with the structural error relating to the statistical errors via: $\varepsilon_t = u_{1t} - \boldsymbol{\alpha}^\top \mathbf{u}_{2t}$. That is, by embedding the structural model (7) in the context of the MLR (10) we will be able to operationalize the conditions $E(\mathbf{X}_t\varepsilon_t) \neq 0$, $E(\mathbf{Z}_t\varepsilon_t) = 0$, in the form of restrictions inducing a reparameterization/restriction on the MLR; while preserving the IV conditions (iii)–(v) (Table 2.1). The result is given in the following theorem.

Theorem 1 Given that $p \geq m$ and $\mathsf{rank}(\mathbf{B}_2) = m$, the structural parameters $(\boldsymbol{\alpha}, \sigma^2)$ take the form:

$$
\begin{aligned}
\boldsymbol{\alpha}_0|_{\boldsymbol{\gamma}_0=0} &= \boldsymbol{\alpha} = (\boldsymbol{\Sigma}_{23}\boldsymbol{\Sigma}_{33}^{-1}\boldsymbol{\Sigma}_{23})^{-1}\boldsymbol{\Sigma}_{23}\boldsymbol{\Sigma}_{33}^{-1}\boldsymbol{\sigma}_{31} \\
\sigma_0^2\Big|_{\boldsymbol{\gamma}_0=0} &= \sigma^2 = \sigma_{11} - \boldsymbol{\sigma}_{12}(\boldsymbol{\Sigma}_{23}\boldsymbol{\Sigma}_{33}^{-1}\boldsymbol{\Sigma}_{23})^{-1}\boldsymbol{\Sigma}_{23}\boldsymbol{\Sigma}_{33}^{-1}\boldsymbol{\sigma}_{31}
\end{aligned}
\tag{14}
$$

Proof Since $\mathsf{rank}(\mathbf{B}_2) = m$, the solution of $\boldsymbol{\beta}_1 - \mathbf{B}_2\boldsymbol{\alpha}_0 = 0$ remains unchanged if it's pre-multiplied by positive definite matrix $\boldsymbol{\Sigma}_{33}^{\frac{1}{2}}$, i.e. $\boldsymbol{\Sigma}_{33}^{\frac{1}{2}}(\boldsymbol{\beta}_1 - \mathbf{B}_2\boldsymbol{\alpha}_0) = 0 \Rightarrow \boldsymbol{\Sigma}_{33}^{-\frac{1}{2}}\boldsymbol{\sigma}_{31} - \boldsymbol{\Sigma}_{33}^{-\frac{1}{2}}\boldsymbol{\Sigma}_{32}\boldsymbol{\alpha}_0 = \boldsymbol{\Sigma}_{33}^{-\frac{1}{2}}\boldsymbol{\sigma}_{31} - \mathbf{H}\boldsymbol{\alpha}_0 = 0$, $\mathbf{H} = \boldsymbol{\Sigma}_{33}^{\frac{1}{2}}\mathbf{B}_2 = \boldsymbol{\Sigma}_{33}^{-\frac{1}{2}}\boldsymbol{\Sigma}_{32}$, $\mathsf{rank}(\mathbf{H}) = m$. Hence, this linear system can be solved uniquely using $\mathbf{H}\left(\mathbf{H}^\top\mathbf{H}\right)^{-1}\mathbf{H}^\top = \boldsymbol{\Sigma}_{33}^{-\frac{1}{2}}\boldsymbol{\Sigma}_{32}\left(\boldsymbol{\Sigma}_{23}\boldsymbol{\Sigma}_{33}^{-1}\boldsymbol{\Sigma}_{32}\right)^{-1}\boldsymbol{\Sigma}_{23}\boldsymbol{\Sigma}_{33}^{-\frac{1}{2}}$, the left inverse of $\mathbf{H}$, giving rise to:

$$
\boldsymbol{\alpha} = \left(\mathbf{H}^\top\mathbf{H}\right)^{-1}\mathbf{H}^\top(\boldsymbol{\Sigma}_{33}^{-\frac{1}{2}}\boldsymbol{\sigma}_{31}) = (\boldsymbol{\Sigma}_{23}\boldsymbol{\Sigma}_{33}^{-1}\boldsymbol{\Sigma}_{23})^{-1}\boldsymbol{\Sigma}_{23}\boldsymbol{\Sigma}_{33}^{-1}\boldsymbol{\sigma}_{31}
$$

Substituting this into σ_0^2 yields σ^2.

In the special case $p = m$, $\boldsymbol{\Sigma}_{23}$ is a non-singular square matrix and $(\boldsymbol{\alpha}, \sigma^2)$ become:

$$
\boldsymbol{\alpha} = \boldsymbol{\Sigma}_{23}^{-1}\boldsymbol{\sigma}_{31}, \quad \sigma^2 = \sigma_{11} - \boldsymbol{\sigma}_{12}\boldsymbol{\Sigma}_{23}^{-1}\boldsymbol{\sigma}_{31}
$$

It is very important to emphasize that the restrictions $\boldsymbol{\gamma}_0 = 0$ are not ordinary constraints on regression coefficients. They are "identification" restrictions that should be imposed in conjunction with $\mathbf{B}_2 \neq 0$, $\boldsymbol{\beta}_1 \neq 0$ to identify the structural parameters in $\boldsymbol{\alpha}$. Solving $\boldsymbol{\beta}_1 - \mathbf{B}_2\boldsymbol{\alpha}_0 = 0$ for $\boldsymbol{\alpha}$ identifies these coefficients by inducing a re-parametrization $\boldsymbol{\alpha}_0 \rightarrow \boldsymbol{\alpha}$ (using up m restrictions) – these restrictions are *non-testable*. As shown in section 5.1, for a given identified $\boldsymbol{\alpha}$, $\boldsymbol{\beta}_1 - \mathbf{B}_2\boldsymbol{\alpha} = 0$ implies $(p - m)$ *testable* restrictions implicitly imposed on the IRF parameters $(\boldsymbol{\beta}_1, \mathbf{B}_2)$ – the so-called *overidentifying restrictions*.

If the restrictions $\boldsymbol{\gamma}_0 = 0$ are treated as ordinary coefficient restrictions and imposed on (13) independently of $(\boldsymbol{\beta}_1, \mathbf{B}_2)$, then the first equation of the statistical model (13) reduces to the well-known linear regression model:

$$y_t = \boldsymbol{\beta}^\top \mathbf{X}_t + u_t,\ u_t \sim \mathsf{N}(0, \sigma_u^2),\ t \in \mathbb{T} \tag{15}$$

where $\boldsymbol{\beta} = \boldsymbol{\Sigma}_{22}^{-1}\boldsymbol{\sigma}_{21}$, $\sigma_u^2 = \sigma_{11} - \sigma_{12}\boldsymbol{\Sigma}_{22}^{-1}\boldsymbol{\sigma}_{21}$ and $E(\mathbf{X}_t u_t) = 0$, based exclusively on:

$$f(y_t \mid \mathbf{x}_t, \mathbf{z}_t; \boldsymbol{\varphi}_3)|_{\boldsymbol{\gamma}_0 = 0} = f(y_t \mid \mathbf{x}_t; \boldsymbol{\varphi}_4) \tag{16}$$

and ignoring the fact that $\boldsymbol{\varphi}_2$ and $\boldsymbol{\varphi}_3$ in (12) are now interrelated via $\boldsymbol{\gamma}_0 = 0$ and $f(\mathbf{x}_t \mid \mathbf{z}_t; \boldsymbol{\varphi}_2)$ cannot be disregarded for inferences concerning $\boldsymbol{\varphi}_3$; see Engle *et al.* (1983). That is, imposing the restriction $\boldsymbol{\gamma}_0 = 0$ on (13) independently of $(\boldsymbol{\beta}_1, \mathbf{B}_2)$ amounts to treating $\mathbf{X}_t$ as exogenous, which contradicts the IVs set up!

In summary, the structural model:

$$y_t = \boldsymbol{\alpha}^\top \mathbf{X}_t + \varepsilon_t,\ \varepsilon_t \sim \mathsf{N}(0, \sigma^2),\ t \in \mathbb{T} \tag{17}$$

subject to the conditions (i)–(v) (Table 2.1), can be viewed as a *reparameterization/restriction* of the **statistical model** (13), the restrictions being:

$$\boldsymbol{\gamma}_0 = \boldsymbol{\beta}_1 - \mathbf{B}_2\boldsymbol{\alpha}_0 = 0, \text{ subject to } \mathbf{B}_2 \neq 0,\ \boldsymbol{\beta}_1 \neq 0 \tag{18}$$

where the statistical model (13) is a reparameterization of the **MLR model** (10).

In order to see this, let us verify the IV conditions (i)–(v) (Table 2.1) in the context of the statistical model (13).

(i) $E(\mathbf{X}_t\varepsilon_t) \neq 0$ follows from the fact that the structural error takes the form:

$$\varepsilon_t = y_t - \boldsymbol{\alpha}^\top \mathbf{X}_t = u_{1t} - \mathbf{u}_{2t}^\top \boldsymbol{\alpha} = y_t - \boldsymbol{\alpha}^\top \mathbf{X}_t - \mathbf{Z}_t^\top (\boldsymbol{\beta}_1 - \mathbf{B}_2\boldsymbol{\alpha})$$

since $(\boldsymbol{\beta}_1 - \mathbf{B}_2\boldsymbol{\alpha}) = 0$ and thus:

$$E(\mathbf{X}_t\varepsilon_t) = E(\mathbf{X}_t u_{1t}) - E(\mathbf{X}_t \mathbf{u}_{2t}^\top)\boldsymbol{\alpha} = \boldsymbol{\omega}_{21} - \boldsymbol{\Omega}_{22}\boldsymbol{\alpha} \neq 0$$

given that $\boldsymbol{\alpha} = (\boldsymbol{\Sigma}_{23}\boldsymbol{\Sigma}_{33}^{-1}\boldsymbol{\Sigma}_{23})^{-1}\boldsymbol{\Sigma}_{23}\boldsymbol{\Sigma}_{33}^{-1}\boldsymbol{\sigma}_{31} \neq \boldsymbol{\alpha}_0 = \boldsymbol{\Omega}_{22}^{-1}\boldsymbol{\omega}_{21}$.
In contrast, since $\boldsymbol{\alpha}_0 = \boldsymbol{\Omega}_{22}^{-1}\boldsymbol{\omega}_{21}$:

$$E(\mathbf{X}_t\varepsilon_{0t}) = E(\mathbf{X}_t u_{1t}) - E(\mathbf{X}_t \mathbf{u}_{2t}^\top)\boldsymbol{\alpha}_0 = \boldsymbol{\omega}_{21} - \boldsymbol{\Omega}_{22}\boldsymbol{\alpha}_0 = 0$$

(ii) $E(\mathbf{Z}_t\varepsilon_t) = 0$ follows from $\varepsilon_t = u_{1t} - \mathbf{u}_{2t}^\top\boldsymbol{\alpha}$:

$$\begin{aligned} E(\mathbf{Z}_t\varepsilon_t) &= E(\mathbf{Z}_t u_{1t}) - E(\mathbf{Z}_t \mathbf{u}_{2t}^\top)\boldsymbol{\alpha} \\ &= (\boldsymbol{\sigma}_{31} - \boldsymbol{\Sigma}_{33}\boldsymbol{\beta}_1) - (\boldsymbol{\Sigma}_{32} - \boldsymbol{\Sigma}_{33}\mathbf{B}_2)\,\boldsymbol{\alpha} = 0 \end{aligned} \tag{19}$$

This holds irrespective of the particular value of $\boldsymbol{\alpha}$.

(iii)–(v) The IV conditions $E(\mathbf{X}_t\mathbf{Z}_t^\top) = \boldsymbol{\Sigma}_{23} \neq 0$, $E(\mathbf{Z}_t\mathbf{Z}_t^\top) = \boldsymbol{\Sigma}_{33} > 0$, $E(y_t\mathbf{Z}_t^\top) = \boldsymbol{\sigma}_{13} \neq 0$ follow from the restrictions:

$$\boldsymbol{\beta}_1 \neq 0, \ \mathbf{B}_2 \neq 0$$

in the context of the MLR model.

3.5 Instrumental Variables and Endogeneity/Exogeneity

The above discussion brought out three important dimensions of the notion of instrumental variables:

1 the endogeneity of $\mathbf{X}_t$,
2 the dependence of all endogenous variables $(y_t, \mathbf{X}_t)$ on $\mathbf{Z}_t$,
3 the view that the structural model constitutes a reparameterization/ restriction of a statistical model.

The endogeneity of $\mathbf{X}_t$ in the IVs context is often understood narrowly in terms of the non-orthogonality $E(\mathbf{X}_t\varepsilon_t) \neq 0$, but in fact the above discussion makes it clear that this coincides with the historically older notion of endogeneity referring to "variables determined within the model in question". The essence of both of these notions is captured by the concept of *weak exogeneity* proposed by Engle *et al.* (1983) which is based on the underlying distributions and their parameterizations. It turns out, however, that one needs to distinguish between two forms of the latter concept, the structural and statistical weak exogeneity.

Structural weak endogeneity In the context of the statistical model (13) based on:

$$f(y_t, \mathbf{x}_t \mid \mathbf{z}_t; \psi_2) = f(y_t \mid \mathbf{x}_t, \mathbf{z}_t; \varphi_3) \cdot f(\mathbf{x}_t \mid \mathbf{z}_t; \varphi_2),\ \forall\, (y_t, \mathbf{x}_t, \mathbf{z}_t) \in \mathbb{R}_W \tag{20}$$

$\mathbf{X}_t$ is *statistically weakly exogenous* with respect to φ_3 because $\varphi_2 \in \Phi_2$ and $\varphi_3 \in \Phi_3$ are *variation free* if no restrictions are imposed. However, when the *identifying restrictions* $(\boldsymbol{\beta}_1 - \mathbf{B}_2\boldsymbol{\alpha}) = 0$ for the structural parameters $(\boldsymbol{\alpha}, \sigma^2)$ are imposed, the variation freeness no longer holds between $\varphi_2^* := (\mathbf{B}_2, \boldsymbol{\Omega}_{22})$ and $\varphi_3^* := (\boldsymbol{\alpha}, \sigma^2)$ in the context of:

$$f(y_t, \mathbf{x}_t \mid \mathbf{z}_t; \psi_2^*) = f(y_t \mid \mathbf{x}_t; \varphi_3^*) \cdot f(\mathbf{x}_t \mid \mathbf{z}_t; \varphi_2^*),\ \forall (y_t, \mathbf{x}_t, \mathbf{z}_t) \in \mathbb{R}_W. \tag{21}$$

This is because $\varphi_3^* = \mathbf{H}(\varphi_2^*)$, $\varphi_2^* \in \Phi_2$, $\varphi_3^* \in \Phi_3^* \subset \Phi_3$, that is φ_2^* and φ_3^* are functionally dependent (see Engle *et al.*, 1983). The imposition of "identifying" restrictions that abnegate variation freeness can be considered as an example where the weak exogeneity is rescinded by *structural* considerations. This is in contrast to revoking weak exogeneity for *statistical* considerations as in the case of the Student's t linear regression model; see Spanos (1994).

The rescinding of weak exogeneity and declaring $\mathbf{X}_t$ endogenous, provides the key to the concept of IVs. The functional dependence between the parameters φ_2^* and φ_3^* arises because of the imposed *conditional independence* between $\mathbf{Z}_t$ and y_t given $\mathbf{X}_t$:

$$f(y_t \mid \mathbf{x}_t, \mathbf{z}_t; \varphi_3) = f(y_t \mid \mathbf{x}_t; \varphi_3^*),\ \forall (y_t, \mathbf{x}_t, \mathbf{z}_t) \in \mathbb{R}_W \tag{22}$$

within the broader context of $f(y_t, \mathbf{x}_t \mid \mathbf{z}_t; \psi_2^*)$, even though $\mathbf{Z}_t$ is *not* (unconditionally) independent of $(y_t, \mathbf{X}_t)$. Hence, the structural model (7) should not be viewed in isolation, but in the context of the **complete model**:

$$\boxed{\begin{array}{c} y_t = \boldsymbol{\alpha}^\top \mathbf{X}_t + \varepsilon_t, \qquad \mathbf{X}_t = \mathbf{B}_2^\top \mathbf{Z}_t + \mathbf{u}_{2t} \\ \begin{pmatrix} \varepsilon_t \\ \mathbf{u}_{2t} \end{pmatrix} \sim \mathsf{N}\left(\begin{pmatrix} 0 \\ 0 \end{pmatrix}, \begin{pmatrix} \sigma^2 & \mathbf{v}_{21}^\top \\ \mathbf{v}_{21} & \boldsymbol{\Omega}_{22} \end{pmatrix} \right),\ t \in \mathbb{T} \end{array}} \tag{23}$$

where $\mathbf{v}_{21} = (\boldsymbol{\omega}_{21} - \boldsymbol{\Omega}_{22}\boldsymbol{\alpha})$. It is interesting to note that $\mathbf{v}_{21} = 0$ only when $E(\mathbf{X}_t\varepsilon_t) = 0$, and this provides the hypothesis for the so-called *exogeneity tests*; see Hausman (1978).

This brings out the crucial role played by the Implicit Reduced Form (IRF) (MLR model) which ties together the other two dimensions of IVs, (2) and (3) above. The MLR is a statistical model which provides the statistical context within which structural inference concerning $(\boldsymbol{\alpha}, \sigma^2)$ takes place. The relationship between the structural $(\boldsymbol{\varphi}_3^* := (\boldsymbol{\alpha}, \sigma^2))$ and statistical $(\boldsymbol{\psi}_2 := (\boldsymbol{\beta}_1, \mathbf{B}_2, \omega_{11}, \boldsymbol{\omega}_{12}, \boldsymbol{\Omega}_{22}))$ parameters being of crucial importance in shedding light on the orthogonality conditions between observables and unobservable error terms. Using the distributions of the observable random variables involved we can revisit the questions of choice and optimality of instruments.

4 The Nature and Choice of Instruments

4.1 The "Implicit Reduced Form"

As argued above, the IRF plays a crucial role in the IVs argument because, when viewed as a statistical on its own right, it provides the statistical context in which the structural model is embedded for statistical inference purposes. In this sense, the MLR has a life of its own as a statistical model, which is related to but also separate from the structural model. The IV conditions (iii)–(v) (Table 2.1) necessitate the estimation of the MLR:

$$y_t = \boldsymbol{\beta}_1^\top \mathbf{Z}_t + u_{1t}, \quad \mathbf{X}_t = \mathbf{B}_2^\top \mathbf{Z}_t + \mathbf{u}_{2t}$$
$$\begin{pmatrix} u_{1t} \\ \mathbf{u}_{2t} \end{pmatrix} \sim \mathsf{N}\left(\begin{pmatrix} 0 \\ 0 \end{pmatrix}, \begin{pmatrix} \omega_{11} & \boldsymbol{\omega}_{12} \\ \boldsymbol{\omega}_{21} & \boldsymbol{\Omega}_{22} \end{pmatrix} \right) \tag{24}$$

in order to ensure that $\boldsymbol{\beta}_1$ and $\mathbf{B}_2$ are well-defined before on can proceed to consider any inference concerning the structural model:

$$y_t = \boldsymbol{\alpha}^\top \mathbf{X}_t + \varepsilon_t, \ \varepsilon_t \sim \mathsf{N}(0, \sigma^2), \ t \in \mathbb{T} \tag{25}$$

$\boldsymbol{\beta}_1$ and $\mathbf{B}_2$ being well-defined has two equally important dimensions. The first is a statistical significance issue $\boldsymbol{\beta}_1 \neq 0$ and $\mathbf{B}_2 \neq 0$, but the second, and more substantive, is that the statistical model in the context of which the estimation and testing relating to $\boldsymbol{\beta}_1 \neq 0$ and $\mathbf{B}_2 \neq 0$ is **statistically adequate,** that is the probabilistic assumptions comprising the model are valid for the data in question. The validity of the premises ensures the reliability of inference concerning the coefficient parameters $\boldsymbol{\beta}_1$ and $\mathbf{B}_2$; see Spanos (1986). The statistical significance issue is concerned with the IV conditions of relevance (iii) $E(\mathbf{X}_t\mathbf{Z}_t^\top) = \boldsymbol{\Sigma}_{23} \neq 0$, (v) $E(y_t\mathbf{Z}_t^\top) = \boldsymbol{\sigma}_{13} \neq 0$, that is the instrumental variables $\mathbf{Z}_t$ that are correlated with $(y_t, \mathbf{X}_t)$. In this sense it involves *potential* factors that influence the process giving rise to the data $(y_t, \mathbf{x}_t,\ t = 1, 2, \ldots, T)$, and economic theory has a crucial role to play in determining these factors. On the other hand, statistical adequacy concerns the validity of the probabilistic assumptions underlying the system of equations in (24) and will ensure that the testing of (iii)–(iv) is reliable.

The proper specification of the implicit reduced form, viewed as a statistical model, is given in Table 2.2; note the notation $\mathbf{y}_t := (y_t, \mathbf{X}_t^\top)^\top, \mathbf{B} = (\boldsymbol{\beta}_1^\top, \mathbf{B}_2^\top)^\top$. The validity of these assumptions ensures the appropriateness of the sampling distributions:

$$\begin{array}{ll} \widehat{\mathbf{B}} = (\mathbf{Z}^\top\mathbf{Z})^{-1}\mathbf{Z}^\top\mathbf{Y}, & \widehat{\mathbf{B}} \sim \mathsf{N}(\mathbf{B}, (\boldsymbol{\Omega} \otimes (Z^\top\mathbf{Z})^{-1})) \\ \widehat{\boldsymbol{\Omega}} = \frac{1}{T}(\mathbf{Y} - \mathbf{Z}^\top\widehat{\mathbf{B}})^\top(\mathbf{Y} - \mathbf{Z}^\top\widehat{\mathbf{B}}), & T\widehat{\boldsymbol{\Omega}} \sim \mathsf{W}(\boldsymbol{\Omega}, T - p) \end{array} \tag{26}$$

and in turn, ensures the reliability of the statistical properties of the estimators, the goodness-of-fit measures and the statistical tests associated with $\boldsymbol{\theta}$.

It is well-known that goodness-of-fit measures are misleading, and inferences are often unreliable, when the estimated model is *misspecified*. Moreover, in view of the fact that the structural model (25) constitutes a reparameterization/restriction of the statistical model, the statistical adequacy of the latter ensures the reliability of inference in the context of the former. The structural and statistical models differ only by the overidentifying restrictions in the case where $p > m$. Hence, when the statistical model is statistically adequate one needs to test the validity of

Table 2.2. *Multivariate linear regression (MLR) model,* $\mathbf{y}_t := (y_t, \mathbf{X}_t^\top)^\top$, $\mathbf{B} = (\beta_1^\top, \mathbf{B}_2^\top)^\top$

$$\boxed{\mathbf{y}_t = \mathbf{B}^\top\mathbf{Z}_t + \mathbf{u}_t,\ t \in \mathbb{T}}$$

(1)	$D(\mathbf{y}_t \mid \mathbf{Z}_t; \boldsymbol{\theta})$ is Normal
(2)	$E(\mathbf{y}_t \mid \mathbf{Z}_t) = \mathbf{Z}_t^\top\mathbf{B}$ – linear in $\mathbf{Z}_t$
(3)	$Cov(\mathbf{y}_t \mid \mathbf{Z}_t) = \boldsymbol{\Omega}$ – homoskedastic (free of $\mathbf{Z}_t$)
(4)	$\boldsymbol{\theta} := (\mathbf{B}, \boldsymbol{\Omega})$ are t-invariant
(5)	$(\mathbf{y}_t \mid \mathbf{Z}_t),\ t = 1, 2, \ldots, T$ are independent r.v's

the overidentifying restrictions to ensure the reliability of inference in the context of the structural model. When the MLR model is misspecified, however, inference in the context of the structural model, including the overidentifying restrictions test, is likely to be unreliable!

4.2 *Weak Instruments*

The problem of *weak instruments*, understood as the correlation between $\mathbf{Z}_t$ and $\mathbf{X}_t$ being insignificant, was first raised by Nelson and Startz (1990a). They showed that IV estimators can be *inconsistent* and *highly biased* in the direction of OLS estimates, giving rise to unreliable IV-based inference; these results were extended by Bounds *et al.* (1995), Hall *et al.* (1996), Staiger and Stock (1997), and Wang and Zivot (1998).

Viewing the problem of weak instruments in the context of (24) we can see that it can be assessed in the context of the "reduced form" of $\mathbf{X}_t$:

$$\mathbf{X}_t = \mathbf{B}_2^\top \mathbf{Z}_t + \mathbf{u}_{2t} \tag{27}$$

by testing the hypothesis:

$$H_0 : \mathbf{B}_2 = 0, \text{ vs. } H_1 : \mathbf{B}_2 \neq 0. \tag{28}$$

This hypothesis can be tested using a likelihood ratio test or some variation thereof; see Anderson (1984). If the null hypothesis is not rejected then one of the IV conditions:

$$\text{(iii) Instrument relevance:} \quad E(\mathbf{X}_t \mathbf{Z}_t^\top) = \mathbf{\Sigma}_{23} \neq 0 \tag{29}$$

is violated and thus the standard inference results associated with the IV estimator $\widehat{\alpha}_{IV} = (\mathbf{X}^\top \mathbf{P}_Z \mathbf{X})^{-1} \mathbf{X}^\top \mathbf{P}_Z \mathbf{y}$ no longer hold. The weak instruments problems of inconsistency and strong bias in the direction of OLS estimates can be easily explained if we return to the **linking up statistical model**:

$$y_t = \boldsymbol{\alpha}_0^\top \mathbf{X}_t + \boldsymbol{\gamma}_0^\top \mathbf{Z}_t + \varepsilon_{0t} \tag{30}$$

where $\boldsymbol{\gamma}_0 = \mathbf{\Sigma}_{33}^{-1} \boldsymbol{\sigma}_{31} - \mathbf{\Sigma}_{33}^{-1} \mathbf{\Sigma}_{32} \boldsymbol{\alpha}_0$ and $\boldsymbol{\alpha}_0 = \mathbf{\Sigma}_{22}^{-1} \boldsymbol{\sigma}_{21} - \mathbf{\Sigma}_{22}^{-1} \mathbf{\Sigma}_{23} \boldsymbol{\gamma}_0$. A moment's reflection suggests that under H_0: $\mathbf{B}_2 = 0$,

(i) the identification restrictions $\boldsymbol{\gamma}_0 = \boldsymbol{\beta}_1 - \mathbf{B}_2 \boldsymbol{\alpha}_0 = 0$ are no longer binding, and

(ii) $\boldsymbol{\gamma}_0|_{\mathbf{B}_2=0} = \boldsymbol{\gamma}_1 = \mathbf{\Sigma}_{33}^{-1} \boldsymbol{\sigma}_{31}$ and $\boldsymbol{\alpha}_0|_{\mathbf{B}_2=0} = \boldsymbol{\alpha}_1 = \mathbf{\Sigma}_{22}^{-1} \boldsymbol{\sigma}_{21}$, that is the implicit parameterization of $\boldsymbol{\alpha}_1$ coincides with the OLS parameterization. These results suggest that weak instruments lead to an *underindentified* model, since $\mathsf{rank}(\boldsymbol{\Sigma}_{23}) < m$, and the probability limit of $\widehat{\boldsymbol{\alpha}}_{IV}$ is now $\boldsymbol{\alpha}_1 = \boldsymbol{\Sigma}_{22}^{-1}\sigma_{21}$, which coincides with the probability limit of the OLS estimator $\widehat{\boldsymbol{\alpha}}_{OLS} = (\mathbf{X}^\top\mathbf{X})^{-1}\mathbf{X}^\top\mathbf{y}$.

Testing $H_0 : \mathbf{B}_2 = 0$, however, can be completely unreliable when the MLR model given in Table 2.2 is statistically misspecified. A certain set of instruments $\mathbf{Z}_t$, when $H_0 : \mathbf{B}_2 = 0$ is tested, might be diagnosed incorrectly as *weak* because of certain forms of misspecifications of the underlying MLR model. It could also happen that a set of instruments is incorrectly diagnosed as *strong* because of the presence of misspecifications. This, for instance, could happen when some of the data series from the variables $(y_t, \mathbf{X}_t, \mathbf{Z}_t)$ are trending, but the estimated MLR does not include any trends; see Spanos (2000). This is because the reliability of the significance test is based on validity of the statistical premises; assumptions (1)–(5) of the MLR model given in Table 2.2. Hence, before any test for weak instruments is performed the modeler should ensure that the MLR model is *statistically adequate.*

4.3 *Statistical Adequacy and the Reliability of Inference*

Statistically Adequate MLR Model Assuming that assumptions (1)–(5) of the MLR model are satisfied by data, we can proceed to estimate $(\boldsymbol{\alpha}, \sigma^2)$ in the context of:

$$\mathbf{y} = \mathbf{X}\boldsymbol{\alpha} + \boldsymbol{\varepsilon} \tag{31}$$

using maximum likelihood (ML) or least-squares (LS) methods. The latter methods are often more intuitive, and thus we will consider the easiest of the LS methods of estimation which will be accomplished in two stages.

Stage 1. Estimate $\mathbf{B}_2$ by least-squares in the context of (24) to get:

$$\mathbf{X} = \mathbf{Z}\widehat{\mathbf{B}}_2 + \widehat{\mathbf{U}}_2 = \widehat{\mathbf{X}} + \widehat{\mathbf{U}}_2, \text{ where } \widehat{\mathbf{B}}_2 = (\mathbf{Z}^\top\mathbf{Z})^{-1}\mathbf{Z}^\top\mathbf{X} \tag{32}$$

and substitute $\mathbf{X} = \mathbf{Z}\widehat{\mathbf{B}}_2 + \widehat{\mathbf{U}}_2$ into (25) to yield:

$$\mathbf{y} = \mathbf{X}\boldsymbol{\alpha} + \boldsymbol{\varepsilon} = (\mathbf{Z}\widehat{\mathbf{B}}_2 + \widehat{\mathbf{U}}_2)\boldsymbol{\alpha} + \boldsymbol{\varepsilon} = \mathbf{Z}\widehat{\mathbf{B}}_2\boldsymbol{\alpha} + (\widehat{\mathbf{U}}_2\boldsymbol{\alpha} + \boldsymbol{\varepsilon}).$$

In view of the fact that $\varepsilon_t = u_{1t} - \mathbf{u}_{2t}^\top\boldsymbol{\alpha}$, $\mathbf{Z}$ is orthogonal to the new error term $\mathbf{U}_2\boldsymbol{\alpha} + \boldsymbol{\varepsilon} = \mathbf{u}_1$. This enables us to proceed to the second stage to estimate $(\boldsymbol{\alpha}, \sigma^2)$ having ensured that $\boldsymbol{\Sigma}_{23} \neq 0$, $\boldsymbol{\sigma}_{31} \neq 0$, and the estimators $(\widehat{\mathbf{B}}, \widehat{\boldsymbol{\Omega}})$ have the sampling distributions (26) we assume they have; see Spanos (1986, pp. 630–1).

Stage 2. Estimate $\boldsymbol{\alpha}$ by least-squares in the context of $\mathbf{y} = \widehat{\mathbf{X}}\boldsymbol{\alpha} + \widehat{\mathbf{U}}_2\boldsymbol{\alpha} + \boldsymbol{\varepsilon}$, giving rise to the IV estimator:

$$\widehat{\boldsymbol{\alpha}}_{IV} = (\widehat{\mathbf{X}}^{\top}\widehat{\mathbf{X}})^{-1}\widehat{\mathbf{X}}^{\top}\mathbf{y} = (\mathbf{X}^{\top}\mathbf{P}_Z\mathbf{X})^{-1}\mathbf{X}^{\top}\mathbf{P}_Z\mathbf{y}, \quad \mathbf{P}_Z = \mathbf{Z}(\mathbf{Z}^{\top}\mathbf{Z})^{-1}\mathbf{Z}^{\top}$$

and then estimate σ^2 using: $\widehat{\sigma}^2 = \frac{1}{T}(\mathbf{y} - \mathbf{X}\widehat{\boldsymbol{\alpha}}_{IV})^{\top}(\mathbf{y} - \mathbf{X}\widehat{\boldsymbol{\alpha}}_{IV})$.

Note that $\widehat{\boldsymbol{\alpha}}_{IV} = \left(\mathbf{X}^{\top}\mathbf{Z}\widehat{\mathbf{B}}_2\right)^{-1}\mathbf{X}^{\top}\mathbf{Z}\widehat{\boldsymbol{\beta}}_1$, is a function of the reduced form OLS estimators $(\widehat{\boldsymbol{\beta}}_1, \widehat{\mathbf{B}}_2)$, and any form of misspecification at the level of the reduced form (24) is likely to affect the sampling distribution and properties of both IV estimators $(\widehat{\boldsymbol{\alpha}}_{IV}, \widehat{\sigma}^2)$; and thus it will affect the reliability of the IV-based inference.

Statistically Inadequate MLR Model Consider the case where the estimated MLR model (Table 2.1) turns out to be statistically misspecified. A particularly common misspecification arises in the case where the data for $(y_t, \mathbf{X}_t, \mathbf{Z}_t)$ are time series and the t-invariance and temporal independence assumptions (4)–(5) of Table 2.2 are often invalid. In such a case the MLR needs to be respecified in order to account for temporal dependence in the data. For the sake of the argument let us assume that the respecified IRF model that turns out to be statistically adequate comes in the form of the Multivariate Dynamic Linear Regression model (see Table 2.3), where we use one lag for simplicity, and $\delta_0(t)$ denotes the constant terms which can be functions of t. The respecified (30)

Table 2.3. *Multivariate dynamic linear regression model,* $\mathbf{y}_t := \left(y_t, \mathbf{X}_t^{\top}\right)^{\top}$

$$\mathbf{y}_t = \delta_0(t) + \mathbf{A}_0^{\top}\mathbf{y}_{t-1} + \mathbf{A}_1^{\top}\mathbf{Z}_t + \mathbf{A}_2^{\top}\mathbf{Z}_{t-1} + \mathbf{u}_t, \; t \in \mathbb{T},$$

(1)	$D(\mathbf{y}_t \mid \mathbf{Z}_t, \mathbf{Z}_{t-1}, \mathbf{y}_{t-1}; \boldsymbol{\theta})$ is Normal
(2)	$E(\mathbf{y}_t \mid \mathbf{Z}_t, \mathbf{Z}_{t-1}, \mathbf{y}_{t-1}) = \delta_0(t) + \mathbf{A}_0^{\top}\mathbf{y}_{t-1} + \mathbf{A}_1^{\top}\mathbf{Z}_t + \mathbf{A}_2^{\top}\mathbf{Z}_{t-1}$
(3)	$Cov(\mathbf{y}_t \mid \mathbf{Z}_t, \mathbf{Z}_{t-1}, \mathbf{y}_{t-1}) = \boldsymbol{\Omega}$ – homoskedastic
(4)	$\boldsymbol{\theta} := (\delta_0, \mathbf{A}_0, \mathbf{A}_1, \mathbf{A}_2, \Omega)$ are t-invariant
(5)	$(\mathbf{y}_t \mid \mathbf{Z}_t, \mathbf{Z}_{t-1})$, $t = 1, 2, \ldots, T$ is a Markov process

will take the form:

$$y_t = \delta_0(t) + \delta_1 y_{t-1} + \boldsymbol{\alpha}_0^\top \mathbf{X}_t + \boldsymbol{\gamma}_0^\top \mathbf{Z}_t + \boldsymbol{\alpha}_1^\top \mathbf{X}_{t-1} + \boldsymbol{\gamma}_1^\top \mathbf{Z}_{t-1}^\top + \varepsilon_{0t},$$

$$\varepsilon_{0t} \sim \mathsf{N}(0, \sigma_0^2), \; t \in \mathbb{T}. \qquad (33)$$

If we compare (33) with (25) we can see that, in addition to the initial identification restrictions $\boldsymbol{\gamma}_0 = 0$, some additional exclusion restrictions are needed to reduce the former to the latter:

$$\boldsymbol{\gamma}_1 = 0, \;\; \boldsymbol{\alpha}_1 = 0, \;\; \delta_1 = 0, \;\; \delta_0(t) = 0. \qquad (34)$$

These restrictions are highly unlikely to be valid in practice, for time series data; raising the possibility that some of these variables might appear explicitly in the context of the structural model.

The important conclusion is that whatever additional variables are included in the respecified IRF to ensure its statistical adequacy, they become relevant instruments and need to be included in an extended set of instruments. Hence, relevant instruments are no longer only the ones suggested by economic theory ($\mathbf{Z}_t$) but the extended set $\mathbf{Z}_t^* := (\mu(t), \mathbf{Z}_t, \mathbf{Z}_{t-1}, \mathbf{y}_{t-1})$, giving rise to the IV estimator:

$$\widehat{\boldsymbol{\alpha}}_{IV}^* = (\mathbf{X}^\top \mathbf{P}_Z^* \mathbf{X})^{-1} \mathbf{X}^\top \mathbf{P}_\mathbf{Z}^* \mathbf{y}, \;\; \mathbf{P}_\mathbf{Z}^* = \mathbf{Z}^*(\mathbf{Z}^{*\top}\mathbf{Z}^*)^{-1}\mathbf{Z}^{*\top}. \qquad (35)$$

Any IV estimator based on a misspecified IRF is likely to give rise to unreliable inferences because the inference propositions in (26) no longer hold!

The Choice of Instruments and Statistical Considerations Addressing the problem of choosing optimal instruments begins with economic theory and factual considerations relating to the observable phenomenon of interest, but it also has a crucial statistical dimension. Armed with the instruments $\mathbf{Z}_t$, as suggested by economic theory considerations the modeller will make the final decision on the set of relevant instruments $\mathbf{Z}_t^*$ by enlarging (if necessary) the initial set with variables which are needed to render the IRF $\mathbf{y}_t = \mathbf{B}^\top \mathbf{Z}_t + \mathbf{u}_t$, $t \in \mathbb{T}$, statistically adequate for the data in question. That is, test assumptions (1)–(5) thoroughly and respecify the model to ensure that no departures from these assumptions are detected. The enlarging of the initial instrument set $\mathbf{Z}_t$ might necessitate including lags, trends or dummy variables to capture any temporal dependence and/or heterogeneity in the data. This will require the modeller to do a thorough job, not only with the misspecification testing of the IRF, but also with the respecification of the statistical model in order to capture the systematic information disregarded by the original model. In some cases, there might not be a statistically adequate model based only on the initial instrument set enlarged by lags and trends. In such cases additional variables might be needed to capture the systematic information in the data and the modeller needs to return to economic theory and the observable phenomenon of interest. Hence, the choice of instruments relates to both theory and statistical information in the sense that their choice involves both theoretical (natural experiments generating $(y_t, \mathbf{X}_t)$) and statistical considerations (no misspecifications).

This raises important questions concerning the reliability of empirical modelling because in practice the IRF is rarely estimated explicitly and even more rarely tested for possible misspecifications. In principle, the statistical model underlying any structural model has a life of its own and should be viewed as providing the statistical framework in the context of which the structural inference takes place. For further discussion on the importance of the reduced form in analyzing the structural form, see Spanos (1986,1990) and Maasoumi (1986).

4.4 2SLS as the Quintessential IV Estimator

The above discussion has revealed that there is substantial phylogenetic relation between the structural model of equations (1) and a single equation, say the first, in a simultaneous equations model (SEM):

$$\left.\begin{aligned} y_{1t} &= \mathbf{y}_{1t}^{\top}\gamma_1 + \mathbf{X}_{1t}^{\top}\delta_1 + \varepsilon_{1t}, \\ \mathbf{Y}_{1t} &= \mathbf{X}_{1t}^{\top}\mathbf{B}_{12} + \mathbf{X}_{(1)t}^{\top}\mathbf{B}_{22} + \mathbf{u}_{1t} = \mathbf{X}_t^{\top}\mathbf{B}_{.2} + \mathbf{u}_{1t}, \end{aligned}\right\} \quad t \in \mathbb{T} \tag{36}$$

where $(y_{1t}, \mathbf{y}_{1t}^{\top}, \mathbf{x}_{1t}^{\top})$ denote the primary endogenous, the included endogenous and the included exogenous variables, respectively. Indeed, one of the purposes of the discussion above has been to make a case that a structural model with stochastic explanatory variables correlated with the error term should been viewed in the context of the IRF which provides the statistical framework for structural inference. As we can see, (36) extends the structural equation model (23) by including some additional exogenous variables $(\mathbf{X}_{1t})$, rendering the structural model more realistic.

What is particularly important from the point of view of choosing optimal instruments, is that the SEM sheds considerable light on the issue because the reduced form is no longer implicitly but explicit. Moreover, it suggests that in choosing instruments the structural form for the explanatory "endogenous" variables should play a major role.

It should come as no surprise that the 2SLS estimation procedure coincides with the IV method discussed above. The first stage:

$$\mathbf{Y}_1 = \mathbf{X}\widehat{\mathbf{B}}_{.2} + \widehat{\mathbf{U}}_1 = \widehat{\mathbf{Y}}_1 + \widehat{\mathbf{U}}_1, \quad \text{where } \widehat{\mathbf{Y}}_1 = \mathbf{X}(\mathbf{X}^\top\mathbf{X})^{-1}\mathbf{X}\mathbf{Y}_1 = \mathbf{P}_X\mathbf{Y}_1 \tag{37}$$

and substitution of $\mathbf{Y}_1 = \widehat{\mathbf{Y}}_1 + \widehat{\mathbf{U}}_1$ gives rise to:
$\mathbf{y}_1 = \widehat{\mathbf{Y}}_1\boldsymbol{\gamma}_1 + \mathbf{X}_1\boldsymbol{\delta}_1 + \widehat{\mathbf{U}}_1\gamma_1 + \boldsymbol{\varepsilon}_1.$
This substitution amounts to a rearrangement that brings back the reduced form errors; see Spanos (1986, pp. 630–1). The 2SLS estimator is an IV estimator:

$$\begin{pmatrix}\widetilde{\boldsymbol{\gamma}}_1\\ \widetilde{\boldsymbol{\delta}}_1\end{pmatrix} = \begin{pmatrix}\mathbf{Y}_1^\top\mathbf{P}_X\mathbf{Y}_1 & \mathbf{Y}_1^\top\mathbf{P}_X\mathbf{X}_1\\ \mathbf{X}_1^\top\mathbf{P}_X\mathbf{Y}_1^\top & \mathbf{X}_1^\top\mathbf{X}_1\end{pmatrix}^{-1}\begin{pmatrix}\mathbf{Y}_1^\top\mathbf{P}_X\mathbf{y}_1\\ \mathbf{X}_1^\top\mathbf{y}_1\end{pmatrix}. \tag{38}$$

The similarity between the IV and the 2SLS arguments can be best brought out by noting that the equation corresponding to the link model (30) is the unrestricted form:

$$y_{1t} = \mathbf{Y}_{1t}^\top\boldsymbol{\gamma}_1 + \mathbf{X}_{1t}^\top\boldsymbol{\delta}_1 + \mathbf{Y}_{(1)t}^\top\boldsymbol{\gamma}_{(1)} + \mathbf{X}_{(1)t}^\top\boldsymbol{\delta}_{(1)} + \varepsilon_{1t}^*$$

where $\left(\mathbf{Y}_{(1)t}, \mathbf{X}_{(1)t}\right)$ denote the excluded endogenous and exogenous variables, the exclusion restrictions being: $\boldsymbol{\gamma}_{(1)} = 0, \;\; \boldsymbol{\delta}_{(1)} = 0$. This gives rise to the following restrictions analogous to the identifying restrictions (18):

$$\mathbf{B}_{12}\boldsymbol{\gamma}_1 + \boldsymbol{\delta}_1 = \boldsymbol{\beta}_{11}, \;\; \mathbf{B}_{22}\boldsymbol{\gamma}_1 = \boldsymbol{\beta}_{12} \tag{39}$$

where $(\boldsymbol{\beta}_{11}, \boldsymbol{\beta}_{12})$ are the parameters of the reduced form associated with y_{1t}:

$$\mathbf{y}_1 = \mathbf{X}_1\boldsymbol{\beta}_{11} + \mathbf{X}_{(1)}\boldsymbol{\beta}_{12} + \mathbf{u}_1. \tag{40}$$

As we can see, the 2SLS estimator is indeed the quintessential IV estimator because it has all the elements of the IV argument as presented above and in addition it has an explicit (not implicit) reduced form! The direct analogy between the IV argument and the estimation of structural equations was first brought out most clearly by Sargan (1958).

5 The Reliability of IV-based Inference

The above discussion has put forward the view that the proper statistical framework for analysing the structural model:

$$y_t = \boldsymbol{\alpha}^\top \mathbf{X}_t + \varepsilon_t,\ E(\mathbf{X}_t \varepsilon_t) \neq 0,\ \ (\varepsilon_t \mid \mathbf{Z}_t) \backsim \mathsf{N}(0, \sigma^2) \tag{41}$$

is provided by the MLR model (Table 2.1) $\left(\mathbf{y}_t := \left(y_t, \mathbf{X}_t^\top\right)^\top, \mathbf{B} = \left(\boldsymbol{\beta}_1^\top, \mathbf{B}_2^\top\right)^\top\right)$:

$$\mathbf{y}_t = \mathbf{Z}_t^\top \mathbf{B} + \mathbf{u}_t,\ E(\mathbf{Z}_t \mathbf{u}_t) = 0,\ (\mathbf{u}_t \mid \mathbf{Z}_t) \backsim \mathsf{N}(0, \boldsymbol{\Omega}),\ t \in \mathbb{T} \tag{42}$$

viewed as an implicit reduced form (IRF). It has been shown that the structural parameters $\left(\boldsymbol{\alpha}, \sigma^2\right)$ can be viewed as a *reparameterization/restriction* of the statistical parameters $(\mathbf{B}, \boldsymbol{\Omega})$ via $\boldsymbol{\beta}_1 - \mathbf{B}_2\boldsymbol{\alpha} = 0$.

The question that naturally arises is whether establishing the *statistical adequacy* of the MLR is sufficient for securing the reliability of IV-based inference concerning $\left(\boldsymbol{\alpha}, \sigma^2\right)$. The answer depends on the identification status of the structural model.

Just-identified case: $p = m$. In this case $\mathbf{B}_2$ is a non-singular square matrix and the structural parameters $(\boldsymbol{\alpha}, \sigma^2)$ constitute a simple *reparameterization* of the statistical coefficients $(\mathbf{B}, \boldsymbol{\Omega})$:

$$\boldsymbol{\alpha} = \mathbf{B}_2^{-1}\boldsymbol{\beta}_1 = \boldsymbol{\Sigma}_{23}^{-1}\boldsymbol{\sigma}_{31},\ \ \sigma^2 = \sigma_{11} - \boldsymbol{\sigma}_{12}\mathbf{B}_2^{-1}\boldsymbol{\beta}_1 = \sigma_{11} - \boldsymbol{\sigma}_{12}\boldsymbol{\Sigma}_{23}^{-1}\boldsymbol{\sigma}_{31}. \tag{43}$$

Hence, in the just-identified case, the statistical adequacy of the MLR model is sufficient to secure the reliability of inference based on the IV estimators:

$$\widehat{\boldsymbol{\alpha}}_{IV} = (\mathbf{Z}^\top \mathbf{X})^{-1} \mathbf{Z}^\top \mathbf{y},\ \ \widehat{\sigma}^2 = \tfrac{1}{T-m}(\mathbf{y} - \mathbf{X}\widehat{\boldsymbol{\alpha}}_{IV})^\top (\mathbf{y} - \mathbf{X}\widehat{\boldsymbol{\alpha}}_{IV}). \tag{44}$$

Overidentified case: $p > m$. In this case the restrictions $\boldsymbol{\beta}_1 - \mathbf{B}_2\boldsymbol{\alpha} = 0$ are more than necessary to identify $\boldsymbol{\alpha}$, and as argued above, they indirectly restrict the statistical parameters $(\mathbf{B}, \boldsymbol{\Omega})$. In this sense the structural model constitutes a reparameterization/restriction of the statistical model, where the over-identifying restrictions are now testable in the context of the statistical model. Hence, the statistical adequacy of the statistical model is not sufficient to secure the reliability of the IV-based inference. The latter also requires the validity of the over-identifying restrictions.

5.1 *Testing Overidentifying Restrictions/Instrument Validity*

As shown in section 3, given the statistical parameters $(\boldsymbol{\beta}_1, \mathbf{B}_2)$ where $\text{rank}(\mathbf{B}_2) = m$, the system of restrictions:

$$\boldsymbol{\Sigma}_{33}^{\frac{1}{2}}(\boldsymbol{\beta}_1 - \mathbf{B}_2\boldsymbol{\alpha}) = 0$$

yields a unique solution for $\boldsymbol{\alpha} = (\boldsymbol{\Sigma}_{23}\boldsymbol{\Sigma}_{33}^{-1}\boldsymbol{\Sigma}_{23})^{-1}\boldsymbol{\Sigma}_{23}\boldsymbol{\Sigma}_{33}^{-1}\boldsymbol{\sigma}_{31}$ based on $\mathbf{P}_H = \mathbf{H}\left(\mathbf{H}^\top\mathbf{H}\right)^{-1}\mathbf{H}^\top$, where $\mathbf{H} = \boldsymbol{\Sigma}_{33}^{-\frac{1}{2}}\boldsymbol{\Sigma}_{32}$, a $p \times m$ idempotent matrix with $\text{rank}(\mathbf{P}_H) = m$. On the other hand, for a given $\boldsymbol{\alpha}$, the restrictions $\boldsymbol{\beta}_1 - \mathbf{B}_2\boldsymbol{\alpha} = 0$ impose $(p - m)$ constraints on the statistical parameters $(\boldsymbol{\beta}_1, \mathbf{B}_2)$. To see this, substitute $\boldsymbol{\alpha}$ back into the identifying restrictions:

$$\left[\boldsymbol{\Sigma}_{33}^{-1} - \boldsymbol{\Sigma}_{33}^{-1}\boldsymbol{\Sigma}_{32}(\boldsymbol{\Sigma}_{23}\boldsymbol{\Sigma}_{33}^{-1}\boldsymbol{\Sigma}_{23})^{-1}\boldsymbol{\Sigma}_{23}\boldsymbol{\Sigma}_{33}^{-1}\right]\boldsymbol{\sigma}_{31} = 0.$$

For a given $\boldsymbol{\alpha}$, this implies the following:

$$\left[\mathbf{I}_p - \boldsymbol{\Sigma}_{33}^{-1}\boldsymbol{\Sigma}_{32}(\boldsymbol{\Sigma}_{23}\boldsymbol{\Sigma}_{33}^{-1}\boldsymbol{\Sigma}_{23})^{-1}\boldsymbol{\Sigma}_{23}\right]\boldsymbol{\beta}_1 = 0, \text{ or } (\mathbf{I} - \mathbf{P}_H)\boldsymbol{\beta}_1 = 0 \quad (45)$$

where $(\mathbf{I}_p - \mathbf{P}_H)$ is also an idempotent matrix with $\text{rank}(\mathbf{I}_p - \mathbf{P}_H) = \text{rank}(\mathbf{I}_p) - \text{rank}(\mathbf{P}_H) = (p - m)$. This indicates most clearly that the overidentifying restrictions are testable because they constitute $(p - m)$ restrictions on $\boldsymbol{\beta}_1$.

The first test for the overidentifying restrictions was proposed by Anderson and Rubin (1949) as a likelihood ratio test:

$$LR = T\ln\left(\frac{\widehat{\boldsymbol{\varepsilon}}_{IV}^\top\widehat{\boldsymbol{\varepsilon}}_{IV}}{\widehat{\boldsymbol{\varepsilon}}_{IV}^\top(\mathbf{I} - \mathbf{P}_Z)\widehat{\boldsymbol{\varepsilon}}_{IV}}\right) \quad (46)$$

where $\widehat{\boldsymbol{\varepsilon}}_{IV} = \mathbf{y} - \mathbf{X}\widehat{\boldsymbol{\alpha}}_{IV}$, $\mathbf{P}_Z = \mathbf{Z}(\mathbf{Z}^\top\mathbf{Z})^{-1}\mathbf{Z}^\top$. Sargan (1958) proposed a Lagrange multiplier form of the same test:

$$LM = T\left(\frac{\widehat{\boldsymbol{\varepsilon}}_{IV}^\top\mathbf{P}_Z\widehat{\boldsymbol{\varepsilon}}_{IV}}{\widehat{\boldsymbol{\varepsilon}}_{IV}^\top\widehat{\boldsymbol{\varepsilon}}_{IV}}\right) \underset{\alpha}{\overset{H_0}{\backsim}} \chi^2(p - m) \quad (47)$$

where $(p-m)$ is the number of *overidentifying restrictions.* This test statistic is equal to the uncentred R^2 from the auxiliary regression of $\widehat{\boldsymbol{\varepsilon}}_{IV}$ on all the instruments $\mathbf{Z}_t$. An F-type form of the overidentifying restrictions test, that has better finite sample properties, was suggested by Basmann (1960):

$$F = \left(\frac{\widehat{\boldsymbol{\varepsilon}}_{IV}^{\top}\mathbf{P}_Z\widehat{\boldsymbol{\varepsilon}}_{IV}}{\widehat{\boldsymbol{\varepsilon}}_{IV}^{\top}(\mathbf{I}-\mathbf{P}_Z)\widehat{\boldsymbol{\varepsilon}}_{IV}}\right)\left(\frac{p-m}{T-p}\right) \underset{appx.}{\overset{H_0}{\backsim}} \mathsf{F}(p-m, T-p). \tag{48}$$

To elucidate the last two test statistics note that the numerator is the square norm of:

$$\mathbf{P}_Z\widehat{\boldsymbol{\varepsilon}}_{IV} = \mathbf{P}_Z\mathbf{y} - \mathbf{P}_Z\mathbf{X}(\mathbf{X}^{\top}\mathbf{P}_z\mathbf{X})^{-1}\mathbf{X}^{\top}\mathbf{P}_z\mathbf{y} \tag{49}$$

which is the sample analogue to (45) since:

$$\mathbf{P}_Z\widehat{\boldsymbol{\varepsilon}}_{IV} = \mathbf{Z}\left[\mathbf{I}_p - (\mathbf{Z}^{\top}\mathbf{Z})^{-1}\mathbf{Z}^{\top}\mathbf{X}(\mathbf{X}^{\top}\mathbf{Z}(\mathbf{Z}^{\top}\mathbf{Z})^{-1}\mathbf{Z}^{\top}\mathbf{X})^{-1}\mathbf{X}^{\top}\mathbf{Z}\right](\mathbf{Z}^{\top}\mathbf{Z})^{-1}\mathbf{Z}^{\top}\mathbf{y}$$

This confirms the above derivation indicating that the hypothesis being tested by the overidentifying restrictions test is:

$$H_0 : (\mathbf{I}_p - \mathbf{P}_H)\boldsymbol{\beta}_1 = 0, \text{ vs. } H_1 : (\mathbf{I}_p - \mathbf{P}_H)\boldsymbol{\beta}_1 \neq 0.$$

(Madgalinos and Symeonides, 1996, have derived a similar result using the non-centrality parameter of the overidentifying restrictions test.) A closer look at $(\mathbf{I}_p - \mathbf{P}_H)$ reveals that any attempt to separate the restrictions into "identifying" and "overidentifying" is completely arbitrary; see also Magdalinos (1988).

What all three overidentifying restrictions tests (46), (47) and (48) have in common is that their size and power properties depend crucially on the statistical adequacy of the implicit reduced form. The validity of their sampling distributions are crucially dependent on assumptions (1)–(5) of the MLR model, being valid for data $(\mathbf{y}, \mathbf{X}, \mathbf{Z})$. In this sense, the overidentifying restrictions tests are not misspecification tests as probing beyond the boundaries of the MLR model, such as those for assumptions (1)–(5). They constitute proper Neyman–Pearson tests probing within the boundaries of the MLR model; see Spanos (1999).

5.2 Testing "Exogeneity"

It was argued in section 3 that the complete structural model should also include the reduced form for $\mathbf{X}_t$ that is, it should be:

$$y_t = \boldsymbol{\alpha}^\top \mathbf{X}_t + \varepsilon_t, \quad \mathbf{X}_t = \mathbf{B}_2^\top \mathbf{Z}_t + \mathbf{u}_{2t}$$

$$\begin{pmatrix} \varepsilon_t \\ \mathbf{u}_{2t} \end{pmatrix} \sim \mathsf{N}\left(\begin{pmatrix} 0 \\ 0 \end{pmatrix}, \begin{pmatrix} \sigma^2 & \mathbf{v}_{21}^\top \\ \mathbf{v}_{21} & \boldsymbol{\Omega}_{22} \end{pmatrix} \right), \quad t \in \mathbb{T}. \tag{50}$$

It was also mentioned that traditional tests for "exogeneity" are based on the hypothesis:

$$H_0 : \mathbf{v}_{21} = 0 \ \text{ vs. } \ H_1 : \mathbf{v}_{21} \neq 0 \tag{51}$$

where $\mathbf{v}_{21} = (\boldsymbol{\omega}_{21} - \boldsymbol{\Omega}_{22}\boldsymbol{\alpha})$. We can now use the statistical parameterizations to elucidate what the "exogeneity" tests are actually assessing.

Expressing $\mathbf{v}_{21}$ in terms of the primary statistical parameters by substituting $\boldsymbol{\alpha}$ reveals that:

$$\begin{aligned} \mathbf{v}_{21} &= \left(\sigma_{21} - \Sigma_{23}\boldsymbol{\Sigma}_{33}^{-1}\sigma_{31}\right) - \left(\Sigma_{22} - \Sigma_{23}\Sigma_{33}^{-1}\Sigma_{32}\right) \\ &\quad \times (\boldsymbol{\Sigma}_{23}\boldsymbol{\Sigma}_{33}^{-1}\boldsymbol{\Sigma}_{23})^{-1}\boldsymbol{\Sigma}_{23}\boldsymbol{\Sigma}_{33}^{-1}\boldsymbol{\sigma}_{31} \\ &= \sigma_{21} - \Sigma_{22}(\boldsymbol{\Sigma}_{23}\boldsymbol{\Sigma}_{33}^{-1}\boldsymbol{\Sigma}_{23})^{-1}\boldsymbol{\Sigma}_{23}\boldsymbol{\Sigma}_{33}^{-1}\boldsymbol{\sigma}_{31} \end{aligned}$$

and thus: $\mathbf{v}_{21} = 0 \ \Leftrightarrow \ (\boldsymbol{\alpha}_1 - \boldsymbol{\alpha}) = 0$, where $\boldsymbol{\alpha}_1 = \Sigma_{22}^{-1}\sigma_{21}$. Hence, testing "exogeneity" can be written in the form of the hypothesis:

$$H_0 : (\boldsymbol{\alpha}_1 - \boldsymbol{\alpha}) = 0 \ \text{ vs. } \ H_1 : (\boldsymbol{\alpha}_1 - \boldsymbol{\alpha}) \neq 0. \tag{52}$$

This formulation sheds light on the Durbin–Wu–Hausman test statistic:

$$DWH = (\widehat{\boldsymbol{\alpha}}_1 - \widehat{\boldsymbol{\alpha}}_{IV})^\top \left[\hat{\sigma}^2[(\mathbf{X}^\top \mathbf{P}_z \mathbf{X})^{-1} - (\mathbf{X}^\top \mathbf{X})^{-1}]\right]^{-1} (\widehat{\boldsymbol{\alpha}}_1 - \widehat{\boldsymbol{\alpha}}_{IV}) \overset{H_0}{\underset{\alpha}{\backsim}} \chi^2(m)$$

(see Durbin, 1954; Wu, 1973; Hausman, 1978), where $\hat{\sigma}^2 = \frac{\widehat{\boldsymbol{\varepsilon}}_{IV}^\top \widehat{\boldsymbol{\varepsilon}}_{IV}}{T}$, $\widehat{\boldsymbol{\alpha}}_1 = (\mathbf{X}^\top \mathbf{X})^{-1}\mathbf{X}^\top \mathbf{y}$ and $\widehat{\boldsymbol{\alpha}}_{IV} = (\mathbf{X}^\top \mathbf{P}_Z \mathbf{X})^{-1}\mathbf{X}^\top \mathbf{P}_Z \mathbf{y}$ are the OLS and IV estimators of $\boldsymbol{\alpha}$ in $\mathbf{y} = \mathbf{X}\boldsymbol{\alpha} + \boldsymbol{\varepsilon}$. The statistic is the square norm of $(\widehat{\boldsymbol{\alpha}}_1 - \widehat{\boldsymbol{\alpha}}_{IV})$, the sample analogue of $(\boldsymbol{\alpha}_1 - \boldsymbol{\alpha})$.

In light of the above discussion, it becomes apparent that the DWH test depends, not only on the MLR model being statistically adequate, but also that the overidentifying restrictions being data acceptable; otherwise the interpretation of its results can be very equivocal (see Dhrymes, 1994). This raises serious questions about the wisdom of applying exogeneity tests in cases where neither the statistical adequacy or the data-acceptability of the overidentifying restrictions have been secured.

6 Conclusions

The primary conclusion of this chapter is that by embedding the structural model in the context of the statistical model suggested by the implicit reduced form (IRF), one can systematize the statistical underpinnings of the IV method. This viewpoint enhances our understanding of the method at both an intuitive as well as a more formal level, and sheds light on a number of issues, including the endogeneity/exogeneity dichotomy, the nature and choice of optimal instruments, the overidentifying restrictions tests, and the weak instruments problem. In particular, the choice and optimality of instruments depends crucially, not only on economic theory, but also on the statistical adequacy of the IRF. Indeed, statistical adequacy considerations play an important role in the choice of instruments in so far as only the set of instruments that give rise to a statistically adequate IRF can be considered "optimal". Hence, the choice of instruments and the optimality of the resulting IV estimator entails both theoretical as well as statistical considerations. The reliability of IV-based inference depends, not only on the statistical adequacy of the IRF and the validity of the overidentifying restrictions, but also on ensuring that the instruments are statistically significant in the context of a statistically adequate IRF; without statistically adequacy, the question of weak or strong instruments cannot even be addressed in a satisfactory manner! A statistically adequate model, specified in terms of a complete and consistent set of specific probabilistic assumptions, gives rise to reliable and incisive structural inference.

3 Nagar-Type Moment Approximations in Simultaneous Equation Models: Some Further Results

Garry D.A. Phillips

1 Introduction

In an important paper, Nagar (1959) analysed the small sample properties of consistent members of the general k-class of simultaneous equation estimators with non-stochastic k and, in particular, found expressions for the bias to the order of T^{-1} where T is the number of observations, and for the second moment matrix to the order of T^{-2}. To obtain the results, Nagar used an asymptotic expansion for the estimation error of the form:

$$(\hat{\alpha} - \alpha) = \sum_{s=1}^{p-1} T^{(-\frac{1}{2}s)} e_s + T^{(-\frac{1}{2}p)} r_p \tag{1}$$

where $\hat{\alpha}$ is an estimator for α and the $e_s, s = 1, 2, \ldots, p - 1$, and remainder term r_p, are all of stochastic order unity as $T \to \infty$. The sum of the retained terms is then assumed to mimic the behaviour of the estimation error and its moments provide the moment approximations for the estimator. To find the moment approximations typically requires the evaluation of the expectations of many, often complex, stochastic terms which can be both lengthy and tedious. In addition, Nagar's results were obtained under relatively restrictive conditions whereby the structural disturbances in each equation were assumed to be normally, independently and identically distributed. However, it is important that the effects of serial correlation in the disturbances be studied and Goldfeld and Quandt (1972) showed through simulations that the impact on estimation efficiency may be quite large. In Phillips (1978) I extended the Nagar results to cover a number of special cases of serial correlation in the disturbances which included the framework used by Goldfeld and Quandt while Magdalinos (1983) considered a model in which there is serial correlation in the equation of interest but not in the other equations. An alternative approach was used by Phillips (2000) where I expressed the k-class estimators as functions of a set underlying random variables, for example reduced form coefficient estimates, whereby the major part of the analysis is concerned with deriving the required partial derivatives in a standard Taylor series expansion. There is relatively little requirement to evaluate the expectations of stochastic terms and results can be obtained under much less restrictive conditions than those imposed by Nagar. In particular, serial correlation and heteroscedasticity of structural disturbances are permitted and and normality is assumed only when deriving the approximation for the second moment. I did not give explicit approximations in terms of structural parameters for particular cases but I do so in this chapter where I examine a case of considerable practical interest in which the disturbances are both contemporaneously and serially correlated and follow the particular generating scheme that was used by Parks (1967) in the context of a system of seemingly unrelated regression equations. The resulting moment approximations are then compared to those obtained by Nagar.

2 Model and Notation

I shall consider a simultaneous equation model containing G equations given by

$$By_t + \Gamma z_t = u_t, \quad t = 1, 2, \ldots \tag{2}$$

in which y_t is a $G \times 1$ vector of endogenous variables, z_t is a $K \times 1$ vector of strongly exogenous variables and u_t is a $G \times 1$ vector of structural parameters with $G \times G$ positive definite covariance matrix Σ. The matrices of structural disturbances, B and Γ are, respectively, $G \times G$ and $G \times K$. It is assumed that B is non-singular so that the reduced form equations corresponding to (2) are:

$$\begin{aligned} y_t &= -B^{-1}\Gamma z_t + B^{-1}u_t \\ &= \Pi z_t + v_t \end{aligned}$$

where Π is a $G \times K$ matrix of reduced form coefficients and v_t is a $G \times 1$ vector of reduced form disturbances with a $G \times G$ positive definite covariance matrix Ω. With T observations we may write the system as:

$$YB' + Z\Gamma' = U. \tag{3}$$

Here, Y is a $T \times G$ matrix of observations on endogenous variables, Z is a $T \times K$ matrix of observations on the strongly exogenous variables and U is a $T \times G$ matrix of structural disturbances all of which may be serially correlated. The first equation of the system will be written as:

$$y_1 = Y_2\beta + Z_1\gamma + u_1 \tag{4}$$

where y_1 and Y_2 are, respectively, a $T \times 1$ vector and a $T \times g$ matrix of observations on $g + 1$ endogenous variables, Z_1 is a $T \times k$ matrix of observations on k exogenous variables, β and γ are, respectively, $g \times 1$ and $k \times 1$ vectors of unknown parameters and u_1 is a $T \times 1$ vector of stationary disturbances with positive definite covariance matrix $E(u_1 u_1') = \Sigma_{11}$ and finite moments up to fourth order. The reduced form of the system includes:

$$Y_1 = Z\Pi_1 + V_1 \tag{5}$$

in which $Y_1 = (y_1 : Y_2), Z = (Z_1 : Z_2)$ is a $T \times K$ matrix of observations on K exogenous variables with an associated $K \times (g+1)$ matrix of reduced form parameters given by $\Pi_1 = (\pi_1 : \Pi_2)$, while $V_1 = (v_1 : V_2)$ is a $T \times (g + 1)$ matrix of reduced form disturbances. The transpose of each row of V_1 has zero mean vector and $(g + 1) \times (g + 1)$ positive definite matrix $\Omega_1 = (\omega_{ij})$ while the $(T \times (g + 1)) \times 1$ vector, $vec V_1$, has a positive definite covariance matrix of dimension $(T \times (g + 1)) \times (T \times (g + 1))$ given by $Cov(vec V_1) = \Omega_1^{vec}$ and finite moments up to fourth order. It is further assumed that:

1 the $T \times K$ matrix Z is strongly exogenous and of rank K with limit matrix $\lim_{T\to\infty} T^{-1}Z'Z = \Sigma_{ZZ}$, which is $K \times K$ positive definite, and that:
2 equation (1) is over-identified so that $K > g + k$, i.e. the number of excluded variables exceeds the number required for the equation to be just identified. In cases where second moments are analysed we shall assume that K exceeds $g + k$ by at least two. These over-identifying restrictions are sufficient to ensure that the Nagar expansion is valid in the case considered by Nagar and that the estimator moments exist: see Sargan (1974).

Following Parks (1967) we shall assume that the G disturbances are generated by the stationary autoregressive process:

$$u_{ti} = \rho_i u_{t-1,i} + \epsilon_{ti}, \quad |\rho_i| < 1, \quad i = 1, 2, \ldots, G \tag{6}$$

where the ε_{ti} are random variables satisfying the conditions:

$$E(\epsilon_{ti}) = 0, i = 1, 2, \ldots, G : t = 1, 2, \ldots, T$$

$$\begin{aligned} E(\varepsilon_{ti}\varepsilon_{t'j}) &= \sigma_{ij}, \text{ for } i, j = 1, 2, \ldots, G \text{ and } t = t' \\ &= 0, \text{ for } i, j = 1, 2, \ldots, G \text{ and } t \neq t'. \end{aligned}$$

The covariance matrix of the $T \times 1$ vectors u_i and u_j is given by

$$E(u_i u_j') = \frac{\sigma ij}{1 - \rho_j \rho_j} \begin{bmatrix} 1 & \rho_j & \rho_j^2 & \cdot & \rho_j^{T-2} & \rho_j^{T-1} \\ \rho_i & 1 & \rho_j & \cdot & \cdot & \rho_j^{T-2} \\ \rho_i^2 & \rho_i & 1 & \cdot & \cdot & \cdot \\ \cdot & \rho_i^2 & & & \cdot & \cdot \\ & & & & \cdot & \cdot \\ & \cdot & & & \cdot & \cdot \\ \cdot & & \cdot & & & \\ & \cdot & & & & \\ & & & \cdot & 1 & \rho_j \\ \cdot\rho_i^{T-1} & \rho_i^{T-2} & & & \rho_i & 1 \end{bmatrix}$$

$$= \sigma_{ij} \Sigma_{ij}, \quad i, j = 1, 2, \ldots\ldots, G. \tag{7}$$

We shall define $vecU$ as the $TG \times 1$ vector that is obtained by stacking the columns of U, and which has a covariance matrix given by:

$$E(vecU(vecU)') = \{\sigma_{ij} \Sigma_{ij}\}$$

$$= \begin{bmatrix} \sigma_{11}\Sigma_{11} & \sigma_{12}\Sigma_{12} & \cdot & \cdot & \cdot & \sigma_{1G}\Sigma_{1G} \\ \sigma_{21}\Sigma_{21} & \sigma_{22}\Sigma_{22} & \cdot & \cdot & \cdot & \cdot \\ \cdot & \cdot & \sigma_{33}\Sigma_{33} & & & \cdot \\ \cdot & \cdot & \cdot & \cdot & & \cdot \\ \cdot & \cdot & \cdot & & \cdot & \cdot \\ \sigma_{G1}\Sigma_{G1} & \sigma_{G2}\Sigma_{G2} & \cdot & \cdot & \cdot & \sigma_{GG}\Sigma_{GG} \end{bmatrix} \tag{8}$$

$$= \overset{vec}{\sum}.$$

Denote by i_p the $G \times 1$ unit vector with unity in the pth position and zeros elsewhere, $p = 1, 2, \ldots, G$. Then we may write the above matrix in the form

$$\sum^{vec} = \sum_{p=1}^{G} \sum_{q=1}^{G} (i_p i_q' \otimes \sigma_{pq} \Sigma_{pq})$$

which is a sum of $G \times G$ Kronecker products.

The matrix of reduced form disturbances is given by $V = U(B^{-1})'$. We are particularly interested in the first $g+1$ columns of V which are given by $V_1 = U(B^{g+1})'$ where $(B^{g+1})'$ denotes the first $g+1$ columns of $(B^{-1})'$. Using the relationship $vec V_1 = vec U(B^{g+1})' = (B^{g+1} \otimes I_T) vec U$ where $vec V_1$ is a $T \times (g+1)$ vector obtained by stacking the first $g+1$ columns of V, we may write the covariance matrix of $vec V_1$ as:

$$\begin{aligned}
E(vec V_1 (vec V_1)') &= E\big((B^{g+1} \otimes I_T) vec U)(vec U)')((B^{g+1})' \otimes I_T)\big) \\
&= (B^{g+1} \otimes I_T) \sum^{vec} \big((B^{g+1})' \otimes I_T\big) \\
&= (B^{g+1} \otimes I_T) \Bigg(\sum_{p=1}^{G} \sum_{q=1}^{G} i_p i_q' \otimes \sigma_{pq} \Sigma_{pq} \Bigg) \big((B^{g+1})' \otimes I_T\big) \\
&= \Bigg(\sum_{p=1}^{G} \sum_{q=1}^{G} B^{g+1} i_p i_q' (B^{g+1})' \otimes \sigma_{pq} \Sigma_{pq} \Bigg) \\
&= \Omega_1^{vec}.
\end{aligned}$$

In the case considered by Nagar, we may put $\Sigma_{pq} = I_T$, whereupon the covariance matrix Ω_1^{vec} takes a much simpler Kronecker product form: $(B^{g+1} \Sigma (B^{g+1})' \otimes I_T) = \Omega \otimes I_T$. As a result it is quite straightforward to find the Nagar moment approximations from Theorems 1 and 2 given in the next section. However, while Ω_1^{vec} does not have such a simple form here, the fact that it can be written in terms of Kronecker products, even a summation of them, makes it possible the find the required approximations.

2.1 An Alternative Approach to Obtaining Approximations for the First and Second Moments

We consider the estimation of the equation given in (4) by the method of 2SLS. It is well-known that the estimator can be written in the form

$$\hat{\alpha} = \begin{pmatrix} \hat{\beta} \\ \hat{\gamma} \end{pmatrix} = \begin{pmatrix} \hat{\Pi}_2' Z'Z\hat{\Pi}_2 & \hat{\Pi}_2' Z'Z_1 \\ Z_1'Z\hat{\Pi}_2 & Z_1'Z_1 \end{pmatrix}^{-1} \begin{pmatrix} \hat{\Pi}_2' Z'Z\hat{\pi}_1 \\ Z_1'Z\hat{\pi}_1 \end{pmatrix} \tag{10}$$

where $\hat{\Pi}_2 = (Z'Z)^{-1}Z'Y_2$ and $\hat{\pi}_1 = (Z'Z)^{-1}Z'y_1$. This representation of 2SLS was considered in Harvey and Phillips (1980). It is apparent that, conditional on the exogenous variables, the 2SLS estimators are functions of the matrix $\hat{\Pi}_1 = (\hat{\pi}_1 : \hat{\Pi}_2)$; hence we may write $\hat{\alpha} = f(vec\hat{\Pi}_1)$. As shown in Phillips (2000), the unknown parameter vector can be written as $\alpha = f(vec\Pi_1)$, so that the estimation error is $f(vec\hat{\Pi}_1) - f(vec\Pi_1)$. A Taylor expansion about the point $vec\Pi_1$ may then be employed directly to find a counterpart of the Nagar expansion. In fact, Phillips considered the general element of the estimation error $\hat{\alpha}_i - \alpha_i = e_i'(\hat{\alpha} - \alpha) = f_i(vec\hat{\Pi}_1) - f_i(vec\Pi_1)$, $i = 1, 2, \ldots, g + k$ where e_i' is a $1 \times (g + k)$ unit vector, and the bias approximation for the general case was found using the expansion:

$$\begin{aligned} f_i(vec\hat{\Pi}_1) =& f_i(vec\Pi_1) + (vec(\hat{\Pi}_1 - \Pi_1))' f_i^{(1)} \\ & + \frac{1}{2!}(vec(\hat{\Pi}_1 - \Pi_1))' f_i^{(2)} (vec(\hat{\Pi}_1 - \Pi_1)) \\ & + \frac{1}{3!}\Sigma_{r=1}^{K}\Sigma_{s=1}^{g+1}(\hat{\pi}_{rs} - \pi_{rs})(vec(\hat{\Pi}_1 - \Pi_1))' f_{i,rs}^{(3)} (vec(\hat{\Pi}_1 - \Pi_1)) \\ & + o_p(T^{-\frac{3}{2}}) \end{aligned}$$

where $f_i^{(1)}$ is a $K(g+1)$ vector of first-order partial derivatives, $\frac{\partial f_i}{\partial vec\hat{\Pi}_1}$: $f_i^{(2)}$ is a $(K(g + 1)) \times (K(g + 1))$ matrix of second-order partial derivatives, $\frac{\partial^2 f_i}{\partial vec\hat{\Pi}_1 (\partial vec\hat{\Pi}_1)'}$: and $f_{i,rs}^{(3)}$ is a $(K(g+1)) \times (K(g+1))$ matrix of third-order partial derivatives defined as $f_{i,rs}^{(3)} = \frac{\partial f_i^{(2)}}{\partial \pi_{rs}}$, $r = 1, \ldots, K$, $s = 1, \ldots, g + 1$. All derivatives are evaluated at $vec\Pi_1$. The bias approximation to order T^{-1} is then obtained by taking expectations of the first two terms of the stochastic expansion to yield:

$$E(\hat{\alpha}_i - \alpha_i) = \frac{1}{2!} tr\left[(f_i^{(2)} (I \otimes (Z'Z)^{-1}Z')\Omega_1^{vec}(I \otimes Z(Z'Z)^{-1}) \right] + o(T^{-1}).$$

When the partial derivatives $f_i^{(2)}$ are introduced the bias approximation is given in the following theorem:

Theorem 1 Let $\hat{\alpha}_i$ be the ith component of the $g+k$ component 2SLS estimator $\hat{\alpha}$ given in (10), then the bias to order T^{-1} is given by

$$E(\hat{\alpha}_i - \alpha_i) = tr\left[(HQe_i\beta_0' \otimes (P_Z - P_X))\Omega_1^{vec}\right] \\ - tr\left[(I^*(XQe_i\beta_0' \otimes H'QX'))\Omega_1^{vec}\right] + o\left(T^{-1}\right) \qquad (11)$$

where I^* is a $T(g+1) \times T(g+1)$ commutation matrix which is partitioned into $T(g+1)$ submatrices of order $(T, g+1)$ such that the p, q^{th} submatrix has unity in its q, p^{th} position and zeroes elsewhere, $p = 1, 2, \ldots, g+1, q = 1, 2, \ldots, T$, (see Magnus and Neudecker (1979)), $H = \begin{bmatrix} 0 & I_g \\ 0 & 0 \end{bmatrix}$ is a $(g+k) \times (g+1)$ selection matrix, $X = (Z\Pi_2 : Z_1)$, $Q = (X'X)^{-1}$, $P_Z = Z(Z'Z)^{-1}Z'$, $P_X = X(X'X)^{-1}X'$ and $\beta_0 = (-1, \beta')'$.

Proof See Phillips (2000).

This Theorem can be used to find the approximate biases for each component of the 2SLS vector $\hat{\alpha}$ under different assumptions concerning the generation of disturbances. From an examination of the bias approximation it is apparent that as the assumptions change, the change in the bias is brought about by changes in Ω_1^{vec}. If Ω_1^{vec} can be expressed as a Kronecker product then the bias expression will reduce to relatively simple form in terms of the structural parameters. However for the generating process considered in (6) this is hardly possible without the use of a double summation of products. Nonetheless it proves possible to find the bias approximation and this is considered further in the next section. The expansion discussed can also be used to approximate the second moment/mean squared error matrix by squaring the terms in the stochastic expansion above and retaining those up to $O_p(T^{-2})$. Taking expectations will then provide an approximation to order T^{-2}. The approximation for the general case is given in the following theorem:

Theorem 2 Let $\hat{\alpha}_i$ be the ith component of the $g+k$ component 2SLS estimator $\hat{\alpha}$ as given in (10), then the second moment of $\hat{\alpha}_i$ to order T^{-2} is given by

$$E(\hat{\alpha}_i - \alpha_i)^2 = tr\left[(\beta_0\beta_0' \otimes XQe_ie_i'QX')\Omega_1^{vec}\right] \\ + tr\left\{\left[(H'Qe_i\beta_0' \otimes (P_X - P_Z)\right]\Omega_1^{vec} \right. \\ \left. - \left(I^*\left[XQe_i\beta_0' \otimes H'QX'\right]\right)\Omega_1^{vec}\right\}$$

$$\times \{(([(H'Qe_i\beta_0' \otimes (P_X - P_Z) - I^*(XQe_i\beta_0' \otimes H'QX')]$$

$$+ [(H'Qe_i\beta_0' \otimes (P_X - P_Z) - I^*(XQe_i\beta_0' \otimes H'QX')]')\Omega_1^{vec}\}]$$

$$+ (tr([H'Qe_i\beta_0' \otimes (P_X - P_Z)] - I^*[XQe_i\beta_0' \otimes H'QX'])\Omega_1^{vec})^2$$

$$+ 2\sum_{r=1}^{K}\sum_{s=1}^{g+1}[(trA_{rs}\Omega_1^{vec})(trB_{rs}\Omega_1^{vec}) + trA_{rs}\Omega_1^{vec}B_{rs}\Omega_1^{vec}$$

$$+ trA_{rs}\Omega_1^{vec}B_{rs}'\Omega_1^{vec}] + o(T^{-2}) \qquad (12)$$

where the terms A_{rs} and B_{rs} which have not been previously defined are given by:

$$A_{rs} = \beta_0 i_s' \otimes XQe_i i_r'(Z'Z)^{-1}Z'$$

$$B_{rs} = ([H'Qe_i\beta_0'E_{rs}'Z'XQH + H'Q(X'ZE_{rs}H' + HE_{rs}'Z'X)Qe_i\beta_0']$$

$$\otimes (P_X - P_Z)) + I^*(XQHE_{rs}'Z'XQe_i\beta_0' \otimes H'QX').$$

Proof See Phillips (2000).

In the above, E_{rs} is a $K \times (g+1)$ matrix with unity in the r, s^{th} position and zero elsewhere, $r = 1, \ldots, K$ and $s = 1, \ldots, g+1$. In what follows we shall find it more convenient to write $E_{rs} = i_r i_s'$ where i_r and i_s are, respectively, $K \times 1$ and $(g+1) \times 1$ unit vectors.

As in the case of the bias approximation, the second-moment approximation takes a much simpler form when Ω_1^{vec} can be expressed in terms of Kronecker products. As noted above, for the disturbance generating process that we wish to specify, we are obliged to use a double summation of such products so that the resulting approximation is relatively complex as will be seen in the next section.

3 Main Results

In this section we present the main theorems which provide bias and second-moment approximations for the disturbance generating process in (6) for which $\Omega_1^{vec} = (\sum_{p=1}^{G}\sum_{q=1}^{G} B^{g+1} i_p i_q' (B^{g+1})' \otimes \sigma_{pq}\Sigma_{pq})$. In principle, this is straightforward since the approximations are found by substituting for Ω_1^{vec} in Theorems 1 and 2 although it requires a considerable amount of manipulation to get the required results. First we consider the bias approximation.

3.1 The Bias Approximation

Theorem 3 Let $\hat{\alpha}_i$ be the ith component of the $g+k$ component 2SLS estimator given in (10) and let the process generating the disturbances be as given in (6), then the bias of $\hat{\alpha}_i$ to order T^{-1} is as follows:

$$E(\hat{\alpha}_i - \alpha_i) = e_i'QH\sum_{p=1}^{G}(tr(P_Z - P_X)\sigma_{p1}\Sigma_{p1})\beta_p^{g+1}$$
$$- e_i'QX'\sum_{p=1}^{G}\sigma_{p1}\Sigma_{p1}XQH\beta_p^{g+1} + o(T^{-1}) \qquad (13)$$

where β_p^{g+1} is the pth column vector in B^{g+1} which is itself formed from the first $g+1$ rows of B^{-1}.

Proof A proof is given in Appendix 1.

Notice that both components of the bias depend on the serial correlation coefficients in all G equations as long as the disturbances are contemporaneously correlated. Also the approximation involves all the column vectors of B^{g+1}. Even if there is no serial correlation in the disturbance of the equation being estimated, the bias will be affected by serial correlation elsewhere in the system. If, however, the disturbances are serially correlated and have the same serial correlation coefficient so that $\Sigma_{pq} = \Sigma_{11}$, all $p, q = 1, \ldots, G$, then the above simplifies to the following:

Corollary 1 If the disturbances are serially correlated and the serial correlation coefficients are all the same, then the bias approximation in Theorem 3 reduces to:

$$E(\hat{\alpha}_i - \alpha_i) = tr((P_Z - P_X)\Sigma_{11})e_i'QHB^{g+1}\Sigma_1$$
$$- e_i'QX'\Sigma_{11}XQHB^{g+1}\Sigma_1 + o(T^{-1}) \qquad (14)$$

where we have used the fact that $\sum_{j=1}^{G}\sigma_{pq}\beta_q^{g+1} = B^{g+1}\Sigma_1$, Σ_1 is the first column of Σ, the covariance matrix of u_t, and we have assumed that $\Sigma_{pq} = \Sigma_{11}, p, q = 1, 2, \ldots, G$.

Now the bias approximation has a relatively simple form but it still involves all the column vectors of B^{g+1}. A further special case arises when the disturbances in the equation under consideration are contemporaneously uncorrelated with the other disturbances (although the other disturbances may be correlated with each other). Now it is seen that only the own equation serial correlation plays a role in the bias:

Corollary 2 If the disturbances are contemporaneously uncorrelated so that $\sigma_{1q} = 0$ for $q \neq 1$, then the result in Theorem 3 becomes:

$$E(\hat{\alpha}_i - \alpha_i) = \sigma_{11} tr((P_Z - P_X)\Sigma_{11})e_i' QHB^{g+1}\Sigma_1$$

$$- \sigma_{11} e_i' QX'\Sigma_{11} XQHB^{g+1}\Sigma_1 \tag{15}$$

$$= \sigma_{11}^2 tr((P_Z - P_X)\Sigma_{11})e_i' QH\beta_1^{g+1}$$

$$- \sigma_{11}^2 e_i' QX'\Sigma_{11} XQH\beta_1^{g+1} + o(T^{-1}) \tag{16}$$

where we have used the fact that in this case the vector Σ_1 has first component σ_{11} and all others zero.

Notice that here the bias approximation depends on only the first column vector of B^{g+1} and none of the others. Finally, we present the approximation obtained by Nagar.

Corollary 3 If the disturbances are serially independent and homoscedastic then we have the situation originally examined by Nagar. Putting $\Sigma_{pq} = I_T$ in Theorem 3 yields the Nagar approximation:

$$E(\hat{\alpha}_i - \alpha_i) = tr(P_Z - P_X - 1)e_i' QHB^{g+1}\Sigma_1 + o(T^{-1}) \tag{17}$$

where B^{g+1} is formed from the first $g + 1$ rows of B^{-1} and we have again used the result that $\sum_{q=1}^{G} \sigma_{pq}\beta_q^{g+1} = B^{g+1}\Sigma_1$.

In fact Nagar set $tr(P_Z - P_X - 1) = K - (k + g) - 1 = L - 1$, where L is the order of overidentication. Hence, for $L = 1$, the bias disappears to $O(T^{-1})$ (it also disappears to order T^{-2} as was shown by Mikhail, 1972). This does not happen, however, when there is serial correlation as is apparent from the corollaries above. As was noted earlier, in Nagar's case we have $\Omega_1^{vec} = (B^{g+1}\Sigma(B^{g+1})' \otimes I_T) = \Omega \otimes I_T$. Hence the Nagar bias approximation above holds whenever Ω_1^{vec} takes this form. This is of some interest since the bias approximation is shown to be valid under much less restricted conditions than might have been thought. Not only is normality not required but even independence is unnecessary. Under Gauss-Markov disturbances, for example, the result is still valid.Thus even under stationary ARCH disturbances the approximation will still hold.

3.2 *The Second-moment Approximation*

Finding the second-moment approximation is quite laborious and the analysis is lengthy. The approximation itself contains many more terms than in Nagar's case and so is correspondingly much longer as is shown in the following:

Theorem 4 Let $\hat{\alpha}_i$ be the ith component of the $g+k$ component 2SLS estimator given in (10) and let the process generating the disturbances be as given in (6), then the second moment to order T^{-2} is given by:

$$E(\hat{\alpha}_i - \alpha_i)^2 =$$

$$\sigma_{11} e_i' QX' \Sigma_{11} XQe_i$$

$$+\sum_{p=1}^{G}\sum_{q=1}^{G} \sigma_{1p}\sigma_{1q} tr\left[(P_X - P_Z)\Sigma_{1p}(P_X - P_Z)\Sigma_{1q}\right]$$

$$\times e_i' QH\beta_p^{g+1}(\beta_q^{g+1})' H' Qe_i$$

$$-2\sum_{p=1}^{G}\sum_{q=1}^{G} \sigma_{1p}\sigma_{1q} e_i' QX' \Sigma_{1p}' (P_X - P_Z)\Sigma_{1q}' XQH\beta_p^{g+1}(\beta_q^{g+1})' H' Qe_i$$

$$+\sum_{p=1}^{G}\sum_{q=1}^{G} \sigma_{1p}\sigma_{1q} e_i' QX' \Sigma_{1q}' XQH\beta_p^{g+1}(\beta_q^{g+1})' H' QX' \Sigma_{1p} XQe_i$$

$$+\sum_{p=1}^{G}\sum_{q=1}^{G} \sigma_{11}\sigma_{pq} tr\left[(P_X - P_Z)\Sigma_{11}(P_X - P_Z)\Sigma_{pq}\right] e_i' QH\beta_p^{g+1}(\beta_q^{g+1})' H' Qe_i$$

$$-2\sum_{p=1}^{G}\sum_{q=1}^{G} \sigma_{11}\sigma_{pq} e_i' QX' \Sigma_{pq}(P_X - P_Z)\Sigma_{11} XQH\beta_p^{g+1}(\beta_q^{g+1})' H' Qe_i$$

$$+\sum_{p=1}^{G}\sum_{q=1}^{G} \sigma_{11}\sigma_{pq} e_i' QX' \Sigma_{pq} XQe_i (\beta_p^{g+1})' H' QX' \Sigma_{11} XQH\beta_q^{g+1}$$

$$+2\sum_{p=1}^{G}\sum_{q=1}^{G} \sigma_{11}\sigma_{pq} tr((P_X - P_Z)\Sigma_{pq}) e_i' QH\beta_p^{g+1}(\beta_q^{g+1})' H' QX' \Sigma_{11} XQe_i$$

$$+2\sum_{p=1}^{G}\sum_{q=1}^{G} \sigma_{1p}\sigma_{1q} tr((P_X - P_Z)\Sigma_{1p}) e_i' QH\beta_p^{g+1}(\beta_q^{g+1})' H' QX' \Sigma_{p1} XQe_i$$

$$+2\sum_{p=1}^{G}\sum_{q=1}^{G}\sigma_{1p}\sigma_{1q}tr((P_X-P_Z)\Sigma_{1p})e_i'QX'\Sigma_{p1}XQe_i\left(\beta_q^{g+1}\right)'H'QH\beta_p^{g+1}$$

$$+2\sum_{p=1}^{G}\sum_{q=1}^{G}\sigma_{1p}\sigma_{1q}e_i'QX'\Sigma_{11}XQe_i\left(\beta_q^{g+1}\right)'H'QX'\Sigma_{1q}XQH\left(\beta_q^{g+1}\right)$$

$$+2\sum_{p=1}^{G}\sum_{q=1}^{G}\sigma_{1p}\sigma_{1q}e_i'QH\beta_q^{g+1}\left(\beta_p^{g+1}\right)'H'QX'\Sigma_{1q}(P_X-P_Z)\Sigma_{p1}XQe_i$$

$$+2\sum_{p=1}^{G}\sum_{q=1}^{G}\sigma_{pq}\sigma_{11}e_i'QH\beta_q^{g+1}\left(\beta_p^{g+1}\right)'H'QX'\Sigma_{pq}(P_X-P_Z)\Sigma_{11}XQe_i$$

$$+2\sum_{p=1}^{G}\sum_{q=1}^{G}\sigma_{pq}\sigma_{11}e_{i'}QX'\Sigma_{pq}(P_X-P_Z)\Sigma_{11}XQe_i\left(\beta_p^{g+1}\right)'H'QH\beta_q^{g+1}$$

$$+2\sum_{p=1}^{G}\sum_{q=1}^{G}\sigma_{pq}\sigma_{11}e_{i'}QX'\Sigma_{pq}XQH\beta_p^{g+1}\left(\beta_q^{g+1}\right)'H'QX'\Sigma_{11}XQe_i$$

$$+2\sum_{p=1}^{G}\sum_{q=1}^{G}\sigma_{1p}\sigma_{1q}e_i'QH\beta_p^{g+1}\left(\beta_q^{g+1}\right)'H'QX'\Sigma_{1q}(P_X-P_Z)\Sigma_{p1}XQe_i$$

$$+2\sum_{p=1}^{G}\sum_{q=1}^{G}\sigma_{1p}\sigma_{1q}e_i'QH\beta_q^{g+1}\left(\beta_p^{g+1}\right)'H'QX'\Sigma_{q1}(P_X-P_Z)\Sigma_{p1}XQe_i$$

$$+2\sum_{p=1}^{G}\sum_{q=1}^{G}\sigma_{1p}\sigma_{1q}e_{i'}QX'\Sigma_{q1}(P_X-P_Z)\Sigma_{p1}XQe_i\left(\beta_q^{g+1}\right)'H'QH\beta_p^{g+1}$$

$$+2\sum_{p=1}^{G}\sum_{q=1}^{G}\sigma_{1p}\sigma_{1q}e_{i'}QX'\Sigma_{p1}XQH\beta_q^{g+1}\left(\beta_p^{g+1}\right)'H'QX'\Sigma_{q1}XQe_i$$

$$+\left(e_i'QH\sum_{p=1}^{G}\left(tr(P_Z-P_X)\sigma_{p1}\Sigma_{p1}\right)\beta_p^{g+1}\right)^2$$

$$+\left(e_i'QX'\sum_{p=1}^{G}\sigma_{p1}\Sigma_{p1}XQH\beta_p^{g+1}\right)^2$$

$$-2e_i'QH\sum_{p=1}^{G}\left(tr(P_Z-P_X)\sigma_{p1}\Sigma_{p1}\right)\beta_p^{g+1}$$

$$\times\left(e_i'QX'\sum_{q=1}^{G}\sigma_{p1}\Sigma_{p1}XQH\beta_p^{g+1}\right)+o(T^{-1}). \tag{18}$$

Proof A proof is given in Appendix 2.

Notice that the first term, which yields the asymptotic covariance matrix, is of order T^{-1} while all the other terms are of order T^{-2}. This approximation to the second moment depends on all the serial correlation coefficients, all the vectors in B^{g+1} and all the structural disturbance parameters. It is difficult to infer any general characteristics of the second moment from such a cumbersome expression although it may be possible with further work to achieve some simplification. Alternatively, numerical analysis is possible and the approximation could be explored under different structures. The Nagar approximation to the second moment follows as a corollary of the above result.

Corollary 4 If the disturbances are serially independent and homoscedastic then we have the situation originally examined by Nagar. Putting $\Sigma_{pq} = I_T$ in Theorem 4 yields the Nagar approximation:

$$\begin{aligned} E(\hat{\alpha}_i-\alpha_i)^2 &= \sigma_{11}e_i'Qe_i + (-2tr(P_Z-P_X)+3)tr\, C_1Q + tr\, C_2Q.e_i'Qe_i \\ &\quad + \{(tr(P_Z-P_X))^2+2)\}e_i'QC_1Qe_1 \\ &\quad - (tr(P_Z-P_X)-2)e_i'QC_2Qe_1 + o(T^{-2}) \end{aligned} \tag{19}$$

where $C_1 = \frac{1}{\sigma_{11}}HB^{g+1}\Sigma_1\Sigma_1'(B^{g+1})'H'$ and $C_2 = HB^{g+1}\Sigma(B^{g+1})' \times H' - C_1$.

Proof The result follows directly on substituting $\Sigma_{pq} = I_T$ in Theorem 4 after some manipulation of terms. In the next section we specialize the bias and second-moment results to the simplest form of structural equation. We shall see that even in this simple case the second-moment approximation remains somewhat complex.

4 A Simple Simultaneous Equation Model

For ease of interpretation of the foregoing results, we shall now consider a very simple version of a simultaneous equation model in which there are two endogenous variables only. We focus on the first equation which contains a single endogenous regressor and a second equation which also contains an endogenous regressor and an arbitrary number of exogenous variables (this framework was recently employed by Hahn and Hausman, 2002). Thus the parameter of interest is overidentified provided at least two exogenous variables (one of which may be the constant term) appear in the second equation while none of the parameters in the second equation are identified. Since we shall require that at least the first two estimator moments exist, we shall assume that the degree of overidentification is at least two. Finally, there are only two structural disturbances and these are assumed to be normally distributed and, possibly, serially correlated; consequently there are just two serial correlation coefficients. The system is:

$$\begin{aligned} y_{1t} &= \beta_{12} y_{2t} + u_{1t} \\ y_{2t} &= \beta_{21} y_{1t} + z_t'\gamma + u_{2t}, \quad t = 1, 2, \ldots, T. \end{aligned} \tag{20}$$

The relevant reduced form equation will be written as:

$$y_{2t} = z_t'\pi_2 + v_{2t}.$$

The disturbances are contemporaneously correlated so that $E(u_{1t}u_{2t}) = \sigma_{12}$ where both u_1 and u_2 are serially correlated with covariance matrices given by (7) and with serial correlation coefficients, respectively, ρ_1 and ρ_2. We now state the bias for the 2SLS estimator of β_{12} as follows.

Theorem 5 For the simple two-equation model given in (20) and the process generating the disturbances (6), the bias of the 2SLS estimator of β_{12} to order T^{-1}as given in Theorem 3 reduces to:

$$\begin{aligned} &E(\hat{\beta}_{12} - \beta_{12}) = \\ &\frac{\beta_{21}}{1-\beta_{12}\beta_{21}} \left\{ \left(\frac{\sigma_{11} tr\,[(P_Z - P_X)\Sigma_{11}]}{\pi_2' Z' Z \pi_2} \right) - \left(\frac{\sigma_{11}\pi_2' Z' \Sigma_{11} Z \pi_2}{(\pi_2' Z' Z \pi_2)^2} \right) \right\} \qquad (21) \\ &+ \frac{1}{1-\beta_{12}\beta_{21}} \left\{ \left(\frac{\sigma_{12} tr\,[(P_Z - P_X)\Sigma_{12}]}{\pi_2' Z' Z \pi_2} \right) - \left(\frac{\sigma_{12}\pi_2' Z' \Sigma_{12} Z \pi_2)}{(\pi_2' Z' Z \pi_2)^2} \right\} \\ &+ o(T^{-1}). \end{aligned}$$

Proof We simply interpret the components of the bias in (13) within the context of the simple model given in (20).

Notice that this bias does not go to zero if β_{21} goes to zero; it also requires the covariance between the structural disturbances to be zero. The Nagar bias is found by setting $\Sigma_{pq} = I_T$, $p, q = 1, 2$. If this is done we have a further corollary:

Corollary 5 For the simple model given in (20) in which the disturbances are normally, independently and identically distributed, the Nagar bias to order T^{-1} is given by:

$$E(\hat{\beta}_{12}-\beta_{12}) = tr\,[(P_Z - P_X - 1)]\,\frac{1}{\pi_2' Z' Z \pi_2}\,\frac{\sigma_{11}\beta_{21}+\sigma_{12}}{1-\beta_{12}\beta_{21}} + o\left(T^{-1}\right). \quad (22)$$

Corollary 6 For the second moment approximation we find that in the simple model given in (20) in which the disturbances are normally distributed and generated by the process in (6), the second moment to order T^{-2} is given by:

$$\begin{aligned}
E(\hat{\beta}_{12}-\beta_{12})^2 = {} & \frac{\sigma_{11}}{(\pi_2' Z' Z \pi_2)} + \left(\frac{\beta_{21}}{1-\beta_{12}\beta_{21}}\right)^2 \\
& \times \Bigg\{ \Bigg(\frac{1}{(\pi_2' Z' Z \pi_2)^2} [(2\sigma_{11}^2 tr((P_Z - P_X)\Sigma_{11}(P_Z - P_X)\Sigma_{11}) \\
& \quad + \sigma_{11}^2 (tr(P_Z - P_X)\Sigma_{11})^2] + \frac{1}{(\pi_2' Z' Z \pi_2)^3} \\
& \quad \times [-8\sigma_{11}^2 \pi_2' Z' \Sigma_{11}(P_Z - P_X)\Sigma_{11} Z \pi_2 \\
& \qquad - 4\sigma_{11}^2 tr((P_Z - P_X)\Sigma_{11})\pi_2' Z' \Sigma_{11} Z \pi_2] \\
& \quad + \frac{1}{(\pi_2' Z' Z \pi_2)^4} (8\sigma_{11}^2 (\pi_2' Z' \Sigma_{11} Z \pi_2)^2) \Bigg) \Bigg\} \\
& + \frac{\beta_{21}}{(1-\beta_{12}\beta_{21})^2} \Bigg\{ \Bigg(\frac{1}{(\pi_2' Z' Z \pi_2)^2} (4\sigma_{11}\sigma_{12} tr((P_Z - P_X) \\
& \quad \times \Sigma_{12}(P_Z - P_X)\Sigma_{11}) + 2\sigma_{11}\sigma_{12} tr((P_Z - P_X)\Sigma_{11}) \\
& \quad \times tr((P_Z - P_X)\Sigma_{12})) + \frac{1}{(\pi_2' Z' Z \pi_2)^3} \\
& \quad \times (-2\,\sigma_{11}\sigma_{12}\,\pi_2' Z' \Sigma_{11}(P_Z - P_X)\Sigma_{12} Z \pi_2
\end{aligned}$$

$$
\begin{aligned}
&-10\sigma_{11}\sigma_{12}\pi_2'Z'\Sigma_{12}(P_Z-P_X)\Sigma_{11}Z\pi_2-2\sigma_{11}^2\\
&\times tr((P_Z-P_X)\Sigma_{11})\,\pi_2'Z'\Sigma_{11}Z\pi_2-4\sigma_{11}\sigma_{12}\\
&\times tr((P_Z-P_X)\Sigma_{12})\pi_2'Z'\Sigma_{11}Z\pi_2)-2\sigma_{11}\sigma_{12}\\
&\times tr((P_Z-P_X)\Sigma_{11}))\pi_2'Z'\Sigma_{21}Z\pi_2)+\frac{1}{(\pi_2'Z'Z\pi_2)^4}\\
&\times(18\sigma_{11}\sigma_{12}\pi_2'Z'\Sigma_{11}Z\pi_2\pi_2'Z'\Sigma_{12}Z\pi_2\Big)\Big\}+\frac{1}{(1-\beta_{12}\beta_{21})^2}\\
&\times\Bigg\{\Bigg(\Bigg(\frac{1}{(\pi_2'Z'Z\pi_2)^2}\Bigg)(4\sigma_{12}^2tr((P_Z-P_X)\Sigma_{12}(P_Z-P_X)\Sigma_{12})\\
&+\sigma_{12}\sigma_{22}tr((P_Z-P_X)\Sigma_{12}(P_Z-P_X)\Sigma_{22})\\
&+\sigma_{12}^2\,[tr(P_Z-P_X)\Sigma_{12}]^2)+\Bigg(\Bigg(\frac{1}{(\pi_2'Z'Z\pi_2)^3}\Bigg)\\
&\times(2\sigma_{11}\sigma_{12}\,\pi_2'Z'\Sigma_{12}(P_Z-P_X)\Sigma_{11}Z\pi_2+6\sigma_{12}^2\,\pi_2'Z'\Sigma_{12}\\
&\times(P_Z-P_X)\Sigma_{21}Z\pi_2-2\sigma_{12}^2tr((P_Z-P_X)\Sigma_{21})\pi_2'Z'\Sigma_{21}Z\pi_2\\
&+2\sigma_{11}\sigma_{22}\,tr((P_Z-P_X)\Sigma_{22})\pi_2'Z'\Sigma_{11}Z\pi_2\Big)\\
&+\Bigg(\Bigg(\frac{1}{(\pi_2'Z'Z\pi_2)^4}\Bigg)((6\sigma_{12}^2(\pi_2'Z'\Sigma_{12}Z\pi_2)^2\\
&+3\sigma_{11}\sigma_{22}\pi_2'Z'\Sigma_{11}Z\pi_2\pi_2'Z'\Sigma_{22}Z\pi_2\Big)\Big)\Bigg\}\\
&+o(T^{-2}). \qquad (23)
\end{aligned}
$$

Proof We reinterpret the result in Theorem 4 in the context of the simple model in (20).

Corollary 7 For the simple model in (20), assuming that the disturbances are independently and normally distributed, the Nagar second-moment approximation is given by:

$$
\begin{aligned}
E(\hat{\beta}_{12}-\beta_{12})^2 &= \frac{\sigma_{11}}{(\pi_2'Z'Z\pi_2)}\\
&\quad+\sigma_{11}^2\left(\frac{\beta_{21}}{1-\beta_{12}\beta_{21}}\right)^2\left\{\left(\frac{1}{(\pi_2'Z'Z\pi_2)^2}\right)(L-3)^2\right\}
\end{aligned}
$$

$$+\sigma_{12}\sigma_{22}\frac{\beta_{21}}{(1-\beta_{12}\beta_{21})^2}\left\{\left(\frac{1}{(\pi_2' Z' Z\pi_2)^2}\right)2(L-3)^2\right\}$$

$$+\sigma_{12}^2\left(\frac{1}{(1-\beta_{12}\beta_{21})^2}\right)\left\{\left(\frac{1}{(\pi_2' Z' Z\pi_2)^2}\right)(L-4)(L-1)\right\}$$

$$+\sigma_{11}\sigma_{22}\left(\frac{1}{(1-\beta_{12}\beta_{21})^2}\right)\left\{\left(\frac{1}{(\pi_2' Z' Z\pi_2)^2}(-(L-3)\right)\right\}$$

$$+o(T^{-2}). \tag{24}$$

Proof We interpret the result in Corollary 6 for the case where the disturbances are serially uncorrelated.

Despite the fact that we have used the simplest possible framework, the second-moment approximation in the context of (6) remains somewhat complicated and difficult to interpret. Notice that it is the fact that the disturbances are contemporaneously correlated that mostly contributes to this. While one can readily see where the individual components are affected by serial correlation it is difficult to say anything about how important they are; hence some numerical evaluation is necessary to make comparisons with the serially independent case.

5 Conclusions

It has proved possible to extend the Nagar approximations to the case of serially correlated disturbances. While the bias approximations are relatively easy to interpret, especially for the simple simultaneous equation model, the second moment approximation is quite complex even in the simple model. Whereas one can see that the serial correlations may have substantial effects on both approximations, it is difficult to make comparisons without some numerical evaluations. In particular it would be interesting to see how the biases and second moments are changed as the degree of serial correlation increases/decreases. In this regard it is possible that more theoretical analysis will be helpful too. Further work will examine these possibilities.

One reason for obtaining bias approximations is to enable bias correction to be carried out. Bias correction based upon the use of the bias approximation is possible but one might need to estimate a lot of parameters in order to carry it through. In particular the bias approximation in the more general model requires the estimation of many parameters and it seems unlikely that bias correction would be successful except in relatively large samples.

Appendix 1

In this Appendix we provide a proof of Theorem 3. We shall show that the expression:

$$tr\left[(HQe_i\beta_0' \otimes (P_Z - P_X))\Omega_1^{vec}\right] - tr\left[(I^*(XQe_i\beta_0' \otimes H'QX')\Omega_1^{vec}\right]$$

reduces to the bias expression in Theorem 3 when we substitute out the covariance term. We shall put $\Omega_1^{vec} = \sum_{p=1}^{G}\sum_{q=1}^{G}(B^{g+1}i_p i_q'(B^{g+1})' \otimes \sigma_{pq}\Sigma_{pq})$ into the above and then with some rearrangement the expression becomes:

$$tr\left[\left(HQe_i\beta_0'\sum_{p=1}^{G}\sum_{q=1}^{G}(B^{g+1}i_p i_q'(B^{g+1})' \otimes (P_Z - P_X)\sigma_{pq}\Sigma_{pq}\right)\right]$$

$$- tr\left[\left(I^*(XQe_i\beta_0' \otimes H'QX')\sum_{p=1}^{G}\sum_{q=1}^{G}(B^{g+1}i_p i_q'(B^{g+1})' \otimes \sigma_{pq}\Sigma_{pq}\right)\right]$$

$$= tr\left[\left(HQe_i\beta_0'\sum_{p=1}^{G}\sum_{q=1}^{G}(B^{g+1}i_p i_q'(B^{g+1})' \otimes (P_Z - P_X)\sigma_{pq}\Sigma_{pq}\right)\right]$$

$$- tr\left[\left(I^*(XQe_i\beta_0'\sum_{p=1}^{G}\sum_{q=1}^{G}B^{g+1}i_p i_q'(B^{g+1})' \otimes H'QX'\sigma_{pq}\Sigma_{pq}\right)\right]$$

$$= tr\left[\left(HQe_i\beta_0'\sum_{p=1}^{G}\sum_{q=1}^{G}(B^{g+1}i_p i_q'(B^{g+1})' \times tr((P_Z - P_X)\sigma_{pq}\Sigma_{pq}\right)\right]$$

$$- tr\left[\left(XQe_i\beta_0'\sum_{p=1}^{G}\sum_{q=1}^{G}B^{g+1}i_p i_q'(B^{g+1})'H'QX'\sigma_{pq}\Sigma_{pq}\right)\right].$$

Noting that $\beta_0' B^{g+1} = i_p'$ and $i_1' i_q = 0$ for $q \neq 1$, the expressions simplify since p takes only the value unity. Hence the double summation is replaced by a single summation over q and the above becomes:

$$\sum_{q=1}^{G}\left[tr(HQe_i i_q'(B^{g+1})') \times tr((P_Z - P_X)\sigma_{1q}\Sigma_{1q})\right]$$

$$-\sum_{q=1}^{G} tr(XQe_i i_q'(B^{g+1})'H'QX'\sigma_{1q}\Sigma_{1q})$$

$$=\sum_{q=1}^{G}\left[e_i'QH'\beta_q^{g+1}\times tr\left((P_Z-P_X)\sigma_{1q}\Sigma_{1q}\right)\right]-\sum_{q=1}^{G}e_i'QX'\Sigma_{q1}\sigma_{1q}XQH\beta_q^{g+1}$$

$$=e_i'QH'\left[\sum_{q=1}^{G}tr\left((P_Z-P_X)\sigma_{1q}\Sigma_{1q}\right)\right]\beta_q^{g+1}-e_i'QX'\sum_{q=1}^{G}\sigma_{1q}\Sigma_{q1}XQH\beta_q^{g+1}. \qquad \text{(A1.1)}$$

This is the bias approximation given in Theorem 3.

Appendix 2

In this Appendix a proof is given for Theorem 4. The proof follows once we substitute for Ω_1^{vec} in the second-moment approximation of Theorem 2. To proceed we shall examine the relevant terms in groups labelled **A** to **G** below.

A $\quad tr\left[(\beta_0\beta_0'\otimes XQe_ie_i'QX')\Omega_1^{vec}\right]$

B $$tr\Big[\Big\{\left[(H'Qe_i\beta_0'\otimes(P_X-P_Z)\right]\Omega_1^{vec} - \left(I^*\left[XQe_i\beta_0'\otimes H'QX'\right]\right)\Omega_1^{vec}\Big\} \times\Big\{\Big(\left[(H'Qe_i\beta_0'\otimes(P_X-P_Z)-I^*\left(XQe_i\beta_0'\otimes H'QX'\right)\right]\Big\}\Big]$$

C $$tr\Big[\Big\{\left[(H'Qe_i\beta_0'\otimes(P_X-P_Z)\right]\Omega_1^{vec}-\left(I^*\left[XQe_i\beta_0'\otimes H'QX'\right]\right)\Omega_1^{vec}\Big\} \times\Big\{\left[(H'Qe_i\beta_0'\otimes(P_X-P_Z)-I^*\left(XQe_i\beta_0'\otimes H'QX'\right)\right]')\Omega_1^{vec}\Big\}\Big]$$

D $$\left(tr\Big(\left[H'Qe_i\beta_0'\otimes(P_X-P_Z)\right]-I^*\left[XQe_i\beta_0'\otimes H'QX'\right]\Big)\Omega_1^{vec}\right)^2$$

E $$+2\sum_{r=1}^{K}\sum_{s=1}^{g+1}(trA_{rs}\Omega_1^{vec})(trB_{rs}\Omega_1^{vec})$$

F $$2\sum_{r=1}^{K}\sum_{s=1}^{g+1}trA_{rs}\Omega_1^{vec}B_{rs}\Omega_1^{vec}$$

G $$2\sum_{r=1}^{K}\sum_{s=1}^{g+1}trA_{rs}\Omega_1^{vec}B_{rs}'\Omega_1^{vec}+o(T^{-2}) \qquad \text{(A2.1)}$$

To find the required approximation, we shall reduce the above to its individual components as follows. We commence from:

$$\mathbf{A} \quad tr\left[(\beta_0\beta_0' \otimes XQe_ie_i'QX')\Omega_1^{vec}\right]$$

$$= tr\left\{\beta_0\beta_0'B^{g+1}\sum_{p=1}^{G}\sum_{q=1}^{G} i_pi_q'(B^{g+1})' \otimes XQe_ie_i'QX'\sigma_{pq}\Sigma_{pq}\right\}$$

$$= \sum_{p=1}^{G}\sum_{q=1}^{G} tr\left(\beta_0\beta_0'B^{g+1}i_pi_q'(B^{g+1})'\right)tr(XQe_ie_i'QX'\sigma_{pq}\Sigma_{pq})$$

$$= \sum_{p=1}^{G}\sum_{q=1}^{G} tr\left(\beta_0'B^{g+1}i_pi_q'(B^{g+1})'\beta_0\right)tr(XQe_ie_i'QX'\sigma_{pq}\Sigma_{pq})$$

$$= tr(XQe_ie_i'QX'\sigma_{11}\Sigma_{11}), \text{ on noting that } \beta_0'B^{g+1}i_p = 1, p = 1,$$

and is zero otherwise.

Finally we have that **A** equals:

$$tr\left[(\beta_0\beta_0' \otimes XQe_ie_i'QX')\Omega_1^{vec}\right] = \sigma_{11}e_i'QX'\Sigma_{11}XQe_i \qquad \text{(A2.2)}$$

which is of order T^{-1}. This is the i, i^{th} term of the asymptotic covariance matrix:

$$\sigma_{11}QX'\Sigma_{11}XQ.$$

Next we have:

$$\mathbf{B} \quad + tr\Bigg[\Bigg\{\left[(H'Qe_i\beta_0' \otimes (P_X - P_Z)\right]\Omega_1^{vec}$$

$$- \left(I^*\left[XQe_i\beta_0' \otimes H'QX'\right]\right)\Omega_1^{vec}\Bigg\}$$

$$\times \left\{\left(\left[(H'Qe_i\beta_0' \otimes (P_X - P_Z) - I^*\left(XQe_i\beta_0' \otimes H'QX'\right)\right]\right\}\Bigg]$$

which has four components as follows:

$$tr\left\{\left[(H'Qe_i\beta_0' \otimes (P_X - P_Z)\right]\Omega_1^{vec}\left[(H'Qe_i\beta_0' \otimes (P_X - P_Z)\right]\Omega_1^{vec}\right\}$$

$$- tr\left\{\left[(H'Qe_i\beta_0' \otimes (P_X - P_Z)\right]\Omega_1^{vec}\left(I^*\left[XQe_i\beta_0' \otimes H'QX'\right]\right)\Omega_1^{vec}\right\}$$

$$- tr\left\{I^*\left[XQe_i\beta_0' \otimes H'QX'\right]\Omega_1^{vec}\left[(H'Qe_i\beta_0' \otimes (P_X - P_Z)\right]\Omega_1^{vec}\right\}$$

$$+ tr\left\{I^*\left[XQe_i\beta_0' \otimes H'QX'\right]\Omega_1^{vec}I^*\left[XQe_i\beta_0' \otimes H'QX'\right]\Omega_1^{vec}\right\}.$$

On substituting for Ω_1^{vec} the first term becomes:

$$tr\left\{\left(H'Qe_i\beta_0'B^{g+1}\sum_{p=1}^{G}\sum_{q=1}^{G} i_p i_q'(B^{g+1})' \otimes (P_X - P_Z)\sigma_{pq}\Sigma_{pq}\right)\right.$$

$$\left.\times\left(H'Qe_i\beta_0'B^{g+1}\sum_{p=1}^{G}\sum_{q=1}^{G} i_p i_q'(B^{g+1})' \otimes (P_X - P_Z)\sigma_{pq}\Sigma_{pq}\right)\right\}$$

$$= tr\sum_{p=1}^{G}\sum_{q=1}^{G}\left\{H'Qe_i i_p'(B^{g+1})'H'Qe_i i_q'(B^{g+1})'\right.$$

$$\left.\otimes (P_X - P_Z)\sigma_{1p}\Sigma_{1p}(P_X - P_Z)\sigma_{1q}\Sigma_{1q}\right\}$$

$$= tr\left\{\sum_{p=1}^{G}\sum_{q=1}^{G} e_i'QHB^{g+1} tr(\sigma_{1p}\sigma_{1q}(P_X - P_Z)\Sigma_{1p}(P_X - P_Z)\Sigma_{1q})\right.$$

$$\left.\times i_p i_q'(B^{g+1})'H'Qe_i\right\}$$

$$= tr\sum_{p=1}^{G}\sum_{q=1}^{G} e_i'QHB^{g+1} i_p i_q'(B^{g+1})'H'Qe_i$$

$$\times tr(\sigma_{1p}\sigma_{1q}(P_X - P_Z)\Sigma_{1p}(P_X - P_Z)\Sigma_{1q})$$

$$= tr\sum_{p=1}^{G}\sum_{q=1}^{G} \sigma_1\sigma_{1q}e_i'QH\beta^{g+1}(\beta_q^{g+1})'H'Qe_i tr((P_X - P_Z)\Sigma_{1p}(P_X - P_Z)\Sigma_{1q}). \tag{A2.3}$$

Substituting for Ω_1^{vec} in the second term yields:

$$-tr\left\{\left(I^*\left[XQe_i\beta_0'B^{g+1}\sum_{p=1}^{G}\sum_{q=1}^{G} i_p i_q'(B^{g+1})' \otimes H'QX'\sigma_{pq}\Sigma_{pq}\right)\right]\right.$$

$$\left.\times\left[\left(H'Qe_i\beta_0'B^{g+1}\sum_{r=1}^{G}\sum_{s=1}^{G} i_r i_s'(B^{g+1})' \otimes (P_X - P_Z)\sigma_{rs}\Sigma_{rs}\right]\right]\right\}$$

$$= -tr\left\{I^*\left(XQe_i\sum_{q=1}^{G} i_q'(B^{g+1})' \otimes H'QX'\sigma_{1q}\Sigma_{1q}\right)\right.$$

$$\times \left(H'Qe_i \sum_{s=1}^{G} i_s'(B^{g+1})' \otimes (P_X - P_Z)\Sigma_{1s} \right) \Big\}$$

$$= -\sum_{q=1}^{G}\sum_{s=1}^{G} e_i'QHB^{g+1} i_q i_s'(B^{g+1})'H'QX'\sigma_{1q}\Sigma_{1q}(P_X - P_Z)\Sigma_{1s}XQe_i$$

$$= -\sum_{p=1}^{G}\sum_{q=1}^{G} \sigma_{1q}\sigma_{1s}e_i'QH\beta_q^{g+1}(\beta_s^{g+1})'H'QX'\Sigma_{1q}(P_X - P_Z)\Sigma_{1s}XQe_i \tag{A2.4}$$

where we have introduced a standard summation notation in p and q.

The third term is the same as the second term. For completeness we write,

$$-tr\left\{ I^* \left[XQe_i\beta_0' \otimes H'QX' \right]) \Omega_1^{vec} \left[(H'Qe_i\beta_0' \otimes (P_X - P_Z) \right] \Omega_1^{vec} \right\}$$

$$= -\sum_{p=1}^{G}\sum_{q=1}^{G} \sigma_{1p}\sigma_{1q}e_i'QH\beta_p^{g+1}(\beta_q^{g+1})'H'QX'\Sigma_{1p}(P_X - P_Z)\Sigma_{1q}XQe_i. \tag{A2.5}$$

Finally the fourth term may be written as:

$$tr\Big\{ \Big(I^* \Big[XQe_i\beta_0'B^{g+1} \sum_{r=1}^{G}\sum_{s=1}^{G} i_r i_s'(B^{g+1})' \otimes H'QX'\sigma_{rs}\Sigma_{rs} \Big]$$

$$\times I^* \Big[XQe_i\beta_0'B^{g+1} \sum_{p=1}^{G}\sum_{q=1}^{G} i_p i_q'(B^{g+1})' \otimes H'QX'\sigma_{pq}\Sigma_{pq} \Big] \Big] \Big\}$$

$$= tr\Big\{ \Big(I^* \Big[XQe_i \sum_{r=1}^{G} i_r'(B^{g+1})' \otimes H'QX'\sigma_{1r}\Sigma_{1r} \Big]$$

$$\times I^* \Big[XQe_i \sum_{q=1}^{G} i_q'(B^{g+1})' \otimes H'QX'\sigma_{1q}\Sigma_{1q} \Big] \Big] \Big\}$$

$$= tr\Big\{ \Big[XQe_i \sum_{r=1}^{G} i_r'(B^{g+1})' \otimes H'QX'\sigma_{1r}\Sigma_{1r} \Big]$$

$$\times tr\Big\{ \Big(\Big[XQe_i \sum_{q=1}^{G} i_q'(B^{g+1})' \otimes H'QX'\sigma_{1q}\Sigma_{1q} \Big\} \Big]$$

$$= tr\Big\{ \sum_{r=1}^{G}\sum_{q=1}^{G} \Big\{ XQe_i i_r'(B^{g+1})'H'QX'\sigma_{1q}\Sigma_{1q}$$

$$\otimes H'QX'\sigma_{1r}\Sigma_{1r}XQe_i i_q'(B^{g+1})' \Big\}$$

$$= \sum_{r=1}^{G}\sum_{q=1}^{G} e_i' QX'\sigma_{1q}\Sigma_{q1}XQHB^{g+1}i_q i_r'(B^{g+1})'H'QX'\sigma_{1r}\Sigma_{1r}XQe_i$$

$$= \sum_{r=1}^{G}\sum_{q=1}^{G} \sigma_{1r}\sigma_{1q}e_i' QX'\Sigma_{q1}XQH\beta_q^{g+1}(\beta_r^{g+1})'H'QX'\Sigma_{1r}XQe_i. \quad \text{(A2.6)}$$

Summing the terms (A2.3–A2.6) yields for **B**:

$$= tr\sum_{r=1}^{G}\sum_{q=1}^{G}\Big\{\sigma_{1r}\sigma_{1q}e_i' QH\beta_r^{g+1}(\beta_q^{g+1})'H'Qe_i tr((P_X-P_Z)\Sigma_{1r}(P_X-P_Z)\Sigma_{1q})$$

$$-\sum_{r=1}^{G}\sum_{q=1}^{G}\sigma_{1r}\sigma_{1q}e_i' QH\beta_r^{g+1}(\beta_q^{g+1})'H'QX'\Sigma_{1r}(P_X-P_Z)\Sigma_{1q}XQe_i$$

$$-\sum_{r=1}^{G}\sum_{q=1}^{G}\sigma_{1r}\sigma_{1q}e_i' QH\beta_r^{g+1}(\beta_q^{g+1})'H'QX'\Sigma_{1r}(P_X-P_Z)\Sigma_{1q}XQe_i$$

$$\sum_{r=1}^{G}\sum_{q=1}^{G}\sigma_{1r}\sigma_{1q}e_i' QX'\Sigma_{q1}XQH\beta_q^{g+1}(\beta_r^{g+1})'H'QX'\Sigma_{1r}XQe\Big\}. \quad \text{(A2.7)}$$

C This has four terms as follows:

$$tr\Big\{[(H'Qe_i\beta_0' \otimes (P_X - P_Z))]\,\Omega_1^{vec}\,[(\beta_0 e_i' QH \otimes (P_X - P_Z))]\,\Omega_1^{vec}\Big\}$$

$$-\, tr\Big\{I^*\,[XQe_i\beta_0' \otimes H'QX']\,\Omega_1^{vec}[(\beta_0 e_i' QH \otimes (P_X - P_Z))]\Omega_1^{vec}\Big\}$$

$$-\, tr\Big\{[(H'Qe_i\beta_0' \otimes (P_X - P_Z))]\Omega_i^{vec}\,[\beta_0 e_i' QX \otimes XQH]\,(I^*)'\Omega_1^{vec}\Big\}$$

$$+\, tr\Big\{I^*\,[XQe_i\beta_0' \otimes H'QX']\,\Omega_1^{vec}\,[\beta_0 e_i' QX \otimes XQH]\,(I^*)'\Omega_1^{vec}\Big\}$$

The first of these can be written:

$$tr\Bigg\{\Bigg(H'Qe_i\beta_0'\Bigg(\sum_{r=1}^{G}\sum_{s=1}^{G}B^{g+1}i_r i_s'(B^{g+1})' \otimes (P_X - P_Z)\sigma_{rs}\Sigma_{rs}\Bigg)$$

$$\times\Bigg(\beta_0 e_i' QH\sum_{p=1}^{G}\sum_{q=1}^{G}B^{g+1}i_p i_q'(B^{g+1})$$

$$\otimes (P_X - P_Z)\sigma_{pq}\Sigma_{pq}\Bigg)\Bigg\}$$

$$= tr\left\{\left(\sum_{p=1}^{G}\sum_{q=1}^{G} HQe_ie_i'QHB^{g+1}i_pi_q'(B^{g+1})'\right.\right.$$

$$\left.\left.\otimes (P_X - P_Z)\sigma_{11}\Sigma_{11}\right)(P_X - P_Z)\sigma_{pq}\Sigma_{pq}\right\}$$

$$= \sum_{p=1}^{G}\sum_{q=1}^{G}\left\{e_i'QHB^{g+1}i_pi_q'(B^{g+1})'HQe_i\sigma_{11}\sigma_{pq}\right.$$

$$\left.\times\, tr[(P_X - P_Z)\Sigma_{11})(P_X - P_Z)\Sigma_{pq}]\right\}$$

$$\sum_{p=1}^{G}\sum_{q=1}^{G}\sigma_{11}\sigma_{pq}tr\left\{(P_X - P_Z)\Sigma_{11})(P_X - P_Z)\Sigma_{pq}\right\}e_i'QH\beta_p^{g+1}(\beta_q^{g+1})'HQe_i. \tag{A2.8}$$

The second term is:

$$- tr\left\{I^*\left[XQe_i\beta_0'\sum_{r=1}^{G}\sum_{s=1}^{G} B^{g+1}i_ri_s'(B^{g+1})' \otimes H'QX'\sigma_{rs}\Sigma_{rs}\right]\right.$$

$$\left.\times\left(\beta_0e_i'QH\sum_{p=1}^{G}\sum_{q=1}^{G} B^{g+1}i_pi_q'(B^{g+1}) \otimes (P_X - P_Z)\sigma_{pq}\Sigma_{pq}\right)\right\}$$

$$= -tr\left\{I^*[XQe_ie_i'QH\sum_{p=1}^{G}\sum_{q=1}^{G} B^{g+1}i_pi_q'(B^{g+1})\right.$$

$$\left.\otimes H'QX'\sigma_{11}\Sigma_{11}(P_X - P_Z)\sigma_{pq}\Sigma_{pq}\right\}$$

$$= -tr\left\{\sum_{p=1}^{G}\sum_{q=1}^{G}[\sigma_{11}\sigma_{pq}XQe_ie_i'QHB^{g+1}i_pi_q'(B^{g+1})H'QX'\right.$$

$$\times\, \Sigma_{11}(P_X - P_Z)\Sigma_{pq}$$

$$-\sum_{p=1}^{G}\sum_{q=1}^{G}\sigma_{11}\sigma_{pq}e_i'QH\beta_p^{g+1}(\beta_q^{g+1})'H'QX'$$

$$\left.\times\, \Sigma_{11}(P_X - P_Z)\Sigma_{pq}XQe_i\right\}. \tag{A2.9}$$

The third term is the same as the previous term so we have:

$$-tr\left\{[(H'Qe_i\beta_0' \otimes (P_X - P_Z)]\,\Omega_1^{vec}[\beta_0 e_i' QX' \otimes XQH](I^*)'\Omega_1^{vec}\right\}$$

$$= \sum_{p=1}^{G}\sum_{p=1}^{G} \sigma_{11}\sigma_{pq} e_i' QH\beta_q^{g+1}(\beta_q^{g+1})'H'QX'$$

$$\times \sum{}_{11}(P_X - P_Z)\sum{}_{pq}XQe_i\Big\} \quad \text{(A2.10)}$$

which is the same as the previous term.

Finally, the fourth term is

$$+tr\left\{I^*\,[XQe_i\beta_0' \otimes H'QX']\,\Omega_1^{vec}\,[\beta_0 e_i' QH \otimes XQH])(I^*)'\Omega_1^{vec}\right\}$$

$$= tr\left\{I^*\left(XQe_i\beta_0' \sum_{r=1}^{G}\sum_{s=1}^{G} B^{g+1}i_r i_s'(B^{g+1})' \otimes H'QX'\sigma_{rs}\Sigma_{rs}\right)\right.$$

$$\left.\times\,(\beta_0 e_i' QX'\sigma_{pq}\Sigma_{pq} \otimes XQH \sum_{p=1}^{G}\sum_{q=1}^{G} B^{g+1}i_p i_q'(B^{g+1})'I^*\right\}.$$

Noting that $I'I^* = I_{T(g+1)}$, we see that the above becomes:

$$tr\sum_{p=1}^{G}\sum_{q=1}^{G}[XQe_i e_i' QX'\sigma_{pq}\Sigma_{pq} \otimes H'QX'\sigma_{11}\Sigma_{11}XQHB^{g+1}i_p i_q'(B^{g+1})']$$

$$= \sum_{p=1}^{G}\sum_{q=1}^{G}\sigma_{11}\sigma_{pq}e_i'QX'\Sigma_{pq}XQe_i.tr(H'QX'\Sigma_{11}XQH\beta_p^{g+1}(\beta_q^{g+1})'. \quad \text{(A2.11)}$$

Gathering the terms in (A2.8)–(A2.11) and using standard summation notation, we have for **C**:

$$\sum_{p=1}^{G}\sum_{q=1}^{G}\sigma_{11}\sigma_{pq}tr\left\{((P_X - P_Z)\Sigma_{11})(P_X - P_Z)\Sigma_{pq}\}e_i'QH(\beta_p^{g+1}(\beta_q^{g+1})'HQe_i\right.$$

$$\left.-\sum_{p=1}^{G}\sum_{q=1}^{G}\sigma_{11}\sigma_{pq}e_i'QH\beta_p^{g+1}(\beta_q^{g+1})'H'QX'\Sigma_{11}(P_X - P_Z)\Sigma_{pq}XQe_i\right\}$$

$$-\sum_{p=1}^{G}\sum_{q=1}^{G}\sigma_{pq}.\sigma_{11}e_i'QX'\Sigma_{pq}(P_X-P_Z)\Sigma_{11}XQH'\beta_p^{g+1}(\beta_q^{g+1})'H'Qe_i$$

$$+\sum_{p=1}^{G}\sum_{q=1}^{G}\sigma_{11}\sigma_{pq}e_i'QX'\Sigma_{pq}XQe_i.tr(H'QX'\Sigma_{11}XQH\beta_p^{g+1}(\beta_q^{g+1})'. \quad \text{(A2.12)}$$

Next we consider the squared bias terms:

$$\mathbf{D} \quad +\left(tr\left(\left[H'Qe_i\beta_0'\otimes(P_X-P_Z)\right]-I^*\left[XQe_i\beta_0'\otimes H'QX'\right]\right)\Omega_1^{vec}\right)^2=$$

$$+\left(e_i'QH\sum_{p=1}^{G}(tr(P_Z-P_X)\sigma_{p1}\Sigma_{r1})\beta_p^{g+1}\right)^2$$

$$-2e_i'QH\sum_{r=1}^{G}(tr(P_Z-P_X)\sigma_{p1}\Sigma_{r1})\beta_p^{g+1}\left(e_i'QX'\sum_{q=1}^{G}\sigma_{q1}\Sigma_{q1}XQH\beta_q^{g+1}\right)$$

$$+\left(e_i'QX'\sum_{p=1}^{G}\sigma_{p1}\Sigma_{p1}XQH\beta_p^{g+1}\right)^2 \quad \text{(A2.13)}$$

$$\mathbf{E} \quad =+2\sum_{r=1}^{K}\sum_{s=1}^{g+1}[(trA_{rs}\Omega_1^{vec})(trB_{rs}\Omega_1^{vec}).$$

We commence by noting that from Theorem 2 we have:

$$A_{rs}=\beta_0 i_s'\otimes XQe_i i_r'(Z'Z)^{-1}Z'.$$

We may then write:

$$A_{rs}\Omega_1^{vec}=\sum_{p=1}^{G}\sum_{q=1}^{G}\left\{\beta_0 i_s' B^{g+1} i_p i_q'(B^{g+1})' \otimes XQe_i i_r'(Z'Z)^{-1}Z'\sigma_{pq}\Sigma_{pq}\right\}$$

$$tr(A_{rs}\Omega_1^{vec})=\sum_{p=1}^{G}i_s'B^{g+1}i_p tr\left(XQe_i i_r'(Z'Z)^{-1}Z'\sigma_{p1}\Sigma_{p1}\right)$$

$$=\sum_{p=1}^{G}i_p'(B^{g+1})'i_s i_r'(Z'Z)^{-1}Z'\sigma_{p1}\Sigma_{p1}XQe_i.$$

Similarly:

$$B_{rs}\Omega_1^{vec} = \Big\{(H'Qe_i\beta_0' i_s i_r' Z'XQH + H'Q(X'Zi_r i_s' H' + HZ' i_s i_r' X)Qe_i\beta_0') \otimes (P_X - P_Z))\Omega_1^{vec}\Big\} + I^*(XQHi_s i_r' Z'XQe_i\beta_0' \otimes H'QX')\Omega_1^{vec}$$

which will be written as four terms as follows:

$$(H'Qe_i\beta_0' i_s i_r' Z'XQH)B^{g+1}\sum_{p=1}^{G}\sum_{q=1}^{G} i_p i_q'(B^{g+1})' \otimes (P_X - P_Z))\sigma_{pq}\Sigma_{pq}$$

$$+ H'Q(X'Zi_s i_r' H'Qe_i\beta_o' \sum_{p=1}^{G}\sum_{q=1}^{G} B^{g+1} i_p i_q'(B^{g+1})' \otimes (P_X - P_Z))\sigma_{pq}\Sigma_{pq}$$

$$+ H'QHZ' i_s i_r' XQe_i\beta_0' \sum_{p=1}^{G}\sum_{q=1}^{G} B^{g+1} i_p i_q'(B^{g+1})' \otimes (P_X - P_Z))\sigma_{pq}\Sigma_{pq}$$

$$+ I^*(XQHi_s i_r' Z'XQe_i\beta_0' \sum_{p=1}^{G}\sum_{q=1}^{G} B^{g+1} i_p i_q'(B^{g+1})' \otimes H'QX'\sigma_{pq}\Sigma_{pq}.$$

We therefore find that:

$$tr(B_{rs}\Omega_1^{vec}) = tr\Big\{(H'Qe_i\beta_0' i_s i_r' Z'XQH)\sum_{p=1}^{G}\sum_{q=1}^{G} B^{g+1} \times tr[(P_X - P_Z)\sigma_{pq}\Sigma_{pq}] i_p i_q'(B^{g+1})'\Big\}$$

$$+ tr\Big\{(H'Q(X'Zi_r i_s' H'Qe_i \sum_{p=1}^{G} tr[(P_X - P_Z)\sigma_{1q}\Sigma_{1q}] i_q'(B^{g+1})'\Big\}$$

$$+ tr\Big\{(Hi_s i_r' Z'X)Qe_i \sum_{q=1}^{G} tr[(P_X - P_Z)\sigma_{1q}\Sigma_{1q}] i_q'(B^{g+1})'\Big\}$$

$$+ tr\Big\{(XQHi_s i_r' Z'XQe \sum_{q=1}^{G} i_q'(B^{g+1})' H'QX'\sigma_{1q}\Sigma_{1q}\Big\}.$$

From the results immediately above, we have that $(trA_{rs}\Omega_1^{vec})(trB_{rs}\Omega_1^{vec})$ is given by the sum of four terms. The first term is:

$$\sum_{p=1}^{G}\left\{\left(i_p'(B^{g+1})'i_s i_r'(Z'Z)^{-1}Z'\sigma_{p1}\Sigma_{p1}XQe_i\right.\right.$$

$$\left.\times\, tr(H'Qe_i\beta_0' i_s i_r' Z'XQH)\right)$$

$$\left.\times\sum_{l=1}^{G}\sum_{m=1}^{G}B^{g+1}tr[(P_X-P_Z)\sigma_{lm}\Sigma_{lm}]i_l i_m'(B^{g+1})'\right\}$$

$$=\sum_{l=1}^{G}\sum_{m=1}^{G}\sum_{p=1}^{G}\left\{i_p'(B^{g+1})'i_s i_s'\beta_0 e_i' QX'\Sigma_{1p}\sigma_{1p}Z(Z'Z)^{-1}i_r i_r' Z'X)\right.$$

$$\left.\times\, QHB^{g+1}tr[(P_X-P_Z)\sigma_{lm}\Sigma_{lm}]i_l i_m'(B^{g+1})'H'Qe_i\right\}.$$

When this is summed over $r = 1,\ldots,K,\ s = 1,2,\ldots,g+1$, it reduces to:

$$\sum_{l=1}^{G}\sum_{m=1}^{G}tr[(P_X-P_Z)\sigma_{lm}\Sigma_{lm}]e_i'QX'\Sigma_{11}\,\sigma_{11}XQH\beta_l^{g+1}(\beta_m^{g+1})'H'Qe_i. \quad \text{(A2.14)}$$

The second term is:

$$\sum_{p=1}^{G}i_p'(B^{g+1})'i_s i_r'(Z'Z)^{-1}Z'\sigma_{p1}\Sigma_{p1}XQe_i$$

$$\times\, tr(H'Q(X'Zi_r i_s' H'Qe_i\sum_{m=1}^{G}tr[(P_X-P_Z)\sigma_{1m}\Sigma_{1m}]i_m'(B^{g+1})'$$

$$=\sum_{p=1}^{G}i_p'(B^{g+1})'i_s i_s' H'Qe_i\sum_{m=1}^{G}tr[(P_X-P_Z)\sigma_{1m}\Sigma_{1m}]i_m'(B^{g+1})'$$

$$\times\, H'Q(X'Zi_r i_r'(Z'Z)^{-1}Z'\sigma_{p1}\Sigma_{p1}XQe_i.$$

Summing over r and s yields:

$$\sum_{p=1}^{G} i_p'(B^{g+1})'H'Qe_i \sum_{m=1}^{G} tr[(P_X - P_Z)\sigma_{1m}\Sigma_{1m}]i_m'(B^{g+1})'$$

$$\times H'Q(X''\sigma_{p1}\Sigma_{p1}XQe_i$$

$$= \sum_{p=1}^{G}\sum_{m=1}^{G} e_i'QHB^{g+1}i_p tr[(P_X - P_Z)\sigma_{1m}\Sigma_{1m}]i_m'(B^{g+1})'$$

$$\times H'Q(X''\sigma_{p1}\Sigma_{p1}XQe_i$$

$$= \sum_{p=1}^{G}\sum_{m=1}^{G} \sigma_{p1}\sigma_{1m}e_i'QHB^{g+1}i_p tr[(P_X - P_Z)\Sigma_{1m}]i_m'(B^{g+1})'$$

$$\times H'Q(X''\Sigma_{p1}XQe_i$$

$$= \sum_{p=1}^{G}\sum_{m=1}^{G} \sigma_{p1}\sigma_{1m} tr[(P_X - P_Z)\Sigma_{1m}]e_i'QH\beta_p^{g+1}(\beta_m^{g+1})'$$

$$\times H'Q(X''\Sigma_{p1}XQe_i. \tag{A2.15}$$

The third term is:

$$\sum_{p=1}^{G}\Big\{i_p'(B^{g+1})'i_s i_r'(Z'Z)^{-1}Z'\sigma_{p1}\Sigma_{p1}XQe_i$$

$$\times tr(H'QHE_{rs}'Z'X)Qe_i \sum_{m=1}^{G} tr[(P_X - P_Z)\sigma_{1m}\Sigma_{1m}]i_m'(B^{g+1})'\Big\}$$

$$= \sum_{p=1}^{G}\Big\{i_p'(B^{g+1})'i_s i_r'(Z'Z)^{-1}Z'\sigma_{p1}\Sigma_{p1}XQe_i i_r'Z'X)Qe_i$$

$$\times \sum_{m=1}^{G} tr[(P_X - P_Z)\sigma_{1m}\Sigma_{1m}]i_m'(B^{g+1})'H'QHi_s\Big\}$$

$$= \sum_{p=1}^{G}\Big\{i_p'(B^{g+1})'i_s i_s'H'QHe_i'QX'Zi_r i_r'(Z'Z)^{-1}Z'\sigma_{p1}\Sigma_{p1}XQe_i$$

$$\times \sum_{m=1}^{G} B^{g+1}i_m tr\big[(P_X - P_Z)\sigma_{1m}\Sigma_{1m}\big]\Big\}$$

Summing over r and s yields:

$$\sum_{p=1}^{G}\left\{i_p'(B^{g+1})'H'QHB^{g+1}\sum_{m=1}^{G}i_m tr[(P_X-P_Z)\sigma_{1m}\Sigma_{1m}]\right.$$
$$\left.\times\,(e_i'QX'\sigma_{p1}\Sigma_{p1}XQe_i)\right\}$$
$$=\sum_{p=1}^{G}\sum_{m=1}^{G}\sigma_{p1}\sigma_{1j}tr[(P_X-P_Z)\Sigma_{1m}]e_i'QX'\Sigma_{p1}XQe_i(\beta_p^{g+1})'H'QH\beta_m^{g+1}. \tag{A2.16}$$

Finally the fourth term is:

$$\sum_{p=1}^{G}i_p'(B^{g+1})'i_s i_r'(Z'Z)^{-1}Z'\sigma_{p1}\Sigma_{p1}XQe_i$$
$$\times\,tr(XQHE_{rs}'Z'XQe\sum_{m=1}^{G}i_j'(B^{g+1})'H'QX'\sigma_{1m}\Sigma_{1m}$$
$$=\sum_{p=1}^{G}\left\{i_p'(B^{g+1})'i_s i_r'(Z'Z)^{-1}Z'\sigma_{p1}\Sigma_{p1}XQe_i\right.$$
$$\left.\times\,tr(XQHi_s i_r'Z'XQe\sum_{m=1}^{G}i_m'(B^{g+1})'H'QX'\sigma_{1m}\Sigma_{1m}\right\}$$
$$=\sum_{p=1}^{G}\left\{i_p'(B^{g+1})'i_s i_r'(Z'Z)^{-1}Z'\sigma_{p1}\Sigma_{p1}XQe_i i_r'Z'XQe\right.$$
$$\left.\times\sum_{m=1}^{G}i_m'(B^{g+1})'H'QX'\sigma_{1m}\Sigma_{1m}XQHi_s\right\}$$
$$=\sum_{p=1}^{G}\left\{i_p'(B^{g+1})'i_s i_s'HQX'\Sigma_{m1}\sigma_{1m}XQHB^{g+1}\right.$$
$$\left.\times\sum_{m=1}^{G}i_m e_i'QX'Zi_r i_r'(Z'Z)^{-1}Z'\sigma_{p1}\Sigma_{p1}XQe_i\right\}.$$

Summing over r and s yields:

$$=\sum_{p=1}^{G}\sum_{m=1}^{G}\sigma_{p1}\sigma_{1m}e_i'QX'\Sigma_{p1}XQe_i(\beta_p^{g+1})'H'QX'\Sigma_{m1}XQH\beta_m^{g+1}. \tag{A2.17}$$

Gathering the terms (A2.14)–(A2.17) and using a standard summation notation, we have shown that:

$$\mathbf{E} \quad = +2\sum_{r=1}^{K}\sum_{s=1}^{g+1}(trA_{rs}\Omega_1^{vec})(trB_{rs}\Omega_1^{vec})$$

$$= 2\sum_{p=1}^{G}\sum_{q=1}^{G} tr[(P_X - P_Z)\sigma_{pq}\Sigma_{pq}]e_i'QX'\Sigma_{11}\ \sigma_{11}XQH\beta_p^{g+1}(\beta_q^{g+1})'H'Qe_i$$

$$+2\sum_{p=1}^{G}\sum_{q=1}^{G}\sigma_{p1}\sigma_{1q}\Big\{tr[(P_X - P_Z)\Sigma_{1q}]$$

$$\times e_i'QH\beta_p^{g+1}(\beta_q^{g+1})'\ H'Q(X''\Sigma_{p1}XQe_i\Big\}$$

$$+2\sum_{p=1}^{G}\sum_{q=1}^{G}\Big\{\sigma_{p1}\sigma_{1q}tr[(P_X - P_Z)\Sigma_{1q}](\beta_p^{g+1})'H'QH\beta_q^{g+1}$$

$$\times e_i'QX'\Sigma_{p1}XQe_i\Big\}$$

$$+2\sum_{p=1}^{G}\sum_{q=1}^{G}\Big\{\sigma_{p1}\sigma_{1q}(\beta_p^{g+1})'H'QX'\Sigma_{q1}XQH\beta_q^{g+1}$$

$$\times e_i'QX'Z\Sigma_{p1}XQe_i\Big\}. \tag{A2.18}$$

The next term to consider is:

$$\mathbf{F} = +2\sum_{r=1}^{K}\sum_{s=1}^{g+1} tr(A_{rs}\Omega_1^{vec}B_{rs}\Omega_1^{vec}).$$

To find $tr(A_{rs}\Omega_1^{vec}B_{rs}\Omega_1^{vec})$ we commence from:

$$A_{rs}\Omega_1^{vec} = \sum_{p=1}^{G}\sum_{q=1}^{G}\beta_0 i_s' B^{g+1} i_p i_q'(B^{g+1})' \otimes XQe_i i_r'(Z'Z)^{-1}Z'\sigma_{pq}\Sigma_{pq}$$

$$B_{rs}\Omega_1^{vec}$$

$$= (H'Qe_i\beta_0'E_{rs}'Z'XQH)B^{g+1}\sum_{l=1}^{G}\sum_{m=1}^{G} i_l i_m'(B^{g+1})' \otimes (P_X - P_Z))\sigma_{lm}\Sigma_{lm}$$

$$+H'Q(X'ZE_{rs}H'Qe_i\beta_o'\sum_{l=1}^{G}\sum_{m=1}^{G}B^{g+1}i_li_m'(B^{g+1})'\otimes(P_X-P_Z))\sigma_{lm}\Sigma_{lm}$$

$$+H'QHE_{rs}'Z'XQe_i\beta_0'\sum_{l=1}^{G}\sum_{m=1}^{G}B^{g+1}i_li_m'(B^{g+1})'\otimes(P_X-P_Z))\sigma_{lm}\Sigma_{lm}$$

$$+I^*(XQHE_{rs}'Z'XQe_i\beta_0'\sum_{l=1}^{G}\sum_{m=1}^{G}B^{g+1}i_li_m'(B^{g+1})'\otimes H'QX'\sigma_{lm}\Sigma_{lm}.$$

There are four terms in $B_{rs}\Omega_1^{vec}$ and so there will be four terms in $A_{rs}\Omega_1^{vec}B_{rs}\Omega_1^{vec}$. We shall examine each in turn. The first is:

$$\sum_{p=1}^{G}\sum_{q=1}^{G}\Bigg\{(\beta_0 i_s' B^{g+1}i_p i_q'(B^{g+1})'\otimes XQe_i i_r'(Z'Z)^{-1}Z'\sigma_{pq}\Sigma_{pq})$$

$$\times((H'Qe_i\beta_0'E_{rs}'Z'XQH)B^{g+1}\sum_{l=1}^{G}\sum_{m=1}^{G}i_li_m'(B^{g+1})'$$

$$\otimes(P_X-P_Z))\sigma_{lm}\Sigma_{lm})\Bigg\}.$$

On putting $E_{rs}=i_ri_s'$, the above may be written as:

$$\sum_{l=1}^{G}\sum_{m=1}^{G}\beta_0'i_si_s'B^{g+1}i_li_m'(B^{g+1})'H'Qe$$

$$\times\sum_{p=1}^{G}i_p'(B^{g+1})'H'QX'Zi_ri_r'(Z'Z)^{-1}Z'\sigma_{lm}\Sigma_{lm}(P_X-P_Z)\Sigma_{p1}XQe_i$$

Summing over $r=1,\ldots,K$ and $s=1,\ldots,g+1$ this becomes

$$\sum_{p=1}^{G}\sum_{m=1}^{G}i_m'(B^{g+1})'H'Qe_ii_p'(B^{g+1})'$$

$$\times H'QX'\sigma_{1m}\Sigma_{1m}(P_X-P_Z)\sigma_{p1}\Sigma_{p1}XQe_i$$

$$\sum_{p=1}^{G}\sum_{m=1}^{G}\sigma_{p1}\sigma_{1m}e_i'QH\beta_m^{g+1}(\beta_p^{g+1})'H'QX'\sigma_{1m}\Sigma_{1m}(P_X-P_Z)\Sigma_{p1}XQe_i. \tag{A2.19}$$

The second term is:

$$\sum_{p=1}^{G}\sum_{q=1}^{G}\Bigg\{(\beta_0 i_s' B^{g+1} i_p i_q'(B^{g+1})' \otimes XQe_i i_r'(Z'Z)^{-1}Z'\sigma_{pq}\Sigma_{pq})$$

$$\times H'Q(X'ZE_{rs}H'Qe_i\beta_o' \sum_{l=1}^{G}\sum_{m=1}^{G} B^{g+1} i_l i_m'(B^{g+1})' \otimes (P_X - P_Z))\sigma_{lm}\Sigma_{lm}\Bigg\}$$

$$= \Bigg\{\sum_{p=1}^{G}\sum_{q=1}^{G}(\beta_0 i_s' B^{g+1} i_p i_q'(B^{g+1})' H'Q(X'Zi_r i_s' H'Qe_i$$

$$\times \sum_{m=1}^{G} i_m'(B^{g+1})') \otimes XQe_i i_r'(Z'Z)^{-1}Z'\sigma_{pq}\Sigma_{pq}(P_X - P_Z))\sigma_{lm}\Sigma_{lm}\Bigg\}.$$

The trace of this is:

$$\sum_{p=1}^{G}\sum_{q=1}^{G} e_{i'} QHi_s i_s' B^{g+1} i_p i_q'(B^{g+1})' H'Q(X'Zi_r i_r'$$

$$\times ((Z'Z)^{-1}Z'\sigma_{pq}\Sigma_{pq}(P_X - P_Z))\sigma_{11}\Sigma_{11}XQe_i)$$

Summing over $r = 1, \ldots, K$ and $s = 1, \ldots, q+1$, this becomes

$$= \sum_{p=1}^{G}\sum_{q=1}^{G}\sigma_{11}\sigma_{pq} e_{i'} QHB^{g+1} i_p i_q'(B^{g+1})' H'Q(X'\Sigma_{pq}(P_X - P_Z))\Sigma_{11}XQe_i$$

$$\times \sum_{p=1}^{G}\sum_{q=1}^{G}\sigma_{11}\sigma_{pq} e_{i'} QH\beta_p^{g+1}(\beta_q^{g+1})' H'QX'\Sigma_{pq}(P_X - P_Z))\Sigma_{11}XQe_i. \tag{A2.20}$$

The third term is:

$$\sum_{p=1}^{G}\sum_{q=1}^{G}\beta_0 i_s' B^{g+1} i_p i_q'(B^{g+1})' \otimes XQe_i i_r'(Z'Z)^{-1}Z'\sigma_{pq}\Sigma_{pq}$$

$$\times H'QHE_{rs}'Z'XQe_i\beta_0' \sum_{l=1}^{G}\sum_{m=1}^{G} B^{g+1} i_l i_m'(B^{g+1})' \otimes (P_X - P_Z))\sigma_{lm}\Sigma_{lm}$$

$$= \sum_{p=1}^{G}\sum_{q=1}^{G}\beta_0 i_s' B^{g+1} i_p i_q'(B^{g+1})' H'QHi_s i_r' Z'XQe_i\beta_0' \sum_{l=1}^{G}\sum_{m=1}^{G} B^{g+1} i_l i_m'(B^{g+1})'$$

$$\otimes XQe_i i_r'(Z'Z)^{-1}Z'\sigma_{pq}\Sigma_{pq}(P_X - P_Z))\sigma_{lm}\Sigma_{lm}.$$

The trace of this is:

$$\sum_{p=1}^{G}\sum_{q=1}^{G} i_q'(B^{g+1})'H'QHi_si_s'B^{g+1}i_pe_{i'}QX'Zi_ri_r'$$

$$\times((Z'Z)^{-1}Z'\sigma_{pq}\Sigma_{pq}(P_X-P_Z))\sigma_{11}\Sigma_{11}XQe_i).$$

Summing over r and K, this becomes:

$$\sum_{p=1}^{G}\sum_{q=1}^{G}\sigma_{11}\sigma_{pq}(\beta_q^{g+1})'H'QH\beta_p^{g+1}e_{i'}QX'\Sigma_{pq}(P_X-P_Z))\Sigma_{11}XQe_i. \quad \text{(A2.21)}$$

Finally, the fourth term is:

$$\sum_{p=1}^{G}\sum_{q=1}^{G}\beta_0 i_s'B^{g+1}i_pi_q'(B^{g+1})'\otimes XQe_ii_r'(Z'Z)^{-1}Z'\sigma_{pq}\Sigma_{pq}$$

$$\times I^*(XQHE_{rs}'Z'XQe_i\beta_0'\sum_{l=1}^{G}\sum_{m=1}^{G}B^{g+1}i_li_m'(B^{g+1})'\otimes H'QX'\sigma_{lm}\Sigma_{lm})$$

$$=\sum_{p=1}^{G}\sum_{q=1}^{G}\beta_0 i_s'B^{g+1}i_pi_q'(B^{g+1})'\otimes XQe_ii_r'(Z'Z)^{-1}Z'\sigma_{pq}\Sigma_{pq}$$

$$\times((H'QX'\sigma_{lm}\Sigma_{lm})\otimes(XQHE_{rs}'Z'XQe_i\beta_0'\sum_{l=1}^{G}\sum_{m=1}^{G}B^{g+1}i_li_m'(B^{g+1})')I^*$$

$$=\sum_{p=1}^{G}\sum_{q=1}^{G}\beta_0 i_s'B^{g+1}i_pi_q'(B^{g+1})'(H'QX'\sigma_{lm}\Sigma_{lm})$$

$$\otimes XQe_ii_r'(Z'Z)^{-1}Z'\sigma_{pq}\Sigma_{pq}(XQHi_si_r'Z'XQe_i\sum_{m=1}^{G}i_m'(B^{g+1})'I^*.$$

The trace of this is:

$$tr\Bigg(\sum_{p=1}^{G}\sum_{q=1}^{G}\sigma_{11}\sigma_{pq}i_s'B^{g+1}i_pi_q'(B^{g+1})'$$

$$\times(H'QX'\Sigma_{11})XQe_ii_r'(Z'Z)^{-1}Z'\Sigma_{pq}(XQHi_si_r'Z'XQe_i)$$

$$=\sum_{p=1}^{G}\sum_{q=1}^{G}\sigma_{11}\sigma_{pq}e_{i'}QX'Zi_r i_r'$$

$$\times((Z'Z)^{-1}Z'\Sigma_{pq}XQHi_s i_s' B^{g+1} i_p i_q'(B^{g+1})'(H'QX'\Sigma_{11})XQe_i\Big).$$

Summing over r and K yields:

$$\sum_{p=1}^{G}\sum_{q=1}^{G}\sigma_{11}\sigma_{pq}e_i'QX'\Sigma_{pq}(XQH\beta_p^{g+1}(\beta_q^{g+1})'(H'QX'\Sigma_{11})XQe_i. \quad \text{(A2.22)}$$

Gathering terms from (A2.19)–(A2.22) and, using standard summation notation, we find:

$$\mathbf{F}=+2\sum_{r=1}^{K}\sum_{s=1}^{g+1}tr(A_{rs}\Omega_1^{vec}B_{rs}\Omega_1^{vec})$$

$$=2\sum_{p=1}^{G}\sum_{q=1}^{G}\sigma_{p1}\sigma_{1q}e_i'QH\beta_q^{g+1}(\beta_p^{g+1})'H'QX'\sigma_{1q}\Sigma_{1q}(P_X-P_Z)\Sigma_{p1}XQe_i$$

$$+2\sum_{p=1}^{G}\sum_{q=1}^{G}\sigma_{11}\sigma_{pq}e_{i'}QH\beta_p^{g+1}(\beta_q^{g+1})'H'QX'\Sigma_{pq}(P_X-P_Z))\Sigma_{11}XQe_i$$

$$+2\sum_{p=1}^{G}\sum_{q=1}^{G}\sigma_{11}\sigma_{pq}(\beta_q^{g+1})'H'QH\beta_p^{g+1}e_{i'}QX'\Sigma_{pq}(P_X-P_Z))\Sigma_{11}XQe_i$$

$$+2\sum_{p=1}^{G}\sum_{q=1}^{G}\sigma_{11}\sigma_{pq}e_i'QX'\Sigma_{pq}(XQHB^{g+1}i_p i_q'(B^{g+1})'(H'QX'\Sigma_{11})XQe_i. \quad \text{(A2.23)}$$

The last term is:

$$\mathbf{G}=+2\sum_{r=1}^{K}\sum_{s=1}^{g+1}tr(A_{rs}\Omega_1^{vec}B_{rs}'\Omega_1^{vec})=2\sum_{r=1}^{K}\sum_{s=1}^{g+1}tr(A_{rs}'\Omega_1^{vec}B_{rs}\Omega_1^{vec}).$$

First note that:

$$A_{rs}=\beta_0 i_s'\otimes XQe_i i_r'(Z'Z)^{-1}Z'$$

$$A_{rs}'=i_s\beta_0'\otimes Z(Z'Z)^{-1}i_r e_i'QX'$$

$$A'_{rs}\Omega_1^{vec} = \sum_{q=1}^{G} i_s i'_q (B^{g+1})' \otimes Z(Z'Z)^{-1} i_r e'_i Q X' \sigma_{1q} \Sigma_{1q}$$

$$B_{rs}\Omega_1^{vec} = \quad H'Qe_i\beta'_0 i_s i'_r Z'XQH)B^{g+1} \sum_{l=1}^{G}\sum_{m=1}^{G} i_l i'_m (B^{g+1})' \otimes (P_X - P_Z))\sigma_{lm}\Sigma_{lm}$$

$$+H'Q(X'Zi_r i'_s H'Qe_i\beta'_o \sum_{l=1}^{G}\sum_{m=1}^{G} B^{g+1} i_l i'_m (B^{g+1})' \otimes (P_X - P_Z))\sigma_{lm}\Sigma_{lm}$$

$$+H'QHZ' i_s i'_r XQe_i\beta'_0 \sum_{l=1}^{G}\sum_{m=1}^{G} B^{g+1} i_l i'_m (B^{g+1})' \otimes (P_X - P_Z))\sigma_{lm}\Sigma_{lm}$$

$$+I^*(XQHi_s i'_r Z'XQe_i\beta'_0 \sum_{l=1}^{G}\sum_{m=1}^{G} B^{g+1} i_l i'_m (B^{g+1})' \otimes H'QX'\sigma_{lm}\Sigma_{lm}.$$

From the above we see that $tr(A'_{rs}\Omega_1^{vec} B_{rs}\Omega_1^{vec})$ has four terms. The first of these is:

$$tr\left\{\sum_{p=1}^{G}\sum_{q=1}^{G} i_s\beta'_0 B^{g+1} i_p i'_q (B^{g+1})' \otimes Z(Z'Z)^{-1} i_r e'_i QX'\sigma_{pq}\Sigma_{pq}\right.$$

$$\left.\times (H'Qe_i\beta'_0 i_s i'_r Z'XQH)B^{g+1} \sum_{l=1}^{G}\sum_{m=1}^{G} i_l i'_m (B^{g+1})' \otimes (P_X - P_Z))\sigma_{lm}\Sigma_{lm}\right\}$$

$$= tr\left\{\sum_{p=1}^{G}\sum_{q=1}^{G} i_s\beta'_0 B^{g+1} i_p i'_q (B^{g+1})'(H'Qe_i\beta'_0 i_s i'_r Z'XQH)B^{g+1}\right.$$

$$\times \sum_{l=1}^{G}\sum_{m=1}^{G} B^{g+1} i_l i'_m (B^{g+1})'$$

$$\left.\otimes Z(Z'Z)^{-1} i_r e'_i QX'\sigma_{pq}\Sigma_{pq}(P_X - P_Z))\sigma_{lm}\Sigma_{lm}\right\}$$

$$= tr\left\{\sum_{p=1}^{G}\sum_{q=1}^{G} e'_i QX'\sigma_{pq}\right.$$

$$\times \Sigma_{pq}(P_X - P_Z))\sigma_{lm}\Sigma_{lm} Z(Z'Z)^{-1} i_r i'_r Z'XQH)$$

$$\left.\times B^{g+1} \sum_{l=1}^{G}\sum_{m=1}^{G} i_l i'_m (B^{g+1})' i_s i'_s \beta_0\beta'_0 B^{g+1} i_p i'_q (B^{g+1})' H'Qe_i\right\}.$$

Summing over r and s yields:

$$\sum_{q=1}^{G} e_i' QX' \sigma_{1q} \Sigma_{1q} (P_X - P_Z)) \sigma_{l1} \Sigma_{l1} XQHB^{g+1} \sum_{l=1}^{G} i_l i_q' (B^{g+1})' H' Qe_i$$

$$= \sum_{l=1}^{G} \sum_{q=1}^{G} \sigma_{l1} \sigma_{1q} e_i' QX' \Sigma_{1q} (P_X - P_Z)) \Sigma_{l1} XQH \beta_l^{g+1} (\beta_q^{g+1})' H' Qe_i. \quad \text{(A2.24)}$$

The second term is:

$$tr\left\{ \sum_{q=1}^{G} i_s i_q' (B^{g+1})' \otimes Z(Z'Z)^{-1} i_r e_i' QX' \sigma_{1q} \Sigma_{1q} \right.$$

$$\left. \times H' Q(X' Z i_r i_s' H' Qe_i \sum_{m=1}^{G} i_m' (B^{g+1})' \otimes (P_X - P_Z)) \sigma_{1m} \Sigma_{1m} \right\}$$

$$= tr\left\{ \sum_{q=1}^{G} \sum_{m=1}^{G} i_s i_q' (B^{g+1})' H' Q(X' Z i_r i_s' H' Qe_i i_m' (B^{g+1})' \right.$$

$$\left. \otimes Z(Z'Z)^{-1} i_r e_i' QX' \sigma_{1q} \Sigma_{1q} (P_X - P_Z)) \sigma_{1m} \Sigma_{1m} \right\}$$

$$= tr\left\{ \sum_{q=1}^{G} \sum_{l=1}^{G} e_i' QH i_s i_s' B^{g+1} i_l e_i' QX' \sigma_{1q} \Sigma_{1q} (P_X - P_Z)) \sigma_{1l} \Sigma_{1l} \right.$$

$$\left. \times Z(Z'Z)^{-1} i_r i_r' Z' XQHB^{g+1} i_q \right\}.$$

Summing over r and s yields:

$$\sum_{q=1}^{G} \sum_{l=1}^{G} \sigma_{1q} \sigma_{1l} e_i' QX' \Sigma_{1q} (P_X - P_Z)) \Sigma_{1l} XQH \beta_q^{g+1} (\beta_l^{g+1})' H' Qe_i. \quad \text{(A2.25)}$$

The third term is:

$$tr\left\{ \sum_{q=1}^{G} i_s i_q' (B^{g+1})' \otimes z(Z'Z)^{-1} i_r e_i' QX' \sigma_{1q} \Sigma_{1q} \right.$$

$$\left. \times H' QH i_s i_r' Z' XQe_i \sum_{m=1}^{G} i_m' (B^{g+1})' \otimes (P_X - P_Z)) \sigma_{lm} \Sigma_{lm} \right\}$$

$$= tr\left\{ \sum_{q=1}^{G} i_s i_q'(B^{g+1})' H' Q H i_s i_r' Z' X Q e_i \sum_{m=1}^{G} i_m'(B^{g+1})' \right.$$

$$\left. \otimes Z(Z'Z)^{-1} i_r e_i' Q X' \sigma_{1q} \Sigma_{1q}(P_X - P_Z))\sigma_{lm}\Sigma_{lm} \right\}$$

$$= \sum_{q=1}^{G}\sum_{m=1}^{G} i_m'(B^{g+1})' i_s i_s' H' Q H B^{g+1} i_q$$

$$\times e_i' Q X' \sigma_{1q} \Sigma_{1q}(P_X - P_Z))\sigma_{lm}\Sigma_{lm} Z(Z'Z)^{-1} i_r i_r' Z' X Q e_i.$$

Summing over r and s yields:

$$\sum_{q=1}^{G}\sum_{m=1}^{G} \sigma_{1q}\sigma_{1m}(\beta_m^{g+1})' H' Q H \beta_q^{g+1} e_i' Q X' \sigma_{1q}\Sigma_{1q}\ (P_X - P_Z))\sigma_{1m}\Sigma_{1m} X Q e_i. \tag{A2.26}$$

The fourth term is:

$$tr\left\{ \sum_{q=1}^{G} i_s i_q'(B^{g+1})' \otimes Z(Z'Z)^{-1} i_r e_i' Q X' \sigma_{1q}\Sigma_{1q} \right.$$

$$\left. \times I^*(XQHi_s i_r' Z' X Q e_i \sum_{m=1}^{G} i_m'(B^{g+1})' \otimes H' Q X' \sigma_{lm}\Sigma_{lm} \right\}$$

$$= tr\left\{ \sum_{q=1}^{G} i_s i_q'(B^{g+1})' \otimes Z(Z'Z)^{-1} i_r e_i' Q X' \sigma_{1q}\Sigma_{1q} \right.$$

$$\left. \times H' Q X' \sigma_{lm}\Sigma_{lm} \otimes (XQHi_s i_r' Z' X Q e_i \sum_{m=1}^{G} i_m'(B^{g+1})' I^* \right\}$$

$$= tr\left\{ \sum_{q=1}^{G} i_s i_q'(B^{g+1})' H' Q X' \sigma_{1m}\Sigma_{1m} \right.$$

$$\left. \otimes Z(Z'Z)^{-1} i_r e_i' Q X' \sigma_{1q}\Sigma_{1q}(XQHi_s i_r' Z' X Q e_i \sum_{m=1}^{G} i_m'(B^{g+1})' I^* \right\}$$

$$=tr\left\{\sum_{q=1}^{G} i_s i_q'(B^{g+1})'H'QX'\sigma_{1m}\Sigma_{1m}\right.$$

$$\left.\otimes Z(Z'Z)^{-1}i_r e_i' QX'\sigma_{1q}\Sigma_{1q}(XQHi_s i_r' Z'XQe_i \sum_{m=1}^{G} i_m'(B^{g+1})'I^*\right\}$$

$$=tr\left\{\sum_{q=1}^{G} i_s\, i_s' H'QX'\Sigma_{q1}\sigma_{q1}XQe_i i_q'(B^{g+1})'H'\right.$$

$$\left.\times QX'\sigma_{1m}\Sigma_{1m}Z(Z'Z)^{-1}i_r i_r' Z'XQe_i \sum_{m=1}^{G} i_m'(B^{g+1})'\right\}.$$

Summing over r and s yields:

$$tr\left\{\sum_{q=1}^{G} H'QX'\Sigma_{q1}\sigma_{q1}XQe_i i_q'(B^{g+1})'H'QX'\sigma_{1m}\Sigma_{1m}XQe_i \sum_{m=1}^{G} i_m'(B^{g+1})'\right\}$$

$$=tr\left\{\left(\sum_{q=1}^{G} H'QX'\Sigma_{q1}\sigma_{q1}XQe_i \sum_{m=1}^{G} i_m'(B^{g+1})\right)i_q'\right.$$

$$\left.\times (B^{g+1})'H'QX'\sigma_{1m}\Sigma_{1m}XQe_i\right\} = tr\left\{\left(\sum_{q=1}^{G}\sum_{m=1}^{G} i_m'(B^{g+1})'H'QX'\right.\right.$$

$$\left.\left.\times \Sigma_{q1}\sigma_{q1}XQe_i\right) i_q'(B^{g+1})'H'QX'\sigma_{1m}\Sigma_{1m}XQe_i\right\}$$

$$=\sum_{q=1}^{G}\sum_{m=1}^{G}\sigma_{q1}\sigma_{1m}e_i'QX'\Sigma_{m1}XQH\beta_q^{g+1}(\beta_m^{g+1})'H'QX'\Sigma_{q1}XQe_i. \quad \text{(A2.27)}$$

Gathering terms from (2.24)–(2.27) and, using standard summation notation, we have shown:

$$\mathbf{G}=2\sum_{r=1}^{K}\sum_{s=1}^{g+1} tr(A_{rs}\Omega_1^{vec}B_{rs}'\Omega_1^{vec})$$

$$=2\sum_{p=1}^{G}\sum_{q=1}^{G}\sigma_{p1}\sigma_{1q}e_i'QX'\Sigma_{1q}(P_X-P_Z))\Sigma_{p1}XQH\beta_p^{g+1}(\beta_q^{g+1})'H'Qe_i$$

$$+2\sum_{p=1}^{G}\sum_{q=1}^{G}\sigma_{1p}\sigma_{1q}e_i'QX'\Sigma_{1p}(P_X-P_Z))\Sigma_{1q}XQH\beta_p^{g+1}(\beta_q^{g+1})'H'Qe_i$$

$$+2\sum_{p=1}^{G}\sum_{q=1}^{G}\sigma_{1p}\sigma_{1q}(\beta_q^{g+1})'H'QH\beta_p^{g+1}e_i'QX'\Sigma_{1p}\,(P_X-P_Z))\Sigma_{1q}XQe_i$$

$$+2\sum_{p=1}^{G}\sum_{q=1}^{G}\sigma_{p1}\sigma_{1q}e_i'QX'\Sigma_{q1}XQH\beta_p^{g+1}(\beta_q^{g+1})'H'QX'\Sigma_{p1}XQe_i. \quad \text{(A2.28)}$$

Gathering terms from (A2.2), (A2.7), (A2.12), (A2.13), (A2.18), A(2.23), (A2.27) and (A2.28) yields Theorem 4.

4 Local GEL Methods for Conditional Moment Restrictions*

Richard J. Smith

1 Introduction

Simulation evidence increasingly indicates that for many models specified by unconditional moment restrictions the generalized method of moments (GMM) estimator (Hansen, 1982) may be substantially biased in finite samples, especially so when there are large numbers of moment conditions. See, for example, Altonji and Segal (1996), Imbens and Spady (2001), Judge and Mittelhammer (2001), Ramalho (2001) and Newey, Ramalho and Smith (2005). Newey and Smith (2004), henceforth NS, provides theoretical underpinning for these findings. Alternative estimators which are first-order asymptotically equivalent to GMM include empirical likelihood (EL) (Owen, 1988; Qin and Lawless, 1994; and Imbens 1997), the continuous updating estimator (CUE) (Hansen, Heaton and Yaron, 1996), and exponential tilting (ET) (Kitamura and Stutzer, 1997 and Imbens, Spady and Johnson, 1998). See also Owen (2001). NS show that these estimators and those from the Cressie and Read (1984) power divergence family of discrepancies are members of a class of generalized empirical likelihood (GEL) estimators and have a common structure; see Brown and Newey (1992, 2002) and Smith (1997, 2001). Correspondingly NS also demonstrate that GEL and GMM estimators are asymptotically equivalent and thus possess the same first-order asymptotic properties. For the unconditional context, NS describe the higher-order efficiency of bias-corrected EL. Also see Kitamura (2001).

The principal aim of this chapter is adapt the GEL method to the conditional moment context and, thereby, to describe GEL estimators

* An earlier version of this chapter also comprised part of the Invited Address "Local GEL Inference for Conditional Moment Restrictions Models" presented at the Econometric Society European Meetings, Madrid, 20–24 August, 2004. Financial support for this research from a 2002 Leverhulme Major Research Fellowship is gratefully acknowledged.

which achieve the semi-parametric efficiency lower bound. In an important recent paper, Kitamura, Tripathi and Ahn (2004), henceforth KTA, develops a semi-parametric efficient estimation method based on EL for models specified by conditional moment restrictions. Like KTA for EL we employ a kernel-weighted version of GEL. The resultant GEL criterion may be regarded as a form of local GEL. We thus term the resultant estimators local GEL estimators. We show that local GEL estimators are asymptotically first-order equivalent to the local EL estimator proposed by KTA. Consequently local GEL estimators achieve the semi-parametric efficiency lower bound; see Chamberlain (1987). The class of local GEL estimators includes local versions of EL as in KTA, the ET estimator and the CUE which is related to the estimator suggested by Bonnal and Renault (2003). Because of their one-step nature a particular advantage of these efficient local methods is the avoidance of the necessity of providing explicit nonparametric estimators for the conditional Jacobian and variance matrices which may require large numbers of observations to be good approximants. See, for example, Robinson (1987) and Newey (1990, 1993) for semi-parametric approaches based on explicit conditional Jacobian and variance matrix estimation. An alternative approach to the local EL and GEL methods suggested here is that in Donald, Imbens and Newey (2001) which employs a sequence of unconditional moment restrictions based, for example, on spline or series approximants, within the standard unconditional GEL set-up as discussed in NS. The first-order conditions arising from this sequence of restrictions approximate those based on semi-parametric efficient conditional moment restrictions from which, therefore, a semi-parametric efficient estimator also results. Their method has the computational virtue of avoiding estimation of nuisance parameter vectors whose number increases directly with sample size although the number of unconditional moment restrictions is required to increase with sample size but at a slower rate. It also incurs the expense of not producing an estimator for the conditional distribution of the data.

A reformulation of the first-order conditions defining the local GEL estimator facilitates an intuition for the semi-parametric efficiency of the local GEL estimator. The structure of these conditions conforms to those describing a semi-parametric efficient GMM estimator, that is, they implicitly incorporate consistent estimators of the conditional Jacobian matrix and conditional variance matrix of the associated conditional moment restrictions.

A test for parametric restrictions may be based on the local GEL criterion function. Unlike asymptotically equivalent Wald or Lagrange multiplier statistics but similar to the fully parametric likelihood ratio statistic this form of statistic does not require an estimator for the asymptotic variance matrix of the local GEL estimator which may be problematic in small samples.

The outline of the chapter then is as follows. In section 2 the conditional moment restrictions model is described. Section 3 details the local GEL method, obtains local EL, ET, CUE and Cressie–Read-type discrepancy estimators as special cases and provides some interpretations for local GEL estimators. Various regularity conditions are given and the consistency, asymptotic normality and semi-parametric efficiency of the local GEL estimator stated in section 4. Section 5 discusses the local GEL criterion function statistic for parametric restrictions. Proofs of the results are given in Appendix A with certain subsidiary results and proofs in Appendix B.

2 The Model

Let (x_i, z_i), $(i = 1, \ldots, n)$, be i.i.d. observations on the s- and d-dimensional data vectors x and z. As in KTA, we assume x to be continuously distributed whereas z may be discrete, mixed or continuous, although the analysis may be straightforwardly adapted for x discrete or mixed, see KTA, section 3. Also, let β be a $p \times 1$ parameter vector which is of inferential interest and $u(z, \beta)$ be a q-vector of known functions of the data observation z and β. The parameter vector β is assumed to lie in the compact parameter space $\mathcal{B}$.

The model is completed by the true parameter value $\beta_0 \in int(\mathcal{B})$ which satisfies the conditional moment restriction

$$E[u(z, \beta_0)|x] = 0 \text{ w.p.1} \tag{1}$$

where $E[\cdot|x]$ denotes expectation taken with respect to the conditional distribution of z given x. In many applications, the conditional moment indicator $u(z, \beta)$ would be a vector of residuals.

From (1), by the law of iterated expectations, any measurable function of the conditioning vector x is uncorrelated with $u(z, \beta_0)$. Therefore, we may construct a $m \times q$ matrix of instruments, $v(x, \beta_0)$ say, with $m \geq p$, and formulate the unconditional moment restrictions

$$E[v(x, \beta_0)u(z, \beta_0)] = 0 \tag{2}$$

from (1), where $E[.]$ denotes expectation taken with respect to the joint unconditional distribution of x and z. Under appropriate regularity conditions, see *inter alia* Newey and McFadden (1994) and NS,

GMM or GEL estimation using $v(x,\beta)u(z,\beta)$ as the vector of (unconditional) moment indicators will deliver consistent estimators for β_0. In general, neither unconditional GMM nor GEL estimation will achieve the semi-parametric efficiency bound because the instrumental variables $v(x,\beta_0)$ are inefficient. Chamberlain (1987) demonstrated that the semi-parametric efficiency lower bound for any $n^{1/2}$-consistent regular estimator of β_0 under (1) is given by $\mathcal{I}^{-1}$ where $\mathcal{I} \equiv \mathcal{I}(\beta_0)$ and $\mathcal{I}(\beta) \equiv E[D(x,\beta)'V(x,\beta)^{-1}D(x,\beta)]$ with the conditional Jacobian matrix $D(x,\beta) \equiv E[\partial u(z,\beta)/\partial\beta'|x]$ and conditional second moment matrix $V(x,\beta) \equiv E[u(z,\beta)u(z,\beta)'|x]$. An optimal GMM or GEL estimator based on the unconditional moment restrictions (2), therefore, would require the infeasible matrix of instrumental variables $v_*(x,\beta) \equiv D(x,\beta)'V(x,\beta)^{-1}$.

Like KTA, this chapter develops estimators for β_0 which achieve the semi-parametric efficiency bound $\mathcal{I}^{-1}$ but which avoid explicit estimation of the conditional Jacobian and conditional variance matrices, $D(x,\beta_0)$ and $V(x,\beta_0)$.

3 Estimators

The principal concern of this chapter then is estimators which achieve the semi-parametric efficiency bound $\mathcal{I}^{-1}$ under (1). We consider a local version of the GEL criterion suggested in Smith (1997, 2001) and more recently reconsidered in Newey and Smith (2004); see also Brown and Newey (1992, 2002). In particular, we are interested in the first order large sample properties of the estimator for β_0 which results from optimising a local GEL criterion. We term the resultant estimator a local GEL estimator for β_0.

Let $u_i(\beta) \equiv u(z_i,\beta)$, $(i = 1,\ldots,n)$. Also let $\rho(v)$ be a function of a scalar v that is concave on its domain, an open interval $\mathcal{V}$ containing zero. Define the positive weights $w_{ij} \equiv \mathcal{K}_{ij}/\sum_{k=1}^{n}\mathcal{K}_{ik}$ where $\mathcal{K}_{ij} \equiv \mathcal{K}(\frac{x_i-x_j}{b_n})$, $\mathcal{K}(.)$ is a symmetric positive kernel and b_n a bandwidth parameter, the properties of which will be described later. Note that $\sum_{j=1}^{n} w_{ij} = 1$. We consider a recentred local GEL criterion, cf. NS, given by

$$\widehat{P}(\beta,\lambda) = \sum_{i=1}^{n} \mathrm{T}_{i,n} \sum_{j=1}^{n} w_{ij}[\rho(\lambda_i' u_j(\beta)) - \rho(0)]/n \qquad (3)$$

where $\lambda = (\lambda_1',\ldots,\lambda_n')'$. The sequence of trimming functions $\mathrm{T}_{i,n}$ is required to bound the denominator of the weights w_{ij} away from zero and are defined as in KTA; that is, $\mathrm{T}_{i,n} \equiv I\{\hat{h}(x_i) \geq b_n^{\tau}\}$ for some

$\tau \in (0,1)$ where $\hat{h}(x_i) \equiv \sum_{j=1}^{n} \mathcal{K}(\frac{x_i - x_j}{b_n})/nb_n^s$ is the standard kernel estimator for the density $h(\cdot)$ of x at $x = x_i$ and $I\{\cdot\}$ is an indicator function. The local GEL criterion $\widehat{P}(\beta, \lambda)$ (3) employs the Nadaraya–Watson estimator $\sum_{j=1}^{n} w_{ij}\rho(\lambda_i' u_j(\beta))$ of the conditional expectation of $\rho(\lambda_i' u_i(\beta))$ given x_i, i.e. $E[\rho(\lambda_i' u_i(\beta))|x_i]$, $(i = 1, \ldots, n)$. Hence, we may consider $\widehat{P}(\beta, \lambda)$ to be an estimator of the centred average conditional expectation $\sum_{i=1}^{n} (E[\rho(\lambda_i' u_i(\beta))|x_i]/n - \rho(0))/n$.

Let $\Lambda_n = \{\lambda \in \mathcal{R}^q : \|\lambda\| \leq Cn^{-1/m}\}$ for some positive integer m and finite constant $C > 0$. The local GEL estimator then is the solution to a saddle-point problem

$$\hat{\beta} = \arg \inf_{\beta \in \mathcal{B}} \sum_{i=1}^{n} \mathrm{T}_{i,n} \sup_{\lambda_i \in \Lambda_n} \widehat{P}_i(\beta, \lambda_i)/n \tag{4}$$

where $\mathcal{B}$ denotes the parameter space and

$$\widehat{P}_i(\beta, \lambda_i) \equiv \sum_{j=1}^{n} w_{ij}[\rho(\lambda_i' u_j(\beta)) - \rho(0)], (i = 1, \ldots, n).$$

Note that the recentring term $\rho(0) \sum_{i=1}^{n} \mathrm{T}_{i,n}/n$ ensures that $\sup_{\lambda_i \in \Lambda_n} \widehat{P}_i(\beta, \lambda_i) \geq 0$ as $\widehat{P}_i(\beta, 0) = 0$ which in turn ensures that $\sum_{i=1}^{n} \mathrm{T}_{i,n} \sup_{\lambda_i \in \Lambda_n} \widehat{P}_i(\hat{\beta}, \lambda_i)$ is a suitable candidate statistic for hypothesis testing.

It will be convenient to impose a normalization on $\rho(v)$ as in NS. Let $\rho_j(v) \equiv \partial^j \rho(v)/\partial v^j$ and $\rho_j \equiv \rho_j(0)$. We normalize so that $\rho_1 = \rho_2 = -1$. We will require $\rho_1 \neq 0$ and $\rho_2 < 0$. This normalization can always be imposed by replacing $\rho(v)$ by $[-\rho_2/\rho_1^2]\rho([\rho_1/\rho_2]v)$, which leaves the estimator of β_0 unaffected.

Specialization of the function $\rho(.)$ provides a number of interesting cases. The local empirical likelihood (EL) estimator suggested by KTA results when $\rho(v) = \log(1 - v)$ and $\mathcal{V} = (-\infty, 1)$; cf. Imbens (1997), Qin and Lawless (1994), NS and Smith (1997). A local exponential tilting (ET) estimator is obtained with $\rho(v) = -\exp(v)$, cf. Imbens, Spady and Johnson (1998), Kitamura and Stutzer (1997), NS and Smith (1997).

Let $\hat{u}_i(\beta) \equiv \sum_{j=1}^{n} w_{ij} u_j(\beta)$ and $\widehat{V}(x_i, \beta) \equiv \sum_{j=1}^{n} w_{ij} u_j(\beta) u_j(\beta)'$, the Nadaraya–Watson estimators of $E[u_i(\beta)|x_i]$ and $E[u_i(\beta)u_i(\beta)'|x_i]$ respectively. A local version of the continuous updating estimator (CUE) of Hansen, Heaton and Yaron (1996), cf. Bonnal and Renault (2003) and Smith (2003), is readily seen to be a local GEL estimator when $\rho(v)$ is quadratic; cf. NS, theorem 2.1, which demonstrates an analogous result for unconditional moment restrictions. The local CUE is constructed as:

$$\hat{\beta}_{CUE} = \arg \min_{\beta \in \mathcal{B}} \sum_{i=1}^{n} \mathrm{T}_{i,n} \hat{u}_i(\beta)' \widehat{V}(x_i, \beta)^{-1} \hat{u}_i(\beta). \tag{5}$$

An alternative local CUE more in the spirit of Hansen, Heaton and Yaron, 1996 would minimize

$$\sum_{i=1}^{n} \mathbb{T}_{i,n} i\hat{u}_i(\beta)]'[\sum_{j=1}^{n} w_{ij} u_j(\beta) u_j(\beta)' - \hat{u}_i(\beta)\hat{u}_i(\beta)']^{-}\hat{u}_i(\beta)]$$

see Bonnal and Renault (2003), and Smith (2003). In contrast to the unconditional moment case, see NS, fn. 1, the resultant CUE does not coincide with $\hat{\beta}_{CUE}$.

Theorem 3.1 If $\rho(v)$ is quadratic, then $\hat{\beta} = \hat{\beta}_{CUE}$.

In contradistinction to the local CUE $\hat{\beta}_{CUE}$ which simultaneously minimizes the objective function over β in $\widehat{V}(x_i, \beta)$, a local GMM estimator is given by

$$\hat{\beta}_{GMM} = \arg\min_{\beta \in \mathcal{B}} \sum_{i=1}^{n} \mathrm{T}_{i,n} \hat{u}_i(\beta)' \widehat{V}(x_i, \tilde{\beta})^{-1} \hat{u}_i(\beta) \tag{6}$$

where $\tilde{\beta}$ denotes an initial consistent estimator for β_0; see, for example, Newey (1990, 1993).

In a similar fashion to NS, we may describe alternative estimators related to the family of discrepancy measures given by Cressie and Read (1984). Recall from NS, theorem 2.2, that the equivalent unconditional GEL criterion to the Cressie–Read discrepancy criterion is given by $\rho(v) = -(1 + \gamma v)^{(\gamma+1)/\gamma}/(\gamma + 1)$, with EL, ET and CUE as special cases obtained by setting $\gamma = -1$, $\gamma = 0$ and $\gamma = 1$ respectively. A local Cressie–Read discrepancy criterion is therefore given by

$$\widehat{P}(\beta, \lambda) = -\sum_{i=1}^{n} \mathrm{T}_{i,n} \left[\sum_{j=1}^{n} w_{ij} (1 + \gamma \lambda_i' u_j(\beta))^{(\gamma+1)/\gamma} / (\gamma + 1) - 1 \right] / n$$

cf. Bonnal and Renault (2003) and Smith (2003).

3.1 Empirical Probabilities

We may also define empirical conditional probabilities for the observations for each member of the GEL class. Let $\hat{u}_i \equiv u_i(\hat{\beta})$ where $\hat{\beta}$ denotes a GEL estimator. Also let $\hat{\lambda}_i(\beta) \equiv \arg\sup_{\lambda_i \in \Lambda_n} \sum_{j=1}^{n} w_{ij} \rho(\lambda_i' u_j(\beta))$ and $\hat{\lambda}_i \equiv \hat{\lambda}_i(\hat{\beta})$, $(i = 1, \ldots, n)$. For a given function $\rho(v)$, the empirical conditional probabilities are defined by:

$$\hat{\pi}_{ij} \equiv w_{ij} \rho_1(\hat{\lambda}_i' \hat{u}_j) / \sum_{k=1}^{n} w_{ik} \rho_1(\hat{\lambda}_i' \hat{u}_k), \; (j = 1, \ldots, n). \tag{7}$$

The empirical probabilities $\hat{\pi}_{ij}$, $(j = 1,\ldots,n; i = 1,\ldots,n)$, sum to one by construction over $j = 1,\ldots,n$, satisfy the sample moment condition $\sum_{i=1}^{n} \hat{\pi}_{ij}\hat{u}_j = 0$ when the first-order conditions for $\hat{\lambda}_i$ hold, and are positive when $\hat{\lambda}_i'\hat{u}_j$ is small uniformly in j; see Lemma B.1 in Appendix B.

For unconditional moment restrictions the (unconditional) probabilities are $\hat{\pi}_i = \rho_1(\hat{\lambda}'\hat{g}_i)/\sum_{k=1}^{n} \rho_1(\hat{\lambda}'\hat{g}_k)$, $(i = 1,\ldots,n)$, see NS, equation (2.4), where $g(z,\beta) \equiv v(x,\beta)u(z,\beta)$ from (2), $\hat{g}_i \equiv g(z_i,\hat{\beta})$ and $\hat{\beta}$ and $\hat{\lambda}$ denote an unconditional GMM or GEL estimator and associated auxiliary parameter estimator respectively. In contrast, the empirical conditional probabilities $\hat{\pi}_{ij}$ employ the differential data-determined kernel weights w_{ij}, $(j = 1,\ldots,n)$, rather than equal weights $1/n$ resulting from the unconditional empirical distribution function.

For EL, see KTA, $\hat{\pi}_{ij} = w_{ij}/(1 - \hat{\lambda}_i'\hat{u}_j)$, cf. Owen (1988), for ET, $\hat{\pi}_{ij} = w_{ij}\exp(\hat{\lambda}_i'\hat{u}_j)/\sum_{k=1}^{n} w_{ik}\exp(\hat{\lambda}_i'\hat{u}_k)$, cf. Kitamura and Stutzer (1997), and for quadratic $\rho(v)$ or CUE, see Bonnal and Renault (2003), $\hat{\pi}_{ij} = w_{ij}(1 + \hat{\lambda}_i'\hat{u}_j)/\sum_{k=1}^{n} w_{ik}(1 + \hat{\lambda}_i'\hat{u}_k)$, cf. Back and Brown (1993) and Smith (2003). See also Brown and Newey (1992, 2002) and Smith (1997).

3.2 *First-order Conditions*

Like NS for the unconditional moment restrictions case, a re-interpretation of the first-order conditions determining the local GEL estimator $\hat{\beta}$ is useful for gaining an intuitive understanding of the reason why $\hat{\beta}$ achieves the semi-parametric efficiency lower bound $\mathcal{I}^{-1}$.

Let $U_j(\beta) \equiv \partial u_j(\beta)/\partial\beta'$, $(j = 1,\ldots,n)$, and $\widehat{D}(x_i,\beta) \equiv \sum_{j=1}^{n} w_{ij}U_j(\beta)$ the Nadaraya–Watson estimator of $E[U_i(\beta)|x_i]$. Initially, consider the first order conditions for the semi-parametric efficient two-step GMM estimator $\hat{\beta}_{GMM}$ defined above in (6); that is,

$$\sum_{i=1}^{n} \widehat{D}(x_i,\hat{\beta}_{GMM})\widehat{V}(x_i,\tilde{\beta})^{-1}\hat{u}_i(\hat{\beta}_{GMM}) = 0 \tag{8}$$

which employs an explicit estimator for the efficient matrix of instrumental variables $v_*(x,\beta_0) = D(x,\beta_0)'V(x,\beta_0)^{-1}$. An analogous expression may also be provided for any GEL estimator $\hat{\beta}$ which mimics that given in NS, Theorem 2.3, for the unconditional moment restrictions case. Let $k(v) = [\rho_1(v) + 1]/v$, $v \neq 0$ and $k(0) = -1$. Also, let $\hat{v}_{ij} \equiv \hat{\lambda}_i'\hat{u}_j$.

Theorem 3.2 The local GEL first-order conditions for $\hat{\beta}$ imply

$$\sum_{i=1}^{n} \mathrm{T}_{i,n}\left[\sum_{j=1}^{n} w_{ij}\rho_1(\hat{v}_{ij})U_j(\hat{\beta})\right]'\left[\sum_{j=1}^{n} w_{ij}k(\hat{v}_{ij})u_j(\hat{\beta})u_j(\hat{\beta})'\right]^{-1}\hat{u}_i(\hat{\beta})=0 \quad (9)$$

where $k(\hat{v}_{ij}) = -1/(1-\hat{v}_{ij})$ for local EL and $k(\hat{v}_{ij}) = -1$ for local CUE.

See also Bonnal and Renault (2003) and Smith (2003) for analogous results for local CUE and efficient information theoretic estimators respectively.

A comparison of the first order conditions determining the semi-parametric efficient infeasible GMM estimator, (8), and those for local GEL, (9), is instructive. Let $\hat{k}_{ij} \equiv w_{ij}k(\hat{v}_{ij})/\sum_{k=1}^{n} w_{ik}k(\hat{v}_{ik})$ and $\hat{\pi}_{ij} \equiv w_{ij}\rho_1(\hat{v}_{ij})/\sum_{k=1}^{n} w_{ik}\rho_1(\hat{v}_{ik})$ as in (7), $(i,j = 1,\ldots,n)$. Similarly to $\hat{\pi}_{ij}$ (7), we may also interpret $\hat{k}_{ij}$ as an empirical conditional probability. Now, Lemma B.1 of Appendix B shows that $\max_{1\le j\le n}\sup_{\lambda_i\in\Lambda_n,\beta\in\mathcal{B}}\lambda_i'g_j(\beta) = o_p(1)$. Therefore, the implicit estimators for the conditional Jacobian and conditional variance matrices in (9) are consistent, i.e., $\sum_{j=1}^{n}\hat{\pi}_{ij}U_j(\hat{\beta}) \xrightarrow{p} D(x_i,\beta_0)$ and $\sum_{j=1}^{n}\hat{k}_{ij}u_j(\hat{\beta})u_j(\hat{\beta})' \xrightarrow{p} V(x_i,\beta_0)$ with $\sum_{k=1}^{n} w_{ik}k(\hat{v}_{ik})/\sum_{k=1}^{n} w_{ik}\rho_1(\hat{v}_{ik}) \xrightarrow{p} 1$. Comparing the GMM and GEL first order conditions, (8) and (9), we see straightforwardly that, asymptotically, local GEL estimators implicitly employ the semi-parametric efficient matrix of instrumental variables and thereby achieve the semi-parametric efficiency lower bound $\mathcal{I}^{-1}$.

It is also interesting to note that the local CUE uses the Nadaraya–Watson kernel regression estimator $\widehat{V}(x_i,\hat{\beta})$ for the conditional variance matrix $V(x_i,\beta_0)$ whereas local EL employs the same weights for the estimation of $V(x_i,\beta_0)$ as for the conditional Jacobian matrix $D(x_i,\beta_0)$, that is, the empirical probabilities $\hat{\pi}_{ij} = 1/(1-\hat{v}_{ij})$. The two-step semi-parametric efficient GMM estimator $\hat{\beta}_{GMM}$ described in (6) utilises Nadaraya–Watson regression estimators for both conditional Jacobian and variance matrices.

4 Asymptotic Theory for Local GEL

This section gives consistency and asymptotic normality results for the local GEL estimator $\hat{\beta}$.

We firstly, however, require some additional notation. Let $h(x)$ denote the density function of x. Elements of vectors and matrices are denoted by superscripts (i) and (ij) respectively.

Next, we provide some regularity conditions. Our assumptions are virtually identical to KTA, Assumptions 3.1–3.7. For a full discussion of these assumptions, see KTA, section 3.

Assumption 4.1 For each $\beta \neq \beta_0$ there exists a set $\mathcal{X}_\beta \subseteq \mathcal{R}^s$ such that $\mathcal{P}\{x \in \mathcal{X}_\beta\} > 0$ and $E[u(z,\beta)|x] \neq 0$ for all $x \in \mathcal{X}_\beta$.

This is the conditional identification condition given in KTA, Assumption 3.1. Together with (1) it crucially ensures that $E[\|E[u(z,\beta)|x]\|^2] = 0$ if and only if $\beta = \beta_0$.

Assumption 4.2 (i) $\rho(v)$ is twice continuously differentiable and concave on its domain, an open interval $\mathcal{V}$ containing 0 and $\rho_1 = \rho_2 = -1$; (ii) $E[\sup_{\beta\in\mathcal{B}} \|u(z,\beta)\|^m] < \infty$ for some $m > 8$.

Assumption 4.2(i) is the condition on $\rho(v)$ adapted from NS, Assumption 1(f).

Assumption 4.3 The kernel $\mathcal{K}(x) = \prod_{k=1}^{s} \kappa(x^{(k)})$, $x = (x^{(1)}, \ldots, x^{(s)})'$, where $\kappa : \mathcal{R} \to \mathcal{R}$, is a continuously differentiable p.d.f. with support $[-1,1]$, symmetric about 0 and bounded away from 0 on $[-a,a]$ for some $a \in (0,1)$.

Assumption 4.4 (i) $0 < h(x) \leq \sup_{x\in\mathcal{R}^s} h(x) < \infty$, $h(x)$ is twice continuously differentiable on $\mathcal{R}^s$, $\sup_{x\in\mathcal{R}^s} \|\partial h(x)/\partial x\| < \infty$ and $\sup_{x\in\mathcal{R}^s} \left\|\partial^2 h(x)/\partial x \partial x'\right\| < \infty$; (ii) $E[\|x\|^{p+1}] < \infty$ for some $p > 0$; (iii) $u(z,\beta)$ is continuous on $\mathcal{B}$ w.p.1 and $E[\sup_{\beta\in\mathcal{B}} \|\partial u(z,\beta)/\partial\beta'\|] < \infty$; (iv) $\left\|\partial^2[E[u^{(i)}(z,\beta)|x]h(x)]/\partial x \partial x'\right\|$ is uniformly bounded on $\mathcal{B} \times \mathcal{R}^s$, $(i = 1, \ldots, q)$.

Let $\mathcal{S}^q \equiv \{\xi : \xi \in \mathcal{R}^q, \|\xi\| = 1\}$ be the unit sphere in $\mathcal{R}^q$.

Assumption 4.5 There exists a non-empty neighbourhood $\mathcal{B}_0$ of β_0 such that (i) $D(x,\beta)$ and $V(x,\beta)$ are continuous on $\mathcal{B}_0$ w.p.1; (ii) $\inf_{(\xi,x,\beta)\in\mathcal{S}^q\times\mathcal{R}^s\times\mathcal{B}_0} \xi' V(x,\beta)\xi > 0$ and $\sup_{(\xi,x,\beta)\in\mathcal{S}^q\times\mathcal{R}^s\times\mathcal{B}_0} \xi' V(x,\beta) \xi > 0$; (iii) $\sup_{\beta\in\mathcal{B}_0} \left|\partial u^{(i)}(z,\beta)/\partial\beta^{(j)}\right| < c(z)$ and $\sup_{\beta\in\mathcal{B}_0} \left|\partial^2 u^{(i)}(z,\beta)/\partial\beta^{(j)}\partial\beta^{(k)}\right| < d(z)$ w.p.1 for some functions $c(z)$ and $d(z)$ such that $E[c(z)^\eta] < \infty$ for some $\eta > 4$ and $E[d(z)] < \infty$; (iv) $\sup_{x\in\mathcal{R}^s} \left\|\partial E[D^{(ij)}(x,\beta_0)h(x)]/\partial x\right\| < \infty$ and $\sup_{(x,\beta)\in\mathcal{R}^s\times\mathcal{B}_0} \left\|\partial^2 E[D^{(ij)}(x,\beta_0)h(x)]/\partial x\partial x'\right\| < \infty$; (v) $\sup_{x\in\mathcal{R}^s} \left\|\partial E[V^{(ij)}(x,\beta_0)h(x)]/\partial x\right\| < \infty$ and $\sup_{(x,\beta)\in\mathcal{R}^s\times\mathcal{B}_0} \left\|\partial^2 E[V^{(ij)}(x,\beta_0)\ h(x)]/\partial x\partial x'\right\| < \infty$.

Assumption 4.6 The parameters λ_i, $(i = 1, \ldots, n)$, are constrained to lie in the set $\Lambda_n = \{\lambda_i : \|\lambda_i\| \leq Dn^{-1/m}\}$ for some $D > 0$.

Assumption 4.7 Let $\tau \in (0,1)$, $\rho \geq \max(1/\eta + 1/2, 2/m + 1/2)$, $b_n \downarrow 0$ and $\sigma \in (0, 1/2)$. Then $n^{1-2\sigma-2/m} b_n^{2s+4\tau} \uparrow \infty$, $n^{\rho} b_n^{2\tau} \uparrow \infty$, $n^{\rho-1/\eta} b_n^{\tau} \uparrow \infty$, $n^{\rho-2/m} b_n^{\tau} \uparrow \infty$, $n^{1-2\sigma} b_n^{5s/2+6\tau} \uparrow \infty$, $n^{2\rho-1/\eta-1/m-1/2} b_n^{2\tau} \uparrow \infty$ and $n^{2\rho-3/m-1/2} b_n^{3\tau} \uparrow \infty$.

As noted by KTA, the presence of the parameter σ is required for the uniform convergence result for kernel estimators given in Ai (1997, Lemma B.1, p. 955) which is central to the proofs of many of the subsidiary results presented in KTA, Appendix B.

These conditions lead to a consistency result.

Theorem 4.1 Let Assumptions 4.1–4.5 and 4.7 hold. Then $\hat{\beta} \xrightarrow{p} \beta_0$.

Asymptotic normality of the local GEL estimator $\hat{\beta}$ requires the additional regularity condition Assumption 4.6.

Theorem 4.2 If Assumptions 4.1–4.7 are satisfied, then $n^{1/2}(\hat{\beta} - \beta_0) \xrightarrow{d} N(0, \mathcal{I}^{-1})$.

Theorem 4.2 emphasizes that all local GEL estimators $\hat{\beta}$ are first order equivalent and achieve the semi-parametric efficiency lower bound $\mathcal{I}^{-1}$. Lemma B.3 below provides a basis for the estimation of the asymptotic variance matrix $\mathcal{I}^{-1}$ of $n^{1/2}(\hat{\beta} - \beta_0)$.

5 Hypothesis Tests

Consider the following null hypothesis which incorporates the parametric restrictions $r(\beta) = 0$:

$$H_0 : r(\beta_0) = 0 \tag{10}$$

where $r(\cdot)$ is an r-vector of twice continuously differentiable functions of β where $p > r$. The alternative hypothesis is defined by $H_1 : r(\beta_0) \neq 0$.

A standard Wald statistic based on the local GEL estimator could be used to test $H_0 : r(\beta_0) = 0$. This form of statistic like others requires the consistent estimation of the semi-parametric information matrix $\mathcal{I}$, cf. Lemma B.3 below. Estimators of $\mathcal{I}$ may be unreliable with the samples typically available in applications. Unlike the Wald statistic the statistic described here is based on the local GEL criterion function (3) and therefore does not require estimation of the conditional Jacobian and variance matrices, $D(x, \beta_0)$ and $V(x, \beta_0)$, which are required for explicit estimation of $\mathcal{I}$.

The local GEL criterion function statistic LR_n^{GEL} is then defined as

$$LR_n^{GEL} = 2n[\widehat{P}(\hat{\beta}, \hat{\lambda}(\hat{\beta})) - \widehat{P}(\tilde{\beta}, \hat{\lambda}(\tilde{\beta}))] \tag{11}$$

where the restricted local GEL estimator $\tilde{\beta} = \arg\inf_{\beta\in\mathcal{B}^r}\sum_{i=1}^{n}\mathrm{T}_{i,n}\sup_{\lambda_i\in\Lambda_n}\widehat{P}_i(\beta,\lambda_i)/n$ with $\mathcal{B}^r = \{\beta : r(\beta) = 0, \beta\in\mathcal{B}\}$.

Similarly to KTA, section 4, to motivate the use of the statistic LR_n^{GEL} (11) consider the situation which arises when the null hypothesis is simple, that is, $H_0^c : \beta_0 = \beta^c$ where β^c is known. By a Taylor expansion about $\hat{\beta}$, as $\partial\widehat{P}(\hat{\beta},\hat{\lambda}(\hat{\beta}))/\partial\beta = 0$,

$$LR_n^{GEL} = 2n[\widehat{P}(\hat{\beta},\hat{\lambda}(\hat{\beta})) - \widehat{P}(\beta^c,\hat{\lambda}(\beta^c))]$$

$$= -n(\hat{\beta}-\beta^c)'\frac{\partial^2\widehat{P}(\beta^*,\hat{\lambda}(\beta^*))}{\partial\beta\partial\beta'}(\hat{\beta}-\beta^c).$$

Now $\partial^2\widehat{P}(\beta^*,\hat{\lambda}(\beta^*))/\partial\beta\partial\beta' = -\mathcal{I} + o_p(1)$ by Lemma B.3 and $n^{1/2}(\hat{\beta}-\beta_0) \xrightarrow{d} N(0,\mathcal{I}^{-1})$ from Theorem 4.2. Therefore, $LR_n^{GEL} \xrightarrow{d} \chi^2(p)$ under H_0^c.

To deal with the general case (10), we make the following assumption:

Assumption 5.1 (i) $r : \mathcal{B} \to \mathcal{R}^r$ is twice continuously differentiable; (ii) $R \equiv \partial r(\beta_0)/\partial\beta'$ is full row rank r.

The following result describes the limiting distribution of the local GEL criterion function statistic LR_n^{GEL} (11).

Theorem 5.1 Let Assumptions 4.1–4.7 and 5.1 be satisfied. Then $LR_n^{GEL} \xrightarrow{d} \chi^2(r)$ under $H_0 : r(\beta_0) = 0$.

A test with given asymptotic size is obtained by comparing the statistic LR_n^{GEL} to an appropriate critical value from the chi-square distribution with r degrees of freedom. Valid asymptotic confidence regions for β_0 may be constructed by inversion of LR_n^{GEL}. In particular, a $(1-\alpha)$ confidence region is $\beta_0 \in \{\beta : 2n[\widehat{P}(\hat{\beta},\hat{\lambda}(\hat{\beta})) - \widehat{P}(\beta,\hat{\lambda}(\beta))] \le \chi^2_{1-\alpha}(p)\}$ where $\chi^2_{1-\alpha}(\cdot)$ is the $100(1-\alpha)$-percentile from the $\chi^2(\cdot)$ distribution. Like KTA, a $(1-\alpha)$ confidence interval for a single parameter, $\beta_0^{(j)}$ say, is given by $\beta_0^{(j)} \in \{\beta : \min_{\beta^{(i)},i\neq j} 2n[\widehat{P}(\hat{\beta},\hat{\lambda}(\hat{\beta})) - \widehat{P}(\beta,\hat{\lambda}(\beta))] \le \chi^2_{1-\alpha}(1)\}$.

Appendix A: Proofs of Results

Throughout these Appendices, C will denote a generic positive constant that may be different in different uses, and CS and T the Cauchy–Schwarz and triangle inequalities respectively. Also, with probability approaching one will be abbreviated as w.p.a.1, UWL will denote a uniform weak law of large numbers such as Lemma 2.4 of Newey and McFadden (1994), and CLT will refer to the Lindeberg–Lévy central limit theorem.

Let $\hat{u}_i(\beta) \equiv \sum_{j=1}^n w_{ij}u_j(\beta)$, $\widehat{D}(x_i,\beta) \equiv \sum_{j=1}^n w_{ij}U_j(\beta)$ and $\widehat{V}(x_i,\beta) \equiv \sum_{j=1}^n w_{ij}u_j(\beta)u_j(\beta)'$. Also let $\hat{\lambda}_{i0} \equiv \hat{\lambda}_i(\beta_0)$, $(i = 1,\ldots,n)$, $\hat{\lambda}_0 = (\hat{\lambda}'_{10},\ldots,\hat{\lambda}'_{n0})'$ and $u_{i0} \equiv u_i(\beta_0)$, $U_{i0} \equiv U_i(\beta_0)$, $(i = 1,\ldots,n)$.

Proof of Theorem 3.1 The proof is very similar to that for NS, theorem 2.1. By $\rho(v)$ quadratic, a second-order Taylor expansion is exact, giving

$$\widehat{P}(\beta,\lambda) = -\sum_{i=1}^n \mathrm{T}_{i,n}\hat{u}_i(\beta)'\lambda_i - \frac{1}{2}\sum_{i=1}^n \mathrm{T}_{i,n}\lambda_i'\widehat{V}(x_i,\beta)\lambda_i.$$

By concavity of $\widehat{P}_i(\beta,\lambda_i) = -\mathrm{T}_{i,n}\hat{u}_i(\beta)'\lambda_i - \mathrm{T}_{i,n}\lambda_i'\widehat{V}(x_i,\beta)\lambda_i/2$ in λ_i, any solution $\hat{\lambda}_i(\beta)$ to the first-order conditions

$$0 = -\mathrm{T}_{i,n}\hat{u}_i(\beta) - \mathrm{T}_{i,n}\widehat{V}(x_i,\beta)\lambda_i$$

will maximize $\widehat{P}_i(\beta,\lambda_i)$ with respect to λ_i holding β fixed. Then, $\hat{\lambda}_i(\beta) = -\widehat{V}(x_i,\beta)^{-1}\hat{u}_i(\beta)$ solves the first-order conditions. Since

$$\widehat{P}_i(\beta,\hat{\lambda}_i(\beta)) = \frac{1}{2}\mathrm{T}_{i,n}\hat{u}_i(\beta)'\widehat{V}(x_i,\beta)^{-1}\hat{u}_i(\beta)$$

the GEL objective function $\widehat{P}(\beta,\hat{\lambda}(\beta))$ is a monotonic increasing function of the CUE objective function.

Proof of Theorem 3.2 Let $\hat{u}_j \equiv u_j(\hat{\beta})$ and $\widehat{U}_j \equiv U_j(\hat{\beta})$. The first-order conditions for $\hat{\lambda}_i \equiv \arg\sup_{\lambda_i\in\Lambda_n}\sum_{j=1}^n w_{ij}\rho(\lambda_i'\hat{u}_j)$ are $\mathrm{T}_{i,n}\sum_{j=1}^n w_{ij}\rho_1(\hat{\lambda}_i'u_j(\hat{\beta}))u_j(\hat{\beta}) = 0$. By the implicit function theorem there is a neighbourhood of $\hat{\beta}$ where the solution $\hat{\lambda}_i(\beta)$ to $\mathrm{T}_{i,n}\sum_{j=1}^n w_{ij}\rho_1(\lambda_i'u_j(\beta))u_j(\beta) = 0$ exists and is continuously differentiable. Then by the envelope theorem, the first-order conditions for GEL are:

$$\sum_{i=1}^n \mathrm{T}_{i,n}\sum_{j=1}^n w_{ij}\rho_1(\hat{\lambda}_i'u_j(\hat{\beta}))U_j(\hat{\beta})'\hat{\lambda}_i = 0, \tag{A.1}$$

$$\mathrm{T}_{i,n}\sum_{j=1}^n w_{ij}\rho_1(\hat{\lambda}_i'u_j(\hat{\beta}))u_j(\hat{\beta}) = 0, (i = 1,\ldots,n).$$

By equation (A.1) and the definition of $k(v)$,

$$0 = \mathrm{T}_{i,n}\sum_{j=1}^n \rho_1(\hat{v}_{ij})w_{ij}\hat{u}_j = \mathrm{T}_{i,n}\left[\sum_{j=1}^n(\rho_1(\hat{v}_{ij})+1)w_{ij}\hat{u}_j - \sum_{j=1}^n w_{ij}\hat{u}_j\right]$$

$$= \mathrm{T}_{i,n}\left[\sum_{j=1}^n k(\hat{v}_{ij})w_{ij}\hat{u}_j\hat{u}_j'\hat{\lambda}_i - \sum_{j=1}^n w_{ij}\hat{u}_j\right], (i = 1,\ldots,n).$$

Plugging the solutions $\mathrm{T}_{i,n}\hat{\lambda}_i = \mathrm{T}_{i,n}[\sum_{j=1}^n k(\hat{v}_{ij})w_{ij}\hat{u}_j\hat{u}_j']^{-1}\sum_{j=1}^n w_{ij}\hat{u}_j$, $(i = 1,\ldots,n)$, into the first part of equation (A.1) $\sum_{i=1}^n \mathrm{T}_{i,n}\sum_{j=1}^n \rho_1(\hat{v}_{ij})w_{ij}\,\widehat{U}_j'\hat{\lambda}_i = 0$

gives the first result. Note that for EL $k(v) = [-(1-v)^{-1}+1]/v = -(1-v)^{-1} = \rho_1(v)$ and for CUE $k(v) = [-(1+v)+1]/v = -1$.

Proof of Theorem 4.1 The structure of the proof closely resembles that of KTA, proof of theorem 3.1. Let $c > 0$ such that $(-c, c) \in \mathcal{V}$. Define $C_n = \{z \in \mathcal{R}^d : \sup_{\beta \in \mathcal{B}} \|u(z, \beta)\| \leq cn^{1/m}\}$ and $u_{nj}(\beta) = I_j u_j(\beta)$, where $I_j = I\{z_j \in C_n\}$. Let $\bar{\lambda}_i(\beta) = -E[u_i(\beta)|x_i]/(1 + \|E[u_i(\beta)|x_i]\|)$. Then,

$$\sup_{\{\lambda_i \in \Lambda_n\}_{i=1}^n} \widehat{P}(\beta, \lambda) \geq Q_n(\beta)$$

$$= \sum_{i=1}^n \mathrm{T}_{i,n} \sum_{j=1}^n w_{ij}[\rho(n^{-1/m}\bar{\lambda}_i(\beta)' u_{nj}(\beta)) - \rho(0)]/n. \tag{A.2}$$

Note that $n^{-1/m}\bar{\lambda}_i(\beta) \in \Lambda_n$.
Now $\rho(n^{-1/m}\bar{\lambda}_i(\beta)' u_{nj}(\beta)) = \rho(0) - n^{-1/m}\bar{\lambda}_i(\beta)' u_j(\beta) + r_{nij}(t)$, for some $t \in (0, 1)$ and:

$$r_{nij}(t) = n^{-1/m}\bar{\lambda}_i(\beta)' u_j(\beta)(1 - I_j)$$

$$+ n^{-1/m}\bar{\lambda}_i(\beta)' u_{nj}(\beta)[\rho_1(tn^{-1/m}\bar{\lambda}_i(\beta)' u_{nj}(\beta)) - \rho_1(0)]. \tag{A.3}$$

From Lemma B.1 $\sup_{\beta \in \mathcal{B}, n^{-1/m}\lambda_i \in \Lambda_n, 1 \leq j \leq n} \left|\rho_1(n^{-1/m}\lambda_i' u_j(\beta)) - \rho_1(0)\right| \xrightarrow{p} 0$. Also $\max_{1 \leq j \leq n}(1 - I_j) = o_p(1)$. Hence, from equation (A.3),

$$n^{1/m} \sum_{i=1}^n \mathrm{T}_{i,n} \sum_{j=1}^n w_{ij} r_{nij}(t)/n = o_p(1) \sum_{i=1}^n \mathrm{T}_{i,n} \bar{\lambda}_i(\beta)' \hat{u}_i(\beta)/n$$

$$+ o_p(1) \sum_{i=1}^n \mathrm{T}_{i,n} \bar{\lambda}_i(\beta)' \hat{u}_i(\beta)/n$$

$$- o_p(1) \sum_{i=1}^n \mathrm{T}_{i,n} \bar{\lambda}_i(\beta)' \sum_{j=1}^n w_{ij} u_j(\beta)(1 - I_j)/n$$

$$= o_p(1) \sum_{i=1}^n \mathrm{T}_{i,n} \bar{\lambda}_i(\beta)' \hat{u}_i(\beta)/n$$

uniformly $\beta \in \mathcal{B}$. Thus,

$$n^{1/m} \sup_{\beta \in \mathcal{B}} \left| \sum_{i=1}^n \mathrm{T}_{i,n} \sum_{j=1}^n w_{ij} r_{nij}(t)/n \right| \leq o_p(1) \sum_{i=1}^n \mathrm{T}_{i,n} \sup_{\beta \in \mathcal{B}} \left\| \hat{u}_i(\beta) \right\| /n$$

$$= o_p(1) O_p(1) = o_p(1)$$

as $\max_{1\le i\le n}\sup_{\beta\in\mathcal{B}}\mathrm{T}_{i,n}\left\|\hat{u}_i(\beta)-E[u_i(\beta)|x_i]\right\| = o_p(1)$; cf. KTA, Proof of Lemma B.8. Therefore, substituting into equation (A.2), $n^{1/m}Q_n(\beta) = -\sum_{i=1}^n \mathrm{T}_{i,n}\sum_{j=1}^n w_{ij}\bar{\lambda}_i(\beta)'u_j(\beta) + o_p(1)$ uniformly $\beta\in\mathcal{B}$ and, from KTA, Lemma B.8,

$$n^{1/m}\sup_{\beta\in\mathcal{B}}\left|Q_n(\beta)-\bar{Q}_n(\beta)\right| = o_p(1) \tag{A.4}$$

as $\sum_{i=1}^n(\mathrm{T}_{i,n}-1)/n = o_p(1)$, see KTA, proof of theorem 3.1, where

$$n^{1/m}\bar{Q}_n(\beta) = -\sum_{i=1}^n \bar{\lambda}_i(\beta)'E[u_i(\beta)|x_i]/n; \tag{A.5}$$

see KTA, equations (A.4) and (A.5). Thus, as in KTA, equation (A.6), from equations (A.2) and (A.4),

$$n^{1/m}\inf_{\beta\in\mathcal{B}}\sup_{\{\lambda_i\in\Lambda_n\}_{i=1}^n}\widehat{P}(\beta,\lambda)\ge n^{1/m}\inf_{\beta\in\mathcal{B}}\bar{Q}(\beta)+o_p(1). \tag{A.6}$$

From the definition of $\bar{\lambda}_i(\beta)$, $(i=1,\ldots,n)$, and (A.5), a UWL gives

$$n^{1/m}\bar{Q}_n(\beta) = E[\|E[u_i(\beta)|x_i]\|^2/(1+\|E[u_i(\beta)|x_i]\|)] + o_p(1) \tag{A.7}$$

uniformly $\beta\in\mathcal{B}$; see KTA, equation (A.7). The function $E[\|E[u_i(\beta)|x_i]\|^2/(1+\|E[u_i(\beta)|x_i]\|)] = E[I\{x_i\in\mathcal{X}_\beta\}\,\|E[u_i(\beta)|x_i]\|^2/(1+\|E[u_i(\beta)|x_i]\|)]$ is continuous in β, has a unique zero β_0 and is strictly positive for all $\beta\ne\beta_0$ by Assumption 4.1.

Now

$$0\le n^{1/m}\sup_{\{\lambda_i\in\Lambda_n\}_{i=1}^n}\widehat{P}(\hat{\beta},\lambda)\le n^{1/m}\sup_{\{\lambda_i\in\Lambda_n\}_{i=1}^n}\widehat{P}(\beta_0,\lambda) \tag{A.8}$$

as $\widehat{P}(\hat{\beta},0)=0$. By the concavity of $\rho(v)$, $\rho(\lambda_{i0}'u_{j0})-\rho(0)\le-\lambda_{i0}'u_{j0}$. Hence,

$$\begin{aligned}
n^{1/m}\sup_{\{\lambda_i\in\Lambda_n\}_{i=1}^n}\widehat{P}(\beta_0,\lambda) &= n^{1/m}\widehat{P}(\beta_0,\hat{\lambda}_0)\\
&= n^{1/m}\sum_{i=1}^n \mathrm{T}_{i,n}\sum_{j=1}^n w_{ij}[\rho(\hat{\lambda}_{i0}'u_{j0})-\rho(0)]/n\\
&\le -n^{1/m}\sum_{i=1}^n \mathrm{T}_{i,n}\sum_{j=1}^n w_{ij}\hat{\lambda}_{i0}'u_{j0}/n\\
&= n^{1/m}\left[o_p\left(\sqrt{\frac{n^\sigma}{nb_n^{s+2\tau}}}\right)+o_p\left(\frac{1}{n^{\rho-1/m}}\right)\right]^2\\
&= o_p(1),
\end{aligned}$$

by Assumption 4.7, by equation (B.3) of Lemma B.2 and KTA, Lemma B.3. Therefore, combining (A.8) and (A.9),

$$n^{1/m} \sup_{\{\lambda_i \in \Lambda_n\}_{i=1}^n} \widehat{P}(\hat{\beta}, \lambda) = o_p(1). \tag{A.9}$$

By T and (A.6):

$$\begin{aligned}
0 &\leq E[-\bar{\lambda}_i(\beta)' E[u_i(\beta)|x_i]]|_{\beta=\hat{\beta}} \\
&\leq \sup_{\beta \in \mathcal{B}} \left\| n^{1/m} \bar{Q}_n(\beta) - E[-\bar{\lambda}_i(\beta)' E[u_i(\beta)|x_i]] \right\| + \left\| n^{1/m} \bar{Q}_n(\hat{\beta}) \right\| \\
&\leq \left\| n^{1/m} \sup_{\{\lambda_i \in \Lambda_n\}_{i=1}^n} \widehat{P}(\hat{\beta}, \lambda) \right\|
\end{aligned}$$

as $\sup_{\{\lambda_i \in \Lambda_n\}_{i=1}^n} \widehat{P}(\beta, \lambda) \geq \bar{Q}_n(\beta) + o_p(1)$ uniformly $\beta \in \mathcal{B}$ from equations (A.2) and (A.4). Hence, from equations (A.9) and (A.10), $E[-\bar{\lambda}_i(\beta)' E[u_i(\beta)|x_i]]|_{\beta=\hat{\beta}} = o_p(1)$. Therefore, $\hat{\beta}$ must lie in any neighbourhood of β_0 w.p.a.1, that is, $\hat{\beta} \xrightarrow{p} \beta_0$, as $E[-\bar{\lambda}_i(\beta)' E[u_i(\beta)|x_i]]$ is continuous and has a unique zero β_0.

Proof of Theorem 4.2 We consider the first-order condition determining the local GEL estimator $\hat{\beta}$; *viz.* $\partial \widehat{P}(\hat{\beta}, \hat{\lambda}(\hat{\beta}))/\partial \beta = 0$. Hence,

$$0 = n^{1/2} \frac{\partial \widehat{P}(\beta_0, \hat{\lambda}_0)}{\partial \beta} + \frac{\partial^2 \widehat{P}(\beta^*, \hat{\lambda}(\beta^*))}{\partial \beta \partial \beta'} n^{1/2} (\hat{\beta} - \beta_0) \tag{A.10}$$

for some β^* on the line segment joining $\hat{\beta}$ and β_0 which may differ row by row. From Lemma B.2 and equation (A.1),

$$n^{1/2} \frac{\partial \widehat{P}(\beta_0, \hat{\lambda}_0)}{\partial \beta} = n^{1/2} \widehat{A} + n^{-1/2} \sum_{i=1}^n \mathrm{T}_{i,n} \sum_{j=1}^n w_{ij} \rho_1(\hat{\lambda}_{i0}' u_{j0}) U_{j0}' r_i \tag{A.11}$$

where

$$\widehat{A} = -\sum_{i=1}^n \mathrm{T}_{i,n} \left[\sum_{j=1}^n w_{ij} \rho_1(\hat{\lambda}_{i0}' u_{j0}) U_{j0} \right]' \widehat{V}(x_i, \beta_0)^{-1} \hat{u}_i(\beta_0)/n. \tag{A.12}$$

From Lemma B.1, $\sup_{\beta\in\mathcal{B},\lambda_i\in\Lambda_n,1\le j\le n}\left|\rho_1(\lambda_i' u_j(\beta)) - \rho_1(0)\right| = o_p(1)$. Therefore, w.p.a.1,

$$n^{-1/2}\left\|\sum_{i=1}^{n}\mathrm{T}_{i,n}\sum_{j=1}^{n}w_{ij}\rho_1(\hat{\lambda}_{i0}'u_{j0})U_{j0}'r_i\right\|$$

$$\le O_p(n^{1/2})\max_{1\le i\le n}\mathrm{T}_{i,n}\|r_i\|\sum_{i=1}^{n}\sum_{j=1}^{n}w_{ij}d(z_j)/n$$

$$= o_p\left(\sqrt{\frac{n^{2\sigma+2/m}}{nb_n^{2s+4\tau}}}\right) + o_p\left(\frac{1}{n^{2\rho-3/m-1/2}}\right) = o_p(1) \qquad \text{(A.13)}$$

uniformly i, j and $\beta \in \mathcal{B}_0$ by Assumption 4.7.

Let

$$\widehat{A} = A + \sum_{i=1}^{n}\mathrm{T}_{i,n}\sum_{j=1}^{n}w_{ij}[\rho_1(\hat{\lambda}_{i0}'u_{j0}) - \rho_1(0)]U_{j0}'\widehat{V}(x_i,\beta_0)^{-1}\hat{u}_i(\beta_0)/n \qquad \text{(A.14)}$$

from (A.12), where:

$$A = \sum_{i=1}^{n}\mathrm{T}_{i,n}\left[\sum_{j=1}^{n}w_{ij}U_{j0}\right]'\widehat{V}(x_i,\beta_0)^{-1}\hat{u}_i(\beta_0)/n. \qquad \text{(A.15)}$$

Now, by Lemma B.1,

$$\left\|\mathrm{T}_{i,n}\sum_{j=1}^{n}w_{ij}[\rho_1(\hat{\lambda}_{i0}'u_{j0}) - \rho_1(0)]U_{j0}\right\| \le O_p(1)\mathrm{T}_{i,n}\left\|\hat{\lambda}_{i0}\right\|$$

$$\times\sum_{j=1}^{n}w_{ij}\sup_{\beta\in\mathcal{B}}\left\|u(z_j,\beta)\right\|d(z_j)$$

uniformly i, j and $\beta \in \mathcal{B}_0$. Moreover, as $\max_{1\le i\le n}\left\|\widehat{V}(x_i,\beta_0)^{-1}\right\| = O_p(1)$, KTA, Lemma B.7, and $\max_{1\le i\le n}\mathrm{T}_{i,n}\left\|\sum_{j=1}^{n}w_{ij}\sup_{\beta\in\mathcal{B}}\right\|u(z_j,\beta)\left\|d(z_j)\right\| = O_p(1)$ by Assumptions 4.2, 4.5 (iii) and 4.7, from (A.14)–(A.16),

$$n^{1/2}\left\|\widehat{A} - A\right\| \le O_p(n^{1/2})\max_{1\le i\le n}\mathrm{T}_{i,n}\left\|\hat{u}_i(\beta_0)\right\|\left[\sum_{i=1}^{n}\mathrm{T}_{i,n}\left\|\hat{\lambda}_{i0}\right\|/n\right]$$

$$= o_p\left(\sqrt{\frac{n^{2\sigma}}{nb_n^{2+4\tau}}}\right) + o_p\left(\frac{1}{n^{2\rho-2/m-1/2}}\right) = o_p(1) \qquad \text{(A.16)}$$

from equation (B.3) and by KTA, Lemma B.3. Therefore, substituting (A.13) and (A.16) into (A.13), $n^{1/2}\partial\widehat{P}(\beta_0,\hat{\lambda}_0)/\partial\beta = n^{1/2}A + o_p(1)$ and the result follows from Lemma B.3 and the continuity of $\mathcal{I}(\beta)$ from Assumption 4.5 (ii) on $\mathcal{B}_0$ as $n^{1/2}A \xrightarrow{d} N(0,\mathcal{I})$ from CLT by KTA, Lemma B.2.

Proof of Theorem 5.1 As $R(\beta_0)$ is full row rank r, by the implicit function theorem there exists neighbourhood $\mathcal{N}$ of β_0, an open set $\mathcal{U} \subseteq \mathcal{R}^{p-r}$ and a twice continuously differentiable function $\beta(\cdot) : \mathcal{U} \to \mathcal{R}^p$ such that $\{\beta \in \mathcal{N} : r(\beta) = 0\} = \{\beta = \beta(\alpha) : \alpha \in \mathcal{U}\}$. Therefore, any $\beta \in \mathcal{N}$ may be expressed as $\beta = \beta(\alpha)$ for some $\alpha \in \mathcal{U}$. In particular, $\beta_0 = \beta(\alpha_0)$ where $\alpha_0 \in \mathcal{U}$. Moreover, $\beta(\cdot)$ is twice continuously differentiable on $\mathcal{U}$ and B is full column rank $p-r$ where $B \equiv B(\alpha_0)$ and $B(\alpha) \equiv \partial\beta(\alpha)/\partial\alpha'$. Cf. the proof of theorem 4.1 of KTA.

The restricted local GEL criterion under H_0: $r(\beta_0) = 0$ (10) becomes

$$\widehat{P}(\beta(\alpha),\lambda) = \sum_{i=1}^{n} \mathrm{T}_{i,n} \sum_{j=1}^{n} w_{ij}[\rho(\lambda_i' u_j(\beta(\alpha))) - \rho(0)]/n \tag{A.17}$$

cf. (3). The restricted GEL estimator is then given by $\tilde{\beta} \equiv \beta(\tilde{\alpha})$ where $\tilde{\alpha} = \arg\inf_{\alpha\in\mathcal{U}} \sum_{i=1}^{n} \mathrm{T}_{i,n} \sup_{\lambda_i\in\Lambda_n} \widehat{P}_i(\beta(\alpha),\lambda_i)/n$. Therefore, as $n^{1/2}(\hat{\beta} - \beta_0) = -\mathcal{I}^{-1}n^{1/2}A + o_p(1) = -\mathcal{I}^{-1}n^{-1/2}\sum_{i=1}^{n} D(x_i,\beta_0)'V(x_i,\beta_0)^{-1}u_i(\beta_0) + o_p(1)$ from the proof of theorem 4.2 and KTA, equation (B.6), under $H_0 : r(\beta_0) = 0$,

$$n^{1/2}(\tilde{\alpha} - \alpha_0) = -(B'\mathcal{I}B)^{-1}B'n^{-1/2}\sum_{i=1}^{n} D(x_i,\beta(\alpha_0))'V(x_i,\beta(\alpha_0))^{-1} \times u_i(\beta(\alpha_0)) + o_p(1) \tag{A.18}$$

where $\mathcal{I} = E[D(x_i,\beta(\alpha_0))'V(x_i,\beta(\alpha_0))^{-1}D(x_i,\beta(\alpha_0))]$, cf. KTA, equation (A.18).

Using a second-order Taylor expansion of $\widehat{P}(\beta_0,\hat{\lambda}(\beta_0))$ around $\hat{\beta}$, by Lemma B.3,

$$\begin{aligned} 2n[\widehat{P}(\hat{\beta},\hat{\lambda}(\hat{\beta})) - \widehat{P}(\beta_0,\hat{\lambda}(\beta_0))] &= -n(\hat{\beta}-\beta_0)'\frac{\partial^2\widehat{P}(\beta^*,\hat{\lambda}(\beta^*))}{\partial\beta\partial\beta'}(\hat{\beta}-\beta_0) \\ &= n(\hat{\beta}-\beta_0)'\mathcal{I}(\hat{\beta}-\beta_0) + o_p(1) \end{aligned}$$

for some β^* between $\hat{\beta}$ and β_0. Similarly, a Taylor expansion of $\widehat{P}(\beta(\alpha_0),\hat{\lambda}(\beta(\alpha_0)))$ around $\tilde{\alpha}$ yields:

$$\begin{aligned} &2n[\widehat{P}(\beta(\tilde{\alpha}),\hat{\lambda}(\beta(\tilde{\alpha}))) - \widehat{P}(\beta(\alpha_0),\hat{\lambda}(\beta(\alpha_0)))] \\ &= -n(\tilde{\alpha}-\alpha_0)'\frac{\partial^2\widehat{P}(\beta(\alpha^*),\hat{\lambda}(\beta(\alpha^*)))}{\partial\alpha\partial\alpha'}(\tilde{\alpha}-\alpha_0) \end{aligned} \tag{A.19}$$

for some α^* between $\tilde{\alpha}$ and α_0. Now,

$$\begin{aligned} \frac{\partial^2\widehat{P}(\beta(\alpha),\hat{\lambda}(\beta(\alpha)))}{\partial\alpha\partial\alpha'} &= B(\alpha)'\frac{\partial^2\widehat{P}(\beta(\alpha),\hat{\lambda}(\beta(\alpha)))}{\partial\beta\partial\beta'}B(\alpha) \\ &\quad + \sum_{k=1}^{p}\frac{\partial^2\beta^{(k)}(\alpha)}{\partial\alpha\partial\alpha'}\frac{\partial\widehat{P}(\beta(\alpha),\hat{\lambda}(\beta(\alpha)))}{\partial\alpha^{(k)}} \end{aligned}$$

and, by Lemmata B.3 and B.8 and Assumption 5.1 (i),

$$\frac{\partial^2 \widehat{P}(\beta(\alpha^*), \hat{\lambda}(\beta(\alpha^*)))}{\partial\alpha\partial\alpha'} = -B'\mathcal{I}B + o_p(1). \tag{A.20}$$

Combining equations (A.19) and (A.20),

$$\begin{aligned} &2n[\widehat{P}(\beta(\tilde{\alpha}), \hat{\lambda}(\beta(\tilde{\alpha}))) - \widehat{P}(\beta(\alpha_0), \hat{\lambda}(\beta(\alpha_0)))] \\ &= n(\tilde{\alpha} - \alpha_0)'B'\mathcal{I}B(\tilde{\alpha} - \alpha_0) + o_p(1). \end{aligned} \tag{A.21}$$

Therefore, from equations (A.15), (A.18), (A.19), (A.21) and KTA, equation (B.6),

$$\begin{aligned} LR_n^{GEL} &= 2n[\widehat{P}(\hat{\beta}, \hat{\lambda}(\hat{\beta})) - \widehat{P}(\beta(\tilde{\alpha}), \hat{\lambda}(\beta(\tilde{\alpha})))] \\ &= nA'(\mathcal{I}^{-1} - B(B'\mathcal{I}B)^{-1}B')A + o_p(1) \\ &\xrightarrow{d} \chi^2(r) \end{aligned}$$

Rao and Mitra (1971, theorem 9.2.1, p. 171), as $\mathcal{I}(\mathcal{I}^{-1} - B(B'\mathcal{I}B)^{-1}B')\mathcal{I}(\mathcal{I}^{-1} - B(B'\mathcal{I}B)^{-1}B')\mathcal{I} = \mathcal{I}(\mathcal{I}^{-1} - B(B'\mathcal{I}B)^{-1}B')\mathcal{I}$ and $tr(\mathcal{I}(\mathcal{I}^{-1} - B(B'\mathcal{I}B)^{-1}B')) = p - (p - r) = r$.

Appendix B: Auxiliary Results

The following Lemma is used extensively in the Proofs of Theorems 4.1, 4.2 and various of the Lemmata given below.
Let $\widehat{\mathrm{T}}_{i,n} \equiv \mathrm{T}_{i,n} h(x_i)/\hat{h}(x_i)$.

Lemma B.1 Suppose Assumptions 4.2 and 4.6 are satisfied. Then for any ζ with $1/m \leq \zeta < 1/2$ and $\Lambda_n = \{\lambda : \|\lambda\| \leq Cn^{-\zeta}, C > 0\}$, $\sup_{\beta\in\mathcal{B},\lambda_i\in\Lambda_n, 1\leq j\leq n} |\lambda_i' u_j(\beta)| \xrightarrow{p} 0$ and w.p.a.1, $\lambda_i' u_j(\beta) \in \mathcal{V}$ for all $1 \leq j \leq n$, $\lambda \in \Lambda_n$ and $\beta \in \mathcal{B}$.

Proof By Assumption 4.2 and KTA, Lemma D.2, $\max_{1\leq j\leq n} \sup_{\beta\in\mathcal{B}} \| u_j(\beta)\| = o_p(n^{1/m})$; also see Owen (1990, Lemma 3). It therefore follows from Assumption 4.6 that

$$\sup_{\beta\in\mathcal{B}} \sup_{\lambda_i\in\Lambda_n} \max_{1\leq j\leq n} |\lambda_i' u_j(\beta)| \leq Cn^{-\zeta} \max_{1\leq j\leq n} \sup_{\beta\in\mathcal{B}} \|u_j(\beta)\| \xrightarrow{p} 0.$$

Therefore, w.p.a.1, $\lambda_i' u_j(\beta) \in \mathcal{V}$ for all $1 \leq j \leq n$, $\lambda_i \in \Lambda_n$ and $\beta \in \mathcal{B}$.

The next Lemma parallels KTA, Lemma B.1, which provides a similar result for local EL.

Lemma B.2 Let Assumptions 4.2–4.5 be satisfied. Also let $n^{1-\sigma-2/m} b_n^{s+2\tau} \uparrow \infty$, $n^{\rho-2/m} \uparrow \infty$ and $n^{1-\sigma} b_n^{(\frac{m+2}{m-2})\frac{s}{2}} \uparrow \infty$ for some $\sigma \in (0, 1)$ and $b_n \downarrow 0$.

Then $T_{i,n}\hat{\lambda}_{i0} = -T_{i,n}\widehat{V}(x_i,\beta_0)^{-1}\hat{u}_i(\beta_0) + T_{i,n}r_i$, where $\max_{1\le i\le n} T_{i,n}\|r_i\| = o_p\left(\frac{n^{\sigma+1/m}}{nb_n^{s+2\tau}}\right) + o_p\left(\frac{1}{n^{2\rho-3/m}}\right)$.

Proof From equation (A.1)

$$0 = T_{i,n}\sum_{j=1}^{n} w_{ij}\rho_1(\hat{\lambda}_{i0}'u_{j0})u_{j0}$$

$$= -T_{i,n}\hat{u}_i(\beta_0) - T_{i,n}\widehat{V}(x_i,\beta_0)\hat{\lambda}_{i0} + T_{i,n}r_{1i}(t) \tag{B.1}$$

for some $t \in (0,1)$, where $r_{1i}(t) = \sum_{j=1}^{n} w_{ij}[\rho_2(t\hat{\lambda}_{i0}'u_{j0}) - \rho_2(0)]u_{j0}u_{j0}'\hat{\lambda}_{i0}$. From Lemma B.1 $\sup_{\beta\in\mathcal{B},\lambda_i\in\Lambda_n,1\le j\le n}\left|\rho_2(\lambda_i'u_j(\beta)) - \rho_2(0)\right| \xrightarrow{p} 0$. Thus, $r_{1i}(t) = o_p(1)\widehat{V}(x_i,\beta_0)\hat{\lambda}_{i0}$ uniformly i and j and

$$T_{i,n}\|r_{1i}(t)\| \le o_p(1)\max_{1\le j\le n}\|u_{j0}\|\, T_{i,n}\left|\hat{u}_i(\beta_0)'\hat{\lambda}_{i0}\right|$$

$$\le o_p(n^{1/m})\max_{1\le j\le n}\|u_{j0}\|\, T_{i,n}\|\hat{u}_i(\beta_0)\|\left\|\hat{\lambda}_{i0}\right\|$$

$$= o_p(n^{1/m})\left[o_p\left(\sqrt{\frac{n^{\sigma}}{nb_n^{s+2\tau}}}\right) + o_p\left(\frac{1}{n^{\rho-1/m}}\right)\right] T_{i,n}\left\|\hat{\lambda}_{i0}\right\| \tag{B.2}$$

where the second inequality follows from CS and $\max_{1\le j\le n}\|u_{j0}\| = o(n^{1/m})$ by KTA, Lemma D.2, and the equality by KTA, Lemma B.3; see KTA, equation (B.3).

Let $\xi_{i0} = \hat{\lambda}_{i0}/\left\|\hat{\lambda}_{i0}\right\|$. Then, multiplying equation (A.1) by $\hat{\lambda}_{i0}$ yields,

$$0 = T_{i,n}\left\|\hat{\lambda}_{i0}\right\|\sum_{j=1}^{n} w_{ij}\rho_1(\hat{\lambda}_{i0}'u_{j0})\xi_{i0}'u_{j0}$$

$$= -T_{i,n}\left\|\hat{\lambda}_{i0}\right\|\xi_{i0}'\hat{u}_i(\beta_0) - T_{i,n}\left\|\hat{\lambda}_{i0}\right\|^2(1+o_p(1))\xi_{i0}'\widehat{V}(x_i,\beta_0)\xi_{i0}$$

uniformly i and j. As $\xi_{i0}'\widehat{V}(x_i,\beta_0)\xi_{i0}$ is bounded below by Assumption 4.5 (ii) solving

$$T_{i,n}\left\|\hat{\lambda}_{i0}\right\| = -T_{i,n}\xi_{i0}'\hat{u}_i(\beta_0)/(1+o_p(1))\xi_{i0}'\widehat{V}(x_i,\beta_0)\xi_{i0} \tag{B.3}$$

$$= o_p\left(\sqrt{\frac{n^{\sigma}}{nb_n^{s+2\tau}}}\right) + o_p\left(\frac{1}{n^{\rho-1/m}}\right)$$

uniformly i by KTA, Lemma B.3, as $\widehat{V}(x_i, \beta_0) = O_p(1)$ from KTA, Lemma B.6. Therefore, from equation (B.2),

$$\mathrm{T}_{i,n} \|r_{1i}(t)\| = o_p\left(\frac{n^{\sigma+1/m}}{nb_n^{s+2\tau}}\right) + o_p\left(\frac{1}{n^{2\rho-3/m}}\right) \tag{B.4}$$

uniformly i.

By Assumption 4.5 (ii), from equations (B.1) and (B.4), as $\max_{1\le i\le n} \mathrm{T}_{i,n} \times \left\|\widehat{V}(x_i, \beta_0)^{-1}\right\| = O_p(1)$ by KTA, Lemma B.7,

$$\begin{aligned}\mathrm{T}_{i,n}\hat{\lambda}_{i0} &= -\mathrm{T}_{i,n}\widehat{V}(x_i, \beta_0)^{-1}\hat{u}_i(\beta_0) + \mathrm{T}_{i,n}\widehat{V}(x_i, \beta_0)^{-1}r_{1i}(t)\\ &= -\mathrm{T}_{i,n}\widehat{V}(x_i, \beta_0)^{-1}\hat{u}_i(\beta_0) + \mathrm{T}_{i,n}r_i.\end{aligned}$$

Lemmata B.3–B.8 given below are the local GEL counterparts of KTA, Lemmas C.1–C.6. Our proofs follow closely those in KTA.

Lemma B.3 Let Assumptions 4.1–4.7 hold. Then $\sup_{\beta\in\mathcal{B}_0}\left\|-\partial^2\widehat{P}(\beta, \hat{\lambda}(\beta))/\partial\beta\partial\beta' - \mathcal{I}(\beta)\right\| = o_p(1)$.

Proof As $\mathrm{T}_{i,n}\sum_{j=1}^n w_{ij}\rho_1(\hat{\lambda}_i(\beta)'u_j(\beta))u_j(\beta) = 0$, $(i = 1, \ldots, n)$, for all $\beta \in \mathcal{B}$ from (A.1),

$$\frac{\partial\widehat{P}(\beta, \hat{\lambda}(\beta))}{\partial\beta} = \sum_{i=1}^n \mathrm{T}_{i,n}\sum_{j=1}^n w_{ij}\rho_1(\hat{\lambda}_i(\beta)'u_j(\beta))U_j(\beta)'\hat{\lambda}_i(\beta)/n. \tag{B.5}$$

Therefore, $\partial^2\widehat{P}(\beta, \hat{\lambda}(\beta))/\partial\beta\partial\beta' = T_1(\beta) + T_2(\beta) + T_3(\beta)$ where:

$$T_1(\beta) = \sum_{i=1}^n \mathrm{T}_{i,n}\sum_{j=1}^n w_{ij}\rho_2(\hat{\lambda}_i(\beta)'u_j(\beta))U_j(\beta)'\hat{\lambda}_i(\beta)\partial[\hat{\lambda}_i(\beta)'u_j(\beta)]/\partial\beta']/n,$$

$$T_2(\beta) = \sum_{i=1}^n \mathrm{T}_{i,n}\sum_{j=1}^n w_{ij}\rho_1(\hat{\lambda}_i(\beta)'u_j(\beta))[U_j(\beta)'\partial\hat{\lambda}_i(\beta)/\partial\beta']/n,$$

$$T_3(\beta) = \sum_{i=1}^n \mathrm{T}_{i,n}\sum_{j=1}^n w_{ij}\rho_1(\hat{\lambda}_i(\beta)'u_j(\beta))\left[\sum_{k=1}^q \hat{\lambda}_i^{(k)}(\beta)\partial^2 u_j^{(k)}(\beta)/\partial\beta\partial\beta'\right]/n.$$

From Lemmata B.4–B.6 the desired result follows.

Lemma B.4 If Assumptions 4.2–4.7 are satisfied, then $\sup_{\beta\in\mathcal{B}_0}\|T_1(\beta)\| = o_p(1)$.

Proof As $\partial[\hat{\lambda}_i(\beta)'u_j(\beta)]/\partial\beta' = \hat{\lambda}_i(\beta)'U_j(\beta) + u_j(\beta)'\partial\hat{\lambda}_i(\beta)/\partial\beta'$, consider

$$T_{1,a}(\beta) = \sum_{i=1}^{n} \mathrm{T}_{i,n} \sum_{j=1}^{n} w_{ij}\rho_2(\hat{\lambda}_i(\beta)'u_j(\beta))U_j(\beta)'\hat{\lambda}_i(\beta)\hat{\lambda}_i(\beta)'U_j(\beta)/n,$$

$$T_{1,b}(\beta) = \sum_{i=1}^{n} \mathrm{T}_{i,n} \sum_{j=1}^{n} w_{ij}\rho_2(\hat{\lambda}_i(\beta)'u_j(\beta))U_j(\beta)'\hat{\lambda}_i(\beta)u_j(\beta)'\partial\hat{\lambda}_i(\beta)/\partial\beta'/n.$$

By Lemma B.1, Assumptions 4.5 (iii) and 4.6 $\sup_{\beta\in\mathcal{B}_0} \|T_{1,a}(\beta)\| \leq o_p(1)\sum_{i=1}^{n} \mathrm{T}_{i,n} \sum_{j=1}^{n} w_{ij} \quad d(z_j)^2/n = o_p(1)$ as $\mathrm{T}_{i,n}\sum_{j=1}^{n} w_{ij}d(z_j)^2 = O_p(1)$ uniformly i by KTA, Lemma D.4. Also, $\sup_{\beta\in\mathcal{B}_0} \|T_{1,b}(\beta)\| \leq o_p(1)\sum_{i=1}^{n} \mathrm{T}_{i,n} \| \partial\hat{\lambda}_i(\beta)/\partial\beta'\| \sum_{j=1}^{n} w_{ij}d(z_j)\|u_j(\beta)\|/n = o_p(1)\sum_{i=1}^{n} \mathrm{T}_{i,n} \|\partial\hat{\lambda}_i(\beta)/\partial\beta'\|/n$ since similarly $\mathrm{T}_{i,n}\sum_{j=1}^{n} w_{ij}d(z_j)\|u_j(\beta)\| \leq (\mathrm{T}_{i,n}\sum_{j=1}^{n} w_{ij}d(z_j)^2)(\mathrm{T}_{i,n}\sum_{j=1}^{n} w_{ij} \|u_j(\beta)\|^2) = O_p(1)$ uniformly i, j and $\beta \in \mathcal{B}_0$. Now, from Lemma B.7 below, $\sup_{\beta\in\mathcal{B}_0}\sum_{i=1}^{n} \mathrm{T}_{i,n} \|\partial\hat{\lambda}_i(\beta)/\partial\beta'\|/n = o_p(1)$. Hence, $\sup_{\beta\in\mathcal{B}_0}\|T_{1,b}(\beta)\| \leq o_p(1)$ from Lemma B.7 as $\sum_{i=1}^{n} \mathrm{T}_{i,n}\|\partial\hat{\lambda}_i(\beta)/\partial\beta'\|/n = O_p(1)$.

Lemma B.5 If Assumptions 4.2–4.7 are satisfied, then $\sup_{\beta\in\mathcal{B}_0} \| - T_2(\beta) - \mathcal{I}(\beta)\| = o_p(1)$.

Proof Using Lemma B.7 below, by a similar argument to that above KTA, equation (C.3), as $\sup_{\beta\in\mathcal{B},\lambda_i\in\Lambda_n,1\leq j\leq n} |\rho_1(\lambda_i'u_j(\beta)) - \rho_1(0)| = o_p(1)$ from Lemma B.1,

$$\sum_{i=1}^{n} \mathrm{T}_{i,n} \sum_{j=1}^{n} w_{ij}\rho_1(\hat{\lambda}_i(\beta)'u_j(\beta))[U_j(\beta)'\partial\hat{\lambda}_i(\beta)/\partial\beta']/n$$
$$= -\sum_{i=1}^{n} \mathrm{T}_{i,n}D(x_i,\beta)'\partial\hat{\lambda}_i(\beta)/\partial\beta'/n + o_p(1)$$

uniformly $\beta \in \mathcal{B}_0$. Again using Lemma B.7,

$$n^{-1}\sup_{\beta\in\mathcal{B}_0}\left\|\sum_{i=1}^{n} \widehat{\mathrm{T}}_{i,n}D(x_i,\beta)'\partial\hat{\lambda}_i(\beta)/\partial\beta' - \sum_{i=1}^{n} \widehat{\mathrm{T}}_{i,n}^2 D(x_i,\beta)'V(x_i,\beta)D(x_i,\beta)\right\|$$
$$= o_p(1).$$

Therefore, from KTA, below equation (C.3),

$$\sum_{i=1}^{n} \mathrm{T}_{i,n} \sum_{j=1}^{n} w_{ij}\rho_1(\hat{\lambda}_i(\beta)'u_j(\beta))[U_j(\beta)'\partial\hat{\lambda}_i(\beta)/\partial\beta']/n$$

$$= -\sum_{i=1}^{n} D(x_i,\beta)'V(x_i,\beta)D(x_i,\beta)/n + o_p(1)$$

uniformly $\beta \in \mathcal{B}_0$, cf. KTA, equation (C.4). The result follows by UWL.

Lemma B.6 If Assumptions 4.3, 4.5 and 4.6 are satisfied, then $\sup_{\beta\in\mathcal{B}_0} \|T_3(\beta)\| = o_p(1)$.

Proof By Assumptions 4.5 (iii) and 4.6 and Lemma B.1, from KTA, Lemma D.4,

$$n^{-1}\sup_{\beta\in\mathcal{B}_0}\left\|\sum_{i=1}^{n}\mathrm{T}_{i,n}\sum_{j=1}^{n} w_{ij}\rho_1(\hat{\lambda}_i(\beta)'u_j(\beta))\left[\sum_{k=1}^{q}\hat{\lambda}_i^{(k)}(\beta)\partial^2 u_j^{(k)}(\beta)/\partial\beta\partial\beta'\right]\right\|$$

$$\le o_p(1)\sum_{i=1}^{n}\mathrm{T}_{i,n}\sum_{j=1}^{n} w_{ij} l(z_j)/n = o_p(1).$$

Lemma B.7 If Assumptions 4.2–4.7 are satisfied, then, for each i and $\beta \in \mathcal{B}_0$,

$$\mathrm{T}_{i,n}\partial\hat{\lambda}_i(\beta)/\partial\beta' = \widehat{\mathrm{T}}_{i,n}V(x_i,\beta)^{-1}D(x_i,\beta) + \widehat{\mathrm{T}}_{i,n}M_{1,i}(\beta)D(x_i,\beta)$$

$$+ \widehat{\mathrm{T}}_{i,n}M_{2,i}(\beta)E[d(z_i)|x_i] + M_{3,i}(\beta)\sum_{j=1}^{n} w_{ij}d(z_j) + M_{4,i}(\beta),$$

where $\max_{1\le i\le n}\sup_{\beta\in\mathcal{B}_0}\|M_{k,i}(\beta)\| = o_p(1)$, $k = 1,\ldots,4$.

Proof Firstly, from differentiating (A.1), we have:

$$\sum_{j=1}^{n} w_{ij}\rho_2(\hat{\lambda}_i(\beta)'u_j(\beta))u_j(\beta)u_j(\beta)'\partial\hat{\lambda}_i(\beta)/\partial\beta'$$

$$= -\sum_{j=1}^{n} w_{ij}\rho_1(\hat{\lambda}_i(\beta)'u_j(\beta))U_j(\beta) - \sum_{j=1}^{n} w_{ij}\rho_2(\hat{\lambda}_i(\beta)'u_j(\beta))u_j(\beta)\hat{\lambda}_i(\beta)'U_j(\beta). \tag{B.6}$$

By Lemma B.1, from Assumption 4.5 (ii) and KTA, Lemma B.6,

$$\max_{1\le i\le n}\sup_{\beta\in\mathcal{B}_0}\mathrm{T}_{i,n}\left\|-\sum_{j=1}^{n} w_{ij}\rho_2(\hat{\lambda}_i(\beta)'u_j(\beta))u_j(\beta)u_j(\beta)' - V(x_i,\beta)\right\| = o_p(1). \tag{B.7}$$

Thus, with $\max_{1\leq i\leq n}\sup_{\beta\in\mathcal{B}_0}\|R_{1,i}(\beta)\| = o_p(1)$, from Assumption 4.5 (ii),

$$\mathrm{T}_{i,n}\left[\sum_{j=1}^{n} w_{ij}\rho_2(\hat{\lambda}_i(\beta)'u_j(\beta))u_j(\beta)u_j(\beta)'\right]^{-1} = -\mathrm{T}_{i,n}V(x_i,\beta)^{-1} + R_{1,i}(\beta) \tag{B.8}$$

cf. KTA, equation (C.6).

Similarly, by Lemma B.1 and KTA, Lemma B.5, an argument like that for KTA, equation (C.7), yields:

$$\mathrm{T}_{i,n}\sum_{j=1}^{n} w_{ij}\rho_1(\hat{\lambda}_i(\beta)'u_j(\beta))U_j(\beta)$$
$$= \widehat{\mathrm{T}}_{i,n}\rho_1(0)D(x_i,\beta) + \widehat{\mathrm{T}}_{i,n}E[d(z_i)|x_i]R_{2,i}(\beta) + R_{3,i}(\beta) \tag{B.9}$$

where $\max_{1\leq i\leq n}\sup_{\beta\in\mathcal{B}_0}\|R_{2,i}(\beta)\| = o_p(1)$ and $\max_{1\leq i\leq n}\sup_{\beta\in\mathcal{B}_0}\|R_{3,i}(\beta)\| = o_p(1)$.

Finally, by Lemma B.1, Assumptions 4.5 (iii) and 4.6, from KTA, Lemma D.2,

$$\mathrm{T}_{i,n}\left\|\sum_{j=1}^{n} w_{ij}\rho_2(\hat{\lambda}_i(\beta)'u_j(\beta))u_j(\beta)\hat{\lambda}_i(\beta)'U_j(\beta)\right\|$$
$$\leq O_p(1)\mathrm{T}_{i,n}\sum_{j=1}^{n} w_{ij}d(z_j)\left\|\hat{\lambda}_i(\beta)\right\|\|u_j(\beta)\| = o_p(1)\sum_{j=1}^{n} w_{ij}d(z_j)$$

uniformly i, j and $\beta\in\mathcal{B}_0$. Therefore, for $\max_{1\leq i\leq n}\sup_{\beta\in\mathcal{B}_0}\|R_{4,i}(\beta)\| = o_p(1)$,

$$\mathrm{T}_{i,n}\sum_{j=1}^{n} w_{ij}\rho_2(\hat{\lambda}_i(\beta)'u_j(\beta))u_j(\beta)\hat{\lambda}_i(\beta)'U_j(\beta) = R_{4,i}(\beta)\sum_{j=1}^{n} w_{ij}d(z_j) \tag{B.10}$$

cf. KTA, equation (C.8).

Substituting equations (B.7)–(B.10) in equation (B.6) and solving for $\mathrm{T}_{i,n}\partial\hat{\lambda}_i(\beta)/\partial\beta'$ yields the desired result.

Lemma B.8 Let Assumptions 4.4, 4.5 and 4.6 hold.
Then $\sup_{\beta\in\mathcal{B}_0}\left\|\partial\widehat{P}(\beta,\hat{\lambda}(\beta))/\partial\beta\right\| = o_p(1)$.

Proof From equation (B.5), Assumptions 4.5 (ii) and 4.6, $\sup_{\beta\in\mathcal{B}_0}\left\|\partial\widehat{P}(\beta,\hat{\lambda}(\beta))/\partial\beta\right\| \leq o_p(1)\sum_{j=1}^{n} w_{ij}d(z_j) = o_p(1)$ uniformly i, j and $\beta\in\mathcal{B}_0$.

5 Limit Theory for Moderate Deviations from a Unit Root under Weak Dependence*

Peter C.B. Phillips and Tassos Magdalinos

This chapter is dedicated to the loving memory of Michael Magdalinos whose enthusiasm for econometrics was an inspiration to us all and was surpassed only by the devotion he had to his family and friends.

1 Introduction

In time-series regression theory, much attention has been given to models with autoregressive roots at unity or in the vicinity of unity. The limit theory has relied on functional laws to Brownian motion and diffusions, and weak convergence to stochastic integrals. The treatment of local to unity roots has relied exclusively on specifications of the form $\rho = 1 + c/n$, where n is the sample size (Phillips, 1987a; Chan and Wei, 1987) or matrix versions of this form (Phillips, 1988). The theory has been particularly useful in defining power functions for unit-root tests (Phillips, 1987a) under alternatives that are immediately local to unity.

To characterize greater deviations from unity Phillips and Magdalinos (2004; hereafter simply PM) have recently investigated time series with an autoregressive root of the form $\rho_n = 1 + c/n^{\alpha}$, where the exponent α lies in the interval $(0, 1)$. Such roots represent moderate deviations from unity in the sense that they belong to larger neighbourhoods of one than conventional local to unity roots. The parameter α measures the radial width of the neighbourhood with smaller values of α being associated with larger neighbourhoods. The boundary value as $\alpha \to 1$ includes the conventional local to unity case, whereas the boundary value as $\alpha \to 0$ includes the stationary or explosive AR(1) process, depending on the value of c.

The limit theory developed in PM was derived under the assumption of independent and identically distributed (i.i.d.) innovations. By combining a functional law to a diffusion with a central limit law to a Gaussian

* Phillips gratefully acknowledges research support from a Kelly Fellowship at the School of Business, University of Auckland, and the NSF under Grant No. SES 04-142254. Magdalinos thanks the EPSRC and the Onassis Foundation for scholarship support.

random variable, the asymptotic distribution of the normalized and centred serial correlation coefficient $h(n)(\hat{\rho}_n - \rho_n)$ was shown to be Gaussian in the near-stationary ($c < 0$) case and Cauchy in the near-explosive ($c > 0$) case. The normalization $h(n)$ depends on the radial parameter α of the width of the neighbourhood of unity and the localizing coefficient c. When $c < 0$, $h(n) = n^{(1+\alpha)/2}$, a rate that bridges the $\sqrt{n}$ and n asymptotics of the stationary ($\alpha = 0$) and conventional local to unity ($\alpha = 1$) cases. When $c > 0$, $h(n) = n^{\alpha}\rho_n^n$, a rate that increases from $O(n)$ when $\alpha \to 1$ to $O((1 + c)^n)$ when $\alpha \to 0$, thereby bridging the asymptotics of local to unity and explosive autoregressions.

The present chapter extends these results to processes with weakly dependent innovations. We impose a linear process structure on the errors and discuss the effect this type of weak dependence has on the limit theory. The results vary significantly according to the sign of c.

In the near-explosive case, the limit theory can be extended without imposing additional restrictions over those in PM beyond a summability condition on the weak dependence structure. The resulting Cauchy limit law for the normalized serial correlation coefficient shows that the limit theory is invariant to both the distribution and the dependence structure of the innovation errors. To our knowledge, this is the first general invariance principle for explosive processes, all earlier results depending explicitly on distributional assumptions as was emphasized in the original paper by Anderson (1959).

The near-stationary case presents more substantial technical difficulties in making the transition from nonstationarity to stationarity. We provide a full extension of the limit theory to the weakly dependent case, a Gaussian limit law obtained for the serial correlation coefficient with normalization $n^{(1+\alpha)/2}$ for $\alpha \in (0, 1)$. An interesting feature of the near stationary case is that Gaussian asymptotics apply, but with a limiting bias that is analogous to the correction (cf. Phillips, 1987b) that is known to apply in the unit-root case. Linkages to the limit theory for the serial correlation coefficient in the stationary case (where $\alpha = 0$) are established.

The chapter is organized as follows. Section 2 briefly summarizes the limit theory obtained in PM for autoregressive processes with moderate deviations from unity and i.i.d. errors. This section provides a foundation for the rest of the chapter since several asymptotic results for the weakly dependent case are derived as approximations of the relevant results under independence using the Phillips–Solo (1992) device and Theorem 2.1 below. The moderate deviations from a unity model under weak dependence is presented in section 3. This section also describes a blocking method that is central to the derivation of the subsequent limit results, based on a segmentation of the sample size and an embedding of a random walk in a Brownian motion. Sections 4 and 5 provide the limit theory for the near-stationary and the near-explosive case respectively. Section 6 includes some discussion and concluding remarks. All proofs are collected in section 7, together with some technical propositions.

2 Moderate Deviations with i.i.d. Errors

Consider the autoregressive time series:

$$x_t = \rho_n x_{t-1} + \varepsilon_t, \quad t = 1, ..., n; \quad \rho_n = 1 + \frac{c}{n^\alpha}, \alpha \in (0,1) \qquad (1)$$

initialized at some $x_0 = o_p(n^{\alpha/2})$ independent of $\sigma(\varepsilon_1, ..., \varepsilon_n)$, where ε_t is a sequence of i.i.d. $(0, \sigma^2)$ random variables with finite ν'th absolute moment,

$$E|\varepsilon_1|^\nu < \infty \text{ for some } \nu > \frac{2}{\alpha}. \qquad (2)$$

PM developed a limit theory for statistics arising from model (1) based on a segmentation of the time series $(x_t)_{t\in\mathbb{N}}$ into blocks, the details of which are provided in section 3. (Subsequently, in a revised version of Phillips and Magdalinos, 2004, it was shown that the main results could be obtained when the innovations ε_t are i.i.d. without using a blocking approach and using only finite second moments. The details of the blocking method and the diffusion approximation used in the original version of PM are included in chapter 2 of Magdalinos, 2004. Giraitis and Phillips, 2004, derived related limit results for the case of martingale difference errors.) The advantage of this blocking method lies on the fact that it provides a way to study the asymptotic behaviour of x_n via that of the component random elements $x_{\lfloor n^\alpha \cdot \rfloor}$ of the Skorohod space $D[0,\infty)$ (see for example Pollard, 1984). Denoting by $W_{n^\alpha}(t) := \frac{1}{n^{\alpha/2}} \sum_{i=1}^{\lfloor n^\alpha t \rfloor} \varepsilon_i$ the partial sum process on $D[0,\infty)$, it is possible to approximate $x_{\lfloor n^\alpha t \rfloor}$ by the Stieltjes integral:

$$U_{n^\alpha}(t) := \int_0^t e^{c(t-r)} dW_{n^\alpha}(r) = \frac{1}{n^{\alpha/2}} \sum_{i=1}^{\lfloor n^\alpha t \rfloor} e^{\frac{c}{n^\alpha}(n^\alpha t - i)} \varepsilon_i.$$

For each $\alpha \in (0,1)$ and $c < 0$,

$$\sup_{t \in [0, n^{1-\alpha}]} \left| \frac{1}{n^{\alpha/2}} x_{\lfloor n^\alpha t \rfloor} - U_{n^\alpha}(t) \right| = o_p(1) \quad \text{as } n \to \infty. \qquad (3)$$

Thus, we are able to operate in the familiar framework of Phillips (1987a) where $U_{n^\alpha}(t)$, and hence the time series x_n with appropriate normalization, converges to the linear diffusion $\int_0^t e^{c(t-s)} dW(s)$, where W is Brownian motion with variance σ^2. However, unlike the local to unity asymptotics of Phillips (1987a), the limiting distribution of the various sample moments of x_n cannot be obtained by the above functional law alone because the series itself is segmented into an asymptotically infinite number of such blocks with this behaviour. Accordingly, this approach is combined with an analysis of asymptotic behaviour as the number of blocks increases.

We use the fact that, by virtue of the moment condition (2), the Hungarian construction (cf. Csörgõ and Horváth, 1993) ensures the existence of a probability space where $W_{n^\alpha}(t) \longrightarrow_{a.s.} W(t)$ and $U_{n^\alpha}(t) \longrightarrow_{a.s.} \int_0^t e^{c(t-s)} dW(s)$ uniformly on $[0, n^{1-\alpha}]$. For the near-stationary case, this embedding then allows the sample moments of the original time series data to be approximated by normalized sums of functionals of the form $\int_0^t e^{c(t-s)} dW(s)$ which obey a law of large numbers in the case of the sample variance and a central limit theorem in the case of the sample covariance. For the near-explosive case, the limit theory is also derived by using the above embedding in conjunction with the martingale convergence theorem.

The following theorem contains a summary of the main results of PM.

Theorem 2.1 For model (1) with $\rho_n = 1 + c/n^a$ and $\alpha \in (0, 1)$, the following limits apply as $n \to \infty$. When $c < 0$,

(a) $n^{-\alpha/2} x_{\lfloor n^\alpha t \rfloor} \Longrightarrow \int_0^t e^{c(t-r)} dW(r)$ on $D[0, \infty)$

(b) $n^{-1-\alpha} \sum_{t=1}^n x_t^2 \longrightarrow_p \frac{\sigma^2}{-2c}$

(c) $n^{-\frac{1+\alpha}{2}} \sum_{t=1}^n x_{t-1}\varepsilon_t \Longrightarrow N\left(0, \frac{\sigma^4}{-2c}\right)$

(d) $n^{\frac{1+\alpha}{2}} \left(\hat{\rho}_n - \rho_n\right) \Longrightarrow N(0, -2c)$

where W is Brownian motion with variance σ^2. When $c > 0$

(e) $\frac{n^\alpha \rho_n^n}{2c} \left(\hat{\rho}_n - \rho_n\right) \Longrightarrow C$

where C is a standard Cauchy variate.

3 Moderate Deviations from Unity with Weakly Dependent Errors

In this chapter we consider the time series

$$y_t = \rho_n y_{t-1} + u_t, \quad t = 1, \ldots, n; \quad \rho_n = 1 + \frac{c}{n^\alpha}, \; \alpha \in (0, 1) \tag{4}$$

initialized at some $y_0 = o_p(n^{\alpha/2})$ independent of $\sigma(u_1, \ldots, u_n)$, with zero mean, weakly dependent errors u_t that satisfy the following condition.

Assumption LP For each $t \in \mathbb{N}$, u_t has the Wold representation:

$$u_t = C(L)\varepsilon_t = \sum_{j=0}^{\infty} c_j \varepsilon_{t-j}, \quad C(1) \neq 0$$

where C is the operator $C(z) = \sum_{j=0}^{\infty} c_j z^j$, $(\varepsilon_t)_{t \in \mathbb{Z}}$ is a sequence of i.i.d. $(0, \sigma^2)$ random variables satisfying the moment condition (2) and $(c_j)_{j \geq 0}$ is a sequence of constants such that $\sum_{j=1}^{\infty} j\,|c_j| < \infty$.

Under **LP**, u_t has variance $\sigma_u^2 = \sigma^2 \sum_{j=0}^{\infty} c_j^2$, finite ν'th moment $E\,|u_1|^{\nu} < \infty$ and its partial sums $S_t := \sum_{i=1}^{t} u_i$ satisfy the functional law (cf. Phillips and Solo, 1992):

$$B_{n^\alpha}(\cdot) := \frac{S_{\lfloor n^\alpha \cdot \rfloor}}{n^{\alpha/2}} = \frac{\sum_{i=1}^{\lfloor n^\alpha \cdot \rfloor} u_i}{n^{\alpha/2}} \Longrightarrow B(\cdot)$$

where $B(\cdot)$ is Brownian motion with variance $\omega^2 = \sigma^2 C(1)^2$. Using the Beveridge Nelson (BN) decomposition, we obtain the following representation for u_t:

$$u_t = C(1)\varepsilon_t - \Delta\tilde{\varepsilon}_t, \quad \text{for } \tilde{\varepsilon}_t = \sum_{j=0}^{\infty} \tilde{c}_j \varepsilon_{t-j},\ \tilde{c}_j = \sum_{k=j+1}^{\infty} c_k \tag{5}$$

where $\sum_{j=0}^{\infty} |\tilde{c}_j| < \infty$ is assured by the summability condition $\sum_{j=1}^{\infty} j\,|c_j| < \infty$. The derivation of (5) as well as the summability of the sequence $(\tilde{c}_j)_{j \geq 0}$ are included in Lemma 2.1 of Phillips and Solo (1992).

A strong approximation over $[0, n^{1-\alpha}]$ for the partial sum process of i.i.d. errors was derived in PM. In the notation of section 2, we can construct an expanded probability space with a Brownian motion $W(\cdot)$ with variance σ^2 for which,

$$\sup_{t \in [0, n^{1-\alpha}]} |W_{n^\alpha}(t) - W(t)| = o_{a.s.}\left(\frac{1}{n^{\frac{\alpha}{2} - \frac{1}{\nu}}}\right) \quad \text{as } n \to \infty. \tag{6}$$

Using the representation (5) and Proposition A3 in the Appendix, it is possible to embed the partial sum process $B_{n^\alpha}(\cdot)$ of the weakly dependent errors in a Brownian motion with variance ω^2, as the following result which is based on Phillips (1999, Lemma D) shows.

Lemma 3.1 Suppose that the sequence $(u_t)_{t\in\mathbb{N}}$ satisfies Assumption **LP**. Then, the probability space which supports $(u_t)_{t\in\mathbb{N}}$ can be expanded in such a way that there exists a process distributionally equivalent to $B_{n^\alpha}(\cdot)$ and a Brownian motion $B(\cdot)$ with variance ω^2 on the new space for which:

$$\sup_{t\in[0,n^{1-\alpha}]} |B_{n^\alpha}(t) - B(t)| = o_p\left(\frac{1}{n^{\frac{\alpha}{2}-\frac{1}{\nu}}}\right) \quad \text{as } n \to \infty. \tag{7}$$

In what follows, we will assume that the probability space has been expanded as necessary in order for (7) to apply. Note that the moment condition $\nu > \frac{2}{\alpha}$ in (2) ensures that $o_p\left(1/n^{\frac{\alpha}{2}-\frac{1}{\nu}}\right) = o_p(1)$ in (7). Note also that the argument used in the proof of Lemma 3.1 describes the expanded probability space on which (7) holds explicitly: it is the same as the probability space on which (6) holds with $B(t) = C(1)W(t)$ *a.s.*

We now employ the same segmentation of the sample size used in PM. The chronological sequence $\{t = 1, ..., n\}$ can be written in blocks of size $\lfloor n^\alpha \rfloor$ as follows. Set $t = \lfloor n^\alpha j \rfloor + k$ for $k = 1, ..., \lfloor n^\alpha \rfloor$ and $j = 0, ..., \lfloor n^{1-\alpha} \rfloor - 1$, so that:

$$y_{\lfloor n^\alpha j \rfloor + k} = \sum_{i=1}^{\lfloor n^\alpha j \rfloor + k} \rho_n^{\lfloor n^\alpha j \rfloor + k - i} u_i + \rho_n^{\lfloor n^\alpha j \rfloor + k} y_0.$$

This arrangement effectively partitions the sample size into $\lfloor n^{1-\alpha} \rfloor$ blocks each containing $\lfloor n^\alpha \rfloor$ sample points. Since the last element of each block is asymptotically equivalent to the first element of the next block, it is possible to study the asymptotic behaviour of the time series $\{y_t : t = 1, ..., n\}$ via the asymptotic properties of the time series $\{y_{\lfloor n^\alpha j \rfloor + k} : j = 0, ..., \lfloor n^{1-\alpha} \rfloor - 1, k = 1, ..., \lfloor n^\alpha \rfloor\}$.

Letting $k = \lfloor n^\alpha p \rfloor$, for some $p \in [0, 1]$, we obtain:

$$\frac{1}{n^{\alpha/2}} y_{\lfloor n^\alpha j \rfloor + \lfloor n^\alpha p \rfloor} = \frac{1}{n^{\alpha/2}} \sum_{i=1}^{\lfloor n^\alpha j \rfloor + \lfloor n^\alpha p \rfloor} \rho_n^{\lfloor n^\alpha j \rfloor + \lfloor n^\alpha p \rfloor - i} u_i + \rho_n^{\lfloor n^\alpha j \rfloor + \lfloor n^\alpha p \rfloor} \frac{y_0}{n^{\alpha/2}}.$$

The random element $y_{\lfloor n^\alpha j \rfloor + \lfloor n^\alpha p \rfloor}$ corresponds to the random element $x_{\lfloor n^\alpha t \rfloor}$ of section 2 (note that $j + p \in \left[0, \lfloor n^{1-\alpha} \rfloor\right]$). As in the case of independent errors, deriving a functional law for $y_{\lfloor n^\alpha j \rfloor + \lfloor n^\alpha p \rfloor}$ provides the first step towards obtaining the limiting distribution of the various statistics arising from (4).

We start with the near stationary case $c < 0$. With a minor abuse of notation, define $x_t := \sum_{i=1}^{t} \rho_n^{t-i} \varepsilon_i$ and

$$V_{n^\alpha}(t) := \int_0^t e^{c(t-r)} dB_{n^\alpha}(r) = \frac{1}{n^{\alpha/2}} \sum_{i=1}^{\lfloor n^\alpha t \rfloor} e^{\frac{c}{n^\alpha}(n^\alpha t - i)} u_i.$$

Here, x_t as defined above is simply the time series x_t defined in section 2 with initialization $x_0 = 0$. Since the limit theory of section 2 is invariant to the initial condition x_0, the asymptotic behaviour of $x_t = \sum_{i=1}^{t} \rho_n^{t-i} \varepsilon_i$ is given by Theorem 2.1. The random element $V_{n^\alpha}(t)$ is a direct extension of $U_{n^\alpha}(t)$ to the weakly dependent error case. The relationship between the random elements $y_{\lfloor n^\alpha \cdot \rfloor}$, $V_{n^\alpha}(\cdot)$ and their counterparts under independence is given below.

Lemma 3.2 For each $\alpha \in (0, 1)$ and $c < 0$

(a) $\sup_{t \in [0, n^{1-\alpha}]} \left| \frac{1}{n^{\alpha/2}} y_{\lfloor n^\alpha t \rfloor} - \frac{C(1)}{n^{\alpha/2}} x_{\lfloor n^\alpha t \rfloor} \right| = o_p(1)$

(b) $\sup_{t \in [0, n^{1-\alpha}]} |V_{n^\alpha}(t) - C(1) U_{n^\alpha}(t)| = o_p(1)$.

Lemma 3.2 together with (3) provide a uniform approximation of $n^{-\alpha/2} y_{\lfloor n^\alpha \cdot \rfloor}$ by $V_{n^\alpha}(\cdot)$ on $[0, n^{1-\alpha}]$. For each $\alpha \in (0, 1)$ and $c < 0$:

$$\sup_{t \in [0, n^{1-\alpha}]} \left| \frac{1}{n^{\alpha/2}} y_{\lfloor n^\alpha t \rfloor} - V_{n^\alpha}(t) \right| = o_p(1) \quad \text{as } n \to \infty. \tag{8}$$

The importance of (8) lies in the fact that an embedding of the random element $V_{n^\alpha}(t)$ to the linear diffusion $\mathcal{J}_c(t) := \int_0^t e^{c(t-r)} dB(r)$ is possible. Using integration by parts (see Lemma 2.1 of the original version of PM or Lemma 2.2.1 of Magdalinos, 2004), it can be shown that:

$$\sup_{t \in [0, n^{1-\alpha}]} |V_{n^\alpha}(t) - \mathcal{J}_c(t)| \leq 2 \sup_{t \in [0, n^{1-\alpha}]} |B_{n^\alpha}(t) - B(t)|.$$

Thus, by Lemma 3.1 we obtain:

$$\sup_{t \in [0, n^{1-\alpha}]} |V_{n^\alpha}(t) - \mathcal{J}_c(t)| = o_p\left(\frac{1}{n^{\frac{\alpha}{2} - \frac{1}{\nu}}}\right) \quad \text{as } n \to \infty \tag{9}$$

and, in view of (8),

$$\sup_{t \in [0, n^{1-\alpha}]} \left| \frac{1}{n^{\alpha/2}} y_{\lfloor n^\alpha t \rfloor} - \mathcal{J}_c(t) \right| = o_p\left(\frac{1}{n^{\frac{\alpha}{2} - \frac{1}{\nu}}}\right) \quad \text{as } n \to \infty \tag{10}$$

on the same probability space that (7) holds.

4 Limit Theory for the Near Stationary Case

We now develop a limit theory for the centred serial correlation coefficient

$$\hat{\rho}_n - \rho_n = \frac{\sum_{t=1}^{n} y_{t-1}u_t}{\sum_{t=1}^{n} y_{t-1}^2} \tag{11}$$

when $\rho_n = 1 + \frac{c}{n^{\alpha}}$ and $c < 0$. The approach follows PM and uses a segmentation of the y_t series into blocks in which we utilize the embedding (10) and apply law of large numbers and central limit arguments to the denominator and numerator of (11).

The sample variance of y_t can be rewritten in terms of block components as:

$$\begin{aligned}
\frac{1}{n^{1+\alpha}}\sum_{t=1}^{n} y_t^2 &= \frac{1}{n^{1+\alpha}}\sum_{j=0}^{\lfloor n^{1-\alpha}\rfloor-1}\sum_{k=1}^{\lfloor n^{\alpha}\rfloor} y_{\lfloor n^{\alpha}j\rfloor+k}^2 + O_p\left(\frac{1}{n^{1-\alpha}}\right) \\
&= \frac{1}{n^{1-\alpha}}\sum_{j=0}^{\lfloor n^{1-\alpha}\rfloor-1}\frac{1}{n^{2\alpha}}\sum_{k=1}^{\lfloor n^{\alpha}\rfloor} y_{\lfloor n^{\alpha}j\rfloor+k}^2 \\
&= \frac{1}{n^{1-\alpha}}\sum_{j=0}^{\lfloor n^{1-\alpha}\rfloor-1}\int_0^1\left(\frac{1}{n^{\alpha/2}}y_{\lfloor n^{\alpha}j\rfloor+\lfloor n^{\alpha}p\rfloor}\right)^2 dp \\
&= \frac{1}{n^{1-\alpha}}\int_0^{\lfloor n^{1-\alpha}\rfloor}\left(\frac{1}{n^{\alpha/2}}y_{\lfloor n^{\alpha}r\rfloor}\right)^2 dr + o_p(1) \\
&= \frac{1}{n^{1-\alpha}}\int_0^{\lfloor n^{1-\alpha}\rfloor}\mathcal{J}_c(r)^2 dr + o_p\left(\frac{1}{n^{\frac{\alpha}{2}-\frac{1}{\nu}}}\right)
\end{aligned} \tag{12}$$

by (10) and Proposition A2. By equation (2.10) of Magdalinos (2004), it is possible to replace the Ornstein–Uhlenbeck process $\mathcal{J}_c(t)$ in (12) by its stationary version $\mathcal{J}_c^*(t)$ with an approximation error of order $O_p\left(n^{-(1-\alpha)}\right)$. If $\mathcal{J}_c^*(0)$ is a $N\left(0, \frac{\omega^2}{-2c}\right)$ random variable independent of $B(\cdot)$, $\mathcal{J}_c^*(t) := e^{ct}\mathcal{J}_c^*(0) + \mathcal{J}_c(t)$ is a strictly stationary process with autocovariance function given by,

$$\gamma_{\mathcal{J}_c^*}(h) = \frac{\omega^2}{-2c}e^{c|h|} \quad h \in \mathbb{Z}.$$

The sample variance then becomes:

$$\frac{1}{n^{1+\alpha}}\sum_{t=1}^{n} y_t^2 = \frac{1}{n^{1-\alpha}}\int_0^{\lfloor n^{1-\alpha}\rfloor} \mathcal{J}_c^*(r)^2 dr + o_p\left(\frac{1}{n^{\frac{\alpha}{2}-\frac{1}{\nu}}}\right)$$

$$= \frac{1}{n^{1-\alpha}}\sum_{j=0}^{\lfloor n^{1-\alpha}\rfloor -1}\int_j^{j+1} \mathcal{J}_c^*(r)^2 dr + o_p\left(\frac{1}{n^{\frac{\alpha}{2}-\frac{1}{\nu}}}\right)$$

$$= \frac{\omega^2}{-2c} + o_p\left(\frac{1}{n^{\frac{\alpha}{2}-\frac{1}{\nu}}}\right) \tag{13}$$

by the weak law of large numbers for stationary processes, since $\gamma_{\mathcal{J}_c^*}(0) = \omega^2/(-2c)$.

The limit distribution of a suitably standardized version of the sample covariance $\sum_{t=1}^{n} y_{t-1}u_t$ is found by expanding this covariance (see (15) below) in terms of components whose asymptotic behaviour can be found directly, such as $\sum_{t=1}^{n} y_{t-1}\varepsilon_t$. The following results help to analyse these components and are proved in the Appendix.

Lemma 4.1 Define $\lambda := Eu_t\tilde{\varepsilon}_t = \sigma^2\sum_{j=0}^{\infty} c_j\tilde{c}_j$. For each $\alpha \in (0,1)$ and $c < 0$

(a) $n^{-\frac{1+\alpha}{2}} y_n\tilde{\varepsilon}_n = o_p(1)$

(b) $n^{-\frac{1+\alpha}{2}}\sum_{t=1}^{n}(u_t\tilde{\varepsilon}_t - \lambda) = o_p(1)$

as $n \to \infty$, where part (b) is valid under the moment condition $E\varepsilon_0^4 < \infty$.

Lemma 4.2 For each $\alpha \in (0,1)$ and $c < 0$

$$\frac{1}{n^{\frac{1+\alpha}{2}}}\sum_{t=1}^{n} y_{t-1}\varepsilon_t \Longrightarrow N\left(0, \frac{C(1)^2\sigma^4}{-2c}\right) \quad \text{as } n \to \infty.$$

For the next result, it is convenient to introduce some notation used throughout the rest of the chapter. Let

$$\gamma_m(h) := E\tilde{\varepsilon}_t u_{t-h} = \sigma^2\sum_{j=0}^{\infty} c_j\tilde{c}_{j+h}, \quad h \geq 0$$

$$m_n := \sum_{i=1}^{\infty} \rho_n^{i-1}\gamma_m(i). \tag{14}$$

Proposition A4 in the Appendix shows that $m_n \to \sum_{i=1}^{\infty}\gamma_m(i)$ as $n \to \infty$.

Lemma 4.3 For each $c < 0$ and $\alpha \in (0,1)$ we have

(a) $\sum_{t=1}^{n} y_{t-1}\tilde{\varepsilon}_t = O_p\left(n^{1+\frac{\alpha}{2}}\right)$

(b) $n^{-\frac{1+3\alpha}{2}} \sum_{t=1}^{n} (y_{t-1}\tilde{\varepsilon}_t - m_n) = o_p(1)$

as $n \to \infty$, where part (b) is valid under the moment condition $E\varepsilon_0^4 < \infty$.

Using the BN decomposition (5) and summation by parts the sample covariance can be decomposed as follows:

$$\begin{aligned}
\frac{1}{n^{\frac{1+\alpha}{2}}}\sum_{t=1}^{n} y_{t-1}u_t &= \frac{C(1)}{n^{\frac{1+\alpha}{2}}}\sum_{t=1}^{n} y_{t-1}\varepsilon_t - \frac{1}{n^{\frac{1+\alpha}{2}}}\sum_{t=1}^{n} y_{t-1}\Delta\tilde{\varepsilon}_t \\
&= \frac{C(1)}{n^{\frac{1+\alpha}{2}}}\sum_{t=1}^{n} y_{t-1}\varepsilon_t - \frac{1}{n^{\frac{1+\alpha}{2}}} y_n\tilde{\varepsilon}_n + \frac{1}{n^{\frac{1+\alpha}{2}}}\sum_{t=1}^{n}\left\{\frac{c}{n^{\alpha}}y_{t-1} + u_t\right\}\tilde{\varepsilon}_t \\
&= \frac{C(1)}{n^{\frac{1+\alpha}{2}}}\sum_{t=1}^{n} y_{t-1}\varepsilon_t + \frac{c}{n^{\frac{1+3\alpha}{2}}}\sum_{t=1}^{n} y_{t-1}\tilde{\varepsilon}_t + \frac{1}{n^{\frac{1+\alpha}{2}}}\sum_{t=1}^{n} u_t\tilde{\varepsilon}_t + o_p(1)
\end{aligned} \tag{15}$$

by Lemma 4.1 (a). From Lemmas 4.1, 4.2 and 4.3 (a), it is clear that the leading term in the above expression for the sample covariance will be $n^{-\frac{1+\alpha}{2}} \sum_{t=1}^{n} u_t\tilde{\varepsilon}_t$ with asymptotic order $O_{a.s.}\left(n^{\frac{1-\alpha}{2}}\right)$ given by the ergodic theorem. Thus, if no correction is made to account for weak dependence, the sample covariance will converge to the constant probability limit of the leading term as follows:

$$\frac{1}{n}\sum_{t=1}^{n} y_{t-1}u_t = \frac{1}{n}\sum_{t=1}^{n} u_t\tilde{\varepsilon}_t + O_p\left(n^{-\frac{\alpha\wedge(1-\alpha)}{2}}\right) = \lambda + o_p(1) \tag{16}$$

by ergodicity of $u_t\tilde{\varepsilon}_t$. The above, together with (13), imply that for each $\alpha \in (0,1)$

$$n^{\alpha}\left(\hat{\rho}_n - \rho_n\right) = \frac{\frac{1}{n}\sum_{t=1}^{n} y_{t-1}u_t}{\frac{1}{n^{1+\alpha}}\sum_{t=1}^{n} y_{t-1}^2} \longrightarrow_p \frac{\lambda}{\frac{\omega^2}{-2c}}. \tag{17}$$

Note that λ is a one sided long run covariance of u_t (cf. Phillips, 1987b) since, denoting the autocovariance function of u_t by $\gamma_u(h)$, we have:

$$\sum_{h=1}^{\infty} \gamma_u(h) = \sigma^2 \sum_{j=1}^{\infty} c_j \sum_{h=1}^{\infty} c_{j+h} = \sigma^2 \sum_{j=1}^{\infty} c_j \sum_{k=j+1}^{\infty} c_k = \sigma^2 \sum_{j=0}^{\infty} c_j \tilde{c}_j = \lambda. \quad (18)$$

Obtaining a non degenerate weak limit for the sample covariance requires centering around the asymptotic mean of the terms $\sum_{t=1}^{n} u_t \tilde{\varepsilon}_t$ and $\sum_{t=1}^{n} y_{t-1} \tilde{\varepsilon}_t$. Then, for each $\alpha \in (0,1)$ (15) gives, up to $o_p(1)$,

$$\begin{aligned}
\frac{1}{n^{\frac{1+\alpha}{2}}} \sum_{t=1}^{n} \left(y_{t-1} u_t - \lambda - \frac{c}{n^{\alpha}} m_n \right) &= \frac{C(1)}{n^{\frac{1+\alpha}{2}}} \sum_{t=1}^{n} y_{t-1} \varepsilon_t + \frac{c}{n^{\frac{1+3\alpha}{2}}} \sum_{t=1}^{n} (y_{t-1} \tilde{\varepsilon}_t - m_n) \\
&\quad + \frac{1}{n^{\frac{1+\alpha}{2}}} \sum_{t=1}^{n} (u_t \tilde{\varepsilon}_t - \lambda) \\
&= \frac{C(1)}{n^{\frac{1+\alpha}{2}}} \sum_{t=1}^{n} y_{t-1} \varepsilon_t + o_p(1) \\
&\Longrightarrow N\left(0, \frac{\omega^4}{-2c}\right) \qquad (19)
\end{aligned}$$

under the moment condition $E\varepsilon_0^4 < \infty$, by Lemmas 4.1 (b), 4.2 and 4.3 (b), recalling that $\omega^2 = C(1)^2 \sigma^2$.

From (13) and (19) it is clear that the weak dependence structure of the innovations induces an asymptotic bias for the least squares estimator $\hat{\rho}_n$, since for each $\alpha \in (0,1)$,

$$\begin{aligned}
n^{\frac{1+\alpha}{2}} \left[\hat{\rho}_n - \rho_n - \frac{n\left(\lambda + \frac{c}{n^{\alpha}} m_n\right)}{\sum_{t=1}^{n} y_{t-1}^2} \right] &= \frac{\frac{1}{n^{\frac{1+\alpha}{2}}} \sum_{t=1}^{n} \left(y_{t-1} u_t - \lambda - \frac{c}{n^{\alpha}} m_n \right)}{\frac{1}{n^{1+\alpha}} \sum_{t=1}^{n} y_{t-1}^2} \\
&\Longrightarrow N(0, -2c). \qquad (20)
\end{aligned}$$

More explicit calculations of the asymptotic bias of $\hat{\rho}_n$ involve analysis of the limiting distribution of the denominator, $\sum_{t=1}^{n} y_{t-1}^2$, of $\hat{\rho}_n$ centered around its asymptotic mean. The left side of (20) can be written as:

$$n^{\frac{1+\alpha}{2}}\left(\hat{\rho}_n-\rho_n-\frac{\lambda+\frac{c}{n^\alpha}m_n}{\frac{1}{n}\sum_{t=1}^n y_{t-1}^2}\right)$$

$$=n^{\frac{1+\alpha}{2}}\left[\hat{\rho}_n-\rho_n-\frac{1}{n^\alpha}\frac{\lambda+\frac{c}{n^\alpha}m_n}{\frac{\omega_n^2}{-2c}+\frac{1}{n}\sum_{t=1}^n\left(\frac{y_{t-1}^2}{n^\alpha}-\frac{\omega_n^2}{-2c}\right)}\right]$$

where

$$\omega_n^2:=\frac{\omega^2+\frac{2c}{n^\alpha}\left(\lambda+\rho_n m_n\right)}{1+\frac{c}{2n^\alpha}}. \tag{21}$$

Part (b) of Theorem 4.1 below gives $n^{-1}\sum_{t=1}^n\left(\frac{y_{t-1}^2}{n^\alpha}-\frac{\omega_n^2}{-2c}\right)=O_p\left(n^{-\frac{1-\alpha}{2}}\right)$, implying that:

$$n^{\frac{1+\alpha}{2}}\left[\hat{\rho}_n-\rho_n-\frac{n\left(\lambda+\frac{c}{n^\alpha}m_n\right)}{\sum_{t=1}^n y_{t-1}^2}\right]$$

$$=n^{\frac{1+\alpha}{2}}\left[\hat{\rho}_n-\rho_n-\frac{1}{n^\alpha}\frac{-2c\left(\lambda+\frac{c}{n^\alpha}m_n\right)}{\omega_n^2}\right]+O_p(1).$$

As we see below, the asymptotic distribution of $\hat{\rho}_n$ depends not only on the probability limit (13) of $n^{-1-\alpha}\sum_{t=1}^n y_t^2$ but also the asymptotic distribution of a centred and standardized version of this sample moment. The latter can be obtained as an approximation of the centred sample covariance, established in the theorem below.

Theorem 4.1 For model (4) with $\rho_n=1+c/n^a$, $c<0$, $\alpha\in(0,1)$ and weakly dependent errors satisfying Assumption **LP** with $E\varepsilon_0^4<\infty$, the following limits apply as $n\to\infty$:

(a) $n^{-\frac{1+\alpha}{2}}\sum_{t=1}^n\left(y_{t-1}u_t-\lambda-\frac{c}{n^\alpha}m_n\right)\Longrightarrow N\left(0,\frac{\omega^4}{-2c}\right)$

(b) $n^{-\frac{1+\alpha}{2}}\sum_{t=1}^n\left(\frac{y_{t-1}^2}{n^\alpha}-\frac{\omega_n^2}{-2c}\right)=\frac{1}{-c}n^{-\frac{1+\alpha}{2}}\sum_{t=1}^n\left(y_{t-1}u_t-\lambda-\frac{c}{n^\alpha}m_n\right)$
$+o_p(1)$

where ω_n^2 is given by (21).

4.1 Remarks

(i) Since by Proposition A4

$$\lim_{n\to\infty} m_n = \sum_{i=1}^{\infty} \gamma_m(i) < \infty$$

we have $n^{-\frac{1+\alpha}{2}} \sum_{t=1}^{n} \frac{c}{n^\alpha} m_n = O\left(n^{-\frac{3\alpha-1}{2}}\right)$. Thus, when $\alpha \in \left(\frac{1}{3}, 1\right)$, part (a) becomes:

$$n^{-\frac{1+\alpha}{2}} \sum_{t=1}^{n} (y_{t-1}u_t - \lambda) \Longrightarrow N\left(0, \frac{\omega^4}{-2c}\right).$$

(ii) Convergence of m_n also implies that $\omega_n^2 = \omega^2 + O\left(n^{-\alpha}\right)$ as $n \to \infty$, giving:

$$\begin{aligned} n^{-\frac{1+\alpha}{2}} & \sum_{t=1}^{n} \left(\frac{y_{t-1}^2}{n^\alpha} - \frac{\omega_n^2}{-2c}\right) \\ &= n^{-\frac{1+\alpha}{2}} \sum_{t=1}^{n} \left(\frac{y_{t-1}^2}{n^\alpha} - \frac{\omega^2}{-2c}\right) + O\left(n^{-\frac{3\alpha-1}{2}}\right). \end{aligned}$$

Thus, when $\alpha \in \left(\frac{1}{3}, 1\right)$, part (b) becomes:

$$n^{-\frac{1+\alpha}{2}} \sum_{t=1}^{n} \left(\frac{y_{t-1}^2}{n^\alpha} - \frac{\omega^2}{-2c}\right) = \frac{1}{-c} n^{-\frac{1+\alpha}{2}} \sum_{t=1}^{n} (y_{t-1}u_t - \lambda) + o_p(1).$$

We are now in a position to provide a nonrandom expression for the asymptotic bias term in (20) and hence derive the limit distribution of the normalized and centred serial correlation coefficient. Letting

$$\bar{\rho}_n := \rho_n + \frac{1}{n^\alpha}\left(\lambda + \frac{c}{n^\alpha} m_n\right) \frac{-2c}{\omega_n^2}$$

we obtain:

$$
\begin{aligned}
\hat{\rho}_n-\bar{\rho}_n &= \frac{\sum_{t=1}^{n} y_t y_{t-1}}{\sum_{t=1}^{n} y_{t-1}^2}-\bar{\rho}_n=\frac{\sum_{t=1}^{n} y_t y_{t-1}-\bar{\rho}_n \sum_{t=1}^{n} y_{t-1}^2}{\sum_{t=1}^{n} y_{t-1}^2} \\
&= \frac{\sum_{t=1}^{n} y_{t-1} u_t-\left(\lambda+\frac{c}{n^\alpha} m_n\right) \frac{-2c}{\omega_n^2} \sum_{t=1}^{n} \frac{y_{t-1}^2}{n^\alpha}}{\sum_{t=1}^{n} y_{t-1}^2} \\
&= \frac{\sum_{t=1}^{n} y_{t-1} u_t-\left(\lambda+\frac{c}{n^\alpha} m_n\right) \frac{-2c}{\omega_n^2} \sum_{t=1}^{n}\left(\frac{y_{t-1}^2}{n^\alpha}-\frac{\omega_n^2}{-2c}\right)-n\left(\lambda+\frac{c}{n^\alpha} m_n\right)}{\sum_{t=1}^{n} y_{t-1}^2} \\
&= \frac{\sum_{t=1}^{n}\left(y_{t-1} u_t-\lambda-\frac{c}{n^\alpha} m_n\right)-\left(\lambda+\frac{c}{n^\alpha} m_n\right) \frac{-2c}{\omega_n^2} \sum_{t=1}^{n}\left(\frac{y_{t-1}^2}{n^\alpha}-\frac{\omega^2}{-2c}\right)}{\sum_{t=1}^{n} y_{t-1}^2} .
\end{aligned} \tag{22}
$$

Normalizing and using Theorem 4.1, yields as $n \to \infty$:

$$
\begin{aligned}
n^{\frac{1+\alpha}{2}}\left(\hat{\rho}_n-\bar{\rho}_n\right) &= \frac{\left[1-\frac{2\left(\lambda+\frac{c}{n^\alpha} m_n\right)}{\omega_n^2}\right] \frac{1}{n^{\frac{1+\alpha}{2}}} \sum_{t=1}^{n}\left(y_{t-1} u_t-\lambda-\frac{c}{n^\alpha} m_n\right)}{\frac{1}{n^{1+\alpha}} \sum_{t=1}^{n} y_{t-1}^2}+o_p(1) \\
&\Longrightarrow\left[1-\frac{2\lambda}{\omega^2}\right] N(0,-2c) \equiv \frac{\sigma_u^2}{\omega^2} N(0,-2c) \equiv N\left(0,-2c \frac{\sigma_u^4}{\omega^4}\right)
\end{aligned}
$$

since $\omega^2 = \sigma_u^2 + 2\lambda$. We have thus obtained the asymptotic distribution of the normalized and centred serial correlation coefficient, presented in the following theorem.

Theorem 4.2 For model (4) with $\rho_n = 1 + c/n^a$, $c < 0$, $\alpha \in (0,1)$ and weakly dependent errors satisfying Assumption **LP** with $E\varepsilon_0^4 < \infty$

$$
n^{\frac{1+\alpha}{2}}\left[\hat{\rho}_n-\rho_n-\frac{1}{n^\alpha} \frac{-2c}{\omega_n^2}\left(\lambda+\frac{c}{n^\alpha} m_n\right)\right] \Longrightarrow N\left(0,-2c \frac{\sigma_u^4}{\omega^4}\right) \quad \text{as } n \to \infty. \tag{23}
$$

4.2 Remarks

(i) Since m_n is a convergent sequence and $\omega_n^2 = \omega^2 + O\left(n^{-\alpha}\right)$ as $n \to \infty$ we have:

$$n^{\frac{1+\alpha}{2}} \left[\frac{1}{n^\alpha} \frac{-2c}{\omega_n^2} \left(\lambda + \frac{c}{n^\alpha} m_n \right) \right] = n^{\frac{1+\alpha}{2}} \left(\frac{1}{n^\alpha} \frac{-2c\lambda}{\omega^2} \right) + O\left(\frac{1}{n^{\frac{3\alpha-1}{2}}} \right)$$

which implies that, for $\alpha \in \left(\frac{1}{3}, 1\right)$, (23) becomes:

$$n^{\frac{1+\alpha}{2}} \left(\hat{\rho}_n - \rho_n - \frac{1}{n^\alpha} \frac{-2c\lambda}{\omega^2} \right) \Longrightarrow N\left(0, -2c\frac{\sigma_u^4}{\omega^4}\right) \quad \text{as } n \to \infty. \tag{24}$$

(ii) By a simple rearrangement, the bias term in (23) can be written as:

$$\begin{aligned} \frac{1}{n^\alpha} \frac{-2c}{\omega_n^2} \left(\lambda + \frac{c}{n^\alpha} m_n \right) &= \frac{\left(1 - \rho_n^2\right)\left[\lambda + (\rho_n - 1)m_n\right]}{\sigma_u^2 + 2\rho_n\left[\lambda + (\rho_n - 1)m_n\right]} \\ &= \frac{\left(1 - \rho_n^2\right)\sum_{i=1}^\infty \rho_n^{i-1}\gamma_u(i)}{\sigma_u^2 + 2\sum_{i=1}^\infty \rho_n^i \gamma_u(i)} \end{aligned}$$

using the identity $\sum_{i=1}^\infty \rho_n^{i-1}\gamma_u(i) = \lambda + (\rho_n - 1)m_n$. This corresponds to the asymptotic bias term of the serial correlation coefficient of a stationary first-order autoregression with linear process errors. To see this, fix $\rho \in (-1, 1)$ and consider the process,

$$y_t = \rho y_{t-1} + u_t, \quad u_t = \sum_{j=0}^\infty c_j \varepsilon_{t-j}, \; \sum_{j=1}^\infty j\left|c_j\right| < \infty$$

where $(\varepsilon_t)_{t\in\mathbb{Z}}$ is a sequence of i.i.d. $\left(0, \sigma^2\right)$ random variables. Then y_t is itself a linear process,

$$y_t = \sum_{j=0}^\infty \bar{c}_j \varepsilon_{t-j}, \quad \bar{c}_j = \sum_{k=0}^j \rho^{j-k} c_k$$

satisfying $\sum_{j=1}^\infty j\left|\bar{c}_j\right| < \infty$. Thus, denoting by $\rho_y(j)$ the autocorrelation function of y_t, equation (29) of Phillips and Solo (1992) implies that $\sqrt{n}\left[\hat{\rho}_n - \rho_y(1)\right]$ has a $N(0, w(1))$ limiting distribution, where

$$w(1) = \sum_{r=1}^{\infty} \left\{\rho_y(r+h) + \rho_y(h-r) - 2\rho_y(h)\rho_y(r)\right\}^2 . \tag{25}$$

It is then an easy matter to obtain,

$$\rho_y(1) = \rho + \frac{Eu_t y_{t-1}}{Ey_t^2} = \rho + \frac{\left(1-\rho^2\right)\sum_{i=1}^{\infty}\rho^{i-1}\gamma_u(i)}{\sigma_u^2 + 2\sum_{i=1}^{\infty}\rho^i\gamma_u(i)}$$

showing that the asymptotic bias term in Theorem 4.2 coincides with the asymptotic bias under stationarity.

(iii) The bias/inconsistency arising from weak dependence, as calculated in (23), has the same order $O\left(n^{-\alpha}\right)$ as the moderate deviation departure from unity itself. When $\alpha \in \left(\frac{1}{3}, 1\right)$ (24) shows that the parameter determining the bias is the one-sided long-run covariance λ of the errors u_t, precisely the same parameter that appears in the limiting bias of the least squares estimator in the unit-root case (cf. Phillips, 1987b). Although the term $\frac{c}{n^\alpha}m_n$ in (23) is of a smaller order than that involving λ, the effect of $m_n = \sum_{i=1}^{\infty}\rho_n^{i-1}E\tilde{\varepsilon}_t u_{t-i}$ on the asymptotic bias increases as ρ_n approaches the stationary region (i.e., as $\alpha \to 0$).

(iv) When the innovation errors u_t are i.i.d., λ and m_n are identically equal to 0, $\sigma_u^2 = \omega^2$, and (23) reduces to:

$$n^{\frac{1+\alpha}{2}}\left(\hat{\rho}_n - \rho_n\right) \Longrightarrow N(0, -2c) \quad \text{as } n \to \infty \tag{26}$$

which is part (d) of Theorem 2.1 from PM. Thus, Theorem 4.2 generalizes that moderate deviation limit theory to the case of weak dependence. Comparing the asymptotic variances between (23) and (26), we conclude that, while weak dependence introduces a limiting bias, it also changes the asymptotic variance of the centered least squares estimator. Indeed, when $\omega^2 > \sigma_u^2$ (or when $\lambda > 0$) the limiting variance is reduced. Thus, stronger long-run dependence in the series reduces the variance in the limit distribution of the serial correlation coefficient, as might be anticipated by heuristic arguments.

4.3 The Stationary Case

When $\alpha = 0$, $\rho_n = \rho = 1 + c$ and the model (4) is stationary for $c \in (-2, 0)$. As we have seen in section 4.2 Remarks (ii), centering in (23) corresponds to the usual centering for the serial correlation coefficient in the stationary case and we have $\hat{\rho}_n \to_p \rho_y(1)$.

For the limit distribution theory we may set, without loss of generality, $c = -1$ and $\rho = 0$, so that $y_t = u_t$ in (4) and then y_t is a weakly dependent time series. We note that equation (22) reduces as follows:

$$\hat{\rho}_n - \rho_u(1)$$

$$= \frac{\sum_{t=1}^{n}\left(y_{t-1}u_t - \lambda - \frac{c}{n^\alpha}m_n\right) - \left(\lambda + \frac{c}{n^\alpha}m_n\right)\frac{-2c}{\omega_n^2}\sum_{t=1}^{n}\left(\frac{y_{t-1}^2}{n^\alpha} - \frac{\omega^2}{-2c}\right)}{\sum_{t=1}^{n} y_{t-1}^2}$$

$$= \frac{\sum_{t=1}^{n}\left(u_t u_{t-1} - \gamma_u(1)\right) - \frac{\gamma_u(1)}{\gamma_u(0)}\sum_{t=1}^{n}\left(u_{t-1}^2 - \gamma_u(0)\right)}{\sum_{t=1}^{n} u_{t-1}^2} \tag{27}$$

so that by standard limit results for serial correlations (e.g. Phillips and Solo, 1992) we have:

$$\sqrt{n}\left(\hat{\rho}_n - \rho_u(1)\right)$$

$$= \frac{n^{-1/2}\sum_{t=1}^{n}\left(u_t u_{t-1} - \gamma_u(1)\right) - \rho_u(1)n^{-1/2}\sum_{t=1}^{n}\left(u_{t-1}^2 - \gamma_u(0)\right)}{n^{-1}\sum_{t=1}^{n} u_{t-1}^2} \tag{28}$$

$$\Longrightarrow N(0, w(1)) \tag{29}$$

where $w(1)$ is as in (25) with ρ_y replaced by ρ_u. Thus, in contrast to the case $\alpha > 0$ where the terms in the numerator of (22) are asymptotically collinear after standardization (as implied by Theorem 4.1(b) and as used in the limit distribution (23) for this case), the terms in the numerator of (28) are no longer asymptotically collinear. Instead, the terms in the numerator of (28) have a common component involving the term $\gamma_u(1)n^{-1/2}\sum_{t=1}^{n}\left(\varepsilon_t^2 - \sigma^2\right)/\sigma^2$ which cancels out, ensuring that the limiting variance (25) depends only on second-order moments.

Thus, the limit distribution theory in Theorem 4.2 for the moderate deviations case does not specialize directly to the stationary case. Instead, when $\alpha = 0$ some additional terms enter the calculations that are $o_p(1)$ when $\alpha > 0$. For instance, when y_t is a moderate deviations from unity process, the sample covariance $\sum_{t=1}^{n} y_{t-1}u_t$ can be approximated, after appropriate centering, by the martingale $\sum_{t=1}^{n} y_{t-1}\varepsilon_t$:

$$\frac{1}{n^{\frac{1+\alpha}{2}}}\sum_{t=1}^{n}\left(y_{t-1}u_t-\lambda-\frac{c}{n^{\alpha}}m_n\right)$$

$$=\frac{C(1)}{n^{\frac{1+\alpha}{2}}}\sum_{t=1}^{n}y_{t-1}\varepsilon_t+\frac{c}{n^{\frac{1+3\alpha}{2}}}\sum_{t=1}^{n}(y_{t-1}\tilde{\varepsilon}_t-m_n)$$

$$+\frac{1}{n^{\frac{1+\alpha}{2}}}\sum_{t=1}^{n}(u_t\tilde{\varepsilon}_t-\lambda)+o_p(1)$$

the last two terms on the right side being asymptotically negligible for each $\alpha>0$. When $\alpha=0$, however, both $n^{-1/2}\sum_{t=1}^{n}(y_{t-1}\tilde{\varepsilon}_t-m_n)$ and $n^{-1/2}\sum_{t=1}^{n}(u_t\tilde{\varepsilon}_t-\lambda)$ contribute to the Gaussian limit distribution of the centered sample covariance.

5 Limit Theory for the Near Explosive Case

We now turn to the limit behaviour of $\hat{\rho}_n-\rho_n$ when $\rho_n=1+c/n^{a}$ and $c>0$. The approach follows PM closely and adjustments in the arguments of that paper are needed only to allow for weakly dependent u_t in the derivations. First, the weak convergence of $V_{n^\alpha}(t)$ to $\mathcal{J}_c(t)$ still holds on $D[0,\infty)$. $\mathcal{J}_c(t)\equiv N\left(0,\frac{\omega^2}{2c}\left(e^{2ct}-1\right)\right)$ is not bounded in probability as $t\to\infty$, so for $t\in\left[0,n^{1-\alpha}\right]$ a normalization of $O\left(\exp\left\{-cn^{1-\alpha}\right\}\right)$ is used to achieve a weak limit for $V_{n^\alpha}(t)$. A similar normalization is needed for $n^{-\alpha/2}y_{\lfloor n^\alpha t\rfloor}$, namely ρ_n^{-n}. The notational conventions introduced in PM, $\kappa_n:=n^{\alpha}\left\lfloor n^{1-\alpha}\right\rfloor$ and $q:=n^{1-\alpha}-\left\lfloor n^{1-\alpha}\right\rfloor$, are used throughout.

The following lemma shows the continued validity of two functional approximations for the near explosive case that were used in PM.

Lemma 5.1 For each $\alpha\in(0,1)$ and $c>0$

(a) $\sup_{t\in[0,n^{1-\alpha}]}\left|\int_0^t\rho_n^{-n^\alpha s}dB_{n^\alpha}(s)-\int_0^t e^{-cs}dB(s)\right|=o_p\left(\frac{1}{n^{\frac{\alpha}{2}-\frac{1}{\nu}}}\right)$

(b) $\sup_{t\in[0,n^{1-\alpha}]}\left|\int_0^t\rho_n^{-(\lfloor n^\alpha t\rfloor-\lfloor n^\alpha s\rfloor)}dB_{n^\alpha}(s)-\mathcal{J}_{-c}(t)\right|=o_p\left(\frac{1}{n^{\frac{\alpha}{2}-\frac{1}{\nu}}}\right)$

as $n\to\infty$, on the same probability space that (7) holds.

For the sample variance, note first that, unlike the near-stationary case, the limit theory is not determined exclusively from the blocks $\{y^2_{\lfloor n^\alpha j\rfloor+k} : j = 0, ..., \lfloor n^{1-\alpha}\rfloor - 1, k = 1, ..., \lfloor n^\alpha\rfloor\}$. We can write:

$$\frac{\rho_n^{-2\kappa_n}}{n^{2\alpha}}\sum_{t=1}^{n} y_t^2 = \frac{\rho_n^{-2\kappa_n}}{n^{2\alpha}}\sum_{j=0}^{\lfloor n^{1-\alpha}\rfloor-1}\sum_{k=1}^{\lfloor n^\alpha\rfloor} y^2_{\lfloor n^\alpha j\rfloor+k} + \frac{\rho_n^{-2\kappa_n}}{n^{2\alpha}}\sum_{t=\lfloor\kappa_n\rfloor}^{n} y_t^2 + O_p\left(\frac{1}{n^\alpha}\right) \tag{30}$$

and denote by U_{1n} and U_{2n} the first and second term on the right side of (30) respectively. Since U_{2n} is almost surely positive with limiting expectation $\frac{\sigma^2}{4c^2}(e^{2cq} - 1) > 0$ when $q > 0$, we conclude that it contributes to the limit theory whenever $n^{1-\alpha}$ is not an integer.

We will analyse each of the two terms on the right of (30) separately. The term containing the block components can be written as:

$$U_{1n} = \rho_n^{-2\kappa_n}\sum_{j=0}^{\lfloor n^{1-\alpha}\rfloor-1}\frac{1}{n^{2\alpha}}\sum_{k=1}^{\lfloor n^\alpha\rfloor} y^2_{\lfloor n^\alpha j\rfloor+k}$$

$$= \rho_n^{-2\kappa_n}\int_0^{\lfloor n^{1-\alpha}\rfloor}\left(\int_0^r \rho_n^{\lfloor n^\alpha r\rfloor - n^\alpha s} dB_{n^\alpha}(s)\right)^2 dr + o_p(1).$$

Taking the inner integral along $[0, r] = [0, \lfloor n^{1-\alpha}\rfloor] \setminus (r, \lfloor n^{1-\alpha}\rfloor]$ we have, up to $o_p(1)$,

$$U_{1n} = \left(\int_0^{\lfloor n^{1-\alpha}\rfloor}\rho_n^{-n^\alpha s} dB_{n^\alpha}(s)\right)^2 \rho_n^{-2\kappa_n}\int_0^{\lfloor n^{1-\alpha}\rfloor}\rho_n^{2\lfloor n^\alpha r\rfloor} dr + R_n \tag{31}$$

where the remainder term R_n is shown in the Appendix to be $o_p(1)$. The second integral on the right side of (31) can be evaluated directly to obtain

$$\int_0^{\lfloor n^{1-\alpha}\rfloor}\rho_n^{2\lfloor n^\alpha r\rfloor} dr = \frac{\rho_n^{2\kappa_n}}{2c}[1 + o(1)] \quad \text{as } n \to \infty. \tag{32}$$

Using (32) and part (a) of Lemma 5.1, (31) yields

$$U_{1n} = \frac{1}{2c}\left(\int_0^{\lfloor n^{1-\alpha}\rfloor} e^{-cs}dB(s)\right)^2 + o_p\left(\frac{1}{n^{\frac{\alpha}{2}-\frac{1}{\nu}}}\right)$$

$$= \frac{1}{2c}\left(\int_0^{\infty} e^{-cs}dB(s)\right)^2 + o_p\left(\frac{1}{n^{\frac{\alpha}{2}-\frac{1}{\nu}}}\right) \tag{33}$$

on the same probability space that (7) holds.

For the second term on the right of (30), noting that $\lfloor n - \kappa_n \rfloor = \lfloor n^\alpha q \rfloor$, $q \in [0, 1)$, we obtain:

$$U_{2n} = \frac{\rho_n^{-2\kappa_n}}{n^{2\alpha}} \sum_{i=0}^{n-\lfloor\kappa_n\rfloor} y_{i+\lfloor\kappa_n\rfloor}^2$$

$$= \frac{\rho_n^{-2\kappa_n}}{n^{2\alpha}} \sum_{i=1}^{\lfloor n^\alpha q\rfloor} y_{i+\lfloor\kappa_n\rfloor-1}^2 + O_p\left(\frac{1}{n^\alpha}\right)$$

$$= \frac{\rho_n^{-2\kappa_n}}{n^{\alpha}} \int_0^q y_{\lfloor\kappa_n\rfloor+\lfloor n^\alpha p\rfloor}^2 dp - \frac{\rho_n^{-2\kappa_n}}{n^{2\alpha}}\left(q - \frac{\lfloor n^\alpha q\rfloor}{n^\alpha}\right) y_{\lfloor\kappa_n\rfloor+\lfloor n^\alpha q\rfloor}^2$$

$$= \int_0^q \left(\frac{\rho_n^{-\kappa_n}}{n^{\alpha/2}} y_{\lfloor\kappa_n\rfloor+\lfloor n^\alpha p\rfloor}\right)^2 dp + O_p\left(\frac{1}{n^{2\alpha}}\right). \tag{34}$$

Now for each $p \in [0, q]$, $q \in [0, 1)$, the following functional approximation is established in the Appendix:

$$\frac{\rho_n^{-\kappa_n}}{n^{\alpha/2}} y_{\lfloor\kappa_n\rfloor+\lfloor n^\alpha p\rfloor} = e^{cp}\int_0^\infty e^{-cs}dW(s) + o_p\left(\frac{1}{n^{\frac{\alpha}{2}-\frac{1}{\nu}}}\right) \quad \text{as } n \to \infty \tag{35}$$

on the same probability space that (7) holds. Thus, applying the dominated convergence theorem to (34) yields:

$$U_{2n} = \left(\int_0^\infty e^{-cs}dW(s)\right)^2 \int_0^q e^{2cp}dp + o_p\left(\frac{1}{n^{\frac{\alpha}{2}-\frac{1}{\nu}}}\right)$$

$$= \frac{1}{2c}\left(\int_0^\infty e^{-cs}dW(s)\right)^2 \left(e^{2cq} - 1\right) + o_p\left(\frac{1}{n^{\frac{\alpha}{2}-\frac{1}{\nu}}}\right). \tag{36}$$

The asymptotic distribution of the sample variance in the near explosive case can be derived directly from the limit results (33) and (36) for the two terms of (30). Letting $X := \int_0^\infty e^{-cs} dB(s) \equiv N\left(0, \frac{\omega^2}{2c}\right)$, and using the asymptotic equivalence $\rho_n^{-2\kappa_n} e^{-2cq} = \rho_n^{-2n}\left[1 + o(1)\right]$, we conclude that,

$$\frac{\rho_n^{-2n}}{n^{2\alpha}} \sum_{t=1}^{n} y_t^2 = \frac{1}{2c} X^2 + o_p\left(\frac{1}{n^{\frac{\alpha}{2} - \frac{1}{\nu}}}\right)$$

on the same probability space that (7) holds, and hence

$$\frac{\rho_n^{-2n}}{n^{2\alpha}} \sum_{t=1}^{n} y_t^2 \Longrightarrow \frac{1}{2c} X^2 \quad \text{as } n \to \infty \tag{37}$$

on the original space.

As in the case of the sample variance, the asymptotic behaviour of the sample covariance is partly determined by elements of the time series $y_{t-1}u_t$ that do not belong to the block components $\left\{y_{\lfloor n^\alpha j\rfloor + k-1} u_{\lfloor n^\alpha j\rfloor + k} : j = 0, \ldots, \lfloor n^{1-\alpha}\rfloor - 1, k = 1, \ldots, \lfloor n^\alpha \rfloor\right\}$. Obtaining limits for the block components and the remaining time series separately in a method similar to that used for the sample variance will work. It is, however, more efficient to derive the limiting distribution of the sample covariance by using a direct argument on $\rho_n^{-n} n^{-\alpha} \sum_{t=1}^{n} y_{t-1}u_t$.

Using the initial condition $y_0 = o_p\left(n^{\alpha/2}\right)$ and equation (45) in the Appendix, the sample variance can be written as:

$$\begin{aligned}
\frac{\rho_n^{-n}}{n^\alpha} \sum_{t=1}^{n} y_{t-1}u_t &= \frac{\rho_n^{-n}}{n^\alpha} \sum_{t=1}^{n-1} y_t u_{t+1} + o_p\left(\frac{\rho_n^{-n}}{n^{\alpha/2}}\right) \\
&= \frac{\rho_n^{-n}}{n^\alpha} \sum_{t=1}^{\left\lfloor n^\alpha\left(n^{1-\alpha} - \frac{1}{n^\alpha}\right)\right\rfloor} y_t u_{t+1} \\
&= \rho_n^{-n} \int_{\frac{1}{n^\alpha}}^{n^{1-\alpha}} \frac{1}{n^{\alpha/2}} y_{\left\lfloor n^\alpha\left(r - \frac{1}{n^\alpha}\right)\right\rfloor} dB_{n^\alpha}(r) \\
&= \rho_n^{-n} \int_{\frac{1}{n^\alpha}}^{n^{1-\alpha}} \int_0^{r - \frac{1}{n^\alpha}} \rho_n^{\lfloor n^\alpha r\rfloor - n^\alpha s - 1} dB_{n^\alpha}(s) dB_{n^\alpha}(r) + o_p(1).
\end{aligned}$$

Taking the inner integral along $\left[0, r - \frac{1}{n^a}\right] = \left[0, n^{1-\alpha}\right] \setminus \left(r - \frac{1}{n^a}, n^{1-\alpha}\right]$ we have, up to $o_p(1)$:

$$\frac{\rho_n^{-n}}{n^\alpha} \sum_{t=1}^{n} y_{t-1} u_t$$

$$= \rho_n^{-1} \int_{\frac{1}{n^\alpha}}^{n^{1-\alpha}} \rho_n^{-n^\alpha s} dB_{n^a}(s) \int_0^{n^{1-\alpha}} \rho_n^{-(\lfloor \kappa_n \rfloor - \lfloor n^\alpha r \rfloor)} dB_{n^a}(r) - I_n \qquad (38)$$

where the remainder term I_n is shown in the Appendix to be $o_p(1)$. Part (b) of Lemma 5.1 implies:

$$\int_0^{n^{1-\alpha}} \rho_n^{-(\lfloor \kappa_n \rfloor - \lfloor n^\alpha r \rfloor)} dB_{n^a}(r) = \mathcal{J}_{-c}\left(n^{1-\alpha}\right) + o_p\left(\frac{1}{n^{\frac{\alpha}{2} - \frac{1}{\nu}}}\right).$$

The rest of the argument is identical to that in PM for the i.i.d. error case. In particular, $\mathcal{J}_{-c}(t)$ is a L_2-bounded martingale on $[0, \infty)$, and the martingale convergence theorem implies that there exists an almost surely finite random variable Y such that

$$\mathcal{J}_{-c}\left(n^{1-\alpha}\right) \longrightarrow_{a.s.} Y \quad \text{as } n \to \infty.$$

Since $\mathcal{J}_{-c}\left(n^{1-\alpha}\right) \equiv N\left(0, \frac{\omega^2}{2c}\left(1 - e^{-2cn^{1-\alpha}}\right)\right)$, we deduce that $Y \equiv N\left(0, \frac{\omega^2}{2c}\right)$. Thus, if $X = \int_0^\infty e^{-cs} dB(s)$ as in (37), (38) yields:

$$\frac{\rho_n^{-n}}{n^\alpha} \sum_{t=1}^{n} y_{t-1} u_t = XY + o_p\left(\frac{1}{n^{\frac{\alpha}{2} - \frac{1}{\nu}}}\right) \quad \text{as } n \to \infty$$

on the same probability space that (7) holds. The latter strong approximation implies that the asymptotic distribution of the sample covariance is given in the original space by:

$$\frac{\rho_n^{-n}}{n^\alpha} \sum_{t=1}^{n} y_{t-1} u_t \Longrightarrow XY \quad X, Y \equiv N\left(0, \frac{\omega^2}{2c}\right). \qquad (39)$$

As in PM, the asymptotic behaviour of the serial correlation coefficient now follows from the strong approximations leading to (37) and (39) and the fact that the limiting random variables X and Y are independent.

Theorem 5.1 For model (4) with $\rho_n = 1 + c/n^a$, $c > 0$, $\alpha \in (0, 1)$ and weakly dependent errors satisfying Assumption **LP**,

$$\frac{n^\alpha \rho_n^n}{2c}\left(\hat{\rho}_n - \rho_n\right) \Longrightarrow C \quad \text{as } n \to \infty \tag{40}$$

where C is a standard Cauchy variate.

5.1 *Remarks*

(i) Other than the allowance for weakly dependent errors, the statement of theorem 5.1 is identical to that of theorem 4.3 of PM. As discussed in PM, the Cauchy limit theory relates to much earlier work (White, 1958; Anderson, 1959; Basawa and Brockwell, 1984) on the explosive Gaussian AR(1) process. In particular, for the first-order autoregressive process with fixed $|\rho| > 1$, i.i.d. Gaussian innovation errors and initialization $y_0 = 0$, White showed that:

$$\frac{\rho^n}{\rho^2 - 1}\left(\hat{\rho}_n - \rho\right) \Longrightarrow C \quad \text{as } n \to \infty. \tag{41}$$

Replacing ρ by $\rho_n = 1+c/n^a$, we obtain $\rho^2 - 1 = \frac{2c}{n^\alpha}[1+o(1)]$. Hence, the normalizations in Theorem 5.1 and (41) are asymptotically equivalent as $n \to \infty$. Anderson (1959) showed that $\frac{\rho^n}{\rho^2-1}\left(\hat{\rho}_n - \rho\right)$ has a limit distribution that depends on the distribution of the errors u_t when $\rho > 1$ and that no central limit theory or invariance principle is applicable.

(ii) By contrast, an invariance principle does apply in Theorem 5.1 and the limit theory is not restricted to Gaussian processes. In particular, the Cauchy limit result (40) holds for $\rho_n = 1 + c/n^a$, $\alpha \in (0, 1)$, and weakly dependent innovations u_t satisfying Assumption **LP**, thereby including a much wider class of processes. At the boundary where $\alpha \to 0$, Theorem 5.1 reduces to (41) with $\rho = 1 + c$ and primitive errors ε_t with infinitely many moments, as under Gaussianity. In summary, the limit theory in the moderate deviation explosive autoregression is invariant to both the distribution and the dependence structure of the innovation errors.

(iii) The limit theory of Theorem 5.1 is also invariant to the initial condition y_0 being any fixed constant value or random variable of smaller asymptotic order than $n^{\alpha/2}$. This property is also not shared by explosive autoregressions where y_0 does influence the limit theory even in the case of i.i.d. Gaussian errors, as shown by Anderson (1959).

5.2 *The Explosive Case*

When $\alpha = 0$, the process (4) has an explosive root $\rho = 1 + c$, $c > 0$. As in the case of explosive autoregressions with independent innovations (cf. Anderson, 1959), the asymptotic behaviour of the serial correlation coefficient can be derived by investigating the limiting properties of the stochastic sequences:

$$Z_n := \sum_{j=1}^{n} \rho^{-j} u_j \text{ and } \Psi_n := \sum_{j=1}^{n} \rho^{-(n-j)-1} u_j. \tag{42}$$

The results of this subsection are valid for $y_0 = 0$ and weakly dependent innovations u_t satisfying assumption **LP** with the moment condition (2) relaxed to $E\varepsilon_1^2 = \sigma^2 < \infty$.

From the monotone convergence theorem,

$$E \sum_{j=1}^{\infty} \left| \rho^{-j} u_j \right| = \sum_{j=1}^{\infty} |\rho|^{-j} E \left| u_j \right| = \frac{E |u_0|}{|\rho| - 1} < \infty$$

which implies that $\sum_{j=1}^{\infty} \left| \rho^{-j} u_j \right| < \infty$ *a.s* so that $Z_n \to_{a.s.} Z = \sum_{j=1}^{\infty} \rho^{-j} u_j$. Next, since $\{u_t\}$ is strictly stationary we may construct another strictly stationary time series $\{u_t'\}$ with identical marginal distributions to those of $\{u_t\}$ and a corresponding sequence $\Psi_n' = \sum_{j=1}^{n} \rho^{-(n-j)-1} u_{n-j+1}' = \sum_{j=1}^{n} \rho^{-j} u_j'$ for which $\Psi_n' =_d \Psi_n$ for all n. Then, $\Psi_n' \to_{a.s.} \Psi = \sum_{j=1}^{\infty} \rho^{-j} u_j'$, and it follows by the Skorohod representation theorem that $\Psi_n \to_d \Psi$. Joint weak convergence of Ψ_n and Z_n then follows and we have $(Z_n, \Psi_n) \Longrightarrow (Z, \Psi)$, as $n \to \infty$, with $Z =_d \Psi$.

The limiting random variables Ψ and Z can be shown to be independent by modifying Anderson's (1959, theorem 2.3) argument adjusted for weakly dependent errors. The idea is that, as $n \to \infty$, Z_n can be approximated by the first $\lfloor L_n \rfloor$ elements of the sum $\sum_{j=1}^{n} \rho^{-j} u_j$ whereas Ψ_n can be approximated by the last $\lfloor L_n \rfloor$ elements of the sum $\sum_{j=1}^{n} \rho^{-(n-j)-1} u_j$ in (42), where $(L_n)_{n \in \mathbb{N}}$ is a sequence increasing to ∞ with $L_n \leq n/3$ for each n. Accordingly, define:

$$Z_n^* := \sum_{j=1}^{\lfloor L_n \rfloor} \rho^{-j} u_j \text{ and } \Psi_n^* := \sum_{j=n-\lfloor L_n \rfloor+1}^{n} \rho^{-(n-j)-1} u_j = \sum_{k=1}^{\lfloor L_n \rfloor - 1} \rho^{-k} u_{n-k+1}.$$

We may further approximate Ψ_n^* as follows:

$$\Psi_n^* = \sum_{k=1}^{\lfloor L_n \rfloor - 1} \rho^{-k} \sum_{s=0}^{\infty} c_s \varepsilon_{n-k+1-s}$$

$$= \sum_{k=1}^{\lfloor L_n \rfloor - 1} \rho^{-k} \sum_{s=0}^{\lfloor L_n \rfloor} c_s \varepsilon_{n-k+1-s} + \sum_{k=1}^{\lfloor L_n \rfloor - 1} \rho^{-k} \sum_{s=\lfloor L_n \rfloor + 1}^{\infty} c_s \varepsilon_{n-k+1-s}$$

$$= \Psi_n^{**} + \sum_{k=1}^{\lfloor L_n \rfloor - 1} \rho^{-k} \sum_{s=\lfloor L_n \rfloor + 1}^{\infty} c_s \varepsilon_{n-k+1-s}$$

where $\Psi_n^{**} = \sum_{k=1}^{\lfloor L_n \rfloor - 1} \rho^{-k} \sum_{s=0}^{\lfloor L_n \rfloor} c_s \varepsilon_{n-k+1-s}$. Now for each $s \leq \lfloor L_n \rfloor$ and $k \leq \lfloor L_n \rfloor - 1$,

$$n - k + 1 - s > n + 1 - 2 \lfloor L_n \rfloor \geq \lfloor L_n \rfloor + 1$$

since $L_n \leq n/3$, showing that Ψ_n^{**} is independent of $\sigma \left(\varepsilon_{\lfloor L_n \rfloor}, \varepsilon_{\lfloor L_n \rfloor - 1}, \ldots \right)$ and hence of Z_n^*. Moreover, $\Psi_n^* - \Psi_n^{**} = o_p(1)$ since,

$$E \left| \sum_{k=1}^{\lfloor L_n \rfloor - 1} \rho^{-k} \sum_{s=\lfloor L_n \rfloor + 1}^{\infty} c_s \varepsilon_{n-k+1-s} \right| \leq E \left| \varepsilon_1 \right| \sum_{k=1}^{\lfloor L_n \rfloor - 1} |\rho|^{-k} \sum_{s=\lfloor L_n \rfloor + 1}^{\infty} |c_s|$$

$$\leq \frac{E \left| \varepsilon_1 \right|}{|\rho| - 1} \sum_{s=\lfloor L_n \rfloor + 1}^{\infty} |c_s| \to 0$$

as $n \to \infty$ in view of **LP**. So, Z_n^* is asymptotically independent of Ψ_n^*. Next, $\Psi_n - \Psi_n^* = \sum_{k=\lfloor L_n \rfloor}^{n} \rho^{-k} u_{n-k+1}$, and so:

$$E \left| \Psi_n - \Psi_n^* \right| \leq E \left| u_1 \right| \sum_{k=\lfloor L_n \rfloor + 1}^{n} |\rho|^{-k} = O\left(|\rho|^{-L_n} \right)$$

so that $\Psi_n - \Psi_n^* = o_p(1)$. In a similar fashion, $Z_n - Z_n^* = o_p(1)$. It follows that Z_n and Ψ_n are asymptotically independent since they differ from the independent variates Z_n^* and Ψ_n^{**} by terms that converge in probability to zero.

The variance of Z (and Ψ) can be calculated directly as:

$$E\left(\sum_{j=1}^{\infty}\rho^{-j}u_j\right)^2 = \sigma_u^2\sum_{j=1}^{\infty}\rho^{-2j} + 2\sum_{j=1}^{\infty}\sum_{k=j+1}^{\infty}\rho^{-j-k}\gamma_u(k-j)$$

$$= \sum_{j=1}^{\infty}\rho^{-2j}\left\{\sigma_u^2 + 2\sum_{i=1}^{\infty}\rho^{-i}\gamma_u(i)\right\} = \frac{\widetilde{\omega}^2}{\rho^2-1}$$

where $\widetilde{\omega}^2 = \sigma_u^2 + 2\sum_{i=1}^{\infty}\rho^{-i}\gamma_u(i)$. Since $E\left|\rho^{-n}\sum_{t=1}^{n}\sum_{j=t}^{n}\rho^{t-j-1}u_ju_t\right| = O(\rho^{-n}n)$ as $n\to\infty$, we can write the sample covariance as,

$$\rho^{-n}\sum_{t=1}^{n}y_{t-1}u_t = \rho^{-n}\sum_{t=1}^{n}\sum_{j=1}^{t-1}\rho^{t-j-1}u_ju_t = Z_n\Psi_n + o_p(1).$$

By a standard argument (e.g. Anderson, 1959), $\rho^{-2n}\sum_{t=1}^{n}y_{t-1}^2 = Z_n^2/(\rho^2-1) + O_p(\rho^{-n})$. Thus, joint convergence of Ψ_n and Z_n implies that:

$$\left(\rho^{-n}\sum_{t=1}^{n}y_{t-1}u_t, \rho^{-2n}\sum_{t=1}^{n}y_{t-1}^2\right) \Longrightarrow (Z\Psi, Z^2) \quad \text{as } n\to\infty. \tag{43}$$

When $(\varepsilon_t)_{t\in\mathbb{Z}}$ is a Gaussian sequence, Z and Ψ are independent Gaussian random variables and (43) yields the standard Cauchy limit:

$$\frac{\rho^n}{\rho^2-1}(\hat{\rho}_n-\rho) \Longrightarrow C. \tag{44}$$

Note that, when $\rho_n = 1 + c/n^{\alpha}$,

$$\sum_{i=1}^{\infty}\rho_n^{-i}\gamma_u(i) \to \sum_{i=1}^{\infty}\gamma_u(i) = \lambda \quad \text{as } n\to\infty$$

for each $c,\alpha > 0$ by an identical argument to that used in the proof of Proposition A4 (b). Thus, when y_t is a near explosive moderate deviations from unity process, (44) agrees with Theorem 5.1 and $\widetilde{\omega}^2 = \sigma_u^2 + 2\sum_{i=1}^{\infty}\rho_n^{-i}\gamma_u(i) \to \omega^2$, the long-run variance of u_t.

6 Discussion

When there are moderate deviations from unity, the derivations of sections 4 and 5 reveal that both functional approximations to a diffusion and standard laws of large numbers and central limit theorems contribute to the limit theory. The functional law provides in each case a limiting subsidiary process whose elements form the components that upon further summation satisfy a law of large numbers and a central limit law. While there is only one limiting process involved as $n \to \infty$, it is convenient to think of the functional law operating within blocks of length $\lfloor n^{\alpha} \rfloor$ and the law of large numbers and central-limit laws operating across the $\lfloor n^{1-\alpha} \rfloor$ blocks. The moment condition in (2) ensures the validity of the embedding argument that makes this segmentation rigorous as $n \to \infty$.

Theorem 4.2 provides a bridge between stationary and local to unity autoregressions with weakly dependent innovation errors. When the innovation error sequence is a linear process, the least squares estimator has been found to satisfy a Gaussian limit theory with an asymptotic bias. A convergence rate of $n^{\frac{1}{2}+\frac{\alpha}{2}}$ has been obtained, which for $\alpha \in (0, 1)$ covers the interval $(n^{1/2}, n)$, providing a link between $\sqrt{n}$ and n asymptotics. As shown in section 4, there is also a close connection between the asymptotic bias in the serial correlation coefficient and the second-order bias that arises in local to unity and unit root asymptotics.

Theorem 5.1 provides a bridge between local to unity and explosive autoregressions with weakly dependent innovation errors. In particular, when $\alpha = 1$,

$$\rho_n^n = \left(1 + \frac{c}{n}\right)^n = e^c[1 + o(1)] \text{ and } \frac{n^{\alpha}\rho_n^n}{2c} = O(n).$$

Thus, ignoring multiplicative constants, the convergence rate of the serial correlation coefficient takes values on (n, ρ^n) as α ranges from 1 to 0, where $\rho := 1 + c$ is an explosive autoregressive root when $\alpha = 0$. Thus, the convergence rate of the serial correlation coefficient covers the interval (n, ρ^n), establishing a link between the asymptotic behaviour of local to unity and explosive autoregressions.

As discussed in PM, the bridging asymptotics are not continuous at the stationary boundary of α, at least without some modification. In the stationary case where $c < 0$ and $\alpha = 0$, the probability limit of the serial correlation coefficient is correctly captured in the limit of the moderate deviation theory as is the $\sqrt{n}$ rate of convergence, but the moderate deviation limit distribution does not continuously merge into the limit theory for the stationary case although the limit distributions are both normal with compatible centering. In the explosive case when $\alpha \to 0$, the bridging asymptotics are continuous at the boundary in the case of weak dependence, yielding the standard Cauchy limit (which applies in the boundary case under Gaussian errors).

For the limit as $\alpha \to 1$, we have $n^{1-\alpha} \to 1$, and so $\lfloor n^{1-\alpha} \rfloor = 1$ for $\alpha = 1$, in which case $j = 0$ necessarily in the blocking scheme of section 3. The invariance principle of Phillips (1987a) $n^{-1/2} y_{\lfloor np \rfloor} \Longrightarrow \mathcal{J}_c(p)$ on $D[0,1]$ together with the argument preceding (31) and (38) with $\alpha = 1$ and $j = 0$ yield the usual local to unity limit result (cf. Phillips, 1987a):

$$n(\hat{\rho}_n - \rho_n) \Longrightarrow \frac{\int_0^1 \mathcal{J}_c(r) dB(r)}{\int_0^1 \mathcal{J}_c(r)^2 dr}.$$

Thus, as in PM, continuity in the limit theory cannot be achieved at the (inside) boundary with the conventional local to unity asymptotics, at least without using the blocking construction.

Appendix and Proofs

Propositions A1 and A2 below are proved in the original version of PM (see also chapter 2 of Magdalinos, 2004). The remainder of this section contains Propositions A3 and A4 as well as the proofs of the various statements made in the chapter.

Proposition A1 For each $x \in [0, M]$, $M > 0$, possibly depending on n, and real valued, measurable function f on $[0, \infty)$,

$$\frac{1}{n^{\alpha/2}} \sum_{i=1}^{\lfloor xn^{\alpha} \rfloor} f\left(\frac{i}{n^{\alpha}}\right) u_i = \int_0^x f(r) dB_{n^{\alpha}}(r).$$

An immediate consequence of Proposition A1 is the following useful identity. For each $x \in \left[0, n^{1-\alpha}\right]$ and $m \in \mathbb{N}$,

$$\frac{1}{n^{\alpha/2}} \sum_{i=1}^{\lfloor xn^{\alpha} \rfloor} f\left(\frac{i}{n^{\alpha}}\right) u_{i+m} = \int_0^x f(r) dB_{n^{\alpha}}\left(r + \frac{m}{n^{\alpha}}\right). \tag{45}$$

Proposition A2 For $c < 0$, $\sup_{t>0} |\mathcal{J}_c(t)| < \infty$ a.s.

Proposition A3 For each $\alpha \in (0, 1)$

$$\max_{0 \le t \le n} \left| \frac{\tilde{\varepsilon}_t}{n^{\alpha/2}} \right| = o_p(1) \quad \text{as } n \to \infty.$$

Proof The argument follows Phillips (1999). Summability of $\sum_{j=1}^{\infty} j \left|c_j\right|$ ensures that $\tilde{\varepsilon}_t = \sum_{j=0}^{\infty} \tilde{c}_j \varepsilon_{t-j}$ converges absolutely almost surely. Thus, Fatou's lemma and the Minkowski inequality give:

$$E\left|\tilde{\varepsilon}_t\right|^{\nu} \leq \operatorname{liminf}_{N\to\infty} E\left|\sum_{j=0}^{N} \tilde{c}_j \varepsilon_{t-j}\right|^{\nu} \leq \operatorname{liminf}_{N\to\infty}\left[\sum_{j=0}^{N}\left(E\left|\tilde{c}_j \varepsilon_{t-j}\right|^{\nu}\right)^{\frac{1}{\nu}}\right]^{\nu}$$

$$= E\left|\varepsilon_0\right|^{\nu} \operatorname{liminf}_{N\to\infty}\left(\sum_{j=0}^{N}\left|\tilde{c}_j\right|\right)^{\nu} = E\left|\varepsilon_0\right|^{\nu}\left(\sum_{j=0}^{\infty}\left|\tilde{c}_j\right|\right)^{\nu} < \infty$$

by (2) since $\sum_{j=0}^{\infty}\left|\tilde{c}_j\right| < \infty$. Thus, for any $\delta > 0$ the Markov inequality gives

$$P\left(\max_{0\leq t\leq n}\left|\tilde{\varepsilon}_t\right| > \delta n^{\alpha/2}\right) \leq \sum_{t=0}^{n} P\left(\left|\tilde{\varepsilon}_t\right| > \delta n^{\alpha/2}\right) \leq \sum_{t=0}^{n} \frac{E\left|\tilde{\varepsilon}_t\right|^{\nu}}{\delta^{\nu} n^{\nu\alpha/2}}$$

$$= \frac{E\left|\tilde{\varepsilon}_0\right|^{\nu}}{\delta^{\nu}} \frac{n+1}{n^{\nu\alpha/2}} = o(1)$$

if and only if $\frac{\nu\alpha}{2} > 1$, which holds by (2).

Proposition A4

(a) Let $y_{nt}^{*} := \sum_{i=0}^{n} \rho_n^i u_{t-i}$. Then for each $\alpha \in (0,1)$

$$\frac{1}{n^{\frac{1+3\alpha}{2}}} \sum_{t=1}^{n} y_{t-1} \tilde{\varepsilon}_t = \frac{1}{n^{\frac{1+3\alpha}{2}}} \sum_{t=1}^{n} y_{nt-1}^{*} \tilde{\varepsilon}_t + o_p(1) \quad \text{as } n \to \infty$$

(b) Let $\gamma_m(h) = E\tilde{\varepsilon}_t u_{t-h} = \sigma^2 \sum_{j=0}^{\infty} c_j \tilde{c}_{j+h}$ for $h \geq 0$ and $m_n = \sum_{i=1}^{\infty} \rho_n^{i-1} \gamma_m(i)$. Then:

$$\lim_{n\to\infty} m_n = \sum_{i=1}^{\infty} \gamma_m(i)$$

Proof For part (a), we can write:

$$\frac{1}{n^{\frac{1+3\alpha}{2}}}\sum_{t=1}^{n}(y_{nt-1}^{*}-y_{t-1})\tilde{\varepsilon}_t = \frac{1}{n^{\frac{1+3\alpha}{2}}}\sum_{t=1}^{n}\left[\left(\sum_{i=t}^{n}\rho_n^i u_{t-i-1}-y_0\rho_n^t\right)\right]\tilde{\varepsilon}_t$$
$$= \frac{1}{n^{\frac{1+3\alpha}{2}}}\sum_{t=1}^{n}\sum_{i=t}^{n}\rho_n^i u_{t-i-1}\tilde{\varepsilon}_t + o_p\left(\frac{1}{n^{\frac{1-\alpha}{2}}}\right)$$

since, by Proposition A3 and the fact that $\sum_{t=1}^{n}|\rho_n|^t = O(n^\alpha)$,

$$\left|\frac{1}{n^{\frac{1+3\alpha}{2}}}\sum_{t=1}^{n}y_0\rho_n^t\tilde{\varepsilon}_t\right| \leq \left|\frac{y_0}{n^{\alpha/2}}\right| \max_{1\leq t\leq n}\left|\frac{\tilde{\varepsilon}_t}{n^{\alpha/2}}\right| \frac{1}{n^{\frac{1+\alpha}{2}}}\sum_{t=1}^{n}|\rho_n|^t = o_p\left(\frac{1}{n^{\frac{1-\alpha}{2}}}\right).$$

Also, the Cauchy–Schwarz inequality yields, for some bounding constant $K \in (0,\infty)$,

$$E\left|\frac{1}{n^{\frac{1+3\alpha}{2}}}\sum_{t=1}^{n}\sum_{i=t}^{n}\rho_n^i u_{t-i-1}\tilde{\varepsilon}_t\right| \leq \frac{1}{n^{\frac{1+3\alpha}{2}}}\sum_{t=1}^{n}\sum_{i=t}^{n}|\rho_n|^i E\left|u_{t-i-1}\tilde{\varepsilon}_t\right|$$
$$\leq \frac{\left\{E(u_1^2)E\left(\tilde{\varepsilon}_1^2\right)\right\}^{1/2}}{n^{\frac{1+3\alpha}{2}}}\sum_{t=1}^{n}\sum_{i=t}^{n}|\rho_n|^i$$
$$= \frac{K}{n^{\frac{1+\alpha}{2}}}\sum_{t=1}^{n}|\rho_n|^t + o\left(n|\rho_n|^n\right) = O\left(\frac{1}{n^{\frac{1-\alpha}{2}}}\right).$$

This completes the proof of part (a).

For part (b), first note that $\gamma_m(\cdot)$ is summable, since

$$\sum_{h=0}^{\infty}|\gamma_m(h)| \leq \sigma^2\sum_{j=0}^{\infty}|c_j|\sum_{h=0}^{\infty}|\tilde{c}_h| < \infty.$$

The limit of m_n is obtained by an application of the Toeplitz lemma (see e.g. Hall and Heyde, 1980), as we now show. Letting for each $i \in \mathbb{N}$,

$S_m(i) = \sum_{k=1}^{i} \gamma_m(k)$, $S_m(0) = 0$ and using summation by parts we obtain:

$$\begin{aligned}\lim_{n\to\infty} m_n &= \lim_{n\to\infty} \sum_{i=1}^{n} \rho_n^{i-1} \Delta S_m(i) \\ &= \lim_{n\to\infty} \rho_n^n S_m(n) - \lim_{n\to\infty} \sum_{i=1}^{n} \left(\rho_n^i - \rho_n^{i-1}\right) S_m(i) \\ &= \lim_{n\to\infty} \frac{-2c}{n^\alpha} \sum_{i=1}^{n} \rho_n^{i-1} S_m(i) = \lim_{n\to\infty} \sum_{i=1}^{n} z_{ni} S_m(i)\end{aligned}$$

where $z_{ni} := \frac{-2c}{n^\alpha} \rho_n^{i-1}$, since $\rho_n^n = o(1)$ and $S_m(n) \to \sum_{k=1}^{\infty} \gamma_m(k) < \infty$. Since $z_{ni} \to 0$ for each fixed i, $\sum_{i=1}^{n} |z_{ni}|$ is bounded by a finite constant, and

$$\sum_{i=1}^{n} z_{ni} = \frac{-2c}{n^\alpha} \sum_{i=1}^{n} \rho_n^{i-1} = \frac{-2c}{n^\alpha} \frac{1-\rho_n^n}{1-\rho_n} = 1 - \rho_n^n = 1 + o(1) \quad \text{as } n \to \infty$$

the Toeplitz lemma implies that:

$$\lim_{n\to\infty} m_n = \lim_{n\to\infty} \sum_{i=1}^{n} z_{ni} S_m(i) = \lim_{n\to\infty} S_m(n) = \sum_{i=1}^{\infty} \gamma_m(i).$$

This completes the proof of the proposition.

Proof of Lemma 3.1 Using the BN decomposition (5) we can write

$$\begin{aligned}B_{n^\alpha}(t) &= \frac{1}{n^{\alpha/2}} \sum_{i=1}^{\lfloor tn^\alpha \rfloor} u_i = \frac{C(1)}{n^{\alpha/2}} \sum_{i=1}^{\lfloor tn^\alpha \rfloor} \varepsilon_i - \frac{1}{n^{\alpha/2}} \sum_{i=1}^{\lfloor tn^\alpha \rfloor} \Delta\tilde{\varepsilon}_i \\ &= C(1) W_{n^\alpha}(t) - \frac{1}{n^{\alpha/2}} \left(\tilde{\varepsilon}_{\lfloor tn^\alpha \rfloor} - \tilde{\varepsilon}_1\right).\end{aligned}$$

Letting $B(t) = C(1) W(t)$ on the probability space where (6) holds, we obtain

$$\sup_{t\in[0,n^{1-\alpha}]} |B_{n^\alpha}(t) - B(t)| \leq C(1) \sup_{t\in[0,n^{1-\alpha}]} |W_{n^\alpha}(t) - W(t)| + 2 \max_{0\leq k\leq n} \left|\frac{\tilde{\varepsilon}_k}{n^{\alpha/2}}\right|,$$

so the lemma follows by (6) and Proposition A3.

Proof of Lemma 3.2 For part (a), we can use the BN decomposition (5) to write

$$\begin{aligned}
\frac{1}{n^{\alpha/2}} y_{\lfloor n^\alpha t \rfloor} &= \frac{1}{n^{\alpha/2}} \sum_{i=1}^{\lfloor n^\alpha t \rfloor} \rho_n^{\lfloor n^\alpha t \rfloor - i} u_i + \frac{y_0}{n^{\alpha/2}} \rho_n^{\lfloor n^\alpha t \rfloor} \\
&= \frac{C(1)}{n^{\alpha/2}} \sum_{i=1}^{\lfloor n^\alpha t \rfloor} \rho_n^{\lfloor n^\alpha t \rfloor - i} \varepsilon_i - \frac{1}{n^{\alpha/2}} \sum_{i=1}^{\lfloor n^\alpha t \rfloor} \rho_n^{\lfloor n^\alpha t \rfloor - i} \Delta \tilde{\varepsilon}_i + \frac{y_0}{n^{\alpha/2}} \rho_n^{\lfloor n^\alpha t \rfloor} \\
&= \frac{C(1)}{n^{\alpha/2}} x_{\lfloor n^\alpha t \rfloor} - \frac{1}{n^{\alpha/2}} \sum_{i=1}^{\lfloor n^\alpha t \rfloor} \rho_n^{\lfloor n^\alpha t \rfloor - i} \Delta \tilde{\varepsilon}_i + \frac{y_0}{n^{\alpha/2}} \rho_n^{\lfloor n^\alpha t \rfloor}.
\end{aligned}$$

Since $\frac{y_0}{n^{\alpha/2}} \rho_n^{\lfloor n^\alpha t \rfloor} = o_p(1)$ uniformly in $t \geq 0$, it is enough to show that:

$$\sup_{t \in [0, n^{1-\alpha}]} \left| \frac{1}{n^{\alpha/2}} \sum_{i=1}^{\lfloor n^\alpha t \rfloor} \rho_n^{\lfloor n^\alpha t \rfloor - i} \Delta \tilde{\varepsilon}_i \right| = o_p(1). \tag{46}$$

Summation by parts gives,

$$\frac{1}{n^{\alpha/2}} \sum_{i=1}^{\lfloor n^\alpha t \rfloor} \rho_n^{\lfloor n^\alpha t \rfloor - i} \Delta \tilde{\varepsilon}_i = \frac{\tilde{\varepsilon}_{\lfloor n^\alpha t \rfloor}}{n^{\alpha/2}} - \frac{1}{n^{\alpha/2}} \sum_{i=1}^{\lfloor n^\alpha t \rfloor} \left(\Delta \rho_n^{\lfloor n^\alpha t \rfloor - i} \right) \tilde{\varepsilon}_i$$

so that:

$$\begin{aligned}
&\sup_{t \in [0, n^{1-\alpha}]} \left| \frac{1}{n^{\alpha/2}} \sum_{i=1}^{\lfloor n^\alpha t \rfloor} \rho_n^{\lfloor n^\alpha t \rfloor - i} \Delta \tilde{\varepsilon}_i \right| \\
&\quad \leq \max_{0 \leq k \leq n} \left| \frac{\tilde{\varepsilon}_k}{n^{\alpha/2}} \right| + \sup_{t \in [0, n^{1-\alpha}]} \left| \frac{1}{n^{\alpha/2}} \sum_{i=1}^{\lfloor n^\alpha t \rfloor} \left(\Delta \rho_n^{\lfloor n^\alpha t \rfloor - i} \right) \tilde{\varepsilon}_i \right| \\
&\quad \leq \max_{0 \leq k \leq n} \left| \frac{\tilde{\varepsilon}_k}{n^{\alpha/2}} \right| + \max_{0 \leq k \leq n} \left| \frac{\tilde{\varepsilon}_k}{n^{\alpha/2}} \right| \sup_{t \geq 0} \frac{|c|}{n^\alpha} \sum_{i=1}^{\lfloor n^\alpha t \rfloor} |\rho_n|^{\lfloor n^\alpha t \rfloor - i} \\
&\quad \leq \max_{0 \leq k \leq n} \left| \frac{\tilde{\varepsilon}_k}{n^{\alpha/2}} \right| \left\{ 1 + \frac{|c|}{n^\alpha} \sup_{t \geq 0} \frac{1 - |\rho_n|^{\lfloor n^\alpha t \rfloor}}{1 - |\rho_n|} \right\} \\
&\quad \leq \max_{0 \leq k \leq n} \left| \frac{\tilde{\varepsilon}_k}{n^{\alpha/2}} \right| \left\{ 1 + \frac{|c|}{(1 - |\rho_n|)\, n^\alpha} \right\} = o_p(1).
\end{aligned}$$

For part (b), the BN decomposition implies that,

$$\sup_{t\in[0,n^{1-\alpha}]} |V_{n^\alpha}(t) - C(1)U_{n^\alpha}(t)|$$

$$= \sup_{t\in[0,n^{1-\alpha}]} \left| \frac{1}{n^{\alpha/2}} \sum_{i=1}^{\lfloor n^\alpha t\rfloor} e^{\frac{c}{n^\alpha}(n^\alpha t - i)} \Delta\tilde{\varepsilon}_i \right| = o_p(1)$$

by an identical argument to the proof of (46).

Proof of Lemma 4.1 For part (a), in view of Proposition A3, it is enough to show that $\frac{y_n}{\sqrt{n}} = o_p(1)$. Using (5) and the fact that $y_0 = o_p\left(n^{\alpha/2}\right)$ we can write:

$$\frac{y_n}{\sqrt{n}} = \frac{1}{\sqrt{n}} \sum_{i=1}^{n} \rho_n^{n-i} u_i + o_p\left(n^{-\frac{1-\alpha}{2}}\right)$$

$$= \frac{C(1)}{\sqrt{n}} \sum_{i=1}^{n} \rho_n^{n-i} \varepsilon_i - \frac{1}{\sqrt{n}} \sum_{i=1}^{n} \rho_n^{n-i} \Delta\tilde{\varepsilon}_i = o_p(1)$$

since $E\left(n^{-1/2}\sum_{i=1}^n \rho_n^{n-i}\varepsilon_i\right)^2 = O\left(n^{-(1-\alpha)}\right)$ and $n^{-\alpha/2}\sum_{i=1}^n \rho_n^{n-i}\Delta\tilde{\varepsilon}_i = o_p(1)$ by (46).

For part (b), denoting by $\gamma_{\tilde{\varepsilon}}(\cdot)$ the autocovariance function of $\tilde{\varepsilon}_t$, the BN decomposition on u_t yields:

$$\frac{1}{n^{\frac{1+\alpha}{2}}} \sum_{t=1}^{n} (u_t\tilde{\varepsilon}_t - \lambda) = \frac{C(1)\tilde{c}_0}{n^{\frac{1+\alpha}{2}}} \sum_{t=1}^{n} \left(\varepsilon_t^2 - \sigma^2\right) + \frac{C(1)}{n^{\frac{1+\alpha}{2}}} \sum_{t=1}^{n} \left(\sum_{j=1}^{\infty} \tilde{c}_j \varepsilon_{t-j}\right) \varepsilon_t$$

$$- \frac{1}{n^{\frac{1+\alpha}{2}}} \sum_{t=1}^{n} \left[\tilde{\varepsilon}_t^2 - \gamma_{\tilde{\varepsilon}}(0)\right] + \frac{1}{n^{\frac{1+\alpha}{2}}} \sum_{t=1}^{n} \left[\tilde{\varepsilon}_t\tilde{\varepsilon}_{t-1} - \gamma_{\tilde{\varepsilon}}(1)\right]. \quad (47)$$

The first term of (47) is $O_p(n^{-\alpha/2})$ from the i.i.d. CLT since $E\varepsilon_1^4 < \infty$. The third and fourth terms of (47) have order $O_p(n^{-\alpha/2})$ from a standard CLT for sample variances and covariances of linear processes (Hall and Heyde, 1980, theorem 6.7) since $E(\varepsilon_0^4) < \infty$ and, for some $\delta \in (0, 1/2)$,

$$\sum_{j=1}^{\infty} j^{\frac{1}{2}} \tilde{c}_j^2 = \sum_{j=1}^{\infty} j^{-1-\delta} \left(j^{\frac{3}{4}+\frac{\delta}{2}} \sum_{k=j+1}^{\infty} c_k\right)^2 \le \sum_{j=1}^{\infty} j^{-1-\delta} \left(\sum_{k=j+1}^{\infty} k^{\frac{3}{4}+\frac{\delta}{2}} |c_k|\right)^2$$

$$\le \left(\sum_{k=2}^{\infty} k\,|c_k|\right)^2 \sum_{j=1}^{\infty} j^{-1-\delta} < \infty.$$

The second term of (47) converges to 0 in L_2 since

$$E\left[\frac{1}{n^{\frac{1+\alpha}{2}}}\sum_{t=1}^{n}\left(\sum_{j=1}^{\infty}\tilde{c}_j\varepsilon_{t-j}\right)\varepsilon_t\right]^2=\frac{\sigma^4}{n^\alpha}\sum_{j=1}^{\infty}\tilde{c}_j^2=O\left(\frac{1}{n^\alpha}\right).$$

This completes the proof of the lemma.

Proof of Lemma 4.2 In view of Theorem 2.1 (c), it is enough to show that,

$$\frac{1}{n^{\frac{1+\alpha}{2}}}\sum_{t=1}^{n}y_{t-1}\varepsilon_t=C(1)\frac{1}{n^{\frac{1+\alpha}{2}}}\sum_{t=1}^{n}x_{t-1}\varepsilon_t+o_p(1) \tag{48}$$

where $x_t=\sum_{i=1}^{t}\rho_n^{t-i}\varepsilon_i$. Using the BN decomposition (5) we can write

$$y_t=\sum_{i=1}^{t}\rho_n^{t-i}u_i+\rho_n^t y_0=C(1)x_t-\sum_{i=1}^{t}\rho_n^{t-i}\Delta\tilde{\varepsilon}_i+\rho_n^t y_0.$$

Summation by parts gives:

$$\sum_{i=1}^{t}\rho_n^{t-i}\Delta\tilde{\varepsilon}_i=\tilde{\varepsilon}_t-\sum_{i=1}^{t}\left(\Delta\rho_n^{t-i}\right)\tilde{\varepsilon}_{i-1}=\tilde{\varepsilon}_t+\frac{c}{n^\alpha}\sum_{i=1}^{t}\rho_n^{t-i}\tilde{\varepsilon}_{i-1}.$$

Since $E\left(\frac{1}{\sqrt{n}}\sum_{t=1}^{n}\rho_n^{t-1}\varepsilon_t\right)^2=\frac{\sigma^2}{n}\sum_{t=1}^{n}\rho_n^{2t-2}=O\left(\frac{1}{n^{1-\alpha}}\right)$ we can write:

$$\frac{1}{n^{\frac{1+\alpha}{2}}}\sum_{t=1}^{n}\left[y_{t-1}-C(1)x_{t-1}\right]\varepsilon_t$$

$$=-\frac{1}{n^{\frac{1+\alpha}{2}}}\sum_{t=1}^{n}\sum_{i=1}^{t-1}\rho_n^{t-i-1}\Delta\tilde{\varepsilon}_i\varepsilon_t+\frac{y_0}{n^{\alpha/2}}\frac{1}{n^{1/2}}\sum_{t=1}^{n}\rho_n^{t-1}\varepsilon_t$$

$$=-\frac{1}{n^{\frac{1+\alpha}{2}}}\sum_{t=1}^{n}\left(\tilde{\varepsilon}_{t-1}+\frac{c}{n^\alpha}\sum_{i=1}^{t-1}\rho_n^{t-i-1}\tilde{\varepsilon}_{i-1}\right)\varepsilon_t+o_p\left(\frac{1}{n^{\frac{1-\alpha}{2}}}\right)$$

$$=-\frac{1}{n^{\frac{1+\alpha}{2}}}\sum_{t=1}^{n}\tilde{\varepsilon}_{t-1}\varepsilon_t-\frac{c}{n^{\frac{1+3\alpha}{2}}}\sum_{t=1}^{n}\left(\sum_{i=1}^{t-1}\rho_n^{t-i-1}\tilde{\varepsilon}_i\right)\varepsilon_t+o_p\left(\frac{1}{n^{\frac{1-\alpha}{2}}}\right).$$

Both terms in the above expression are martingales. For the first term, we have:

$$E\left(\frac{1}{n^{\frac{1+\alpha}{2}}}\sum_{t=1}^{n}\tilde{\varepsilon}_{t-1}\varepsilon_t\right)^2=\frac{\sigma^2}{n^{1+\alpha}}\sum_{t=1}^{n}E\tilde{\varepsilon}_{t-1}^2=\frac{\sigma^2E\tilde{\varepsilon}_0^2}{n^\alpha}=O\left(n^{-\alpha}\right).$$

The second term also converges to 0 in L_2 since, by Minkowski's inequality, we have:

$$E\left[\frac{1}{n^{\frac{1+3\alpha}{2}}}\sum_{t=1}^{n}\left(\sum_{i=1}^{t-1}\rho_n^{t-i-1}\tilde{\varepsilon}_i\right)\varepsilon_t\right]^2 = \frac{\sigma^2}{n^{1+3\alpha}}\sum_{t=1}^{n}E\left(\sum_{i=1}^{t-1}\rho_n^{t-i-1}\tilde{\varepsilon}_i\right)^2$$

$$\leq \frac{\sigma^2}{n^{1+3\alpha}}\sum_{t=1}^{n}\left[\sum_{i=1}^{t-1}\left\{E\left(\rho_n^{2(t-i-1)}\tilde{\varepsilon}_i^2\right)\right\}^{1/2}\right]^2$$

$$= \frac{\sigma^2 E\tilde{\varepsilon}_0^2}{n^{1+3\alpha}}\sum_{t=1}^{n}\left(\sum_{i=1}^{t-1}\left|\rho_n^{t-i-1}\right|\right)^2$$

$$= \frac{\sigma^2 E\tilde{\varepsilon}_0^2}{n^{1+3\alpha}(1-\rho_n)^2}\left[n + O(n^{\alpha})\right] = O(n^{-\alpha}).$$

This shows (48) and the lemma follows.

Proof of Lemma 4.3 For part (a), using the Cauchy–Schwarz inequality we can write:

$$\left|\frac{1}{n^{1+\frac{\alpha}{2}}}\sum_{t=1}^{n}y_{t-1}\tilde{\varepsilon}_t\right| \leq \frac{1}{n^{1+\frac{\alpha}{2}}}\sum_{t=1}^{n}\left|y_{t-1}\tilde{\varepsilon}_t\right| \leq \left(\frac{1}{n^{1+\alpha}}\sum_{t=1}^{n}y_{t-1}^2\right)^{1/2}\left(\frac{1}{n}\sum_{t=1}^{n}\tilde{\varepsilon}_t^2\right)^{1/2}$$

$$= \left(\frac{\omega^2}{-2c}E\tilde{\varepsilon}_0^2\right)^{1/2} + o_p\left(\frac{1}{n^{\frac{\alpha}{2}-\frac{1}{\nu}}}\right)$$

by the ergodic theorem applied to $\tilde{\varepsilon}_t^2$ and by (13). The proof of part (b) is lengthy and has been omitted. It is available from the authors upon request.

Proof of Theorem 4.1 Part (a) is given by (19). The moment condition $E\varepsilon_0^4 < \infty$ is essential for all $\alpha \in (0,1)$ as a consequence of using Lemma 4.1 (b).

For part (b), by squaring (4) we obtain:

$$\left(1-\rho_n^2\right)\sum_{t=1}^{n}y_{t-1}^2 = y_0^2 - y_n^2 + 2\rho_n\sum_{t=1}^{n}y_{t-1}u_t + \sum_{t=1}^{n}u_t^2$$

$$= 2\rho_n\sum_{t=1}^{n}y_{t-1}u_t + \sum_{t=1}^{n}u_t^2 + O_p(n^{\alpha})$$

since $y_n = O_p\left(n^{\alpha/2}\right)$ by (10). Writing $1-\rho_n^2 = \frac{-2c}{n^\alpha}\left(1+\frac{c}{2n^\alpha}\right)$ we obtain:

$$\begin{aligned}
\sum_{t=1}^{n}\frac{y_{t-1}^2}{n^\alpha} &= \frac{1}{-2c\left(1+\frac{c}{2n^\alpha}\right)}\left\{2\rho_n\sum_{t=1}^{n} y_{t-1}u_t + \sum_{t=1}^{n} u_t^2\right\} + O_p\left(n^\alpha\right) \\
&= \frac{1}{-2c\left(1+\frac{c}{2n^\alpha}\right)}\left\{2\rho_n\sum_{t=1}^{n}\left(y_{t-1}u_t - \lambda - \frac{c}{n^\alpha}m_n\right) + \sum_{t=1}^{n}\left(u_t^2-\sigma_u^2\right)\right\} \\
&\quad + \frac{n}{-2c}\frac{2\rho_n\left(\lambda+\frac{c}{n^\alpha}m_n\right)+\sigma_u^2}{1+\frac{c}{2n^\alpha}} + O_p\left(n^\alpha\right) \\
&= \frac{1+o(1)}{-2c}\left\{2\rho_n\sum_{t=1}^{n}\left(y_{t-1}u_t - \lambda - \frac{c}{n^\alpha}m_n\right) + O_p\left(n^{1/2}\right)\right\} \\
&\quad + \frac{n\omega_n^2}{-2c} + O_p\left(n^\alpha\right) \qquad (49)
\end{aligned}$$

since, under the assumption $E\varepsilon_0^4 < \infty$, $n^{-1/2}\sum_{t=1}^{n}\left(u_t^2-\sigma_u^2\right)$ satisfies a CLT for sample variances (theorem 3.8 of Phillips and Solo, 1992). Hence, as $n\to\infty$

$$\begin{aligned}
\frac{1}{n^{\frac{1+\alpha}{2}}}\sum_{t=1}^{n}\left(\frac{y_{t-1}^2}{n^\alpha} - \frac{\omega_n^2}{-2c}\right) &= \frac{1+o(1)}{-c}\sum_{t=1}^{n}\left(y_{t-1}u_t - \lambda - \frac{c}{n^\alpha}m_n\right) \\
&\quad + O_p\left(n^{-\frac{\alpha\wedge(1-\alpha)}{2}}\right).
\end{aligned}$$

Proof of Lemma 5.1 For part (a) we can write, using Proposition A1 and the BN decomposition (5),

$$\begin{aligned}
\int_0^t \rho_n^{-n^\alpha s}dB_{n^\alpha}(s) &= \frac{1}{n^{\alpha/2}}\sum_{i=1}^{\lfloor tn^\alpha\rfloor}\rho_n^{-i}u_i = \frac{C(1)}{n^{\alpha/2}}\sum_{i=1}^{\lfloor tn^\alpha\rfloor}\rho_n^{-i}\varepsilon_i - \frac{1}{n^{\alpha/2}}\sum_{i=1}^{\lfloor tn^\alpha\rfloor}\rho_n^{-i}\Delta\tilde{\varepsilon}_i \\
&= C(1)\int_0^t \rho_n^{-n^\alpha s}dW_{n^\alpha}(s) - \frac{1}{n^{\alpha/2}}\sum_{i=1}^{\lfloor tn^\alpha\rfloor}\rho_n^{-i}\Delta\tilde{\varepsilon}_i.
\end{aligned}$$

By Lemma 4.1 of the original version of PM (Lemma 2.4.1 of Magdalinos, 2004),

$$\sup_{t\in[0,n^{1-\alpha}]}\left|\int_0^t \rho_n^{-n^\alpha s}dW_{n^\alpha}(s) - \int_0^t e^{-cs}dW(s)\right| = o_p\left(\frac{1}{n^{\frac{\alpha}{2}-\frac{1}{\nu}}}\right)$$

on the probability space that (6) holds, which is the same space that (7) holds with $B(t) = C(1)W(t)$ (see the proof of Lemma 3.1). Therefore, it is enough to show that

$$\frac{1}{n^{\alpha/2}}\max_{0\le k\le n}\left|\sum_{i=1}^{k}\rho_n^{-i}\Delta\tilde{\varepsilon}_i\right| = o_p(1). \tag{50}$$

Summation by parts gives

$$\sum_{i=1}^{k}\rho_n^{-i}\Delta\tilde{\varepsilon}_i = \rho_n^{-k}\tilde{\varepsilon}_k - \sum_{i=1}^{k}\left(\Delta\rho_n^{-i}\right)\tilde{\varepsilon}_{i-1} = \rho_n^{-k}\tilde{\varepsilon}_k + \frac{c}{n^{\alpha}}\sum_{i=1}^{k}\rho_n^{-i}\tilde{\varepsilon}_{i-1}$$

so that:

$$\frac{1}{n^{\alpha/2}}\max_{0\le k\le n}\left|\sum_{i=1}^{k}\rho_n^{-i}\Delta\tilde{\varepsilon}_i\right| \le \max_{0\le k\le n}\left|\frac{\tilde{\varepsilon}_k}{n^{\alpha/2}}\right|\left\{\max_{0\le k\le n}\left|\rho_n^{-k}\right| + \frac{|c|}{n^{\alpha}}\sum_{i=1}^{n}\left|\rho_n^{-i}\right|\right\}$$

$$\le 2\max_{0\le k\le n}\left|\frac{\tilde{\varepsilon}_k}{n^{\alpha/2}}\right| = o_p(1)$$

by Proposition A3. For part (b) a similar argument gives

$$\int_0^t \rho_n^{-(\lfloor n^{\alpha}t\rfloor - \lfloor n^{\alpha}s\rfloor)}dB_{n^{\alpha}}(s) = C(1)\int_0^t \rho_n^{-(\lfloor n^{\alpha}t\rfloor - \lfloor n^{\alpha}s\rfloor)}dW_{n^{\alpha}}(s)$$
$$- \frac{1}{n^{\alpha/2}}\sum_{i=1}^{\lfloor tn^{\alpha}\rfloor}\rho_n^{-(\lfloor n^{\alpha}t\rfloor - i)}\Delta\tilde{\varepsilon}_i.$$

By Lemma 4.2 of PM (Lemma 2.4.2 of Magdalinos, 2004),

$$\sup_{t\in[0,n^{1-\alpha}]}\left|\int_0^t \rho_n^{-(\lfloor n^{\alpha}t\rfloor - \lfloor n^{\alpha}s\rfloor)}dW_{n^{\alpha}}(s) - \int_0^t e^{-c(t-s)}dW(s)\right| = o_p\left(\frac{1}{n^{\frac{\alpha}{2}-\frac{1}{\nu}}}\right)$$

again on the probability space that (6) and (7) with $B(t) = C(1)W(t)$ hold. Summation by parts again shows that:

$$\frac{1}{n^{\alpha/2}}\max_{0\le k\le n}\left|\sum_{i=1}^{k}\rho_n^{-(k-i)}\Delta\tilde{\varepsilon}_i\right| \le 2\max_{0\le k\le n}\left|\frac{\tilde{\varepsilon}_k}{n^{\alpha/2}}\right| = o_p(1)$$

and part (b) follows.

Proof of (35) Proposition A1 and Lemma 5.1 (a) give for each $p \in [0, q]$:

$$\frac{\rho_n^{-\kappa_n}}{n^{\alpha/2}} y_{\lfloor \kappa_n \rfloor + \lfloor n^\alpha p \rfloor} = \frac{1}{n^{\alpha/2}} \sum_{i=1}^{\lfloor n^\alpha (\lfloor n^{1-\alpha} \rfloor + p) \rfloor} \rho_n^{\lfloor n^\alpha p \rfloor - i} u_i + o_p(1)$$

$$= \rho_n^{\lfloor n^\alpha p \rfloor} \int_0^{\lfloor n^{1-\alpha} \rfloor + p} \rho_n^{-n^\alpha s} dB_{n^\alpha}(s)$$

$$= e^{cp} \int_0^\infty e^{-cs} dB(s) + o_p\left(\frac{1}{n^{\frac{\alpha}{2} - \frac{1}{\nu}}} \right)$$

on the probability space that (7) holds.

Proof of asymptotic negligibility of R_n Write $R_n = R_{1n} - 2R_{2n}$, where:

$$R_{1n} = \rho_n^{-2\kappa_n} \int_0^{\lfloor n^{1-\alpha} \rfloor} \left(\int_r^{\lfloor n^{1-\alpha} \rfloor} \rho_n^{-n^\alpha (s-r)} dB_{n^\alpha}(s) \right)^2 dr$$

$$R_{2n} = \left(\int_0^{\lfloor n^{1-\alpha} \rfloor} \rho_n^{-n^\alpha (s-r)} dB_{n^\alpha}(s) \right) \overline{R}_{2n}$$

where $\overline{R}_{2n} := \rho_n^{-2\kappa_n} \int_0^{\lfloor n^{1-\alpha} \rfloor} \int_r^{\lfloor n^{1-\alpha} \rfloor} \rho_n^{-n^\alpha (s-r)} dB_{n^\alpha}(s) dr$. In PM (also Proposition 2.8.5 of Magdalinos, 2004), it is shown that:

$$\int_r^{\lfloor n^{1-\alpha} \rfloor} \rho_n^{-n^\alpha (s-r)} dW_{n^\alpha}(s) = O_p(1), \quad \text{uniformly on } r \in \left[0, \lfloor n^{1-\alpha} \rfloor\right].$$

Using Proposition A1 and the BN decomposition we obtain:

$$\int_r^{\lfloor n^{1-\alpha} \rfloor} \rho_n^{-n^\alpha (s-r)} dB_{n^\alpha}(s) = \frac{1}{n^{\alpha/2}} \sum_{i=1}^{\lfloor \kappa_n \rfloor - \lfloor n^\alpha r \rfloor} \rho_n^{-i} u_{\lfloor n^\alpha r \rfloor + i}$$

$$= \frac{C(1)}{n^{\alpha/2}} \sum_{i=1}^{\lfloor \kappa_n \rfloor - \lfloor n^\alpha r \rfloor} \rho_n^{-i} \varepsilon_{\lfloor n^\alpha r \rfloor + i} - \frac{1}{n^{\alpha/2}} \sum_{i=1}^{\lfloor \kappa_n \rfloor - \lfloor n^\alpha r \rfloor} \rho_n^{-i} \Delta \tilde{\varepsilon}_{\lfloor n^\alpha r \rfloor + i}$$

$$= C(1) \int_r^{\lfloor n^{1-\alpha} \rfloor} \rho_n^{-n^\alpha (s-r)} dW_{n^\alpha}(s) - \frac{1}{n^{\alpha/2}} \sum_{i=1}^{\lfloor \kappa_n \rfloor - \lfloor n^\alpha r \rfloor} \rho_n^{-i} \Delta \tilde{\varepsilon}_{\lfloor n^\alpha r \rfloor + i}$$

where, from (50),

$$\frac{1}{n^{\alpha/2}} \sup_{r \in [0, \lfloor n^{1-\alpha} \rfloor]} \left| \sum_{i=1}^{\lfloor \kappa_n \rfloor - \lfloor n^\alpha r \rfloor} \rho_n^{-i} \Delta \tilde{\varepsilon}_{\lfloor n^\alpha r \rfloor + i} \right| \leq \frac{1}{n^{\alpha/2}} \max_{0 \leq k \leq n} \left| \sum_{i=1}^{k} \rho_n^{-i} \Delta \tilde{\varepsilon}_i \right| = o_p(1).$$

Thus,

$$\int_r^{\lfloor n^{1-\alpha}\rfloor} \rho_n^{-n^\alpha(s-r)} dB_{n^\alpha}(s) = O_p(1), \quad \text{uniformly on } r \in \left[0, \left\lfloor n^{1-\alpha}\right\rfloor\right]. \tag{51}$$

The uniform boundedness in (51) together with the fact that $\rho_n^{-\kappa_n} = o(n^{-1})$ give

$$\begin{aligned} R_{1n} &= \rho_n^{-2\kappa_n} \int_0^{\lfloor n^{1-\alpha}\rfloor} \left(\int_r^{\lfloor n^{1-\alpha}\rfloor} \rho_n^{-n^\alpha(s-r)} dB_{n^\alpha}(s) \right)^2 dr \\ &= O_p(1) \times O\left(\rho_n^{-2\kappa_n} \int_0^{\lfloor n^{1-\alpha}\rfloor} dr \right) = O_p\left(\rho_n^{-2\kappa_n} \left\lfloor n^{1-\alpha} \right\rfloor \right) = o_p\left(\frac{1}{n^\alpha} \right). \end{aligned}$$

For the second remainder term, we obtain from (51),

$$\begin{aligned} \overline{R}_{2n} &= \rho_n^{-2\kappa_n} \int_0^{\lfloor n^{1-\alpha}\rfloor} \int_r^{\lfloor n^{1-\alpha}\rfloor} \rho_n^{-n^\alpha(s-r)} dB_{n^\alpha}(s) dr \\ &= O_p\left(\rho_n^{-2\kappa_n} \int_0^{\lfloor n^{1-\alpha}\rfloor} dr \right) = o_p\left(\frac{1}{n^\alpha} \right) \end{aligned}$$

so that

$$R_{2n} = \left(\int_0^{\lfloor n^{1-\alpha}\rfloor} \rho_n^{-n^\alpha(s-r)} dB_{n^\alpha}(s) \right) \overline{R}_{2n} = o_p\left(\frac{1}{n^\alpha} \right)$$

by part (b) of Lemma 5.1. Thus, $R_n = R_{1n} - 2R_{2n} = o_p(1)$ follows.

Proof of asymptotic negligibility of I_n Using Proposition A1,

$$\begin{aligned} I_n &= \rho_n^{-n-1} \int_{\frac{1}{n^a}}^{n^{1-\alpha}} \int_{r-\frac{1}{n^a}}^{n^{1-\alpha}} \rho_n^{\lfloor n^a r\rfloor - n^a s} dB_{n^a}(s) dB_{n^a}(r) \\ &= \rho_n^{-n-1} \int_{\frac{1}{n^a}}^{n^{1-\alpha}} \frac{1}{n^{\alpha/2}} \sum_{i=\lfloor n^\alpha r\rfloor}^{n} \rho_n^{\lfloor n^a r\rfloor - i} u_i dB_{n^a}(r) \\ &= \rho_n^{-n-1} \frac{1}{n^\alpha} \sum_{j=2}^{n} \sum_{i=j}^{n} \rho_n^{j-i} u_i u_j. \end{aligned}$$

Thus, the Cauchy–Schwarz inequality yields

$$\begin{aligned} E\left|I_n\right| &\leq \rho_n^{-n-1} \frac{1}{n^\alpha} \sum_{j=2}^{n} \sum_{i=j}^{n} \rho_n^{j-i} E\left|u_i u_j\right| \\ &\leq \rho_n^{-n-1} \frac{\sigma_u^2}{n^\alpha} \sum_{j=2}^{n} \sum_{i=j}^{n} \rho_n^{j-i} = O\left(\rho_n^{-n} n\right) = o(1) \end{aligned}$$

since $\rho_n^{-n} = o(n^{-1})$ and $\sigma_u^2 < \infty$. Thus, $I_n \to 0$ in L_1.

Proof of Theorem 5.1 This follows precisely as in theorem 4.3 of PM. In particular, since (37) and (39) have been established, it simply remains to show that the Gaussian random variables X and Y are independent, or equivalently, that $E(XY) = 0$. Since $X = \lim_{n\to\infty} \int_0^{n^{1-\alpha}} e^{-cs} dB(s)$ *a.s.*, $Y = \lim_{n\to\infty} \mathcal{J}_{-c}(n^{1-\alpha})$ *a.s.* the dominated convergence theorem gives:

$$E(XY) = \lim_{n\to\infty} E\left(\int_0^{n^{1-\alpha}} e^{-cs} dB(s) \mathcal{J}_{-c}\left(n^{1-\alpha}\right)\right)$$

$$= \lim_{n\to\infty} e^{-cn^{1-\alpha}} E\left(\int_0^{n^{1-\alpha}} e^{-cs} dB(s) \int_0^{n^{1-\alpha}} e^{cr} dB(r)\right)$$

$$= \omega^2 \lim_{n\to\infty} e^{-cn^{1-\alpha}} \int_0^{n^{1-\alpha}} dr = \omega^2 \lim_{n\to\infty} e^{-cn^{1-\alpha}} n^{1-\alpha} = 0$$

so X and Y are independent.

6 The Structure of Multiparameter Tests

Christopher L. Cavanagh and Thomas J. Rothenberg

1 Introduction

For many econometric problems there exist alternative inference procedures that are asymptotically equivalent. Since these procedures often behave rather differently in small samples, it seems reasonable to use higher-order asymptotic approximations to distinguish among them. This idea was pursued in the context of simultaneous equations testing in a series of papers by Michael Magdalinos. In this chapter we use higher-order approximations to compare general likelihood-based tests of hypotheses in smooth parametric models where the test statistics are asymptotically chi square. These results extend previous work by Hayakawa (1975), Peers (1971) and Pfanzagl (1980).

2 Likelihood-based Inference

We assume that the probability distribution of the observed data is a known smooth function of the p-dimensional parameter vector θ. We denote the log likelihood function for a sample of size n by $L_n(\theta)$ and define the p-dimensional standardized score vector:

$$S(\theta) = n^{-1/2} \frac{\partial L_n(\theta)}{\partial \theta}$$

and the $p \times p$ average Hessian matrix,

$$H(\theta) = n^{-1} \frac{\partial^2 L_n(\theta)}{\partial \theta \partial \theta'}.$$

The $p \times p$ average information matrix $\Sigma(\theta)$ is defined as:

$$\Sigma(\theta) = E[S(\theta)S(\theta)'] = -E[H(\theta)]$$

and assumed to be positive definite. We consider the null hypothesis that θ satisfies the equation $G\theta = g$, where G is a known $q \times p$ matrix having full row rank and g is a known q-dimensional vector in the column space of G.

Let $\hat{\theta}$ be the maximum-likelihood estimate of θ and let $\tilde{\theta}$ be the constrained maximum-likelihood estimate satisfying the equation $G\tilde{\theta} = g$. One estimate of the information matrix is $\hat{\Sigma} = \Sigma(\hat{\theta})$. Another estimate is minus the Hessian evaluated at the mle: $-\hat{H} = -H(\hat{\theta})$. Many commonly used test statistics turn out to be simple functions of the observable statistics

$$d = \sqrt{n}(\hat{\theta} - \tilde{\theta}) \quad \text{and} \quad Y = \sqrt{n}(\hat{\Sigma} + \hat{H}).$$

We assume that, when the null hypothesis is true, both $\sqrt{n}(\hat{\theta} - \theta)$ and $\sqrt{n}(\tilde{\theta} - \theta)$ are asymptotically normal. Since the set of parameter values yielding moderate power shrinks as the sample size increases, we shall consider alternatives close to satisfying the null hypothesis and assume the standardized difference $\sqrt{n}(G\theta - g)$ is of moderate size for all n. For such local alternatives, d is asymptotically normal with mean vector

$$\delta = \Sigma^{-1}G'(G\Sigma^{-1}G')^{-1}\sqrt{n}(G\theta - g)$$

and (generally singular) $p \times p$ covariance matrix

$$\Omega = \Sigma^{-1}G'(G\Sigma^{-1}G')^{-1}G\Sigma^{-1}.$$

A value for d far from the origin is then evidence against the null hypothesis.

In typical linear problems with data distributions in the exponential family, Y is identically zero. In most nonlinear and nonexponential problems, however, Y is nonzero and plays a key role in distinguishing among alternative asymptotically equivalent tests. We shall consider the "regular" case where the joint limiting distribution of the first four standardized derivatives of the log likelihood function is normal and possesses a valid Edgeworth expansion with error $o(n^{-1})$. This implies that the joint distribution of d and Y is asymptotically normal and also possesses a valid Edgeworth expansion.

3 Main Results

Many different statistics have been proposed for testing the null hypothesis $G\theta = g$. These include the Wald statistic

$$W = n(G\hat{\theta} - g)'(G\hat{\Sigma}^{-1}G')^{-1}(G\hat{\theta} - g), \tag{1a}$$

the likelihood ratio statistic

$$LR = 2[L_n(\hat{\theta}) - L_n(\tilde{\theta})], \tag{1b}$$

the Lagrange multiplier (or score) statistic

$$LM = S(\tilde{\theta})'\tilde{\Sigma}^{-1}S(\tilde{\theta}), \tag{1c}$$

where $\tilde{\Sigma} \equiv \Sigma(\tilde{\theta})$, and the standardized estimator difference

$$d'\hat{\Sigma}d. \tag{1d}$$

Under our regularity conditions, all four of these test statistics behave in large samples like $d'\Sigma d$ and are asymptotically noncentral chi square with q degrees of freedom and noncentrality parameter $\delta'\Sigma\delta$. Additional asymptotically equivalent tests can be obtained by using alternative consistent estimates of Σ. Using higher-order asymptotic approximations, we find that these test statistics generally also depend on the random variable Y and on the individual components of d. Consider the family of test statistics:

$$T = d'\left(\hat{\Sigma} - \frac{\gamma Y}{\sqrt{n}}\right)d + \frac{a_{ijk}d_i d_j d_k}{\sqrt{n}} + \frac{b_{ij}d_i d_j + c_{ijkl}d_i d_j d_k d_l}{n} \tag{2}$$

where γ, the a's, the b's, and the c's are scalars, possibly functions of $\hat{\theta}$ but converging to constants as the sample size tends to infinity. (Note we use the tensor summation convention where repeated subscripts are summed from 1 to p.) We have the following result:

Proposition 1 Each of the usual test statistics has the same approximate distribution to order $o(n^{-1})$ as a member of the family (2). The Wald statistic (1a) and the estimator difference statistic (1d) behave like members with $\gamma = 0$. The likelihood ratio statistic (1b) behaves like a member with $\gamma = 1$. The Lagrange multiplier statistic (1c) behaves like a member with $\gamma = 2$. If the Hessian estimate $-\hat{H}$ is used in place of $\hat{\Sigma}$ in (1a) and (1d) and in place of $\tilde{\Sigma}$ in (1c), the resulting statistics behave like members with $\gamma = 1$.

Since all of the usual test statistics behave like members of the same family, it is reasonable to ask if there is a best member. We consider tests with rejection regions of the form $T > x$, where x is the appropriate critical value. We then approximate the rejection probabilities under local alternatives by an expansion of the form

$$\Pr[T > x] = 1 - F_q(x, \lambda) + \frac{A_T(x, \delta)}{\sqrt{n}} + \frac{B_T(x, \delta)}{n} + o(n^{-1})$$

where $F_q(\cdot, \lambda)$ is the cumulative distribution function for a noncentral chi square variate with q degrees of freedom and noncentrality parameter $\lambda = \delta'\Sigma\delta$; the correction terms A_T and B_T depend on the particular test statistic T. After insuring that each test has (with error $o(n^{-1})$) the same probability of a type I error, their $o(n^{-1})$ approximate local powers can be compared. Note that the terms of order $n^{-1/2}$ in the stochastic expansion (2) are odd functions of asymptotically normal variates. Since the asymptotic critical region is symmetric, the size correction of order $n^{-1/2}$ is therefore zero. Hence the size adjustment can be made by modifying only the n^{-1} term in the stochastic expansion.

In general, the approximate power surfaces for the various tests are found to cross so that no one test dominates the others. This is not surprising given that each test weights the components of d differently. However, in nonlinear and nonexponential families where Y is nonzero, some common tests are dominated. In particular, we have the following result:

Proposition 2 Suppose $Y\Omega$ is nondegenerate with at least one element having positive asymptotic variance. Then tests based on statistics of the form (2) are admissible only if $\gamma < 2$. If $\gamma \geq 2$, there exist other members of the family having to order $o(n^{-1})$ the same probability of a type I error but with uniformly greater power to that order of approximation. For example, the Lagrange multiplier test (where the variance estimate is based on $\tilde{\Sigma}$) is dominated.

4 Comments

In the one-dimension case where a scalar null hypothesis is tested against a one-sided alternative, all of the usual tests (including the Lagrange multiplier test based on the square root of (1c)) are known to be admissible to order n^{-1}. See, for example, Pfanzagl (1980). The inadmissibility of tests with $\gamma \geq 2$ for two-sided and multidimensional alternatives seems to arise from the particular curvature properties of their power functions at the origin resulting from the term $n^{-1/2}\gamma d'Yd$.

Needless to say, proofs of the above results require numerous technical regularity conditions to ensure the validity of the asymptotic expansions.

Under i.i.d. sampling, the results of Bhattacharya and Ghosh (1978) and Chandra and Ghosh (1980) can be used to establish validity. Stronger conditions are needed with dependent sampling, but they seem not to be restrictive in practice. Two potentially more serious weaknesses of the above theory should be mentioned:

1 The power differences between asymptotically equivalent tests are typically small unless $d'Yd$ has large variance. After adjustment for size, the inadmissible tests may not in practice be very different from the admissible ones.
2 The probability calculations underlying the results use the unconditional distributions of the data. It can be argued that Y is an approximate ancillary statistic and that the appropriate distributions should condition on Y (cf. Cox, 1980). In that case, the inadmissibility result stated above no longer holds. Since most econometricians base their inference on the unconditional distribution and since Y is only ancillary to order $o(n^{-1/2})$, our results seem relevant.

Appendix: The Derivations

Notation We assume that the average log likelihood function possess continuous partial derivatives with respect to θ up to the fourth order. When evaluated at the actual parameter value θ these derivatives are denoted by:

$$L_i = \frac{\partial n^{-1} L_n(\theta)}{\partial \theta_i}, \; L_{ij} = \frac{\partial^2 n^{-1} L_n(\theta)}{\partial \theta_i \partial \theta_j}, \; L_{ijk} = \frac{\partial^3 n^{-1} L_n(\theta)}{\partial \theta_i \partial \theta_j \partial \theta_k}, \; \dots$$

where the subscripts $i, j, k, l \dots$ range from 1 to p. When evaluated at the mle $\hat{\theta}$, these derivatives are written as $\hat{L}_i$, $\hat{L}_{ij}$, $\hat{L}_{ijk}, \dots$. Assuming these dervatives have finite moments, we define

$$\lambda_{ij} = EL_{ij}, \; \lambda_{ijk} = EL_{ijk}, \text{ and } \lambda_{ijkl} = EL_{ijkl}.$$

These moments are assumed to be differentiable functions of θ. When evaluated at $\hat{\theta}$ they are denoted by $\hat{\lambda}_{ij}, \hat{\lambda}_{ijk}$, and $\hat{\lambda}_{ijkl}$. (Note that $\lambda_i = EL_i = 0$, $S(\theta)$ is the vector whose ith element is $S_i = \sqrt{n} L_i$, and $H(\theta)$ is the matrix whose ij-element is L_{ij}. Further, $\lambda_{ij} = -\sigma_{ij}$.)

Finally, we define

$$y_{ij} = \sqrt{n}(\hat{L}_{ij} - \hat{\lambda}_{ij}), \; y_{ijk} = \sqrt{n}(\hat{L}_{ijk} - \hat{\lambda}_{ijk}), \text{ and } y_{ijkl} = \sqrt{n}(\hat{L}_{ijkl} - \hat{\lambda}_{ijkl}).$$

We assume that these variables, along with the $d_i - \delta_i$, are jointly asymptotically normal with mean zero. (Of course, if some of the derivatives L_{ij}, L_{ijk}, L_{ijkl} are nonrandom, this joint distribution will have a singular covariance matrix.) It can be shown that the y's are asymptotically independent of the d's. We will use the fact that the conditional mean of y_{ij} given d has the form

$$E[y_{ij}|d] = \frac{1}{2\sqrt{n}}[\alpha_{ij} + \sigma_{ij.kl}(d_k - \delta_k)(d_l - \delta_l)] + O_p(n^{-1})$$

where the α_{ij} are constants and $\sigma_{ij.kl}$ is the asymptotic covariance between y_{ij} and y_{kl}.

The derivations that follow are based on algorithms developed in Cavanagh (1983) and described in Rothenberg (1984) and (1988). To save space, some of the more tedious details have been omitted. A key step in simplifying the calculations is the following fact: If a statistic T has a stochastic expansion,

$$T_n = f(d_n) + \frac{P_n}{\sqrt{n}} + \frac{Q_n}{n}$$

where the scalars P_n and Q_n and the elements of the vector d_n have a joint limiting distribution, then, if the distribution of T_n has a valid asymptotic expansion (to order $o(n^{-1})$), it is unaffected if Q_n is replaced by its asymptotic expectation given d_n. In particular, if Q_n contains terms of the form $a(\hat{\theta})$ where a is continuous and $\hat{\theta}$ is a consistent estimate of θ, the expansion is unaffected if $\hat{\theta}$ is replaced by θ.

Proposition 1 By Taylor-series expansion, the likelihood-ratio test statistic (1b) can be written as,

$$\begin{aligned} LR &= 2[L_n(\hat{\theta}) - L_n(\tilde{\theta})] \\ &= -\hat{L}_{ij} d_i d_j + \frac{1}{3\sqrt{n}} \hat{L}_{ijk} d_i d_j d_k - \frac{1}{12n} \hat{L}_{ijkl} d_i d_j d_k d_l + o_p(n^{-1}) \\ &= \hat{\sigma}_{ij} d_i d_j + \frac{1}{\sqrt{n}} \left(\frac{1}{3} \hat{\lambda}_{ijk} d_i d_j d_k - y_{ij} d_i d_j \right) \\ &\quad - \frac{1}{12n} (\hat{\lambda}_{ijkl} d_i d_j d_k d_l - 4 y_{ijk} d_i d_j d_k) + o_p(n^{-1}) \end{aligned}$$

which has the same approximate distribution as,

$$\hat{\sigma}_{ij} d_i d_j + \frac{1}{\sqrt{n}} \left(\frac{1}{3} \hat{\lambda}_{ijk} d_i d_j d_k - y_{ij} d_i d_j \right) - \frac{1}{12n} \hat{\lambda}_{ijkl} d_i d_j d_k d_l$$

since the asymptotic expectation of y_{ijk} given d is 0. This has the same form as (2) with $\gamma = 1$, $a_{ijk} = \frac{1}{3}\hat{\lambda}_{ijk}$, $b_{ij} = 0$, and $c_{ijkl} = -\frac{1}{12}\hat{\lambda}_{ijkl}$.

The constrained mle $\tilde{\theta}$ satisfies the first-order condition $\tilde{S} = G'\lambda$, where λ is a vector of Lagrange multipliers and $\tilde{S} = S(\tilde{\theta})$. It follows that, for any positive definite matrix Q, $\lambda = (GQG')^{-1}GQ\tilde{S}$ and $[I - G'(GQG')^{-1}GQ]\tilde{S} = 0$. Defining the matrix $\hat{\Phi} = [\hat{\varphi}_{ij}]$ as:

$$\hat{\Phi} = \hat{\Sigma}^{-1} - \hat{\Omega} = \hat{\Sigma}^{-1} - \hat{\Sigma}^{-1}G'(G\hat{\Sigma}^{-1}G')^{-1}G\hat{\Sigma}^{-1}$$

it follows that $\hat{\Phi}\tilde{S} = 0$. Furthermore, by Taylor-series expansion, the ith element of $\tilde{S}$ is given by:

$$\begin{aligned}\tilde{S}_i = \sqrt{n}\tilde{L}_i &= -\hat{L}_{ij}d_j + \frac{1}{2\sqrt{n}}\hat{L}_{ijk}d_jd_k - \frac{1}{6n}\hat{L}_{ijkl}d_jd_kd_l + o_p(n^{-1}) \\ &\approx \hat{\sigma}_{ij}d_j + \frac{1}{\sqrt{n}}\left(\frac{1}{2}\hat{\lambda}_{ijk}d_jd_k - y_{ij}d_j\right) + \frac{1}{6n}(3y_{ijk}d_jd_k - \hat{\lambda}_{ijkl}d_jd_kd_l)\end{aligned} \tag{3}$$

and hence $\hat{\Sigma}d = \tilde{S} - n^{-1/2}b + o_p(n^{-1/2})$, where the ith element of the vector b is given by $b_i = \frac{1}{2}\hat{\lambda}_{ijk}d_jd_k - y_{ij}d_j$. The Wald statistic $(1a)$ can be written as:

$$W = d'G'(G\hat{\Sigma}^{-1}G')^{-1}Gd = d'\hat{\Sigma}d - d'\hat{\Sigma}\hat{\Phi}\hat{\Sigma}d.$$

Since $\hat{\Phi}\tilde{S} = 0$, it follows that the $o(n^{-1})$ approximate distribution of W is the same as that of

$$d'\hat{\Sigma}d - \frac{1}{n}b'\hat{\Phi}b = d'\hat{\Sigma}d - \frac{1}{n}\left[\frac{1}{4}\hat{\lambda}_{pij}\hat{\varphi}_{pq}\hat{\lambda}_{qkl}d_id_jd_kd_l + \hat{\sigma}_{pi.qj}\hat{\varphi}_{pq}d_id_j\right]. \tag{4}$$

This has the same form as (2) with $\gamma = 0$, $a_{ijk} = 0$, $b_{ij} = -\hat{\sigma}_{pi.qj}\hat{\varphi}_{pq}$ and $c_{ijkl} = -\frac{1}{4}\hat{\lambda}_{pij}\hat{\varphi}_{pq}\hat{\lambda}_{qkl}$. If $\hat{\Sigma}$ is replaced by $-\hat{H}$ in the definition of W and $\hat{\Phi}$, the leading term in (4) becomes $-d'\hat{H}d = d'\hat{\Sigma}d - n^{-1/2}d'Yd$, so γ changes to 1.

Let $\tilde{\sigma}^{pq}$ be the pq element of $\tilde{\Sigma}^{-1}$. Then, by Taylor expansion, we have

$$\tilde{\sigma}^{pq} = \hat{\sigma}^{pq} - \frac{1}{\sqrt{n}}\hat{\gamma}_{pq.i}d_i + \frac{1}{2n}\hat{\gamma}_{pq.ij}d_id_j + o_p(n^{-1})$$

where $\gamma_{pq.i} = \partial\sigma^{pq}/\partial\theta_i$ and $\gamma_{pq.ij} = \partial^2\sigma^{pq}/\partial\theta_i\partial\theta_j$. From (3) and (4), the LM statistic (1c) has the same approximate distribution as,

$$\begin{aligned}LM = \tilde{S}_p\tilde{\sigma}^{pq}\tilde{S}_q &= d'\hat{\Sigma}d + \frac{1}{\sqrt{n}}[(\hat{\lambda}_{ijk} - \hat{\sigma}_{pi}\hat{\gamma}_{pq.k}\hat{\sigma}_{qj})d_id_jd_k - 2y_{ij}d_id_j] \\ &+ \frac{1}{n}\left[\frac{1}{2}\left(\hat{\sigma}_{pq.kl}\hat{\sigma}_{pi}\hat{\sigma}_{qj} + \hat{\lambda}_{pjl}\hat{\gamma}_{pq.k}\hat{\sigma}_{pi} + \frac{1}{4}\hat{\lambda}_{pij}\hat{\lambda}_{qkl}\hat{\sigma}^{pq} - \frac{1}{3}\hat{\lambda}_{ijkl}\right)d_id_jd_kd_l \right. \\ &\left. + \hat{\omega}_{pi.qj}\hat{\sigma}^{pq}d_id_j\right].\end{aligned}$$

This has the same form as (2) with $\gamma = 2$. Note that

$$-\hat{H}^{-1} = [\hat{\Sigma} - n^{-1/2}Y]^{-1} = \hat{\Sigma}^{-1} + n^{-1/2}\hat{\Sigma}^{-1}Y\hat{\Sigma}^{-1} + O_p(n^{-1}).$$

If $\tilde{\sigma}^{pq}$ is replaced by $-\hat{L}^{pq}$ in defining the LM statistic, the coefficient on y_{ij} changes to -1 and the terms involving the γ's disappear.

Proposition 2 Consider the test statistic:

$$T_1 = d'\hat{\Sigma}d - \frac{\gamma_1 d'Yd}{\sqrt{n}}$$

with approximate moment-generating function,

$$M_1(t) = Ee^{tT_1} \approx Ee^{td'\hat{\Sigma}d}\left[1 - \frac{t\gamma_1 d'Yd}{\sqrt{n}} + \frac{t^2\gamma_1^2(d'Yd)^2}{2n}\right]$$

where the expectation is taken with respect to the $o(n^{-1})$ approximate distributions of d, Y, and $\hat{\Sigma}$. Since $\sqrt{n}(\hat{\Sigma} - \Sigma)$ is asymptotically independent of Y, we have:

$$M_1(t) \approx Ee^{td'\hat{\Sigma}d}\left[1 - \frac{t\gamma_1 E(d'Yd|d)}{\sqrt{n}} + \frac{t^2\gamma_1^2 E[(d'Yd)^2|d]}{2n}\right]$$

$$\approx Ee^{td'\Sigma d}\left[1 - \frac{t\gamma_1 d_i d_j[\alpha_{ij} + \sigma_{ij.kl}(d_k - \delta_k)(d_l - \delta_l)]}{2n} - \frac{t^2\gamma_1^2\sigma_{ij.kl}d_i d_j d_k d_l}{2n}\right].$$

Let x be the $1-\alpha$ quantile for a central chi-square distribution with q degrees of freedom. Consider the test statistic

$$T_2 = d'\hat{\Sigma}d - \frac{\gamma_2 d'Yd}{\sqrt{n}} + \frac{(\gamma_2 - \gamma_1)}{2n}[\hat{\alpha}_{ij}d_i d_j + Q(d)]$$

where

$$Q(d) = \left(1 - \frac{\gamma_1 + \gamma_2}{2}\right)\hat{\sigma}_{ij.kl}d_i d_j d_k d_l + \frac{\gamma_1 + \gamma_2}{2}\hat{\sigma}_{ij.kl}(d_i d_j \hat{\omega}_{kl} + 2d_i d_k \hat{\omega}_{jl})$$
$$- \left(\frac{q+2}{x} - 2 + \frac{\gamma_1 + \gamma_2}{2}\right)\hat{\sigma}_{ij.kl}\hat{\omega}_{kl}\left(d_i d_j - \frac{x}{q}\hat{\omega}_{ij}\right)$$
$$- (\gamma_1 + \gamma_2 - 4)\hat{\sigma}_{ij.kl}\omega_{ik}\left(d_j d_l - \frac{x}{q}\hat{\omega}_{jl}\right).$$

To order $o(n^{-1})$, the difference in moment generating functions is found to be:

$$M_1(t) - M_2(t) = \frac{t}{2n}(\gamma_2 - \gamma_1)Ee^{td'\Sigma d}h(d)$$

where

$$h(d) = \sigma_{ij.kl}d_i d_j[\delta_k\delta_l - 2d_k\delta_l + d_k d_l - t(\gamma_1 + \gamma_2)d_k d_l] - Q(d)$$

Since d is asymptotically normal, we find by completing the square that

$$Ee^{td'\hat{\Sigma}d}h(d) \approx \int e^{td'\Sigma d}f(d)h(d)\mathrm{d}d = M_0(t)\int g(d)h(d)\mathrm{d}d$$

where $M_0(t) = (1-2t)^{-q/2}\exp[\delta'\Sigma\delta t/(1-2t)]$ and g is the density function of a multivariate normal random variable with mean $\delta(1-2t)^{-1}$ and covariance matrix $\Omega(1-2t)^{-1}$. Thus, to order $o(n^{-1})$, the difference in moment generating functions is given by:

$$\begin{aligned}M_1(t)-M_2(t) = {} & \frac{t}{2n}(\gamma_2-\gamma_1)M_0(t)\sigma_{ij.kl} \\ & \times\left[\frac{\delta_i\delta_j\delta_k\delta_l}{(1-2t)^2}+\frac{\omega_{ij}\delta_k\delta_l}{1-2t}-\frac{\delta_i\delta_j\delta_k\delta_l}{(1-2t)^3}-2\frac{\omega_{ij}\delta_k\delta_l+2\omega_{ik}\delta_j\delta_l}{(1-2t)^2}\right. \\ & +\frac{\gamma_1+\gamma_2}{2}\left(\frac{\delta_i\delta_j\delta_k\delta_l}{(1-2t)^2}+\frac{\omega_{ij}\delta_k\delta_l+2\omega_{ik}\delta_j\delta_l}{(1-2t)^2}\right) \\ & -\left(\frac{q+2}{x}-2+\frac{\gamma_1+\gamma_2}{2}\right)\omega_{kl}\left(\frac{\delta_i\delta_j}{(1-2t)^2}+\frac{\omega_{ij}}{1-2t}-\frac{x}{q}\hat{\omega}_{ij}\right) \\ & \left.-(\gamma_1+\gamma_2-4)\omega_{ik}\left(\frac{\delta_j\delta_l}{(1-2t)^2}+\frac{\omega_{jl}}{1-2t}-\frac{x}{q}\hat{\omega}_{jl}\right)\right].\end{aligned}$$

Let $f_r(x,\lambda)$ be the density function for a noncentral chi-square random variable with $q+r$ degrees of freedom and noncentrality parameter $\lambda = \delta'\Sigma\delta$. Inverting the moment generating functions and using the identity

$$xf_0(x,\lambda) = qf_2(x,\lambda) + \lambda f_4(x,\lambda)$$

we find:

$$\begin{aligned}\Pr(T_1>x)-\Pr(T_2>x) = {} & \frac{1}{2n}(\gamma_2-\gamma_1) \\ \times\Bigg\{ & \frac{1}{x}\left[\lambda a_1\frac{q+2}{q}+b_2(\delta)\right]f_4(x,\lambda)+\frac{1}{x}\lambda b_1(\delta)f_6(x,\lambda) \\ & -\left(2-\frac{\gamma_1+\gamma_2}{2}\right)\left[\frac{\lambda}{q}(a_1+2a_2)f_4(x,\lambda)+b_2(\delta)f_6(x,\lambda)\right]\Bigg\}+o(n^{-1}) \qquad (5)\end{aligned}$$

where

$$a_1 = \sigma_{ij.kl}\omega_{ij}\omega_{kl} = E[tr^2(Y\Omega)]$$

$$a_2 = \sigma_{ij.kl}\omega_{ik}\omega_{jl} = E[tr(Y\Omega Y\Omega)]$$

$$b_1(\delta) = \sigma_{ij.kl}\omega_{ij}\delta_k\delta_l = E[\delta Y\delta tr(Y\Omega)]$$

$$b_2(\delta) = \sigma_{ij.kl}\delta_i\delta_j\delta_k\delta_l = E[(\delta Y\delta)^2].$$

Under the null hypothesis where $\delta = 0$, the two test statistics have the same rejection probability. Otherwise, equation (5) can be rewritten as

$$\Pr(T_1 > x) - \Pr(T_2 > x) = \frac{1}{2n}(\gamma_2 - \gamma_1)\left[C\left(\frac{D}{C} - 2 + \frac{\gamma_1 + \gamma_2}{2}\right)\right] + o(n^{-1})$$

where,

$$C = \frac{\lambda}{q}(a_1 + 2a_2) f_4(x, \lambda) + b_2(\delta) f_6(x, \lambda)$$

$$D = \left[\frac{1}{x}\lambda a_1 \frac{q+2}{q} + b_2(\delta)\right] f_4(x, \lambda) + \frac{1}{x}\lambda b_1(\delta) f_6(x, \lambda).$$

When $Y\Omega$ is nondegenerate, a_2 is positive and a_1 and $b_2(\delta)$ are nonnegative. Thus, C is necessarily positive for all δ. Although $b_1(\delta)$ can take negative values, $|b_1| \leq \sqrt{a_1 b_2}$. Moreover, using the properties of the modified Bessel function,

$$I_n(z) = \sum_{j=0}^{\infty} \frac{(\frac{z}{2})^{n+2j}}{j!\Gamma(n+1+j)}$$

(see, for example, Lebedev, 1972, chapter 5), we find that:

$$\sqrt{\frac{\lambda}{x}\frac{f_6(x,\lambda)}{f_4(x,\lambda)}} = \frac{I_{(q+6)/2}(\sqrt{\lambda x})}{I_{(q+4)/2}(\sqrt{\lambda x})} < 1.$$

It follows that:

$$D \geq \left[\lambda a_1 \frac{q+2}{qx} + b_2\right] f_4 - \frac{1}{x}\lambda\sqrt{a_1 b_2} f_6$$

$$\geq f_4 \left(\sqrt{\frac{\lambda a_1 (q+2)}{xq}} - \sqrt{b_2}\right)^2 + f_4 \sqrt{\frac{\lambda a_1 b_2}{x}} \left(2\sqrt{\frac{q+2}{q}} - \sqrt{\frac{\lambda}{x}\frac{f_6}{f_4}}\right) > 0$$

when $\delta \neq 0$. Furthermore, D/C is bounded away from zero. Thus, T_1 has uniformly lower power than T_2 if $\gamma_2 < \gamma_1$ and $2 - (\gamma_2 + \gamma_1)/2 < \min(D/C)$. It follows that, if $\gamma_1 \geq 2$, T_1 is inadmissible. Numerical calculations suggest that $\min(D/C)$ is much less than one so tests with $\gamma \leq 1$ are admissible.

7 Cornish–Fisher Size Corrected t and F Statistics for the Linear Regression Model with Heteroscedastic Errors*

Spyridon D. Symeonides, Helen Kandilorou and Elias Tzavalis

1 Introduction

The linear regression model with a nonscalar error covariance matrix is usually estimated by Generalized Least Squares (GLS). Conventional F and t-testing procedures of any linear hypotheses on the parameters for this model is justified under the implicit assumption that the sample size is large enough to permit inference on the parameters estimates based on the chi-square or normal distributions. However, the possibility of erroneous inferences in finite samples is always present, and it can be attributed to the existence of considerable discrepancy between the actual and the nominal size of the asymptotic chi-square or normal tests. Since the differences between the actual and nominal size tend to be large in finite samples, compared with the differences in power (see Rothenberg, 1982), size corrections are suggested to eliminate most of the probability of conflict among the alternative testing procedures (see Rothenberg, 1984b, 1988, and Magdalinos and Symeonides, 1995). In particular, Rothenberg (1984b, 1988) derived general formulae giving the Edgeworth-corrected critical values for the Wald and t-test statistics based on Edgeworth expansions of their corresponding asymptotic, chi-square and normal distributions, respectively. This is done for a wide class of regression models used in practice. Instead of using the asymptotic form of the tests, Magdalinos and Symeonides (1995, 1996) recommended to use the degrees of freedom adjusted forms of the above statistics and derived expansions in terms of the F and t distributions, respectively. Both of the above approximations have an error of the same order of magnitude but the degrees of freedom adjusted test statistics are found to have better finite sample performance. An explanation for this

* The authors would like to thank George Mitsopoulos and Athanasios Stavrakoudis for computation assistance.

is that, when the model is sufficiently simplified, the degrees of freedom adjusted approximations reduce to the (known) exact distributions of the test statistics. This is consistent with the notion of "local exactness"(see Magdalinos, 1985), which can be extended to the framework of the GLS estimation.

In this chapter we suggest Cornish–Fisher size-corrected tests based on the degrees of freedom adjusted t and F statistics for the generalized linear regression model, with heteroscedastic errors. Compared with the Edgeworth size corrections, the Cornish–Fisher corrections have two advantages (see Cornish and Fisher, 1937; Fisher and Cornish, 1960; Hill and Davis, 1968; Magdalinos, 1985; and Magdalinos and Symeonides, 1995, 1996, *inter alia*). First, the Cornish–Fisher-corrected statistics are proper random variables with well-behaved distribution tails, compared with the Edgeworth approximation which often assigns negative tail "probabilities". Second, the notion of "local exactness" can be easily extended to Cornish–Fisher expansions.

The structure of this chapter is as follows. In section 2 we derive the analytic formulae of the Edgeworth and Cornish–Fisher second order corrections of the t and F tests for the linear model with heteroscedastic errors. In section 3, we present the analytic formulae of the tests for a parametric model of heteroscedasticity often used in practice. In section 4 we report results of Monte Carlo experiments evaluating the small-sample performance of the tests. As a demonstration of how to apply the tests, in section 5 we present an empirical example. Some concluding remarks are given in section 6.

2 Cornish–Fisher Size-corrected Test Statistics

We start our analysis by introducing all the necessary notations and assumptions made to derive the Cornish–Fisher size adjusted test statistics for the linear model with scalar variance-covariance matrix. The proposed statistics are locally exact in the sense that, if the vector of parameters of the variance-covariance matrix coefficients is known to belong to a ball of radius δ, they reduce to their exact formulae as $\delta \to 0$. All the proofs of the chapter are given in the Appendix.

2.1 Notation and Assumptions

Consider the linear regression model,

$$y = X\beta + \sigma u \tag{1}$$

where y is a $(T \times 1)$ vector of observations of the dependent variable, X is a $(T \times n)$ matrix of observations of n exogenous regressors, β is a $(n \times 1)$ vector of unknown parameters and σu (σ is a positive scalar) is a $(T \times 1)$ vector of disturbance terms. We assume that the random vector u is distributed as $N(0, \Omega^{-1})$, where the elements of the $(T \times T)$ matrix Ω are known functions of a $(k \times 1)$ vector of parameters, γ, and of a $(T \times m)$ matrix Z of observations of a set of exogenous variables which may include some of the explanatory variables of model (1). The vector γ belongs to the parameter space Θ, which is an open subset of the k-dimensional Euclidean space.

Let $\hat{\gamma}$ be a consistent estimator of γ. For any function $f = f(\gamma)$, we can write $\hat{f} = f(\hat{\gamma})$. The feasible GLS estimators of β and σ^2 are given by

$$\hat{\beta} = (X'\widehat{\Omega}X)^{-1}X'\widehat{\Omega}y \tag{2}$$

and

$$\hat{\sigma}^2 = (y - X\hat{\beta})'\widehat{\Omega}(y - X\hat{\beta})/(T - n) \tag{3}$$

respectively.

Denote as Ω_i, Ω_{ij}, etc. the $(T \times T)$ matrices of the first, second and higher-order derivatives of Ω with respect to the elements of γ, and define a $((k + 1) \times 1)$ vector δ, with elements

$$\delta_0 = (\hat{\sigma}^2 - \sigma^2)/\tau\sigma^2, \quad \delta_i = (\hat{\gamma}_i - \gamma_i)/\tau \quad (i = 1, ..., k) \tag{4}$$

where $\tau = 1/\sqrt{T}$ stands for the asymptotic scale of our expansions. Then, the formulas of the test statistics can be derived based on the following assumption.

Assumption 1 Let the following regularity conditions hold:

(i) the elements of Ω and Ω^{-1} are bounded in all T and $\gamma \in \Theta$, and the matrices

$$A = X'\Omega X/T, \quad F = X'X/T \tag{5}$$

converge to non-singular limits, as $T \longrightarrow \infty$.

(ii) The partial derivatives of the elements of Ω with respect to the elements of γ up to the fourth order are bounded for all T and all $\gamma \in \Theta$.

(iii) The estimator $\hat{\gamma}$ is an even function of u and is functionally unrelated to the vector of parameters β, implying that it can be written only as a function of X, Z and σu.

(iv) The vector δ admits a stochastic expansion of the form

$$\delta = d_1 + \tau d_2 + \omega(\tau^2) \tag{6}$$

where $\omega(\cdot)$ is an order of magnitude defined in the Appendix which has the same operational properties with $O(\cdot)$, and the expectations

$$E(d_1 d_1') \quad \text{and} \quad E(\sqrt{T} d_1 + d_2)$$

exist and have finite limits, as $T \longrightarrow \infty$.

The first two conditions of the assumption imply that the following matrices

$$A_i = X'\Omega_i X/T \quad A_{ij} = X'\Omega_{ij} X/T \quad \text{and} \quad A_{ij}^* = X'\Omega_i \Omega^{-1} \Omega_j X/T \tag{7}$$

are bounded, which in turn implies that the Taylor series expansion of $\hat{\beta}$ constitutes a stochastic expansion (see Magdalinos, 1986). Since the parameters β and γ are functionally unrelated, condition (iii) is satisfied for a wide class of estimators of γ including the maximum likelihood (ML) estimators and the simple or iterative estimators based on the regression residuals [see Breusch (1980), Rothenberg (1984a)]. For these estimators, it can be shown that condition (iv) is satisfied provided that a similar to condition (i) is satisfied for matrix Z. Finally, note that we do not need to assume that the estimator $\hat{\gamma}$ is asymptotically efficient.

Next, define the scalars λ_0 and μ_0, the $(k \times 1)$ vectors λ and μ, and the $(k \times k)$ matrix Λ, such as

$$\begin{bmatrix} \lambda_0 & \lambda' \\ \lambda & \Lambda \end{bmatrix} = \lim_{T \to \infty} E(d_1 d_1'), \quad \begin{bmatrix} \mu_0 \\ \mu \end{bmatrix} = \lim_{T \to \infty} E(\sqrt{T} d_1 + d_2) \tag{8}$$

and denote any $(n \times m)$ matrix L with elements l_{ij}, such as

$$L = \left[(l_{ij})_{i=1,\ldots,n;\, j=1,\ldots,m} \right] \tag{9}$$

with obvious modifications for the vectors and square matrices. If l_{ij} are $(n_i \times m_j)$ matrices, then matrix L is the $\left(\left(\sum n_i\right) \times \left(\sum m_j\right) \right)$ partitioned matrix with submatrices l_{ij}. Throughout the paper, P_X and $\overline{P}_X$ will stand for the orthogonal projectors of y into the space spanned by the columns of the matrix X and its orthogonal complement, respectively.

2.2 The t Test

Let e_0 be a known scalar and e be a known $(n \times 1)$ vector. A test of the null hypothesis

$$H_0: e'\beta = e_0 \tag{10}$$

against its one-sided alternatives can be conducted based on the statistic

$$t = (e'\hat{\beta} - e_0) / \left[\hat{\sigma}^2 e'(X'\widehat{\Omega}X)^{-1} e\right]^{1/2} \tag{11}$$

which takes into account the degrees of freedom of the t distribution.

Define a $(k \times 1)$ vector l and a $(k \times k)$ matrix L as:

$$l = \left[(l_i)_{i=1,...,k}\right], \quad L = \left[(l_{ij})_{i,j=1,...,k}\right] \tag{12}$$

where

$$l_i = e'GA_iGe/e'Ge, \quad l_{ij} = e'GC_{ij}Ge/e'Ge, \text{ and} \tag{13}$$

$$G = (X'\Omega X/T)^{-1}, \quad C_{ij} = A^*_{ij} - 2A_iGA_j + A_{ij}/2. \tag{14}$$

Based on Rothemberg (1988), we can prove the following Lemma (see Appendix for more details).

Lemma 1 Let Assumption 1 hold. Then, under the null hypothesis (10), the following results hold.

(i) The distribution function of the t-statistic, given by (11), admits the Edgeworth expansion:

$$\Pr\{t \le x\} = I(x) - \frac{\tau^2}{2}\left[\left(p_1 + \frac{1}{2}\right) + \left(p_2 + \frac{1}{2}\right)x^2\right] x i(x) + O(\tau^3) \tag{15}$$

where

$$p_1 = tr(\Lambda L) + l'\Lambda l/4 + l'(\mu + \lambda/2) - \mu_0 + (\lambda_0 - 2)/4 \tag{16}$$

$$p_2 = (l'\Lambda l - 2l'\lambda + \lambda_0 - 2)/4$$

and $I(x)$ and $i(x)$ stand for the standard normal distribution and density functions of a random variable x, respectively.

(ii) The distribution function of the t-statistic admits the Edgeworth expansion:

$$\Pr\{t \leq x\} = I_{T-n}(x) - \frac{\tau^2}{2}(p_1 + p_2 x^2) x i_{T-n}(x) + O(\tau^3) \qquad (17)$$

where the quantities p_1 and p_2 are defined in (16), and $I_{T-n}(x)$ and $i_{T-n}(x)$ stand for the distribution and density functions of a t-distributed random variable with $T - n$ degrees of freedom, respectively.

The first result of Lemma 1 enables us to calculate the Edgeworth corrected $\alpha\%$ critical value of the t-statistic as

$$\hat{n}_\alpha = n_\alpha + \frac{\tau^2}{2}\left[\left(p_1 + \frac{1}{2}\right) + \left(p_2 + \frac{1}{2}\right) n_\alpha^2\right] n_\alpha \qquad (18)$$

where n_α is the $\alpha\%$ significant point of the standard normal distribution, or as

$$\hat{t}_\alpha = t_\alpha + \frac{\tau^2}{2}(p_1 + p_2 t_\alpha^2) t_\alpha \qquad (19)$$

where t_α is the $\alpha\%$ significant point of the t distribution with $T-n$ degrees of freedom.

The Edgworth corrected critical values $\hat{n}_\alpha$ and $\hat{t}_\alpha$ can be employed to conduct inference for hypothesis (10) (see Rothenberg, 1984b, 1988). However, the Edgeworth approximation used to derive $\hat{n}_\alpha$ and $\hat{t}_\alpha$ is not a proper distribution function. In fact, it often assigns negative "probabilities" in the tails of the distribution. To overcome this problem, we can use a Cornish–Fisher expansion to correct the test statistics of interest, instead of an Edgeworth expansion to correct the critical values. The Cornish–Fisher expansion is simply the inversion of the Edgeworth correction of the critical values and it is expected to have very similar properties in the main body of the approximated distribution. However in the tail area, which is of outmost importance in hypothesis testing, the properties are quite different. The Cornish–Fisher corrected statistics are proper random variables with well-behaved tails: they never assign negative tail "probabilities". In addition, these statistics can be readily implemented using the tables of standard distributions. The calculation of the significance level (p-value) of the statistics is straightforward, and it requires the integration of standard density functions only.

Based on the second result of Lemma 1 (see equation 17), we can prove the following theorem.

Theorem 1 Let Assumption 1 hold. Then, under the null hypothesis (10), the Cornish–Fisher corrected t-statistic is given by

$$\hat{t} = t - \frac{\tau^2}{2}(p_1 + p_2 t^2)t \tag{20}$$

and it follows a t-distribution with $T - n$ degrees of freedom up to an approximation error of order $O(\tau^3)$.

The result of theTheorem 1 implies that the size corrected $\hat{t}$-statistic can be employed to test one or two-sided hypotheses on a typical coefficient (say the kth) of the linear model (1) based on the tables of the t distribution, with $T - n$ degrees of freedom. For a one-sided hypothesis, the p-value of the $\hat{t}$-statistic can be computed based on

$$\Pr\{t > t_0\} = 1 - I_{T-n}(\hat{t}_0) + O(\tau^3), \tag{21}$$

for any value of t (say t_0), using the tables of the t-distribution. To implement the test statistic $\hat{t}$ for a two-sided hypothesis, vector e should take 1 in its kth position and 0's elsewhere. Then, the elements of $\hat{l}$ and $\widehat{L}$ become

$$\hat{l}_i = \hat{g}_k' \widehat{A}_i \hat{g}_k / \hat{g}_{kk}, \quad \hat{l}_{ij} = \hat{g}_k' \widehat{C}_{ij} \hat{g}_k / \hat{g}_{kk} \tag{22}$$

respectively, where $\hat{g}_k$ is the kth column of matrix $\widehat{G} = (X'\widehat{\Omega}X/T)^{-1}$, with k^{th} diagonal element denoted as $\hat{g}_{kk}$. Finally, note that since the parameters p_1 and p_2 are functions of the unknown vector of parameters γ, in practice one has to substitute γ with its estimates in order to implement the test statistic $\hat{t}$, making the approximation:

$$\hat{p}_i = p_i(\hat{\gamma}) = p_i + \omega(\tau) \quad (i = 1, 2). \tag{23}$$

2.3 *The F Test*

To derive the Cornish–Fisher corrected F-statistic, define a $(r \times n)$ known matrix H of rank r and a $(r \times 1)$ known vector h. A test of the joint null hypothesis

$$H_0 : H\beta - h = 0 \tag{24}$$

can be conducted using the the familiar F statistic

$$v = (H\hat{\beta} - h)' \left[H(X'\widehat{\Omega}X)^{-1}H\right]^{-1} (H\hat{\beta} - h)/r\hat{\sigma}^2 \tag{25}$$

which adjusts for the degrees of freedom, or on the Wald test statistic

$$w = (H\hat{\beta} - h)' \left[H(X'\hat{\Omega}X)^{-1}H \right]^{-1} (H\hat{\beta} - h)/\hat{\sigma}^2 \qquad (26)$$

which does not take into account the degrees of freedom.

Define a $(k \times 1)$ vector c and the $(k \times k)$ matrices C and D as

$$c = \left[(trA_iP)_{i=1,\ldots,k} \right], \quad C = \left[(trC_{ij}P)_{i,j=1,\ldots,k} \right] \quad \text{and} \qquad (27)$$
$$D = \left[(trD_{ij}P)_{i,j=1,\ldots,k} \right]$$

respectively, where the matrices A_i and C_{ij} involved in (27) are defined in equations (7) and (14), and

$$P = GQG, \quad Q = H'(HGH')^{-1}H \quad \text{and} \quad D_{ij} = A_iPA_j/2. \qquad (28)$$

To derive the Cornish–Fisher corrected F-statistic, we will rely on the following lemma, corresponding to Lemma 1 for the $\hat{t}$-statistic.

Lemma 2 Let Assumption 1 hold. Then, under the null hypothesis (24), the following results hold:

(i) The distribution function of the w-statistic, given by (26), admits the Edgeworth-type expansion:

$$\Pr\{w \leq x\} = F_r(x) - \tau^2 \left(h_1 + h_2 \frac{x}{r+2} \right) \frac{x}{r} f_r(x) + O(\tau^3) \qquad (29)$$

where

$$h_1 = tr[\Lambda(C+D)] - c'\Lambda c/4 + c'\mu + r[c'\lambda/2 - \mu_0 - (r-2)\lambda_0/4] \qquad (30)$$
$$h_2 = tr(\Lambda D) + [c'\Lambda c - (r+2)(2c'\lambda - r\lambda_0)]/4$$

and $F_r(x)$ and $f_r(x)$ stand for the distribution and density functions of a chi-square distributed random variable x with r degrees of freedom, respectively.

(ii) The distribution function of the v-statistic, given by (25), admits the Edgeworth-type expansion:

$$\Pr\{v \leq x\} = F^r_{T-n}(x) - \tau^2(q_1 + q_2x)xf^r_{T-n}(x) + O(\tau^3) \qquad (31)$$

where

$$q_1 = h_1/r + (r-2)/2 \tag{32}$$

$$q_2 = h_2/(r+2) - r/2$$

and $F^r_{T-n}(x)$ and $f^r_{T-n}(x)$ stand for the distribution and density functions of an F distributed random variable x with r and $T-n$ degrees of freedom, respectively.

The first result of the lemma enables us to calculate the Edgeworth corrected $a\%$ critical value of the Wald test statistic w as

$$\hat{\chi}_\alpha = \chi_\alpha + \tau^2 \left[(h_1/r) + (h_2/r(r+2))\chi_\alpha\right] \chi_\alpha \tag{33}$$

where χ_α denotes the $\alpha\%$ significant point of a chi-square distributed variable with r degrees of freedom. The parameters h_1 and h_2 can be substituted with their estimates, implying the approximation

$$\hat{h}_i = h_i(\hat{\gamma}) = h_i + \omega(\tau) \quad (i = 1, 2). \tag{34}$$

From the second result of the lemma (see equation 31), we can calculate the Edgeworth corrected $\alpha\%$ critical value of the v statistic as

$$\widehat{F}_\alpha = F_\alpha + \tau^2(q_1 + q_2 F_\alpha)F_\alpha \tag{35}$$

where F_α denotes the $\alpha\%$ significant point of the F-distribution with r and $T-n$ degrees of freedom.

Based on the second result of the lemma, next we derive the formula of the Cornish–Fisher corrected F-statistic, denoted as $\hat{v}$.

Theorem 2 Let Assumption 1 hold. Then, under the null hypothesis (24) the Cornish–Fisher corrected F-statistic is given by

$$\hat{v} = v - \tau^2(q_1 + q_2 v)v \tag{36}$$

and it follows an F distribution with r and $T-n$ degrees of freedom up to an approximation error of order $O(\tau^3)$.

The results of the theorem imply that the $\hat{v}$-statistic can be implemented to test the null hypothesis against a two sided alternative using the table of the F-distribution. To implement the test, the parameters q_1 and q_2 can be substituted with their estimates given by

$$\hat{q}_1 = \hat{h}_1/r + (r-2)/2, \quad \hat{q}_2 = \hat{h}_2/(r+2) - r/2 \tag{37}$$

implying (as before) an approximation error of order $\omega(\tau)$. The p-value of the $\hat{v}$-statistic can be computed based on

$$\Pr\{v > v_0\} = 1 - F^r_{T-n}(\hat{v}_0) + O(\tau^3) \tag{38}$$

for any value of v (say v_0), using the tables of the F-distribution.

As an example of the Cornish–Fisher corrected F-statistic, $\hat{v}$, consider a test for the joint null hypothesis $\beta_1 = \beta_2 = ... = \beta_n = 0$. Then, $r = n$, H becomes an $(n \times n)$ identity matrix and the elements of the vector c and matrices D and $C^* = C + D$ are given as follows:

$$c_i = tr(A_i G), \quad d_{ij} = trA_i GA_j G/2, \quad c^*_{ij} = tr[(A^*_{ij} + A_{ij}/2)G] - 3d_{ij}, \tag{39}$$

while the coefficients q_1 and q_2 of the Cornish–Fisher expansion can be calculated as

$$q_1 = tr[\Lambda C^* - c'\Lambda c/4 + c'\mu]/n + c'\lambda/2 - \mu_0 - (n-2)(\lambda_0 - 2)/4 \tag{40}$$

$$q_2 = \frac{1}{n+2}[tr(\Lambda D) + \frac{1}{4}[c'\Lambda c - (n+2)(2c'\lambda - n(\lambda_0 - 2))]].$$

3 Cornish–Fisher Corrected $\hat{t}$ and $\hat{v}$-statistics for a Parametric Model of Heteroscedasticity

The Cornish–Fisher test statistics $\hat{t}$ and $\hat{v}$ derived in the previous section allow for the variance of the disturbance terms of the linear regression model (1) to have a general specification. This can include many models of heteroscedasticity or random coefficients suggested in the literature for model (1) (see Hildreth and Houck, 1968; Goldfeld and Quandt, 1972; and Amemiya 1977; *inter alia*). In this section, we show how to implement the statistics for a parametric model of heteroscedasticity often used in empirical work. Specifically, we consider that the disturbances of model (1) are independent normal variables with zero mean and variances given by the function

$$\sigma^2_t = z'_t\gamma, \quad t = 1, ..., T \tag{41}$$

where $z'_t = (1, z_{t2}, ..., z_{tk})$ is a set of k exogenous variables, with slope coefficients collected in the vector $\gamma = (\gamma_1, ..., \gamma_k)'$.

The above specification of σ_t^2 implies that the parameters σ and γ are not simultaneously identified. Thus, in order to derive the Cornish–Fisher size-corrected statistics we will set $\sigma = 1$. Under this restriction, the transformed, GLS model will have disturbances with identity variance matrix, only if γ can be estimated exactly, which can be done for infinite samples. In small samples the estimate of the variance matrix of the transformed disturbances will differ from the identity matrix. A reasonable method to overcome this difficulty is to estimate the variance of the transformed residuals and, then, use the standard formulas of the t and F-test statistics instead of the normal and chi-square tests, respectively. The resulting tests are locally exact and, as will be shown later by simulation experiments, they have size which is closer to the nominal than the asymptotic tests.

To implement the $\hat{t}$ and $\hat{v}$-statistics in the case that the variance of u_t are given by equation (41), we need an estimator of γ and estimates of the parameters p_i and q_i involved in the Cornish–Fisher expansions, given by equations (16) and (32), respectively. To estimate γ, we can use one of the following estimators: Goldfeld–Quandt's (1972) estimator (hereafter GQ), Amemiya's (1977) standard and iterative estimators (hereafter A and IA) respectively, and the Maximum likelihood (ML) estimator.[1] The above estimators satisfy the regularity conditions (i)–(iv) of Assumption 1, if the quantities $|z_{tj}|$, $|\sigma_t^{-2}|$ and $|\sigma_t^2|$ are bounded and the following matrices

$$A = \sum_{t=1}^{T} \sigma_t^{-2} x_t x_t'/T, \quad \overline{A} = \sum_{t=1}^{T} \sigma_t^{-4} z_t z_t'/T \tag{42}$$

$$F = \sum_{t=1}^{T} x_t x_t'/T, \quad \text{and} \quad \overline{F} = \sum_{t=1}^{T} z_t z_t'/T$$

converge to non-singular limits, as $T \to \infty$.

To estimate p_i and q_i, below we will present two propositions. To this end, we first define the following matrices:

$$\Gamma = \sum_{t=1}^{T} \sigma_t^2 x_t x_t'/T, \quad \overline{\Gamma} = \sum_{t=1}^{T} \sigma_t^4 z_t z_t'/T, \tag{43}$$

$$G = A^{-1}, \quad \overline{G} = \overline{A}^{-1}, \quad B = F^{-1} \quad \text{and} \quad \overline{B} = \overline{F}^{-1}.$$

Proposition 1 For the variance function given by the parametric model (41), the vector l and matrix L, defined by equation (12), can be computed as

$$l = -L(h)\gamma, \quad L = 2[L(h) - C(h)GC'(h)] \tag{44}$$

where $h = Ge/(e'Ge)^{1/2}$, while the vector c, and the matrices C and D, defined by equation (27), can be computed as:

$$c = -C_1\gamma, \quad C = 2(C_1 - C_2), \quad D = C_3/2 \tag{45}$$

$$C_1 = \sum_{i=1}^{r} L(h_i), \quad C_2 = \sum_{i=1}^{r} C(h_i)GC'(h_i) \quad C_3 = \sum_{i=1}^{r} C(h_i)PC'(h_i)$$

with $h_i = \lambda_i^{1/2} w_i$, where λ_i and w_i $(i = 1, ..., r)$ are the non-zero eigenvalues and the corresponding orthonormalised eigenvectors of P.

Remark 1 The computation of the vectors l and c, and the matrices L, C and D (see equations 12 and 27) involved in the formulas of p_i and q_i is straightforward, but it can be computationally demanding when the dimension of vector γ, k, is large. To overcome this difficulty, we recommend the following computational procedure. Given an arbitrary $(n \times 1)$ vector h, define the matrices

$$L(h) = \sum_{t=1}^{T} \sigma_t^{-6}(x_t'h)^2 z_t z_t'/T, \quad C(h) = \sum_{t=1}^{T} \sigma_t^{-4}(x_t'h) z_t x_t'/T. \tag{46}$$

These matrices constitute the sample moment matrices of the transformed variables

$$z_t^* = z_t(x_t'h)\sigma_t^3, \quad x_t^* = x_t/\sigma_t$$

and thus can be computed using standard procedures.

Remark 2 Note that the differences between the formulas of the vectors l and c for the general scalar specification of the variance function, σ_t^2, given by formulas (12) and (27), respectively, and their corresponding formulas (44) and (45) for the parametric specification of σ_t^2 given by equation (41) are of order $O(\tau^2)$, and thus are negligible to the order of our approximation.

To calculate p_i and q_i, it remains to compute the set of parameters involved in definitions (8); that is $\lambda, \lambda_0, \Lambda, \mu$ and μ_0. Notice that these parameters can be expressed in terms of the matrices (42), (43) and of the vectors:

$$\xi = \sum_{t=1}^{T} v_t z_t / T, \quad \xi_1 = \sum_{t=1}^{T} \sigma_t^{-4} v_t z_t / T, \quad \xi_2 = \sum_{t=1}^{T} \sigma_t^{-4} x_t' G x_t z_t / T \tag{47}$$

where $v_t = 2\sigma_t^2 x_t' B x_t - x_t' B \Gamma B x_t$.

The next proposition shows how to calculate $\lambda, \lambda_0, \Lambda, \mu$ and μ_0 for the estimators of vector γ, mentioned above.

Proposition 2 Let Assumption 1 hold. Then, the parameters involved in the definitions of equation (8) for the parametric specification of the variance function given by equation (41) can be calculated as:

$$\Lambda = 2\overline{B\Gamma B}, \quad \mu = -\overline{B}\xi, \quad \lambda = 2\gamma - \Lambda\overline{A}\gamma \tag{48}$$

$$\lambda_0 = 2(1 - \gamma'\overline{A}\gamma) - \gamma'\overline{A}\lambda, \quad \mu_0 = tr(\Lambda\overline{A}) - 2k - \gamma'\overline{A}\mu$$

for the GQ estimator of γ, and as

$$\Lambda = 2\overline{G}, \quad \lambda = 0, \quad \lambda_0 = 2(1 - \gamma'\overline{A}\gamma), \quad \mu_0 = -\gamma'\overline{A}\mu \tag{49}$$

$$\mu = -\overline{G}\xi_1 - 4\sum_{i=1}^{k} \overline{G}[\overline{A}_i\overline{g}_i - (Z\Omega_i\Omega^{-1}Z/T)\overline{b}_i]$$

for the A estimator of γ. For the IA and ML estimators of γ, they can be estimated based on (49), with

$$\mu = -\overline{G}\xi_2 \tag{50}$$

where $\overline{g}_i$ is the ith column of matrix $\overline{G}$, $\overline{b}_i$ is the ith column of matrices $\overline{B}$ and $\overline{A}_i = (Z'\Omega\Omega_i Z/T)$.

From a computation point of view, the formulas given by the above two propositions can substantially simplify the calculation of both the Edgeworth and Cornish–Fisher corrections. Note that all the matrices defined in the above propositions are of dimension $(n \times n)$, or $(k \times k)$, and, apart from $\overline{A}_i$ and $(Z'\Omega_i\Omega^{-1}Z/T)$, they can be calculated in the GLS estimation procedure. The trace of matrix $\Lambda\overline{A}$ can be easily computed, while the matrices $\overline{A}_i$ and $(Z'\Omega_i\Omega^{-1}Z/T)$ can be computed using the following formulas:

$$\overline{A}_i = -\sum_{t=1}^{T} z_{ti}\,\sigma_t^{-6} z_t z_t'/T, \quad Z'\Omega_i\Omega^{-1}Z/T = -\sum_{t=1}^{T} z_{ti}\,\sigma_t^{-2} z_t z_t'/T. \quad (51)$$

4 Simulation Experiments

The goal of this section is to evaluate the small-sample performance of the Cornish–Fisher corrected $\hat{t}$ and $\hat{v}$-statistics (denoted as CF-$\hat{t}$ and CF-$\hat{F}$, respectively), compared with their corresponding standard test statistics, based on the normal/t and chi-squared/F-distributions (denoted as N/t and χ^2/F, respectively), and the tests suggested by Rothenberg (1984b, 1988) based on the Edgeworth approximations of the critical values of the normal/t and chi-square/F distributions (denoted as E-$\hat{N}$/E-$\hat{t}$ and E-$\hat{\chi}^2$/E-$\hat{F}$, respectively). To this end, we present the results of a Monte Carlo simulation study based on 5,000 iterations.

Our experiments are based on the following four-parameters linear regression model:

$$y_t = \sum_{j=1}^{4} x_{tj}\beta_j + u_t, \quad u_t \sim N(0, \sigma_t^2), \quad t = 1, \ldots, T \quad (52)$$

with $\sigma_t^2 = z_t'\gamma$ and $z_t' = (1, x_{t2}, x_{t3}, z_{t4})$ where the regressors are generated as

$$x_{tj} = 1, \quad (t = 1, \ldots, T \text{ and } j = 1) \quad (53)$$

$$x_{tj} = (1-\phi)^{1/2} z_{t(j-1)} + \phi^{1/2} z_{t4}, \quad (t = 1, \ldots, T \text{ and } j = 2, 3, 4)$$

where z_{tj} $(j = 1, 2, 3, 4)$ are independent $N(0, 1)$ pseudo-random numbers and ϕ stands for the correlation coefficient between any pair of regressors (x_{ti}, x_{tj}). The above procedure for generating the regressors enables us to evaluate the performance of the Cornish–Fisher test statistics in the presence of different degrees of multicollinearity between the regressors, often observed in practice (see McDonald and Galarneau, 1975). For the correlation coefficient, we consider the following set of values: $\phi = \{0.0, 0.5, 0.9\}$.

Without loss of generality, we confine ourselves to the case that $\sigma_t^2 \geq 1$ and we consider the following six vectors of values of $\gamma : \gamma_{(1)}' = (\gamma_1, 0, 0, 0)$, $\gamma_{(2)}' = (\gamma_1, 1, 0, 0)$, $\gamma_{(3)}' = (\gamma_1, 0, 0, 1)$,

$\gamma'_{(4)} = (\gamma_1, 1, 1, 0)$, $\gamma'_{(5)} = (\gamma_1, 1, 0, 1)$ and $\gamma'_{(6)} = (\gamma_1, 1, 1, 1)$. Cases like $0 \leq \sigma_t^2 \leq 1$ can be tackled by using the inverse of σ_t^2, instead of σ_t^2. As vector z_t, we assume $z_t = (1, x_{t2}, x_{t3}, z_{t4})'$. To guarantee that $\sigma_t^2 = z_t'\gamma \geq 1$, γ_1 is calculated so that $\sigma_t^2 = z_t'\gamma \geq 1$, for all z_t'. The heteroscedastic disturbances are calculated as

$$u_t = \sigma_t \epsilon_t \tag{54}$$

where ϵ_t $(t = 1, \ldots, T)$ are independent $N(0, 1)$ pseudo-random numbers.

For the sake of simplicity, we assume that $\beta_j = 0$ $(j = 1, \ldots, 4)$, which implies

$$y_t = u_t, \quad u_t \sim N(0, \sigma_t^2), \quad \sigma_t^2 = z_t'\gamma \geq 1, \quad (t = 1, \ldots, T). \tag{55}$$

For testing the individual coefficients, we consider four hypotheses of the form (10):

$$\beta_1 = 0, \beta_2 = 0, \beta_3 = 0, \beta_4 = 0, \tag{56}$$

while for testing the significance of the model we consider the null hypothesis: $\beta_2 = \beta_3 = \beta_4 = 0$, which means that H and h are defined as follows:

$$H = \begin{bmatrix} 0 & 1 & 0 & 0 \\ 0 & 0 & 1 & 0 \\ 0 & 0 & 0 & 1 \end{bmatrix}, \quad h = \begin{bmatrix} 0 \\ 0 \\ 0 \end{bmatrix}. \tag{57}$$

In each iteration, β is estimated by least squares (LS). The residuals of the LS regression are used to obtain the value of the GQ estimator for γ, and hence the value of Amemiya's estimator, denoted $\hat{\gamma}_A$. We use Amemiya's estimator of γ because it is simpler than all the other asymptotically efficient estimators of γ. Given $\hat{\gamma}_A$, we calculate the GLS estimator of β as:

$$\hat{\beta} = \left[\sum_{t=1}^{T} (z_t'\hat{\gamma}_A)^{-1} x_t x_t' \right]^{-1} \sum_{t=1}^{T} (z_t'\hat{\gamma}_A)^{-1} x_t y_t. \tag{58}$$

The estimates of $\hat{\beta}$ are used to compute the null rejection probabilities (known as the actual size) of the statistics of interest, namely (11), (20),

(26), (25), (36) and the Edgeworth-corrected critical values (18), (19), (33) and (35). This is done at the nominal levels of 1%, 5% and 10%.

The results of our experiments are reported in Tables 7.1 through 7.4. Tables 7.1 and 7.2 report results for a very small sample of $T = 20$ observations and different values of ϕ, that is $\phi = \{0.0, 0.5, 0.9\}$, for the hypothesis $H_0 : \beta_3 = 0$ and the joint hypothesis $H_0 : \beta_2 = \beta_3 = \beta_4 = 0$, respectively. The results for the null hypotheses $H_0 : \beta_1 = 0$, $H_0 : \beta_2 = 0$, and $H_0 : \beta_4 = 0$ are similar to those for $H_0 : \beta_3 = 0$, and thus are omitted. Tables 7.3 and 7.4 present results for the above two hypotheses for a medium value of the correlation coefficient, $\phi = 0.50$, and a set of different values of the sample size, i.e. $T = \{15, 20, 30, 50, 100, 500, 1000\}$. This set of experiments can reveal if there is any sample size within which the Cornish–Fisher corrected test statistics should be preferred than the other finite or asymptotic test statistics. Since the t-test of the null hypotheses (56) against two-sided alternatives is a special case of the F-test, we examine the performance of the t-test for one-sided alternatives. Thus, in Tables 7.1 and 7.3 we report the actual size for the positive values of the t-statistics. For the negative values of the t-statistics, we obtain similar results. These results are not presented for reasons of space.

The results of both Tables 7.1 and 7.2 clearly indicate that the Cornish–Fisher corrected t and F test statistics (CF-$\hat{t}$ and CF-$\hat{F}$) outperform the other tests, as their differences between the actual and nominal sizes are the smallest ones. This is true for any level of nominal size, that is 1%, 5% and 10%, and degree of multicollinearity considered. The E-$\hat{t}$ and E-$\hat{F}$ test statistics, based on the Edgeworth correction of the critical values, are found to have satisfactory performance, which is analogous to that of the standard t and F-statistics. Note that in the case where the degree of multicollinearity is very high (i.e. $\phi = 0.9$), the t-statistic seems to slightly outperform the E-$\hat{t}$ statistic. The test statistics based on the Edgeworth expansion of the normal and chi-square distributions seems to perform less satisfactorily than their corresponding standard (t/F) and approximated E-$\hat{t}$ and E-$\hat{F}$ test statistics. The worst performing test is found to be the normal statistic, N. Obviously, this can be attributed to the fact that this statistic neither adjusts for the degrees of freedom nor uses correct critical values in small samples. Note that the performance of the above all test statistics for the join hypothesis $\beta_2 = \beta_3 = \beta_4 = 0$ are found to be worse than those for the single hypothesis $\beta_3 = 0$, especially at the lower significance levels 1% and 5%. The actual rejection probabilities of these tests are found to be double or much higher of their nominal levels, with the Cornish–Fisher statistics performing better than the other tests.

Table 7.1. *Null rejection probability estimates* ($H_0: \beta_3 = 0$), $T = 20$ *(positive alternative)*

Nominal size:		1%					5%					10%				
$\gamma_{(i)}$	ϕ	N	E-$\hat{N}$	t	E-$\hat{t}$	CF-$\hat{t}$	N	E-$\hat{N}$	t	E-$\hat{t}$	CF-$\hat{t}$	N	E-$\hat{N}$	t	E-$\hat{t}$	CF-$\hat{t}$
	0.0	5.2	3.7	2.3	2.2	1.4	11.8	8.3	8.0	6.2	5.3	17.7	13.1	13.7	10.7	9.7
$\gamma_{(1)}$	0.5	5.4	4.2	2.5	2.6	1.4	12.2	8.6	8.3	6.5	5.8	17.9	13.3	14.0	11.3	10.5
	0.9	5.8	4.4	2.8	2.9	1.6	12.0	9.2	8.6	7.1	5.5	17.7	13.6	14.1	11.6	10.3
	0.0	5.8	4.3	2.6	2.3	1.3	12.6	9.2	9.5	6.5	5.2	17.9	14.0	14.6	12.0	10.7
$\gamma_{(2)}$	0.5	5.3	4.0	2.6	2.4	1.4	12.3	9.3	8.6	6.8	5.7	16.6	12.9	13.2	10.8	9.9
	0.9	5.2	4.3	2.4	2.7	1.9	12.7	9.2	8.3	6.7	5.9	18.4	14.7	14.7	12.0	10.7
	0.0	5.5	4.6	2.6	3.2	1.7	11.8	9.0	8.1	6.7	5.3	17.2	13.3	13.6	11.0	9.5
$\gamma_{(3)}$	0.5	5.5	3.7	2.5	1.9	1.3	12.7	9.0	9.3	6.6	5.6	18.4	13.8	14.6	11.5	10.8
	0.9	6.5	5.1	2.9	3.4	2.2	13.3	10.6	9.4	7.9	6.5	19.0	14.8	15.2	12.6	11.6
	0.0	5.7	3.4	2.3	1.9	1.4	12.4	8.6	8.6	6.3	5.4	17.2	13.3	13.9	11.3	10.3
$\gamma_{(4)}$	0.5	4.8	4.8	2.2	3.2	1.8	11.4	9.3	7.7	7.2	6.2	17.2	13.9	13.7	11.7	10.7
	0.9	6.0	4.9	2.5	3.2	2.1	13.2	10.3	9.1	7.7	6.6	18.5	15.2	14.8	12.7	11.8
	0.0	5.0	3.5	2.4	2.1	1.3	10.1	8.0	7.8	5.9	5.0	16.2	12.4	13.1	10.5	9.6
$\gamma_{(5)}$	0.5	6.3	4.9	2.9	3.2	2.0	12.4	9.6	8.9	7.1	5.7	18.6	13.9	14.6	11.8	10.6
	0.9	4.5	3.5	1.8	2.2	1.4	11.5	8.2	7.4	5.8	4.9	17.8	13.3	13.6	10.9	9.9
	0.0	4.8	4.9	2.0	3.2	2.2	11.6	9.5	7.4	7.3	6.3	17.0	14.1	13.2	11.7	10.9
$\gamma_{(6)}$	0.5	5.3	3.8	2.3	2.0	1.5	11.7	8.6	8.4	6.3	5.5	17.5	13.7	13.9	10.9	9.9
	0.9	6.5	4.8	3.0	3.5	1.6	13.7	9.7	9.2	7.3	5.4	19.3	14.6	15.7	11.9	10.4

Table 7.2. *Null rejection probability estimates* ($H_0 : \beta_2 = \beta_3 = \beta_4 = 0$), $T = 20$

Nominal size:		1%					5%					10%				
$\gamma(i)$	ϕ	χ^2	E-$\hat{\chi}^2$	F	E-$\hat{F}$	CF-$\hat{F}$	χ^2	E-$\hat{\chi}^2$	F	E-$\hat{F}$	CF-$\hat{F}$	χ^2	E-$\hat{\chi}^2$	F	E-$\hat{F}$	CF-$\hat{F}$
	0.0	22.4	16.3	9.4	7.8	2.3	35.2	25.0	19.9	15.0	8.4	44.3	31.0	28.8	21.3	14.8
$\gamma(1)$	0.5	25.3	18.6	10.7	9.4	2.6	37.5	27.5	22.6	16.9	8.5	45.8	33.4	31.4	24.4	14.8
	0.9	24.4	17.9	10.1	8.5	2.6	36.9	26.6	21.8	16.2	8.7	45.2	32.8	30.7	23.5	15.0
	0.0	25.5	19.2	10.4	9.3	3.0	39.7	28.4	23.5	17.2	8.3	48.2	35.5	33.0	24.9	13.5
$\gamma(2)$	0.5	24.4	18.3	10.1	8.8	2.0	38.2	26.9	22.1	16.4	7.4	46.5	33.6	31.5	23.3	13.9
	0.9	23.4	19.0	9.4	9.6	3.2	35.8	27.7	21.1	17.9	10.6	44.9	33.6	29.4	24.6	16.6
	0.0	22.8	18.4	9.5	9.4	3.3	36.0	26.0	20.5	16.6	8.9	44.6	32.6	29.3	23.3	14.9
$\gamma(3)$	0.5	24.5	17.6	9.5	8.3	2.3	37.0	27.0	21.5	15.8	7.5	46.0	33.5	30.3	23.2	13.4
	0.9	26.5	20.2	10.8	9.8	3.3	39.2	29.3	23.7	18.8	10.2	47.8	35.3	32.7	25.3	16.3
	0.0	25.3	18.5	10.24	9.0	3.2	37.6	27.5	23.0	17.2	9.8	46.4	33.9	31.4	24.2	16.0
$\gamma(4)$	0.5	22.7	19.0	9.2	10.1	3.8	34.5	27.5	20.0	17.4	9.6	42.6	33.8	28.5	24.7	16.0
	0.9	23.6	17.5	9.1	8.4	2.8	36.8	27.4	21.2	16.4	9.1	45.1	34.5	30.1	24.1	16.2
	0.0	24.2	17.2	9.9	8.4	2.7	37.0	26.1	22.3	16.0	7.7	45.8	32.7	31.9	22.7	13.4
$\gamma(5)$	0.5	24.7	20.6	10.2	10.8	4.3	37.4	29.6	22.1	19.2	11.3	45.9	35.9	30.9	26.0	17.5
	0.9	23.7	18.6	9.8	9.3	2.9	37.0	28.1	21.0	17.0	9.9	45.9	34.2	29.7	24.3	16.1
	0.0	22.6	18.1	8.7	8.9	3.8	34.8	27.3	19.9	16.5	9.6	42.7	33.6	28.3	23.8	16.5
$\gamma(6)$	0.5	24.0	20.3	9.6	9.7	3.6	37.5	29.1	21.3	17.9	10.7	46.0	35.5	30.5	25.4	17.5
	0.9	25.0	18.9	9.9	9.2	2.8	38.3	28.2	22.5	17.0	8.6	47.3	34.8	31.5	24.2	13.7

The results of Tables 7.3 and 7.4, for the case that T increases, indicate that the Cornish–Fisher corrected test statistics CF-$\hat{t}$ and CF-$\hat{F}$ have better size performance up to samples of size $T = 100$, compared with the other tests. For sufficiently large T, for example $T = \{500, 1000\}$, the actual size of all tests reaches the correct nominal size. Note that the actual size of all the statistics which are adjusted for the degrees of freedom , that is the CF-$\hat{t}$, CF-$\hat{F}$, E-$\hat{t}$, E-$\hat{F}$, t and F statistics, converge to the nominal size in a non-linear way, as T increases. That is, for very small T (e.g. $T = 15$), they have an actual size which is much closer to the nominal than for $T = 50$. The nonlinear pattern of convergence of the actual size of these tests to their nominal size may be jointly attributed to the effects of the degrees of freedom adjustments in small samples and the fact that the rate of convergence of the estimators of the structural parameters to their true values is not as fast as the increase of the sample size.

Overall, the results of our simulation study show that the locally exact, degrees of freedom-adjusted Cornish–Fisher corrected tests outperform the standard and Edgeworth corrected asymptotic tests in small samples. The performance of the locally exact, degrees of freedom-adjusted Edgeworth corrected tests, is analogous especially for the t-test. These results highlight the important role that degrees of freedom adjustments can play in finite sample inference procedures.

5 Empirical Example: Productivity Gains from in-company Training

As an illustration of how to implement the Cornish–Fisher size-corrected test statistics $\hat{t}$ and $\hat{F}$, suggested in the previous sections, we here present the results of an empirical study conducted to investigate whether there is a positive relationship between in-company training and labour productivity for small-medium manufacturing Greek enterprises (SMEs), employing more than 10 people. Our data comes from a sample survey conducted by Athens University of Economics & Business, during October–November of year 2002. A designed questionnaire was sent to a randomly selected number of 15 SMEs from which 11 usable returns were obtained.

To measure productivity, we consider a Gobb–Douglas production function in capital (denoted K) and effective labour (denoted L), that is

$$Y = AK^{\beta}L^{\gamma} \tag{59}$$

Table 7.3. *Null rejection probability estimates ($H_0: \beta_3 = 0$), as T increases (positive alternative)*

Nominal size:		1%					5%					10%				
$\gamma_{(i)}$	T	N	E-$\hat{N}$	t	E-$\hat{t}$	CF-$\hat{t}$	N	E-$\hat{N}$	t	E-$\hat{t}$	CF-$\hat{t}$	N	E-$\hat{N}$	t	E-$\hat{t}$	CF-$\hat{t}$
	15	6.4	3.9	2.2	1.9	0.7	12.9	8.7	8.2	5.7	4.4	18.5	12.8	13.7	10.0	8.7
	30	4.2	3.8	2.5	3.0	2.1	10.2	8.2	8.1	7.1	6.2	16.1	12.3	13.6	11.2	10.4
$\gamma_{(1)}$	50	3.5	3.0	2.2	2.4	1.8	8.8	7.3	7.4	6.4	6.0	14.5	12.3	13.0	11.7	11.3
	100	2.1	1.5	1.8	1.3	1.3	6.8	5.7	6.4	5.5	5.4	11.7	10.2	11.1	10.0	9.9
	500	1.0	0.9	0.9	0.9	0.9	5.1	4.8	5.1	4.8	4.8	9.8	9.5	9.8	9.5	9.5
	1000	0.9	0.9	0.9	0.9	0.9	4.9	4.7	4.9	4.7	4.7	10.2	10.0	10.1	10.0	10.0
	15	7.0	4.9	2.4	3.1	1.6	14.2	9.9	8.7	6.6	5.0	19.3	14.3	14.4	11.3	9.2
	30	4.6	4.3	2.7	3.1	2.5	11.2	9.4	8.6	7.7	6.8	16.6	14.0	13.9	12.4	11.7
$\gamma_{(2)}$	50	3.3	3.4	2.3	2.6	2.1	8.7	7.5	7.3	6.8	6.5	13.6	12.0	12.0	11.0	10.8
	100	2.7	2.5	2.0	2.1	1.9	8.3	7.4	7.1	6.8	6.7	13.8	12.5	12.7	12.1	12.0
	500	1.3	1.2	1.2	1.2	1.2	5.1	4.8	5.0	4.8	4.7	10.3	10.0	10.2	10.0	10.0
	1000	1.0	0.9	1.0	0.9	0.9	4.8	4.8	4.8	4.8	4.8	9.8	9.6	9.7	9.6	9.6
	15	6.2	4.1	2.3	2.1	0.9	13.0	9.3	8.0	6.0	4.7	18.6	13.4	13.9	10.5	9.1
	30	4.5	4.1	2.5	3.0	2.2	11.4	9.1	8.2	7.6	7.0	16.9	13.7	14.3	12.1	11.6
$\gamma_{(3)}$	50	4.0	3.5	2.6	2.9	2.3	9.8	8.3	7.9	7.2	6.9	15.0	13.3	13.3	12.2	12.0
	100	3.4	3.5	2.6	2.8	2.6	8.7	8.0	7.6	7.3	7.1	13.8	12.9	12.6	12.0	11.9
	500	1.2	1.1	1.1	1.1	1.1	5.2	4.8	5.0	4.8	4.8	10.0	9.6	9.8	9.6	9.6
	1000	1.0	1.0	1.0	1.0	1.0	5.5	5.4	5.5	5.4	5.4	10.6	10.3	10.6	10.3	10.3

	15	6.1	4.0	1.8	2.0	1.2	12.7	8.4	7.6	5.0	4.1	18.7	13.2	13.4	9.7	8.2
	30	4.6	3.4	2.6	2.0	1.5	10.6	8.4	8.3	6.6	6.2	16.8	13.2	13.6	11.2	10.6
$\gamma(4)$	50	3.8	3.8	2.3	2.7	2.1	9.4	8.3	7.6	7.0	6.9	15.4	13.4	13.4	12.2	11.9
	100	2.5	2.6	2.0	2.1	2.0	8.4	7.7	7.1	7.1	6.9	13.8	12.9	12.6	12.2	12.2
	500	1.3	1.3	1.3	1.2	1.2	5.4	5.2	5.2	5.0	5.0	10.4	10.4	10.3	10.2	10.2
	1000	1.2	1.0	1.1	1.0	1.0	5.3	5.2	5.2	5.2	5.2	10.6	10.5	10.5	10.5	10.5
	15	5.9	3.4	1.9	1.7	0.8	12.7	8.1	7.3	5.1	4.0	19.2	12.6	13.7	9.5	8.3
	30	6.0	5.3	3.2	3.7	2.6	12.2	10.7	9.6	9.0	8.3	17.6	15.0	15.0	13.2	12.8
$\gamma(5)$	50	4.1	3.9	2.7	3.0	2.6	9.8	8.5	8.0	7.4	7.2	15.3	13.6	13.3	12.4	12.0
	100	2.4	2.0	1.8	1.6	1.5	7.6	6.5	6.7	6.0	5.8	13.4	11.9	12.4	11.3	11.3
	500	1.4	1.3	1.2	1.2	1.2	5.8	5.7	5.8	5.6	5.6	11.0	10.5	10.7	10.4	10.4
	1000	1.0	1.0	0.9	1.0	1.0	4.9	4.9	4.9	4.9	4.9	9.6	9.4	9.5	9.4	9.4
	15	7.5	6.5	2.6	3.9	1.8	14.8	11.6	8.9	8.1	6.0	20.9	16.2	15.4	12.5	10.7
	30	4.9	5.6	2.6	3.9	2.9	10.8	10.0	8.3	8.3	7.5	17.2	14.5	14.2	12.8	12.0
$\gamma(6)$	50	4.1	5.1	2.8	3.9	3.1	10.0	9.7	8.2	8.5	8.1	15.1	14.6	13.5	13.7	13.4
	100	2.8	3.5	2.0	2.9	2.3	7.7	7.6	6.8	7.1	6.6	13.2	12.7	12.1	12.0	11.9
	500	1.6	1.5	1.5	1.4	1.4	6.0	5.7	5.7	5.6	5.6	10.8	10.3	10.5	10.2	10.2
	1000	1.2	1.1	1.1	1.0	1.0	5.3	5.3	5.3	5.2	5.2	10.4	10.2	10.3	10.2	10.2

Table 7.4. *Null rejection probability estimates ($H_0: \beta_2 = \beta_3 = \beta_4 = 0$), as T increases*

Nominal size:		1%					5%					10%				
$\gamma_{(i)}$	T	χ^2	E-$\hat{\chi}^2$	F	E-$\hat{F}$	CF-$\hat{F}$	χ^2	E-$\hat{\chi}^2$	F	E-$\hat{F}$	CF-$\hat{F}$	χ^2	E-$\hat{\chi}^2$	F	E-$\hat{F}$	CF-$\hat{F}$
	15	28.8	19.1	7.0	7.2	0.6	41.4	28.0	20.4	11.5	2.3	49.9	34.4	29.5	19.5	5.8
	30	16.9	14.9	9.8	10.1	6.2	27.7	22.0	18.5	16.8	12.8	36.3	27.7	26.0	22.4	18.6
$\gamma_{(1)}$	50	11.1	9.6	7.3	7.6	5.9	20.4	15.9	15.1	13.5	11.7	28.1	21.8	22.3	19.0	17.0
	100	3.7	2.5	2.6	2.2	1.9	10.5	7.6	8.5	6.8	6.3	17.7	12.9	14.8	12.1	11.3
	500	1.0	0.8	0.9	0.7	0.7	5.5	4.8	5.1	4.8	4.8	10.9	9.6	10.3	9.5	9.4
	1000	1.1	1.0	1.0	1.0	1.0	4.7	4.5	4.6	4.5	4.5	9.6	9.0	9.4	9.0	9.9
	15	28.4	18.4	7.3	7.5	0.7	42.1	28.3	19.8	11.9	3.0	50.1	34.9	29.8	19.3	7.1
	30	18.7	15.8	10.2	10.4	6.2	29.9	24.3	20.9	18.2	13.5	38.6	30.3	28.5	24.7	20.3
$\gamma_{(2)}$	50	13.7	13.7	9.3	11.3	8.6	23.9	20.2	17.7	17.5	15.3	31.9	26.4	25.3	23.3	21.5
	100	7.8	8.1	5.8	6.8	5.6	15.7	13.9	12.7	12.3	11.2	22.8	19.9	19.4	18.5	17.8
	500	1.7	1.6	1.6	1.5	1.5	6.4	5.7	6.0	5.6	5.6	12.1	10.9	11.5	10.8	10.8
	1000	1.2	1.1	1.2	1.1	1.1	5.2	4.9	5.1	4.9	4.9	10.9	10.3	10.7	10.3	10.2
	15	28.4	18.2	6.6	7.3	1.1	41.3	28.6	20.1	11.4	3.5	50.6	35.2	30.4	19.5	7.7
	30	20.3	16.9	11.0	11.0	7.4	32.2	25.5	21.7	19.6	15.3	40.6	32.2	30.1	25.7	21.9
$\gamma_{(3)}$	50	15.0	14.6	9.5	11.6	9.0	25.1	22.0	18.9	18.7	16.7	32.8	27.9	26.4	24.8	22.8
	100	10.3	10.9	7.9	9.7	8.0	18.4	16.6	14.8	15.0	13.9	25.5	22.8	21.9	20.8	19.8
	500	1.7	1.5	1.6	1.4	1.4	6.4	5.7	6.0	5.7	5.7	11.7	10.5	11.1	10.5	10.5
	1000	1.2	1.2	1.2	1.2	1.2	5.4	5.1	5.3	5.1	5.0	10.5	10.0	10.3	10.0	10.0

	15	28.9	20.5	7.0	8.3	1.7	42.1	29.9	20.0	13.4	5.5	50.7	36.6	29.5	20.5	9.8
	30	20.0	16.7	10.7	10.7	6.4	30.8	24.8	20.8	18.9	14.4	39.2	31.2	28.5	25.5	21.4
$\gamma(4)$	50	14.7	15.0	9.4	12.2	9.2	24.8	21.6	19.1	19.0	16.8	32.6	28.1	25.9	24.9	22.8
	100	9.6	10.4	7.2	9.1	7.7	16.8	15.9	14.1	14.6	13.7	23.7	21.6	20.1	19.7	18.9
	500	2.2	2.3	2.0	2.1	2.0	7.0	6.7	6.6	6.6	6.5	11.7	11.0	11.3	10.8	10.8
	1000	1.3	1.3	1.2	1.2	1.2	5.6	5.2	5.4	5.2	5.1	11.2	10.6	10.8	10.4	10.4
	15	26.9	19.6	6.8	7.6	0.8	40.6	28.4	19.0	12.2	3.4	49.2	34.3	28.1	19.3	7.9
	20	24.7	20.6	10.2	10.8	4.3	37.4	29.6	22.1	19.2	11.3	45.9	35.9	30.9	26.0	17.5
	30	21.4	19.3	11.4	12.7	8.5	33.6	28.2	22.5	21.7	17.4	41.9	34.6	31.4	28.4	24.9
$\gamma(5)$	50	14.5	13.7	8.9	10.6	8.1	24.5	21.3	17.9	17.8	15.8	32.1	27.2	25.1	23.6	22.0
	100	8.6	9.1	6.3	8.1	6.7	16.4	15.3	13.6	13.9	12.8	23.4	20.9	20.4	19.5	18.6
	500	2.4	2.3	2.0	2.1	2.0	6.8	6.5	6.5	6.2	6.2	12.2	11.5	11.8	11.4	11.3
	1000	1.1	0.9	1.0	0.9	0.8	5.2	4.9	4.9	4.9	4.9	10.7	10.2	10.4	10.0	10.0
	15	28.6	20.6	6.8	8.0	1.3	41.7	30.7	19.6	13.3	5.3	50.0	37.0	29.1	20.5	10.7
	30	20.2	19.9	10.9	13.5	8.3	31.4	27.9	20.7	21.2	16.9	40.3	33.9	28.7	27.5	23.6
$\gamma(6)$	50	17.0	19.1	11.2	15.7	12.0	27.2	26.4	20.7	22.9	20.7	34.8	32.4	28.5	28.7	26.7
	100	9.4	10.1	7.1	8.6	7.2	17.0	15.7	13.3	13.8	12.7	23.9	21.5	20.1	19.7	18.7
	500	2.6	2.7	2.4	2.4	2.3	7.6	7.1	7.0	6.9	6.8	12.9	12.1	12.4	11.9	11.9
	1000	1.3	1.3	1.2	1.3	1.2	6.2	6.0	6.1	6.0	5.9	10.8	10.3	10.6	10.2	10.2

where Y denotes output per enterprise (i). The effective labour is measured as a function of the number of workers employed (W) and the training (T) per worker, measured by the number of training days per worker in year 1999, that is

$$L = W(1 + \lambda T), \text{ with } \lambda > 0. \tag{60}$$

Substituting (60) into (59), taking logarithms and, then, differences, leads to the following regression model:

$$\Delta\left(\log \frac{Y_i}{W_i}\right) = c + \beta\Delta(\log K_i) + \delta\Delta \log W_i + kT_i + u_i$$

$$i = 1, 2, \ldots, \quad N = 11 \tag{61}$$

where $\delta = \gamma - 1$ and $k = \gamma\lambda$, $\Delta(\cdot)$ stands for the differences of data between the years 2001 and 1999, and T_i is measured in year 1999. The above regression model is often used in practice to estimate the relationship between productivity per worker (Y_i/W_i) and the input variables in (59) (see Bartel, 1994).

In Table 7.5(a) we report GLS estimates of the parameters of regression model (61) corrected for heteroscedasticity using Amemiya's (1977) A method. Our estimates are based on measures of Y_i by the total amount of sales per firm and of K_i by the value of the fixed assets. In addition to the GLS estimates and their related standard t and F-statistics, the table reports the estimates of the Cornish–Fisher size-corrected statistics CF-$\hat{t}$ and CF-$\hat{F}$, calculated following the steps described in section 3.[2] As expected by the results of our simulation study, the estimates of the CF corrected statistics are smaller than the uncorrected ones, thus implying smaller rejection probabilities.

The estimates of both the standard and the Cornish–Fisher size corrected t-statistic clearly indicate that there is no positive relationship between labour productivity and in-company training for the Greek SMEs. The only variable which seems to explain labour productivity is the total number of workers. This can be confirmed by both the values of the CF-$\hat{t}$ and CF-$\hat{F}$ test statistics. This variable is found to have a negative impact on labour productivity which may be attributed to the unproductive use of labour of the Greek SMEs. Note that the negative value of the CF-$\hat{F}$ statistic should not be interpreted as evidence of insignificance of model (61). According to our formula (36), for CF-$\hat{F}$, this can be attributed to the fact that $v < \tau^2(q_1 + q_2 v)v$ which is the result of the very small number of degrees of freedom ($11 - 4 = 7$) relative to the

Table 7.5. *GLS estimates and CF test statistics*

(a)

Parameters	Estimates	St. errors	t	CF-$\hat{t}$
c	0.14132	0.04264	3.31416	2.37171
β	0.11301	0.13025	0.86761	0.74098
δ	−1.82644	0.22414	−8.14851	−5.06915
k	0.00299	0.04449	0.06729	0.05105
R^2	0.9859			
$\overline{R}^2$	0.9798			
F	161.5481			
CF-$\hat{F}$	−3242.3236			

(b)

Parameters	Estimates	St. errors	t	CF-$\hat{t}$
c	0.14150	0.03305	4.28093	0.56012
δ	−1.92001	0.32419	−5.95101	−5.43848
R^2	0.8150			
$\overline{R}^2$	0.78021			
F	38.18214			
CF-$\hat{F}$	109.84070			

very high value of the F-statistic (large value of v) determining the term $\tau^2(q_1 + q_2 v)v$. In general, a negative CF-$\hat{F}$ can only be encountered if the standard F-statistic assumes very large positive values. This happens when the null hypothesis of model insignificance is rejected with very high probability by the uncorrected (standard) F-test. Thus, a negative value of CF-$\hat{F}$ should be interpreted as a clear cut evidence that the sample size is too small relative to the observed correlation (very high $\overline{R}^2$) between the dependent and any subset of the explanatory variables. Under these circumstances, the asymptotic methods and their derived size corrected tests are not applicable. To confirm this, in Table 7.5(b) we report estimates for model (61) excluding the insignificant regressors. This results in an increase of the degrees of freedom. The results of this table reveal that increasing the degrees of freedom renders positive the value of the CF-$\hat{F}$ statistic, which also rejects the hypothesis that model (61) is insignificant. The new estimates of the CF-$\hat{t}$ statistics also support that the number of employees in Greek SMEs have a significant negative effect on labour productivity.

6 Conclusions

In this chapter, we suggest Cornish–Fisher size corrected t and F-statistics to draw inferences in small samples on the coefficients of the normal linear regression model with heteroscedastic errors. Since the t and F-tests are adjusted for the degrees of freedom, the size corrected statistics that we introduce are found to have better finite sample size performance than asymptotic testing procedures (standard or Edgeworth corrected) which do not adjust for the degrees of freedom. This is confirmed through a simulation study. The test statistics that we propose follow the t and F-distributions up to an approximation error of order $O(\tau^3)$. This approximation is of the same order of magnitude as that of the standard normal and Wald test statistics suggested by Rothenberg (1984b, 1988), based on Edgeworth expansions of the normal and chi-square distributions. Monte Carlo experiments reveal that our tests can lead to substantial size improvements for samples up to 100 observations. The results of the paper highlight the important role that Cornish–Fisher corrections and adjustments for the degrees of freedom can play in finite-sample testing procedures. As an empirical illustration, we employ our tests to examine whether there is a positive relationship between in-company training and productivity for 11 Greek small–medium-sized enterprises. Our evidence provides no support of such a relationship.

Notes

1. The closed form formulae of these estimators are as follows:

$$\hat{\gamma}_{GQ} = \left[\sum_{t=1}^{T} z_t z_t'\right]^{-1} \sum_{t=1}^{T} z_t (y_t - x_t'\tilde{\beta})^2$$

where $\tilde{\beta}$ is the ordinary least squares (OLS) estimator of β,

$$\hat{\gamma}_A = \left[\sum_{t=1}^{T} (z_t'\hat{\gamma}_{GQ})^{-2} z_t z_t'\right]^{-1} \sum_{t=1}^{T} (z_t'\hat{\gamma}_{GQ})^{-2} z_t (y_t - x_t'\tilde{\beta})^2, \text{ and}$$

$$\hat{\gamma}_{IA} = \left[\sum_{t=1}^{T} (z_t'\hat{\gamma}_{i-1})^{-2} z_t z_t'\right]^{-1} \sum_{t=1}^{T} (z_t'\hat{\gamma}_{i-1})^{-2} z_t (y_t - x_t'\tilde{\beta}_{i-1})^2$$

where i denotes the number of iteration, $\hat{\gamma}_{i-1}$ and $\widetilde{\beta}_{i-1}$ $(i = 2, 3, 4, \ldots)$ denote the estimator of γ and the feasible GLS estimator of β taken from the previous iteration, using as $\hat{\gamma}_1 = \hat{\gamma}_A$. The ML estimator of γ can be obtained by maximizing the log-likelihood function:

$$L(\beta, \gamma) = -\frac{1}{2}\sum_{t=1}^{T} \log(z_t'\gamma) - \frac{1}{2}\sum_{t=1}^{T}(y_t - x_t'\beta)^2/(z_t'\gamma).$$

2. A statistical package calculating the Cornish–Fisher corrected test statistics are available from the authors upon request.

Appendix

In this Appendix we provide brief proofs of the main results of the chapter. Detailed proofs is available upon request.

In our proofs, we adopt the following definition of the stochastic order of magnitude $\omega(\cdot)$. For any stochastic quantity (scalar, vector, or matrix) Y_τ, we write $Y_\tau = \omega(\tau^i)$ if for every $n > 0$ there exists an $\epsilon > 0$, such that

$$\Pr\left\{\left|Y_\tau/\tau^i\right| > (-\ln\tau)^\epsilon\right\} = o(\tau^n) \text{ as } \tau \to 0 \tag{A.1}$$

where $|\cdot|$ is the Euclidean norm. The use of this order is motivated by the fact that, if two stochastic quantities differ by an order of $\omega(\tau^i)$, then under general conditions the distribution function of the one provides an asymptotic approximation to the distribution function of the other, with an error of order $O(\tau^i)$. Moreover, the orders $\omega(\cdot)$ and $O(\cdot)$ have similar operational properties. For details see Magdalinos (1986).

Proof of Lemma 1 Result (i) of the lemma can be proved along the same lines as Rothenberg (1988). That is, to obtain the constants (13) we expand the corresponding constants given by Rothenberg and we retain the first term in the expansion. The second result of the lemma follows from result (i) and the following asymptotic approximations (see Fisher, 1925):

$$I_{T-n}(x) = I(x) - (\tau^2/4)(1 + x^2)xi(x) + O(\tau^4) \tag{A.2}$$

$$i_{T-n}(x) = i(x) + O(\tau^2).$$

Proof of Lemma 2 To prove this lemma we follow similar steps with those in the proof of Lemma 1. Result (i) of the lemma can be proved along the same lines as Rothenberg (1984b). In order to obtain the constants (27) we expand the corresponding constants given by Rothenberg and we retain the first term in the expansion. To prove result (ii), we rely on the following asymptotic approximations:

$$F^r_{T-n}(x) = F_r(rx) + (\tau^2/2)(r - 2 - rx)rxf_r(rx) + O(\tau^4) \tag{A.3}$$

$$f^r_{T-n}(x) = rf_r(rx) + O(\tau^2).$$

Note that both approximations (see equations 17 and 31) given by Lemmas 1 and 2 are locally exact. This can be easily seen as follows. As $\delta \to 0$, γ becomes a fixed, known vector which implies that

$$\Lambda = 0, \quad \lambda = \mu = 0, \quad \lambda_0 = 2, \quad \mu_0 = 0 \tag{A.4}$$

$$h_1 = -r(r-2)/2 \quad h_2 = r(r+2)/2$$

and hence $p_1 = p_2 = q_1 = q_2 = 0$.

Proof of Theorem 1 To prove the theorem, first notice that, under the null hypothesis (10), the t-statistic, given by (11), admits a stochastic expansion of the form

$$t = t_0 + \tau t_1 + \tau^2 t_2 + \omega(\tau^3) \tag{A.5}$$

where the first term in the expansion is given by

$$t_0 = e'b(e'Ge)^{1/2}, \quad b = GX'\Omega u/\sqrt{T}.$$

The result given by equation (A.5) implies that the Cornish–Fisher corrected test statistic, $\hat{t}$, admits a stochastic expansion of the form

$$\hat{t} = t_0 + \tau t_1 + \tau^2(t_2 - t_3) + \omega(\tau^3) \tag{A.6}$$

where $t_3 = (p_1 + p_2 t_0^2)t_0/2$.

Let s be an imaginary number, and $\psi(s)$ and $\phi(s)$ denote the characteristic functions of the t-statistic and of a standard normal variable, respectively. Using (A.6) and

$$E[\exp(st_0)t_0] = s\phi(s), \quad E[\exp(st_0)t_0^3] = (3s + s^3)\phi(s)$$

we can show that the characteristic function of the $\hat{t}$-statistic, denoted as $\hat{\psi}(s)$, can be approximated as:

$$\hat{\psi}(s) = \psi(s) - \tau^2 s\, E[\exp(st_0)t_3] + O(\tau^3)$$

$$= \psi(s) - \frac{\tau^2}{2} s\, [p_1 s + p_2(3s + s^3)]\phi(s) + O(\tau^3).$$

Dividing $\hat{\psi}(s)$ by $-s$, applying the inverse Fourier transform and using the second result of Lemma 1, we can show that:

$$\Pr\left\{\hat{t} \le x\right\} = \Pr\{t \le x\} + \frac{\tau^2}{2}(p_1 + p_2 x^2)x i_{T-n}(x) + O(\tau^3)$$

$$= I_{T-n}(x) - \frac{\tau^2}{2}(p_1 + p_2 x^2)x i_{T-n}(x)$$

$$+ \frac{\tau^2}{2}(p_1 + p_2 x^2)x i_{T-n}(x) + O(\tau^3)$$

$$= I_{T-n}(x) + O(\tau^3). \tag{A.7}$$

When $\delta \to 0$, then $p_1 = p_2 = 0$, and thus equation (20) implies that $\hat{t} = t$. That is, the $\hat{t}$-statistic is distributed as a t variable with $T - n$ degrees of freedom.

Proof of Theorem 2 To prove the theorem, first notice that, under the null hypothesis (24), the v-statistic, given by (25), admits a stochastic expansion of the form

$$v = v_0 + \tau v_1 + \tau^2 v_2 + \omega(\tau^3) \tag{A.8}$$

where the first term in the expansion is $v_0 = b'Qb/r$, $\quad b = GX'\Omega u/\sqrt{T}$.
The result given by equation (A.8) implies that the Cornish–Fisher corrected statistic (36) admits a stochastic expansion of the form

$$\hat{v} = v_0 + \tau v_1 + \tau^2(v_2 - v_3) + \omega(\tau^3) \tag{A.9}$$

where $v_3 = (q_1 + q_2 v_0)v_0$.

Let s be an imaginary number, and $\psi(s)$ and $\phi_r(s)$ now denote the characteristic functions of the F-statistic, given by (25), and of a chi-square distributed variable with r degrees of freedom, respectively. Using (A.9) and

$$E[\exp(sv_0)v_0] = \phi_{r+2}(s/r), \quad E[\exp(sv_0)v_0^2] = \frac{r+2}{r}\phi_{r+4}(s/r)$$

we can show that the characteristic function of the Cornish–Fisher corrected $\hat{F}$-statistic, denoted as $\hat{\psi}(s)$, can be approximated as

$$\hat{\psi}(s) = \psi(s) - \tau^2 s\, E[\exp(sv_0)v_3] + O(\tau^3)$$

$$= \psi(s) - \tau^2 s\left[q_1\phi_{r+2}(s/r) + q_2\frac{r+2}{r}\phi_{r+4}(s/r)\right] + O(\tau^3). \tag{A.10}$$

For the chi-square density $f_r(x)$, the following results can be shown:

$$(rx)f_r(rx) = rf_{r+2}(rx), \quad (rx)^2 f_r(rx) = r(r+2)f_{r+4}(rx). \tag{A.11}$$

Dividing (A.10) by $-s$, applying the inverse Fourier transform and using the second result of Lemma 2, and the results of equations (A.3b) and (A.11), we can show that the following approximations hold:

$$\begin{aligned}
\Pr\{\hat{v} \le x\} &= \Pr\{v \le x\} + \tau^2\left[(q_1 rf_{r+2}(rx) + q_2\frac{r+2}{r}rf_{r+4}(rx)\right] + O(\tau^3) \\
&= \Pr\{v \le x\} + \tau^2[(q_1 rxf_r(rx) + q_2 rx^2 f_r(rx)] + O(\tau^3) \\
&= \Pr\{v \le x\} + \tau^2(q_1 + q_2 x)rxf_r(rx) + O(\tau^3) \\
&= F^r_{T-n}(x) - \tau^2(q_1 + q_2 x)xf^r_{T-n}(x) \\
&\quad + \tau^2(q_1 + q_2 x)xf^r_{T-n}(x) + O(\tau^3) \\
&= F^r_{T-n}(x) + O(\tau^3)
\end{aligned} \tag{A.12}$$

which proves Theorem 2. Following similar steps with those in the proof of Theorem 1, we can show that the $\hat{v}$-statistic is locally exact.

Proof of Proposition 1 To derive the formulas of the proposition, first notice that we can write the columns and elements of matrix A in terms of product matrices of z_{ti} and x_t as

$$A_i = -\sum_{t=1}^{T} \sigma_t^{-4} z_{ti} x_t x_t' / T, \quad A_{ij} = 2A_{ij}^*, \quad \text{with} \quad A_{ij}^* = \sum_{t=1}^{T} \sigma_t^{-6} z_{ti} z_{tj} x_t x_t' / T.$$

Next, notice that matrix P is a semidefinite matrix with r positive eigenvalues. Thus, it can be decomposed as

$$P = WL_* W' = \sum_{i=1}^{r} \lambda_i w_i w_i' = \sum_{i=1}^{r} h_i h_i', \quad h_i = \lambda_i^{1/2} w_i$$

where λ_i $(i = 1, \ldots, r)$ are the r positive eigenvalues of P, L_* is a diagonal matrix consisting of the eigenvalues λ_i and W is a matrix with columns the standardized eigenvectors of P. In matrix notation, the above decomposition can be written as

$$P = (WL_*^{1/2})(W\lambda_r^{1/2})' = \mathcal{Y}\mathcal{Y}', \quad \mathcal{Y} = W\lambda_r^{1/2}$$

where $\mathcal{Y}$ is a $(n \times r)$ matrix with columns the vectors h_i. Based on the above decomposition, it can be easily shown that

$$x_t' P x_s = x_t' \mathcal{Y}\mathcal{Y}' x_s = \sum_{i=1}^{r} x_t{}' h_i h_i' x_s. \tag{A.13}$$

Using (A.13) and the definitions given by equation (27), we can show that the jth element of the vector c can be calculated as

$$c_j = trA_j P = -\sum_{t=1}^{T} \sigma_t^{-4} z_{tj} x_t' P x_t / T$$

$$= -\sum_{i=1}^{r} \sum_{t=1}^{T} \sigma_t^{-6} (h_i' x_t)^2 z_{tj} z_t' \gamma / T$$

which gives the first formula of (45), for c. The remaining formulas can be derived following similar steps with those above, and thus are omitted.

Proof of Proposition 2 To derive the formulas given by the proposition, define the $(T \times 1)$ vectors $\bar{u}$, ϵ and $\bar{\epsilon}$, with elements:

$$\bar{u}_t = u_t^2 - \sigma_t^2$$

$$\epsilon_t = 2u_t e_t - \tau e_t^2, \quad e_t = x_t' B X' u / \sqrt{T}$$

$$\bar{\epsilon}_t = 2u_t \bar{e}_t - \tau \bar{e}_t^2, \quad \bar{e}_t = x_t' G X' \Omega u / \sqrt{T}.$$

Expanding the Goldfeld–Quandt estimator of γ as a Taylor series and collecting terms of the same order of magnitude, we can show that the sampling error of $\hat{\gamma}_{GQ}$ is given as:

$$\delta_*^{GQ} = \sqrt{T}(\hat{\gamma}_{GQ} - \gamma) = d_{*1}^{GQ} - \tau d_{*2}^{GQ}, \text{ with} \tag{A.14}$$

$$d_{*1}^{GQ} = \overline{B}Z'\overline{u}/\sqrt{T}, \quad d_{*2}^{GQ} = \overline{B}Z'\epsilon/\sqrt{T}.$$

Expanding Amemiya's estimator of γ as a Taylor series and collecting terms of the same order of magnitude, we can show that the sampling error of $\hat{\gamma}_A$ can be written as:

$$\delta_*^{A} = \sqrt{T}(\hat{\gamma}_A - \gamma) = d_{*1}^{A} - \tau d_{*2}^{A} + \omega(\tau^2), \text{ with} \tag{A.15}$$

$$d_{*1}^{A} = \overline{G}(Z'\Omega^2\overline{u}/\sqrt{T}),$$

$$d_{*2}^{A} = \overline{G}(Z'\Omega^2\epsilon/\sqrt{T}) - 2\sum_{i=1}^{k}\overline{G}(Z'\Omega\Omega_i\overline{u}/\sqrt{T})d_{1i}^{GQ}$$

$$+ 2\sum_{i=1}^{k}\overline{GA_i G}(Z'\Omega^2\overline{u}/\sqrt{T})d_{1i}^{GQ}$$

and d_{1i}^{GQ} is the ith element of the vector d_{*1}^{GQ}. Following similar steps, we can show that the sampling error of Amemiya's iterative estimator of γ can be written as:

$$\delta_*^{IA} = \sqrt{T}(\hat{\gamma}_{IA} - \gamma) = d_{*1}^{A} - \tau d_{*2}^{IA} + \omega(\tau^2) \tag{A.16}$$

$$d_{*1}^{A} = \overline{G}(Z'\Omega^2\overline{u}/\sqrt{T})$$

$$d_{*2}^{IA} = \overline{G}(Z'\Omega^2\overline{\epsilon}/\sqrt{T}) - 2\sum_{i=1}^{k}\overline{G}(Z'\Omega\Omega_i\overline{u}/\sqrt{T})d_{1i}^{A}$$

$$+ 2\sum_{i=1}^{k}\overline{GA_i G}(Z'\Omega^2\overline{u}/\sqrt{T})d_{1i}^{A}$$

and d_{1i}^{A} is the ith element of vector d_{*1}^{A}. As the number of iterations goes to infinity, the IA estimator of γ converges to the ML estimator, and thus the sampling error of the ML estimator admits the same stochastic expansion as the IA estimator, given by (A.16).

Taking expectations of (A.14) and (A.15), it can be easily shown that

$$E(d_{*1}^{GQ}) = E(d_{*1}^{A}) = 0, \quad E(d_{*2}^{GQ}) = \overline{B}\xi, \quad E(d_{*2}^{IA}) = \overline{G}\xi_2,$$

$$E(d_{*2}^{A}) = \overline{G}\xi_1 + 4\sum_{i=1}^{k}\overline{G}[\overline{A}_i\overline{g}_i - (Z'\Omega_i\Omega^{-1}Z/T)\overline{b}_i] \tag{A.17}$$

$$E(d_{*1}^{GQ}d_{*1}^{GQ\prime}) = 2\overline{B\Gamma B}, \quad E(d_{*1}^{A}d_{*1}^{A\prime}) = 2\overline{G},$$

where $\overline{g}_i$ is the ith column of matrix $\overline{G}$, $\overline{b}_i$ is the ith column of matrix $\overline{B}$, and $\overline{A}_i = (Z'\Omega\Omega_i Z/T)$.

Using the results of equation (A.17), we can derive the formulas (48), (49) and (50) for Λ and μ, given by the proposition. To derive the remaining formulas for λ_0, λ and μ_0, we will base on the GLS estimator of $\hat{\sigma}$, given by equation (3). This can be written as

$$\hat{\sigma}^2 = [u'\widehat{\Omega}u - b'(X'\widehat{\Omega}X/T)b + \omega(\tau)]/(T-n) \tag{A.18}$$

where $b = GX'\Omega u/\sqrt{T} = \sqrt{T}(\hat{\beta}-\beta) + \omega(\tau)$, and $\hat{\beta}$ is the feasible GLS estimator of β.

Define the scalars

$$\theta_0 = \sqrt{T}(u'\Omega u/T - 1) \quad \text{and} \quad \theta_i = \sqrt{T}(u'\Omega_i u/T + a_i)$$

where

$$a_i = -E(u'\Omega_i u/T) = \sum_{t=1}^{T} \sigma_t^{-2} z_{ti}/T$$

and the $(k \times 1)$ vectors θ and a, with elements θ_i and a_i respectively. Expanding (A.18) as a Taylor series and collecting terms of the same order of magnitude, we can show that, for any estimator of γ whose sampling error admits a stochastic expansion of the forms (A.14)–(A.16), the estimator of $\hat{\sigma}$ admits the following expansion

$$\delta_0 = \sqrt{T}(\hat{\sigma}^2 - 1) = \sigma_0 + \tau\sigma_1 + \omega(\tau^2)$$

where

$$\sigma_0 = \theta_0 - a'd_{*1}, \quad \sigma_1 = \theta' d_{*1} + d'_{*1}\overline{A}d_{*1} + a'd_{*2} - b'Ab + n.$$

Results (A.14)–(A.16) imply that for all the estimators of γ considered, we can calculate the following expectations as

$$E(\theta_0 d_{*1}) = 2\gamma, \quad E(\theta' d_{*1}) = -2k. \tag{A.19}$$

Using the results of equation (A.19), we can show:

$$\lambda_0 = 2 - 4a'\gamma + a'\Lambda a$$

$$\lambda = 2\gamma - \Lambda a$$

$$\mu_0 = tr\overline{A}\Lambda - 2k - a'\mu$$

Substituting $a = \overline{A}\gamma$ and the values of Λ and μ into the different estimators of γ gives the formulas of the proposition for λ_0, λ and μ.

8 Non-Parametric Specification Testing of Non-Nested Econometric Models

*Qi Li and Thanasis Stengos**

1 Introduction

This chapter proposes a testing procedure for discriminating between alternative sets of regressors in a non-parametric context. The literature on non-parametric testing of regression models is quite extensive. Non-parametric methods have been used for specification testing of a parametric model against a non-parametric alternative, see Eubank and Spiegelman (1990), Hall and Hart (1990), Hong and White (1991), Wooldridge (1992), Härdle and Mammen (1993), Whang and Andrews (1993), Horowitz and Härdle (1994), de Jong and Bierens (1994), Fan and Li (1996) and Delgado and Stengos (1994), to mention only a few.

Discriminating between non-nested sets of regressors is a well-motivated problem. Existing tests assume a particular functional form of the regression function and are consistent in the direction of precisely parameterized alternatives, see Cox (1961, 1962), Pesaran (1974), Davidson and MacKinnon (1981) and Fisher and McAleer (1981), also see MacKinnon (1992) for a survey. Recently Delgado and Stengos (1994) have proposed an extension of the *J*-test of Davidson and MacKinnon that is consistent against non-parametric alternatives. The above test still assumes a particular parametric regression curve under the null hypothesis. Hence, it is still not robust to functional misspecification. In this chapter, we propose to test a non-parametric regression model in the direction of a non-parametric non-nested alternative. As in Delgado and Stengos (1994), our work is an extension of the *J*-test to the non-parametric environment. The proposed test relies on the use of double kernel estimation and is, after being multiplied by the $\sqrt{n}$ factor, normally distributed. Double kernel estimation was used in

* The second author is grateful for financial support from the Social Sciences and Humanities Research Council of Canada.

the estimation of a semiparametric regression model by by Stengos and Yan (2001).

In the next section we present a consistent non-parametric test for non-nested models; the proofs of the main results are collected in Appendix A. Section 3 presents results of some Monte Carlo simulations.

2 The Test Statistic and Its Asymptotic Distribution

Our data consist of independent observations $\{(x_i, z_i, y_i), i = 1, ..., n\}$ identically distributed as the $R^p \times R^q \times R$-valued multivariate random variable (x, z, y). The researcher faces the problem of choosing between the alternative sets of explanatory variables x and z which are non-nested, in the sense that none of the σ-algebras corresponding to x and z are contained in the other. Our selection rule is based on a non-parametric model specification procedure. Under the null hypothesis H_0: $E[y|x, z] = m(x)$, we have

$$y_i = m(x_i) + u_i, \qquad i = 1, ..., n \tag{1}$$

where $E(u_i|x_i, z_i) = 0$. Under the alternative hypothesis H_a: $E[y|x, z] = m_a(z)$, we have

$$y_i = m_a(z_i) + \epsilon_i, \qquad i = 1, ..., n \tag{2}$$

where $E(\epsilon_i|x_i, z_i) = 0$. Proceeding in the way suggested by Davidson and MacKinnon (1981), we nest the null and the alternative hypothesis in the artificial nested regression model,

$$y_i = (1 - \alpha)m(x_i) + \alpha\, m_a(z_i) + \eta_i$$

where α is the nesting parameter and $\eta_i = (1 - \alpha)u_i + \alpha\epsilon_i$ is the composite error. The null hypothesis is reformulated as H_0: $\alpha = 0$, and the alternative as H_a: $\alpha = 1$.

The analog of the $\mathcal{J}$-regression of Davidson and MacKinnon (1981) in the case of the two non-parametric regression functions examined here is given by

$$y_i = \theta(x_i) + \alpha\, \hat{m}_a(z_i) + \eta_i^* \tag{3}$$

where $m_a(z)$ is replaced by its non-parametric kernel estimator $\hat{m}_a(z_i) = \widehat{E}(y_i|x_i)$, $\theta(x_i) = (1 - \alpha)m(x_i)$ and $\eta_i^* = \eta_i + \alpha(m_a(z_i) - \hat{m}_a(z_i))$ is the composite error.

Following Robinson's (1988) semi-parametric estimation approach, α in (3) could be estimated by

$$\hat{\alpha} = \frac{\sum_i (\hat{m}_a(z_i) - \widehat{E}(\hat{m}_a(z_i)|x_i))(y_i - \widehat{E}(y_i|x_i))}{\sum_i (\hat{m}_a(z_i) - \widehat{E}(\hat{m}_a(z_i)|x_i))^2}$$

where $\widehat{E}(\cdot|x)$ is a nonparametric estimate of $E(\cdot|x)$. Our proposed test statistic is based on the numerator of $\hat{\alpha}$, given by:

$$T_n = \frac{1}{n}\sum_i (\hat{m}_a(z_i) - \widehat{E}(\hat{m}_a(z_i)|x_i))(y_i - \widehat{E}(y_i|x_i)).$$

A direct application of Robinson's (1988) method in (3) requires two trimming parameters (in addition to the two smoothing parameters) to overcome the random denominator problem that arises in kernel estimation. Moreover, the technical difficulties of using a trimming method in the context of double kernel estimation prove difficult to overcome. Therefore, we choose to estimate a density-weighted relationship to avoid the random denominator problem, see Powell *et al.* (1989). A density-weighted approach leads to a wider range of choices of smoothing parameters than the trimming method and the regularity conditions needed are weaker. We estimate $E(y_i|x_i)f(x_i)$ by

$$\hat{y}_i = \frac{1}{(n-1)a^p}\sum_{j\neq i} y_j K_{ij} \tag{4}$$

and $f(x_i)$, the probability density function (p.d.f) of x_i, by $\hat{f}(x_i) = \frac{1}{(n-1)a^p}\sum_{j\neq i} K_{ij}$, where $K_{ij} = K\left(\frac{x_i - x_j}{a}\right)$ is the kernel function and a is the smoothing parameter. We use a product kernel, $K(u) = \prod_{l=1}^{p} k(u_l)$; u_l is the lth component of u.

We estimate $m_a(z_i)f_a(z_i) = E(y_i|z_i)f_a(z_i)$ by

$$\tilde{y}_i = \frac{1}{(n-1)b^q}\sum_i y_j \overline{K}_{ij} \tag{5}$$

and $f_a(z_i)$ is estimated by $\tilde{f}_a(z_i) = \frac{1}{(n-1)b^q}\sum_{j\neq i} \overline{K}_{ij}$, where $\overline{K}_{ij} = \overline{K}\left(\frac{z_i - z_j}{b}\right)$ is the kernel function associated with z and b is the corresponding smoothing parameter ($\overline{K}(\cdot)$ is a product kernel). We also need to estimate $E\{m_a(z_i)f_a(z_i)|x_i\}f(x_i) = E\{[E(y_i|z_i)f_a(z_i)]|x\}f(x)$. Its kernel estimate is given by:

$$\hat{\tilde{y}}_i = \frac{1}{(n-1)a^p}\sum_{j\neq i}\tilde{y}_j K_{ij} \equiv \frac{1}{(n-1)a^p}\sum_{j\neq i}\left[\frac{1}{(n-1)b^q}\sum_{l\neq j} y_l \bar{K}_{lj}\right]K_{ij}. \quad (6)$$

Our density-weighted test statistic will be based on

$$I_n = \frac{1}{n}\sum_i (\tilde{y}_i\hat{f}_i - \hat{\tilde{y}}_i)(y_i\hat{f}_i - \hat{y}_i) \quad (7)$$

which is, roughly speaking, a sample analogue of $I = E\{[\gamma(z) - E(\gamma(z)|x)]f(x)[y - E(y|x)]f(x)\}$, where $\gamma(z) = E(y|z)f_a(z)$.

To derive the asymptotic distribution of I_n, the following definitions and assumptions will be used. Let $\mathcal{G}_l^\alpha$ denote the class of functions such that if $g \in \mathcal{G}_l^\alpha$ ($\alpha > 0$ and $l \geq 1$ is an integer), then g is l times differentiable, g and its derivatives (up to order l) are all bounded by some function that has αth order finite moments. Also $\mathcal{K}_l$, $l \geq 1$, denote the class of even functions $k : R \to R$ satisfying $\int k(u)u^m du = \delta_{0m}$ for $m = 0, 1, \ldots, l-1$ and $k(u) = O((1 + |u|^{l+1+\delta})^{-1})$, some $\delta > 0$. Denote $g(z) = E(y|z)$, $\gamma(z) = g(z)f_a(z)$ and $\xi = E(\gamma(z)|x)$.

Assumption A1 (y_i, x_i, z_i) are independently distributed as (y, x, z), x admits a pdf $f(x) \in \mathcal{G}_\nu^\infty$, also $m(x) \in \mathcal{G}_\nu^4$ and $\xi(x) \in \mathcal{G}_\nu^4$, where $\nu \geq 2$ is a positive integer. $\sigma^2(x)f(x)$ is uniformly bounded, where $\sigma^2(x) = E(u^2|x)$. Moreover z admits a pdf $f_a(z) \in \mathcal{G}_\mu^\infty$, $g(z) \in \mathcal{G}_\mu^4$, $m_a(z) \in \mathcal{G}_1^4$ and $E(m_a(z)|x) \in \mathcal{G}_1^4$, where $\mu \geq 2$ is a positive integer.

Assumption A2 $k \in \mathcal{K}_\nu$. As $n \to \infty$, $na^{2p} \to \infty$, $na^{4\nu} \to 0$; $\bar{k} \in \mathcal{K}_\mu$. As $n \to \infty$, $nb^{2q} \to \infty$ and $nb^{4\mu} \to 0$.

Assumption **A1** presents some smoothness and moments conditions. **A2** is similar to the conditions used by Robinson (1988) or Fan, Li and Stengos (1995). It requires a higher-order kernel to be used for $k(\bar{k})$ if $p \geq 4$ $(q \geq 4)$.

The following theorems justify I_n as an asymptotic test. The proofs are presented in the Appendix.

Theorem 2.1 Under assumptions **A1** and **A2**, if H_0 is true, then as $n \to \infty$, $\mathcal{J}_n \xrightarrow{d} N(0,1)$, where $\mathcal{J}_n = \sqrt{n}I_n/\sqrt{\hat{\sigma}_0^2}$, $\hat{\sigma}_0^2 = \frac{1}{n}\sum(\tilde{y}_i\hat{f}_i - \hat{\tilde{y}}_i)^2(y_i\hat{f}_i - \hat{y}_i)^2$ is a consistent estimator for $\sigma_0^2 = E\{[g(z_1) - E(g(z_1)|x_1)]^2 f^2(x_1)u_1^2 f^2(x_1)]$, where $g(z_1) = E(y_1|z_1)$.

Theorem 2.2 Under assumptions **A1** and **A2**, if H_a is true, then as $n \to \infty$, $Prob[|\mathcal{J}_n| > c] \to 1$ for any positive constant c.

3 Monte Carlo Results

In this section we investigate the small sample performance of the test statistic $\mathcal{J}_n$ in the context of some Monte Carlo experiments. We take the null model and the alternative model as given by H_0: $y_i = \beta_0 + (\beta_1 x_{1i} + \beta x_{2i})^2 + u_{0i}$ and H_a: $y_i = \gamma_0 + (\gamma_1 z_{1i} + \gamma_2 z_{2i})^2 + u_{1i}$ respectively. The parameters β_0, β_1, β_2, γ_0, γ_1, γ_2 are all set to unity. The x's and u's are generated as independent normal variates $N(0, 1)$. We generate the z's as $z_{li} = \rho x_{li} + v_{li}$ $(l = 1, 2)$, where v_{li} is distributed independently as $N(0, 1)$. By varying ρ we control the correlation coefficients between z_i's and x_i's. Similar Monte Carlo designs have been considered by Davidson and MacKinnon (1982), Godfrey and Pesaran (1983) and Delgado and Stengos (1994).

The sample size was chosen as $n = 50, 100, 200$ and the number of replications is 2000. We used a second-order normal kernel and we set the bandwidth as $a_l = cx_{l,sd}n^{-1/6}$ and $b_l = cz_{l,sd}n^{-1/6}$, where $x_{l,sd}(z_{l,sd})$ is the sample standard deviation of x_l $(z_l, l = 1, 2)$ and c is a constant. We chose $c = 0.8, 1.0, 1.2$. Table 8.1 reports the size results. It can be seen that the results for our non-parametric test statistic are quite encouraging. In samples as small as $n = 50$, the size performance of the proposed test is quite good. Also the estimated size is not sensitive to the different c values used. For comparison purposes we also report the conventional $\mathcal{J}$ and $\mathcal{J}A$ test statistics that are computed based on the assumptions that the null and the alternative models are linear in x's and z's respectively.

The power results are presented in Table 8.2. The powers for different c values are virtually the same, hence we will only report the results for $c = 1$ to save space. Again the proposed non-parametric test performs quite well. As expected the test is asymptotically powerful. Also different values of ρ do not seem to affect the results considerably. Note that as ρ increases the correlation between the x's and z's increases as well and hence the two models become less distinguishable. As expected we also observe that the conventional $\mathcal{J}$ and $\mathcal{J}A$ tests are inconsistent, the number of rejections for both the $\mathcal{J}$ and the $\mathcal{J}A$ tests decreases as n increases.

The limited Monte Carlo results suggest that the proposed test performs adequately with respect to its size and power characteristics especially when compared to the traditional $\mathcal{J}$ and $\mathcal{J}A$ tests.

Table 8.1. *Size results: proportion of rejections when H_0 is true*

	$\lambda = 0.1$		$\lambda = 0.4$		$\lambda = 0.7$	
	5%	1%	5%	1%	5%	1%
			[n = 50]			
$NP(c = 0.8)$	0.054	0.006	0.052	0.005	0.056	0.009
$NP(c = 1.0)$	0.050	0.005	0.051	0.003	0.060	0.009
$NP(c = 1.2)$	0.043	0.006	0.046	0.005	0.065	0.008
J	0.180	0.065	0.159	0.055	0.125	0.033
JA	0.065	0.019	0.068	0.019	0.061	0.020
			[n = 100]			
$NP(c = 0.8)$	0.048	0.010	0.061	0.009	0.053	0.009
$NP(c = 1.0)$	0.046	0.005	0.055	0.007	0.055	0.009
$NP(c = 1.2)$	0.040	0.004	0.042	0.007	0.060	0.013
J	0.164	0.052	0.133	0.031	0.114	0.035
JA	0.060	0.011	0.062	0.010	0.060	0.015
			[n = 200]			
$NP(c = 0.8)$	0.056	0.014	0.057	0.009	0.058	0.016
$NP(c = 1.0)$	0.051	0.012	0.054	0.009	0.053	0.013
$NP(c = 1.2)$	0.049	0.010	0.047	0.007	0.060	0.016
J	0.146	0.045	0.133	0.029	0.110	0.025
JA	0.053	0.009	0.056	0.014	0.057	0.011

Table 8.2. *Power results: proportion of rejections when H_a is true*

	$\lambda = 0.1$		$\lambda = 0.4$		$\lambda = 0.7$	
	5%	1%	5%	1%	5%	1%
			[n = 50]			
NP	0.260	0.062	0.275	0.068	0.240	0.060
J	0.373	0.203	0.348	0.197	0.301	0.133
JA	0.173	0.081	0.142	0.073	0.140	0.060
			[n = 100]			
NP	0.511	0.219	0.477	0.223	0.401	0.165
J	0.364	0.182	0.326	0.176	0.301	0.131
JA	0.143	0.061	0.144	0.070	0.132	0.053
			[n = 200]			
NP	0.840	0.634	0.754	0.523	0.651	0.421
J	0.341	0.162	0.310	0.160	0.290	0.130
JA	0.139	0.060	0.137	0.070	0.130	0.050

Appendix A

Similar to (4)–(6), for any sequence $\{A_i, i = 1, \ldots, n\}$, we define $\widehat{A}_i = \frac{1}{(n-1)a^p}\sum_{j\neq i} A_j K_{ij}$, $\widetilde{A}_i = \frac{1}{(n-1)b^q}\sum_{j\neq i} A_j \overline{K}_{ij}$, and $\widehat{\widetilde{A}}_i = \frac{1}{(n-1)a^p}\sum_{j\neq i}[\frac{1}{(n-1)b^q}\sum_{l\neq j} A_l \overline{K}_{jl}]K_{ij}$; they are kernel estimators for $E(A_i|x_i)f(x_i)$, $E(A_i|z_i)f_a(z_i)$ and $E[E(A_i|z_i)f_a(z_i)|x_i]f(x_i)$ respectively. Define $w(x_i, z_i) = m(x_i) - g(z_i)$. We will write $m_i = m(x_i)$, $g_i = g(z_i)$, $\gamma_i = \gamma(z_i)$, $\xi_i = \xi(x_i)$, $w_i = m_i - g_i$, $f_i = f(x_i)$ and $f_{ai} = f_a(z_i)$. There should be no confusion about these because when we define a function, it is clear from the context whether its argument is x, z or (x, z).

Proof of Theorem 1 We first give a decomposition of I_n under H_0. Recall that $g_i = E(y_i|z_i)$ and $w_i = m_i - g_i$. We have, under H_0, $y_i = m_i + u_i = g_i + w_i + u_i$. Thus:

$$y_i = m_i + u_i, \quad \hat{y}_i = \hat{m}_i + \hat{u}_i$$

$$\tilde{y}_i = \tilde{m}_i + \tilde{u}_i = \tilde{g}_i + \tilde{w}_i + \tilde{u}_i = \gamma_i + (\tilde{g}_i - \gamma_i) + \tilde{w}_i + \tilde{u}_i$$

$$\hat{\tilde{y}}_i = \hat{\tilde{m}}_i + \hat{\tilde{u}}_i = \hat{\tilde{g}}_i + \hat{\tilde{w}}_i + \hat{\tilde{u}}_i = \hat{\gamma}_i + (\hat{\tilde{g}}_i - \hat{\gamma}_i) + \hat{\tilde{w}}_i + \hat{\tilde{u}}_i \tag{A.1}$$

where $\gamma_i = g_i f_{ai}$. Substituting (A.1) into (7), we get

$$I_n = I_{1n} + I_{2n}$$

where

$$I_{1n} = \frac{1}{n}\sum_i [\gamma_i \hat{f}_i - \hat{\gamma}_i][(m_i \hat{f}_i - \hat{m}_i) + u_i \hat{f}_i - \hat{u}_i]$$

and

$$I_{2n} = \frac{1}{n}\sum_i [(\tilde{g}_i - \gamma_i)\hat{f}_i + \tilde{w}_i \hat{f}_i + \tilde{u}_i \hat{f}_i - (\hat{\tilde{g}}_i - \hat{\gamma}_i) - \hat{\tilde{w}}_i - \hat{\tilde{u}}_i][(m_i \hat{f}_i - \hat{m}_i)$$
$$+ u_i \hat{f}_i - \hat{u}_i].$$

We will prove $\sqrt{n} I_n \xrightarrow{d} N(0, \sigma_0^2)$ by showing that $\sqrt{n} I_{1n} \xrightarrow{d} N(0, \sigma_0^2)$ and $I_{2n} = o_p(n^{-1/2})$.

Proof of $\sqrt{n} I_{1n} \xrightarrow{d} N(0, \sigma_0^2)$ Recall that $\xi_i = E[\gamma_i|x_i]$ and define $v_i = \gamma_i - \xi_i$. Denote $S_{A\hat{f},B\hat{f}} = \frac{1}{n}\sum_i A_i \hat{f}_i B_i \hat{f}_i$, $S_{A,B} = \frac{1}{n}\sum_i A_i B_i$, $S_{A\hat{f},B} = \frac{1}{n}\sum_i A_i \hat{f}_i B_i$. Also $S_A = S_{A,A}$. Then I_{1n} can be written as:

$$I_{1n} = \frac{1}{n}\sum_i [(\xi_i \hat{f}_i - \hat{\xi}_i) + v_i \hat{f}_i - \hat{v}_i][(m_i \hat{f}_i - \hat{m}_i) + u_i \hat{f}_i - \hat{u}_i]$$

$$\equiv S_{(\xi\hat{f}-\hat{\xi})+v\hat{f}-\hat{v},(m\hat{f}-\hat{m})+u\hat{f}-\hat{u}} = S_{u\hat{f},v\hat{f}} + \{S_{\xi\hat{f}-\hat{\xi},m\hat{f}-\hat{m}} + S_{\xi\hat{f}-\hat{\xi},u\hat{f}}$$
$$- S_{\xi\hat{f}-\hat{\xi},\hat{u}} + S_{v\hat{f},m\hat{f}-\hat{m}} - S_{v\hat{f},\hat{u}} - S_{\hat{v},m\hat{f}-\hat{m}} - S_{\hat{v},u\hat{f}} + S_{\hat{v},\hat{u}}\}. \tag{A.2}$$

All the terms inside the curly bracket of (A.2) are $o_p(n^{-1/2})$ by lemma B.4. $\sqrt{n}(S_{\hat{uf},\hat{vf}} - S_{uf,vf}) = O_p(n^{-1}a^{-p} + a^{2\nu}) = o_p(1)$ by proposition 7 of Fan, Li and Stengos (1995). Hence $\sqrt{n}I_{1n} = \sqrt{n}S_{uf,vf} + o_p(1) \to N(0, \sigma_0^2)$ by the Levi–Linderberg central limit theorem.

Proof of $I_{2n} = o_p(n^{-1/2})$:

$$I_{2n} = \frac{1}{n}\sum_i [(\tilde{g}_i - \gamma_i)\hat{f}_i + \hat{\tilde{w}}_i\hat{f}_i + \hat{\tilde{u}}_i\hat{f}_i - (\hat{\tilde{g}}_i - \hat{\gamma}_i) - \hat{\tilde{w}}_i - \hat{\tilde{u}}_i][(m_i\hat{f}_i - \hat{m}_i)$$

$$+ u_i\hat{f}_i - \hat{u}_i]$$

$$= S_{(\tilde{g}-\gamma)\hat{f}+\tilde{w}\hat{f}+\tilde{u}\hat{f}-(\hat{\tilde{g}}-\hat{\gamma})-\hat{\tilde{w}}-\hat{\tilde{u}},\,(m\hat{f}-\hat{m})+u\hat{f}-\hat{u}}$$

We need to show that $S_{(\tilde{g}-\gamma)\hat{f},\, m\hat{f}-\hat{m}}$, $S_{(\tilde{g}-\gamma)\hat{f},\, u\hat{f}}$, $S_{(\tilde{g}-\gamma)\hat{f},\, \hat{u}}$, $S_{\hat{\tilde{g}}-\hat{\gamma},\, m\hat{f}-\hat{m}}$, $S_{\hat{\tilde{g}}-\hat{\gamma},\, u\hat{f}}$, $S_{\hat{\tilde{g}}-\hat{\gamma},\, \hat{u}}$, $S_{\tilde{r}\hat{f},\, m\hat{f}-\hat{m}}$, $S_{\tilde{r}\hat{f},\, u\hat{f}}$, $S_{\tilde{r}\hat{f},\, \hat{u}}$ $S_{\hat{\tilde{r}},\, m\hat{f}-\hat{m}}$, $S_{\hat{\tilde{r}},\, u\hat{f}}$, $S_{\hat{\tilde{r}},\, \hat{u}}$ are all $o_p(n^{-1/2})$, where $r = w$ or u. It suffices to show that

(i) $S_{(\tilde{g}-\hat{\gamma})\hat{f}} = o_p(n^{-1/2})$;

(ii) $S_{\hat{\tilde{g}}-\hat{\gamma}} = o_p(n^{-1/2})$;

(iii) $S_{(\tilde{g}-\hat{\gamma})\hat{f},\, u\hat{f}} = o_p(n^{-1/2})$;

(iv) $S_{\hat{\tilde{g}}-\hat{\gamma},\, u\hat{f}} = o_p(n^{-1/2})$;

(v) $S_{\tilde{r}\hat{f}} = o_p(n^{-1/2})$;

(vi) $S_{\hat{\tilde{r}}} = o_p(n^{-1/2})$;

(vii) $S_{\tilde{r}\hat{f},\, u\hat{f}} = o_p(n^{-1/2})$;

(viii) $S_{\hat{\tilde{r}},\, u\hat{f}} = o_p(n^{-1/2})$, $(r = w$ or $u)$.

Because (i)–(viii), together with lemma B.4 and the Cauchy inequality imply that all the other terms in I_{2n} are also $o_p(n^{-1/2})$, we prove (i)–(viii) in Propositions 3.1 to 3.8 below.

Proposition 3.1 $S_{(\tilde{g}-\gamma)\hat{f}} = O((nb^q)^{-1} + b^{2\mu})$.

Proof First by adding and subtracting term, we have $(\tilde{g}_i - \gamma_i)\hat{f}_i = (\tilde{g}_i - g_i\tilde{f}_{ai})\hat{f}_i + g_i(\tilde{f}_{ai} - f_{ai})\hat{f}_i \overset{\Delta}{=} F_i + H_i$, where $F_i = (\tilde{g}_i - g_i\tilde{f}_{ai})\hat{f}_i$ and $H_i = g_i(\tilde{f}_{ai} - f_{ai})\hat{f}_i$. Thus we have $S_{(\tilde{g}-\gamma)\hat{f}} \equiv S_{F+H}$. By Cauchy inequality, it suffices to show that $S_F = o_p(n^{-1/2})$ and $S_H = o_p(n^{-1/2})$. We prove these below.

Proof of $S_F = O((nb^q)^{-1} + b^{2\mu})$:

$$E|S_F| = \frac{1}{n}\sum E(F_i^2) = E(F_1^2). \text{ Using } F_1 = (\tilde{g}_1 - g_1\tilde{f}_a(z_1))\hat{f}_1$$

$$= \left[((n-1)b^q)^{-1}\sum_{i\neq 1}(g_i - g_1)\overline{K}_{1i}\right]\left[((n-1)a^p)^{-1}\sum_{j\neq 1}K_{1j}\right], \text{ we have}$$

$$E|S_F| = E\left\{\left[((n-1)b^q)^{-1}\sum_{i\neq 1}(g_i - g_1)\overline{K}_{1i}\right]\left[((n-1)b^q)^{-1}\sum_{i'\neq 1}(g_{i'} - g_1)\overline{K}_{1i'}\right]\right.$$

$$\left.\times\left[((n-1)a^p)^{-1}\sum_{j\neq 1}K_{1j}\right]\left[((n-1)a^p)^{-1}\sum_{j'\neq 1}K_{1j'}\right]\right\} \qquad \text{(A.3)}$$

If i, i', j, j' are all different from each other, then conditional on 1, the terms in different square brackets in (A.3) are independent, using lemmas B.1 and B.3. In this case, (A.3) is

$$E\{[b^{-q}E_1(g_2 - g_1)\overline{K}_{12}][b^{-q}E_1(g_3 - g_1)\overline{K}_{13}][a^{-p}E_1(K_{14})][a^{-p}E_1(K_{15})]\}$$

$$\le E\{[D(z_1)b^{\mu}][D(z_1)b^{\mu}][O(1)][O(1)]\} = O(b^{2\mu}).$$

Next we consider the case that i, i', j, j' (in (A.3)) take three different values. There are six different combinations, but symmetry reduces it to three different cases. (1) $i = i'$, (2) $j = j'$ and (3) $i = j$, or $i = j'$, or $i' = j$, or $i' = j'$. We first consider case (1): $i = i'$, and in this case using lemmas B.1 and B.3 (A.3) becomes:

$$E\left\{\left[((n-1)b^q)^{-2}\sum_{i\neq 1}(g_i - g_1)^2\overline{K}_{1i}^2\right]\left[((n-1)a^p)^{-1}\sum_{j\neq 1}K_{1j}\right]\right.$$

$$\left.\times\left[((n-1)a^p)^{-1}\sum_{j'\neq 1}K_{1j'}\right]\right\}$$

$$= E\left\{\left[n^{-1}b^{-2q}E_1(g_2 - g_1)^2\overline{K}_{12}^2\right][a^{-p}E_1(K_{13})][a^{-p}E_1(K_{14})]\right\}$$

$$= O((nb^q)^{-1})O(1)O(1) = O((nb^q)^{-1}).$$

For case (2): $j = j'$, and (A.3) becomes (using lemmas B.1 and B.3):

$$E\left\{\left[((n-1)b^q)^{-1}\sum_{i\neq 1}(g_i - g_1)\overline{K}_{1i}\right]\left[((n-1)b^q)^{-1}\sum_{i'\neq 1}(g_{i'} - g_1)\overline{K}_{1i'}\right]\right.$$

$$\left.\times\left[((n-1)a^p)^{-2}\sum_{j\neq 1}K_{1j}^2\right]\right\}$$

$$= E\{[b^{-q}E_1(g_2 - g_1)\overline{K}_{12}][b^{-q}E_1(g_3 - g_1)\overline{K}_{13}][na^{-2p}E_1(K_{14}^2)]$$

$$\leq E\{[D(z_1)b^{\mu}][D(z_1)b^{\mu}][n^{-1}a^{-q}O(1)]\} = O((na^p)^{-1}b^{2\mu}) = o(b^{2\mu}).$$

For case (3), the two subcases are symmetric, we only consider $j' = i$, then (A.3) becomes:

$$E\left\{\left[((n-1)a^p)^{-1}((n-1)b^q)^{-1}\sum_{i\neq 1}(g_i - g_1)\overline{K}_{1i}K_{1i}\right]\left[((n-1)b^q)^{-1}\right.\right.$$

$$\left.\left.\times\sum_{j\neq 1}(g_j - g_1)\overline{K}_{1j}\right]\left[((n-1)a^p)^{-1}\sum_{i'\neq 1}K_{1i'}\right]\right\}$$

$$= E\left\{\left[((n-1)a^p)^{-1}b^{-q}E_1(g_2 - g_1)\overline{K}_{12}K_{12}\right]\left[b^{-q}E_1(g_3 - g_1)\overline{K}_{13}\right]\right.$$

$$\left.\times [a^{-p}E_1(K_{14})]\right\}$$

$$\leq E\{[n^{-1}D(z_1)b^{\mu}O(1)][D(z_1)b^{\mu}][O(1)]\} = O(n^{-1}b^{2\mu}) = o(b^{2\mu})$$

where we used $E_1[(g_2 - g_1)\overline{K}_{12}K_{12}] = E_1[(g(z_2) - g(z_1))\overline{K}_{12}E_{1,z_2}(K(\frac{x_1-x_2}{a}))] = E_1[(g_2 - g_1)\overline{K}_{12}O(a^p)] \leq D(z_1)b^{q+\mu}a^p$ by lemma B.3.

When i, i', j, j' take no more than two values, we will have at most two summations, and using similar arguments as above, it is easy to show that in this case (A.3) will have a smaller order. Hence $E|S_F| = O((nb^q)^{-1} + b^{2\mu})$.

Proof of $S_H = O((nb^q)^{-1} + b^{2\mu})$:

$$E|S_H| = \frac{1}{n}\sum_i E(H_i^2) = E(H_1^2). \text{ Using} H_1 = g(z_1)(\tilde{f}_a(z_1) - f_a(z_1))\hat{f}_1,$$

we have

$$E|S_H| = E\left\{\left[g(z_1)n^{-1}\sum_{i\neq 1}(b^{-q}\overline{K}_{1i} - f_a(z_1))\right]\left[g(z_1)n^{-1}\right.\right.$$

$$\times\sum_{i'\neq 1}(b^{-q}\overline{K}_{1i'} - f_a(z_1))\left]\left[((n-1)a^p)^{-1}\sum_{j\neq 1}K_{1j}\right]\right.$$

$$\left.\times\left[((n-1)a^p)^{-1}\sum_{j'\neq 1}K_{1j'}\right]\right\} \tag{A.4}$$

Comparing (A.4) with (A.3), the main difference is that $(\tilde{g}_1 - g_1\tilde{f}_a(z_1))$ in (A.3) is replaced by $(\tilde{f}_a(z_1) - f_a(z_1))$ here. This amounts to replacing lemma B.3 by lemma B.2 in the proof. Hence (A.4) has the same order as (A.3), and $S_H = O_p((nb^q)^{-1} + b^{2\mu})$.

Proposition 3.2 $S_{\hat{\tilde{g}}-\hat{\gamma}} = O((nb^q)^{-1} + b^{2\mu})$.

Proof By adding and subtracting terms, we can rewrite $\hat{\tilde{g}}_i$ as

$$\hat{\tilde{g}}_i \equiv \frac{1}{(n-1)a^p} \sum_{j\neq i} \left[\frac{1}{(n-1)b^q} \sum_{l\neq j} g(z_l)\overline{K}_{jl} \right] K_{ij}$$

$$= \frac{1}{(n-1)a^p} \sum_{j\neq i} g(z_j) f_a(z_j) K_{ij} + \frac{1}{(n-1)a^p} \sum_{j\neq i} g(z_j)((\tilde{f}_a(z_j)$$

$$- f_a(z_j))K_{ij} + \frac{1}{(n-1)a^p} \sum_{j\neq i} \left[\frac{1}{(n-1)b^q} \sum_{l\neq j} (g(z_l) - g(z_j))\overline{K}_{jl} \right] K_{ij}$$

$$\triangleq \hat{\gamma}(z_i) + M_i + T_i$$

where $M_i = \frac{1}{(n-1)a^p} \sum_{j\neq i} g(z_j)((\tilde{f}_a(z_j) - f_a(z_j))K_{ij}$ and $T_i = \frac{1}{(n-1)a^p} \sum_{j\neq i}[\frac{1}{(n-1)b^q} \sum_{l\neq j}(g(z_l) - g(z_j))\overline{K}_{jl}]K_{ij}$. Hence $S_{\hat{\tilde{g}}-\hat{\gamma}} \equiv S_{M+T}$. By the Cauchy inequality, we only need to show that $S_M = o_p(n^{-1/2})$ and $S_T = o_p(n^{-1/2})$. We prove them below.

Proof of $S_M = O((nb^q)^{-1} + b^{2\mu})$:

$$E|S_M| = \frac{1}{n}\sum_i E(M_i^2) = E(M_1^2). \text{Using } M_1 = ((n-1)a^p)^{-1}$$

$$\times \sum_{i\neq 1} g(z_i)(\tilde{f}_a(z_i) - f_a(z_i))K_{i1}$$

$$= \left[((n-1)a^p)^{-1} n^{-1} \sum_{i\neq 1}\sum_{j\neq i} g(z_i) K_{i1}(b^{-q}K_{ij} - f_a(z_i)) \right],$$

we have

$$E|S_M| = E\left\{ \left[((n-1)a^p)^{-1} n^{-1} \sum_{i\neq 1}\sum_{j\neq i} g_i K_{1i}(\overline{b^{-q}}K_{ij} - f_a(z_i)) \right] \right.$$

$$\left. \times \left[((n-1)a^p)^{-1} n^{-1} \sum_{i'\neq 1}\sum_{j'\neq i'} g_{i'} K_{1i'}(b^{-q}\overline{K}_{i'j'} - f_a(z_{i'})) \right] \right\}. \quad \text{(A.5)}$$

We consider two different situations: (I) j and j' are both different from 1 and (II) at least one of the j and j' equals 1. The proof for case (I) is the same as in the proof of (A.3). For example, if i, j, i', j' are all different from each other, then using lemmas B.1 and B.3, (A.5) is $O(b^{2\mu})$, and if some of the i, j, i', j' take the same values, then (A.5) is of the order $O_p((nb^q)^{-1}) + o_p(b^{2\mu})$. The detailed proof is identical to the proof of (A.3) and is thus omitted here.

For case (II), The two subcases are symmetric, hence we only consider $j' = 1$, we still have different situations: (1) i, i', j take three different values, (2) i, i', j take two different values, (3) i, i', j all take the same value.
For (1), first assume $j \neq 1$, then (A.5) becomes (using lemmas B.1 and B.2):

$$((n-1)a^p)^{-2}n^{-2}\sum_{i\neq 1}\sum_{j\neq i,1}\sum_{i'\neq 1,i,j} E[g(z_i)g(z_{i'})K_{1i}$$

$$\times (b^{-q}\overline{K}_{ij} - f_a(z_i))K_{1i'}(b^{-q}\overline{K}_{i'1} - f_a(z_{i'}))]$$

$$= n^{-1}a^{-2p}E[g(z_2)g(z_3)(E_{1,z_2}K_{12})(E_{1,z_3}K_{13})(b^{-q}E_2(\overline{K}_{24}) - f_a(z_2))$$

$$\times (b^{-q}E_{3,x_1}(\overline{K}_{31}) - f_a(z_3))]$$

$$= n^{-1}E[g(z_2)g(z_3)G(z_2)G(z_3)O(b^{2\mu})] = O(n^{-1}b^{2\mu}) = o(b^{2\mu}).$$

Next if $j = 1$, then (A.5) becomes:

$$((n-1)a^p)^{-2}n^{-2}\sum_{i\neq 1}\sum_{i'\neq i,1} E[g(z_i)g(z_{i'})K_{1i}(b^{-q}\overline{K}_{i1}$$

$$- f_a(z_i))K_{1i'}(b^{-q}\overline{K}_{i'1} - f_a(z_{i'}))]$$

$$= n^{-2}a^{-2p}E[g(z_2)g(z_3)(E_{1,z_2}K_{12})(E_{1,z_3}K_{13})(b^{-q}(\overline{K}_{21})$$

$$- f_a(z_2))(b^{-q}(\overline{K}_{31}) - f_a(z_3))]$$

$$= n^{-2}O(1)E\{E_1[g(z_1)(b^{-q}(\overline{K}_{21}) - f_a(z_2))]E_1[g(z_3)(b^{-q}(\overline{K}_{31})$$

$$- f_a(z_3))]\} = O(n^{-2}).$$

For cases (2) and (3) there are at most two summations, and using the same arguments as above it is easy to show that in these cases (A.5) will have a smaller order. Hence for case (II), (A.5) is of the order $O(n^{-1}b^{2\mu} + n^{-2})$. Summarizing the results for cases (I) and (II) above, we have shown that $E|S_M| = O((nb^q)^{-1} + b^{2\mu})$.

Proof for $S_T = O((nb^q)^{-1} + b^{2\mu})$: Using $T_1 = [((n-1)a^p)^{-1}((n-1)b^q)^{-1}\sum_{i\neq 1}\sum_{j\neq i} K_{1i}(g(z_j) - g_a(z_i))\overline{K}_{ij}]$, we have

$$E|S_T| = E(T_1^2) = E\left\{\left[((n-1)a^p)^{-1}\sum_{i\neq 1} K_{1i}\right]\left[((n-1)b^q)^{-1}\right.\right.$$

$$\left.\times \sum_{j\neq i}(g(z_j) - g_a(z_i))\overline{K}_{ij}\right]\left[((n-1)a^p)^{-1}\sum_{i'\neq 1} K_{1i'}\right]$$

$$\left.\times \left[((n-1)b^q)^{-1}\sum_{j\neq i}(g(z_j') - g_a(z_i'))\overline{K}_{ij'}\right]\right\}. \tag{A.6}$$

Comparing (A.6) and (A.5), the main difference is that $\widetilde{f}_a(z_i) - f_a(z_i)$ in (A.5) is replaced by $\widetilde{g}(z_i) - g(z_i)\hat{f}_a(z_i)$. This amounts to replacing lemma B.2 by lemma B.3 in the proof. Thus, it is obvious that (A.6) has the same order as (A.5) and $S_T = O_p((nb^q)^{-1} + b^{2\mu})$.

Proposition 3.3 $S_{(\widetilde{g}-\hat{\gamma})\hat{f},\, u\hat{f}} = o_p(n^{-1/2})$.

Proof $S_{(\widetilde{g}-\hat{\gamma})\hat{f},\, u\hat{f}} \equiv S_{F+H,\, u\hat{f}}$. Let $A = F$ or H, we have $S_{A,u\hat{f}} = S_{A,uf} + S_{A,u(\hat{f}-f)}$. We will show that both $S_{A,uf}$ and $S_{A,u(\hat{f}-f)}$ are $o_p(n^{-1/2})$. $E[(S_{A,uf})^2] = \frac{1}{n^2}\sum_i\sum_j E[(A_iu_if_i)(A_ju_jf_j)] = \frac{1}{n^2}\sum_i E[A_i^2u_i^2f_i^2] = n^{-1}E[A_1^2u_1^2f_1^2] = n^{-1}O(E(A_1^2)) = n^{-1}O(E|S_A|) = n^{-1}O((nb^q)^{-1} + b^{2\mu})$ by proposition 1. $E|S_{u(\hat{f}-f)}| = \frac{1}{n}\sum_i E[u_i^2(\hat{f}_i - f_i)^2] = E[u_1^2(\hat{f}_1 - f_1)^2] = O(E[(\hat{f}_1 - f_1)^2]) = O((na^p)^{-1} + a^{2\nu})$ by lemma B.4. Also $S_A = o_p(n^{-1/2})$ by proposition 1, hence $S_{A,u(\hat{f}-f)} = o_p(n^{-1/2})$ by the Cauchy inequality.

Proposition 3.4 $S_{\hat{\widetilde{g}}-\hat{\gamma},\, u\hat{f}} = o_p(n^{-1/2})$.

Proof $S_{\hat{\widetilde{g}}-\hat{\gamma},\, u\hat{f}} \equiv S_{M+T,\, u\hat{f}} = S_{M+T,\, uf} + S_{M+T,\, u(\hat{f}-f)}$. Let $B = M$ or T, then by a similar proof as proposition 3 (using proposition 2 and the Cauchy inequality), one can show that $S_{B,\, u\hat{f}} = o_p(n^{-1/2})$.

Proposition 3.5 $S_{\widetilde{r}\hat{f}} = O_p(n^{-1/2})$, ($r = w$, or u).

Proof We first consider the case of $r = w$. $S_{\widetilde{w}\hat{f}} = S_{\widetilde{w}f} + S_{\widetilde{w}(\hat{f}-f)}$.

$$
\begin{aligned}
E|S_{\widetilde{w}f}| &= \frac{1}{n}\sum_i E[\widetilde{w}_i^2 f_i^2] = E[\widetilde{w}_1^2 f_1^2] = E\Bigg\{f_1^2\Bigg[((n-1)b^q)^{-1} \\
&\quad \times \sum_{i\neq 1} w_i\overline{K}_{1i}\Bigg]\Bigg[((n-1)b^q)^{-1}\sum_{j\neq 1} w_j\overline{K}_{1j}\Bigg]\Bigg\} \\
&= E\Bigg\{f_1^2\Bigg[((n-1)b^q)^{-2}\sum_{i\neq 1} w_i^2\overline{K}_{1i}^2\Bigg]\Bigg\} = E\{f_1^2[n^{-1}b^{-2q} \\
&\quad \times E_1(w_2^2\overline{K}_{12}^2)]\} = O((nb^q)^{-1})
\end{aligned}
\tag{A.7}
$$

by lemma B.1. We also used the fact that $E(w_i|Z, X_{-i}) = 0$, where $X_{-i} = (x_1, \ldots, x_{i-1}, x_{i+1}, \ldots, x_n)$.

Obviously (A.7) also proves $S_{\widetilde{w}} = O_p((nb^q)^{-1})$ (by removing f_1^2). From $S_{\widetilde{w}} = o_p(n^{-1/2})$ and $S_{\hat{f}-f} = o_p(n^{-1/2})$ (see lemma B.4) and the the Cauchy inequality, we know that $S_{\widetilde{w}(\hat{f}-f)} = o_p(n^{-1/2})$.

The proof is identical to the case of $r = w$. Simply replacing w by u in the above proof.

Proposition 3.6 $S_{\hat{\tilde{r}}} = o_p(n^{-1/2})$, ($w = r$ or u).

Proof $E|S_{\hat{\tilde{w}}}| = \frac{1}{n}\sum_i E[\hat{\tilde{r}}_i^2] = E[\hat{\tilde{w}}_1^2] = [(n-1)^4 a^{2p} b^{2q}]^{-1} \sum_{i\neq 1} \sum_{j\neq i} \sum_{i'\neq 1} \sum_{j'\neq i'} E[w_j w_{j'} \overline{K}_{ij} \overline{K}_{i'j'} \ K_{1i} K_{1i'}] = [(n-1)^4 a^{2p} b^{2q}]^{-1} \sum_{i\neq 1} \sum_{j\neq i,i'} \sum_{i'\neq 1} E[w_j^2 \overline{K}_{ij} \overline{K}_{i'j} K_{1i} K_{1i'}] = [(n-1)^4 a^{2p} b^{2q}]^{-1} \{\sum_{i\neq 1} \sum_{j\neq i,i'} \sum_{i'\neq 1} (n-1)(n-1)(n-3) E[w_3^2 \overline{K}_{23} \overline{K}_{43} K_{12} K_{14}] + (n-1)(n-2) E[w_3^2 \overline{K}_{23}^2 K_{12}^2] = O(n^{-1} + (n^2 a^p b^q)^{-1}) = O(n^{-1})$. The same proof leads to $E|S_{\hat{\tilde{u}}}| = O(n^{-1})$.

Proposition 3.7 $S_{\widetilde{rf},u\hat{f}} = o_p(n^{-1/2})$, ($r = w$ or u).

Proof $S_{\widetilde{rf},u\hat{f}} = S_{\widetilde{rf},uf} = S_{\widetilde{rf},u(\hat{f}-f)}$. Then similar to the proof of proposition 3, one can show that $E|S^2_{\widetilde{rf},uf}| = n^{-1}O(E[(\tilde{r}_1\hat{f}_1)^2]) = o(n^{-1})$. Also $S_{u(\hat{f}-f)} = o_p(n^{-1/2})$ (by the proof of proposition 3) and $S_{\widetilde{rf}} = o_p(n^{-1/2})$ by proposition 5. Hence $S_{\widetilde{rf},u(\hat{f}-f)} = o_p(n^{-1/2})$ by the Cauchy inequality.

Proposition 3.8 $S_{\hat{\tilde{r}},u\hat{f}} = o_p(n^{-1/2})$, ($r = w$ or u).

Proof $S_{\hat{\tilde{r}},u\hat{f}} = S_{\hat{\tilde{r}},uf} + S_{\hat{\tilde{r}},u(\hat{f}-f)}$. Then similar to the proof of proposition 7, using propositions 3, 6 and the Cauchy inequality, it is to see that $S_{\hat{\tilde{r}},u\hat{f}} = o_p(n^{-1/2})$.

Summarizing the above results, we have shown that $\sqrt{n}I_n \xrightarrow{d} N(0, \sigma_0^2)$ under H_0.

Proof of Theorem 2 Using similar arguments as in Theorem 1, it follows that, under H_a, $I_n \xrightarrow{p} E\{[m_a(z)f_a(z) - E(m_a(z)f_a(z)|x)][m_a(z) - E(m_a(z)|x)]f^2(x)\} \neq 0$, and $\hat{\sigma}_0^2 \xrightarrow{p} E\{(g(z)f_a(z) - E(g(z)f_a(z)|x)^2 f^2(x)\,[(m_a(z) - E(m_a(z)|x))^2 + \epsilon^2] f^2(x)\}$ which is positive and finite. Hence $Prob[|\mathcal{J}_n| > c] \to 1$ for any non-negative constant c.

Appendix B

In this Appendix we give some useful lemmas. Lemmas B.1–B.3 are from Robinson (1988), and the proof of lemma B.4 can be found in Fan, Li and Stengos (1995). In lemmas B.1–B.3 below, we assume that $x \in R^p$, $k \in \mathcal{K}_\nu$ (some $\nu \geq 1$), $f(v) \in \mathcal{G}_\nu^\infty$, $g(v) \in \mathcal{G}_\nu^\alpha$ for some $\alpha > 0$. E_1 denote the conditional expectation (conditional on x_1). K_{ij} denote $K(\frac{x_i - x_j}{a})$. Note that lemmas B.1–B.3 hold when changing (x, f, K, p, a, ν) to $(z, f_a, \overline{K}, q, b, \mu)$.

Lemma B.1

(i) $E_1(\hat{f}_1) = \frac{1}{(n-1)a^p} \sum_{i\neq 1} E_1(K_{1i}) = a^{-p} E_1(K_{12}) = O(1)$

(ii) $a^{-p}|E_1[(g(= x_2)K_{12}]| \leq \Phi(x_1)$

where $\Phi(x)$ has finite αth moment.

Lemma B.2

$$E_1(\hat{f}_1 - f_1) = E_1(((n-1)a^p)^{-1}\sum_{i\neq 1} K_{i1}) - f(x_1)$$

$$= a^{-p}E_1(K_{12}) - f_1 \leq G(x_1)a^{\nu}$$

where $G(\cdot)$ has finite moments of any order.

Lemma B.3

$$E_1(g_1\hat{f}_1 - \hat{g}_1) = \frac{1}{(n-1)a^p}\sum_{i\neq 1} E_1(g_1 - g_i)K_{1i}$$

$$= a^{-p}E_1[(g(x_1) - g(x_2))K_{12}] \leq D(x_1)(a^{\nu}),$$

where $D(\cdot)$ has finite αth moment.

Lemma B.4 Let m, ξ, f, f_a, u and v all defined as in the paper. Let $g = m$ or ξ and $\epsilon = u$ or v, then:

(i) $S_{g\hat{f}-\hat{g},\epsilon\hat{f}} = O_p((na^p)^{-1})$, $S_{g\hat{f}-\hat{g},\hat{\epsilon}} = O_p((na^p)^{-1})$,
(ii) $S_{g\hat{f}-\hat{g}} = O_p((na^p)^{-1} + a^{2\mu})$, $S_{\hat{f}-f} = O_p((na^p)^{-1} + a^{2\mu})$,
(iii) $S_{v,\hat{u}} = O_p((na^p)^{-1})$, $S_{\hat{v},u\hat{f}} = O_p((na^p)^{-1})$, $S_{\hat{v},\hat{u}} = O_p((na^p)^{-1})$.

9 Testing for Autocorrelation in Systems of Equations

Phoebus J. Dhrymes

1 Introduction

Consider the model

$$y_{t\cdot} = y_{t-1\cdot}A + x_{t\cdot}B + u_{t\cdot}, \quad t = 1, 2, 3, \ldots, T \tag{1}$$

where $y_{t\cdot}$ is an m-element row vector of dependent, and $x_{t\cdot}$ is a k-element vector of independent variables, respectively; $u_{t\cdot}$, $t = 1, 2, \ldots, T$ is the structural error vector. We assume:

(i) $\{u_{t\cdot} : t = 1, 2, 3, \ldots, T\}$ is a sequence of independent identically distributed (i.i.d.) random vectors with

$$E\, u_{t\cdot} = 0, \quad \mathrm{Cov}(u_{t\cdot}) = \Sigma > 0 \tag{2}$$

defined on some probability space $(\Omega, \mathcal{A}, \mathcal{P})$.

(ii) It is further assumed that

$$\operatorname*{plim}_{T\to\infty} \frac{X'X}{T} = M_{xx} > 0 \tag{3}$$

and that the elements in X and U are mutually independent.

(iii) The system of equations (1) is **stable,** that is the characteristic roots of A are less than one in absolute value.

Regarding the errors, the alternative hypothesis we entertain is

$$u_{t\cdot} = u_{t-1\cdot}R + \epsilon_{t\cdot}. \tag{4}$$

We require, for stationarity, the following assumptions:

1 the matrix R is non-singular and stable, that is its characteristic roots are less than one in absolute value; and

2 with little loss of generality, and certainly no loss of relevance, we further assume that the matrix R is diagonalizable, that is it has the representation $R = P\Lambda P^{-1}$, where Λ is the (diagonal) matrix of its characteristic roots.

This problem, for the case $m = 1$, (and R a scalar) was dealt with by Durbin (1970a), (1970b). A search of widely used econometrics textbooks such as Greene (1999) and Davidson and MacKinnon (1993) discloses no mention of its generalization to VARs.

Remark 1 If one were to write down a VAR one would normally not be concerned about the behaviour of the "error", since **by definition** the errors in such a system are assumed to be i.i.d. If not, in empirical applications, one simply specifies a VAR of a higher order. Notwithstanding this observation, in many applied contexts the logic of the economic model requires the presence of a specific number of lagged endogenous variables, in addition to the exogenous variables required by the specification. In such a case, the problem we are examining here may arise.

Remark 2 When the structural error, $u_{t\cdot}$, is in fact a first order autoregression, the OLS estimators for the parameters of the model in equation (1) are inconsistent **because of the presence of lagged endogenous variables**, which are therefore correlated with the structural error.

Thus, if we suspect that the form given in equation (4) may be appropriate, we may wish to test the hypothesis

$H_0: \quad R = 0$
as against the alternative
$H_1: \quad R \neq 0$

when ordinary least squares (OLS) is used to estimate the unknown parameters of equation (1).

2 Derivation of the Test Statistic

Writing the sample as

$$Y = Y_{-1}A + XB + U = ZC + U, \quad Z = (Y_{-1}, X), \quad C = (A', B')' \tag{5}$$

the OLS estimator of C is given by:

$$\tilde{C} = (Z'Z)^{-1}Z'Y = C + (Z'Z)^{-1}Z'U. \tag{6}$$

It may be shown that, under the assumptions above, a central limit theorem (CLT) is applicable, see Dhrymes (1994), pp. 73–80, Dhrymes (1989), pp. 271*ff* and pp. 328–37. Thus, the limiting distribution of the OLS estimator may be obtained from (the notation $X \sim W$ below means, in this context, that X has the same limiting distribution as W):

$$\sqrt{T}(\tilde{c}-c) \sim \frac{1}{\sqrt{T}}\sum_{t=2}^{T}(I \otimes Sz'_{t\cdot})u'_{t\cdot}, \quad c = \mathrm{vec}(C) \quad \text{where} \tag{7}$$

$$S = \operatorname*{plim}_{T\to\infty}(Z'Z/T)^{-1} = \begin{bmatrix} S_{11} & S_{12} \\ S_{21} & S_{22} \end{bmatrix} = \begin{bmatrix} S_1 \\ S_2 \end{bmatrix}. \tag{8}$$

As is easily seen from equation (7), the summands therein form a sequence of martingale difference (MD) vectors that satisfy the conditions of Proposition 21 in Dhrymes (1989) p. 337. Consequently,

$$\sqrt{T}(\tilde{c}-c) \xrightarrow{\mathrm{d}} N(0, \Sigma \otimes S). \tag{9}$$

Since

$$\sqrt{T}\mathrm{vec}(\tilde{A}-A) \sim \frac{1}{\sqrt{T}}\mathrm{vec}(S_1 Z'U) = \frac{1}{\sqrt{T}}\sum_{t=2}^{T}[I_m \otimes S_1 z'_{t\cdot}]u'_{t\cdot} \tag{10}$$

using the same arguments as above we conclude that,

$$\sqrt{T}\mathrm{vec}(\tilde{A}-A) = \sqrt{T}(\tilde{a}-a) \xrightarrow{\mathrm{d}} N(0, \Sigma \otimes S_{11}). \tag{11}$$

Let

$$\tilde{U} = Y - Z\tilde{C} = U - Y_{-1}(\tilde{A}-A) - X(\tilde{B}-B) \tag{12}$$

be the matrix of OLS residuals and consider the estimator of R:

$$\tilde{R} = (\tilde{U}'_{-1}\tilde{U}_{-1})^{-1}\tilde{U}'_{-1}\tilde{U}, \quad \tilde{U} = U - Z(\tilde{C}-C). \tag{13}$$

Using equations (12) and (13), and omitting terms that converge to zero in probability, we may write, see Dhrymes (1989), pp. 161*ff*,

$$\sqrt{T}(\tilde{R}-R) \sim \Sigma^{-1}\frac{1}{\sqrt{T}}\left(U'_{-1}U - \frac{U'_{-1}Y_{-1}}{T}\sqrt{T}(\tilde{A}-A)\right) \tag{14}$$

either because $Z'Z/T$ converges, or because $\tilde{C}$ is consistent and has a well-defined limiting distribution, or both. Moreover, using the result again, and bearing in mind that

$$\frac{1}{T}U'_{-1}Y_{-1} \xrightarrow{\mathrm{P}} \Sigma$$

we finally obtain,

$$\sqrt{T}(\tilde{R} - R) \sim \Sigma^{-1}\frac{1}{\sqrt{T}}U'_{-1}U - \sqrt{T}(\tilde{A} - A). \tag{15}$$

Using equation (10), and giving more details, we note that

$$\sqrt{T}(\tilde{A} - A) \sim S_1\frac{1}{\sqrt{T}}Z'U, \quad S_1 = (S_{11},\ S_{12}).$$

Vectorizing, we have the expression:

$$\sqrt{T}\mathrm{vec}(\tilde{R} - R) = \sqrt{T}(\tilde{r} - r) \sim \frac{1}{\sqrt{T}}\mathrm{vec}[(\Sigma^{-1}U'_{-1} - S_1Z')U] \tag{16}$$

$$= \frac{1}{\sqrt{T}}\mathrm{vec}\left[\sum_{t=2}^{T}(\Sigma^{-1}u'_{t-1\cdot} - S_1z'_{t\cdot})u_{t\cdot}\right]$$

$$= \frac{1}{\sqrt{T}}\sum_{t=2}^{T}\left[I_m \otimes (\Sigma^{-1}u'_{t-1\cdot} - S_1z'_{t\cdot})\right]u'_{t\cdot}. \tag{17}$$

The summands in the rightmost member above are recognized as a MD sequence that obeys the Lindeberg condition, as noted above. Let

$$\mathcal{A}_t = \sigma(u_{s\cdot}, s \le t) \tag{18}$$

be the σ-algebra generated by the u's up to t, and note that

$$\frac{1}{T}E\left(\left[I_m \otimes (\Sigma^{-1}u'_{t-1\cdot} - S_1z'_{t\cdot})\right]u'_{t\cdot}u_{t\cdot}\left[I_m \otimes (u_{t-1\cdot}\Sigma^{-1} - z_{t\cdot}S'_1)\right] | \mathcal{A}_{t-1}\right) \tag{19}$$

$$= \frac{1}{T}\left[\Sigma \otimes (\Sigma^{-1}u'_{t-1\cdot} - S_1z'_{t\cdot}\right]\left[I_m \otimes (u_{t-1\cdot}\Sigma^{-1} - z_{t\cdot}S'_1)\right] \tag{20}$$

which, upon summation, obeys

$$\frac{1}{T}\sum_{t=2}^{T}\left[\Sigma \otimes (\Sigma^{-1}u'_{t-1\cdot} - S_1 z'_{t\cdot})\right]$$

$$\left[I_m \otimes (u_{t-1\cdot}\Sigma^{-1} - z_{t\cdot}S'_1)\right] \xrightarrow{\mathrm{P}} \Sigma \otimes (\Sigma^{-1} - S_{11}). \qquad (21)$$

Thus, one of the sufficient conditions of Proposition 21, Dhrymes (1989) p. 327, is satisfied and, consequently, under the null $R = 0$,

$$\sqrt{T}\tilde{r} \xrightarrow{\mathrm{d}} N(0, \Sigma \otimes (\Sigma^{-1} - S_{11})). \qquad (22)$$

It is interesting to note that, **if** the elements of U were **known,** we could obtain the estimator $\hat{R} = (U'_{-1}U_{-1})^{-1}U'_{-1}U$, which, under the null, obeys:

$$\sqrt{T}\hat{r} = \frac{1}{\sqrt{T}}\sum_{t=2}^{T}(I_m \otimes (U'_{-1}U_{-1})^{-1}u'_{t-1\cdot})u'_{t\cdot} \xrightarrow{\mathrm{d}} N(0, \Sigma \otimes \Sigma^{-1}). \qquad (23)$$

We have therefore proved:

Theorem 1 Given the model in equation (1) and the assumptions stated in (i) through (iii), the following are true:

1 If the elements of the matrix U are known, we can estimate the unknown matrix R by means of equation (23), which yields a consistent estimator whose limiting distribution is $N(0, \Sigma \otimes \Sigma^{-1})$.
2 If the elements of U are not known but are estimated by means of the matrix of the OLS residuals from the regression of Y on Z, the limiting distribution of the estimator exhibited in equation (6) is given by

$$\sqrt{T}(\tilde{c} - c) \xrightarrow{\mathrm{d}} N(0, \Sigma \otimes S)$$

and thus the limiting distribution of the OLS estimator of the (vectorized matrix of) coefficients of the lagged dependent variable is given by:

$$\sqrt{T}(\tilde{a} - a) \xrightarrow{\mathrm{d}} N(0, \Sigma \otimes S_{11}).$$

3 The limiting distribution of the least squares estimator of the first-order autocorrelation (matrix) exhibited in equation (13) is, under the **null** hypothesis $H_0 : R = 0$, given by:

$$\sqrt{T}\mathrm{vec}(\tilde{R}) = \sqrt{T}\tilde{r} \xrightarrow{\mathrm{d}} N(0, \Sigma \otimes (\Sigma^{-1} - S_{11})).$$

4 The estimator in 3 above is efficient relative to the estimator in 1.

Corollary 1 A test statistic, under the null, for testing the hypothesis of (first-order) autocorrelation in the residuals is given by:

$$\delta = T\tilde{r}'[\tilde{\Sigma}^{-1} \otimes (\tilde{\Sigma}^{-1} - \tilde{S}_{11})^{-1}]\tilde{r}) \xrightarrow{\text{d}} \chi^2_{m^2}. \tag{24}$$

Proof Evident from Theorem 1.

Remark 3 Notice that the conclusion in parts 1 and 3 above reveal a somewhat counter-intuitive result viz. that **knowing more, results in inefficiency** relative to the case where we know less; more specifically, the estimator of R, assuming that U is **known, is inefficient** relative to a similar estimator obtained when U is **not known, but is estimated** by means of the matrix of OLS residuals from the regression of Y on Z. As it will be made clear below, this is also true when $m = 1$ and $R = \rho$, a scalar.

Remark 4 If, in a given application, the estimated matrix $\tilde{\Sigma}^{-1} - \tilde{S}_{11}$ is **not at least positive semi-definite,** the test fails. If it is positive semi-definite but not positive definite we may use in equation (24) the **generalized inverse,** instead of the inverse. If the matrix itself (not only the estimated one) is positive semi-definite **but not** positive definite, the distribution is still asymptotically χ^2, but with degrees of freedom equal to the rank of $\Sigma^{-1} - S_{11}$. Notice that these matrices can easily be estimated consistently by:

$$\tilde{\Sigma} = \frac{1}{T}\tilde{U}'\tilde{U}, \quad \tilde{S}_{11} = (I, 0)\left(\frac{Z'Z}{T}\right)^{-1}(I, 0)'.$$

Remark 5 If the model of equation (1) contains more than one lag of the dependent variable, the test procedure **remains the same,** as it is clear from the derivation given above, because under the null $u_{t-1\cdot}$ is independent of $u_{t-j\cdot}$, for $j \geq 2$.

Remark 6 When the alternative is of the form

$$u_{t\cdot} = u_{t-2\cdot}R_2 + \epsilon_{t\cdot}$$

the analog of the δ-test will be applicable, but it would involve the limiting distribution of $A\sqrt{T}(\tilde{A} - A)$ instead of that of $\sqrt{T}(\tilde{A} - A)$. If the specification were $u_{t\cdot} = u_{t-3\cdot}R_3 + \epsilon_{t\cdot}$, it would involve the limiting distribution of $A^2\sqrt{T}(\tilde{A} - A)$, and so on. This is so because $(U'_{-p}Y_{-1}/T)$ converges, at least in probability, to ΣA^p.

Remark 7 Note that in the case $m = 1$, and consequently $\tilde{R} = \tilde{\rho}$, the test statistic of equation (23) reduces to

$$T\text{vec}(\tilde{R})'[\tilde{\Sigma}^{-1} \otimes (\tilde{\Sigma}^{-1} - \tilde{S}_{11})^{-1}]\text{vec}(\tilde{R}) = \frac{T\tilde{\rho}^2}{1 - \text{AVar}(\tilde{a}_{11})} \tag{25}$$

where $\text{Avar}(\tilde{a}_{11})$ is the variance of the limiting distribution of the OLS estimated coefficient of the lagged dependent variable. Thus, the δ statistic reduces to the square of the h-statistic, as given by Durbin (1970a), because basically $\Sigma \otimes \Sigma^{-1}$ reduces to unity in the case $m = 1$. Thus, the case where $\Sigma^{-1} - S_{11}$ **is not at least positive semi-definite** corresponds to the case where the asymptotic variance in question is equal to or greater than 1. When this is so one should employ an alternative procedure to be derived below.

Notice, further, that in the scalar case the estimator of ρ when U is **known** converges to $N(0, 1)$, while the corresponding estimator when U is **not known** but is estimated by means of the OLS residuals from the regression Y on Z converges to a $N(0, 1 - \text{AVar}(\tilde{a}_{11}))$!

3 An Alternative Test when the δ Test Fails

The δ statistic occasionally yields inadmissible results, and is thus desirable to obtain another test that "always works". To this end write the model in equation (1) as:

$$Y = ZC + U_{-1}R + E = WD + E$$
$$E = (\epsilon_{t\cdot}), \quad W = (Y_{-1}, X, U_{-1}) = (Z, U_{-1}), \quad D = (C', R')' \tag{26}$$

where we have merely made use of the alternative specification in equation (4). If we could observe U we would simply estimate R by OLS and then carry out a test on R as we would with any other OLS-estimated parameter. Since we cannot, we take a page out of two stage least squares procedures and estimate it by using the OLS residuals from the regression of Y on Z. The estimator thus obtained is,

$$\tilde{D} = (\tilde{W}'\tilde{W})^{-1}\tilde{W}'Y = (\tilde{W}'\tilde{W})^{-1}\tilde{W}'WD$$
$$+ (\tilde{W}'\tilde{W})^{-1}\tilde{W}'E, \quad \tilde{W} = (Z, \tilde{U}_{-1}). \tag{27}$$

Under the null $R = 0$, we obtain

$$(\tilde{W}'\tilde{W})^{-1}\tilde{W}'WD = \begin{bmatrix} Z'Z & Z'\tilde{U}_{-1} \\ \tilde{U}'_{-1}Z & \tilde{U}'_{-1}\tilde{U}_{-1} \end{bmatrix}^{-1} \begin{bmatrix} Z'Z & Z'U_{-1} \\ \tilde{U}'_{-1}Z & \tilde{U}'_{-1}U_{-1} \end{bmatrix} D = \begin{bmatrix} I \\ 0 \end{bmatrix} C \tag{28}$$

so that

$$\sqrt{T}(\tilde{D} - D) \sim \frac{1}{\sqrt{T}} S^* \tilde{W}'E \sim \frac{1}{\sqrt{T}} S^* W'E, \quad S^* = \operatorname*{plim}_{T\to\infty} (\tilde{W}'\tilde{W}/T)^{-1}. \tag{29}$$

Vectorizing, we have under the null:

$$\sqrt{T}\text{vec}(\tilde{D} - D) \sim \frac{1}{\sqrt{T}} \sum_{t=1}^{T} (I_m \otimes S^* w'_{t\cdot}) \epsilon'_{t\cdot}. \tag{30}$$

Using the same arguments as in the derivation of δ we conclude that, under the null,

$$\sqrt{T}\text{vec}(\tilde{D} - D) \xrightarrow{\text{d}} N(0, \Sigma \otimes S^*), \quad S^* = \begin{bmatrix} S^*_{11} & S^*_{12} \\ S^*_{21} & S^*_{22} \end{bmatrix}, \text{ where} \tag{31}$$

$$S^{*-1} == \begin{bmatrix} S^{-1} & \Sigma'_* \\ \Sigma_* & \Sigma \end{bmatrix}, \quad \Sigma_* = (\Sigma, 0), \text{ so that } S^*_{22} = (\Sigma - \Sigma S_{11} \Sigma)^{-1}$$

The preceding also implies that, under the null,

$$\tilde{D} \xrightarrow{\text{P}} D. \tag{32}$$

so that D is estimated consistently and has a well-defined limiting distribution.

Using the same arguments as we did in the discussion immediately following equation (9), we conclude that the estimator of R obeys:

$$\sqrt{T}\text{vec}(\tilde{R}) = \sqrt{T}\tilde{r} \xrightarrow{\text{d}} N(0, \Sigma \otimes S^*_{22}). \tag{33}$$

We have therefore proved:

Theorem 2 Under the conditions of Theorem 1, write the model of equation (1), as

$$Y = ZC + U_{-1}R + E = WD + E$$

$$E = (\epsilon_{t\cdot}), \quad W = (Y_{-1}, X, U_{-1}) = (Z, U_{-1}), \quad D = (C', R')'.$$

The following statements are true:

1 Regressing Y on $\tilde{W} = (Y_{-1}, X, \tilde{U}_{-1}) = (Z, \tilde{U}_{-1})$, where $\tilde{U}_{-1}$ is the lagged matrix of the OLS residuals from the regression of Y on Z, yields the estimator of equation (26) which, under the null, obeys:

$$\sqrt{T}\mathrm{vec}(\tilde{D} - D) \sim \frac{1}{\sqrt{T}} \sum_{t=1}^{T} (I_m \otimes S^* w_{t\cdot}')\epsilon_{t\cdot}'. \tag{34}$$

2 This estimator of D is consistent and its limiting distribution is given by

$$\sqrt{T}\mathrm{vec}(\tilde{D} - D) \stackrel{\mathrm{d}}{\to} N(0, \Sigma \otimes S^*) \tag{35}$$

where S^* is as defined in equation (29).

3 The limiting distribution of the autocorrelation matrix estimator $\tilde{R}$ is given by:

$$\sqrt{T}\mathrm{vec}(\tilde{R}) = \sqrt{T}\tilde{r} \stackrel{\mathrm{d}}{\to} N(0, \Sigma \otimes S_{22}^*), \quad S_{22}^* = (\Sigma - \Sigma S_{11} \Sigma)^{-1}. \tag{36}$$

4 If U were known and we employed the same procedure embedded in Theorem 2, we should get exactly the same results as in part ii, although we would have the option of estimating R directly from U, as we did in Theorem 1.

Corollary 2 A test of the null hypothesis

$H_0: \ R = 0$
as against the alternative
$H_1: \ R \neq 0$

may be carried out by means of the statistic

$$\delta^* = T\tilde{r}'[\tilde{\Sigma}^{-1} \otimes (\tilde{\Sigma} - \tilde{\Sigma}\tilde{S}_{11}\tilde{\Sigma})^{-1}]\tilde{r} \stackrel{\mathrm{d}}{\to} \chi^2_{m^2} \tag{37}$$

where

$$\tilde{\Sigma} = \frac{1}{T}\tilde{U}'\tilde{U}, \text{ and } \tilde{S}^*_{22} \text{ is the appropriate submatrix of } (\tilde{W}'\tilde{W}/T)^{-1}.$$

Remark 8 Since under the null the process $u_{t\cdot}$ is strictly stationary, we could as well estimate,

$$\tilde{\Sigma} = \frac{1}{T-1}\tilde{U}'_{-1}\tilde{U}_{-1}.$$

The loss of one observation is inconsequential if the sample is at all large.

Remark 9 Because $\tilde{S}^{*-1}_{22}$ is a (principal) submatrix of $(\tilde{W}'\tilde{W}/T)^{-1}$ and the latter must be invertible for estimators to exist, we conclude that **if estimators can be obtained in this context** $\tilde{S}^*_{22}$ **is invertible** and, thus, this test can **always** be carried out. Consequently, this should become the standard test of choice, and there is no particular reason one should employ the test based on δ. Perhaps in an era of less powerful computing capabilities the lower dimensions of the relevant regressions made δ appealing; this is no longer true, however, and consequently there is no reason to employ it, given that it does not always produce conclusive results – even if all estimators required can be obtained! The only possible reason to employ it may be deduced from Proposition 1, below.

Remark 10 The two δ tests (δ and δ^*) discussed above are not identical (or equivalent), although their (respective) test statistics have the same limiting distribution. The first version, δ, is a **conformity** test, that is we estimate under the null and the test asks whether the results "conform" with the null. (For reasons that are not clear to me such tests are often termed *Wald* tests). The second test, δ^*, is a likelihood ratio type of test, that is we estimate using the form of the alternative and we ask of the results whether they support the null. This should explain why sometimes the first does not produce a definitive answer, while the second always does.

4 Diagonal *R*

When the autoregression matrix R is diagonal, the situation is more complex than that of the simple Durbin context, **unless**

$$\mathrm{Cov}(\epsilon_{t\cdot}) = \mathrm{diag}(\sigma_{11}, \sigma_{22}, \ldots, \sigma_{mm}) \tag{38}$$

in which case we are reduced to doing m h-tests *seriatim*.

We could deal with this case by simply using the results above and taking into account only the diagonal elements of the estimator of R, as defined in the previous discussion, that is for the diagonal specification we set $\tilde{r}_D = H'\tilde{R}$ and derive the limiting distribution in the diagonal case by using he results of Theorems 1 and 2 (this notation will be clarified immediately below). To do so, however, entails potential loss of efficiency in that we do not fully take into account all available information and, in particular, the assertion that

$$r_{ij} = 0, \quad i \neq j.$$

Thus, we shall employ a new framework using the **fact** that R is diagonal and the covariance matrix of the structural error, ϵ, is **unrestricted**, that is we produce the analog of the δ and δ^*-statistics when R is diagonal but the elements of $u_{t\cdot}$ are cross correlated. Specifically, the alternative dealt with is

$$u_{t\cdot} = u_{t-1\cdot}R + \epsilon_{t\cdot}, \quad R = \mathrm{diag}(r_{11}, r_{22}, \ldots, r_{mm}), \quad \mathrm{Cov}(\epsilon_{t\cdot}) = \Sigma > 0 \tag{39}$$

where,

$$\Sigma = (\sigma_{ij}), \quad \sigma_{ij} \neq 0, \quad \text{for} \quad i \neq j.$$

If the u's could be observed, we would write the model as

$$u = Vr_D + e, \quad u = \mathrm{vec}(U), \quad V = \mathrm{diag}(v_{\cdot 1}, v_{\cdot 2}, \ldots, v_{\cdot m}) \tag{40}$$

where $v_{\cdot i}$ is the ith column of U_{-1}, $r_D = (r_{11}, r_{22}, \ldots, r_{mm})'$, and estimate

$$\hat{r}_D = [V'(\Sigma^{-1} \otimes I_T)V]^{-1} V'(\Sigma^{-1} \otimes I_T)u \tag{41}$$

the limiting distribution of which is given by

$$\sqrt{T}\hat{r}_D \xrightarrow{\mathrm{d}} N(0, \Omega_*^{-1}), \quad \Omega_* = (\sigma_{ij}\sigma^{ij}). \tag{42}$$

In connection with the result above we have:

Lemma 1 The matrix $\Omega_* = (\sigma^{ij}\sigma_{ij})$ is positive (semi) definite if and only if $\Sigma \otimes \Sigma^{-1}$ has this property.

Proof Define the matrix

$$H = \text{diag}(e_{\cdot 1}, e_{\cdot 2}, \ldots, e_{\cdot m}) \tag{43}$$

where $e_{\cdot i}$ is an m-element column vector all of whose element are zero save the ith, which is unity. Note that H is $m^2 \times m$, of rank m and its columns are orthonormal. It may be easily verified that:

$$\Omega_* = H'(\Sigma \otimes \Sigma^{-1})H. \tag{44}$$

Let α be an arbitrary m-element vector and consider

$$g = \alpha'\Omega_*\alpha = (\alpha' H)(\Sigma \otimes \Sigma^{-1})(H\alpha). \tag{45}$$

Necessity: Since $H\alpha = 0$ if an only if $\alpha = 0$ and $\Omega_* > 0$ by assumption, this implies that $\Sigma \otimes \Sigma^{-1} > 0$. Sufficiency: Suppose that $(\Sigma \otimes \Sigma^{-1}) > 0$, then for arbitrary non-null α

$$g = \alpha'\Omega_*\alpha = (\alpha' H)(\Sigma \otimes \Sigma^{-1})(H\alpha) > 0$$

owing to the fact that if $\alpha \neq 0$, $H\alpha \neq 0$.

Remark 11 Notice that for a block matrix, say P, the operation $H'PH$ simply creates a matrix whose (ij) element is the (ij) element of the (ij) block of the matrix P. Thus, for example the (ij) block of $\Sigma \otimes \Sigma^{-1}$ is $\sigma_{ij}\Sigma^{-1}$ and the (ij) element of this block is $\sigma_{ij}\sigma^{ij}$. It is thus quite apparent that $H'(\Sigma^{-1} \otimes \Sigma)H = H'(\Sigma \otimes \Sigma^{-1})H$.
The estimator in equation (41) is infeasible because in fact the u's are not observed. Since they are not, we may try using instead the corresponding OLS residuals from the regression of Y on Z. When we do so we have, under the null,

$$\sqrt{T}\tilde{r}_D = \left(\frac{\tilde{V}'(\tilde{\Sigma}^{-1} \otimes I_T)\tilde{V}}{T} \right)^{-1} \frac{1}{\sqrt{T}} \tilde{V}'(\tilde{\Sigma}^{-1} \otimes I_T)\tilde{u}. \tag{46}$$

To determine its limiting distribution we need a slightly different approach than the one employed in previous discussions. To this end note that

$$\tilde{V}'(\tilde{\Sigma}^{-1} \otimes I_T)\tilde{V} = [\tilde{\sigma}^{ij}\tilde{v}_{\cdot i}'\tilde{v}_{\cdot j}] \tag{47}$$

that is, it is an $m \times m$ matrix with typical element $\tilde{\sigma}^{ij}\tilde{v}'_{\cdot i}\tilde{v}_{\cdot i}$. Evidently,

$$\frac{1}{T}\tilde{\sigma}^{ij}\tilde{v}'_{\cdot i}\tilde{v}_{\cdot j} \overset{\mathrm{P}}{\to} \sigma_{ij}\sigma^{ij}$$

and thus

$$\frac{1}{T}\tilde{V}'(\tilde{\Sigma}^{-1} \otimes I_T)\tilde{V} \overset{\mathrm{P}}{\to} \Omega_* \tag{48}$$

as was the case when the elements of U were assumed to be known. Recalling that

$$\tilde{v}_{\cdot i} = v_{\cdot i} - Z_{-1}(\tilde{c}_{\cdot i} - c_{\cdot i}), \quad \tilde{u}_{\cdot j} = u_{\cdot j} - Z(\tilde{c}_{\cdot j} - c_{\cdot j})$$

we have

$$\frac{1}{\sqrt{T}}\tilde{v}'_{\cdot i}\tilde{u}_{\cdot j} \sim \frac{1}{\sqrt{T}}(v_{\cdot i} - ZS'_1\sigma_{\cdot i})'u_{\cdot j} = \frac{1}{T}v^{*\prime}_{\cdot i}u_{\cdot j}, \quad v^*_{\cdot i} = v_{\cdot i} - ZS'_1\sigma_{\cdot i}. \tag{49}$$

We can now write the rightmost term of equation (46) as

$$\frac{1}{\sqrt{T}}\tilde{V}'(\tilde{\Sigma}^{-1} \otimes I_T)\tilde{u} \sim \frac{1}{\sqrt{T}}V^{*\prime}(\Sigma^{-1} \otimes I_T)u, \quad V^* = \mathrm{diag}(v^*_{\cdot 1}, v^*_{\cdot 2}, \ldots, v^*_{\cdot m}) \tag{50}$$

the ith element of the right vector above being:

$$\sum_{j=1}^{m}\sigma^{ij}v^{*\prime}_{\cdot i}u_{\cdot j} = \sum_{t=2}^{T}v^*_{ti}\sum_{j=1}^{m}\sigma^{ij}u_{tj}$$

$$= \sum_{t=2}^{T}v^*_{ti}\sigma^{i\cdot}u'_{t\cdot}. \tag{51}$$

Define the vector:

$$\zeta^*_{(T)} = \frac{1}{\sqrt{T}}\sum_{t=2}^{T}\zeta_t, \quad \zeta_t = \begin{bmatrix} v^*_{t1}\sigma^{1\cdot} \\ v^*_{t2}\sigma^{2\cdot} \\ \vdots \\ v^*_{tm}\sigma^{m\cdot} \end{bmatrix} u'_{t\cdot}.$$

It is easily seen that the summands above, the *zeta*'s, are a zero mean MD sequence obeying the Lindeberg condition, just as in the earlier discussion. They also obey the sufficient condition for Proposition 21, Dhrymes (1989), p. 327, because,

$$\operatorname*{plim}_{T\to\infty} \frac{1}{T}\sum_{t=2}^{T} E[\zeta_t\zeta_t'|\mathcal{A}_{t-1}] = (\sigma^{ij}\omega_{ij}), \quad \omega_{ij} = \sigma_{ij} - \sigma_{i\cdot}S_{11}\sigma_{\cdot j}. \tag{52}$$

Since the sequence obeys a sufficient condition for the application of a MD CLT, $\zeta^*_{(T)}$ converges in distribution, and we conclude that under the null, for the case of diagonal R,

$$\sqrt{T}\tilde{r}_D \xrightarrow{\text{d}} N(0, \Phi), \quad \Phi = \Omega_*^{-1} - \Omega_*^{-1}(\sigma^{ij}\sigma_{i\cdot}S_{11}\sigma_{\cdot j})\Omega_*^{-1}, \text{ or} \tag{53}$$

$$\Phi = (\sigma^{ij}\sigma_{ij})^{-1}\Omega_1(\sigma^{ij}\sigma_{ij})^{-1}, \quad \Omega_1 = [\sigma^{ij}(\sigma_{ij} - \sigma_{i\cdot}S_{11}\sigma_{\cdot j})]. \tag{54}$$

If the matrix Ω_1 is at least positive semi-definite, we may carry out a test of the null by means of the test statistic:

$$\delta_D = T\tilde{r}_D'\tilde{\Phi}^{-1}\tilde{r}_D \xrightarrow{\text{d}} \chi^2_m, \quad \text{or, more generally,} \quad \delta_D \xrightarrow{\text{d}} \chi^2_{\text{rank}(\Omega_1)}. \tag{55}$$

We have therfore proved:

Theorem 3 Under the conditions of Theorem 1, and the additional specification that $R = \text{diag}(r_{11}, r_{22}, \ldots, r_{mm})$, the following statements are true:

1 If the elements of U are **known** we may estimate

$$\hat{r}_D = [V'(\Sigma^{-1} \otimes I_T)V]^{-1}V'(\Sigma^{-1} \otimes I_T)u$$

which, under the null, obeys

$$\sqrt{T}\hat{r}_D \xrightarrow{\text{d}} N(0, \Omega_*^{-1}), \quad \Omega_* = (\sigma_{ij}\sigma^{ij}).$$

2 Because we do not generally know the matrix of the structural error observations, the estimator above, though consistent, is infeasible. Instead we obtain, under the null, the feasible estimator

$$\tilde{r}_D = \left(\frac{\tilde{V}'(\tilde{\Sigma}^{-1}\otimes I_T)\tilde{V}}{T}\right)^{-1} \frac{1}{T}\tilde{V}'(\tilde{\Sigma}^{-1}\otimes I_T)\tilde{u} \xrightarrow{\text{P}} 0, \text{ obeying}$$

$$\sqrt{T}\tilde{r}_D \sim \left(\frac{V'(\Sigma^{-1}\otimes I_T)V}{T}\right)^{-1} \frac{1}{\sqrt{T}}V^{*\prime}(\Sigma^{-1}\otimes I_T)u$$

which has the limiting distribution

$$\sqrt{T}\tilde{r}_D \xrightarrow{\text{d}} N(0, \Phi), \quad \Phi = \Omega_*^{-1} - \Omega_*^{-1}(\sigma^{ij}\sigma_{i\cdot}S_{11}\sigma_{\cdot j})\Omega_*^{-1}$$

as defined in equations (42) through (54).

3 The estimator given in 2 is **efficient** relative to that given in 1.

Corollary 3 A test of the null hypothesis

$H_0: \ R = 0$
as against the alternative
$H_1: \ R \neq 0$

may be carried out by means of the statistic

$$\delta_D = T\tilde{r}_D'\tilde{\Phi}^{-1}\tilde{r}_D \xrightarrow{\text{d}} \chi_m^2$$

or more generally

$$\delta_D = T\tilde{r}_D'\tilde{\Phi}_g\tilde{r}_D \xrightarrow{\text{d}} \chi^2_{\text{rank}(\Phi)}$$

where $\Phi_{(g)}$ is the **generalized inverse** of Φ.

Remark 12 A comparison of equations (42) and (53) discloses the same phenomenon noted in Remark 3, that is that **knowing more,** results in inefficiency relative to the case where we know less or, more specifically, **knowing** U results in an estimator which is **inefficient** relative to a similar estimator obtained when U is **not known** but is estimated by the matrix of the least squares residuals in the regression of Y on Z.

Remark 13 Notice that in the case $m = 1$, δ_D reduces to the square of the h-statistic because $\Omega_* = 1$ and $\Omega_1 = 1 - \text{Avar}(\hat{a}_{11})$, as in Durbin (1970a).

If the (estimated) matrix Ω_1 is **indefinite, or negative definite,** the test above is inoperable and an alternative test may be undertaken as follows. Write (the observations on) the ith equation of the model as

$$y_{\cdot i} = Y_{-1}a_{\cdot i} + Xb_{\cdot i} + r_{ii}v_{\cdot i} + \epsilon_{\cdot i} = Zc_{\cdot i} + r_{ii}v_{\cdot i} + \epsilon_{\cdot i}, \quad i = 1, 2, 3, \ldots, m \tag{56}$$

and stack them so that the observations on the entire model can be written as

$$y = (I_m \otimes Z)c + Vr_D + e, \quad r_D = (r_{11}, r_{22}, \ldots, r_{mm})',$$
$$V = \text{diag}(v_{\cdot 1}, v_{\cdot 2}, \ldots, v_{\cdot m}). \tag{57}$$

Since V is not observable we use instead the columns $(\tilde{v}_{\cdot i})$ of the matrix of the OLS residuals $\tilde{U}_{-1}$, that is,

$$\tilde{V} = \mathrm{diag}(\tilde{v}_{\cdot 1}, \tilde{v}_{\cdot 2}, \tilde{v}_{\cdot 3}, \ldots, \tilde{v}_{\cdot m}) \tag{58}$$

and estimate

$$\tilde{d} = [(\tilde{W}'(\tilde{\Sigma}^{-1} \otimes I_T)\tilde{W}]^{-1}\tilde{W}'(\tilde{\Sigma}^{-1} \otimes I_T)y, \;\; \tilde{W} = [(I_m \otimes Z), \tilde{V}], \;\; d = (c', r')'. \tag{59}$$

As in the discussion above we can show that, under the null,

$$[(\tilde{W}'(\tilde{\Sigma}^{-1} \otimes I_T)\tilde{W}]^{-1}\tilde{W}'(\tilde{\Sigma}^{-1} \otimes I_T)Wd = (I, 0)'c \tag{60}$$

so that the estimator of d and hence of r_D is consistent. We can further show that, under the null,

$$\sqrt{T}(\tilde{d} - d) \sim \Psi \frac{1}{\sqrt{T}} W'(\Sigma^{-1} \otimes I_m)e \xrightarrow{\mathrm{d}} N(0, \Psi) \tag{61}$$

where

$$\Psi^{-1} = \operatorname*{plim}_{T\to\infty} \frac{1}{T} W'(\Sigma^{-1} \otimes I_T)W. \tag{62}$$

It follows then that, under the null,

$$\sqrt{T}\tilde{r} \xrightarrow{\mathrm{d}} N(0, \Psi_{22}) \tag{63}$$

where Ψ_{22} is the $m \times m$ principal submatrix of Ψ, consisting of its last m rows and columns. Consequently, to test the null $H_0 : r_D = 0$ we may use the test statistic

$$\delta_D^* = T\tilde{r}_D'\tilde{\Psi}_{22}^{-1}\tilde{r}_D \xrightarrow{\mathrm{d}} \chi_m \tag{64}$$

where

$$\tilde{\Psi}_{22}^{-1} = \frac{1}{T}\left(\tilde{V}'(\tilde{\Sigma}^{-1} \otimes I_T)\tilde{V} - \tilde{V}'(\tilde{\Sigma}^{-1} \otimes Z(Z'Z)^{-1}Z')\tilde{V}\right) \tag{65}$$

and $\tilde{\Sigma} = \tilde{U}'\tilde{U}/T$.

If an estimator for r_D is obtainable, the matrices of equations (62) and (65) will be **positive definite**, and hence invertible, so that this test is always operational in practice.
We have therefore proved:

Theorem 4 Under the conditions of Theorem 1, and the additional specification that $R = \text{diag}(r_{11}, r_{22}, \ldots, r_{mm})$, let the elements of U be estimated by means of the residuals of the regression of Y on Z, that is $\tilde{U} = Y - Z\tilde{C}$. Using generalized least squares with estimated covariance matrix $\tilde{\Sigma} = (\tilde{U}'\tilde{U}/T)$, regress $y = \text{vec}(Y)$ on $\tilde{W}$ to obtain:

$$\tilde{d} = [(\tilde{W}'(\tilde{\Sigma}^{-1} \otimes I_T)\tilde{W}]^{-1}\tilde{W}'(\tilde{\Sigma}^{-1} \otimes I_T)y, \; \tilde{W} = [(I_m \otimes Z), \tilde{V}], \; d = (c', r')'.$$

Then the following statements are true:

1 Under the null,

$$\tilde{d} - d \sim \tilde{\Psi}\left(\frac{1}{T}\right)\tilde{W}'(\tilde{\Sigma}^{-1} \otimes I_T)u \xrightarrow{\text{P}} 0$$

and

$$\sqrt{T}\tilde{d} \xrightarrow{\text{d}} N(0, \Psi), \quad \Psi = \underset{T \to \infty}{\text{plim}} \left(\frac{\tilde{W}'(\tilde{\Sigma} \otimes I_T)\tilde{W}}{T}\right)^{-1}.$$

2 In addition,

$$\sqrt{T}\tilde{r}_D \xrightarrow{\text{d}} N(0, \Psi_{22}), \quad \Psi = \begin{bmatrix} \Psi_{11} & \Psi_{12} \\ \Psi_{21} & \Psi_{22} \end{bmatrix}$$

where $\Psi_{22} = \Omega_1^{-1}$ as the latter is defined in equation (54). The estimator of Ψ_{22}^{-1} is defined in equation (65).

Corollary 4 A test of the null hypothesis

$H_0: \; r_D = 0$
as against the alternative
$H_1: \; r_D \neq 0$

may be carried out by means of the statistic

$$\delta_D^* = T\tilde{r}_D'(\tilde{\Psi}_{22})^{-1}\tilde{r}_D \xrightarrow{\text{d}} \chi_m^2$$

or more generally

$$\delta_D^* = T\tilde{r}_D'\tilde{\Psi}_{(22)g}\tilde{r}_D \xrightarrow{\text{d}} \chi^2_{\text{rank}(\Psi_{22})}.$$

We now consider the relative efficiencies among the estimators obtained in Theorems 1 through 4. Since all estimators converge in distribution to a zero mean **normal** vector, questions of relative efficiency are completely resolved by considering differences of the covariance matrices of the respective limiting distributions.
We have

Proposition 1 The following statements are true:

1 The estimator of Theorem 1 is efficient relative to the estimator in Theorem 2.
2 The estimator of Theorem 3 is efficient relative to the estimator of Theorem 4.

Proof Let

$$\Delta_{12} = \Sigma \otimes F, \quad F = (\Sigma - \Sigma S_{11} \Sigma)^{-1} - (\Sigma^{-1} - S_{11}) \tag{66}$$

and note that Δ_{12} is positive (semi) definite if and only if F is. Using the result in Dhrymes (2000) p. 44, we have that:

$$F = \Sigma^{-1} + (S_{11}^{-1} - \Sigma)^{-1} - (\Sigma^{-1} - S_{11}) = S_{11} + (S_{11}^{-1} - \Sigma)^{-1}. \tag{67}$$

Assuming that $\Sigma^{-1} - S_{11}$ is positive (semi) definite, so that the test of Theorem 1 is applicable, we conclude from Dhrymes (2000), Proposition 2.66 p. 89, that $(S_{11}^{-1} - \Sigma) \geq 0$, which shows that $\Delta_{12} \geq 0$, thus proving 1.

To prove 2, consider

$$\Delta_{34} = \Omega_1^{-1} - \Omega_*^{-1} \Omega_1 \Omega_*^{-1}, \quad \Omega_1 = \Omega_* - G, \quad G = [\sigma^{ij}(\sigma_{i\cdot} S_{11} \sigma_{\cdot j})] \tag{68}$$

so that using again the results in Dhrymes (2000) p. 44 and p. 89, we obtain

$$\Omega_1^{-1} = \Omega_*^{-1} + \Omega_*^{-1}(G^{-1} - \Omega_*^{-1})^{-1} \Omega_*^{-1} \text{ and, consequently} \tag{69}$$

$$\Delta_{34} = \Omega_*^{-1}(G^{-1} - \Omega_*^{-1})^{-1} \Omega_*^{-1} + \Omega_*^{-1} G \Omega_*^{-1} \geq 0. \tag{70}$$

That G is a positive definite matrix follows from the fact that,

$$G = H'(\Sigma^{-1} \otimes \Sigma S_{11} \Sigma) H. \qquad \text{q.e.d.}$$

Remark 14 Because $r_D = H'\text{vec}(R)$, it may be interesting to compare the results of Theorem 1 to those of Theorem 3, and those of Theorem 2 to those of Theorem 4. The issue is the relation between the limiting covariance matrices $H'[\Sigma \otimes (\Sigma^{-1} - S_{11})]H$ implied by Theorem 1 and Ω_*^{-1} of Theorem 3; similarly an interesting comparison would be between $H'(\Sigma \otimes S_{22}^*)H$ implied by Theorem 2, and the limiting covariance matrix Ψ_{22} of Theorem 4.

A direct comparison cannot be easily made owing to the complexity of the expressions; on the other hand, from the standard theory of restricted least squares, the **unrestricted estimator is inefficient relative to the restricted estimator**, when the restriction is valid. Consequently, estimating $\tilde{r}_D = H'\text{vec}(\tilde{R})$ is inefficient relative to the direct estimator of r_D.

10 Alternative Approaches to Estimation and Inference in Large Multifactor Panels: Small Sample Results with an Application to Modelling Asset Returns

*George Kapetanios and M. Hashem Pesaran**

1 Introduction

Panel data-sets have been increasingly used in economics to analyse complex economic phenomena. One of their attractions is the ability to use an extended data-set to obtain information about parameters of interest which are assumed to have common values across panel units. Most of the work carried out on panel data has usually assumed some form of cross-sectional independence to derive the theoretical properties of various inferential procedures. However, such assumptions are often suspect and as a result recent advances in the literature have focused on estimation of panel data models subject to error cross-sectional dependence.

A number of different approaches have been advanced for this purpose. In the case of spatial data-sets where a natural immutable distance measure is available the dependence is often captured through "spatial lags" using techniques familiar from the time series literature. In economic applications, spatial techniques are often adapted using alternative measures of "economic distance". This approach is exemplified in work by Lee and Pesaran (1993), Conley and Dupor (2003), Conley and Topa (2002) and Pesaran, Schuermann, and Weiner (2004), as well as the literature on spatial econometrics recently surveyed by Anselin (2001). In the case of panel data models where the cross-section dimension (N) is small (typically $N < 10$) and the time-series dimension (T) is large the standard approach is to treat the equations from the different cross-section units as a system of seemingly unrelated regression equations (SURE) and then estimate the system by the Generalized Least Squares (GLS) techniques.

* We are grateful to Til Schuermann and Bejorn Treutler for providing us with the company data used in the empirical section. We have also benefited from comments and discussions with Ron Smith and Takashi Yagamata.

In the case of panels with large cross-section dimension, the SURE approach is not practical and has led a number of investigators to consider unobserved factor models, where the cross-section error correlations are defined in terms of the factor loadings. Use of factor models is not new in economics and dates back to the pioneering work of Stone (1947) who applied the principal components (PC) analysis of Hotelling to US macroeconomic time series over the period 1922–38 and was able to demonstrate that three factors (namely total income, its rate of change and a time trend) explained over 97 percent of the total variations of all the 17 macro variables that he had considered. Until recently, subsequent applications of the PC approach to economic times series has been primarily in finance. See, for example, Chamberlain and Rothschild (1983), Connor and Korajzcyk (1986, 1988). But more recently the unobserved factor models have gained popularity for forecasting with a large number of variables as advocated by Stock and Watson (2002). The factor model is used very much in the spirit of the original work by Stone, in order to summarize the empirical content of a large number of macroeconomics variables by a small set of factors which, when estimated using principal components, is then used for further modelling and/or forecasting. A related literature on dynamic factor models has also been put forward by Forni and Reichlin (1998) and Forni, Hallin, Lippi, and Reichlin (2000).

Recent uses of factor models in forecasting focus on consistent estimation of unobserved factors and their loadings. Related theoretical advances by Bai and Ng (2002) and Bai (2003) are also concerned with estimation and selection of unobserved factors and do not consider the estimation and inference problems in standard panel data models where the objects of interest are slope coefficients of the conditioning variables (regressors). In such panels the unobserved factors are viewed as nuisance variables, introduced primarily to model the cross section dependencies of the error terms in a parsimonious manner relative to the SURE formulation.

Despite these differences, knowledge of factor models could still be useful for the analysis of panel data models if it is believed that the errors might be cross-sectionally correlated. Disregarding the possible factor structure of the errors in panel data models can lead to inconsistent parameter estimates and incorrect inference. Coakley, Fuertes, and Smith (2002) suggest a possible solution to the problem using the method of Stock and Watson (2002). But, as Pesaran (2006) shows, the PC approach proposed by Coakley, Fuertes, and Smith (2002) can still yield inconsistent estimates. Pesaran (2006) suggests a new approach by noting that linear combinations of the unobserved factors can be well approximated by cross-section averages of the dependent variable and the observed regressors. This leads to a new set of estimators, referred to as the Common Correlated Effects (CCE) estimators, that can be computed by running standard panel regressions augmented with the cross-section averages of the dependent and independent variables. The CCE procedure is applicable to panels with a single or multiple unobserved factors so long as the number of unobserved factors is fixed.

In this chapter we consider an alternative two-stage estimation method where in the first stage principal components of all the economic variables in the panel data model are obtained as in Stock and Watson (2002), and in the second stage the model is estimated augmenting the observed regressors with the estimated PCs. Unlike the CCE method the implementation of the PC augmented procedure requires the determination of the number of factors to be included in the second stage. This can be done using the criteria advanced in Bai and Ng (2002).

The small sample properties of the CCE and the PC augmented estimators will be investigated by means of Monte Carlo experiments, allowing for up to four factors and regressors. We find that augmenting the panel data model with cross-sectional averages of the dependent and explanatory variable works well in the multiple factor case. This is line with the results of Monte Carlo experiments reported by Pesaran (2006) and Coakley, Fuertes, and Smith (2006). On the other hand the PC augmented method does not perform as well, and can lead to substantial size distortions. This could be partly due to the small sample errors in the number of factors selected by the Bai and Ng procedure. To shed light on such a possibility we also conduct a number of Monte Carlo experiments where the factors are taken as observed, but it is not known which of the factors should actually be included in the PC augmented procedure. Using alternative regressor selection procedures it is shown that even in this setting the PC augmented method could be subject to substantial bias in small samples. We also provide an empirical application to a large panel of company returns with a wide geographical coverage where we estimate asset return regressions that include observed as well as unobserved regressors. The standard asset return equations routinely estimated in the finance literature either allow for unobserved factors or observed factors, but not both. We extend this literature by including both types of regressors in the analysis.

The plan of the chapter is as follows: section 2 sets out the multi-factor residual model, its assumptions and the CCE estimators; section 3 sets out the PC augmented estimators; section 4 describes the Monte Carlo design and discusses the results; while section 5 presents the empirical application, and finally, section 6 concludes.

2 Panel Data Models with Observed and Unobserved Common Effects

In this section we review the methodology introduced in Pesaran (2006). Let y_{it} be the observation on the ith cross-section unit at time t for $i = 1, 2, \ldots, N$; $t = 1, 2, \ldots, T$, and suppose that it is generated according to the following linear heterogeneous panel data model

$$y_{it} = \alpha_i' \mathbf{d}_t + \beta_i' \mathbf{x}_{it} + \gamma_i' \mathbf{f}_t + \varepsilon_{it} \tag{1}$$

where $\mathbf{d}_t$ is a $n \times 1$ vector of observed common effects (including deterministic components such as intercepts or seasonal dummies), $\mathbf{x}_{it}$ is a $k \times 1$ vector of observed individual-specific regressors on the ith cross-section unit at time t, $\mathbf{f}_t$ is the $m \times 1$ vector of unobserved common effects, and ε_{it} are the individual-specific (idiosyncratic) errors assumed to be independently distributed of $(\mathbf{d}_t, \mathbf{x}_{it})$, but allowed to follow general covariance stationary processes. The unobserved factors, $\mathbf{f}_t$, could be correlated with $(\mathbf{d}_t, \mathbf{x}_{it})$, and to allow for such a possibility the following specification for the individual specific regressors will be considered

$$\mathbf{x}_{it} = \mathbf{A}_i' \mathbf{d}_t + \Gamma_i' \mathbf{f}_t + \mathbf{v}_{it} \tag{2}$$

where $\mathbf{A}_i$ and Γ_i are $n \times k$ and $m \times k$, factor loading matrices with fixed components, $\mathbf{v}_{it}$ are the specific components of $\mathbf{x}_{it}$ distributed independently of the common effects and across i, but assumed to follow general covariance stationary processes. (For more details on the conditions assumed about ε_{it} and $\mathbf{v}_{it}$ see Pesaran, 2006.) In this chapter we assume that the common factors, $\mathbf{d}_t$ and $\mathbf{f}_t$, are covariance stationary, although the results obtained here can be readily extended to cases where one or more elements of the common factors could have unit roots and/or deterministic trends.

Combining (1) and (2) we now have

$$\underset{(k+1)\times 1}{\mathbf{z}_{it}} = \begin{pmatrix} y_{it} \\ \mathbf{x}_{it} \end{pmatrix} = \underset{(k+1)\times n}{\mathbf{B}_i'} \underset{n\times 1}{\mathbf{d}_t} + \underset{(k+1)\times m}{\mathbf{C}_i'} \underset{m\times 1}{\mathbf{f}_t} + \underset{(k+1)\times 1}{\mathbf{u}_{it}} \tag{3}$$

where

$$\mathbf{u}_{it} = \begin{pmatrix} \varepsilon_{it} + \beta_i' \mathbf{v}_{it} \\ \mathbf{v}_{it} \end{pmatrix} \tag{4}$$

$$\mathbf{B}_i = \begin{pmatrix} \alpha_i & \mathbf{A}_i \end{pmatrix} \begin{pmatrix} 1 & \mathbf{0} \\ \beta_i & \mathbf{I}_k \end{pmatrix}, \mathbf{C}_i = \begin{pmatrix} \gamma_i & \Gamma_i \end{pmatrix} \begin{pmatrix} 1 & \mathbf{0} \\ \beta_i & \mathbf{I}_k \end{pmatrix} \tag{5}$$

$\mathbf{I}_k$ is an identity matrix of order k, and the rank of $\mathbf{C}_i$ is determined by the rank of the $m \times (k+1)$ matrix of the unobserved factor loadings

$$\widetilde{\Gamma}_i = \begin{pmatrix} \gamma_i & \Gamma_i \end{pmatrix}. \tag{6}$$

As discussed in Pesaran (2006), the above set-up is sufficiently general and renders a variety of panel data models as special cases. In the panel literature with T small and N large, the primary parameters of interest are the means of the individual specific slope coefficients, $\beta_i, i = 1, 2, \ldots, N$. The common factor loadings, α_i and γ_i, are generally treated as nuisance parameters. In cases where both N and T are large, it is also possible to consider consistent estimation of the factor loadings. The presence of the unobserved factors in (1) implies that estimation of β_i and its cross-sectional mean cannot be undertaken using standard methods. Pesaran (2006) has suggested using cross-section averages of y_{it} and $\mathbf{x}_{it}$ as proxies for the unobserved factors in (1). To see why such an approach could work, consider simple cross-section averages of the equations in (3) (Pesaran (2006) considers cross-section weighted averages that are more general; but to simplify the exposition we confine our discussion to simple averages throughout):

$$\overline{\mathbf{z}}_t = \overline{\mathbf{B}}'\mathbf{d}_t + \overline{\mathbf{C}}'\mathbf{f}_t + \overline{\mathbf{u}}_t \tag{7}$$

where

$$\overline{\mathbf{z}}_t = \frac{1}{N}\sum_{i=1}^{N} \mathbf{z}_{it}, \overline{\mathbf{u}}_t = \frac{1}{N}\sum_{i=1}^{N} \mathbf{u}_{it}$$

and

$$\overline{\mathbf{B}} = \frac{1}{N}\sum_{i=1}^{N} \mathbf{B}_i, \overline{\mathbf{C}} = \frac{1}{N}\sum_{i=1}^{N} \mathbf{C}_i. \tag{8}$$

Suppose that,

$$Rank(\overline{\mathbf{C}}) = m \leq k+1, \text{ for all } N. \tag{9}$$

Then, we have,

$$\mathbf{f}_t = \left(\overline{\mathbf{C}}\overline{\mathbf{C}}'\right)^{-1} \overline{\mathbf{C}} \left(\overline{\mathbf{z}}_t - \overline{\mathbf{B}}'\mathbf{d}_t - \overline{\mathbf{u}}_t\right). \tag{10}$$

But since

$$\overline{\mathbf{u}}_t \overset{q.m.}{\rightarrow} \mathbf{0}, \text{ as } N \rightarrow \infty, \text{ for each } t \tag{11}$$

and

$$\overline{\mathbf{C}} \overset{p}{\rightarrow} \mathbf{C} = \widetilde{\Gamma} \begin{pmatrix} 1 & \mathbf{0} \\ \beta & \mathbf{I}_k \end{pmatrix}, \text{ as } N \rightarrow \infty \tag{12}$$

where

$$\widetilde{\Gamma} = \left(E(\gamma_i), E(\Gamma_i)\right) = (\gamma, \Gamma) \tag{13}$$

it follows, assuming that $Rank(\widetilde{\Gamma}) = m$, that

$$\mathbf{f}_t - \left(\mathbf{C}\mathbf{C}'\right)^{-1} \mathbf{C} \left(\overline{\mathbf{z}}_t - \overline{\mathbf{B}}'\mathbf{d}_t\right) \overset{p}{\rightarrow} \mathbf{0}, \text{ as } N \rightarrow \infty.$$

This suggests using $\overline{\mathbf{h}}_t = (\mathbf{d}_t', \overline{\mathbf{z}}_t')'$ as observable proxies for $\mathbf{f}_t$, and is the basic insight that lies behind the Common Correlated Effects estimators developed in Pesaran (2006). It is further shown that the CCE estimation procedure in fact holds even if $\widetilde{\Gamma}$ turns out to be rank deficient.

We now discuss the two estimators for the means of the individual specific slope coefficients proposed by Pesaran (2006). One is the Mean Group (MG) estimator proposed in Pesaran and Smith (1995) and the other is a generalization of the fixed-effects estimator that allows for the possibility of cross-section dependence. The former is referred to as the "Common Correlated Effects Mean Group" (CCEMG) estimator, and the latter as the "Common Correlated Effects Pooled" (CCEP) estimator.

The CCEMG estimator is a simple average of the individual CCE estimators, $\hat{\mathbf{b}}_i$ of β_i,

$$\hat{\mathbf{b}}_{MG} = N^{-1} \sum_{i=1}^{N} \hat{\mathbf{b}}_i. \tag{14}$$

where

$$\hat{\mathbf{b}}_i = (\mathbf{X}_i'\overline{\mathbf{M}}\mathbf{X}_i)^{-1}\mathbf{X}_i'\overline{\mathbf{M}}\mathbf{y}_i \tag{15}$$

and $\mathbf{X}_i = (\mathbf{x}_{i1}, \mathbf{x}_{i2}, \ldots, \mathbf{x}_{iT})'$, $\mathbf{y}_i = (y_{i1}, y_{i2}, \ldots, y_{iT})'$, and $\overline{\mathbf{M}}$ is defined by

$$\overline{\mathbf{M}} = \mathbf{I}_T - \overline{\mathbf{H}}\left(\overline{\mathbf{H}}'\overline{\mathbf{H}}\right)^{-1}\overline{\mathbf{H}}' \tag{16}$$

$\overline{\mathbf{H}} = (\mathbf{D}, \overline{\mathbf{Z}})$, $\mathbf{D}$ and $\overline{\mathbf{Z}}$ being, respectively, the $T \times n$ and $T \times (k+1)$ matrices of observations on $\mathbf{d}_t$ and $\overline{\mathbf{z}}_t$.

Under certain conditions, Pesaran (2006) has shown that:

$$\sqrt{N}\left(\hat{\mathbf{b}}_{MG} - \beta\right) \xrightarrow{d} N(\mathbf{0}, \Sigma_{MG}), \text{ as } (N, T) \xrightarrow{j} \infty \tag{17}$$

where Σ_{MG} can be consistently estimated non-parametrically by

$$\widehat{\Sigma}_{MG} = \frac{1}{N-1}\sum_{i=1}^{N}\left(\hat{\mathbf{b}}_i - \hat{\mathbf{b}}_{MG}\right)\left(\hat{\mathbf{b}}_i - \hat{\mathbf{b}}_{MG}\right)'. \tag{18}$$

Efficiency gains from pooling of observations over the cross-section units can be achieved when the individual slope coefficients, β_i, are the same. Such a pooled estimator of β, denoted by CCEP, has been developed by Pesaran (2006) and is given by

$$\hat{\mathbf{b}}_P = \left(\sum_{i=1}^{N}\mathbf{X}_i'\overline{\mathbf{M}}\mathbf{X}_i\right)^{-1}\sum_{i=1}^{N}\mathbf{X}_i'\overline{\mathbf{M}}\mathbf{y}_i. \tag{19}$$

Again, Pesaran (2006) has shown that

$$N^{-1/2}\left(\hat{\mathbf{b}}_P - \beta\right) \xrightarrow{d} N(\mathbf{0}, \Sigma_P^*)$$

where Σ_P^* can be consistently estimated by

$$\widehat{AVar}\left(N^{-1/2}\left(\hat{\mathbf{b}}_P - \beta\right)\right) = \widehat{\Psi}^{*-1}\widehat{\mathbf{R}}^*\widehat{\Psi}^{*-1} \tag{20}$$

where

$$\widehat{\mathbf{R}}^* = \frac{1}{N-1}\sum_{i=1}^{N}\left(\frac{\mathbf{X}_i'\overline{\mathbf{M}}\mathbf{X}_i}{T}\right)\left(\hat{\mathbf{b}}_i - \hat{\mathbf{b}}_{MG}\right)\left(\hat{\mathbf{b}}_i - \hat{\mathbf{b}}_{MG}\right)'\left(\frac{\mathbf{X}_i'\overline{\mathbf{M}}\mathbf{X}_i}{T}\right) \tag{21}$$

and

$$\widehat{\Psi}^* = \frac{1}{N}\sum_{i=1}^{N}\left(\frac{\mathbf{X}_i'\overline{\mathbf{M}}\mathbf{X}_i}{T}\right). \tag{22}$$

3 A Principal Components Augmentation Approach

In this section we explore an alternative method of estimating the model given by (1) and (2) based on principal component analysis as discussed in the work of Stock and Watson (2002). Our approach is first to apply the Bai and Ng (2002) procedure to $\mathbf{z}_{it} = (y_{it}, \mathbf{x}'_{it})'$ to obtain consistent estimates of the unobserved factors, and then use these factor estimates to augment the regression (1), and thus produce consistent estimates of β. A formal justification for such an approach is as follows. Recall from (3) that

$$\mathbf{z}_{it} = \begin{pmatrix} y_{it} \\ \mathbf{x}_{it} \end{pmatrix} = \Theta' \mathbf{g}_t + \mathbf{u}_{it}$$

where $\Theta'_i = \left(\mathbf{B}'_i, \mathbf{C}'_i\right)$, $\mathbf{g}_t = (\mathbf{d}'_t, \mathbf{f}'_t)'$. The errors $\mathbf{u}_{it}$, can be serially correlated but do not have common factors and are cross-sectionally independent by assumption. Therefore, under Assumptions 1–5 of Pesaran (2006), this model satisfies assumptions of Bai (2003) and the common factors $\mathbf{g}_t$, can be consistently estimated (up to a non-singular transformation) from the principal components of $\mathbf{z}_{it}$ for $i = 1, 2, \ldots, N$, and $t = 1, 2, \ldots, T$.

The estimated factors at time t, denoted by $\hat{\mathbf{f}}_t$ will be linear combinations of the $(m + n) \times 1$ vector $\mathbf{g}_t$. It is important to note that $m + n$, rather than just m factors, must be extracted from $\mathbf{z}_{it}$. In practice, m is not known and must be replaced by an estimate using the selection procedure in Bai and Ng (2002), for example. This in turn can introduce a certain degree of sampling uncertainty into the analysis.

Once these factors are extracted we can use the results of Bai (2003) and in particular Comment 2 (p. 146) to justify augmenting (1) by the estimated factors. In particular, Bai (2003) shows that as long as $\sqrt{T}/N \to 0$ the error in the estimated factor is negligible for estimating the regression

$$y_{it} = \alpha'_i \mathbf{d}_t + \beta'_i \mathbf{x}_{it} + \gamma'_i \hat{\mathbf{f}}_t + \eta_{it}. \qquad (23)$$

Again we consider both mean group and pooled estimators. The mean group and pooled estimators are given respectively by

$$\hat{\mathbf{b}}_{MGPC} = N^{-1} \sum_{i=1}^{N} \hat{\mathbf{b}}_{MGPC,i} \qquad (24)$$

and

$$\hat{\mathbf{b}}_{PPC} = \left(\sum_{i=1}^{N} \mathbf{X}_i' \mathbf{M}_{\widehat{g}} \mathbf{X}_i \right)^{-1} \sum_{i=1}^{N} \mathbf{X}_i' \mathbf{M}_{\widehat{g}} \mathbf{y}_i \tag{25}$$

where

$$\mathbf{M}_{\widehat{g}} = \mathbf{I}_T - \widehat{\mathbf{G}} \left(\widehat{\mathbf{G}}' \widehat{\mathbf{G}} \right)^{-1} \widehat{\mathbf{G}}' \tag{26}$$

$\widehat{\mathbf{G}} = (\mathbf{D}, \widehat{\mathbf{F}})$, $\widehat{\mathbf{F}}$ is the $T \times (m+n)$ matrix of observations on $\hat{\mathbf{f}}_t$, and $\hat{\mathbf{b}}_{MGPC,i}$ is the estimator of β_i in (23). The variance for the mean group estimator is given by

$$\widehat{AVar}(\hat{\mathbf{b}}_{MGPC}) = \frac{1}{N-1} \sum_{i=1}^{N} \left(\hat{\mathbf{b}}_{MGPC,i} - \hat{\mathbf{b}}_{MGPC} \right) \left(\hat{\mathbf{b}}_{MGPC,i} - \hat{\mathbf{b}}_{MGPC} \right)' \tag{27}$$

and for the pooled estimator, in the case where $\beta_i = \beta$, by

$$\widehat{AVar}(\hat{\mathbf{b}}_{PPC}) = \frac{1}{N} \left(\sum_{i=1}^{N} \mathbf{X}_i' \mathbf{M}_{\widehat{g}} \mathbf{X}_i \right)^{-1} \left(\sum_{i=1}^{N} \widehat{\sigma}_i^2 \mathbf{X}_i' \mathbf{M}_{\widehat{g}} \mathbf{X}_i \right) \left(\sum_{i=1}^{N} \mathbf{X}_i' \mathbf{M}_{\widehat{g}} \mathbf{X}_i \right)^{-1} \tag{28}$$

where $\hat{\sigma}_i^2$ is the estimated error variance of (23). The principal components are computed based on standardized observations, namely $(y_{it} - \overline{y}_i)/s_i$ and $(x_{it\ell} - \overline{x}_{i\ell})/s_{il}$ where $\overline{y}_i$ and $\overline{x}_{i\ell}$ are sample means of y_{it} and the ℓth element of $\mathbf{x}_{it}$, and s_i and $s_{i\ell}$ are the associated sample standard deviations.

Finally, we also consider an alternative principal-component-based estimation strategy. This consists of extracting the principal component estimates of the unobserved factors from y_{it} and $\mathbf{x}_{it}$ separately, regressing y_{it} and $\mathbf{x}_{it}$ on their respective factor estimates separately, and then applying the standard pooled estimator, with no cross-sectional dependence adjustments, to the residuals of these regressions. We refer to this estimator as *PCPOOL*.

4 Small Sample Properties of the Various Estimators

4.1 Monte Carlo Design

The data-generating processes used in the Monte Carlo experiments are different parameterizations of (1) and (2) which we reproduce here for convenience

$$y_{it} = \alpha_i' \mathbf{d}_t + \beta_i' \mathbf{x}_{it} + \gamma_i' \mathbf{f}_t + \varepsilon_{it} \tag{29}$$

and

$$\mathbf{x}_{it} = \mathbf{A}_i' \mathbf{d}_t + \Gamma_i' \mathbf{f}_t + \mathbf{v}_{it} \tag{30}$$

where $\mathbf{A}_i = [\alpha_{isl}]$ and $\Gamma_i = [\gamma_{isl}]$ are $n \times k$ and $m \times k$, factor loading matrices with fixed components, $\mathbf{v}_{it}$ are the specific components of $\mathbf{x}_{it}$ distributed independently of the common effects and across i, but assumed to follow general covariance stationary processes.

In the calibration of the Monte Carlo design, it is important that the population value of R^2 for (29) is controlled across the different experiments. Otherwise, comparisons of the power properties of the different estimators can be misleading in the case of models with different numbers of observed and unobserved factors. In what follows we show how the average population R^2 of the y_{it} equation varies with the model parameter and hence find values of the error variances, σ_i^2, that ensure the population R^2 is around .60 irrespective of the number of regressors included in the model. We shall assume that unconditionally

$$\mathbf{f}_t \sim (\mathbf{0}, \Sigma_f), \mathbf{d}_t \sim (\mathbf{0}, \Sigma_d)$$

$$\varepsilon_{it} \sim IID(0, \sigma_i^2), \mathbf{v}_{it} \sim IID(\mathbf{0}, \Sigma_{vi}).$$

We choose not to introduce any serial correlation in ε_{it} and $\mathbf{v}_{it}$ for simplicity, but results available upon request suggest that introducing serial correlation does not affect the results. The variables, $\mathbf{f}_t, \mathbf{d}_t, \varepsilon_{it}, \mathbf{v}_{it}$ are also assumed to be distributed independently of the parameters, $\alpha_i, \beta_i, \Gamma_i, \mathbf{A}_i$, and γ_i. Using (30) in (29) we have

$$y_{it} = \alpha_i' \mathbf{d}_t + \beta_i' \left(\mathbf{A}_i' \mathbf{d}_t + \Gamma_i' \mathbf{f}_t + \mathbf{v}_{it} \right) + \gamma_i' \mathbf{f}_t + \varepsilon_{it}$$

$$y_{it} = \varphi_i' \mathbf{g}_t + e_{it}$$

where

$$\varphi_i = \begin{pmatrix} \alpha_i + \mathbf{A}_i\beta_i \\ \gamma_i + \Gamma_i\beta_i \end{pmatrix}, \mathbf{g}_t = \begin{pmatrix} \mathbf{d}_t \\ \mathbf{f}_t \end{pmatrix}$$

and

$$e_{it} = \varepsilon_{it} + \beta_i'\mathbf{v}_{it}.$$

The population R^2 of (29), conditional on φ_i and β_i, is given by

$$R_i^2 = 1 - \frac{\sigma_i^2}{Var(y_{it} \mid \varphi_i, \beta_i)}$$

where

$$Var(y_{it} \mid \varphi_i, \beta_i) = \varphi_i'\Sigma_g\varphi_i + \beta_i'\Sigma_{vi}\beta_i + \sigma_i^2$$

and

$$\Sigma_g = \begin{pmatrix} \Sigma_d & \Sigma_{df} \\ \Sigma_{fd} & \Sigma_f \end{pmatrix}.$$

Since, $E(y_{it} \mid \varphi_i, \beta_i) = 0$, then on average (integrating out the individual effects)

$$Var(y_{it}) = E\left(\varphi_i'\Sigma_g\varphi_i + \beta_i'\Sigma_{vi}\beta_i + \sigma_i^2\right)$$

$$Var(\varepsilon_{it}) = E\left(\sigma_i^2\right)$$

and the average population R^2 value will be given by

$$R^2 = 1 - \frac{E(\sigma_i^2)}{E\left(\varphi_i'\Sigma_g\varphi_i + \beta_i'\Sigma_{vi}\beta_i + \sigma_i^2\right)}.$$

Suppose that the individual-specific parameters, σ_i^2, φ_i and β_i, are distributed independently of Σ_g, and β_i is distributed independently of Σ_{vi} with constant means and variances, $\sigma^2 = E(\sigma_i^2)$, $\varphi = E(\varphi_i)$, $\beta = E(\beta_i)$,

$Var(\varphi_i) = \Sigma_\varphi$, $Var(\beta_i) = \Sigma_\beta$, and $\Sigma_v = E(\Sigma_{vi})$. Then it is easily seen that

$$R^2 = 1 - \frac{\sigma^2}{\varphi'\Sigma_g\varphi + Tr\left(\Sigma_g\Sigma_\varphi\right) + \beta'\Sigma_v\beta + Tr\left(\Sigma_v\Sigma_\beta\right) + \sigma^2}$$

where $\Sigma_\varphi = E(\varphi_i\varphi_i') - \varphi\varphi'$. To derive $E(\varphi_i\varphi_i')$, let $\mathbf{A}_i' = (\mathbf{a}_{i1}, \mathbf{a}_{i2}, \ldots, \mathbf{a}_{in})$, $\gamma_i' = (\gamma_{i1}, \gamma_{i2}, \ldots, \gamma_{im})$ and note that

$$\varphi_i\varphi_i' = \begin{pmatrix} (\alpha_i + \mathbf{A}_i\beta_i)(\alpha_i + \mathbf{A}_i\beta_i)' & (\alpha_i + \mathbf{A}_i\beta_i)(\gamma_i + \Gamma_i\beta_i)' \\ (\gamma_i + \Gamma_i\beta_i)(\alpha_i + \mathbf{A}_i\beta_i)' & (\gamma_i + \Gamma_i\beta_i)(\gamma_i + \Gamma_i\beta_i)' \end{pmatrix},$$

$$E\left(\mathbf{A}_i\beta_i\beta_i'\mathbf{A}_i'\right) =$$

$$= \begin{pmatrix} E(\beta_i'\mathbf{a}_{i1}\mathbf{a}_{i1}'\beta_i) & E(\beta_i'\mathbf{a}_{i1}\mathbf{a}_{i2}'\beta_i) & & E(\beta_i'\mathbf{a}_{i1}\mathbf{a}_{in}'\beta_i) \\ E(\beta_i'\mathbf{a}_{i1}\mathbf{a}_{i2}'\beta_i) & E(\beta_i'\mathbf{a}_{i2}\mathbf{a}_{i2}'\beta_i) & & E(\beta_i'\mathbf{a}_{i2}\mathbf{a}_{in}'\beta_i) \\ \vdots & \vdots & \vdots & \vdots \\ E(\beta_i'\mathbf{a}_{in}\mathbf{a}_{i1}'\beta_i) & \cdots & & E(\beta_i'\mathbf{a}_{in}\mathbf{a}_{in}'\beta_i) \end{pmatrix}.$$

Assuming β_i is distributed independently of $\mathbf{a}_{ir}$ for $r = 1, 2, \ldots, n$, we have

$$E(\beta_i'\mathbf{a}_{ir}\mathbf{a}_{is}'\beta_i) = \beta' E(\mathbf{a}_{ir}\mathbf{a}_{is}')\beta + Tr[E(\mathbf{a}_{ir}\mathbf{a}_{is}')\Sigma_\beta]$$

for $r, s = 1, 2, \ldots, n$. Similarly, assuming β_i is distributed independently of γ_{ir}

$$E(\beta_i'\gamma_{ir}\gamma_{is}'\beta_i) = \beta' E(\gamma_{ir}\gamma_{is}')\beta + Tr[E(\gamma_{ir}\gamma_{is}')\Sigma_\beta]$$

for $r, s = 1, 2, \ldots, m$. The remaining elements of $E(\varphi_i\varphi_i')$ can also be obtained in a similar fashion.

For the Monte Carlo experiments we used the following parameterizations

$$\Sigma_\beta = \mathbf{0},\ \Sigma_g = \begin{pmatrix} \mathbf{I}_n & \mathbf{0} \\ \mathbf{0} & \Sigma_f \end{pmatrix},\ \Sigma_v = \mathbf{I}_k$$

$$\Sigma_f = \begin{pmatrix} 1 & \theta & \cdots & \theta \\ \theta & 1 & \cdots & \theta \\ \vdots & \vdots & \vdots & \vdots \\ \theta & \theta & \cdots & 1 \end{pmatrix}$$

θ is the pair-wise correlation coefficient of the unobserved factors and

$$\varphi = \begin{pmatrix} \alpha + \mathbf{A}\beta \\ \gamma + \Gamma\beta \end{pmatrix}.$$

Also since the parameters are generated independently we have

$$E(\alpha_i \beta_i' \mathbf{A}_i') = \alpha\beta'\mathbf{A}'$$
$$E(\alpha_i \beta_i' \Gamma_i') = \alpha\beta'\Gamma'$$

and

$$E(\alpha_i \alpha_i') = \Sigma_\alpha + \alpha\alpha'$$
$$E(\gamma_i \gamma_i') = \Sigma_\gamma + \gamma\gamma'.$$

$$\begin{aligned} E(\mathbf{a}_{ir}\mathbf{a}_{is}') &= \mathbf{a}_r\mathbf{a}_s' \text{ if } r \neq s \\ &= \Sigma_{a_r} + \mathbf{a}_r\mathbf{a}_r' \end{aligned}$$

assuming that $\mathbf{a}_{ir}$ are identically distributed. Similarly,

$$\begin{aligned} E(\gamma_{ir}\gamma_{is}') &= \gamma_r\gamma_s' \text{ if } r \neq s \\ &= \Sigma_{\gamma_r} + \gamma_r\gamma_r'. \end{aligned}$$

Using the above framework we carried out two different sets of experiments. In the first set, which we denote by A, we consider the small sample properties of the CCE and PC-augmented estimators. In a second set, denoted as experiments B, we also investigate the small sample properties of estimators obtained from regressing y_{it} on $\mathbf{d}_t$, $\mathbf{x}_{it}$ and a sub-set of $\mathbf{f}_t$ obtained using two different information criteria, namely the Akaike-type criterion where the objective function to be minimized is given by

$$IC_1(f) = \frac{T}{2}\sum_{i=1}^{N} \ln(\hat{\varepsilon}_i'\hat{\varepsilon}_i/T) + NK \tag{31}$$

where $\hat{\varepsilon}_i$ are the residuals of (29) for cross-sectional unit i, and K denotes the total number of regressors in (29). The second criterion is a Theil-type criterion defined by,

$$IC_2(f) = \frac{\frac{T}{2}\sum_{i=1}^{N} \ln(\hat{\varepsilon}_i'\hat{\varepsilon}_i/T)}{N(T-m_y)-k} \tag{32}$$

where $m_y < m$ denotes the number of factors entering (29). The criteria are minimized over all possible factor combinations. These experiments are intended to highlight the dependence of the PC augmented procedure on the choice of the factors, even if satisfactory estimates of $\mathbf{f}_t$ can be obtained using the PC procedure.

For all experiments $T, N = 30, 50, 100, 200$, $n = 3$, $\beta = (1, 1, \ldots, 1)'$. For experiments A, $k = 1, 3$. For experiments B, $k = 1$. Partition $\mathbf{d}_t$ as follows: $\mathbf{d}_t = (d_{1t}, d_{2t}, d_{3t})'$ and partition conformably α_i and $\mathbf{A}_i$. $d_{1t} = 1$. For experiments A, $m = 1, 2, 3, 4$. For experiments B, $m = 5$. Further, we set

$$\alpha_i = (\alpha_{i1}, \alpha_{i2}, \ldots, \alpha_{ik+1}, 0, \ldots, 0)', \alpha_{ij} \sim IIDU(0.5, 1.5),\ j = 1, \ldots, k+1$$

$$\alpha_{isl} = 0;\ s = 1, \ldots, n;\ l = 1, \ldots, k+1$$

$$\alpha_{isl} \sim U(0.5, 1.5);\ s = 1, \ldots, n;\ l = k+2, \ldots, n$$

d_{jt} is given by

$$d_{jt} = \rho_{d_j} d_{jt-1} + \varepsilon_{d_j t},\ j = 2, \ldots, n$$

where $\rho_{d_j} = 0.4$, $j = 2, \ldots, n$ and $\varepsilon_{d_j t} \sim IIDN(0, 1 - \rho_{d_j}^2)$. $\gamma_i = (\gamma_{1i}, \ldots, \gamma_{mi})'$ where $\gamma_{ji} \sim IIDN(1, 0.04)$ for experiment A. For experiment B $\gamma_{ji} \sim IIDN(1, 0.04), j = 1, 2, 3$ and $\gamma_{ji} = 0$ for $j = 4, 5$.

$$\gamma_{isl} \sim IIDU(0.5, 1.5).$$

$\mathbf{v}_{it}$ is given by

$$\mathbf{v}_{it} = \Phi_i \mathbf{v}_{it-1} + \varepsilon_{i\mathbf{v}t}$$

where $\Phi_i = diag(\rho_{v1i}, \ldots, \rho_{vki})$, $\varepsilon_{i\mathbf{v}t} \sim N(0, \Sigma_{iv})$, $\rho_{vji} \sim U(0.2, 0.9)$, $\Sigma_{iv} = diag(1 - \rho_{v1i}^2, \ldots, 1 - \rho_{vki}^2)$. Finally, $\mathbf{f}_t = (f_{1t}, \ldots, f_{mt})'$

$$f_{jt} = \rho_{f_j} f_{jt-1} + \varepsilon_{f_j t},\ j = 2, \ldots, m$$

where $\rho_{d_j} \sim IIDU(0.2, 0.9)$, $j = 2, \ldots, m$, $\varepsilon_{f_j t} = \sqrt{1 - \rho_{f_j}^2}\,\omega_{jt}$, $\omega_{jt} = \sqrt{\theta}\omega_t + (1 - \theta)\varpi_{jt}$ and $\omega_t, \varpi_{jt} \sim N(0, 1)$. Hence, $Var(f_{it}) = 1$, and $Corr(f_{it}, f_{jt}) = \theta$, as required.

To ensure a constant average R^2 of around 0.6 for all experiments we generated the equation-specific errors according to

$$\varepsilon_{it} \sim IIDN(0, \sigma_i^2), \ \sigma_i^2 \sim IID \frac{h(k,m)}{2} \chi_2^2$$

where the scalar $h(k, m)$ is set in terms of m and k as

m	k	$h(k,m)$
1	1	8
1	2	16
1	3	26
2	1	11
2	2	32
2	3	53
3	1	22
3	2	48
3	3	74
4	1	29
4	2	70
4	3	155
5	1	40
5	2	100
5	3	190

Finally, all parameters are set at the beginning of each experiment and 2,000 replications are run. The only exception to that is γ_i for which new parameter draws occur for every replication.

4.2 Alternative Estimators Considered

In the case of experiments A, we considered five different types of estimators. First, a misspecified procedure that ignores the common unobserved effects and for efficiency purposes considers a pooled estimator under the slope homogeneity assumption, $\beta = \beta_i$. We denote this as the "Naive" estimator. Second, we consider the *CCEMG* and *CCEP* estimators defined by (14) and (19). Third, we consider the PC-augmented estimators defined by (24) and (25), which we denote by *MGPC* and *PPC*, respectively. Fourth, we consider the principal component estimator proposed by Coakley, Fuertes, and Smith (2002). For this estimator the following steps are taken. We estimate (1), using a standard pooled estimator for β_i, without proxying for the factors. Then, we obtain the residuals from (1) normalize them and extract $m + n$ factors from them. We use these factors in (23) and obtain the relevant Mean Group and Pooled estimators. These are denoted *MGCFS* and *PCFS*. Finally, we consider the *PCPOOL* estimator defined at the end of section 3. Again, $m + n$ factors are separately extracted from y_{it} and $\mathbf{x}_{it}$ for this estimator.

As noted earlier, the estimators under experiments B, assume that all the factors are observed. In one case, there is uncertainty as to which factors enter (29) as opposed to (30). The criteria described earlier are used to select the set of factors to be included in (29). All possible combinations are considered. These are infeasible estimators since the factors are not actually observed. However, they serve the purposes of showing that using principal components does not only introduce a factor estimation problem but a model selection problem as well, which is not present with the CCE estimators. These estimators are denoted by *MG*(*IC*) and *P*(*IC*) where *IC* stands for either Theil or AIC-type criteria. Finally, we consider the infeasible estimators where both the factors, and the identities of the factors entering (29), are known. These estimators are denoted by *MGT* and *PT*, respectively. We present results on the Bias ($\times$10,000) and RMSE($\times$100) for all these estimators. We also provide size and power estimates of the different estimators for testing the hypothesis that $\beta = 1$. The power of the tests are computed under the alternative $\beta = 1.05$.

Compared to the Monte Carlo study reported in Coakley, Fuertes, and Smith (2006), our design allows for the failure of the rank condition (9), and provides a comparative analysis of the *CCEMG* and *CCEP* estimators. Coakley, Fuertes, and Smith (2006) find that the *CCEMG* performs best across a number of alternative estimators. However, they do not consider the *CCEP* estimator, although their Monte Carlo design imposes the homogeneity restrictions $\beta_i = \beta$. We also consider a more extensive analysis of multifactor and multiregressor models since we consider models of up to four factors in conjunction with up to three individual specific regressors. Further, we control for the R^2 of the models which as explained earlier is of great importance for the validity of the Monte Carlo analysis. Fourthly, we consider new principal component-based estimators. These estimators take into account the possibility that (30) contains unobserved common components not contained in (29) by extracting the number of factors in both (30) and (29) rather than just (29) as discussed in the previous section. More generally, via experiments B, we explore the important issue of factor selection when principal components are used for the estimation of the common effects.

4.3 Monte Carlo Results

The results for experiment A are summarized in Tables 10.1–10.8, and for experiments B are given in Tables 10.9 and 10.10. It is clear from Table 10.1 that the "Naive" estimator that ignores the unobserved common effects is substantially biased and over-rejects the null hypothesis often by a 80–95 percent margin! Considering the estimators that attempt to account for the presence of the unobserved common effects, we first note that cross-section averages work as expected for the case of a single unobserved common factor. Tests using both the MG and PC estimators are correctly sized reflecting the fact that the estimated variance is a consistent estimate of the true variance. Further, the *CCEMG* estimator has marginally worse RMSEs than the *CCEP* estimator as expected given the efficiency gains of pooling. The improvement when *CCEP* is used is of the order of 10–15 percent. When we move to experiments with more than one unobserved common factors similar conclusions are reached concerning the *CCEMG* and *CCEP* estimators. The most obvious difference relates to the size of the test that $\beta = 1$ under the null hypothesis. For both estimators there are cases where the test over-rejects slightly under the null. Most of these cases, however, relate to small N experiments and the over-rejection disappears as N is increased. Also, both the bias and RMSE of the estimators increase as more factors are introduced. For comparable population R^2, the power of the tests based on *CCEMG* and *CCEP* estimators also tend to decline as the number of unobserved factors are increased. This is due to the fact that the cross section averages, $\overline{y}_t$ and $\overline{x}_t$, capture smaller proportion of the time variations of the unobserved factors as the number of unobserved factors is increased. This feature could not have been observed if the population R^2 had not been kept fixed across the different experiments.

Moving on to the PC-augmented estimators we note that they perform considerably worse than the *CCE* type estimators. The biases are dramatically larger. Although the bias is reduced with increased sample sizes (both N and T) they still remain much larger than the bias observed for the cross sectional average estimators. The RMSEs also tell the same story. Both *MGPC* and *PPC* perform badly, and substantially over-reject the null hypothesis. The *MGCFS* and *PCFS* estimators perform considerably worse that the other PC augmented estimators.

Moving on to Experiments B we note several striking features. The cross-sectional average estimators work as expected. They have relatively small biases and RMSE. The size performance is reasonable even for five factors. The estimators when the true factors are known but the

Table 10.1. *Naïve estimator*

		One factor				Two factors			
# *x*	*N*/*T*	30	50	100	200	30	50	100	200
Bias									
1	30	2731.1	2535.7	2648.3	2781.2	5516.9	5250.6	5163.0	5124.6
	50	2675.2	2722.7	2874.8	2660.2	5270.2	5084.6	5187.1	5387.0
	100	2729.7	2732.6	2688.7	2660.6	4874.1	5491.7	5363.7	5904.4
	200	2814.9	2738.9	2602.4	2743.4	5941.5	4977.3	5749.6	5615.7
3	30	1195.2	1133.3	1198.2	1160.4	2261.5	2302.0	2100.7	2032.9
	50	1210.6	1190.5	1146.1	1153.1	2056.7	2100.8	2152.4	2076.8
	100	1154.9	1280.3	1191.2	1200.7	2046.2	2097.5	2139.9	2089.8
	200	1244.8	1160.3	1153.9	1158.4	2019.4	2063.2	2113.6	2161.1
RMSE									
1	30	29.2	26.5	27.0	28.1	56.3	53.2	52.0	51.4
	50	28.2	28.2	29.2	26.8	53.7	51.5	52.2	54.0
	100	28.5	28.1	27.3	26.8	49.8	55.4	53.9	59.2
	200	29.3	28.1	26.4	27.6	60.1	50.3	57.7	56.3
3	30	19.6	17.5	14.4	12.9	32.7	28.8	23.7	21.6
	50	17.9	14.7	13.1	12.5	26.9	24.2	23.2	21.6
	100	14.7	14.8	12.8	12.4	23.6	22.8	22.2	21.4
	200	14.2	12.6	12.1	11.8	22.0	21.6	21.6	21.8
Size									
1	30	91.0	97.7	100.0	100.0	100.0	100.0	100.0	100.0
	50	97.1	99.2	100.0	100.0	100.0	100.0	100.0	100.0
	100	99.2	100.0	100.0	100.0	100.0	100.0	100.0	100.0
	200	99.8	100.0	100.0	100.0	100.0	100.0	100.0	100.0
3	30	70.7	76.2	99.4	100.0	95.3	99.9	100.0	100.0
	50	79.0	96.8	100.0	100.0	97.8	100.0	100.0	100.0
	100	92.5	99.2	100.0	100.0	99.7	100.0	100.0	100.0
	200	98.8	99.9	100.0	100.0	100.0	100.0	100.0	100.0
Power									
1	30	82.0	92.1	100.0	100.0	100.0	100.0	100.0	100.0
	50	92.7	97.2	100.0	100.0	100.0	100.0	100.0	100.0
	100	97.0	99.5	100.0	100.0	99.9	100.0	100.0	100.0
	200	98.0	99.9	100.0	100.0	100.0	100.0	100.0	100.0
3	30	40.4	38.8	77.0	93.8	84.3	98.2	99.9	100.0
	50	48.7	71.1	84.0	96.7	90.0	99.2	100.0	100.0
	100	65.2	83.9	96.9	99.9	97.9	100.0	100.0	100.0
	200	84.1	91.8	98.6	100.0	99.3	100.0	100.0	100.0

Table 10.1. *(cont.)*

		Three factors				Four factors			
# x	N/T	30	50	100	200	30	50	100	200
Bias									
1	30	7030.9	7007.8	6742.8	7187.6	7776.8	7975.1	7721.5	7839.8
	50	6919.5	7141.9	6585.5	7151.4	8143.6	7462.9	7740.1	7879.7
	100	6247.5	6858.1	6785.6	6704.2	7515.4	7433.3	8082.8	7913.0
	200	7034.4	6590.4	7326.2	7223.1	7983.9	8055.9	8039.8	8373.7
3	30	2558.5	2532.6	2729.7	2669.0	2818.1	2849.3	2838.3	2758.1
	50	2568.3	2618.9	2706.2	2640.4	2839.9	2725.2	2854.4	2864.6
	100	2517.6	2747.9	2525.3	2428.1	2846.2	2874.4	2893.2	2870.4
	200	2584.7	2680.1	2618.7	2603.4	2822.2	2773.3	2884.4	2886.9
RMSE									
1	30	71.0	70.6	67.7	72.0	78.4	80.1	77.4	78.5
	50	69.9	71.8	66.1	71.6	81.9	75.0	77.5	78.9
	100	63.2	69.0	68.1	67.1	75.7	74.6	80.9	79.2
	200	70.9	66.3	73.4	72.3	80.2	80.7	80.5	83.8
3	30	36.9	29.7	30.0	28.1	47.5	37.0	32.6	29.2
	50	33.0	30.0	28.9	27.4	40.3	31.9	31.9	30.2
	100	28.7	29.4	26.2	24.7	33.9	31.4	30.3	29.5
	200	27.6	27.8	26.6	26.2	31.2	29.5	29.6	29.3
Size									
1	30	100.0	100.0	100.0	100.0	100.0	100.0	100.0	100.0
	50	100.0	100.0	100.0	100.0	100.0	100.0	100.0	100.0
	100	100.0	100.0	100.0	100.0	100.0	100.0	100.0	100.0
	200	100.0	100.0	100.0	100.0	100.0	100.0	100.0	100.0
3	30	98.9	100.0	100.0	100.0	97.8	100.0	100.0	100.0
	50	99.6	100.0	100.0	100.0	99.9	100.0	100.0	100.0
	100	100.0	100.0	100.0	100.0	100.0	100.0	100.0	100.0
	200	100.0	100.0	100.0	100.0	100.0	100.0	100.0	100.0
Power									
1	30	100.0	100.0	100.0	100.0	100.0	100.0	100.0	100.0
	50	100.0	100.0	100.0	100.0	100.0	100.0	100.0	100.0
	100	100.0	100.0	100.0	100.0	100.0	100.0	100.0	100.0
	200	100.0	100.0	100.0	100.0	100.0	100.0	100.0	100.0
3	30	94.6	100.0	100.0	100.0	93.3	99.8	100.0	100.0
	50	98.5	100.0	100.0	100.0	98.9	100.0	100.0	100.0
	100	99.7	100.0	100.0	100.0	100.0	100.0	100.0	100.0
	200	100.0	100.0	100.0	100.0	100.0	100.0	100.0	100.0

Notes: The naïve estimator is given by $\beta = \left(\sum_{i=1}^{N} \mathbf{X}_i'\mathbf{M}\mathbf{X}_i\right)^{-1} \sum_{i=1}^{N} \mathbf{X}_i'\mathbf{M}\mathbf{y}_i$ where $\mathbf{M} = \mathbf{I}_T - \mathbf{D}(\mathbf{D}'\mathbf{D})^{-1}\mathbf{D}'$. Bias and RMSE estimates are scaled up by 10,000 and 100, respectively.

Table 10.2. *Mean group estimator*

		One factor				Two factors			
# *x*	*N*/*T*	30	50	100	200	30	50	100	200
Bias									
1	30	−1.1	202.4	155.8	155.5	160.8	−64.2	−24.7	−62.0
	50	−5.6	112.1	115.0	19.2	−6.6	70.6	30.7	8.3
	100	27.0	15.9	14.3	38.7	45.9	−19.3	25.9	−31.0
	200	−31.6	10.6	−24.6	10.0	41.4	10.5	17.5	−5.9
3	30	87.1	117.0	−106.3	36.7	166.8	160.0	−52.2	−184.8
	50	72.4	−48.1	−5.9	−0.6	−117.9	−21.2	74.8	138.3
	100	20.6	−3.3	−9.4	27.0	−68.1	−7.1	42.4	−95.9
	200	−57.4	−32.9	−8.1	−0.1	4.9	0.0	2.4	26.2
RMSE									
1	30	13.7	8.8	4.8	4.4	13.3	9.9	6.9	3.9
	50	9.0	7.1	5.0	2.9	11.4	8.2	4.9	3.5
	100	6.4	5.0	3.0	2.0	8.3	5.4	3.7	2.3
	200	4.7	3.3	2.2	1.5	6.2	3.8	2.5	1.8
3	30	23.8	18.7	10.3	6.9	40.9	25.1	14.6	9.4
	50	21.0	11.9	8.1	5.9	28.7	17.1	11.7	7.6
	100	14.1	9.8	5.7	3.7	19.3	13.0	7.4	5.6
	200	10.0	6.2	4.3	2.7	14.0	9.2	5.5	3.8
Size									
1	30	6.8	6.0	6.2	7.3	6.6	6.6	6.2	6.7
	50	6.3	5.7	6.2	5.0	6.1	6.2	6.4	5.1
	100	5.6	5.8	5.2	5.9	5.6	5.3	6.0	5.0
	200	5.1	4.8	5.8	5.5	5.5	5.7	5.5	5.2
3	30	9.3	8.5	10.1	9.4	7.5	10.5	10.4	9.5
	50	7.8	7.9	7.2	6.9	7.4	6.3	6.6	7.3
	100	7.0	5.5	6.1	6.3	5.5	7.0	5.7	5.3
	200	5.1	5.8	5.1	4.5	5.9	5.1	6.0	5.5
Power									
1	30	8.1	8.1	14.7	16.9	6.9	11.1	15.3	35.4
	50	11.1	9.4	15.4	38.9	8.5	9.3	18.2	30.1
	100	12.5	18.5	36.5	65.1	9.6	16.1	26.4	62.3
	200	20.0	31.9	69.0	91.3	12.6	26.5	50.8	81.7
3	30	10.2	10.0	19.0	23.2	8.2	11.1	14.6	25.2
	50	8.3	12.8	17.5	25.7	8.2	8.8	9.8	13.8
	100	9.8	10.8	27.6	48.1	7.4	10.0	13.5	34.4
	200	11.8	22.1	38.9	78.2	8.8	12.2	25.7	42.6

Table 10.2. *(cont.)*

		Three factors				Four factors			
# *x*	*N*/*T*	30	50	100	200	30	50	100	200
Bias									
1	30	−186.2	−216.5	78.7	−8.1	42.6	−122.5	92.9	304.8
	50	−35.5	148.4	81.2	−287.1	36.5	−66.2	191.8	99.5
	100	−78.0	75.3	−80.6	35.4	−56.5	−137.1	−7.9	21.5
	200	−19.1	−17.9	20.3	−10.0	−48.6	−29.7	23.5	21.8
3	30	−100.5	47.4	−238.8	4.8	−87.9	157.1	132.8	−88.6
	50	407.0	−17.0	−60.7	−19.4	−158.6	72.5	−171.6	185.7
	100	187.5	−17.5	0.6	46.0	23.4	−89.5	−118.0	24.5
	200	11.3	−57.9	−25.9	−1.0	−113.5	−0.4	81.2	−72.6
RMSE									
1	30	19.1	14.4	8.1	6.6	22.8	14.5	10.0	8.2
	50	15.3	9.5	7.6	6.0	16.6	13.0	8.0	5.6
	100	10.0	7.3	4.9	3.6	12.5	8.7	6.5	3.7
	200	7.4	5.1	3.7	2.5	9.0	6.3	3.9	2.8
3	30	44.7	23.5	17.5	11.8	63.8	35.6	22.6	13.2
	50	36.1	22.4	13.9	9.9	48.5	26.0	20.5	13.4
	100	23.7	16.0	9.3	5.8	32.9	19.6	13.2	9.3
	200	15.9	11.8	6.6	4.2	23.0	15.6	9.4	6.5
Size									
1	30	5.9	6.4	6.8	5.4	6.5	5.2	5.5	6.6
	50	5.9	5.4	5.7	7.2	5.3	4.7	7.4	5.0
	100	5.1	5.2	6.2	5.5	5.1	5.4	5.1	5.2
	200	5.1	5.1	5.1	5.1	5.2	5.5	4.7	5.5
3	30	10.7	8.7	10.8	9.7	8.5	8.3	9.3	9.7
	50	8.5	7.8	7.5	9.5	7.5	8.2	7.9	9.2
	100	5.3	5.9	4.7	6.6	5.6	5.4	6.1	5.2
	200	4.9	5.3	5.5	5.8	5.6	6.3	5.3	5.5
Power									
1	30	7.8	9.5	10.7	12.3	7.0	8.2	8.1	6.6
	50	8.0	7.6	10.5	30.5	6.3	7.5	8.8	10.4
	100	8.9	9.2	23.9	28.8	8.2	11.5	13.1	25.7
	200	10.2	18.2	27.0	54.2	10.3	14.6	22.9	43.0
3	30	11.1	10.0	14.7	16.1	8.6	9.0	9.9	15.2
	50	8.3	8.6	11.1	16.2	8.1	8.7	9.8	10.8
	100	5.5	7.5	11.2	20.2	6.2	7.6	11.1	11.6
	200	7.1	9.9	19.8	38.9	7.5	7.6	9.5	21.9

Notes: The mean group estimator is given by (14). Its estimated variance is given by (18). Bias and RMSE estimates are scaled up by 10,000 and 100, respectively.

Table 10.3. *Pooled estimator*

		One factor				Two factors			
# x	N/T	30	50	100	200	30	50	100	200
Bias									
1	30	−51.4	206.8	141.2	160.7	101.6	−43.9	−26.8	−54.0
	50	−17.4	117.6	107.7	18.9	−16.3	49.2	26.6	3.9
	100	34.6	22.0	11.2	35.7	37.0	−19.6	22.1	−33.9
	200	−28.7	13.8	−25.1	10.0	30.3	9.8	17.7	−5.4
3	30	84.0	130.0	−123.3	35.3	99.9	177.8	−50.0	−174.6
	50	74.1	−31.7	6.7	3.1	−120.1	−29.0	85.6	146.7
	100	18.4	6.8	−13.2	34.1	−44.4	−21.4	52.4	−103.2
	200	−54.2	−34.1	−8.7	−0.5	−3.2	2.9	−0.7	26.0
RMSE									
1	30	12.0	8.3	4.5	4.4	12.5	9.6	6.6	3.8
	50	8.2	6.7	4.8	2.9	9.9	7.8	4.8	3.4
	100	6.0	4.6	2.9	2.0	7.7	5.1	3.6	2.3
	200	4.2	3.1	2.1	1.4	5.4	3.7	2.4	1.8
3	30	20.7	17.2	10.0	6.7	33.5	23.3	14.0	9.2
	50	17.9	11.1	7.7	5.8	23.5	15.4	11.0	7.3
	100	11.9	9.2	5.5	3.6	15.9	11.9	7.2	5.5
	200	8.4	5.7	4.1	2.7	11.6	8.1	5.2	3.7
Size									
1	30	5.2	6.2	6.1	7.0	5.8	6.1	5.7	6.7
	50	6.1	5.9	5.4	4.5	5.7	6.2	5.9	4.9
	100	5.2	5.5	5.7	6.4	5.5	4.7	5.9	5.1
	200	4.2	5.0	5.4	5.5	5.4	5.3	5.4	5.3
3	30	8.9	7.8	9.7	9.0	7.0	9.3	9.5	8.7
	50	7.0	7.3	6.0	6.5	7.1	5.9	5.9	7.0
	100	6.9	5.8	6.0	6.4	6.1	6.3	5.5	5.5
	200	5.3	5.1	5.2	4.5	6.1	5.2	5.1	5.7
Power									
1	30	8.1	7.2	15.2	16.2	7.6	10.1	15.3	34.0
	50	11.9	9.9	15.3	39.2	9.1	9.8	18.6	31.1
	100	13.0	18.8	38.3	66.6	10.5	16.7	27.2	64.4
	200	22.4	35.5	71.0	92.2	14.9	28.5	53.0	82.0
3	30	9.8	9.0	20.3	21.6	7.5	9.7	14.6	24.4
	50	8.5	12.8	17.3	25.6	9.2	8.2	9.4	12.3
	100	10.6	11.6	30.6	46.9	8.3	10.6	15.6	36.0
	200	14.1	26.0	41.4	79.0	10.4	13.4	26.9	43.8

Table 10.3. *(cont.)*

		Three factors				Four factors			
# x	N/T	30	50	100	200	30	50	100	200
Bias									
1	30	−206.9	−277.0	53.3	−5.3	13.1	−121.2	93.8	314.9
	50	−3.9	139.5	77.2	−288.9	115.5	−140.6	203.0	110.4
	100	−81.1	45.7	−75.4	32.6	−53.4	−131.1	0.2	19.9
	200	−10.0	−15.0	17.7	−10.3	−36.6	−33.9	25.0	20.7
3	30	−101.6	55.2	−270.4	0.4	−28.2	160.3	146.7	−177.8
	50	382.2	−18.3	−71.6	−23.7	−179.5	45.0	−219.9	220.3
	100	146.4	−23.8	−9.1	39.7	27.3	−86.4	−144.0	33.9
	200	20.7	−37.7	−21.7	0.5	−116.9	11.4	83.2	−76.4
RMSE									
1	30	17.4	13.5	7.8	6.6	22.2	13.8	9.8	8.0
	50	13.6	9.1	7.4	5.9	15.8	12.6	7.7	5.6
	100	9.3	6.9	4.9	3.5	11.6	8.1	6.3	3.6
	200	6.8	4.9	3.5	2.4	8.2	5.9	3.8	2.8
3	30	38.1	21.2	17.0	11.6	55.0	32.3	21.3	13.0
	50	30.9	19.9	13.2	9.9	41.7	23.6	19.4	13.4
	100	19.4	14.5	8.9	5.6	27.5	17.9	12.6	9.0
	200	13.4	10.5	6.3	4.1	19.6	14.0	9.0	6.4
Size									
1	30	6.5	5.9	6.2	5.5	6.0	4.7	4.8	6.0
	50	5.5	5.5	5.3	7.1	5.3	3.8	7.4	4.7
	100	4.9	4.9	5.9	5.3	5.1	5.1	5.0	5.1
	200	4.3	5.1	5.0	5.7	5.0	5.0	4.2	5.2
3	30	9.2	8.5	9.8	8.3	7.6	7.6	8.1	8.3
	50	7.5	6.9	7.4	8.8	7.3	7.3	7.1	9.0
	100	6.2	4.9	4.5	5.5	6.6	5.3	6.8	5.7
	200	5.1	4.9	5.3	5.6	5.5	5.8	5.5	5.1
Power									
1	30	7.5	9.6	10.5	12.7	6.4	7.6	6.9	5.9
	50	6.9	7.5	10.6	29.8	6.3	7.7	9.2	9.8
	100	9.3	9.7	24.1	29.4	8.8	12.2	13.0	26.0
	200	10.7	19.2	28.1	55.5	11.2	15.2	23.8	43.5
3	30	10.2	9.0	15.8	15.5	8.6	7.2	8.8	14.5
	50	7.4	7.5	11.4	16.1	7.3	8.2	10.0	10.7
	100	6.8	8.3	11.3	21.0	6.8	7.8	12.2	11.7
	200	7.4	10.8	20.3	40.6	7.5	8.6	9.4	22.6

Notes: The Pooled estimator is given by (19). Its estimated variance is given by (20). Bias and RMSE estimates are scaled up by 10,000 and 100, respectively.

Table 10.4. *MGPC estimator*

		One factor				Two factors			
# x	N/T	30	50	100	200	30	50	100	200
Bias									
1	30	−1877.3	−1506.8	−864.4	−838.1	−2738.5	−2469.0	−2309.2	−1708.0
	50	−965.3	−920.6	−710.7	−458.7	−1960.2	−1710.8	−1307.8	−1085.9
	100	−519.3	−440.1	−250.8	−190.9	−1111.3	−950.8	−709.3	−543.9
	200	−334.9	−240.0	−134.7	−99.9	−683.0	−441.2	−334.1	−274.7
3	30	−1316.3	−1172.1	−925.7	−840.8	−3103.8	−2581.6	−2327.2	−2055.3
	50	−977.6	−629.1	−563.0	−569.7	−1794.1	−1346.7	−1257.1	−1141.8
	100	−454.1	−382.7	−264.0	−223.4	−858.0	−730.2	−567.4	−507.4
	200	−284.2	−186.9	−141.5	−117.5	−440.4	−378.7	−267.0	−245.8
RMSE									
1	30	23.8	17.6	10.0	9.5	30.9	26.7	24.2	17.6
	50	13.8	11.9	8.9	5.5	23.3	19.3	14.0	11.4
	100	8.7	6.9	4.0	2.8	14.4	11.3	8.1	5.9
	200	6.2	4.3	2.6	1.8	10.0	6.1	4.2	3.3
3	30	28.8	22.9	14.1	11.0	54.0	36.5	28.0	22.9
	50	24.2	13.9	10.1	8.3	36.7	23.2	17.9	14.0
	100	15.2	10.7	6.4	4.3	23.4	16.0	9.7	7.7
	200	10.9	6.7	4.6	3.0	16.3	10.7	6.3	4.7
Size									
1	30	28.2	38.9	40.2	50.7	51.5	66.1	87.4	91.6
	50	19.8	24.4	30.6	33.9	37.0	47.7	71.9	81.0
	100	12.9	15.3	12.3	16.4	23.8	36.4	44.4	60.2
	200	10.3	10.3	9.5	10.9	16.9	19.4	26.0	32.8
3	30	16.6	16.1	27.7	41.4	21.8	33.8	58.5	75.8
	50	11.5	13.7	17.0	26.6	14.3	19.9	30.8	51.8
	100	8.1	7.4	10.2	13.2	8.9	13.2	16.0	23.4
	200	6.7	7.8	6.6	8.2	7.4	7.3	9.0	14.1
Power									
1	30	39.6	62.3	77.5	85.7	65.3	81.2	97.2	99.5
	50	36.9	48.5	66.0	88.8	50.7	69.5	94.2	99.2
	100	34.1	45.9	67.5	92.7	43.9	67.1	87.9	99.5
	200	36.3	56.6	82.0	97.8	39.8	61.6	91.0	98.8
3	30	23.8	27.4	55.8	79.8	26.8	44.7	77.7	93.1
	50	17.6	29.4	46.4	74.2	19.4	32.6	53.9	84.5
	100	16.2	24.1	51.0	82.7	14.2	24.4	49.5	75.4
	200	17.2	32.0	55.9	91.7	13.9	22.6	49.7	79.5

Table 10.4. *(cont.)*

		Three factors				Four factors			
# *x*	*N*/*T*	30	50	100	200	30	50	100	200
Bias									
1	30	−4314.2	−3592.8	−2765.2	−2715.0	−4983.8	−4425.2	−3710.9	−3216.8
	50	−3000.3	−2351.1	−2277.3	−1647.5	−3506.5	−3231.9	−2487.2	−2103.8
	100	−1775.9	−1529.4	−1261.9	−1048.8	−2490.2	−1963.1	−1660.2	−1268.0
	200	−1134.3	−877.5	−755.9	−606.6	−1626.8	−1311.2	−976.3	−733.2
3	30	−4279.5	−3433.0	−3279.3	−2924.4	−5472.5	−4863.3	−4106.5	−4141.1
	50	−2690.1	−2549.2	−2179.6	−2031.2	−4207.6	−3260.3	−3375.8	−2675.5
	100	−1366.1	−1452.1	−1064.6	−704.0	−2591.5	−2163.3	−1927.6	−1667.4
	200	−757.1	−692.4	−479.5	−405.4	−1350.0	−1114.0	−981.3	−949.1
RMSE									
1	30	47.0	38.2	28.7	27.9	53.9	46.3	38.3	32.9
	50	34.2	25.4	24.0	17.2	38.9	34.7	25.9	21.7
	100	21.1	17.3	13.6	11.1	28.6	21.5	17.7	13.2
	200	14.3	10.5	8.4	6.6	19.5	14.7	10.6	7.8
3	30	63.0	42.8	37.1	31.3	80.4	59.1	45.7	43.5
	50	47.3	35.2	26.1	22.6	66.6	42.9	39.2	29.4
	100	31.4	23.4	14.6	9.4	46.6	31.1	23.8	19.2
	200	20.5	15.1	8.5	6.0	30.9	21.5	14.2	11.7
Size									
1	30	66.1	78.0	91.5	97.4	71.1	89.9	96.7	99.1
	50	49.8	69.0	85.3	89.3	56.0	71.5	91.6	97.0
	100	34.8	49.6	71.9	82.8	44.6	58.6	75.5	93.7
	200	24.7	34.6	51.9	68.7	35.4	51.5	68.4	75.3
3	30	31.4	52.0	79.3	93.0	32.0	58.2	84.3	99.0
	50	18.3	33.8	56.9	85.2	24.6	38.1	69.9	87.8
	100	11.2	20.8	31.4	35.2	16.0	28.4	50.5	73.1
	200	8.2	10.5	15.7	24.8	10.8	14.2	25.9	49.5
Power									
1	30	73.6	86.4	97.7	99.8	78.5	94.8	99.0	99.9
	50	61.9	83.8	95.3	99.0	68.1	82.7	98.0	99.9
	100	51.2	73.1	94.2	99.2	58.4	78.6	92.7	99.9
	200	45.5	67.7	91.8	99.4	53.9	78.0	95.4	99.2
3	30	36.9	63.8	89.8	98.7	36.5	66.0	91.6	99.9
	50	23.2	45.1	77.5	96.8	28.8	49.2	82.0	97.2
	100	16.3	33.2	61.1	82.7	21.4	40.9	71.9	93.2
	200	15.5	23.4	51.2	86.6	15.4	24.8	55.8	87.6

Notes: The MGPC estimator is given by (24). Its estimated variance is given by (27). Bias and RMSE estimates are scaled up by 10,000 and 100, respectively.

Table 10.5. *MGCFS estimator*

		One factor				Two factors			
# x	N/T	30	50	100	200	30	50	100	200
Bias									
1	30	1978.2	1538.2	1599.3	1575.1	4630.8	3942.8	3965.2	3836.3
	50	1801.9	1793.0	1730.4	1645.1	4018.8	3795.7	3906.6	4126.9
	100	1614.9	1702.2	1619.7	1661.7	3685.1	4248.5	3860.1	4193.3
	200	1845.4	1722.0	1516.4	1549.1	4578.0	3639.0	3710.2	3529.6
3	30	1007.6	991.5	1015.0	923.7	2170.4	2193.5	1898.8	1860.1
	50	1092.8	1027.7	949.0	933.3	1917.8	1983.0	1941.0	1889.6
	100	974.8	1081.6	960.9	930.9	1873.4	1962.2	1910.0	1830.3
	200	1034.7	944.5	919.3	950.8	1838.3	1841.6	1885.1	1924.1
RMSE									
1	30	23.4	17.3	16.8	16.4	47.9	40.6	40.3	38.6
	50	20.3	19.6	18.1	16.8	41.8	39.0	39.5	41.5
	100	17.8	18.1	16.7	16.9	38.2	43.1	38.9	42.1
	200	19.8	18.0	15.6	15.7	46.5	36.9	37.3	35.4
3	30	21.9	19.2	13.7	11.2	38.3	30.3	23.0	20.4
	50	19.9	14.4	12.0	10.8	29.6	24.5	22.0	20.1
	100	15.1	13.8	10.9	9.9	24.4	22.5	20.2	19.0
	200	13.3	11.0	10.0	9.9	21.5	20.1	19.5	19.6
Size									
1	30	70.2	76.2	97.4	98.4	99.2	99.8	100.0	100.0
	50	81.2	87.7	98.2	100.0	99.1	100.0	100.0	100.0
	100	87.5	95.7	99.9	100.0	99.7	100.0	100.0	100.0
	200	95.9	99.5	100.0	100.0	100.0	100.0	100.0	100.0
3	30	54.0	62.9	89.6	96.8	88.5	98.4	99.8	100.0
	50	59.2	83.9	93.2	99.0	89.1	99.2	100.0	100.0
	100	73.7	90.8	99.6	100.0	96.5	100.0	100.0	100.0
	200	90.0	96.1	99.7	100.0	99.1	100.0	100.0	100.0
Power									
1	30	54.9	56.1	84.5	87.5	98.2	98.9	100.0	100.0
	50	65.8	73.8	88.1	98.8	97.7	99.5	100.0	100.0
	100	70.3	83.1	96.0	100.0	97.9	100.0	100.0	100.0
	200	86.6	94.6	98.3	100.0	100.0	100.0	100.0	100.0
3	30	33.5	36.5	55.0	62.5	76.4	92.2	97.3	99.7
	50	33.3	49.4	55.9	66.8	73.4	95.0	99.1	100.0
	100	40.9	58.7	72.4	89.2	86.4	98.2	100.0	100.0
	200	57.5	65.6	79.5	96.2	94.7	99.6	100.0	100.0

Table 10.5. *(cont.)*

		Three factors				Four factors			
# x	*N/T*	30	50	100	200	30	50	100	200
Bias									
1	30	6296.5	5910.7	5636.6	6304.7	6843.9	7350.1	6940.5	7000.9
	50	6136.7	5681.3	5462.4	6054.7	7450.9	6418.1	6900.7	6966.7
	100	5084.7	5789.9	5617.7	5334.9	6518.3	6556.3	7084.1	6643.9
	200	5681.8	5209.1	5660.9	5080.3	6781.6	6903.4	6454.9	5811.4
3	30	2478.7	2420.8	2594.4	2492.3	2763.9	2727.2	2713.3	2657.8
	50	2436.1	2500.8	2563.8	2509.8	2759.7	2648.8	2721.6	2680.6
	100	2407.7	2591.5	2336.2	2212.3	2759.4	2779.2	2709.6	2744.7
	200	2429.9	2532.0	2432.0	2418.7	2711.9	2586.8	2731.4	2768.9
RMSE									
1	30	64.2	60.1	56.8	63.3	69.9	74.0	69.8	70.2
	50	62.5	57.4	55.1	60.7	75.2	65.0	69.2	69.8
	100	51.9	58.4	56.4	53.5	66.0	66.0	71.0	66.5
	200	57.5	52.5	56.7	50.9	68.3	69.2	64.7	58.2
3	30	42.7	30.9	29.8	27.0	57.4	40.1	33.3	29.0
	50	37.6	30.9	28.2	26.5	47.7	34.0	32.3	29.1
	100	30.5	29.2	24.8	22.7	38.6	32.3	29.3	28.6
	200	27.6	27.1	25.0	24.5	32.8	29.1	28.5	28.3
Power									
1	30	99.8	100.0	100.0	100.0	99.7	100.0	100.0	100.0
	50	100.0	100.0	100.0	100.0	100.0	100.0	100.0	100.0
	100	100.0	100.0	100.0	100.0	100.0	100.0	100.0	100.0
	200	100.0	100.0	100.0	100.0	100.0	100.0	100.0	100.0
3	30	93.7	100.0	100.0	100.0	93.0	99.9	100.0	100.0
	50	96.8	100.0	100.0	100.0	98.2	100.0	100.0	100.0
	100	99.8	100.0	100.0	100.0	99.6	100.0	100.0	100.0
	200	100.0	100.0	100.0	100.0	99.9	100.0	100.0	100.0
Power									
1	30	99.6	99.9	100.0	100.0	99.4	100.0	100.0	100.0
	50	99.9	100.0	100.0	100.0	100.0	100.0	100.0	100.0
	100	99.7	100.0	100.0	100.0	100.0	100.0	100.0	100.0
	200	100.0	100.0	100.0	100.0	100.0	100.0	100.0	100.0
3	30	85.4	99.1	100.0	100.0	85.9	98.7	100.0	100.0
	50	91.6	99.7	100.0	100.0	94.9	99.7	100.0	100.0
	100	97.9	100.0	100.0	100.0	98.2	100.0	100.0	100.0
	200	99.7	100.0	100.0	100.0	99.9	100.0	100.0	100.0

Notes: The MGCFS estimator is given by (24), where the factor in (23) has been constructed as described in Section 3.2. Its estimated variance is given by (27). Bias and RMSE estimates are scaled up by 10,000 and 100, respectively.

Table 10.6. *PPC estimator*

		One factor				Two factors			
# x	N/T	30	50	100	200	30	50	100	200
Bias									
1	30	−1706.2	−1426.7	−816.2	−817.5	−2726.8	−2449.1	−2252.5	−1598.6
	50	−901.4	−861.1	−683.1	−448.8	−1772.2	−1633.8	−1275.3	−1067.5
	100	−485.9	−408.4	−243.9	−188.2	−1070.5	−871.5	−683.3	−533.9
	200	−306.6	−215.2	−130.5	−97.5	−606.5	−406.2	−319.9	−269.2
3	30	−1194.2	−1064.5	−878.7	−808.3	−2769.1	−2469.3	−2204.4	−1962.2
	50	−837.6	−558.6	−515.1	−544.3	−1544.2	−1203.1	−1161.1	−1098.1
	100	−402.8	−356.7	−249.2	−211.1	−711.5	−648.8	−521.9	−488.7
	200	−253.6	−173.4	−133.0	−113.5	−381.9	−331.1	−254.2	−236.6
RMSE									
1	30	21.4	16.6	9.4	9.3	30.4	26.5	23.5	16.5
	50	12.6	11.1	8.5	5.4	20.8	18.3	13.7	11.2
	100	8.1	6.4	3.9	2.8	13.7	10.4	7.8	5.8
	200	5.5	3.9	2.5	1.7	8.7	5.7	4.1	3.2
3	30	25.0	21.2	13.5	10.7	44.9	34.3	26.6	21.9
	50	20.6	12.8	9.5	8.0	29.9	20.5	16.5	13.4
	100	12.8	10.1	6.1	4.2	19.0	14.4	9.1	7.4
	200	9.1	6.1	4.4	2.9	13.3	9.2	6.0	4.5
Size									
1	30	26.7	42.0	43.0	51.1	58.0	69.4	92.2	98.6
	50	19.1	23.5	29.9	33.6	38.5	50.0	75.7	88.4
	100	12.4	13.9	13.5	16.2	25.1	34.2	43.5	62.8
	200	9.8	10.2	9.4	10.7	17.8	19.1	25.0	33.0
3	30	11.6	11.9	21.8	35.3	19.4	30.7	60.0	89.1
	50	9.2	10.5	14.1	23.4	11.7	15.8	29.3	57.0
	100	7.4	6.8	9.2	11.6	8.1	10.9	14.4	21.8
	200	6.9	5.5	6.2	7.6	6.9	7.2	8.8	13.2
Power									
1	30	41.5	65.0	82.3	87.2	71.6	83.3	98.5	100.0
	50	39.2	48.9	68.3	89.4	56.5	74.3	95.5	99.6
	100	34.5	47.4	70.4	94.3	45.2	68.7	88.2	99.5
	200	41.7	58.5	83.2	98.4	44.9	62.6	91.1	99.1
3	30	18.6	20.5	48.3	77.5	24.8	41.9	77.3	97.7
	50	16.0	24.0	41.8	72.2	17.8	29.6	53.8	87.5
	100	17.7	22.8	49.1	82.7	14.4	22.8	48.4	73.7
	200	19.7	35.5	57.8	92.7	16.2	23.5	49.9	79.7

Table 10.6. *(cont.)*

		Three factors				Four factors			
# x	N/T	30	50	100	200	30	50	100	200
Bias									
1	30	−4226.6	−3570.6	−2714.9	−2722.1	−5059.8	−4391.2	−3680.7	−3150.6
	50	−2882.2	−2335.7	−2244.0	−1645.0	−3478.5	−3255.2	−2423.7	−2085.1
	100	−1722.6	−1477.2	−1254.3	−1040.8	−2426.5	−1906.8	−1637.2	−1258.4
	200	−1072.0	−834.6	−744.5	−599.1	−1526.6	−1278.4	−960.8	−731.9
3	30	−4073.5	−3173.2	−3211.5	−2903.4	−5342.3	−4699.9	−4029.9	−4174.5
	50	−2475.2	−2318.8	−2095.2	−1983.0	−3934.3	−3149.9	−3280.7	−2706.3
	100	−1191.2	−1285.7	−1005.0	−683.5	−2312.8	−1970.8	−1848.8	−1641.1
	200	−663.1	−603.2	−436.9	−388.1	−1198.8	−1008.4	−925.4	−921.6
RMSE									
1	30	45.6	37.8	28.2	28.0	54.3	45.8	38.0	32.3
	50	32.5	25.1	23.6	17.1	38.2	34.8	25.2	21.5
	100	20.2	16.6	13.5	11.0	27.5	20.8	17.5	13.1
	200	13.4	10.0	8.3	6.5	18.0	14.3	10.4	7.8
3	30	57.7	39.2	36.2	31.0	74.2	56.1	44.6	43.7
	50	41.1	31.3	25.0	22.1	59.1	40.4	37.8	29.6
	100	24.9	20.8	13.9	9.1	38.9	28.1	22.7	18.8
	200	17.1	13.1	8.0	5.8	26.1	19.1	13.4	11.4
Size									
1	30	70.4	83.8	96.9	99.1	75.9	93.5	98.6	99.8
	50	53.3	73.4	88.2	94.0	60.2	75.3	94.7	98.2
	100	39.0	52.2	72.9	85.4	49.4	63.0	77.1	95.6
	200	24.6	34.2	53.9	70.3	39.0	52.0	69.5	77.5
3	30	29.1	53.0	84.8	98.8	29.4	63.1	89.9	100.0
	50	17.5	35.1	61.7	89.5	23.7	41.5	74.5	94.3
	100	11.4	19.7	30.9	34.2	16.1	28.0	53.0	75.4
	200	8.9	10.5	13.2	22.6	10.7	13.4	24.6	50.0
Power									
1	30	80.3	92.0	99.4	99.9	81.9	97.7	99.6	100.0
	50	66.0	86.9	97.2	99.5	71.0	86.4	99.0	99.9
	100	56.3	77.5	94.8	99.4	65.0	82.4	94.0	100.0
	200	49.4	68.7	93.2	99.2	58.2	80.3	96.0	99.5
3	30	36.1	64.1	92.9	99.9	35.5	71.8	95.7	100.0
	50	22.9	48.5	81.6	98.3	28.5	52.3	86.2	98.8
	100	17.6	34.6	60.7	81.8	22.6	43.2	73.7	94.2
	200	15.9	23.7	50.8	86.3	17.2	25.9	55.9	87.8

Notes: The PPC estimator is given by (25). Its estimated variance is given by (28). Bias and RMSE estimates are scaled up by 10,000 and 100, respectively.

Table 10.7. *PCFS estimator*

		One factor				Two factors			
# x	N/T	30	50	100	200	30	50	100	200
Bias									
1	30	1875.6	1491.1	1574.0	1554.9	4466.1	3822.6	3890.2	3758.7
	50	1728.1	1738.4	1695.6	1625.9	3880.7	3676.8	3815.0	4067.3
	100	1538.8	1638.8	1587.0	1632.3	3533.3	4109.9	3780.7	4166.3
	200	1755.5	1658.1	1482.0	1526.5	4422.2	3534.4	3672.7	3520.8
3	30	986.2	970.8	1015.5	921.8	2158.9	2176.3	1900.8	1858.4
	50	1064.6	1022.1	948.4	938.3	1889.2	1951.5	1940.0	1887.7
	100	957.2	1071.5	961.6	935.4	1848.2	1958.9	1912.4	1827.2
	200	1017.0	942.2	918.8	952.6	1817.1	1831.7	1878.5	1921.1
RMSE									
1	30	22.2	16.9	16.5	16.1	46.2	39.4	39.5	37.9
	50	19.4	18.9	17.8	16.6	40.3	37.8	38.6	40.9
	100	17.0	17.5	16.4	16.5	36.7	41.7	38.1	41.8
	200	18.8	17.3	15.2	15.4	44.9	35.8	36.9	35.3
3	30	19.6	17.9	13.3	11.0	34.2	29.0	22.6	20.2
	50	18.0	13.8	11.8	10.7	27.0	23.6	21.6	20.0
	100	13.8	13.3	10.8	9.9	22.7	22.0	20.1	18.9
	200	12.5	10.8	10.0	9.9	20.6	19.6	19.4	19.5
Size									
1	30	69.0	75.2	97.8	99.5	99.4	99.9	100.0	100.0
	50	82.9	89.9	98.0	100.0	99.4	100.0	100.0	100.0
	100	86.7	96.3	100.0	100.0	99.7	100.0	100.0	100.0
	200	96.2	99.5	100.0	100.0	100.0	100.0	100.0	100.0
3	30	53.2	62.4	90.3	97.7	89.8	98.1	100.0	100.0
	50	65.0	87.4	94.2	99.5	91.5	99.3	100.0	100.0
	100	77.5	92.0	99.6	100.0	98.0	100.0	100.0	100.0
	200	92.8	98.0	99.9	100.0	99.7	100.0	100.0	100.0
Power									
1	30	54.9	53.5	85.2	91.5	98.4	98.9	100.0	100.0
	50	66.3	75.2	87.5	99.1	97.9	99.4	100.0	100.0
	100	67.8	83.5	96.5	100.0	98.2	100.0	100.0	100.0
	200	87.1	94.8	98.6	100.0	100.0	100.0	100.0	100.0
3	30	31.3	34.8	53.2	60.6	78.0	94.1	98.0	100.0
	50	38.6	51.2	57.5	70.5	78.5	96.3	99.5	100.0
	100	45.5	62.5	75.6	91.8	90.0	99.1	100.0	100.0
	200	63.0	70.5	82.6	97.2	96.5	99.9	100.0	100.0

Table 10.7. *(cont.)*

		Three factors				Four factors			
# x	N/T	30	50	100	200	30	50	100	200
Bias									
1	30	6074.4	5790.8	5532.9	6212.3	6657.4	7177.3	6869.6	6912.7
	50	5952.6	5555.0	5348.9	5990.5	7300.6	6272.0	6799.5	6883.0
	100	4905.1	5653.3	5516.6	5262.3	6330.6	6405.8	6974.2	6617.6
	200	5485.0	5088.9	5589.3	5090.6	6596.4	6777.7	6404.3	5854.1
3	30	2477.9	2423.6	2611.9	2493.0	2771.2	2733.3	2764.8	2675.2
	50	2433.4	2505.1	2553.5	2505.4	2777.4	2664.7	2740.7	2679.2
	100	2392.1	2589.5	2337.2	2213.0	2764.3	2788.5	2710.6	2738.0
	200	2417.4	2535.9	2431.3	2417.7	2706.2	2577.6	2730.3	2777.1
RMSE									
1	30	62.0	58.8	55.8	62.3	68.0	72.3	69.1	69.3
	50	60.6	56.2	54.0	60.1	73.7	63.5	68.2	69.0
	100	50.1	57.1	55.4	52.7	64.1	64.4	69.9	66.3
	200	55.5	51.3	56.0	51.0	66.4	68.0	64.2	58.6
3	30	39.3	29.9	29.6	26.9	52.4	38.5	32.9	28.9
	50	34.4	29.9	27.8	26.4	43.3	32.7	31.8	28.8
	100	28.5	28.5	24.6	22.7	35.1	31.4	29.0	28.5
	200	26.6	26.7	24.9	24.4	31.2	28.3	28.3	28.2
Size									
1	30	99.9	100.0	100.0	100.0	99.9	100.0	100.0	100.0
	50	100.0	100.0	100.0	100.0	100.0	100.0	100.0	100.0
	100	100.0	100.0	100.0	100.0	100.0	100.0	100.0	100.0
	200	100.0	100.0	100.0	100.0	100.0	100.0	100.0	100.0
3	30	96.5	99.9	100.0	100.0	95.0	99.9	100.0	100.0
	50	97.2	100.0	100.0	100.0	99.1	100.0	100.0	100.0
	100	99.7	100.0	100.0	100.0	99.8	100.0	100.0	100.0
	200	100.0	100.0	100.0	100.0	100.0	100.0	100.0	100.0
Power									
1	30	99.7	100.0	100.0	100.0	99.7	100.0	100.0	100.0
	50	100.0	100.0	100.0	100.0	100.0	100.0	100.0	100.0
	100	99.7	100.0	100.0	100.0	100.0	100.0	100.0	100.0
	200	100.0	100.0	100.0	100.0	100.0	100.0	100.0	100.0
3	30	90.5	99.6	100.0	100.0	90.0	99.2	100.0	100.0
	50	93.0	99.9	100.0	100.0	96.8	99.8	100.0	100.0
	100	98.3	100.0	100.0	100.0	99.2	100.0	100.0	100.0
	200	100.0	100.0	100.0	100.0	99.9	100.0	100.0	100.0

Notes: The PCFS estimator is given by (25), where the factor in (23) has been constructed as described in Section 3.2. Its estimated variance is given by (28). Bias and RMSE estimates are scaled up by 10,000 and 100, respectively.

Table 10.8. *PCPOOL estimator*

		One factor				Two factors			
# x	N/T	30	50	100	200	30	50	100	200
Bias									
1	30	−1987.1	−1642.4	−1188.7	−1009.4	−2896.1	−2340.8	−1787.6	−1373.8
	50	−1553.9	−1312.5	−948.3	−665.3	−2266.2	−1771.6	−1342.2	−995.1
	100	−1261.6	−956.5	−600.1	−363.0	−1915.8	−1374.8	−992.2	−632.9
	200	−982.7	−686.5	−371.5	−210.4	−1521.3	−1040.9	−682.2	−443.1
3	30	−2147.4	−1745.4	−1299.3	−1069.8	−2949.6	−2383.6	−1900.9	−1474.6
	50	−1799.8	−1382.6	−1029.5	−787.7	−2466.1	−1904.0	−1381.9	−1082.8
	100	−1385.3	−1069.1	−756.1	−498.0	−1956.4	−1477.8	−1006.7	−733.2
	200	−1148.2	−800.0	−524.1	−314.7	−1632.2	−1204.9	−769.7	−512.1
RMSE									
1	30	23.2	18.3	12.7	10.8	31.8	25.4	19.0	14.2
	50	17.6	14.8	10.6	7.3	24.9	19.4	14.3	10.4
	100	14.2	10.8	6.7	4.2	20.8	14.8	10.6	6.7
	200	10.9	7.7	4.4	2.6	16.3	11.1	7.3	4.8
3	30	28.6	23.6	15.8	12.4	41.6	31.5	22.9	16.8
	50	24.9	17.3	12.7	9.6	33.1	24.0	17.1	12.8
	100	17.9	13.9	9.2	6.1	25.2	18.8	12.2	9.0
	200	14.2	9.9	6.6	4.1	19.9	14.5	9.3	6.3
Size									
1	30	43.8	56.2	78.7	76.3	67.7	69.6	80.0	96.4
	50	53.5	51.7	52.7	63.9	64.1	64.0	82.2	88.2
	100	56.6	56.7	52.4	46.4	68.3	73.8	78.8	80.5
	200	61.4	58.8	42.5	30.5	78.8	79.5	79.4	71.0
3	30	45.0	37.6	56.5	70.7	35.9	40.8	59.9	77.9
	50	41.3	52.0	51.0	52.9	42.1	51.8	48.0	62.6
	100	52.4	42.2	57.8	53.0	52.3	47.3	55.9	52.9
	200	58.0	55.5	47.7	38.0	61.8	61.6	58.1	49.7
Power									
1	30	58.6	79.3	97.8	97.7	80.0	83.9	94.6	100.0
	50	75.2	78.6	87.1	97.2	80.0	83.8	96.8	99.7
	100	82.1	87.6	96.3	99.1	86.8	94.2	98.2	99.9
	200	91.1	95.0	97.4	99.9	95.2	98.4	99.7	100.0
3	30	61.0	57.6	84.0	96.4	45.6	55.1	80.9	95.9
	50	57.2	79.0	86.9	93.5	55.9	73.0	78.3	92.9
	100	75.6	76.1	94.4	99.3	72.0	74.7	89.6	94.3
	200	87.8	93.2	97.2	99.7	83.5	90.3	95.8	98.6

Table 10.8. *(cont.)*

		Three factors				Four factors			
# x	N/T	30	50	100	200	30	50	100	200
Bias									
1	30	−3650.4	−2871.7	−2190.4	−2022.3	−4437.8	−3468.5	−2835.7	−2378.0
	50	−2944.3	−2277.4	−1767.7	−1348.2	−3587.3	−2900.5	−2023.8	−1642.3
	100	−2463.0	−1783.6	−1295.9	−933.3	−3073.4	−2152.1	−1574.2	−1070.7
	200	−2075.8	−1449.1	−964.5	−656.9	−2515.2	−1828.6	−1174.1	−795.3
3	30	−3787.6	−3061.2	−2455.6	−1967.1	−4457.0	−3629.1	−2895.0	−2422.9
	50	−3053.8	−2347.3	−1768.1	−1422.7	−3855.5	−2940.0	−2245.9	−1695.9
	100	−2464.9	−1880.1	−1309.9	−938.3	−3130.7	−2239.9	−1538.3	−1181.0
	200	−2157.4	−1515.1	−976.5	−662.0	−2626.1	−1884.6	−1219.5	−847.3
RMSE									
1	30	40.7	31.6	23.1	21.2	49.7	37.8	29.9	24.8
	50	32.9	24.6	19.1	14.4	39.9	31.9	21.6	17.3
	100	26.7	19.2	13.9	10.0	33.3	23.2	17.0	11.3
	200	22.2	15.4	10.3	7.0	26.8	19.4	12.4	8.4
3	30	51.2	36.2	28.6	21.9	65.1	45.9	34.1	26.8
	50	41.6	29.8	21.4	16.7	56.0	37.0	28.9	20.3
	100	31.1	23.8	15.8	10.9	41.9	29.0	19.8	14.7
	200	25.7	18.5	11.6	7.8	33.2	23.9	15.3	10.6
Size									
1	30	56.0	62.0	87.2	89.1	56.6	68.2	84.5	93.2
	50	58.3	70.7	70.2	79.4	58.1	60.9	80.9	86.0
	100	70.3	71.2	76.8	77.1	71.8	73.4	69.2	85.1
	200	78.9	80.2	77.5	77.0	81.7	81.9	85.0	82.2
3	30	42.5	66.4	70.7	84.2	33.5	49.0	65.5	88.2
	50	42.2	48.4	54.9	67.8	35.5	49.8	41.2	59.0
	100	56.4	50.1	58.7	68.7	43.7	46.9	44.6	48.8
	200	72.7	58.5	65.0	65.0	56.0	50.9	49.8	48.5
Power									
1	30	66.1	74.2	95.9	98.2	65.1	79.0	93.3	98.5
	50	70.5	85.5	88.6	96.8	69.5	73.8	93.5	98.0
	100	84.8	89.8	95.3	98.6	82.2	88.8	90.2	99.2
	200	92.0	96.0	98.2	99.7	93.5	95.6	98.6	99.7
3	30	50.5	80.0	87.5	97.1	38.9	59.6	80.3	97.4
	50	53.0	64.5	78.6	92.3	41.8	62.9	59.6	83.9
	100	71.2	70.7	86.6	97.9	56.6	63.7	68.0	81.3
	200	86.9	83.4	94.9	99.2	69.8	72.0	79.8	87.8

Notes: The PCPOOL estimator is defined at the end of section 3. Bias and RMSE estimates are scaled up by 10,000 and 100, respectively.

Table 10.9. *Mean group (MG) estimators for experiments B*

		CCEMG estimator				MG(Theil) estimator			
# *x*	*N*/*T*	30	50	100	200	30	50	100	200
Bias									
1	30	3.4	−27.8	106.1	−252.0	2071.7	1796.8	1880.7	−3.5
	50	184.4	−35.9	−247.4	153.0	2862.7	1440.6	547.2	1.1
	100	17.6	8.5	−143.4	−3.3	3203.4	2849.7	676.3	4.3
	200	−3.5	3.1	7.7	−10.3	2877.8	2597.8	1604.2	−0.2
RMSE									
1	30	24.0	18.2	13.6	7.8	24.1	20.8	21.0	5.2
	50	20.6	13.3	9.4	6.3	30.4	18.1	11.6	4.0
	100	14.2	9.8	6.4	4.2	33.0	29.7	12.0	2.7
	200	10.0	7.0	4.8	3.1	30.5	27.7	17.1	2.0
Size									
1	30	6.3	5.1	6.5	7.8	51.5	54.4	71.9	5.6
	50	5.1	5.8	4.3	6.8	84.8	53.9	33.6	7.0
	100	5.1	5.3	5.9	5.8	98.8	97.5	44.1	6.2
	200	4.7	5.6	5.7	5.2	94.0	97.9	97.1	5.7
Power									
1	30	6.6	6.5	8.0	17.2	37.6	37.8	54.8	20.1
	50	6.7	8.6	12.8	9.6	75.9	37.3	33.1	27.8
	100	6.7	8.3	18.7	24.6	96.0	94.5	54.6	48.4
	200	8.2	12.0	18.4	39.2	88.5	92.5	88.6	71.3
		MG(AIC) estimator				MGT estimator			
Bias									
1	30	1802.4	1367.2	731.8	−3.6	6.3	−58.3	−29.0	−3.8
	50	1210.0	547.4	9.2	0.7	−34.5	−26.3	5.8	1.1
	100	641.5	405.8	−26.0	4.3	24.5	−33.2	−26.0	4.3
	200	1369.4	105.8	71.9	−0.2	−17.8	−1.6	2.3	−0.2
RMSE									
1	30	22.8	18.6	12.2	5.2	16.7	11.5	8.6	5.2
	50	20.7	10.4	6.0	4.0	13.3	8.5	5.9	4.0
	100	16.4	10.5	4.3	2.7	9.2	6.1	4.3	2.7
	200	17.7	6.0	4.5	2.0	7.1	4.3	3.1	2.0
Size									
1	30	45.1	41.7	25.8	5.3	5.0	5.8	5.8	5.7
	50	36.7	17.0	5.5	6.9	5.5	5.5	5.3	7.0
	100	23.6	25.9	6.3	6.2	4.5	5.3	6.3	6.2
	200	61.5	12.7	10.0	5.7	6.5	5.7	5.3	5.7

Table 10.9. *(cont.)*

Power									
1	30	32.9	29.5	15.0	19.8	6.5	9.7	11.3	20.1
	50	31.6	9.9	14.5	27.8	7.8	11.8	14.2	27.8
	100	26.0	25.2	25.7	48.4	8.6	15.0	25.7	48.4
	200	46.7	27.4	40.9	71.3	12.2	22.8	37.3	71.3

Notes: The *CCEMG* estimator is given by (14); its estimated variance is given by (18). The MG (Theil) estimator is given by (24); its estimated variance is given by (27). The factors included in (23) are chosen by the criterion in (32). The MG(AIC) estimator is given by (24); its estimated variance is given by (27). The factors included in (23) are chosen by the criterion in (31). The *MGT* estimator is the MG estimator that uses the true unobserved factor and is, therefore, infeasible in practice.

identity of the factors entering (29) is not and needs to be determined via a selection criterion, are performing rather poorly. Further, they do not seem to improve when N grows, but only when T grows. Of course, for large T they outperform the *CCE* estimators since the factors get selected perfectly. This can be seen if one compares the result for the *MGT* and *PT* estimators that include the true factors. This feature is shared by both pooled and mean group estimators. We also note that the Akaike-type criterion performs better in selecting the appropriate factors compared to the Theil-type criterion. This is the case both for the *CCEP* and *CCEMG* estimators. Overall, it appears that even if one knows the factors, the small sample bias in the model selection aspect of the PC-augmented procedure is important enough to adversely affect the performance of the estimators for moderate values of T, even if one abstracts from the small sample bias in estimation of the unobserved factors.

5 An Empirical Application

In this section we present the results of an empirical application to a panel-data set of company returns to the following stock return equations

$$y_{it} = \alpha_{i1} + \alpha_{i2}\pi_{ot} + \mathbf{x}_{it}'\beta + \mathbf{f}_t'\gamma_i + \varepsilon_{it} \tag{33}$$

where here y_{it} denotes the individual company stock returns, π_{ot} is the rate of change of oil prices in US dollars (representing the observed common factor of the model), $\mathbf{x}_{it}$ is a vector of observed macroeconomic factors $\mathbf{x}_{it} = (\Delta q_{it}, \Delta\pi_{it}, \Delta r_{it}, \Delta m_{it}, \Delta e_{it})'$, where q_{it} is (log of) real output of the country of company i at time t, π_{it} is the inflation rate of the country of

Table 10.10. *Pooled estimators for experiments B*

		CCEP estimator				P(Theil) estimator			
# *x*	*N*/*T*	30	50	100	200	30	50	100	200
Bias									
1	30	106.4	−18.1	138.3	−265.1	1994.7	1745.6	1839.0	−6.8
	50	237.4	−23.7	−240.1	156.9	2781.7	1375.7	530.4	0.1
	100	20.6	−4.0	−133.4	−2.9	3090.8	2757.4	660.1	3.2
	200	2.8	−7.6	7.7	−11.0	2754.0	2510.5	1564.4	−1.4
RMSE									
1	30	22.9	17.1	13.1	7.7	23.3	20.2	20.5	4.7
	50	20.0	12.5	9.5	6.2	29.6	17.4	11.2	4.0
	100	13.0	9.5	6.2	4.1	31.8	28.8	11.7	2.6
	200	9.0	6.5	4.5	3.0	29.2	26.8	16.7	1.9
Size									
1	30	5.6	5.7	6.2	7.1	47.0	53.8	71.5	4.8
	50	5.5	5.3	4.8	6.2	83.5	51.2	33.1	5.8
	100	4.9	5.3	5.5	5.2	98.5	97.5	44.0	5.3
	200	5.1	6.0	5.5	5.1	94.5	97.8	97.2	5.0
Power									
1	30	6.2	6.6	7.1	17.5	32.9	35.6	53.0	18.2
	50	6.0	8.1	11.5	9.3	73.6	35.2	33.0	24.6
	100	6.9	9.3	18.9	25.1	96.0	94.2	56.4	50.0
	200	8.5	13.5	19.6	39.7	88.4	91.8	88.3	74.8
		P(AIC) estimator				PT estimator			
Bias									
1	30	1734.6	1325.4	716.0	−6.6	−8.9	−52.8	−22.6	−7.2
	50	1165.1	514.3	6.0	−0.3	−44.0	−34.3	2.6	0.1
	100	609.3	388.1	−24.3	3.2	16.6	−37.9	−24.3	3.2
	200	1301.2	106.9	70.8	−1.4	−18.1	3.6	3.3	−1.4
RMSE									
1	30	22.0	18.0	11.9	4.7	16.0	10.7	8.3	4.7
	50	20.1	9.9	5.6	4.0	13.2	8.1	5.5	4.0
	100	15.7	10.2	3.9	2.6	8.5	5.9	3.9	2.6
	200	16.8	5.7	4.4	1.9	6.5	4.0	3.0	1.9
Size									
1	30	39.8	40.8	22.1	4.5	4.4	4.7	4.7	4.8
	50	35.4	14.6	4.8	5.7	4.6	5.2	4.6	5.8
	100	23.5	25.1	5.7	5.3	4.3	4.7	5.7	5.3
	200	62.0	12.1	10.0	5.0	5.7	4.8	5.2	5.0

Table 10.10. *(cont.)*

Power									
1	30	28.4	27.4	12.6	17.9	5.1	7.2	9.6	18.2
	50	29.1	9.0	14.3	24.6	6.9	11.2	14.1	24.6
	100	25.6	24.4	27.7	50.0	8.6	14.5	27.7	50.0
	200	47.6	28.5	42.2	74.8	13.6	24.2	38.9	74.8

Notes: The *CCEP* estimator is given by (19). Its estimated variance is given by (20). The P(Theil) estimator is given by (25). Its estimated variance is given by (28). The factors included in (23) are chosen by the criterion in (32). The P(AIC) estimator is given by (25). Its estimated variance is given by (28). The factors included in (23) are chosen by the criterion in (31). The *PT* estimator is the pooled estimator that uses the true unobserved factor and is therefore, infeasible in practice.

company i at time t, r_{it} is the real interest rate of the country of company i at time t, m_{it} is the real money supply of the country of company i at time t, and e_{it} is the real exchange rate of the country of company i at time t with respect to the US dollar. The model is also assumed to contain m unobserved common effects, $\mathbf{f}_t$ that could be correlated with $\mathbf{x}_{it}$ and/or π_{ot}. We also assume that m is fixed but unknown. This model is clearly a generalization of a standard APT model. It allows individual stock returns to be affected both by observed macroeconomic variables and by unobserved common factors. We report results for subsets of the above macroeconomic explanatory variables as well.

The data-set contains 243 companies from France, Germany, Italy, Japan, the UK, the USA, Southeast Asia, the Middle East and Latin America. The sample periods differ across companies and cover the period 1979Q1–1999Q1. Table 10.11 gives details of the geographical coverage of the companies included in the panel and the associated sample periods. Note that the structure of the panel data-set is very rich. 10 different regions of the world are considered where each region is represented by at least 10 companies each (with the exception of Middle East). The macroeconomic variables for each company in a given region are the same. Therefore, the model in (33), can be viewed as a mixture of an APT model with observed regional macroeconomic factors and an APT model with global unobserved common effects represented by the unobserved factors and proxied by the global cross-sectional averages used by the *CCEMG* and *CCEP* estimators.

There is reduced coverage over time for some countries and companies. As a result this is an unbalanced panel and so our estimation methods must be modified to address this. The *CCEMG* estimator is

Table 10.11. *Number of companies and the sample periods*

Region	No. of Companies	Sample periods
USA	63	79Q1–99Q1
UK	24	79Q1–99Q1
Germany	21	79Q1–99Q1
France	14	79Q1–99Q1
Italy	10	79Q1–99Q1
W. Europe	24	79Q1–99Q1
Middle East	4	90Q3–99Q1
S.E. Asia	34	89Q3–99Q1
Japan	35	79Q1–99Q1
L. America	14	89Q3–99Q1
Total	243	

Notes: Western Europe is made up of Spain, the Netherlands, Belgium and Switzerland. The Middle East contains firms from Turkey. Southeast Asia contains firms from Indonesia, Korea, Malaysia, Philippines, Singapore and Thailand. Finally, Latin America contains firms from Argentina, Brazil, Chile, Mexico and Peru.

Source: Company data is from Datastream, with more details provided in Pesaran, Schuermann, and Treutler (2004). The macroeconomic data are the same as those in Pesaran, Schuermann, and Weiner (2004) and we refer the reader to that paper for details.

readily modified. The *CCEP* estimator is in this case still given by (19) but the matrices $\mathbf{X}_i' \mathbf{y}_i$ and $\bar{\mathbf{M}}$ are defined so as to include only available observations for the i-th unit. In the unbalanced panel case the dimension of the $\bar{\mathbf{M}}$ now depends on i.

We report the coefficient estimates, and the test results for the null hypothesis that the coefficients are equal to zero, in Tables 10.12–10.15. Tables 10.12–10.13 report results for the pooled (*CCEP*) estimators. Tables 10.14–10.15 report the results for the MG estimators (*CCEMG*). We consider a number of specifications whereby subsets of the explanatory variables are dropped from the regression to investigate the effect of such omissions on the remaining coefficients.

The coefficients of the $\mathbf{x}_{it}$ variables have the expected signs and are for the most part significantly different from zero. One exception is the coefficient of the inflation variable which is generally found to be insignificant. The oil price variable does not seem to be statistically significant either. This could be due to the highly heterogeneous nature of the effect of oil prices on different company returns, being positive for companies with large oil interests such as oil or petrochemical companies, and being

Table 10.12. *Empirical application 1: pooled estimator*

Spec.	Δq	$\Delta\pi$	Δr	Δm	Δe	const	$\Delta\pi_o$
1	$1.251_{(4.45)}$	$0.335_{(1.63)}$	$-1.594_{(-1.94)}$	$0.185_{(2.21)}$	$-0.366_{(-5.12)}$	$-0.002_{(-0.45)}$	$0.042_{(1.07)}$
2	—	$0.277_{(1.35)}$	$-1.763_{(-2.02)}$	$0.283_{(3.30)}$	$-0.411_{(-5.75)}$	$0.003_{(0.83)}$	$0.073_{(1.76)}$
3	$1.254_{(4.43)}$	—	$-1.464_{(-1.77)}$	$0.164_{(2.03)}$	$-0.356_{(-4.95)}$	$-0.003_{(-0.67)}$	$0.039_{(0.98)}$
4	$1.243_{(4.30)}$	$0.187_{(0.67)}$	—	$0.167_{(1.95)}$	$-0.395_{(-5.51)}$	$-0.002_{(-0.50)}$	$0.040_{(0.98)}$
5	$1.261_{(4.51)}$	$0.265_{(1.35)}$	$-1.678_{(-1.89)}$	—	$-0.336_{(-4.79)}$	$-0.004_{(-1.00)}$	$0.039_{(1.01)}$
6	$1.669_{(5.67)}$	$0.087_{(0.41)}$	$-1.923_{(-2.43)}$	$0.115_{(1.30)}$	—	$-0.003_{(-0.70)}$	$0.032_{(0.80)}$
7	$1.252_{(4.49)}$	—	$-1.583_{(-1.80)}$	—	$-0.329_{(-4.64)}$	$-0.004_{(-0.99)}$	$0.038_{(0.98)}$

Table 10.13. *Empirical application 2: pooled estimator*

Spec.	$\overline{ret}$	$\overline{\Delta q}$	$\overline{\Delta \pi}$	$\overline{\Delta r}$	$\overline{\Delta m}$	$\overline{\Delta e}$	$\overline{\sigma}_i^2$
1	1.021 (26.14)	−0.482 (−0.90)	−0.654 (−1.68)	2.022 (3.35)	−0.377 (−1.43)	0.360 (4.45)	0.0328 (0.0440)
2	1.040 (26.21)	—	−0.593 (−1.61)	2.132 (3.48)	−0.552 (−2.08)	0.362 (4.35)	0.0334 (0.0443)
3	1.016 (25.67)	−0.489 (−0.95)	—	1.689 (3.70)	−0.240 (−0.91)	0.324 (4.08)	0.0327 (0.0429)
4	1.011 (25.29)	−0.598 (−1.18)	−0.167 (−0.76)	—	−0.267 (−0.99)	0.376 (4.71)	0.0326 (0.0421)
5	1.018 (27.82)	−0.446 (−0.83)	−0.515 (−1.35)	2.070 (3.33)	—	0.319 (3.96)	0.0327 (0.0440)
6	1.005 (28.47)	−0.564 (−1.04)	−0.433 (−1.18)	2.415 (3.57)	−0.337 (−1.29)	—	0.0335 (0.0439)
7	1.015 (27.43)	−0.440 (−0.85)	—	1.808 (3.72)	—	0.295 (3.71)	0.0327 (0.0432)

Table 10.14. *Empirical application 1: mean group estimator*

Spec.	Δq	$\Delta \pi$	Δr	Δm	Δe	const	$\Delta \pi_o$
1	$1.163_{(3.68)}$	$0.303_{(0.98)}$	$-3.041_{(-5.62)}$	$0.139_{(0.96)}$	$-0.268_{(-4.02)}$	$0.001_{(0.19)}$	$0.055_{(1.48)}$
2	—	$0.308_{(1.04)}$	$-3.634_{(-6.62)}$	$0.194_{(1.54)}$	$-0.354_{(-6.03)}$	$0.007_{(1.76)}$	$0.116_{(2.54)}$
3	$1.048_{(3.40)}$	—	$-2.789_{(-4.89)}$	$0.119_{(0.89)}$	$-0.284_{(-4.70)}$	$-0.000_{(-0.06)}$	$0.043_{(1.18)}$
4	$1.053_{(3.39)}$	$0.041_{(0.14)}$	—	$0.042_{(0.27)}$	$-0.348_{(-4.84)}$	$-0.000_{(-0.07)}$	$0.040_{(1.07)}$
5	$1.366_{(4.33)}$	$0.388_{(1.32)}$	$-3.490_{(-6.35)}$	—	$-0.198_{(-3.10)}$	$-0.005_{(-0.94)}$	$0.015_{(0.38)}$
6	$1.347_{(4.81)}$	$0.100_{(0.36)}$	$-2.917_{(-5.37)}$	$0.091_{(0.64)}$	—	$-0.000_{(-0.08)}$	$0.055_{(1.44)}$
7	$1.253_{(4.20)}$	—	$-3.174_{(-5.56)}$	—	$-0.188_{(-3.23)}$	$-0.004_{(-0.90)}$	$0.015_{(0.40)}$

Table 10.15. *Empirical application 2: mean group estimator*

Spec.	$\overline{ret}$	$\overline{\Delta q}$	$\overline{\Delta \pi}$	$\overline{\Delta r}$	$\overline{\Delta m}$	$\overline{\Delta e}$	χ^2_k
1	$1.018_{(24.23)}$	$-0.668_{(-1.21)}$	$-0.700_{(-1.36)}$	$-0.148_{(-0.24)}$	$-0.285_{(-1.01)}$	$0.170_{(2.23)}$	0.00
2	$1.058_{(24.97)}$	—	$-0.965_{(-1.99)}$	$0.178_{(0.29)}$	$-0.610_{(-2.15)}$	$0.170_{(2.27)}$	0.00
3	$1.013_{(23.32)}$	$-0.595_{(-1.05)}$	—	$-0.272_{(-0.43)}$	$-0.131_{(-0.49)}$	$0.146_{(2.00)}$	0.00
4	$1.001_{(23.30)}$	$-0.440_{(-0.80)}$	$-0.655_{(-1.53)}$	—	$-0.064_{(-0.23)}$	$0.187_{(2.51)}$	0.00
5	$0.995_{(26.19)}$	$-0.826_{(-1.60)}$	$-0.680_{(-1.44)}$	$-0.243_{(-0.40)}$	—	$0.143_{(1.89)}$	0.00
6	$0.993_{(27.57)}$	$-0.542_{(-1.00)}$	$-0.162_{(-0.34)}$	$-0.484_{(-0.76)}$	$-0.159_{(-0.61)}$	—	0.00
7	$0.991_{(25.37)}$	$-0.691_{(-1.29)}$	—	$-0.390_{(-0.69)}$	—	$0.136_{(1.91)}$	0.00

negative on those with significant dependence on oil, such as airlines or automobile industries. Overall, the *CCEP* and the *CCEMG* estimators yield very similar results, the exception being the coefficient of the interest rate variable which is much larger (in absolute value) when estimated by *CCEMG* as compared to *CCEP*. Deletion of some of the macro variables from return equation does not change the remaining estimated coefficients significantly, and the results seem to be quite robust. The coefficients of the cross sectional averages of the explanatory variables are generally less significant than the region specific variables. In contrast, the cross section average of the dependant variable is highly significant and its coefficient is very close to one. Its inclusion is clearly critical in dealing with the unobserved common factors and can be viewed as proxying for the market index as in Capital Asset Pricing Models (CAPM).

6 Conclusions

Much of the empirical research carried out on panels assume some form of cross-section error independence. However, such assumptions are usually suspect, in practice, and as a result recent advances in the theoretical literature have focused on the analysis of cross sectional dependence.

In this chapter we have explored further some aspects of the work by Pesaran (2006) who has developed methods for estimation and inference in panel data models with multifactor error structures. The method is based on proxying unobserved factors with cross-sectional averages. We compare this method with alternative methods that aim to augment panel regressions with factor estimates using principal components. We reach a major conclusion. Methods based on principal components do not seem to work as well as the methods based on cross-sectional averages. The estimation error for the factor estimates seems to be one, but not the only, reason for this inferior performance. Using Monte Carlo experiments we show that the PC-augmented estimators could still be subject to substantial small-sample bias due to the need to select a sub-set of factors for inclusion in the model to be estimated.

The relevance of CCE-type estimators is illustrated by an empirical application to a rich panel of company returns with a wide geographical coverage. The CCE approach allows us to estimate asset return equations with observed as well as unobserved common factors; thus going beyond CAPM and asset-pricing models that focus exclusively on observed or unobserved factors. The empirical results clearly show the importance of country-specific macro variables for the analysis of company returns beyond the market indices.

11 Judging Contending Estimators by Simulation: Tournaments in Dynamic Panel Data Models

Jan F. Kiviet

1 Introduction

The joint occurrence in dynamic panel data models of individual specific effects and of lagged dependent variables complicates the statistical inference on the model parameters considerably. A great number of alternative techniques for the estimation of dynamic panel data models have been suggested over the last few decades, see *inter alia* Balestra and Nerlove (1966), Anderson and Hsiao (1981, 1982), Holtz-Eakin *et al.* (1988), Arellano and Bond (1991), Ahn and Schmidt (1995, 1997), Blundell and Bond (1998) and Hsiao *et al.* (2002). As a rule these techniques claim particular desirable asymptotic properties under specific circumstances. Various Monte Carlo studies have been undertaken in order to find out how well (variants of) these methods work in finite samples, see inter alia Nerlove (1967, 1971), Bhargava and Sargan (1983), Arellano and Bond (1991), Kiviet (1995), Blundell and Bond (1998), Judson and Owen (1999), Blundell *et al.* (2000), Harris and Mátyás (2000, 2004), Andrews and Lu (2001), Doornik *et al.* (2002), Hsiao *et al.* (2002), Alvarez and Arellano (2003), Bun and Kiviet (2003, 2005) and Doran and Schmidt (2005). The main purpose of this study is to clarify that in most of these simulation studies the focus has been too narrow, at least regarding particular aspects, to enable fair and fully informative conclusions on the qualities of the alternative inference procedures examined. Progress in this line of research could have been more efficient, as we shall argue, if the designs of these Monte Carlo studies had been less restrictive and more transparent.

Usually the finite sample distribution of individual coefficient estimators and test statistics does not involve just the parameters affecting their asymptotic distribution. However, exact or almost exact finite sample results are usually hard to obtain by analytic derivation. Therefore, examination of the effects of nuisance parameters and initial conditions on inference in finite samples constitutes the main motivation for performing simulation experiments. As we shall illustrate, the design of such experiments requires a justification built on both analytical and empirical considerations regarding the choices made on the model specifications included in the simulation study, the particular parameter values chosen and any further conditions set and possibly varied. Although any Monte Carlo design will have limitations regarding its size and scope, we shall show that in addition there are particular qualitative aspects – say aspects of proper Monte Carlo methodology – which should always be respected in order to make a simulation exercise really worthwhile. Already for many decades a great number of studies in econometric theory are supplemented by simulation findings, but usually without much explicit reference to simulation methodology. Monte Carlo has become part of the standard toolkit, and seems to be very user-friendly, because researchers use it without reference to any user-manual. In fact, not much has been published in econometrics about Monte Carlo methodology since Hendry (1984). Indeed, this is still the state-of-the-art study. It provides the necessary background to Monte Carlo simulation, but only as far as it concerns the fundamentals of the techniques for assessing in an efficient and effective way by random experimentation on a programmable computer the finite sample characteristics of one particular estimator or test procedure. It does not address explicitly the various issues that are relevant when a further purpose of the Monte Carlo study is to make a comparison between different inference techniques. Here we will argue that particular improvements in the practice of designing Monte Carlo contests seems to be called for. We shall illustrate this in the context of the comparison by simulation of different method of moment estimators for dynamic panel data models.

We focus on a very simple example of the dynamic panel data model, viz. the stable first-order autoregressive panel relationship with an unknown intercept, random unobserved individual effects, and i.i.d. disturbances. Hence, there are no further external regressors. Its full specification is:

$$\left.\begin{aligned} y_{it} &= \beta + \gamma y_{i,t-1} + \eta_i + \varepsilon_{it} \\ y_{i0} &= \alpha_0 + \alpha_1 \eta_i + \alpha_2 \varepsilon_{i0} \\ \eta_i &\sim \text{i.i.d.}(0, \sigma_\eta^2) \\ \varepsilon_i &= (\varepsilon_{i0}, \varepsilon_{i1}, \ldots, \varepsilon_{iT})' \sim \text{i.i.d.}(0, \sigma_\varepsilon^2 I_{T+1}) \end{aligned}\right\} \quad i = 1, \ldots, N; t = 1, \ldots, T. \tag{1}$$

The model has two random error components, viz. the individual specific effects η_i and the white-noise innovations ε_{it}. For any $i, j \in \{1, \ldots, N\}$ the vector ε_i and scalar effect η_j are independent. The start-up values y_{i0} are mutually independent, are determined by the two types of random error components and a non-random component too, and are independent of all ε_{jt} for $t > 0$. Note that we have seven unknown parameters: $\alpha_0, \alpha_1, \alpha_2, \beta, \gamma, \sigma_\eta^2$ and σ_ε^2. These are all similar for the N cross-section units. We shall only examine here the stable case $|\gamma| < 1$, which will yield weakly-stationary y_{it} series (time-invariant mean and auto-covariances) under particular initial conditions only. Inference on the parameter of primary interest γ can only be based on the N observed time-series $\{y_{it};\ t = 0, \ldots, T\}$, which are identically and independently distributed over the N cross-sections. Various alternative implementations of GMM estimators are available for the estimation of model (1). In illustrations below some of these will be used in our attempt to constitute some explicit methodological standards for designing Monte Carlo experiments when the purpose is to compare and to rate alternative competing inference techniques.

The structure of this chapter is as follows. In section 2 we list a number of important general qualitative aspects for a simulation study, when the aim is to draw conclusions on the relative and absolute qualities of alternative inference methods under relevant circumstances. Before we can fully substantiate by illustrations the importance of the rules we set for such studies, we have to discuss some further details on panel AR(1) models and their estimation. Therefore, in section 3 we first examine some consequences for data transformations occurring in GMM procedures which stem from particular specifications of the start-up values y_{i0} via the coefficients α_0, α_1 and α_2. Next, in section 4 we introduce the range of estimators to be considered here. Special attention is paid to the weight matrices used in GMM implementations. In section 5 we discuss aspects of a number of the earlier Monte Carlo studies referred to above and confront them with the rules discussed in section 2. To illustrate some of their deficiencies we produce a few further Monte Carlo results from an alternative design. Finally, section 6 concludes.

2 Rules for Simulation Contests

Inevitably any simulation study is limited in scope and detail. One simply cannot produce results for all parameter values deemed relevant and for all inference techniques that might be of interest for the type of model under study. On the contrary, if one does not want to put off consumers of the results of simulation studies, one has to restrict the number and size of resulting tables severely. Also one should try to condense the information as much as possible to enhance its palatability, for instance by using graphical methods or possibly by producing so-called response surfaces,[1] although these never became widely popular. Hence, it is simply unavoidable to put restrictions on the design of the experiments, such as the chosen density of the grid of discrete numerical values of both the model parameters and further design parameters, such as: the examined actual sample sizes, nominal significance levels of tests, the chosen number of included exogenous variables and the actual parametrizations of their generating schemes, and so on. Apart from that, also the actual number of executed Monte Carlo replications for each separate experiment will be limited, implying that Monte Carlo results do not deliver the exact characterizations of estimators and test statistics, such as their moments and quantiles, but only estimates of these which have error margins. These aspects and various methods to economize on computer time, while reducing at the same time as much as possible the specificity and imprecision of the simulation results, are all addressed in Hendry (1984), when the focus is to examine one single specific estimator or test statistic for a particular class of data-generating process.

However, when comparisons are to be made between competing inference techniques, then next to the primarily quantitative aspects just indicated there are particular more qualitative facets to the justification of the chosen design, to the range of techniques included and to the final presentation of the results of the executed experiments, which are of paramount importance too. Their neglect may in fact have much more serious consequences than the unavoidable imposed restrictions on the primarily quantitative aspects. Below, we list eight such more qualitative aspects. First we merely give a succinct characterization, and in the remainder of this section we give some further explanation. A more tangible clarification follows later when we discuss and criticize aspects of earlier simulation studies on panel AR(1) models and produce some further illustrative simulation results.

2.1 *Methodologic Aspirations for an Adequate and Impartial Design of Simulation Studies that Aim to Rank Various Alternative Inference Techniques*

1 Explicit exploitation of any invariance properties;
2 Exploration of the non-invariance properties, both analytically and experimentally;
3 No dimensional restrictions on the relevant nuisance parameter space;
4 "Orthogonal" reparametrization of the parameter space to enhance interpretability;

5 Well-argued choice of the examined design parameter values;
6 Any contending techniques should play both at home and away;
7 Inclusion of (non-)operational full information techniques;
8 Full documentation with respect to accuracy, interpretability and reproducibility.

Most of the points mentioned above are strongly interrelated. Some of these aspirations do also refer to the simulation efficiency issues discussed in Hendry (1984); some are also mentioned in Davidson and MacKinnon (1993, chapter 21).

The first six points focus on the construction and delineation of the set of designs to be examined in the simulation experiments. Point 1 is simply a matter of simulation efficiency, and is easily illustrated as follows. For most techniques for analysing γ in model (1) the actual value of β is inconsequential under particular initial conditions. Of course, it is useless then to perform Monte Carlo experiments for various values of β, as long as we are only interested in the qualities of inference methods for γ. Moreover, the study should mention that the actual value chosen for β, for instance zero, does not limit the scope for conclusions from this design. As a complement to a successful extraction of all – if any – invariance properties, the nuisance parameters, which inflict non-invariance properties, as mentioned in point 2, remain. Again, simulation efficiency is enhanced when theoretical evidence is exploited on the effects of particular parameters on the statistics of interest, as we shall illustrate later. As a rule, however, such analytical small sample evidence is scarce or incomplete, and the primary goal of the simulation study is exactly to disclose experimentally whether and how the various parameters do have effects in finite samples. This requires a deliberate strategy when choosing the actual parameter values in the experiments, in order to be able to reveal the essentials of the actual dependencies. This is reiterated by point 3. If restrictions are imposed on the dimensionality of the experimental design then it is impossible to reveal the independent effects from all parameters separately, and consequently what is supposed to be an impartial simulation contest between various estimators may actually be a handicap race for particular competitors.

Although the parameters as they appear in the model specification may provide a straightforward base for the nuisance parameter space, it can be very useful to find a transformation for this base, such that it becomes both easier to select empirically relevant values for the nuisance parameters and to interpret their effects. As we shall illustrate below this base should consist of autonomous parameters and thus be orthogonal in a particular sense, as is stated in point 4. The related point 5 reemphasizes that the actual choice of and variation in the design parameter values should be thoroughly justified, both in the light of the before mentioned goal to reveal yet unknown (in)dependencies, but also with respect to empirical relevance. Since it is simply practically impossible to examine a grid of parameter values which reasonably well represents the full usually unbounded parameter space, it seems much more important to make sure that the chosen grid covers that part of the parameter space which seems empirically most relevant. Points 4 and 5 can be illustrated as follows for model (1). Below, we shall argue more extensively that it is very beneficial for the simulation study if one does not select particular fixed values for α_1, but for another parameter ϕ, and select for instance $\phi \in \{0, 0.5, 1\}$ and $\gamma \in \{0, 0.4, 0.8\}$ to determine $\alpha_1 = \phi(1-\gamma)$. Now ϕ is a base parameter "orthogonal" to γ expressing and procuring the degree in which the start-up value y_{i0} has attained the equilibrium level of the individual effect component in y_{it}, irrespective of the value of γ.

Points 6 and 7 have to do with the techniques to be included in a simulation contest in relation to further particulars of the simulation design. Both points are easily clarified by illustration in the context of model (1) too. Comparing the behaviour of various 1-step GMM implementations for this model differing in, for instance, the weight matrix used and in the nature and number of moment conditions exploited, it seems worthwhile to generate data under various situations covering all particular situations that in turn renders each of the examined weight matrices optimal or not, and the exploited moment conditions either valid or not. Point 6 highlights that a fair competition requires that the range of simulation designs examined should be such that all contending techniques can demonstrate their qualities under the conditions for which they were specifically designed, but have to expose as well their possible failures under the conditions that may better suit the other techniques examined. Point 7 approaches the same issue from opposite direction. Whereas point 6 says that, given the techniques included, the various designs should be such that all techniques have to perform under each others most favourable circumstances, point 7 states, that given the designs that are to be covered because of their practical relevance, one should also include techniques that exploit a considerable amount of the information incorporated in the simulated data generating processes, even if such techniques appear non-operational from a practical point of view. Their inclusion is useful nevertheless, because it generates information on the costs of being deprived of particular information. For instance, it seems useful in the context of 1-step GMM estimation to include techniques that exploit the optimal weight matrix, even if this includes parameters which are unknown in practice, simply because that yields a yardstick against which the performance of the operational techniques can be judged, whereas it offers insights also into what at best can be achieved by an operational 2-step GMM estimator.

The final point 8 refers to obvious quality criteria such as reporting all relevant information regarding the reproducibility of the simulation study, and with respect to the accuracy of the resulting Monte Carlo estimates. It also stresses the importance that the presentation of Monte Carlo studies should allow a full and proper interpretation of their findings, mentioning clearly its unavoidable limitations. To further substantiate and illustrate the above, some further analysis of the panel AR(1) model is required first.

3 Initial Conditions

According to the scheme $y_{it} = \beta + \gamma y_{i,t-1} + \eta_i + \varepsilon_{it}$ all y_{it} contain, in addition to $\gamma y_{i,t-1}$, three types of components, viz. a deterministic component β and two random error components, the individual specific η_i and the idiosyncratic ε_{it} respectively. Therefore it seems reasonable and fully general that we assumed the y_{i0} to be generated by three such types of components as well. By defining ε_{i0} in (1) all conceivable options for a specification of the start-up values are represented by $y_{i0} = \alpha_0 + \alpha_1\eta_i + \alpha_2\varepsilon_{i0}$, where $\alpha = (\alpha_0, \alpha_1, \alpha_2)'$ are three extra unobservable parameters. By repeated substitution we find that model (1) implies for $t > 0$:

$$
\begin{aligned}
y_{it} &= \beta\sum_{s=0}^{t-1}\gamma^s + \alpha_0\gamma^t + \left(\sum_{s=0}^{t-1}\gamma^s + \alpha_1\gamma^t\right)\eta_i + \sum_{s=0}^{t-1}\gamma^s\varepsilon_{i,t-s} + \gamma^t\alpha_2\varepsilon_{i0} \\
&= \left[\frac{\beta}{1-\gamma} + \gamma^t\left(\alpha_0 - \frac{\beta}{1-\gamma}\right)\right] + \left[\frac{1}{1-\gamma} + \gamma^t\left(\alpha_1 - \frac{1}{1-\gamma}\right)\right]\eta_i \\
&\quad + \left(\sum_{s=0}^{t-1}\gamma^s\varepsilon_{i,t-s} + \gamma^t\alpha_2\varepsilon_{i0}\right) \qquad (2)
\end{aligned}
$$

exposing for each y_{it} its three constituent components, viz. a non-random part, an individual effects part, and a component determined by the idiosyncratic disturbances $(\varepsilon_{i0}, \ldots, \varepsilon_{it})$.

From the first component of the final expression of (2) we find that y_{it} will have constant mean through time only if

$$\alpha_0 = \frac{\beta}{1-\gamma}. \qquad (3)$$

The second component shows that the impact of η_i on y_{it} will be constant through time only if

$$\alpha_1 = \frac{1}{1-\gamma}. \tag{4}$$

When (4) is not fulfilled this will have far-reaching consequences, because of the following. An important issue in the estimation of dynamic panel data models with individual effects is whether it is possible to remove these individual effects from the model, or from the regressors, or from any variable that may be used as an instrument. A transformation often employed in this context is first-differencing. Although it may seem, at first sight, that taking first differences in (1), which results (for $t > 1$) in

$$\Delta y_{it} = \gamma \Delta y_{i,t-1} + \Delta \varepsilon_{it} \tag{5}$$

has completely removed the individual effects, this is only really the case under (4). This is seen as follows. From (2) we find (for $t > 1$):

$$\begin{aligned}\Delta y_{it} &= \gamma^{t-1}\left[\beta - (1-\gamma)\alpha_0\right] + \gamma^{t-1}\left[1 - (1-\gamma)\alpha_1\right]\eta_i \\ &\quad + \varepsilon_{it} - (1-\gamma)\left(\sum_{s=1}^{t-1} \gamma^{s-1}\varepsilon_{i,t-s} + \gamma^{t-1}\alpha_2\varepsilon_{i0}\right).\end{aligned} \tag{6}$$

Hence, estimators involving Δy_{it} will in general not be invariant with respect to the elements of α, nor to β, γ, σ_ε^2 and σ_η^2. However, from (6) we find that under (3) and (4) Δy_{it} is invariant with respect to α_0, α_1, β and σ_η^2. For other transformations that are used in this context, such as taking differences from individual means (taken over time) or orthogonal forward deviations (see Arellano and Bover, 1995), one easily finds similar invariance properties, provided (3) and (4) hold.

From (2) we can also derive that (for $t \geq 0$):

$$\begin{aligned}\mathrm{Var}(y_{it}) &= \left[\frac{1}{1-\gamma} + \gamma^t\left(\alpha_1 - \frac{1}{1-\gamma}\right)\right]^2 \sigma_\eta^2 \\ &\quad + \left[\frac{1}{1-\gamma^2} + \gamma^{2t}\left(\alpha_2^2 - \frac{1}{1-\gamma^2}\right)\right]\sigma_\varepsilon^2.\end{aligned} \tag{7}$$

Therefore, variance constancy of y_{it} through time requires both (4) and

$$\alpha_2 = \pm\sqrt{\frac{1}{1-\gamma^2}} \tag{8}$$

and then yields

$$\text{Var}(y_{it}) = \frac{\sigma_\eta^2}{(1-\gamma)^2} + \frac{\sigma_\varepsilon^2}{1-\gamma^2}, \qquad t = 0, \ldots, T. \tag{9}$$

When the two conditions (4) and (8) hold jointly then we obtain for the auto-covariance (for $0 \leq s \leq t$):

$$\text{Cov}(y_{it}, y_{i,t-s}) = \frac{\sigma_\eta^2}{(1-\gamma)^2} + \frac{\gamma^s \sigma_\varepsilon^2}{1-\gamma^2}. \tag{10}$$

Like (9) these are not determined by t either, thus the three conditions on α jointly imply weak-stationarity of y_{it}.

From the above we conclude that the distribution of the untransformed y_{it} (for $t > 0$) is always determined by β, γ, σ_η^2 and σ_ε^2, irrespective of the properties of y_{i0} (the values of the α parameters), whereas for particular α values, viz. under the three above special conditions, Δy_{it} is determined by γ and σ_ε^2 only. Because in panel data often T is rather small and asymptotics concerns $N \to \infty$, the effects of the initial conditions are not asymptotically diminishing, and hence they are of major importance.

In addition we want to remark that the three special conditions on α, though mathematically convenient, are not necessarily very realistic cases. There does not seem much reason to assume that in actual empirical panel data observations the accumulated impact of the disturbances, of the random individual effects and of the deterministic components all three happen to be constant in magnitude (or variance) through time. Therefore, in principle, in a Monte Carlo study of model (1) one should vary α_0, α_1, α_2, β, γ, σ_η^2 and σ_ε^2, which after scaling with respect to for instance σ_ε^2 implies dimensionality six of the parameter space. However, in most earlier studies all α parameters have been set at their stationarity values. Although weak stationarity implies invariance of inference on γ with respect to β for some techniques only, β is often set at zero nevertheless. Moreover, $\sigma_\eta^2/\sigma_\varepsilon^2$ is usually fixed at unity[2] and only γ is varied, so that the dimensionality of the nuisance parameter space is restricted from six to just one.

Below, when we address the three stationarity assumptions regarding the initial values that may hold in addition to the *stability condition* $|\gamma| < 1$, we will indicate (3) as *deterministic stationarity*, which implies that $\mathsf{E}(y_{it})$ is constant; (4) will be called *accumulated effect stationarity*, which implies that $\mathsf{E}(y_{it} \mid \eta_i) - \mathsf{E}(y_{it})$ is constant; and (8) will be called *accumulated noise stationarity*, which implies that $\text{Var}(y_{it} \mid \eta_i)$ is constant for all i and t.

4 Various GMM Implementations

4.1 Generic Framework

The GMM (system) estimators we will examine all fit into the following simple generic setup, which allows further regressors. After appropriate manipulation (transformation and stacking) of the panel data observations one has

$$y_i^{**} = X_i\theta + \upsilon_i, \quad i = 1, \ldots, N \tag{11}$$

where y_i^{**} is a $T^{**} \times 1$ vector that may contain $\Delta y_i^* = (\Delta y_{i2}, \ldots, \Delta y_{iT})'$ or $y_i^* = (y_{i2}, \ldots, y_{iT})'$ or both stacked, hence T^{**} is either $T^* = T-1$ or $2T^*$, and υ_i contains the corresponding vector of error components. The $T^{**} \times K^{**}$ matrix X_i and $K^{**} \times 1$ coefficient vector θ follow straightforwardly from the choice regarding y_i^{**}. In case of our panel AR(1) model θ equals $(\beta, \gamma)'$ if y_i^{**} contains y_i^* (i.e. $K^{**} = 2$) and if it just contains Δy_i^* then $\theta = \gamma$ (i.e. $K^{**} = 1$), with $X_i = \Delta y_{i,-1}^*$.

The unknown vector θ is estimated by employing $L \geq K^{**}$ moment conditions that hold for $i = 1, \ldots, N$, viz.

$$\mathsf{E}[Z_i'(y_i^{**} - X_i\theta)] = 0 \tag{12}$$

where Z_i, which will be substantiated in the next subsection, is $T^{**} \times L$. Exploiting the assumption that the individuals are i.i.d. the GMM estimator using the $L \times L$ semi-positive definite weight matrix W is found by minimizing the quadratic form

$$\left(\sum_{i=1}^{N} Z_i'(y_i^{**} - X_i\theta)\right)' W \left(\sum_{i=1}^{N} Z_i'(y_i^{**} - X_i\theta)\right) \tag{13}$$

which yields

$$\hat{\theta}_W = (X'ZWZ'X)^{-1}X'ZWZ'y^{**} \tag{14}$$

where $y^{**} = (y_1^{**\prime}, \ldots, y_N^{**\prime})'$, $X = (X_1', \ldots, X_N')'$ and $Z = (Z_1', \ldots, Z_N')'$. We only consider cases where convenient regularity conditions hold, including the existence of

$$\operatorname*{plim}_{N\to\infty} \frac{1}{N}Z'X \quad \text{and} \quad \operatorname*{plim}_{N\to\infty} \frac{1}{N}Z'Z$$

whereas $\text{rank}(N^{-1}Z'X)$ and $\text{rank}(N^{-1}Z'Z)$ are K^{**} and L with probability 1, respectively, implying that the estimator $\hat{\theta}_W$ exists.

According to (12) the instruments are valid, thus $\text{plim}_{N\to\infty} N^{-1} \sum_{i=1}^{N} Z_i' v_i = 0$, so that $\hat{\theta}_W$ is consistent.

The asymptotically efficient GMM estimator[3] in the class of estimators exploiting instruments Z is obtained if W is chosen such that, after appropriate scaling, it has probability limit proportional to the inverse of the covariance of the limiting distribution of $N^{-1/2} \sum_{i=1}^{N} Z_i' v_i$. This implies,

$$W^{opt} \propto \left(\underset{N\to\infty}{\text{plim}} \frac{1}{N} \sum_{i=1}^{N} Z_i' v_i v_i' Z_i \right)^{-1} \tag{15}$$

and we shall denote the asymptotically efficient GMM estimator as $\hat{\theta}_{W^{opt}}$.

For the special case $v_i \sim \text{i.i.d.}(0, \sigma_v^2 I_{T^{**}})$ one would obtain $W_{iid}^{opt} \propto (Z'Z)^{-1}$, which yields the familiar 2SLS or GIV result,

$$\hat{\theta}_{GIV} = [X'Z(Z'Z)^{-1}Z'X]^{-1}X'Z(Z'Z)^{-1}Z'y^{**} \tag{16}$$

which in case $K^{**} = L$ simplifies to the simple instrumental variable estimator

$$\hat{\theta}_{IV} = (Z'X)^{-1}Z'y^{**}. \tag{17}$$

However, $v_i \sim \text{i.i.d.}(0, \sigma_v^2 I_{T^{**}})$ does usually not hold in panel data, either due to the occurrence of the two error components, or due to the effects of the transformation applied to remove the individual specific component. Also (but we shall not consider these cases here) there may be further complications, such as cross-sectional heteroskedasticity, cross-sectional dependence or serial correlation.

If, under particular assumptions on the distribution of v_i, the matrix W^{opt} is not directly available then one may use some arbitrary initial weight matrix W that produces a consistent (though inefficient) 1-step GMM estimator $\hat{\theta}_W$, and then exploit the 1-step residuals $\hat{v}_i = y_i^{**} - X_i\hat{\theta}_W$ to construct the empirical weight matrix

$$\widehat{W}^{opt} \propto \left(\frac{1}{N} \sum_{i=1}^{N} Z_i' \hat{v}_i \hat{v}_i' Z_i \right)^{-1} \tag{18}$$

which yields the 2-step GMM estimator:

$$\hat{\theta}_{\widehat{W}^{opt}} = (X'Z\widehat{W}^{opt}Z'X)^{-1}X'Z\widehat{W}^{opt}Z'y^{**}. \tag{19}$$

This 2-step GMM estimator $\hat{\theta}_{\hat{W}^{opt}}$ is asymptotically equivalent to $\hat{\theta}_{W^{opt}}$, and hence it is efficient in the class of estimators exploiting instruments Z.

Note that, provided the moment conditions are valid, $\hat{\theta}_{GIV}$ is consistent thus could be employed as a 1-step GMM estimator. When $K^{**} = L$ using a weight matrix is redundant, because the criterion function (13) will be zero for any W, because all moment conditions can be imposed on the sample observations.

4.2 Instruments for Panel AR(1) Models

We now consider a range of GMM estimators that have been suggested for linear dynamic panel data models, but we specialize them to our very specific model (1). It is obvious that estimating model (1) by OLS will yield inconsistent estimators, because it follows from (2) that

$$\mathsf{E}[y_{i,t-1}(\varepsilon_{it} + \eta_i)] = \sigma_\eta^2 \left[\frac{1}{1-\gamma} + \gamma^t \left(\alpha_1 - \frac{1}{1-\gamma} \right) \right] \tag{20}$$

and this differs from zero for any α_1 and $|\gamma| < 1$, unless $\sigma_\eta^2 = 0$. Also the least-squares estimator for γ obtained after removing the individual effects from the model by taking deviations from the mean per individual over the time-series observations, known as the least-squares dummy variable estimator (LSDV) or within groups estimator, is inconsistent unless $T \to \infty$.

To obtain valid moment conditions many techniques actually estimate the transformed model

$$\Delta y_{it} = \gamma \Delta y_{i,t-1} + \Delta\varepsilon_{it}, \qquad i = 1, \ldots, N;\ t = 2, \ldots, T. \tag{21}$$

Applying least-squares would again yield an inconsistent estimator (also for $T \to \infty$) because

$$\mathsf{E}(\Delta y_{i,t-1} \Delta\varepsilon_{it}) = -\mathsf{E}(y_{i,t-1}\varepsilon_{i,t-1}) = -\sigma_\varepsilon^2 \neq 0$$

but, given $\varepsilon_{it} \sim$ i.i.d.$(0, \sigma_\varepsilon^2)$, it is obvious that in (21) the $(T-2)(T-1)/2$ moment conditions

$$\mathsf{E}(\Delta y_{ir} \Delta\varepsilon_{it}) = 0, \qquad r = 1, \ldots, t-2;\ t = 3, \ldots, T \tag{22}$$

can be exploited. In fact, the even more extensive set of $(T-1)T/2$ conditions hold.

$$\mathsf{E}(y_{ir} \Delta\varepsilon_{it}) = 0, \qquad r = 0, \ldots, t-2;\ t = 2, \ldots, T \tag{23}$$

Note that all conditions of set (22), where the instruments are lagged first differences, are implied by set (23), where the instruments are lagged levels. So, we cannot exploit these two sets jointly, because they would lead to a Z matrix that does not have full column rank. Set (23) implies for the ith partition $\Delta\varepsilon_i^* = (\Delta\varepsilon_{i2}, \ldots, \Delta\varepsilon_{iT})'$ of the stacked disturbance vector of model (21) the corresponding block Z_i of the $N(T-1) \times (T-1)T/2$ matrix of instruments Z that is given (and here denoted) by:

$$Z_i^{AB} = \begin{bmatrix} y_{i,0} & 0,\ 0 & \cdots & 0' & 0' \\ 0 & y_{i,0}, y_{i,1} & & 0' & 0' \\ \vdots & & \ddots & & \vdots \\ 0 & 0,\ 0 & & y_{i,0}, \ldots, y_{i,T-3} & 0' \\ 0 & 0,\ 0 & \cdots & 0' & y_{i,0}, \ldots, y_{i,T-2} \end{bmatrix}. \quad (24)$$

For the instrument matrix Z^{AB} to have full column rank it is required that $N \geq T/2$ and $T \geq 2$. Exploiting the instrument set Z_i^{AB} was suggested by Arellano and Bond (1991).

It has been found, however, that using Z^{AB} may lead to bias problems, especially when N is moderate and T not very small. Bun and Kiviet (2005) found that the leading term of this bias has magnitude $O(N^{-1}T^0)$. They suggest using fewer instruments in order to mitigate the bias problems, and prove that GMM using a subset of $2T - 3$ instruments, viz.

$$Z_i^{BK} = \begin{bmatrix} y_{i,0} & 0,\ 0 & \cdots & 0,\ 0 & 0,\ 0 \\ 0 & y_{i,0}, y_{i,1} & & 0,\ 0 & 0,\ 0 \\ \vdots & & \ddots & & \vdots \\ 0 & 0,\ 0 & & y_{i,T-4}, y_{i,T-3} & 0,\ 0 \\ 0 & 0,\ 0 & \cdots & 0,\ 0 & y_{i,T-3}, y_{i,T-2} \end{bmatrix} \quad (25)$$

reduces the order of the bias to $O(N^{-1}T^{-1})$. Note that $Z_i^{BK} = Z_i^{AB}C_{AB}^{BK}$, where C^{BK} is a $(T-1)T/2 \times (2T-3)$ matrix that annihilates instruments from Z_i^{AB}.

Anderson and Hsiao (1981, 1982) originated removing the individual effects from the model by first-differencing and then applying IV to (21). They suggested using either a lagged first-difference as instrument, i.e. exploiting (22) just for $r = t - 2$, or a lagged level variable as instrument, that is exploiting (23) just for $r = t - 2$, giving either

$$Z_i^{AHd} = \begin{bmatrix} 0 \\ \Delta y_{i,1} \\ \vdots \\ \Delta y_{i,T-2} \end{bmatrix} \text{ or } Z_i^{AHl} = \begin{bmatrix} y_{i,0} \\ y_{i,1} \\ \vdots \\ y_{i,T-2} \end{bmatrix} \tag{26}$$

as instruments. These entail a much more drastic reduction of the valid instruments available than Z_i^{BK}. Note that $Z_i^{AHl} = Z_i^{BK} C_{BK}^{AHl}$ and $Z_i^{AHd} = Z_i^{BK} C_{BK}^{AHd}$, where both C_{BK}^{AHl} and C_{BK}^{AHd} are simple transformation matrices of just one column.

Blundell and Bond (1998), on the other hand, attempted to mitigate the bias problems associated with Z^{AB} by extending the set of instruments. Upon checking the validity of lags of differenced variables as instruments in the untransformed model (1) in levels, one finds using (6),

$$\mathsf{E}[\Delta y_{ir}(\eta_i + \varepsilon_{it})] = \gamma^{r-1}[1 - (1-\gamma)\alpha_1]\sigma_\eta^2, \qquad r = 1, \ldots, t-1;\ t = 2, \ldots, T. \tag{27}$$

Hence, under the condition of stationary accumulated effects (4) these expectations are zero, and then they imply the $(T-1)T/2$ moment conditions

$$\mathsf{E}[\Delta y_{ir}(\eta_i + \varepsilon_{it})] = 0, \qquad r = 1, \ldots, t-1;\ t = 2, \ldots, T. \tag{28}$$

This set can be transformed linearly into two sub-sets of $T - 1$ and $(T-2)(T-1)/2$ conditions respectively, viz.

$$\left.\begin{array}{ll} \mathsf{E}[\Delta y_{i,t-1}(\eta_i + \varepsilon_{it})] = 0, & t = 2, \ldots, T \\ \mathsf{E}[\Delta y_{ir}\Delta\varepsilon_{it}] = 0, & r = 1, \ldots, t-2;\ t = 3, \ldots, T \end{array}\right\}. \tag{29}$$

Note that the second sub-set conforms to (22) and hence is found to be implied by (23) already. Nevertheless, we see that assuming stationary accumulated effects generates $T - 1$ moment conditions in addition to (22). Arellano and Bover (1995) and Blundell and Bond (1998)[4] exploit these in a system comprising both equations

$$\left.\begin{array}{r} \Delta y_{it} = \gamma \Delta y_{i,t-1} + \Delta\varepsilon_{it} \\ y_{it} = \beta + \gamma y_{i,t-1} + u_{it} \end{array}\right\} \tag{30}$$

for $t = 2, \ldots, T$, with $u_{it} = \eta_i + \varepsilon_{it}$. Here the ith block has the disturbances

$$v_i = (\Delta\varepsilon_{i2}, \ldots, \Delta\varepsilon_{iT}, u_{i2}, \ldots, u_{iT})', \tag{31}$$

and the instrument matrix has i^{th} block

$$Z_i^{BB} = \begin{bmatrix} Z_i^{AB} & & & O & \\ & \Delta y_{i1} & 0 & \cdots & 0 \\ & 0 & \Delta y_{i2} & & 0 \\ O & \vdots & & \ddots & \vdots \\ & 0 & 0 & \cdots & \Delta y_{i,T-1} \end{bmatrix} \tag{32}$$

whereas $Z^{BB} = (Z_1^{BB'}, \ldots, Z_N^{BB'})'$ is $2N(T-1) \times (T+2)(T-1)/2$. Applying GMM to the system (30) exploiting the instruments (32) will be labelled below as GMMs. For Z^{BB} to have full column rank $T \geq 2$ and $N \geq (T+2)/4$ are required.

Due to the i.i.d. assumption regarding ε_i further (non-linear) moment conditions are valid in the dynamic panel data model, see Ahn and Schmidt (1995, 1997), but below we will only consider the instrument matrices (24), (25), (26) and (32).

4.3 *Weight Matrices*

To establish the optimal weight matrix W^{opt} of (15) for the generic model (11) we have to find an expression that has probability limit equivalent to $\lim_{N\to\infty} \frac{1}{N}\sum_{i=1}^{N} \mathsf{E}(Z_i' v_i v_i' Z_i)$, which is a symmetric matrix. Note that when Z_i^{AB} is used the individual elements of the matrix $Z_i' v_i v_i' Z_i$ are all of the form $y_{ir}\Delta\varepsilon_{it}\Delta\varepsilon_{is}y_{ip}$, with $t, s = 2, \ldots, T$ and $r = 0, \ldots, t-2$; $p = 0, \ldots, s-2$. When Z_i^{BK} is used only the cases $r = \max(0, t-3), t-2$ and $p = \max(0, s-3), s-2$ occur. Because of the symmetry we shall focus on the expression $y_{ir}\Delta\varepsilon_{it}\Delta\varepsilon_{is}y_{ip}$ for the cases $t \geq s$ only. Using E_q to denote expectation conditional on information available at time period q, we obtain (under both time-series and cross-section homoskedasticity and independence of the disturbances) for $t = s$,

$$\mathsf{E}_{s-2}(y_{ir}\Delta\varepsilon_{is}\Delta\varepsilon_{is}y_{ip}) = y_{ir}y_{ip}\mathsf{E}_{s-2}(\Delta\varepsilon_{is})^2 = 2\sigma_\varepsilon^2 y_{ir}y_{ip}$$

and for $t = s+1$ we find

$$\mathsf{E}_{s-1}(y_{ir}\Delta\varepsilon_{i,s+1}\Delta\varepsilon_{is}y_{ip}) = y_{ir}y_{ip}\mathsf{E}_{s-1}[(\varepsilon_{i,s+1}-\varepsilon_{is})(\varepsilon_{is}-\varepsilon_{i,s-1})] = -\sigma_\varepsilon^2 y_{ir}y_{ip}$$

whereas $\mathsf{E}(y_{ir}\Delta\varepsilon_{it}\Delta\varepsilon_{is}y_{ip}) = 0$ for $t > s+1$. Employing both the law of large numbers and the law of iterated expectations we have,

$$\underset{N\to\infty}{\text{plim}} \frac{1}{N}\sum_{i=1}^{N} \mathsf{E}_q(y_{ir}\Delta\varepsilon_{it}\Delta\varepsilon_{is}y_{ip}) = \lim_{N\to\infty} \frac{1}{N}\sum_{i=1}^{N} \mathsf{EE}_q(y_{ir}\Delta\varepsilon_{it}\Delta\varepsilon_{is}y_{ip})$$
$$= \lim_{N\to\infty} \frac{1}{N}\sum_{i=1}^{N} \mathsf{E}(y_{ir}\Delta\varepsilon_{it}\Delta\varepsilon_{is}y_{ip})$$

for any q. Using this with the obtained (conditional) expectations we establish,

$$\lim_{N\to\infty} \frac{1}{N}\sum_{i=1}^{N} \mathsf{E}(y_{ir}\Delta\varepsilon_{it}\Delta\varepsilon_{is}y_{ip}) = \sigma_\varepsilon^2 h_{ts} \underset{N\to\infty}{\text{plim}} \frac{1}{N}\sum_{i=1}^{N} y_{ir}y_{ip}$$

where h_{ts} is the typical element of the $(T-1)\times(T-1)$ matrix

$$H = \begin{bmatrix} 2 & -1 & 0 & \dots & 0 \\ -1 & 2 & -1 & \ddots & \vdots \\ 0 & -1 & 2 & \ddots & 0 \\ \vdots & \ddots & \ddots & \ddots & -1 \\ 0 & \dots & 0 & -1 & 2 \end{bmatrix}. \tag{33}$$

From the above we find that for GMM estimation of model (21), when the DGP (data-generating process) is given by (1) and the instruments Z_i^k (for $k = AB, BK$) are being employed, the optimal weight matrix W_k^{opt} is given by:

$$W_k^{opt} \propto \left[\sum_{i=1}^{N} Z_i^{k\prime} H Z_i^k\right]^{-1} = [Z^{k\prime}(I_N \otimes H)Z^k]^{-1}. \tag{34}$$

Using it in 1-step GMM we will indicate as GMM_1^{AB} (or GMM_1^{BK}), whereas GMM_2^{AB} employs the residuals of GMM_1^{AB} in 2-step GMM and similarly for GMM_2^{BK}. Self-evidently, the weight matrix for the Anderson-Hsiao implementations is of no concern, because the number of instruments equals the number of regressors.

The derivation of the optimal weight matrix for the GMMs estimator is much more involved. Although its matrix $Z_i^\prime v_i v_i^\prime Z_i$ still contains the elements just examined, it now also has elements of the hybrid type $y_{ir}\Delta\varepsilon_{it}(\varepsilon_{is}+\eta_i)\Delta y_{i,s-1}$, for $t, s = 2, \ldots, T$ and $r = 0, \ldots, t-2$, and of the type $\Delta y_{i,t-1}(\varepsilon_{it}+\eta_i)(\varepsilon_{is}+\eta_i)\Delta y_{i,s-1}$, where $t, s = 2, \ldots, T$. To date the GMMs optimal weight matrix has only been derived for the specific no individual effects case $\sigma_\eta^2 = 0$ by Windmeijer (2000), who finds

$$W^{opt}_{BB,\sigma_\eta^2=0} \propto \left[Z^{BB\prime}\left(I_N \otimes D^{opt}_{\sigma_\eta^2=0}\right)Z^{BB}\right]^{-1} \tag{35}$$

with

$$D^{opt}_{\sigma_\eta^2=0} = \begin{pmatrix} H & C \\ C' & I_{T-1} \end{pmatrix} \tag{36}$$

where C is the $(T-1)\times(T-1)$ matrix

$$C = \begin{bmatrix} 1 & 0 & 0 & \ldots & 0 \\ -1 & 1 & 0 & \ddots & \vdots \\ 0 & -1 & 1 & \ddots & 0 \\ \vdots & \ddots & \ddots & \ddots & 0 \\ 0 & \ldots & 0 & -1 & 1 \end{bmatrix}. \tag{37}$$

We re-establish this result with respect to the matrix C by observing that for $s > t$ and for $t > s+1$ we have $\mathsf{E}(y_{ir}\Delta\varepsilon_{it}\varepsilon_{is}\Delta y_{i,s-1}) = 0$, whereas for $t = s$ we find

$$\mathsf{E}_{s-1}(y_{ir}\Delta\varepsilon_{is}\varepsilon_{is}\Delta y_{i,s-1}) = y_{ir}\Delta y_{i,s-1}\mathsf{E}_{s-1}(\varepsilon_{is}^2 - \varepsilon_{is}\varepsilon_{i,s-1}) = \sigma_\varepsilon^2 y_{ir}\Delta y_{i,s-1}$$

and for $t = s+1$ we obtain

$$\begin{aligned}\mathsf{E}_{s-1}(y_{ir}\Delta\varepsilon_{i,s+1}\varepsilon_{is}\Delta y_{i,s-1}) &= y_{ir}\Delta y_{i,s-1}\mathsf{E}_{s-1}(\varepsilon_{i,s+1}\varepsilon_{is} - \varepsilon_{is}^2) \\ &= -\sigma_\varepsilon^2 y_{ir}\Delta y_{i,s-1}.\end{aligned}$$

The identity matrix in the South-East block of (36) follows from $\mathsf{E}(\Delta y_{i,t-1}\varepsilon_{it}\varepsilon_{is}\Delta y_{i,s-1}) = 0$ for $t \neq s$, whereas for $t = s$ we obtain $\mathsf{E}_{s-1}(\Delta y_{i,s-1}\varepsilon_{is}^2\Delta y_{i,s-1}) = \sigma_\varepsilon^2(\Delta y_{i,s-1})^2$.

When allowing for individual effects, we find with respect to the elements $\Delta y_{i,t-1}(\varepsilon_{it}+\eta_i)(\varepsilon_{is}+\eta_i)\Delta y_{i,s-1}$ for $t=s$ that

$$\mathsf{E}_{s-1}(\Delta y_{i,s-1}(\varepsilon_{is}+\eta_i)^2\Delta y_{i,s-1}) = (\Delta y_{i,s-1})^2(\sigma_\varepsilon^2+\eta_i^2)$$

and for $t>s$

$$\begin{aligned}\mathsf{E}_{t-1}&[\Delta y_{i,t-1}(\varepsilon_{it}+\eta_i)(\varepsilon_{is}+\eta_i)\Delta y_{i,s-1}]\\ &= \Delta y_{i,t-1}\Delta y_{i,s-1}(\varepsilon_{is}+\eta_i)[\mathsf{E}_{t-1}(\varepsilon_{it})+\eta_i]\\ &= \Delta y_{i,t-1}\Delta y_{i,s-1}(\varepsilon_{is}\eta_i+\eta_i^2).\end{aligned}$$

Since $\text{plim}_{N\to\infty}\frac{1}{N}\sum_{i=1}^N \eta_i^2 = \sigma_\eta^2$ and $\text{plim}_{N\to\infty}\frac{1}{N}\sum_{i=1}^N \varepsilon_{is}\eta_i = 0$ it follows that in case $\sigma_\eta^2 \neq 0$ we should replace the I_{T-1} matrix in the South-East block of (36) by $I_{T-1}+\frac{\sigma_\eta^2}{\sigma_\varepsilon^2}\iota_{T-1}\iota_{T-1}'$.

Without having analysed the effects of $\sigma_\eta^2 \neq 0$ on the non-diagonal block, from the above we already note that, when the ratio $\sigma_\eta^2/\sigma_\varepsilon^2$ is unknown (which it usually is), the optimal weight matrix is infeasible. Therefore, various feasible but (even under i.i.d. disturbances) non-optimal weight matrices have been suggested. Blundell, Bond and Windmeijer (2000, footnote 11), and Doornik *et al.* (2002, p. 9) in the computer program DPD, use in 1-step GMMs the operational weight matrix $W_{BB}^{DPD} \propto [Z^{BB\prime}(I_N \otimes D^{DPD})Z^{BB}]^{-1}$, with

$$D^{DPD} = \begin{pmatrix} H & O \\ O & I_{T-1}\end{pmatrix}. \tag{38}$$

The motivation for the chosen block diagonality of D^{DPD}, which does not lead to an interesting reduction of computational requirements, is unclear. There is no specific parametrization for which these weights are optimal. Blundell and Bond (1998) did use (see p. 130, 7 lines from bottom) in their first step of 2-step GMMs

$$D^{GIV} = \begin{pmatrix} I_{T-1} & O \\ O & I_{T-1}\end{pmatrix} = I_{2T-2} \tag{39}$$

which yields the simple GIV estimator. This is certainly not optimal, but it is easy and suits well perhaps as a first step (to be indicated below as GMMs $_1^{GIV}$) in a 2-step procedure (GMMs$_2^{GIV}$). Blundell and Bond (1998) mention that, in most of the cases they examined, GMMs$_1^{GIV}$

gave similar results as GMMs_2^{GIV}, suggesting that the weight matrix to be used in combination with Z^{BB} under homoskedasticity seems of minor concern. However, in our less restrained simulation experiments below, we will find that different weight matrices can lead to huge differences in the performance of GMMs_1. Although we find too that GMMs_1^{GIV} and GMMs_2^{GIV} give very similar results, we also establish that both perform poorly in finite sample in comparison to other operational weight matrices.

A more promising operational alternative to D^{DPD} and D^{GIV} could be the following. Instead of capitalizing on the assumption $\sigma_\eta^2 = 0$, as in $D^{opt}_{\sigma_\eta^2=0}$, one could employ a weight matrix which presupposes a particular (not necessarily zero) value of the ratio $\sigma_\eta^2/\sigma_\varepsilon^2$, that is:

$$D^{subopt}_{\sigma_\eta^2/\sigma_\varepsilon^2} = \begin{pmatrix} H & C \\ C' & I_{T-1} + \frac{\sigma_\eta^2}{\sigma_\varepsilon^2}\iota_{T-1}\iota_{T-1}' \end{pmatrix}. \tag{40}$$

We make explicit that the resulting weight matrix

$$W_{BB}^{subopt} \propto [Z^{BB\prime}(I_N \otimes D^{subopt}_{\sigma_\eta^2/\sigma_\varepsilon^2})Z^{BB}]^{-1} \tag{41}$$

is not optimal (unless $\sigma_\eta^2 = 0$) even when a correct non-zero value of $\sigma_\eta^2/\sigma_\varepsilon^2$ is substituted, because the non-diagonal blocks have been obtained under the assumption of no individual effects.

Above an already rather wide collection of competing 1-step and 2-step GMM estimators have been presented. They are consistent (provided the employed moment conditions are valid), and some may claim optimality properties under particular circumstances asymptotically for $N \to \infty$. Below we will make an initial attempt to rank the performance of these estimators by employing Monte Carlo simulation for the situation where both T and N are small or moderate.

5 A Limited Monte Carlo Contest

In the experiments below we have severely restricted ourselves regarding the generality of the Monte Carlo design, simply for practical reasons. The main purpose here is to illustrate particular pitfalls in estimator comparisons by Monte Carlo. This study is certainly not meant to produce the "final" in a Monte Carlo tournament on dynamic panel data estimators. At this stage we only considered the fully homoskedastic case, where $\varepsilon_i \sim \text{i.i.d.}(0, \sigma_\varepsilon^2 I_{T+1})$, whereas 2-step GMM is especially meant to cope with cross-section heteroskedasticity. According to aspiration 7, as set out before, we should have included estimators that exploit the homoskedasticity restriction, since it implies further moment conditions and corresponding asymptotically more efficient GMM implementations. However, if we had included them, we should also have performed experiments involving heteroskedasticity in order to satisfy aspiration 6 and make all estimators play both at home and away. Also, in all the present experiments ε_{it} and η_i are Gaussian. This situation too could have been exploited by including maximum-likelihood estimators in the set of competing techniques,[5] but we didn't at this stage, so we do not fully respect aspirations 6 and 7. Not only did we not examine dynamic panel data models with any further exogenous regressors, but we also imposed $\beta = 0$ so that deterministic stationarity is in fact not an issue here, and all GMM estimators have $K^{**} = 1$. We also restricted ourselves to models with accumulated noise stationarity, that is (8) holds and $\alpha_2 = \pm(1-\gamma^2)^{-1/2}$.

Thus, apart from illustrating some of the individual aspirations for an impartial Monte Carlo contest, the main object of study will be limited here to examine whether under accumulated noise stationarity, homoskedasticity, cross-section independence and normality of both error components there is much impact on the bias and RMSE (root-mean-squared error) in zero-mean panel AR(1) models of:

(i) the effects of various different weight matrices in GMMs;
(ii) the effects of skipping from Z^{BB} the instruments related to accumulated effect stationarity, that is using Z^{AB};
(iii) the effects of skipping valid moment conditions from Z^{AB} and using either Z^{BK} or even Z^{AHl} or Z^{AHd}.

We will investigate just a few particular small values for N and T, only positive stable values of γ, a few different values of $\sigma_\eta^2/\sigma_\varepsilon^2$ and of α_1. Note that GMMs will be inconsistent for $\alpha_1 \neq (1-\gamma)^{-1}$.

5.1 *An Orthogonal Monte Carlo Design*

Due to the above-mentioned restrictions, we lose the parameters β, α_0 and α_2, and retain γ, α_1, σ_η^2, and σ_ε^2 only. Note that our data series y_{it} and Δy_{it} are now such that:

$$\mathsf{E}(y_{it}) = 0 \qquad\qquad \mathsf{E}(\Delta y_{it}) = 0$$

$$\mathsf{E}(y_{it} \mid \eta_i) = \left[\tfrac{1}{1-\gamma} + \gamma^t\left(\alpha_1 - \tfrac{1}{1-\gamma}\right)\right]\eta_i \qquad \mathsf{E}(\Delta y_{it} \mid \eta_i) = \gamma^{t-1}[1-(1-\gamma)\alpha_1]\eta_i$$

$$\text{Var}(y_{it}) = \left[\tfrac{1}{1-\gamma} + \gamma^t\left(\alpha_1 - \tfrac{1}{1-\gamma}\right)\right]^2 \times\sigma_\eta^2 + \tfrac{\sigma_\varepsilon^2}{1-\gamma^2} \qquad \text{Var}(\Delta y_{it}) = \gamma^{2t-2}[1-(1-\gamma)\alpha_1]^2 \times\sigma_\eta^2 + \tfrac{2\sigma_\varepsilon^2}{1-\gamma^2}$$

$$\text{Var}(y_{it} \mid \eta_i) = \tfrac{\sigma_\varepsilon^2}{1-\gamma^2} \qquad \text{Var}(\Delta y_{it} \mid \eta_i) = \tfrac{2\sigma_\varepsilon^2}{1-\gamma^2}$$

Since all estimators to be examined include level and/or differenced variables in a highly non-linear way, we do not expect that more general invariance properties can be exploited in the Monte Carlo than the one with respect to the scale parameter σ_ε. So, next to items such as N, T and the adopted normality of both random components, the only design parameters are γ, α_1 and $\sigma_\eta^2/\sigma_\varepsilon^2$. However, we shall not use these as a base for the Monte Carlo grid, but γ, ϕ and ψ, where:

$$\phi \equiv \alpha_1(1-\gamma) \tag{42}$$

$$\psi^2 \equiv \frac{1+\gamma}{1-\gamma}\frac{\sigma_\eta^2}{\sigma_\varepsilon^2}. \tag{43}$$

Note that for $\phi = 1$ we have accumulated effect stationarity,[6] for $\phi = 0$ the individual effect component in y_{i0} is zero, and for $\phi = 0.5$ the effect component in y_{i0} is 50 percent of the stationary magnitude $1/(1-\gamma)$. Hence, by fixing ϕ instead of α_1 we can control the effect component in y_{i0} in proportion to the stationary magnitude, irrespective of the chosen value for γ, whereas when we fix α_1 this characteristic would vary with γ. Therefore we may call the parameters γ and ϕ autonomous and orthogonal: γ is just about speed of adjustment and ϕ exclusively about the initial disequilibrium condition with respect to the individual effects, whereas α_1 is an ambiguous parameter because the consequences for y_{it} of its magnitude can only be understood when either γ or ϕ are known too.

The parameter ψ expresses the following basic characteristic of the observations from the DGP independently from γ and ϕ. We find that when $\phi = 1$ or otherwise for $t \to \infty$ when accumulated effect stationarity has been attained:

$$\text{Var}(y_{it}) = \frac{\sigma_\eta^2}{(1-\gamma)^2} + \frac{\sigma_\varepsilon^2}{1-\gamma^2} = \left(\frac{1+\gamma}{1-\gamma}\frac{\sigma_\eta^2}{\sigma_\varepsilon^2} + 1\right)\frac{\sigma_\varepsilon^2}{1-\gamma^2}$$
$$= (\psi^2+1)\frac{\sigma_\varepsilon^2}{1-\gamma^2}. \tag{44}$$

Hence, ψ^2 expresses under accumulated effect stationarity the magnitude of the variance component in $\mathrm{Var}(y_{it})$ stemming from the individual effects in terms of the magnitude of the variance of $\mathrm{Var}(y_{it})$ originating from the other error component, the accumulated noise. If we would fix $\sigma_\eta^2/\sigma_\varepsilon^2$ the characteristic ψ^2 would vary with γ. By fixing ψ we can control the relative size of the variance of the accumulated two error components in a stationary y_{it}, irrespective of the value of γ, by choosing

$$\sigma_\eta^2 = \frac{1-\gamma}{1+\gamma}\psi^2\sigma_\varepsilon^2. \tag{45}$$

Although $\sigma_\eta^2/\sigma_\varepsilon^2$ directly characterizes the relative magnitude of the incremental error components in the right-hand side of $y_{it} = \beta + \gamma y_{i,t-1} + \eta_i + \varepsilon_{it}$, it does not characterize the data, unless γ is known too. Therefore we find that ψ is an autonomous parameter (like γ and ϕ), whereas $\sigma_\eta/\sigma_\varepsilon$ and α_1 are not. The reparametrization makes it easier to chose and to cover the relevant values of the parameters and it will enhance the interpretability of the Monte Carlo results too, because we can change γ now while keeping the two other basic characteristics expressed by ϕ and ψ fixed, whereas otherwise changing γ would imply changing the relative prominence and closeness to stationarity of the accumulated individual effects too.[7]

Most published Monte Carlo studies on (generalizations of) the above panel AR(1) model assume that all stationarity conditions hold. And in addition most of them consider only one value for $\sigma_\eta^2/\sigma_\varepsilon^2$ (often one), which is a further restriction on the dimensionality of the parameter space.[8] This restriction makes it quite likely that important properties of the estimators will be overlooked, and one cannot distinguish between the effects of increasing γ and decreasing ψ^2. Even if the value of $\sigma_\eta^2/\sigma_\varepsilon^2$ is varied, relationship (43) implies that from such simulations one cannot easily disentangle the effects due to a high (low) γ and those due to a high (low) ψ value.[9]

What would be reasonable values for ψ? In Blundell and Bond (1998, model A) it varies from 1 when $\gamma = 0$ to 19 when $\gamma = 0.9$. In Blundell and Bond (1998, model B)[10] it is 1 again for $\gamma = 0$ but only 0.19 for $\gamma = 0.9$. Hence, neither in model A nor B ψ is held constant when γ is changed, which hampers the interpretation of the Monte Carlo results. It would be interesting to know the actual estimates of σ_η^2 and σ_ε^2 in the application of the AR(1) model in Bond (2002) or in similar empirical exercises. In Blundell, Bond, Windmeijer (2000), for instance p. 16, it is discussed what happens "at high values of γ and high values of $\sigma_\eta^2/\sigma_\varepsilon^2$". Note that this implies doubly high values of ψ^2 in their model A. Thus, we should know whether it is really likely to occur that $\psi = 5\sqrt{1.8/0.2} = 15$ or even higher. Below, we will restrict ourselves to values $0 \leq \psi \leq 5$ and $0.1 \leq \gamma \leq 0.9$, implying $0 \leq \sigma_\eta/\sigma_\varepsilon \leq 4.52$.

Choosing in a Monte Carlo exclusively equivalent values for σ_η^2 and σ_ε^2 is deceiving from a theoretical point of view as well. Recently, Bun and Kiviet (2005) derived a first-order-asymptotic approximation to the bias of the GMMs estimator when use is made of the simple weight matrix involving $D^{GIV} = I$ in first-order autoregressive panel data models with another weakly exogenous regressor. When we specialize that result for the case of a pure AR(1) panel model we obtain that the leading term of the bias, which is $O(N^{-1})$, is in fact proportional to

$$\frac{1}{N}\frac{1}{1-\gamma}\left(1 - \frac{\sigma_\eta^2}{\sigma_\varepsilon^2}\right). \tag{46}$$

Hence, in all Monte Carlo studies restricted to the case $\sigma_\eta^2 = \sigma_\varepsilon^2$ this leading term is zero, which may explain the relatively small bias that has been established for the GMMs estimator in such restricted simulation studies.

5.2 *Some New Monte Carlo Findings*

Using the design suggested above we ran simulations (1,000 replications for each parametrization, using the same η_i and ε_{it} realizations for different parameter values and different techniques) for various GMM implementations for $N = 100$ and $T = 3(+1)10$, over $\gamma = 0.1(+0.2)0.9$ and choosing $\phi \in \{1, 0.5\}$ and $\psi \in \{0 \text{ or } 0.5, 1, 5\}$. The chosen N may seem small for some applications, but it is large for other. Moreover, finding serious problems and quality differences for modest N values, usually quite well indicates where similar problems may still be looming for larger though finite N. Of course, for $N \to \infty$ there is no bias and the RMSE will be zero for any consistent GMM estimator.

Below, results are presented in the form of diagrams above each other, for all the particular parametrizations and implementations of GMM examined: the upper diagrams present relative bias, that is the Monte Carlo estimate of $\mathsf{E}(\hat{\gamma} - \gamma)/\gamma$; the lower diagrams depict relative efficiency, which is RMSE$(\hat{\gamma})/\gamma$. Both are given in percent. Where the relative bias is larger than, say, 25 percent in absolute value there is a serious bias problem, and where relative RMSE is larger than, say, 50 percent there seems a serious problem regarding efficient and useful inference. Naturally, extreme values of these relative measures will always occur for values of γ very close to zero. However, for a particular estimator (at the sample sizes examined) to show satisfying behaviour it seems reasonable to require that its relative RMSE does not exceed 50 percent for, say, $\gamma > 0.2$, although this criterion should not be taken too strictly.

GMMs Under Accumulated Effect Stationarity ($\phi = 1$) We first examine the system estimator GMMs for the situation where $\phi = 1$, hence the extra instruments for the equation in levels are valid. Given that observations are available on y_{it} for $t = 0, \ldots, T$, GMMs exploits $(T + 2)(T - 1)/2$ instruments, viz. $T(T - 1)/2$ instruments as in the Arellano–Bond implementation plus $T - 1$ non-redundant "level instruments". In Figure 11.1 we first investigate the simple weight matrix $D^{GIV} = I_{2T-2}$ in GMMs$_1^{GIV}$ for $\psi = 0, 1$ and 5 (from left to right) respectively. Similar results for GMMs$_2^{GIV}$, which exploits the empirical weight matrix (18) based on GMMs$_1^{GIV}$ residuals, are given in Figure 11.2. Both these estimators are examined in Blundell and Bond (1998) too. Note that in their design A $\psi = \sqrt{1.9/0.1} = 4.36$ when $\gamma = 0.9$ and $\psi = \sqrt{1.1/0.9} = 1.1$ when $\gamma = 0.1$, but they did not examine large ψ in combination with small or moderate γ (nor vice versa). From our figures

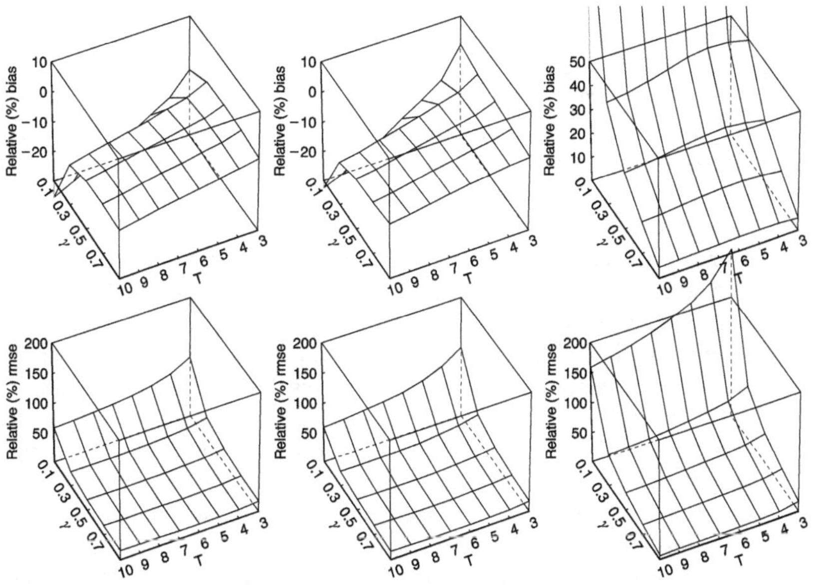

Figure 11.1 *GMMs*$_1^{GIV}$ *at* $N = 100; \phi = 1; \psi = 0, 1, 5$

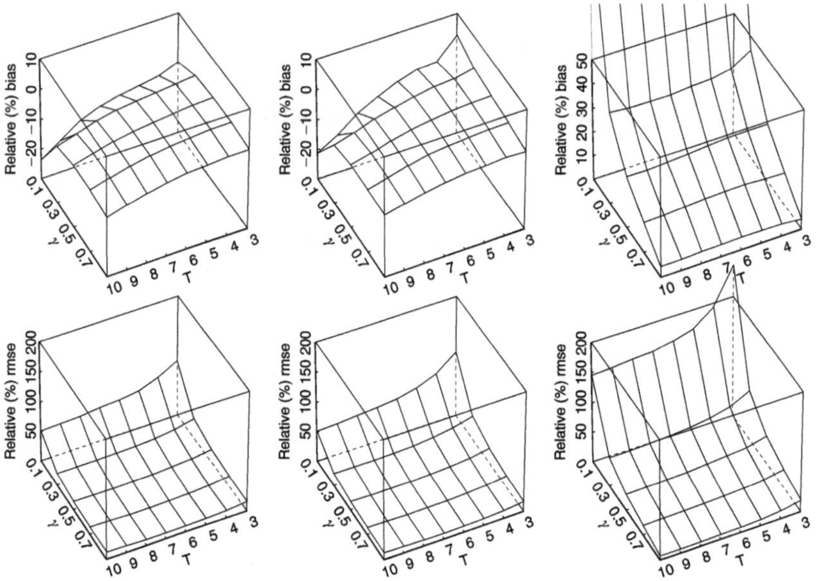

Figure 11.2 $GMMs_2^{GIV}$ *at* $N = 100; \phi = 1; \psi = 0, 1, 5$

we see that the effect on bias and RMSE of γ and T is almost similar, both for $\psi = 0$ and $\psi = 1$ and for one and two step GMMs^{GIV}, the latter being only slightly better.

However, at $\psi = 5$ the sign of the bias has changed (which may explain the very small bias at $\gamma = 0.5$ and $\psi = \sqrt{1.5/0.5} = 1.73$ in table 5 of Blundell and Bond, 1998) and the bias is dramatically high for moderate and small values of γ. At $\psi = 5$ the bias and RMSE results are satisfactory for large values of γ only (which are the only large ψ cases examined in earlier Monte Carlo's). In table 5 of Blundell and Bond (1998), for $\gamma = 0.5$ and $\psi = 1.73$, the 1-step and 2-step estimators show both their consistency (by a small bias), and the 2-step estimator shows a just slightly lower variance. Examining the nuisance parameter space over an extra dimension, we find only minor differences between one and two step GMMs^{GIV} too; the 2-step procedure seems to lead to a very moderate improvement of efficiency over the whole parameter space. However, this correspondence should not be interpreted as though the weight matrix has only minor effects, as we will see from further experiments.

In Figures 11.3 and 11.4 we examine what the quality is of the operational weights used in DPD. We do not find much difference between the D^{DPD} and D^{GIV} results in 1-step GMMs, although for $\psi = 0$

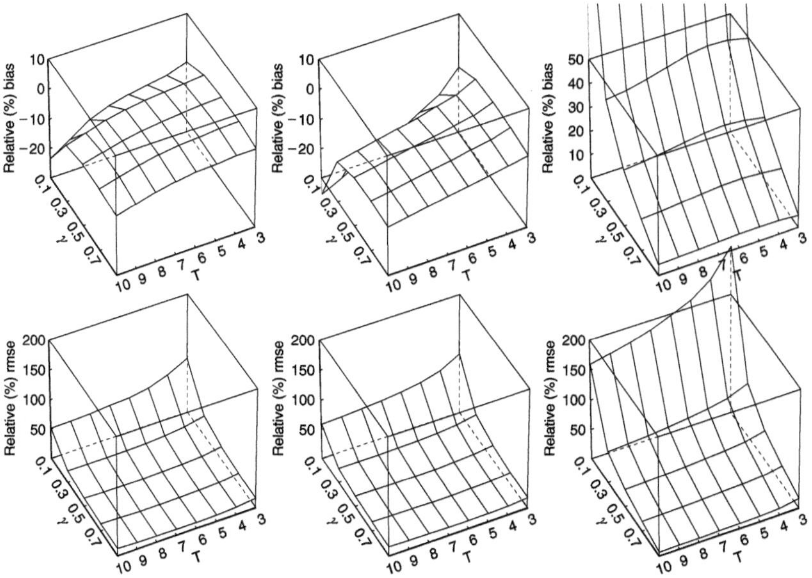

Figure 11.3 $GMMs_1^{DPD}$ *at* $N = 100; \phi = 1; \psi = 0, 1, 5$

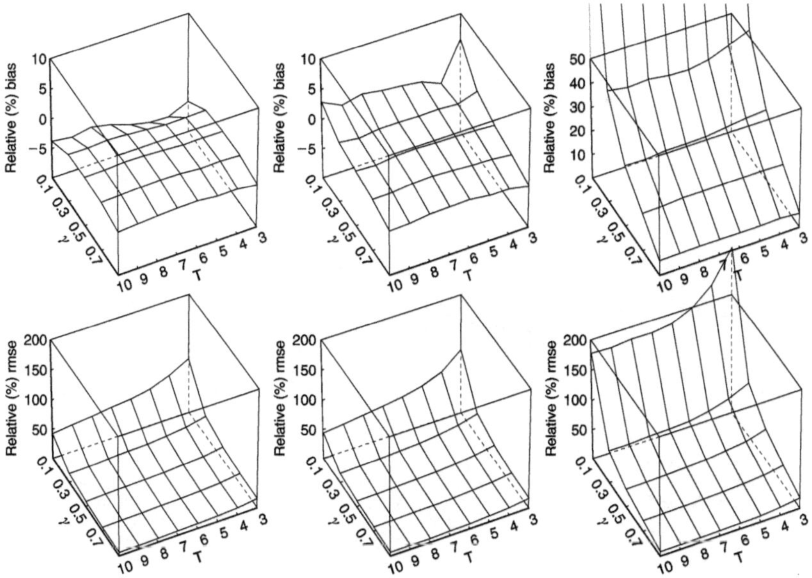

Figure 11.4 $GMMs_2^{DPD}$ *at* $N = 100; \phi = 1; \psi = 0, 1, 5$

we find that the DPD weights work slightly better than the simple GIV weights. However, for $\psi = 5$ and γ not very large, using D^{DPD} in the weight matrix works even worse than D^{GIV}.

Next we examine the effects on bias and RMSE of GMMs when using the non-operational weights W_{BB}^{subopt} given in (41), in which we substituted the true value of $\sigma_\eta^2/\sigma_\varepsilon^2$ in 1-step estimation, giving what we denote as $\text{GMMs}_1^{\sigma_\eta^2/\sigma_\varepsilon^2}$ (Figure 11.5), and employing its residuals in 2-step estimation to give $\text{GMMs}_2^{\sigma_\eta^2/\sigma_\varepsilon^2}$ (Figure 11.6). Note that for $\psi = 0$ (no individual effects) these are the optimal weights. We see that for $\sigma_\eta^2/\sigma_\varepsilon^2 = 0$ estimator $\text{GMMs}_1^{\sigma_\eta^2/\sigma_\varepsilon^2}$ has much smaller bias than both GMMs_1^{GIV} and GMMs_1^{DPD}, and also its RMSE is much smaller, especially for larger values of T (even more than four times smaller at $T = 10$ and $\gamma = 0.9$). Self-evidently at $\psi = 0$ $\text{GMMs}_2^{\sigma_\eta^2/\sigma_\varepsilon^2}$ does not outperform the already optimal $\text{GMMs}_1^{\sigma_\eta^2/\sigma_\varepsilon^2}$, which is also notably better than the asymptotically equivalent GMMs_2^{DPD} and GMMs_2^{GIV}, which have larger (double and triple respectively)

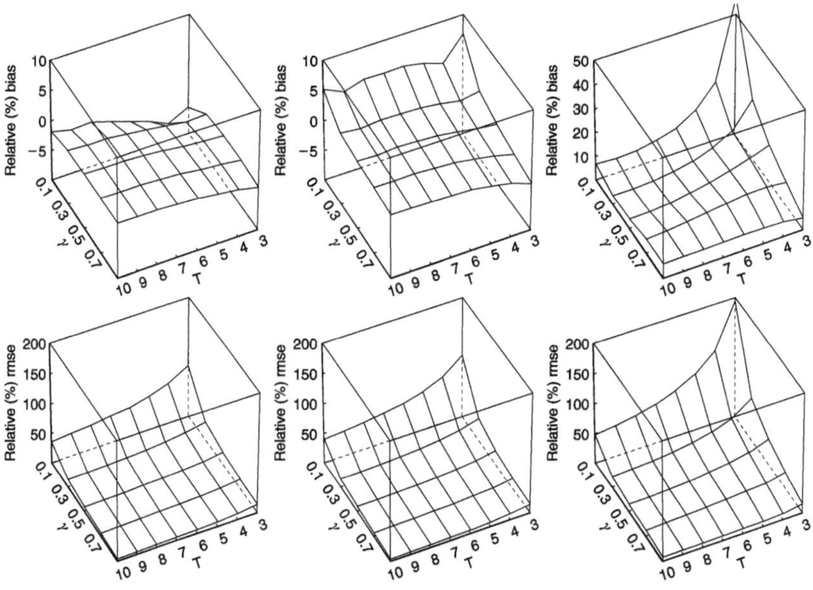

Figure 11.5 $GMMs_1^{\sigma_\eta^2/\sigma_\varepsilon^2}$ at $N = 100; \phi = 1; \psi = 0, 1, 5$

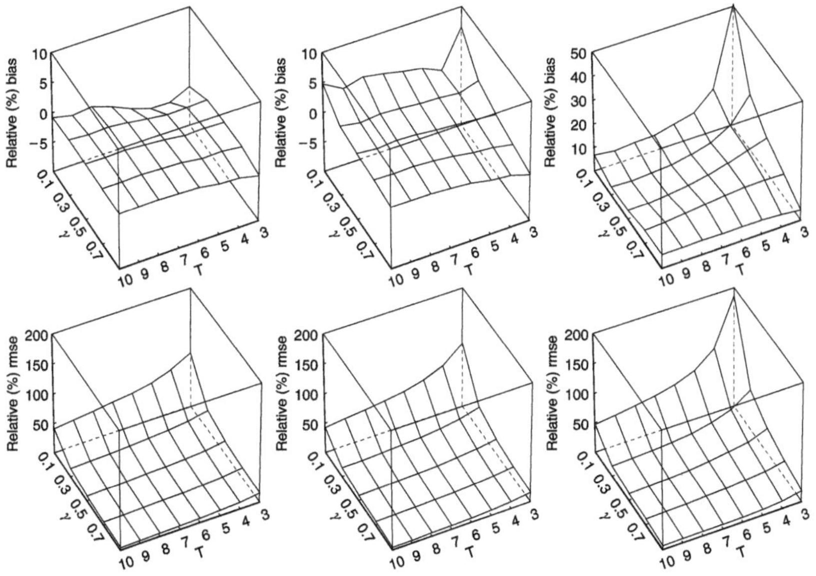

Figure 11.6 $GMMs_2^{\sigma_\eta^2/\sigma_\varepsilon^2}$ *at* $N = 100; \phi = 1; \psi = 0, 1, 5$

RMSE at $\psi = 0$, $\gamma = 0.9$ and $T = 10, N = 100$. For $\psi > 0$ $\text{GMMs}_1^{\sigma_\eta^2/\sigma_\varepsilon^2}$ is sub-optimal, but we see that it has very moderate bias and behaves well, whereas both GIV and DPD weights lead to very poor performance when ψ is large and γ moderate or small. For this non-operational 1-step estimator we find too that (under i.i.d. disturbances) 2-step estimation does not yield worthwhile improvements.

Looking into the options for making the attractive properties of weight matrix W_{BB}^{subopt} operational, we examined using it while taking in 1-step estimation for the unknown $\sigma_\eta^2/\sigma_\varepsilon^2$ a value of 10, irrespective of the true value, and indicate it as GMMs_1^{10} in Figure 11.7. Note that in our simulations the actual value of $\sigma_\eta^2/\sigma_\varepsilon^2$ is zero when $\psi = 0$, and when $\psi = 1$ or 5, $\sigma_\eta^2/\sigma_\varepsilon^2$ decreases from 0.81 to 0.05 and from 20.5 to 1.32 respectively, when γ moves from 0.1 to 0.9. We see that the easy and operational GMMs_1^{10} procedure yields results almost as good as the non-operational $\text{GMMs}_1^{\sigma_\eta^2/\sigma_\varepsilon^2}$ when ψ is large. This is not the case when $\psi \leq 1$, but then it still has smaller RMSE than GMMs_1^{GIV} and GMMs_1^{DPD}, except for T very small and γ very large. Employing the GMMs_1^{10} residuals to obtain GMMs_2^{10} (see Figure 11.8) the performance of the estimator has improved slightly.

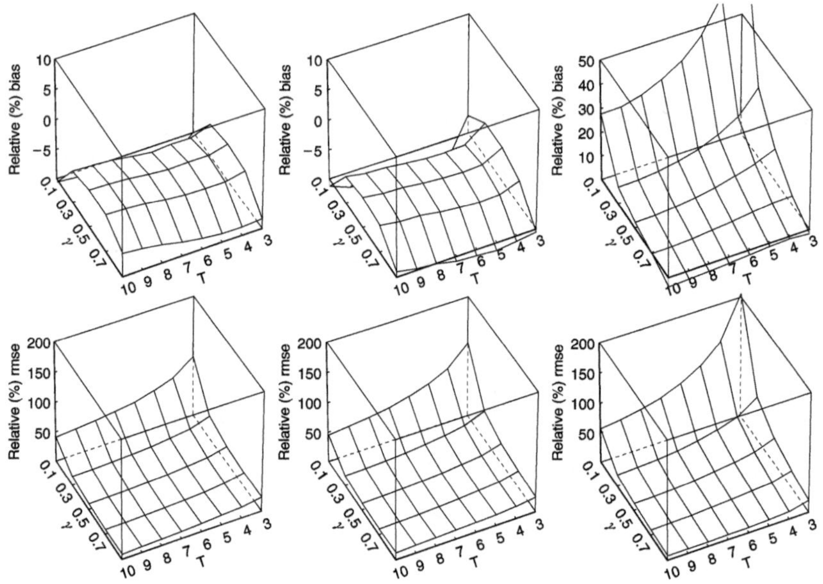

Figure 11.7 $GMMs_1^{10}$ *at* $N = 100; \phi = 1; \psi = 0, 1, 5$

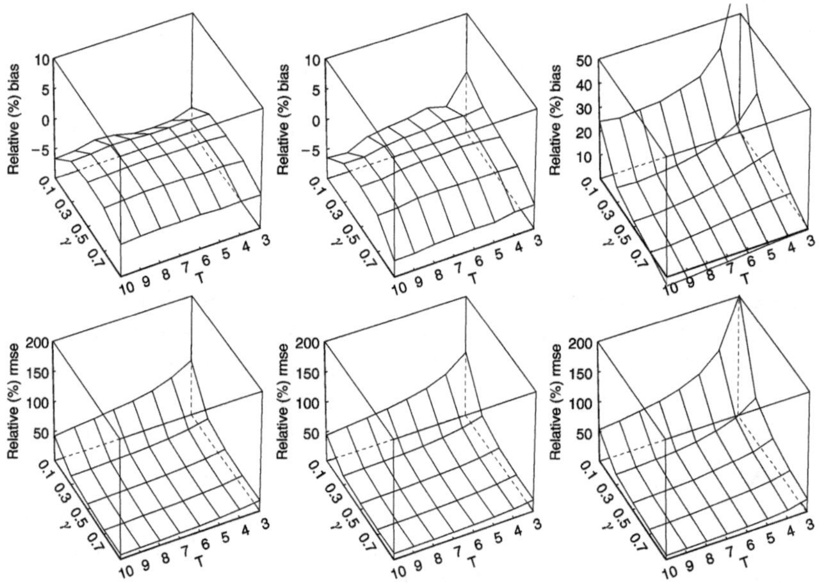

Figure 11.8 $GMMs_2^{10}$ *at* $N = 100; \phi = 1; \psi = 0, 1, 5$

Hence, with respect to the system estimator we conclude that the quality of the weight matrix used in 1-step GMMs is of much more importance for its resulting bias and efficiency than was recognized previously. Also the widespread reputation of GMMs as yielding only very moderate bias needs correction: when GIV or DPD weights are used in the system estimator then a moderate bias is obtained only when γ is large.

GMM Not Exploiting All Valid Instruments, While $\phi = 1$ It seems interesting now to examine similar results for GMM in this context while omitting the $T - 1$ differenced instruments in the level equation. Still having $\alpha_1 = 1/(1 - \gamma)$, we find in Figure 11.9 for the Arellano–Bond implementation that it works best for intermediate values of γ. The bias is negative now for all ψ values and is not large for intermediate γ values. However, it is substantial for large and for small positive γ, especially for large ψ and small T. For large values of γ all GMMs implementations achieve a smaller RMSE. However, we also find that even in the case of accumulated effect stationarity, adding the level equation with differenced instruments and form a system, while using the poor weight matrices based on D^{GIV} or D^{DPD}, is counterproductive when γ is small and ψ large. Irrespective of the weights used in the first step, 2-step GMMs is

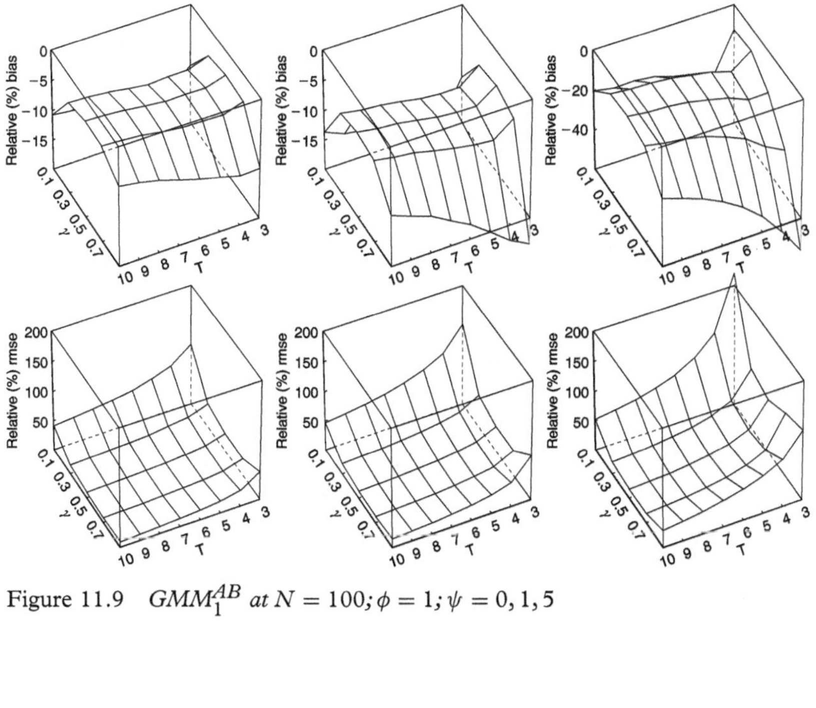

Figure 11.9 GMM_1^{AB} *at* $N = 100; \phi = 1; \psi = 0, 1, 5$

asymptotically efficient. However in finite sample we find, that when poor weights are used in 1-step GMMs, the Arellano-Bond implementation is often better.

From Figure 11.10 we note that omitting more valid instruments by using the matrix Z^{BK} yields slightly less bias and higher efficiency than for Z^{AB} only when $\psi \leq 1$, and the other way around when $\psi = 5$. The latter is surprising, because in Bun and Kiviet (2005) we found that when Z^{BK} is used instead of Z^{AB} then the leading term of the bias is of smaller order in T by a factor T. Earlier we found that it yields a smaller bias indeed in a model with further regressors and $T = 10$ and $N = 20$. Apparently, this does not occur in the pure AR(1) model for $T \leq 10$ at $N = 100$.

Reducing the number of instruments to just one and employing the Anderson–Hsiao implementation with the lagged level instrument Z_i^{AHl} of (26) leads to curious results presented in Figure 11.11. Here we notice a phenomenon that has already undermined so many earlier simulation findings. Because the number of instruments equals the number of regressors this estimator has no finite moments. Therefore, the Monte Carlo sample average of the 1,000 estimates (and also the RMSE) do not converge to a constant for an increasing number of Monte Carlo replications,

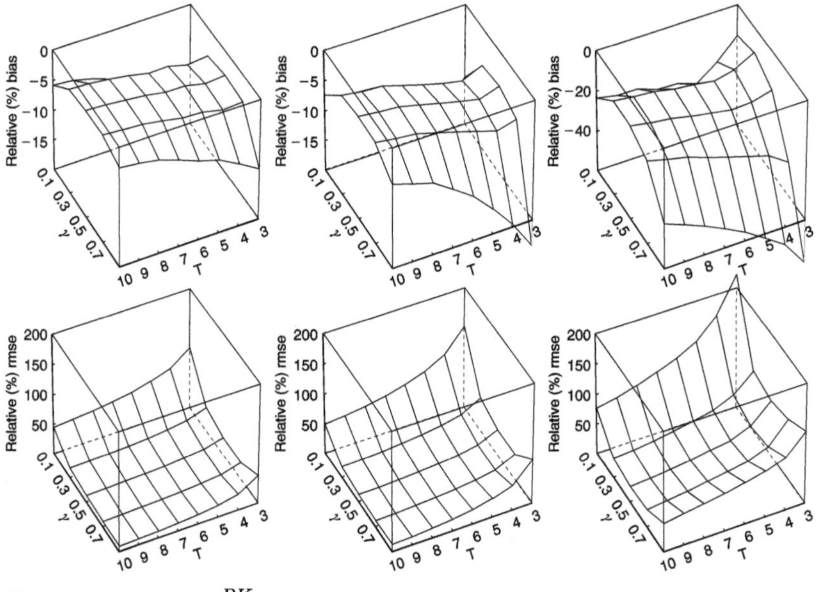

Figure 11.10 GMM_1^{BK} at $N = 100; \phi = 1; \psi = 0, 1, 5$

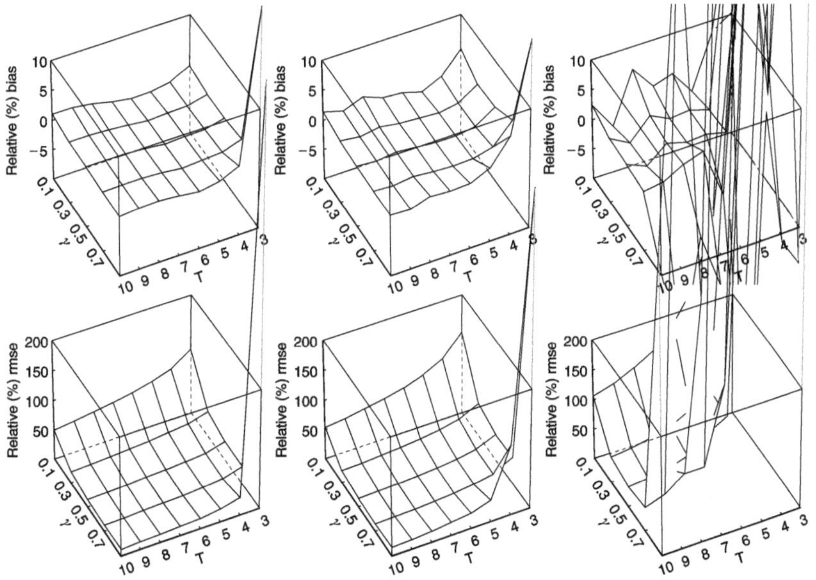

Figure 11.11 MM^{AHl} *at* $N = 100; \phi = 1; \psi = 0, 1, 5$

but to a random variable. The ostensible small bias for $\psi \leq 1$ (apart from the outlying value at $T = 3$ and $\gamma = 0.9$) would change in a jumble as for $\psi = 5$ when we would use a much larger number of replications. The density at zero for the denominator in the expression of the estimator is apparently larger for smaller T, larger γ and larger ψ, but at $\psi \leq 1$ the probability of huge outliers in just 1,000 trials is still moderate. The results for Z_i^{AHd} (not included in the figures) proved to be even more vulnerable in this respect. To represent the behaviour of these estimators appropriately the median and interquartile range could and should have been used.[11] Note that the GMM^{AB} and GMM^{BK} estimators have an equal number of instruments and regressors for $T = 2$ only, so by examining $T \geq 3$ we avoided similar confusing results in the Figures 11.9 and 11.10. At $T = 3$ they exploit 3 instruments for one regressor and hence their first two moments exist.

Results for Non-stationary Accumulated Effects ($\phi = 0.5$) Next we examine various of the estimators when applied to data series where accumulated effect stationarity does not hold. Of course, this is of no interest when $\psi = 0$ and no effects are present. Therefore we examined $\psi = 0.5$ instead. Figure 11.12 shows that the finite sample properties

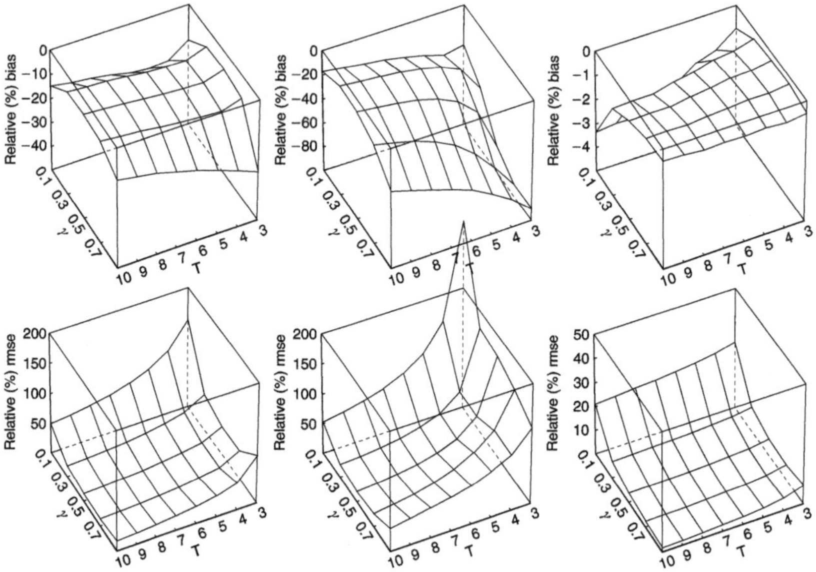

Figure 11.12 GMM_1^{AB} at $N = 100; \phi = 0.5; \psi = 0.5, 1, 5$

of GMM_1^{AB} are much worse than those of the $\phi = 1$ case when $\psi = 1$. When $\psi = 0.5$ or 5, however, GMM_1^{AB} works much better under $\phi = 0.5$ than it does under $\phi = 1$. Similar results (not presented) were found for GMM_1^{BK}.

Finally we examine what happens when GMMs is applied when $\phi \neq 1$. Of course, for any weight matrix both 1-step and 2-step implementations are inconsistent now. In Figure 11.13 we see that the inconsistency of GMMs is evident only when ψ is not small and γ not very large. In fact, when $\psi = 1$ and γ large GMMs_2^{DPD} behaves better than the consistent estimator GMM^{AB}. For larger ψ, however, GMM^{AB} is much more efficient. Figure 11.14 shows that $\text{GMMs}_1^{\sigma_\eta^2/\sigma_\varepsilon^2}$ seems less vulnerable when ψ is large. These results make clear that it is of great importance to test for the validity of accumulated effect stationarity, before its orthogonality conditions are imposed in estimation.

6 Concluding Remarks

We performed Monte Carlo experiments in the context of a very specific simple dynamic panel data model and examined and compared the results

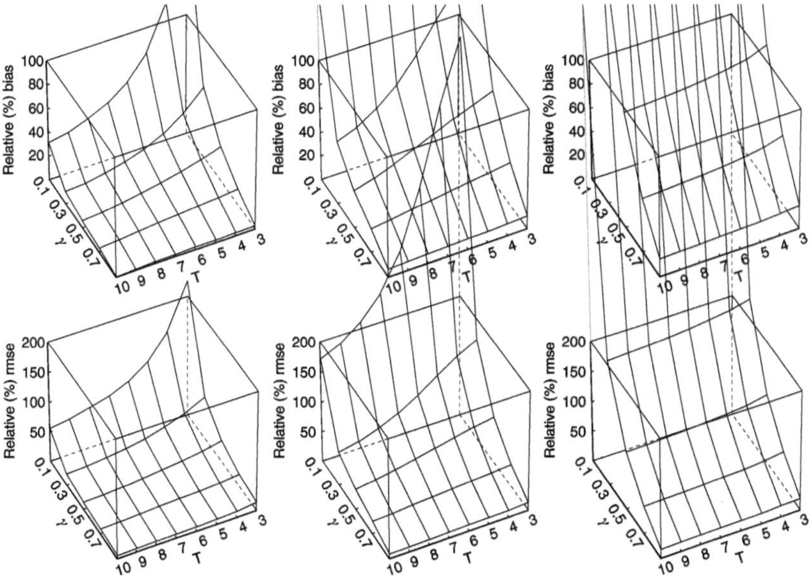

Figure 11.13 *Inconsistent* $GMMs_2^{DPD}$ *at* $N = 100; \phi = 0.5; \psi = 0.5, 1, 5$

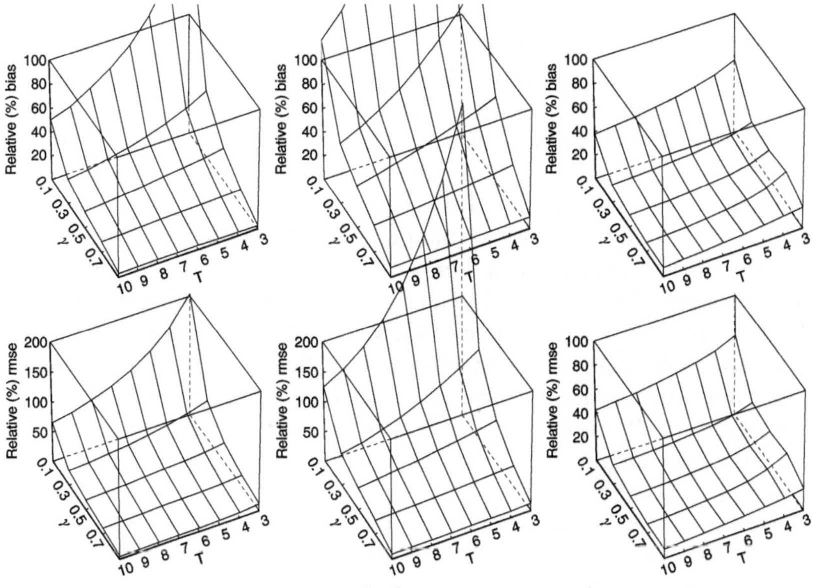

Figure 11.14 *Inconsistent* $GMMs_1^{\sigma_\eta^2/\sigma_\varepsilon^2}$ *at* $N = 100; \phi = 0.5; \psi = 0.5, 1, 5$

of a few implementations of 1 and 2-step GMM, which differ in the number of moment conditions exploited and in the weight matrix employed. This Monte Carlo study as such was not designed to enable a serious competition between the full range of alternative techniques available for dynamic panel data models. It has only been used here to illustrate the importance of the eight distinct methodological aspirations listed in section 2 for the design and conduct of a fair tournament. In particular, we illustrated that in Monte Carlo comparisons one should always examine what the restrictions are that have been put on the parameter space of the design, and whether these seem reasonable. We gave attention to the dimensionality of the parameter space of the Monte Carlo design, but also to the actual parameter values chosen in the experiments. Moreover, we demonstrated that it is very useful to create a base for the parameter space which is orthogonal with respect to separately interpretable characteristics of the generated data processes. Otherwise, the marginal effects of numerical changes in the design parameters are hard to disentangle. We also showed that it can be useful to examine non-operational techniques, which exploit information that is usually not available in practice, but self-evidently is in simulation experiments.

With respect to the qualities of various GMM estimators in zero-mean stable panel AR(1) models we found the following. Most existing studies have been misleading, because they did not include parametrizations where both the individual effects are prominent (ψ high) and the lagged dependent variable coefficient (γ) moderate. We demonstrate that these are cases where the quality of GMMs (the system estimator) is extremely dependent on the weight matrix used. Both the GIV and DPD weight matrices work poorly here, and performing a second iteration step is of little or no help. It is shown that aiming to get closer to the non-operational optimal weight matrix yields substantial improvements. This finding is in line with results obtained recently in Doran and Schmidt (2005). Earlier simulation studies paid little or no attention to data series where the initial conditions deviate from accumulated effect stationarity. Then GMMs is inconsistent and GMM_1^{AB} is the asymptotically efficient estimator. Although we re-establish that in finite sample this estimator may show substantial bias, we also find that GMM_1^{AB} may work surprisingly well. We note that the bias is affected non-monotonically by the long-run magnitude of the effects ψ when the effect in the initial observation is moderate ($\phi = 0.5$).

We should reemphasize that our present experimental findings just pertain to the highly specific simple panel AR(1) model without any further explanatory variables. The simplicity of this DGP should in principle enable one to obtain analytic evidence on the actual dependence on the model parameters of the quality of alternative instrument and weight matrices and resulting estimator efficiency. Blundell and Bond (1998) obtained such evidence for the simple case $T = 2$ (in our notation) where the weight matrix is not a complicating factor. Probably, due to the simplicity of the AR(1) DGP, a relatively good performance is achieved by instrument matrices incorporating very few lags, because it seems likely that higher-order lagged variables will establish weak instruments here. To rate estimators for empirically more relevant but much more complex DGP's (i.e. including higher-order lags, further weakly exogenous regressors, cross-sectional heteroskedasticity, non-normality, non-stationary initial values) the only practicable option seems to run appropriately designed simulation experiments, for which in our opinion the design in Bun and Kiviet (2005) establishes a reasonable starting point to meet the eight aspirations mentioned in section 2. However, in conclusion we want to remark that it seems highly unlikely that it will ever happen that single winners can be celebrated in fully fledged simulation contests between alternative inference techniques, because of the following truism: techniques that build on many assumptions, though efficient when these assumptions do hold, usually are not robust to situations where they are false, whereas more robust techniques will not beat full information techniques on their home ground.

Notes

1. In designing reponse surfaces, see Hendry (1984), one is faced with inevitable specification problems that might corrupt the simulation findings; see Davidson and MacKinnon (1993) for further references.
2. Notable exceptions are Nerlove (1967, 1971), initiating this line of research. Nerlove uses in his design the so-called "intra-class correlation", the transformed parameter $\rho \equiv \sigma_\eta^2/(\sigma_\varepsilon^2 + \sigma_\eta^2)$, which he varies over its entire domain $0 \leq \rho < 1$.
3. See Hansen (1982) and, in the context of dynamic panel data, Arellano (2003) and Baltagi (2005).
4. They speak about mean-stationarity instead of accumulated effect stationarity. We prefer the latter, because (4) does not lead to constant (conditional) mean in a model where (3) does not hold.
5. Hsiao *et al.* (2002) examines ML and GMM estimators under both normal and nonnormal errors.
6. This parameter is also used in Andrews and Lu (2001, p. 49).
7. Note that ψ differs from the design parameter $\mu = (1-\gamma)^{-1}\sigma_\eta/\sigma_\varepsilon$ introduced in the Monte Carlo in Kiviet (1995, p. 65) and also practiced in Harris and Mátyás (2004). Like ψ this μ serves to break away from the habitual designs where $\sigma_\eta/\sigma_\varepsilon$ is constant. Its rationalization bears on the arguments given in Nerlove (1967, footnote 2) and is also in line with the parameter

orthogonalization achieved by Lancaster (2002, p. 655). However, regarding designing a DGP we find that ψ has a more solid underpinning and interpretation than μ has. The latter compares the accumulated magnitude of the individual effect with that of the current idiosyncratic disturbance, whereas ψ^2 (already used in Bun and Kiviet, 2005) captures the accumulated variance of both error components and thus seems closer to a basic characteristic of the generated data orthogonal to γ.

8. This offence of aspiration 3 occurs in, for instance, Bhargava and Sargan (1983), Arellano and Bond (1991), Blundell and Bond (1998), Blundell *et al.* (2000), Harris and Mátyás (2000), Andrews and Lu (2001), Bond (2002), Bowsher (2002), Doornik *et al.* (2002), Bond and Windmeijer (2005) and Windmeijer (2005). Little or no information on the actual magnitude of the individual effects in their experiments is given by Judson and Owen (1999), Hansen (2001) and Hsiao *et al.* (2002), which is at odds with aspiration 8.
9. For instance, Alvarez and Arellano (2003, p. 1133) examine $\gamma \in \{0.2, 0.5, 0.8\}$ and $\sigma_\eta^2/\sigma_\varepsilon^2 \in \{0.2, 1.0\}$. They infer that $\sigma_\eta^2/\sigma_\varepsilon^2$ has little effect, but since their design does not cover cases where ψ is large (say 5) and γ small, this limited grid cannot reveal the full effect of ψ and γ. Doran and Schmidt (2005) use a wider grid including $\sigma_\eta^2/\sigma_\varepsilon^2 = 4$, so at moderate $\gamma = 0.5$ they cover $\psi = 3.5$. They report, as do Alonso-Borrego and Arellano (1999), that the effects of increasing γ and $\sigma_\eta^2/\sigma_\varepsilon^2$ are qualitatively similar. Note that these findings underscore the non-orthogonality of these two parameters.
10. Stephen Bond informed me that there is a typo in Blundell and Bond (1998, pp. 129–30) regarding the specification of simulation model B. Their published simulation results for model B have actually been obtained by (their notation) $y_{it} = \alpha y_{i,t-1} + (1-\alpha)\eta_i + v_{it}$, with start-up value $y_{it} = \eta_i + u_{i1}$, so that accumulated effect stationarity is obtained indeed (which would not when using the initial condition mentioned on p. 130).
11. Studies in which Monte Carlo estimates on moments of Anderson–Hsiao estimators have been presented which (due to the limited number of simulation replications) seem meaningful but are in fact all will o' the wisps include: Arellano and Bond (1991), Arellano and Bover (1995), Kiviet (1995), Judson and Owen (1999), Doornik *et al.* (2002) and Hsiao *et al.* (2002).

12 A Statistical Proof of the Transformation Theorem

*Karim M. Abadir and Jan R. Magnus**

1 Introduction

Let $\boldsymbol{x} \in \mathcal{X}$ be an $m \times 1$ variate with a known distribution. Suppose $\boldsymbol{x}$ is transformed into a new $n \times 1$ variate defined by the deterministic function $\boldsymbol{y} := \boldsymbol{g}(\boldsymbol{x}) \in \mathcal{Y}$. What are the statistical properties of $\boldsymbol{y}$? More specifically, how can we express the distribution of $\boldsymbol{y}$ in terms of the (known) distribution of $\boldsymbol{x}$? Three main methods are available: the moment-generating function (m.g.f.) or characteristic function (c.f.) technique, the cumulative distribution function (c.d.f.) technique, and the probability density function (p.d.f.) technique.

The transformation theorem relates to the p.d.f. technique when the variates are continuous, and is our focus here. The theorem is difficult and lengthy to prove, typically relying on advanced results in analysis, on differential forms and changes of variables of integration, see for example Wilks (1962, pp. 53–9) and Rao (1973, pp. 156–7) for statements and discussions, and Rudin (1976, ch. 10) for a proof. It is one of the very few major statistical theorems for which there is no proof in the statistics literature. Here, we provide a simple proof, by exploiting the statistical context that it is a density function whose arguments are being transformed. The proof uses the idea of conditioning for continuous random variables. It also illustrates how conditioning can provide shortcuts to proofs by reducing the dimensionality of some statistical problems.

In the following two sections, we introduce then prove the theorem, respectively. We use the notation proposed by Abadir and Magnus (2002).

* We are grateful to Adi Ben-Israel, David Cox, Anders Hald, Samuel Kotz, Peter Lee, Jan van Maanen and Stephen Stigler for helping us with the historical details. Karim Abadir acknowledges support from the British ESRC grant R000239538.

2 The Transformation Theorem

The first general statement and proof of the transformation theorem is due to Jacobi, who wrote a long memoir in 1841 devoted to the "functional determinant" (that is, the Jacobian). The memoir ends by restating the main result (in Jacobi's notation):

$$\int U\,\partial f\,\partial f_1 \ldots \partial f_n = \int U \left(\sum \pm \frac{\partial f}{\partial x}\frac{\partial f_1}{\partial x_1}\cdots\frac{\partial f_n}{\partial x_n} \right) \partial x\,\partial x_1 \ldots \partial x_n$$

and remarking that

> "Quam formulam pro duabus et tribus variabilibus eodem fere tempore Eulerus et Lagrange invenerunt, sed ille paullo prius." (Jacobi, 1841, p. 438)

Thus, Jacobi acknowledges that Euler (for $n = 2$) and Lagrange ($n = 3$) discovered this formula before him, Euler a little earlier than Lagrange, but he provides no references. In fact, Euler's paper was first presented to the St. Petersburg Academy on August 18, 1768, and published as Euler (1770), while Lagrange's result is the solution of the second of four problems raised in Lagrange (1773); see also Hairer and Wanner (1996, p. 338).

The results for $n = 2$ and $n = 3$ must have been known to Laplace, when he published his monumental *Théorie Analytique des Probabilités* in 1812, but he carefully avoids two-dimensional change of variables. For example, in Book 1, Part 2, Chapter 1, Section 24, Laplace proves the "résultat remarquable" that $\int_0^\infty \mathrm{e}^{-t^2}\mathrm{d}t = \sqrt{\pi}/2$. Instead of the now common proof of squaring and using polar coordinates (thus using the transformation theorem), Laplace uses a clever trick based on the two ingredients $\int_0^\infty \mathrm{e}^{-\lambda x}\mathrm{d}x = 1/\lambda$ and $\int_0^\infty \mathrm{d}x/(1+x^2) = \pi/2$.

The fact that functional dependence between variables implies that the functional determinant vanishes was probably known to Cauchy in 1815 (see Grimmett and Stirzaker, 2001, p. 108), but the opposite implication was not known to him.

The French naval officer Auguste Bravais (1811–1863) used Jacobi's result in 1846, when he considered a random vector $\boldsymbol{x} \sim \mathrm{N}_n(\mathbf{0}, \boldsymbol{\Sigma})$, where $\boldsymbol{\Sigma}$ is a diagonal $n \times n$ matrix, and obtained the density of $\boldsymbol{y} = \boldsymbol{A}\boldsymbol{x}$, where $\boldsymbol{A}$ is an $m \times n$ matrix of rank m. This is achieved by first enlarging $\boldsymbol{A}$ to a nonsingular $n \times n$ matrix using $n - m$ auxiliary variables, then applying the transformation theorem, and finally integrating out the auxiliary variables. For $m = 2$ and $m = 3$ Bravais proved that $\boldsymbol{y}$ is normally distributed, for $m = 4$ he claims the same, and for $m > 4$ he predicts that the same result holds but admits (p. 301) that he cannot prove it.

In order to state the transformation theorem for continuous variates, we make two assumptions. First, we assume that the function $\boldsymbol{g}(\boldsymbol{x})$ is continuously differentiable (implying inter alia that $\boldsymbol{x}$ is continuous too) and that $n = m$. The latter condition is not restrictive, because we may always augment the case $n < m$ with some identities. We further assume that the augmented transformation is nonsingular, that is having Jacobian of the transformation $\det(\partial \boldsymbol{x}/\partial \boldsymbol{y}') \neq 0$ for some $\boldsymbol{x} \in \mathcal{X}$. The role of this assumption is to rule out redundant variates in the vector $\boldsymbol{y}$.

With these two assumptions, we can now state the transformation theorem for continuous variates. In the case of an invertible function, that is a function which can be written as $\boldsymbol{x} = \boldsymbol{g}^{-1}(\boldsymbol{y})$, the transformation theorem states that

$$f_y(\boldsymbol{w}_y) = \left|\det\left(\frac{\partial \boldsymbol{g}^{-1}(\boldsymbol{w}_y)}{\partial \boldsymbol{w}_y'}\right)\right| f_x\left(\boldsymbol{g}^{-1}(\boldsymbol{w}_y)\right) \qquad (\boldsymbol{w}_y \in \mathcal{Y}),$$

where $\partial \boldsymbol{g}^{-1}(\boldsymbol{w}_y)/\partial \boldsymbol{w}_y'$ is $\partial \boldsymbol{x}/\partial \boldsymbol{y}'$ evaluated at $\boldsymbol{y} = \boldsymbol{w}_y$ and $\boldsymbol{x} = \boldsymbol{g}^{-1}(\boldsymbol{w}_y)$. The absolute value of the determinant ensures that probabilities cannot be negative. In the more general case, the function does not possess a unique inverse over all $\boldsymbol{x} \in \mathcal{X}$. We then assume that the function is invertible (with probability 1) within each of the subsets $\mathcal{X}_i$ of some partition $\bigcup_{i=1}^{p} \mathcal{X}_i = \mathcal{X}$. Note that the term "partition" implies that the sets $\mathcal{X}_i$ are non-overlapping. The transformation theorem then generalizes to

$$f_y(\boldsymbol{w}_y) = \sum_{i=1}^{p} \left|\det\left(\frac{\partial \boldsymbol{g}_i^{-1}(\boldsymbol{w}_y)}{\partial \boldsymbol{w}_y'}\right)\right| f_x(\boldsymbol{g}_i^{-1}(\boldsymbol{w}_y)) \qquad (\boldsymbol{w}_y \in \mathcal{Y}),$$

where $\boldsymbol{g}_i^{-1}(\boldsymbol{w}_y)$ is the inverse function within partition $\boldsymbol{\mathcal{X}}_i$.

3 A Statistical Proof, Using Conditioning and Induction

We shall only prove the case where the function $\boldsymbol{g}(\boldsymbol{x})$ is invertible. The general case, where $\boldsymbol{y} = \boldsymbol{g}(\boldsymbol{x})$ is piece-wise (that is over non-overlapping sets) invertible, then follows easily (for example from the first line of (3) below).

We proceed by induction, starting with $m = 1$. First, assume that $g(x)$ is an increasing function. By the c.d.f. method,

$$F_y(w_y) = \Pr(y \le w_y) = \Pr\left(x \le g^{-1}(w_y)\right) = \int_{-\infty}^{g^{-1}(w_y)} f_x(s)\mathrm{d}s.$$

Differentiating both sides with respect to w_y, by Leibniz' rule, gives the required result. Alternatively, the change of variable of integration $t = g(s)$ gives

$$F_y(w_y) = \int_{-\infty}^{w_y} f_x\left(g^{-1}(t)\right) \mathrm{d}g^{-1}(t) = \int_{-\infty}^{w_y} f_x\left(g^{-1}(t)\right) \frac{\mathrm{d}g^{-1}(t)}{\mathrm{d}t}\mathrm{d}t \qquad (1)$$

which identifies $f_y(t)$ as the integrand. A variant of this alternative approach will be used in the vector case, later in the proof. Next, for $g(x)$ a decreasing function,

$$F_y(w_y) = \Pr(y \le w_y) = \Pr(x \ge g^{-1}(w_y)) = 1 - \int_{-\infty}^{g^{-1}(w_y)} f_x(s)\mathrm{d}s$$

and we get the required result by differentiating both sides. Notice that $\mathrm{d}g^{-1}(w_y)/\mathrm{d}w_y$ is negative in this case, because the function (hence its inverse) is decreasing in its argument, which explains the appearance of the absolute value in the transformation theorem. We have to be careful that, in general, $\boldsymbol{g}(\boldsymbol{x}) \le \boldsymbol{y}$ is *not* the same as either of $\boldsymbol{x} \le \boldsymbol{g}^{-1}(\boldsymbol{y})$ or $\boldsymbol{x} \ge \boldsymbol{g}^{-1}(\boldsymbol{y})$ in the vector case. For example,

$$\begin{pmatrix} -1 & 1 \\ 1 & 0 \end{pmatrix} \begin{pmatrix} x_1 \\ x_2 \end{pmatrix} \le \begin{pmatrix} 0 \\ 0 \end{pmatrix} \qquad (2)$$

is not equivalent to either

$$\begin{pmatrix} x_1 \\ x_2 \end{pmatrix} \le \begin{pmatrix} 0 \\ 0 \end{pmatrix} \quad \text{or} \quad \begin{pmatrix} x_1 \\ x_2 \end{pmatrix} \ge \begin{pmatrix} 0 \\ 0 \end{pmatrix}$$

because the regions of the plane $\mathbb{R}^2$ defined by these inequalities are all different.

We now assume that the relation holds for some m, where $m \ge 1$, and prove it for $m+1$. We decompose the joint density into the product of the marginal density for the last component times the conditional density for the first m components. Define the $(m+1) \times m$ selection matrix $\boldsymbol{C}_1$ and the $(m+1) \times 1$ vector $\boldsymbol{c}_2$ by

$$\boldsymbol{I}_{m+1} = \begin{pmatrix} \boldsymbol{I}_m & \boldsymbol{0}_m \\ \boldsymbol{0}'_m & 1 \end{pmatrix} = (\boldsymbol{C}_1, \boldsymbol{c}_2)$$

so that

$$\boldsymbol{x} := \begin{pmatrix} x_1 \\ \vdots \\ x_m \\ x_{m+1} \end{pmatrix} = \begin{pmatrix} \boldsymbol{C}'_1 \boldsymbol{x} \\ \boldsymbol{c}'_2 \boldsymbol{x} \end{pmatrix}$$

and similarly for the other vectors. We have

$$\begin{aligned} F_{\boldsymbol{y}}(\boldsymbol{w}_{\boldsymbol{y}}) &= \int_{\boldsymbol{g}(\boldsymbol{s}) \leq \boldsymbol{w}_{\boldsymbol{y}}} f_{\boldsymbol{x}}(\boldsymbol{s}) \mathrm{d}\boldsymbol{s} \\ &= \int_{B_2} f_{\boldsymbol{c}'_2 x}(\boldsymbol{c}'_2 \boldsymbol{s}) \int_{B_1} f_{\boldsymbol{C}'_1 \boldsymbol{x} | \boldsymbol{c}'_2 \boldsymbol{s}}(\boldsymbol{C}'_1 \boldsymbol{s}) \mathrm{d}(\boldsymbol{C}'_1 \boldsymbol{s}) \mathrm{d}(\boldsymbol{c}'_2 \boldsymbol{s}) \end{aligned} \tag{3}$$

where $B_2 := \{\boldsymbol{c}|'_2 \boldsymbol{s} : \boldsymbol{g}(\boldsymbol{s}) \leq \boldsymbol{w}_{\boldsymbol{y}}\}$ and $B_1 := \{\boldsymbol{C}'_1 \boldsymbol{s} : \boldsymbol{g}(\boldsymbol{s}) \leq \boldsymbol{w}_{\boldsymbol{y}}\}$. The transformation theorem holds for variates of dimensions 1 (by proof) and m (by induction assumption), so it can be applied to both densities in this formula.

We now need to work out the Jacobians of the two transformations

$$\boldsymbol{c}'_2 \boldsymbol{x} \mapsto \boldsymbol{c}'_2 \boldsymbol{y} \quad \text{and} \quad \boldsymbol{C}'_1 \boldsymbol{x} \,(\text{given } \boldsymbol{c}'_2 \boldsymbol{x}) \mapsto \boldsymbol{C}'_1 \boldsymbol{y} \,(\text{given } \boldsymbol{c}'_2 \boldsymbol{y})$$

where $\boldsymbol{x} = \boldsymbol{g}^{-1}(\boldsymbol{y})$ and, similarly to (1), evaluated at the point $(\boldsymbol{x}, \boldsymbol{y}) = (\boldsymbol{s}, \boldsymbol{t})$.

To obtain the Jacobians of these transformations, a Taylor-series linearization near the point $\boldsymbol{y} = \boldsymbol{t}$ gives

$$\boldsymbol{x} = \boldsymbol{g}^{-1}(\boldsymbol{y}) = \boldsymbol{g}^{-1}(\boldsymbol{t}) + \boldsymbol{A}(\boldsymbol{y} - \boldsymbol{t}) + \boldsymbol{r}$$

where

$$\boldsymbol{A} := \begin{pmatrix} \boldsymbol{A}_{11} & \boldsymbol{a}_{12} \\ \boldsymbol{a}'_{21} & a_{22} \end{pmatrix} = \frac{\partial \boldsymbol{g}^{-1}(\boldsymbol{t})}{\partial \boldsymbol{t}'}$$

and $\boldsymbol{r}$ contains the remainder terms. This linearization can be rewritten as $\boldsymbol{z} = \boldsymbol{A}\boldsymbol{y}$, where $\boldsymbol{z}$ differs from $\boldsymbol{x}$ by a constant and by $\boldsymbol{r}$. For the first integral of (3), the Jacobian is simply

$$\left.\frac{\partial x_{m+1}}{\partial y_{m+1}}\right|_{y=t} = \frac{\partial z_{m+1}}{\partial y_{m+1}} = a_{22}.$$

For the second integral, matters are more elaborate because of the dependence of the integral on $\boldsymbol{c}_2'\boldsymbol{s}$ (that is on s_{m+1}). We write

$$\boldsymbol{A}^{-1} = \begin{pmatrix} \boldsymbol{B}_{11} & \boldsymbol{b}_{12} \\ \boldsymbol{b}_{21}' & b_{22} \end{pmatrix}$$

where $\boldsymbol{B}_{11} = \left(\boldsymbol{A}_{11} - \frac{1}{a_{22}}\boldsymbol{a}_{12}\boldsymbol{a}_{21}'\right)^{-1}$. Then, $\boldsymbol{C}_1'\boldsymbol{A}^{-1} = (\boldsymbol{B}_{11}, \boldsymbol{b}_{12})$, and hence

$$\boldsymbol{C}_1'\boldsymbol{y} = \boldsymbol{C}_1'\boldsymbol{A}^{-1}\boldsymbol{z} = \boldsymbol{B}_{11}\boldsymbol{C}_1'\boldsymbol{z} + \boldsymbol{b}_{12}\boldsymbol{c}_2'\boldsymbol{z}.$$

Since we have conditioned on $\boldsymbol{c}_2'\boldsymbol{x}$ (that is on x_{m+1}) in the inner integral of (3), it can be treated as a constant when calculating the Jacobian, and

$$\left.\frac{\partial(\boldsymbol{C}_1'\boldsymbol{x})}{\partial(\boldsymbol{C}_1'\boldsymbol{y})'}\right|_{y=t} = \frac{\partial(\boldsymbol{C}_1'\boldsymbol{z})}{\partial(\boldsymbol{C}_1'\boldsymbol{y})'} = \boldsymbol{B}_{11}^{-1}.$$

Substituting both Jacobians into (3) yields:

$$\begin{aligned} F_{\boldsymbol{y}}(\boldsymbol{w}_{\boldsymbol{y}}) &= \int_{\boldsymbol{c}_2'\boldsymbol{t} \le \boldsymbol{c}_2'\boldsymbol{w}_{\boldsymbol{y}}} |a_{22}| f_{\boldsymbol{c}_2'\boldsymbol{x}}\left(\boldsymbol{c}_2'\boldsymbol{g}^{-1}(\boldsymbol{t})\right) \\ &\quad \times \int_{\boldsymbol{C}_1'\boldsymbol{t} \le \boldsymbol{C}_1'\boldsymbol{w}_{\boldsymbol{y}}} \left|\det\left(\boldsymbol{B}_{11}^{-1}\right)\right| f_{\boldsymbol{C}_1'\boldsymbol{x}|\boldsymbol{c}_2'\boldsymbol{g}^{-1}(\boldsymbol{t})}\left(\boldsymbol{C}_1'\boldsymbol{g}^{-1}(\boldsymbol{t})\right) \mathrm{d}\boldsymbol{t} \\ &= \int_{\boldsymbol{t} \le \boldsymbol{w}_{\boldsymbol{y}}} |\det(\boldsymbol{A})| f_{\boldsymbol{x}}\left(\boldsymbol{g}^{-1}(\boldsymbol{t})\right) \mathrm{d}\boldsymbol{t} \end{aligned}$$

because $f_{\boldsymbol{c}_2'\boldsymbol{x}}(\boldsymbol{c}_2'\boldsymbol{s}) f_{\boldsymbol{C}_1'\boldsymbol{x}|\boldsymbol{c}_2'\boldsymbol{s}}(\boldsymbol{C}_1'\boldsymbol{s}) = f_{\boldsymbol{x}}(\boldsymbol{s})$, and

$$a_{22}\det\left(B_{11}^{-1}\right) = \det(\boldsymbol{A}) \equiv \det\left(\frac{\partial \boldsymbol{g}^{-1}(\boldsymbol{t})}{\partial \boldsymbol{t}'}\right).$$

The result follows by differentiating both sides of $F_{\boldsymbol{y}}(\boldsymbol{w}_{\boldsymbol{y}})$ with respect to $\boldsymbol{w}_{\boldsymbol{y}}$, which is equivalent to evaluating the integrand at $\boldsymbol{t} = \boldsymbol{w}_{\boldsymbol{y}}$. Notice that we have assumed implicitly that $a_{22} \neq 0$ and $\det(\boldsymbol{B}_{11}^{-1}) \neq 0$. This is not a restrictive assumption since, for $\det(\boldsymbol{A}) \neq 0$, we can always find a permutation of the elements of $\boldsymbol{x}$ or $\boldsymbol{y}$ to achieve this; for example see (2). The absolute value of the determinant of a permutation (hence orthogonal) matrix is always 1, so the result is unaltered.

We can interpret the transformation theorem in a similar way to Leibniz' rule. The Jacobian factor provides the change in the volume of the domain covered by the limits of integration of $\boldsymbol{x}$ as $\boldsymbol{y}$ changes infinitesimally: the determinant is the volume of the parallelotope of dimension $m+1$ formed by the vectors $\partial x_i/\partial \boldsymbol{y}'$, evaluated at $\boldsymbol{y} = \boldsymbol{w}_{\boldsymbol{y}}$ and $\boldsymbol{x} = \boldsymbol{g}^{-1}(\boldsymbol{w}_{\boldsymbol{y}})$.

13 On the Joint Density of the Sum and Sum of Squares of Non-Negative Random Variables

Grant Hillier

1 Introduction

In statistical models for which either or both of the statistics

$$S_{n1} = \Sigma_{i=1}^{n} x_i, \text{ and } S_{n2} = \Sigma_{i=1}^{n} x_i^2$$

is(are) minimal sufficient, the joint density of (S_{n1}, S_{n2}) is likely to be of interest. If the sample space for $x = (x_1, x_2, \ldots, x_n)'$ is all of R^n, this joint density is easily obtained, but if, as is frequently the case, the sample space consists of just non-negative values of x, that is R_+^n, the problem is far from trivial, and there appears to be no known closed-form expression for the joint density in the literature. This chapter provides an expression for that joint density. In doing so we shall see that the density cannot be characterized by a single function, but has a different functional form on each of $n - 1$ disjoint intervals. This situation arises elsewhere, and has been discussed by, among others, Mulholland (1965, 1970). Examples with similar characteristics to the problem studied here include the statistic $Q_1 = y'Ay/y'y$, with $y \sim N(0, I_n)$ (studied by many authors, but see in particular von Neumann, 1941; Koopmans, 1942; Anderson, 1971; Saldanha and Tomei, 1996; and Hillier, 2001), and the more general form $Q_2 = y'Ay/y'By$, again with $y \sim N(0, I_n)$ and B positive definite (also studied by many, but see in particular Forchini, 2002).

Our approach to the problem is differential-geometric in character. In particular, our starting point will be Theorem 8.3.1 from Tjur (1981), which gives an expression for the density of a suitably behaved statistic as a surface integral over the manifold in the sample space on which the statistic is constant (see also Hillier and Armstrong, 1999). For a general, continuously differentiable, p-dimensional statistic $S = S(x)$ defined on an open subset X of R^n, and having the property that the $p \times n$ matrix $DS(x) = \{\partial S_i(x)/\partial x_j\}_{i=1,\ldots,p}^{j=1,\ldots,n}$ has rank p whenever $S(x) = s$, the s-level set of S,

$$M(s) = \{x; x \in X, S(x) = s\} \tag{1}$$

is an $(n - p)$-dimensional manifold embedded in R^n (Spivak (1965), Theorem 5-1, p. 111). The density of S at the point s is then given by:

$$pdf_S(s) = \int_{M(s)} |DS(x)DS(x)'|^{-\frac{1}{2}} pdf(x)(dM(s)) \tag{2}$$

where $pdf(x)$ is the density of the underlying random vector x, $|\cdot|$ denotes the determinant of the indicated matrix, and $dM(s)$ denotes the (canonical) volume element on $M(s)$ (defined more precisely below).

For $S(x) = (S_{n1}, S_{n2})'$ it is easy to see that the hypotheses above are satisfied, and that $|DS(x)DS(x)'| = 4(ns_2 - s_1^2)$ is constant on $M(s)$, which in this case is an $(n-2)$-dimensional manifold. Here, of course, we must have $s_1^2 < ns_2$ (Cauchy–Schwarz). And if, as we shall assume, $pdf(x)$ is a member of the exponential family with minimal sufficient statistic S, the density of x (with respect to Lebesgue measure) has the form

$$pdf(x; \theta) = \exp\{\theta_1 S_{n1} + \theta_2 S_{n2} + \kappa(\theta)\}, \; x \in X \subseteq R^n \tag{3}$$

and is therefore also constant on $M(s)$. In this case (2) gives at once,

$$pdf_S(s; \theta) = [4(ns_2 - s_1^2)]^{-\frac{1}{2}} \exp\{\theta_1 s_1 + \theta_2 s_2 + \kappa(\theta)\} \int_{M(s)} (dM(s)). \tag{4}$$

The integral in (4) is simply the surface content of the $(n - 2)$-dimensional manifold

$$M(s) = \{x : x \in X, \Sigma_{i=1}^n x_i = s_1, \Sigma_{i=1}^n x_i^2 = s_2\} \tag{5}$$

that is, that part of the surface formed by the intersection of the hyperplane $\Sigma_{i=1}^n x_i = s_1$ with the hypersphere $\Sigma_{i=1}^n x_i^2 = s_2$ that lies in X. In case X is all of R^n this is easily evaluated because the hypersphere $\Sigma_{i=1}^n x_i^2 = s_2$ intersects the hyperplane $\Sigma_{i=1}^n x_i = s_1$ in an $(n - 1)$-dimensional hypersphere of radius $\sqrt{(ns_2 - s_1^2)/n}$, and the content of this surface is simply the surface content of an $(n-1)$-sphere with this radius, namely,

$$C_{n-1}[(ns_2 - s_1^2)/n]^{(n-2)/2} \tag{6}$$

where $C_k = 2\pi^{\frac{k}{2}}/\Gamma\left(\frac{k}{2}\right)$ denotes the surface content of the unit sphere in k dimensions.

Thus, equation (4) immediately yields, for instance, familiar results for the case where the x_i are $i.i.d.$ $N(\mu, \sigma^2)$ (which, of course, are usually expressed in terms of the joint density of S_{n1} and $S_{n2}^* = (nS_{n2} - S_{n1}^2)/n)$.

However, in the case where the x_i are restricted to be non-negative (as, for instance, in the censored or truncated normal model, or when the x_i are $i.i.d.$ with an exponential distribution, see below), the manifold $M(s)$ is much more complicated: it consists of that part of the surface of the hypersphere $\Sigma_{i=1}^n x_i^2 = s_2$ that intersects the hyperplane $\Sigma_{i=1}^n x_i = s_1$ *in the non-negative orthant*. Thus, our problem will be to evaluate the integral in (4) for this case. Naturally, the marginal densities of S_{n1} and S_{n2} can be obtained from the joint density, but may also be obtainable by direct application of (2) with $S(x)$ one-dimensional. Whether or not this latter approach is straightforward depends on the context.

Before proceeding, we note an important implication of (4). For any two members of the exponential family (3), indexed by parameter vectors θ_a and θ_b respectively, (4) holds for both. Eliminating the surface integral from this pair of equations we obtain the result:

$$pdf_S(s;\theta_b) = \left[\frac{pdf(x;\theta_b)}{pdf(x;\theta_a)}\right] pdf_S(s;\theta_a) \tag{7}$$

(*cf.*, Durbin (1980)). That is, the density of S induced by any member of this family can be (trivially) obtained from that induced by any other. Thus, for instance, the density of S under censored normal sampling, when the conditional density for $n \geq 2$ uncensored observations, given n, is reasonably complicated (and both S_{n1} and S_{n2} are minimal sufficient) can be obtained from that under the much simpler independent exponential sampling (when S_{n1} alone is sufficient).

The plan of the chapter is as follows. In section 2 we first simplify the manifold over which the integral is to be evaluated slightly, and mention some of its more obvious properties. We then provide some background information on, first, the regular simplex in k dimensions (because this turns out to be the key to the result), and, second, integration on manifolds. The main result, and its derivation, are given in section 3, and section 4 briefly discusses its application to the censored normal model.

The more routine and tedious aspects of the derivation of the main result are relegated to the Appendix.

2 Preliminaries

2.1 *Simplifications*

The manifold $M(s)$ may be simplified slightly by replacing the x_i by x_i/s_1, $i = 1,\ldots,n$. $M(s)$ is thereby transformed into the manifold $M(u) = \{x > 0, \Sigma_{i=1}^n x_i = 1, \Sigma_{i=1}^n x_i^2 = u\}$, where $u = s_2/s_1^2$, and it is easy to check that under this rescaling the volume elements, $dM(u)$ and $dM(s)$, are related by $dM(s) = s_1^{n-2}dM(u)$. We may therefore confine attention to the integral:

$$V_n^*(u) = \int_{M(u)} (dM(u)) \tag{8}$$

where

$$M(u) = \{x > 0, \Sigma_{i=1}^n x_i = 1, \Sigma_{i=1}^n x_i^2 = u\}. \tag{9}$$

Note that if, in (4), $\theta_2 = 0$ (so that the x_i are independent exponential variates), and we transform from (S_{n1}, S_{n2}) to (S_{n1}, U_n), with $U_n = S_{n2}/S_{n1}^2$, we have at once from (4) that S_{n1} and U_n are independent (because the integral does not involve s_1), that S_{n1} is exponentially distributed, and that $pdf_{U_n}(u) = [4(nu-1)]^{-\frac{1}{2}} V_n^*(u)$. This result is useful in its own right, and also for checking the results to follow. Also, in view of (2), $V_n^*(u)$ is proportional to the density of the sum of squares $U_n = \Sigma_{i=1}^n x_i^2$, at the point $U_n = u$, when x is uniformly distributed on the set $X = \{x; x > 0, \Sigma_{i=1}^n x_i = 1\}$.

In the case $n = 2$ it is easy to see that, for $1/2 < u < 1$, the circle $x_1^2 + x_2^2 = u$ cuts the line $x_1 + x_2 = 1$ in two points in the non-negative quadrant, and in this case we take $V_2^*(u) = 2$. We henceforth assume that $n \geq 3$. We denote the *surface* of a hypersphere in k-dimensions with radius ρ by $S_k(\rho)$. $S_k(\rho)$ is itself a $(k-1)$-dimensional manifold, and, as above, we denote the content of the surface $S_k(1)$ by:

$$C_k = 2\pi^{\frac{k}{2}}/\Gamma\left(\tfrac{k}{2}\right). \tag{10}$$

We shall also need to integrate over (parts of) the *interior* of various hyperspheres. With a slight abuse of terminology, we refer to the interior of the hypersphere with the same radius and centre as $S_k(\rho)$ as the interior of $S_k(\rho)$.

The squared distance from the origin to the hyperplane $\Sigma_{i=1}^n x_i = 1$ is n^{-1}, and the hyperplane meets the coordinate axes where each $x_i = 1$, so the hypersphere $S_n(\sqrt{u}) = \{x \in R^n;\ x'x = u\}$ can only intersect the hyperplane $\Sigma_{i=1}^n x_i = 1$ in the non-negative orthant if $n^{-1} < u < 1$. That is,

Proposition 1 $V_n^*(u) = 0$ for $u \leq n^{-1}$ or $u \geq 1$.
(At $u = n^{-1}$ and $u = 1$, $S_n(\sqrt{u})$ intersects the hyperplane in one point, and in n isolated points, respectively. Thus, in these cases $M(u)$ is a 0-dimensional manifold, and has content zero.)

Now, the hyperplane $\Sigma_{i=1}^n x_i = 1$ intersects the non-negative orthant in a *regular simplex* of dimension $n-1$, Σ_{n-1} say, with sides of length $\sqrt{2}$. The vertices of this simplex lie on the surface of an $(n-1)$-dimensional hypersphere whose centre, c_{n-1} say, is at the point on the hyperplane nearest the origin (c_{n-1} is called the *centroid* of Σ_{n-1}). Since the hyperplane is orthogonal to the line joining the origin to c_{n-1}, for any point x in the simplex, $x'x = n^{-1} + \rho_{n-1}^2$, where ρ_{n-1}^2 is the squared distance from x to c_{n-1}. Thus, the intersection of $S_n(\sqrt{u})$ with the hyperplane $\Sigma_{i=1}^n x_i = 1$ consists of that part of the $S_{n-1}(\rho_{n-1})$ (with centre at c_{n-1}) that lies *inside* the simplex Σ_{n-1}, with

$$\rho_{n-1} = \sqrt{u - n^{-1}}. \tag{11}$$

That is:

Proposition 2 For $n^{-1} < u < 1$, $V_n^*(u)$ is the content of that part of the surface of an $(n-1)$-dimensional hypersphere with radius ρ_{n-1} and centre at the centroid of Σ_{n-1} that lies inside Σ_{n-1}. Denoting this quantity by $V_{n-1}(\rho_{n-1})$, $V_n^*(u) = V_{n-1}(\rho_{n-1})$.

Before seeking to evaluate $V_{n-1}(\rho_{n-1})$ for $n^{-1} < u < 1$ we briefly describe those properties of the regular simplex that bear on the calculation.

2.2 *The Regular Simplex*

A k-dimensional regular simplex, Σ_k, is determined by $k+1$ points (its *vertices*), each equidistant from the remainder. Thus, the vertices lie on the surface of a k-dimensional hypersphere, the centre of which is the *centroid* of the simplex, c_k say. In the case of a simplex of side length s, the lines joining the centroid to the vertices are of length $r_k = s\sqrt{k/2(k+1)}$, the radius of the hypersphere containing the simplex. In our case, $s = \sqrt{2}$, so in future we take $r_k = \sqrt{k/(k+1)}$, and Σ_k will always denote a regular simplex of side-length $\sqrt{2}$.

Each choice of k vertices from the original $(k+1)$ determines a *face* of Σ_k, itself a $(k-1)$-dimensional regular simplex with the same side length as the original Σ_k. The distance from the centroid c_k of Σ_k to any of its faces is:

$$f_k = 1/\sqrt{k(k+1)}. \tag{12}$$

Thus, f_k is the radius of the largest hypersphere (with centre at the centroid of Σ_k) that lies entirely inside Σ_k. Setting $k = n-1$, the entire surface $S_{n-1}(\rho_{n-1})$ lies inside Σ_{n-1} if $0 < \rho_{n-1} < f_{n-1}$, or $n^{-1} < u < (n-1)^{-1}$, so we can state our first result for $V_{n-1}(\rho_{n-1})$ immediately:

Case 1 For $n^{-1} < u < (n-1)^{-1}$,

$$V_n^*(u) = V_{n-1}(\rho_{n-1}) = C_{n-1}\rho_{n-1}^{n-2} \tag{13}$$

These results for a face determined by k points generalize as follows. Any $r+1 \geq 1$ of the original $k+1$ vertices of Σ_k determine a regular simplex, Σ_r, of dimension r, with the same side length as Σ_k. We call this an r-face of Σ_k; there are obviously $\binom{k+1}{r+1}$ distinct such r-faces. The $k+1$ 0-faces are single points, the vertices of Σ_k, while the $k(k+1)/2$ 1-faces are line segments, its sides. The line joining the origin (the centroid of the original Σ_k) to the centroid of any r-face is orthogonal to all points in the r-face, and has length

$$f_{k,r} = \sqrt{\frac{k}{k+1} - \frac{r}{r+1}}. \tag{14}$$

Note that the f_k defined above are, in this notation, the $f_{k,k-1}$. We omit the extra subscript for the special case $r = k-1$.

Since $f_{k,r}$ increases as r decreases, *faces of lower dimension are further from the centroid of the original simplex.* Thus, an $S_k(\rho)$ with centre at the centroid of Σ_k intersects just those r-faces for which $\rho > f_{k,r}$. In particular, for $f_{k,r} < \rho < f_{k,r-1}$, $S_k(\rho)$ intersects all r-faces, but no r'-face with $r' < r$. That is, $S_k(\rho)$ lies "inside" the set of $(r-1)$-faces of Σ_k, but partly "outside" the set of its r-faces.

Setting $k = n-1$ and $\rho = \rho_{n-1} = \sqrt{u - n^{-1}}$, the interval $f_{n-1,r} < \rho_{n-1} < f_{n-1,r-1}$ corresponds to the interval $(r+1)^{-1} < u < r^{-1}$.

As u passes through a point seperating two of these intervals, the surface $S_{n-1}(\rho_{n-1})$ passes "outside" a new set of r-faces of Σ_{n-1} (but remains "inside" the set of lower dimensional faces), and $V_{n-1}(\rho_{n-1})$ thus becomes a different function of u. Therefore:

Proposition 3 $V_n^*(u)$, thought of as a function of u, has a different functional form on each of the $n-1$ intervals:

$$(r+1)^{-1} < u < r^{-1}\ ,\ r = 1, \ldots, n-1. \tag{15}$$

Our approach to the evaluation of the content of $M(u)$ will be based on the observation that both the surface of an $S_k(\rho)$, and its interior, can be partitioned into disjoint "pieces" corresponding to the faces of Σ_k, and that points in R^k can be assigned local coordinates which reflect that fact. Before introducing this partitioning we briefly describe the key ideas relating to integration on manifolds that will be needed later.

2.3 *Surface Integration*

The surfaces we are concerned with are *differentiable manifolds* embedded in R^k (where, initially, $k = n-1$). In the case of a manifold M of dimension $p < k$, this means that, in the neighbourhood of each point $x \in M$, there is an open set $A \subset R^k$ containing x, an open set $B \subset R^p$, and a one-to-one differentiable function $f : B \mapsto R^k$ such that (a) $f(B) = M \cap A$, (b) $f^{-1} : f(B) \mapsto B$ is continuous, and (c) the matrix $Df(y) = \{\partial f_i(y)/\partial y_j\}_{i=1,k}^{j=1,p}$ has rank p for each $y \in B$. Such a function is called a *local coordinate chart* for M near x. Given a local coordinate chart f near a point $x \in M$, the (canonical) volume element on M, (dM), is defined locally by:

$$(dM) = \left|Df(y)'Df(y)\right|^{\frac{1}{2}} (dy) \tag{16}$$

where (dy) denotes ordinary Lebesgue measure on R^p. M can be equipped with a system of such (overlapping) local coordinate charts (an *atlas*) that cover it, so that (dM) is well-defined everywhere on M, and one can therefore integrate functions defined on M in a natural way. It is straightforward to show that the integral of a function defined on the manifold is independent of the system of local coordinate charts used.

Now, the surface of a simplex Σ_k (that is, the set of its $(k-1)$-faces) is evidently in one-to-one correspondence with a surface $S_k(\rho)$ centered at the centroid of Σ_k. In particular, the $(k+1)$ faces of Σ_k partition $S_k(\rho)$

into $(k+1)$ disjoint pieces, each piece being in the "direction" (from the centroid of Σ_k) of a single face. (We say that points in R^k are *in the direction of* a particular face of Σ_k if the line joining the centroid of Σ_k to the point in question intersects that face, or would do so if extended positively). Thus, we can use the faces of Σ_k to construct (local) coordinates for points on $S_k(\rho)$, as follows.

Choose one $(k-1)$-face of Σ_k, a Σ_{k-1}. Coordinate axes in R^k, with c_k as origin, can be chosen so that this face is parallel to one axis, say the first, so that the first coordinate of each point on the Σ_{k-1} is constant, and this is obviously f_k, the length of the line joining c_k to the centroid of the face, c_{k-1}. Let $y_{k-1} \in R^{k-1}$ denote the coordinates of a point in the R^{k-1} containing Σ_{k-1}, with its centroid, c_{k-1}, as origin. Then points in R^k in the direction of Σ_{k-1} can be written in the form:

$$x = \alpha \begin{pmatrix} f_k \\ y_{k-1} \end{pmatrix}, \ \alpha > 0, \ y_{k-1} \in \Sigma_{k-1} \tag{17}$$

and it is easy to see that for points of this form on $S_k(\rho)$, $\alpha = \rho(f_k^2 + y_{k-1}'y_{k-1})^{-\frac{1}{2}}$. This defines, locally (for points in the direction of one $(k-1)$-face of Σ_k), a coordinate chart for $S_k(\rho)$ given by:

$$x = f(y_{k-1}) = \rho(f_k^2 + y_{k-1}'y_{k-1})^{-\frac{1}{2}} \begin{pmatrix} f_k \\ y_{k-1} \end{pmatrix}, y_{k-1} \in \Sigma_{k-1} \tag{18}$$

and it is straightforward to check that, with these coordinates, the volume element defined in (16) is given by:

$$(dS_k(\rho)) = f_k \rho^{k-1}(f_k^2 + y_{k-1}'y_{k-1})^{-\frac{k}{2}}(dy_{k-1}). \tag{19}$$

Clearly, the union of such coordinate charts over all $(k+1)$ faces of Σ_k completely covers $S_k(\rho)$, and, by construction, they overlap only in spaces of dimension $(k-2)$ (the Σ_{k-2} where two $(k-1)$-faces intersect), which have ($(k-1)$-dimensional Lebesgue) measure zero.

In fact, if we replace ρ by $r > 0$, in (18), and allow r to vary, *all* points in $x \in R^k$ in the direction of one face of Σ_k can be represented uniquely in the form:

$$x = r(f_k^2 + y_{k-1}'y_{k-1})^{-\frac{1}{2}} \begin{pmatrix} f_k \\ y_{k-1} \end{pmatrix}, \ r > 0, \ y_{k-1} \in \Sigma_{k-1} \tag{20}$$

and it is easy to see that the Euclidean volume element (Lebesgue measure), (dx), on R^k factors (locally) as:

$$(dx) = f_k r^{k-1}(f_k^2 + y'_{k-1}y_{k-1})^{-\frac{k}{2}} dr(dy_{k-1})$$
$$= (dS_k(r))dr, \; r > 0, \; y_{k-1} \in \Sigma_{k-1}. \tag{21}$$

That is, locally, Lebesgue measure on R^k factors into the product of a measure on part of the surface of the hypersphere $S_k(r)$ and Lebesgue measure on R^+. This, of course, is well-known from the polar coordinate representation of points in R^k. In the present context, though, the coordinates (20) prove more useful, and will enable us to integrate over the interior of an S_k, as well as over its surface.

3 Main Results

Consider an $S_k(\rho)$ with centre at the centroid of a Σ_k, which we take as the origin, and with $f_k < \rho < r_k$, so that part, but not all of, $S_k(\rho)$ lies inside Σ_k. We denote the surface content of $S_k(\rho)$ that is inside Σ_k by $V_k(\rho)$, and its *complement*, the surface content *outside* Σ_k, by:

$$\overline{V}_k(\rho) = C_k\rho^{k-1} - V_k(\rho). \tag{22}$$

Clearly, because of the symmetry of both Σ_k and $S_k(\rho)$, to evaluate $\overline{V}_k(\rho)$, and hence $V_k(\rho)$, we need only consider the content of $S_k(\rho)$ that is in the direction of, but outside, *one* face of Σ_k.

The surface, $S_k(\rho)$ intersects each face of Σ_k in (at least part of) a hyperspherical surface $S_{k-1}(\rho_{k-1})$ centered at the centroid of that face, and having radius $\rho_{k-1} = \sqrt{\rho^2 - f_k^2}$. If $\rho_{k-1} < f_{k-1}$ each such $S_{k-1}(\rho_{k-1})$ lies entirely inside its respective Σ_{k-1}. But if $\rho_{k-1} > f_{k-1}$ each $S_{k-1}(\rho_{k-1})$, in turn, intersects each of the faces of the Σ_{k-1} in (at least part of) yet another (lower dimensional) hypersphere $S_{k-2}(\rho_{k-2})$, with $\rho_{k-2} = \sqrt{\rho_{k-1}^2 - f_{k-1}^2}$, and so on. The radii of the successively lower-dimensional hyperspheres ocurring in this process are given by the recursive relation:

$$\rho_{k-r-1}^2 = \rho_{k-r}^2 - f_{k-r}^2, \; r = 0, \ldots, k-1, \; \rho_k \equiv \rho. \tag{23}$$

For ρ in the interval $f_{k,k-r} < \rho < f_{k,k-r-1}$, $\rho_{k-s} > f_{k-s}$ for $s = 1, \ldots, r-1$, but $\rho_{k-r} < f_{k-r}$. That is, in the above process it is not until we arrive at a face of dimension $k-r$, a Σ_{k-r}, that the entire $S_{k-r}(\rho_{k-r})$ lies inside the Σ_{k-r}. This is the basis of the calculations to follow.

Suppose first that $f_k < \rho < f_{k,k-2}$, so that $\rho > f_k$ but $\rho_{k-1} < f_{k-1}$. Then $S_k(\rho)$ intersects each $(k-1)$-face of the original Σ_k, but none of the r-faces with $r < k-1$. Thus, in the direction of a single face of Σ_k, the part of $S_k(\rho)$ outside that face is a (complete) "cap" on $S_k(\rho)$. Using the coordinates (18), we therefore have, for the content *outside* a single face,

$$f_k \rho^{k-1} \int_{y'_{k-1}y_{k-1} \leq \rho^2_{k-1}} (f_k^2 + y'_{k-1}y_{k-1})^{-\frac{k}{2}} (dy_{k-1})$$

$$= f_k C_{k-1} \rho^{k-1} \int_0^{\rho_{k-1}} r_1^{k-2} (f_k^2 + r_1^2)^{-\frac{k}{2}} dr_1 \tag{24}$$

on converting y_{k-1} to polar coordinates and integrating over the surface $S_{k-1}(1)$. Note that the integral here is over the *interior* of $S_{k-1}(\rho_{k-1})$. Adding these $(k+1)$ equal components, and subtracting the result from the original surface content of $S_k(\rho)$, we obtain for $f_k < \rho < f_{k,k-2}$:

$$V_k(\rho) = C_k \rho^{k-1} - (k+1) f_k C_{k-1} \rho^{k-1} \int_0^{\rho_{k-1}} r_1^{k-2} (f_k^2 + r_1^2)^{-\frac{k}{2}} dr_1. \tag{25}$$

The integral here can, of course, be evaluated explicitly, but we defer the evaluation of all integrals until later.

Applying this result for the case $k = n-1$, $\rho = \rho_{n-1}$, with $f_{n-1} < \rho_{n-1} < f_{n-1,n-3}$, we obtain:

Case 2 For $(n-1)^{-1} < u < (n-2)^{-1}$,

$$V_{n-1}(\rho_{n-1}) = C_{n-1} \rho_{n-1}^{n-2} - n f_{n-1} C_{n-2} \rho_{n-1}^{n-2} \int_0^{\rho_{n-2}} r_1^{n-3} (f_{n-1}^2 + r_1^2)^{-\frac{n-1}{2}} dr_1. \tag{26}$$

where $\rho^2_{n-2} = \rho^2_{n-1} - f^2_{n-1} = u - (n-1)^{-1}$.

Suppose next that $f_{k,k-2} < \rho < f_{k,k-3}$, so that $\rho_{k-1} > f_{k-1}$, but $0 < \rho_{k-2} < f_{k-2}$. In this case equation (24) *overstates* the content of $S_k(\rho)$ outside Σ_k but in the direction of one of its faces, because only part of the (interior of) $S_{k-1}(\rho_{k-1})$ over which the integral in the first line of (24) is evaluated actually lies inside the Σ_{k-1}: we need to restrict the integral in the first line of (24) to the part of the interior of $S_{k-1}(\rho_{k-1})$ that is inside the face.

To calculate the content to be *excluded* from (24) we can proceed much as above: we now partition the interior of $S_{k-1}(\rho_{k-1})$ into k pieces, each piece corresponding to one face of the Σ_{k-1}, a Σ_{k-2}. In one of these, we use the analogue of the coordinates (20) for y_{k-1} itself. That is, we put, for points y_{k-1} in the direction of one of the faces of Σ_{k-1},

$$y_{k-1} = r_1(f_{k-1}^2 + y_{k-2}'y_{k-2})^{-\frac{1}{2}} \begin{pmatrix} f_{k-1} \\ y_{k-2} \end{pmatrix}, \; r_1 > 0, \; y_{k-2} \in \Sigma_{k-2} \tag{27}$$

and, from (21), the volume element becomes:

$$(dy_{k-1}) = f_{k-1} r_1^{k-2} (f_{k-1}^2 + y_{k-2}'y_{k-2})^{-\frac{k-1}{2}} dr_1 (dy_{k-2}). \tag{28}$$

In these coordinates, points y_{k-1} are in the interior of $S_{k-1}(\rho_{k-1})$ if $r_1 < \rho_{k-1}$. And, since the $S_{k-1}(\rho_{k-1})$ intersects a face of Σ_{k-1}, a Σ_{k-2}, in an entire $S_{k-2}(\rho_{k-2})$ (under the hypothesis $\rho_{k-2} < f_{k-2}$), such points are outside Σ_{k-1} in the direction of one of its faces if $y_{k-2}'y_{k-2} < \rho_{k-2}^2$ and $r_1 > \sqrt{f_{k-1}^2 + y_{k-2}'y_{k-2}}$. The latter inequality arises because the radius of the hyperspherical surface with centre at the centroid c_k of the original Σ_k and containing the point $y_{k-2} \in \Sigma_{k-2}$ is $\sqrt{f_{k-1}^2 + y_{k-2}'y_{k-2}}$, while the point (27) lies on a hypersphere of radius r_1, and is therefore outside Σ_{k-1} (in the direction of this face) only when $r_1 > \sqrt{f_{k-1}^2 + y_{k-2}'y_{k-2}}$. Hence, in these coordinates, the portion of the interior of $S_{k-1}(\rho_{k-1})$ in (24) to be excluded is, for each of the k faces of Σ_{k-1}, of the form:

$$\{(r_1, y_{k-2}); \sqrt{f_{k-1}^2 + y_{k-2}'y_{k-2}} < r_1 < \rho_{k-1}, \; y_{k-2}'y_{k-2} < \rho_{k-2}^2\}$$

so that, for each $(k-2)$-face of the Σ_{k-1}, the content to be excluded from (24) is:

$$\begin{aligned} & f_k f_{k-1} \rho^{k-1} \int_{y_{k-2}'y_{k-2} \le \rho_{k-2}^2} \int_{\sqrt{f_{k-1}^2 + y_{k-2}'y_{k-2}}}^{\rho_{k-1}} r_1^{k-2} (f_k^2 + r_1^2)^{-\frac{k}{2}} \\ & \times (f_{k-1}^2 + y_{k-2}'y_{k-2})^{-\frac{k-1}{2}} dr_1 (dy_{k-2}) \\ & \quad = f_k f_{k-1} C_{k-2} \rho^{k-1} \int_0^{\rho_{k-2}} \int_{\sqrt{f_{k-1}^2 + r_2^2}}^{\rho_{k-1}} r_1^{k-2} r_2^{k-3} \\ & \qquad \times (f_k^2 + r_1^2)^{-\frac{k}{2}} (f_{k-1}^2 + r_2^2)^{-\frac{k-1}{2}} dr_1 dr_2 \end{aligned} \tag{29}$$

on again converting y_{k-2} to polar coordinates and integrating over $S_{k-2}(1)$. Since, for each $(k-1)$-face of Σ_k, there are k such $(k-2)$-faces, we have for $f_{k,k-2} < \rho < f_{k,k-3}$:

$$V_k(\rho) = C_k\rho^{k-1} - (k+1)f_kC_{k-1}\rho^{k-1}\int_0^{\rho_{k-1}} r_1^{k-2}(f_k^2+r_1^2)^{-\frac{k}{2}}\,dr_1$$

$$+ k(k+1)f_kf_{k-1}C_{k-2}\rho^{k-1}\int_0^{\rho_{k-2}}\int_{\sqrt{f_{k-1}^2+r_2^2}}^{\rho_{k-1}} r_1^{k-2}r_2^{k-3}$$

$$\times (f_k^2+r_1^2)^{-\frac{k}{2}}(f_{k-1}^2+r_2^2)^{-\frac{k-1}{2}}\,dr_1\,dr_2. \tag{30}$$

Applying this result for the case $k = n-1$, $\rho_{n-1} = \sqrt{u - n^{-1}}$, we have:

Case 3 For $(n-2)^{-1} < u < (n-3)^{-1}$,

$$V_{n-1}(\rho_{n-1}) = C_{n-1}\rho_{n-1}^{n-2} - nf_{n-1}C_{n-2}\rho_{n-1}^{n-2}\int_0^{\rho_{n-2}} r_1^{n-3}(f_{n-1}^2+r_1^2)^{-\frac{n-1}{2}}\,dr_1$$

$$+ n(n-1)f_{n-1}f_{n-2}C_{n-3}\rho_{n-1}^{n-2}\int_0^{\rho_{n-3}}\int_{\sqrt{f_{n-2}^2+r_2^2}}^{\rho_{n-2}} r_1^{n-3}r_2^{n-4}$$

$$\times (f_{n-1}^2+r_1^2)^{-\frac{n-1}{2}}(f_{n-2}^2+r_2^2)^{-\frac{n-2}{2}}\,dr_1\,dr_2. \tag{31}$$

Example 1 $k = 3$.

In the case $k = 3$, Σ_3 is a regular tetrahedron with four equilateral triangles as faces. The three possible cases (a) $0 < \rho < f_3$, (b) $f_3 < \rho < f_{3,1}$, and (c) $f_{3,1} < \rho < f_{3,0} = r_3$ are depicted in Figure 13.1(a)–(c).

The results so far obtained yield:

Case 1 for $0 < \rho < 1/2\sqrt{3}$:

$$V_3(\rho) = 4\pi\rho^2 \tag{32}$$

Case 2 for $1/2\sqrt{3} < \rho < 1/2$:

$$V_3(\rho) = 4\pi\rho^2 - (4\pi/\sqrt{3})\rho^2\int_0^{\rho_2} r_1(f_3^2+r_1^2)^{-\frac{3}{2}}\,dr_1$$

$$= 4\pi\rho/\sqrt{3} - 4\pi\rho^2 \tag{33}$$

(a) $k = 3, 0 < \rho < 1/2\sqrt{3}$

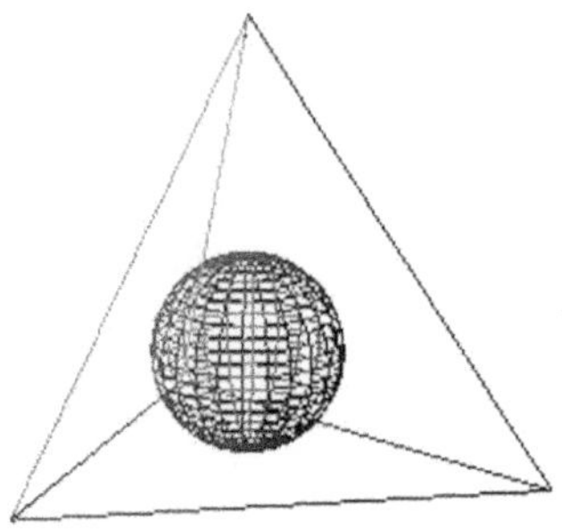

(b) $k = 3, 1/2\sqrt{3} < \rho < 1/2$

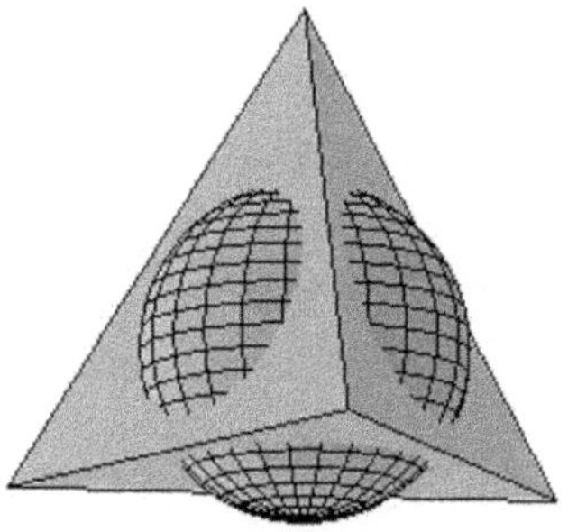

(c) $k = 3, 1/2 < \rho < \sqrt{3}/2$

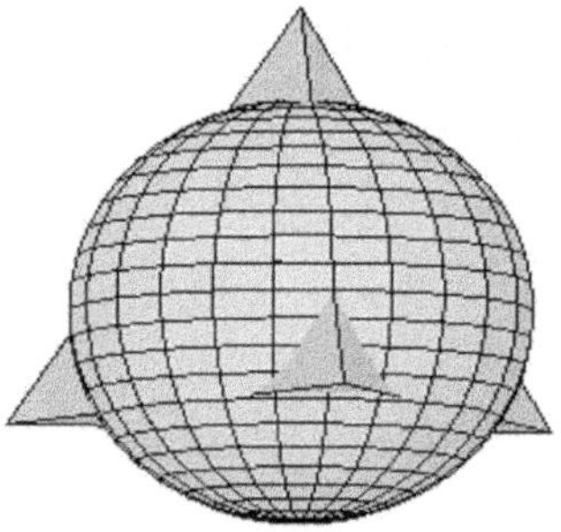

Figure 13.1 *The sphere and the simplex*

Case 3 for $1/2 < \rho < \sqrt{3}/2$:

$$
\begin{aligned}
V_3(\rho) &= 4\pi\rho^2 - (4\pi/\sqrt{3})\rho^2 \int_0^{\rho_2} r_1 (f_3^2 + r_1^2)^{-\frac{3}{2}} dr_1 \\
&\quad + (2\sqrt{2})\rho^2 \int_0^{\rho_1} \int_{\sqrt{f_2^2+r_2^2}}^{\rho_2} r_1 (f_3^2 + r_1^2)^{-\frac{3}{2}} (f_2^2 + r_2^2)^{-1} dr_1 dr_2 \\
&= 4\pi\rho/\sqrt{3} - 4\pi\rho^2 \\
&\quad + (2\sqrt{2})\rho^2 \int_0^{\rho_1} (f_2^2 + r_2^2)^{-1} \left\{ (f_2^2 + f_3^2 + r_2^2)^{-\frac{1}{2}} - \frac{1}{\rho} \right\} dr_2 \\
&= 4\pi\rho/\sqrt{3} - 4\pi\rho^2 - 4\sqrt{3}\rho \arctan(\rho_1/f_2) \\
&\quad + 24\rho^2 \arctan(\rho_1/\rho\sqrt{2})
\end{aligned} \tag{34}
$$

with $\rho_1^2 = \rho^2 - f_2^2 - f_3^2$.

The function $V_3(\rho)$ is plotted as a function of ρ in Figure 13.2, where the three different functional forms evident in equations (32)–(34) are clearly discernable.

One further case will illustrate the structure of the general result. Thus, consider the case $f_{k,k-3} < \rho < f_{k,k-4}$, so that both $\rho_{k-1} > f_{k-1}$ and $\rho_{k-2} > f_{k-2}$, but $\rho_{k-3} < f_{k-3}$. In this case the integral in the second term in (29) is now too large, because not all points y_{k-2} in the region

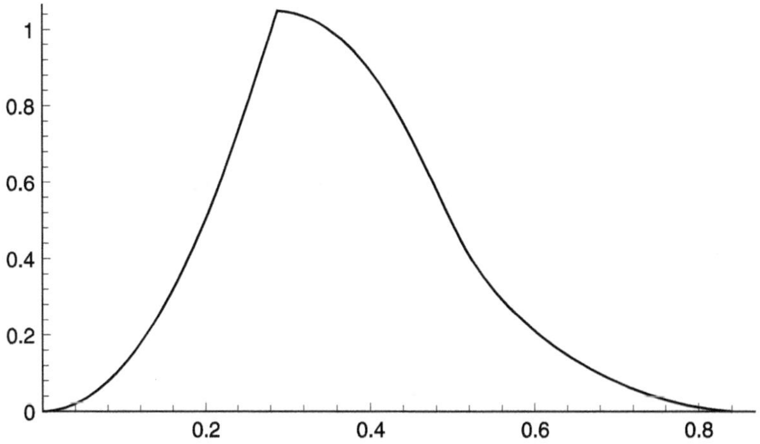

Figure 13.2 *$V_k(\rho)$ for the case $k = 3$*

$y'_{k-2}y_{k-2} \leq \rho^2_{k-2}$, over which that integral is evaluated, lie in the $(k-2)$-face Σ_{k-2}. Again, though, we can partition the Σ_{k-2} into its $(k-3)$-faces ($(k-1)$ of them), use the analogue of the coordinates (20) for y_{k-2}, and evaluate the contribution to the integral for one such face as before. To simplify the notation, let us define the sequence of constants

$$a_{k,s} = \Pi_{i=1}^{s}(k-i+2)f_{k-i+1} = \sqrt{\tfrac{k+1}{k-s+1}},\ s = 1, \ldots, k \tag{35}$$

and the functions

$$H_{k,s}(\rho) = \int_0^{\rho_{k-s}} \int_{\sqrt{f^2_{k-s+1}+r_s^2}}^{\rho_{k-s+1}} \cdots \int_{\sqrt{f^2_{k-1}+r_2^2}}^{\rho_{k-1}} \left[\Pi_{i=1}^{s} r_i^{k-i-1}\right]$$
$$\times \left[\Pi_{i=1}^{s}(f^2_{k-i+1}+r_i^2)^{-\frac{k-s+1}{2}}\right]\left[dr_1 dr_2 \ldots dr_s\right] \tag{36}$$

where the ρ_{k-i} are as defined in equation (23) above. Series expansions for the functions $H_{k,s}(\rho)$, as well as some of their properties, are given in the Appendix.

In this notation, (25) and (30) become:

$$V_k(\rho) = C_k\rho^{k-1} - a_{k,1}C_{k-1}\rho^{k-1}H_{k,1}(\rho) \tag{37}$$
$$f_k < \rho < f_{k,k-2}$$

and

$$V_k(\rho) = C_k\rho^{k-1} - a_{k,1}C_{k-1}\rho^{k-1}H_{k,1}(\rho) + a_{k,2}C_{k-2}\rho^{k-1}H_{k,2}(\rho) \tag{38}$$
$$f_{k,k-2} < \rho < f_{k,k-3}.$$

The content to be excluded from (29), for each of the $(k-3)$-faces of the Σ_{k-2}, is:

$$f_k f_{k-1} f_{k-2} C_{k-3}\rho^{k-1} \int_0^{\rho_{k-3}} \int_{\sqrt{f^2_{k-2}+r_3^2}}^{\rho_{k-2}} \int_{\sqrt{f^2_{k-1}+r_2^2}}^{\rho_{k-1}} r_1^{k-2} r_2^{k-3} r_3^{k-4}$$
$$\times (f_k^2 + r_1^2)^{-\frac{k}{2}}(f^2_{k-1}+r_2^2)^{-\frac{k-1}{2}}(f^2_{k-2}+r_3^2)^{-\frac{k-2}{2}}\, dr_1 dr_2 dr_3.$$
$$= f_k f_{k-1} f_{k-2} C_{k-3}\rho^{k-1}H_{k,3}(\rho). \tag{39}$$

There are $(k-1)$ such terms, so that, subtracting these from the second term in (29), for $f_{k,k-3} < \rho < f_{k,k-4}$,

$$\overline{V}_k(\rho) = a_{k,1}C_{k-1}\rho^{k-1}H_{k,1}(\rho) - a_{k,2}C_{k-2}\rho^{k-1}H_{k,2}(\rho) + a_{k,3}C_{k-3}\rho^{k-1}H_{k,3}(\rho) \tag{40}$$

and so for $f_{k,k-3} < \rho < f_{k,k-4}$,

$$V_k(\rho) = C_k\rho^{k-1} - a_{k,1}C_{k-1}\rho^{k-1}H_{k,1}(\rho) + a_{k,2}C_{k-2}\rho^{k-1}H_{k,2}(\rho) - a_{k,3}C_{k-3}\rho^{k-1}H_{k,3}(\rho). \tag{41}$$

In general, for the case $f_{k,k-r} < \rho < f_{k,k-r-1}$,we need to continue this process of iteratively modifying the calculation at the previous step – the contribution to $\overline{V}_k(\rho)$ from faces of dimension higher than $k-r$ – and only at the last stage (for the $(k-r)$-faces of each Σ_{k-r+1}) integrating over the complete interior of an $S_{k-r}(\rho_{k-r})$. We state the result in:

Theorem 1 Let $S_k(\rho)$ denote the surface of a hypersphere in k dimensions with centre at the centroid of the k-dimensional simplex Σ_k. Let $V_k(\rho)$ denote the surface content of the part of $S_k(\rho)$ that lies inside Σ_k, and let $f_{k,r}$ and ρ_{k-r} be as defined in equations (14) and (23) respectively. Then:

(a) $V_k(\rho)$ is a different function of ρ on each interval,

$$f_{k,k-r} < \rho < f_{k,k-r-1},\ r = 0, 1, \ldots, k-1,\ f_{k,k} = 0 \tag{42}$$

(b) In the interval $f_{k,k-r} < \rho < f_{k,k-r-1}$, $V_k(\rho)$ is given by,

$$V_k(\rho) = C_k\rho^{k-1} + \rho^{k-1}\sum_{s=1}^{r}(-1)^s a_{k,s}C_{k-s}H_{k,s}(\rho) \tag{43}$$

where $a_{k,s}$, C_{k-s} , and $H_{k,s}(\rho)$ are as defined in equations (35), (10), and (36) respectively.

Applying the theorem to the case $k = n-1$, $\rho = \rho_{n-1} = \sqrt{u - n^{-1}}$, and noting that $\rho^2_{n-r-1} = u - (n-r)^{-1}$ we have:

Corollary 1 For each $r = 0, 1, \ldots, n-2$, for u in the interval

$$(n-r)^{-1} < u < (n-r-1)^{-1} \tag{44}$$

$$V_n^*(u) = \int_{M(u)} (dM(u))$$

$$= C_{n-1}\rho_{n-1}^{n-2} + \rho_{n-1}^{n-2}\sum_{s=1}^{r}(-1)^s a_{n-1,s}C_{n-s-1}H_{n-1,s}(\rho_{n-1}) \quad (45)$$

where $M(u) = \{x > 0, \Sigma_{i=1}^n x_i = 1, \Sigma_{i=1}^n x_i^2 = u\}$ and $\rho_{n-1} = \sqrt{u - n^{-1}}$.

4 Example: Censored Normal Model

Let z_i, $i = 1, \ldots, n$ be N independent $N(0,1)$ variates, and let $Y_i^* = (\gamma + z_i)/\theta$, with $-\infty < \gamma < \infty$, $\theta > 0$. Assume that we observe not the latent variates Y_i^* but the censored variates

$$Y_i = Y_i^* \text{ if } Y_i^* > 0$$

$$= 0 \text{ if } Y_i^* \leq 0. \quad (46)$$

The data then consist of the number, n, of uncensored observations, and their (necessarily positive) values, together with the configuration of the uncensored values in the sample. Since, in this simple case, the configuration is unimportant we may, for each n, sum over those configurations, and it is easy to see that the conditional density of the uncensored observations is given by:

$$pdf(y_+|n) = (2\pi)^{-\frac{n}{2}}(\theta/F(\gamma))^n \exp\{-\tfrac{1}{2}\Sigma_+(\theta y_i - \gamma)^2\} \quad (47)$$

where $F(\cdot)$ denotes the *cdf* of the standard normal distribution, y_+ denotes the n-vector of positive observations, and Σ_+ denotes the sum over the indices for which $y_i > 0$. The marginal density of n is Binomial $(N, F(\gamma))$. Of interest, at least initially, is the conditional joint density, given n, of the (conditionally) sufficient statistics in (47), $S_{n1} = \Sigma_+ y_i$ and $S_{n2} = \Sigma_+ y_i^2$.

For $n = 0, 1, 2$ there is nothing to prove, but for $n > 2$ the conditional density (47) is a member of the exponential family (3). The earlier results thus give the conditional joint density of $S_{n1} = \Sigma_+ y_i$ and $S_{n2} = \Sigma_+ y_i^2$, given n:

$$pdf_{S|n}(s|n; \gamma, \theta)) = [4(ns_2 - s_1^2)]^{-\frac{1}{2}} s_1^{n-2} \exp\{-(\theta^2 s_2 + n\gamma^2 - 2\theta\gamma s_1)/2\}$$

$$\times V_n^*(u), \; n > 2 \quad (48)$$

with $V_n^*(u)$ as given in Corollary 1.

Because the number, n, of uncensored observations is not ancillary in this model, it would usually be the unconditional density of S_n, and of functions of S, such as the maximum likelihood estimator for (γ, θ), that would be of interest. Unfortunately, converting this conditional result into its unconditional counterpart is not at all straightforward because, as we have seen, $V_n^*(u)$ has a different functional form on intervals that depend on the conditioning variate, n. This problem, among others, is addressed in a seperate paper dealing with the properties of the maximum likelihood estimators for γ and θ in this model.

Appendix: The Integrals $H_{k,s}(\rho)$

Let

$$H_{k,s} = \int_{R_s} \cdots \int \left[\prod_{i=1}^{s} r_i^{k-i-1} (f_{k-i+1}^2 + r_i^2)^{-\frac{k-i+1}{2}} \right] (dr_1 dr_2 \ldots dr_s) \qquad \text{(A.1)}$$

where R_s is the region:

$$\sqrt{f_{k-i}^2 + r_{i+1}^2} < r_i < \rho_{k-i}, \; i = 1, \ldots, s-1 \qquad \text{(A.2)}$$

$$0 < r_s < \rho_{k-s}. \qquad \text{(A.3)}$$

Transform to the new variables $q_i = r_i^2, i = 1, \ldots, s$, so that $r_i = q_i^{\frac{1}{2}}, i = 1, \ldots, s$. The Jacobian is $2^{-s} \prod_{i=1}^{s} q_i^{-\frac{1}{2}}$, the integrand becomes:

$$2^{-s} \left[\prod_{i=1}^{s} q_i^{\frac{k-i}{2}-1} (f_{k-i+1}^2 + q_i)^{-\frac{k-i+1}{2}} \right] \qquad \text{(A.4)}$$

and the region of integration becomes:

$$f_{k-i}^2 + q_{i+1} < q_i < \rho_{k-i}^2, \; i = 1, \ldots, s-1, \qquad \text{(A.5)}$$

$$0 < q_s < \rho_{k-s}^2. \qquad \text{(A.6)}$$

Now define

$$b_i = (\rho_{k-i}^2 - q_i)/(\rho_{k-i-1}^2 - q_{i+1}), \; i = 1, \ldots, s-1 \qquad \text{(A.7)}$$

$$b_s = (\rho_{k-s}^2 - q_s)/\rho_{k-s}^2. \qquad \text{(A.8)}$$

Then $0 < b_i < 1$ for $i = 1, \ldots, s$, the Jacobian of the transformation is $\rho_{k-s}^{2s} \prod_{i=1}^{s} b_i^{i-1}$, and

$$q_i = \rho_{k-i}^2 - \rho_{k-s}^2 \prod_{j=i}^{s} b_j \tag{A.9}$$

$$= \rho_{k-i}^2 \left(1 - \psi_s(i) \prod_{j=i}^{s} b_j\right) \; i = 1, \ldots, s \tag{A.10}$$

where

$$\psi_s(i) = \rho_{k-s}^2 / \rho_{k-i}^2, \; i = 0, \ldots, s; \; \psi_s(s) = 1. \tag{A.11}$$

Also,

$$f_{k-i+1}^2 + q_i = \rho_{k-i+1}^2 - \rho_{k-s}^2 \prod_{j=i}^{s} b_j$$

$$= \rho_{k-i+1}^2 \left(1 - \psi_s(i-1) \prod_{j=i}^{s} b_j\right), \; i = 1, \ldots, s. \tag{A.12}$$

Note that

$$0 < \psi_s(0) < \psi_s(1) < \ldots < \psi_s(s-1) < \psi_s(s) = 1. \tag{A.13}$$

In terms of the variables $b_1, \ldots, b_s$,

$$H_{k,s} = 2^{-s} \rho_k^{-k} \rho_{k-s}^{k+s} \left[\prod_{i=1}^{s} \rho_{k-i}^2\right]^{-1} \cdots \int_{C_s} \left[\prod_{i=1}^{s} b_i^{i-1}\right]$$

$$\times \left[\prod_{i=1}^{s} (1 - \psi_s(i) p_i)^{\frac{k-i}{2} - 1}\right] \left[\prod_{i=1}^{s} (1 - \psi_s(i-1) p_i)^{-\frac{k-i+1}{2}}\right] (db_1 \ldots db_s), \tag{A.14}$$

where C_s denotes the unit s-cube, $C_s = \{b_i; i = 1, \ldots, s; 0 < b_i < 1\}$, and we have put

$$p_i = \prod_{j=i}^{s} b_j, \; i = 1, \ldots, s. \tag{A.15}$$

Now, the integral of the term involving b_1 is, from standard results,

$$\sum_{j_1=0}^{\infty} \frac{(\frac{k}{2})_{j_1}(1)_{j_1}}{j_1!(2)_{j_1}}(\psi_s(0)p_2)^{j_1}\,{}_2F_1\left(j_1+1, 1-\frac{k-1}{2}; j_1+2; \psi_s(1)p_2\right)$$

$$= (1-\psi_s(1)p_2)^{\frac{k-1}{2}} \sum_{j_1,j_2=0}^{\infty} \frac{\left(\frac{k}{2}\right)_{j_1}\left(j_1+\frac{k+1}{2}\right)_{j_2}}{j_1!j_2!\Gamma(j_1+j_2+2)}$$

$$\times (1)_{j_1}(1)_{j_2}\psi_s(0)^{j_1}\psi_s(1)^{j_2}p_2^{j_1+j_2} \tag{A.16}$$

where $(c)_j = c(c+1)\ldots(c+j-1)$ is the usual Pocchammer symbol, and we have used the Gaussian transformation of the hypergeometric function:

$${}_2F_1(a, b; c; z) = (1-z)^{c-a-b}\,{}_2F_1(c-a, c-b; c; z). \tag{A.17}$$

Multiplying (A.16) by $b_2(1-\psi_s(2)p_2)^{\frac{k-2}{2}-1}(1-\psi_s(1)p_2)^{-\frac{k-1}{2}}$ and integrating out b_2 gives:

$$(1-\psi_s(2)p_3)^{\frac{k-2}{2}} \sum_{j[3]=0}^{\infty} \frac{\left(\frac{k}{2}\right)_{j_1}\left(j_1+\frac{k+1}{2}\right)_{j_2}\left(j_1+j_2+\frac{k+2}{2}\right)_{j_3}}{j_1!j_2!j_3!\Gamma(j_1+j_2+j_3+3)}$$

$$\times (1)_{j_1}(1)_{j_2}(1)_{j_3}\psi_s(0)^{j_1}\psi_s(1)^{j_2}\psi_s(2)^{j_3}p_3^{j_1+j_2+j_3}. \tag{A.18}$$

Let

$$\alpha_i = \sum_{l=1}^{i} j_l,\ i = 1, \ldots, s,\ \alpha_0 \equiv 0, \tag{A.19}$$

$$\nu(j[s]) = \prod_{l=1}^{s} j_l!, \tag{A.20}$$

$$(c)_{j[s]} = \prod_{l=1}^{s} (c)_{j_l}, \tag{A.21}$$

$$\psi_s^{j[s]} = \prod_{l=1}^{s} \psi_s(l-1)^{j_l} \tag{A.22}$$

Continuing as above to integrate out $b_3, \ldots, b_{s-1}$ we obtain:

$$(1-\psi_s(s-1)b_s)^{\frac{k-s+1}{2}} \sum_{j[s]=0}^{\infty} \frac{\left[\prod_{i=1}^{s}(\alpha_{i-1}+\frac{k+i-1}{2})_{j_i}\right]}{\nu(j[s])]\Gamma(\alpha_s+s)}(1)_{j[s]}\psi_s^{j[s]}b_s^{\alpha_s}. \quad \text{(A.23)}$$

Multiplying this by $b_s^{s-1}(1-\psi_s(s)b_s)^{\frac{k-s}{2}-1}(1-\psi_s(s-1)b_s)^{-\frac{k-s+1}{2}}$ and integrating out b_s we thus obtain:

$$H_{k,s} = \frac{\rho_{k-s}^{k+s}}{\left(\frac{k-s}{2}\right)_s 2^s \rho^k \left[\prod_{i=1}^{s}\rho_{k-i}^2\right]} \sum_{j[s]=0}^{\infty} \frac{\left[\prod_{i=1}^{s}\left(\alpha_{i-1}+\frac{k+i-1}{2}\right)_{j_i}\right]}{\nu(j[s])\left(\frac{k+s}{2}\right)_{\alpha_s}}(1)_{j[s]}\psi_s^{j[s]}. \quad \text{(A.24)}$$

14 Conditional Response Analysis

*Grayham E. Mizon and Anna Staszewska**

1 Introduction

We are pleased to have this opportunity to make a contribution to this book in memory of a distinguished Greek econometrician. Michael Magdalinos, from the early years as a PhD student to more recent years when he made important contributions to the literature on hypothesis testing and in particular the role of higher-order approximations to improve inference, impressed the first author by his considerable technical abilities, his tenacity in solving problems, and his warmth as a friend and colleague. Though it was to theoretical econometrics that Michael made his contributions, ultimately the value of many theoretical results lies in applications. We review an issue in applied econometrics in this chapter, namely the efficacy of alternative methods of response analysis in economic policy investigations.

From the 1950s, dynamic simultaneous equations models (DSEM) were a major tool in applied macroeconometric modelling (see for example Klein, Ball, Hazlewood and Vandome, 1961; Klein, 1969), with dynamic multipliers (Goldberger, 1964) being the construct used to measure policy responses. However, following the critiques of economic time-series analysis made by Box and Jenkins (1976) and Granger and Newbold (1974), namely that ignoring non-stationarity in data has serious consequences, time-series models involving differences of data became prevalent. Sims (1980) also criticized DSEMs for employing incredible untested identifying restrictions, and proposed that vector autoregressions (VAR) be used instead. Indeed Sims (1980) was a major influence leading to the VAR becoming the dominant class of model for macroeconometric modelling, and to impulse response analysis being the conventional form of response analysis. Sims (1980, p. 22) wrote, "the best descriptive device appears to be analysis of the system's response to

* We are grateful to Hashem Pesaran for comments on an earlier version of this chapter.

typical random shocks". Several distinct versions of the device have been proposed, and it has been adapted to more recent formulations such as the vector equilibrium correction model (VECM) (see Lütkepohl and Reimers, 1992). Apart from investigating dynamic properties of the fitted model, as originally suggested by Sims, impulse response analysis also has been used as a tool for policy analysis and model evaluation. Moreover, after Sims (1981, 1986), Bernanke (1986) and Shapiro and Watson (1988) introduced the "structural VAR" (SVAR) impulse response analysis became a primary tool used to draw inferences from this type of model.

Econometricians based at the LSE between the 1960s and 1980s developed and advocated the use of an alternative methodology for modelling economic time-series data. This LSE methodology had its origins in Sargan (1964) and has had a more recent comprehensive presentation in Hendry (1995). This methodology, by requiring that an econometric model is coherent with and has fully exploited the available information (congruence) as well as being able to account for the relevant results of rival models and is thus inferentially dominant (encompassing), can be seen to have responded to the criticisms of ignoring the non-stationarity of economic time series and adopting untested restrictions. Indeed the recommendation of Box and Jenkins (1976) that non-stationary data be modelled in differenced format without testing the appropriateness of this transformation was criticized by Hendry and Mizon (1978). Further, Hendry and Mizon (2000) use the basic tenets of the LSE methodology to criticize many of the commonly adopted techniques of economic policy analysis, and propose an alternative approach to economic policy analysis using macroeconomic time-series data. We review and extend some of their analysis in this chapter. In particular, we emphasize the difference between responses to unanticipated or unknown shocks (for example the OPEC oil price hike in the 1970s, the Asian crisis in the 1990s, or September 11, 2001) and to known policy changes (such as changes in tax rates and central bank interest rates). We also draw attention to the value of conditional models for analysing and estimating responses to both types of change. VAR models are closed in that they only condition on the history of the process under investigation and so are used for estimating responses to unknown shocks or impulses. On the other hand open models that condition on some contemporaneous variables, in addition to the history of all variables, enable responses to known changes in the conditioning variables to be estimated via dynamic multipliers as well as the response to impulses in the conditional system to be estimated. We argue that in a policy context the conditional sub-model can be interpreted as a model of the target variables $\mathbf{y}_t$

(e.g. inflation, exchange, and unemployment rates) conditional on the policy instruments $\mathbf{z}_t$ (e.g. tax rates and central bank interest rates), and that as such they contain precisely the response parameters of interest in policy analysis. Whether the estimated policy responses will be accurate and reliable will depend on how well the model characterizes the relevant sectors of the economy, and whether there are any structural breaks in the model or regime shifts affecting these sectors of the economy that are not taken account of. Requiring an econometric model to be congruent and encompassing ensures that it is the best characterization of the relevant sectors of the economy given the available information. However, nothing other than serendipity can render estimated policy responses accurate in the face of post-estimation unknown structural breaks or regime shifts.

Section 2 defines concepts and notation, with the data-generation process (DGP) and econometric model defined in sections 2.1 and 2.2 respectively, the underlying closed (no contemporaneous conditioning variables) and open (some contemporaneous conditioning variables) models for the stationary case are defined in section 2.3, and the stationary VAR is presented in section 2.4. Section 3 discusses different types of response analysis and illustrates some of them graphically for a numerical example in section 3.3. The non-stationary case is considered in section 4 using the vector equilibrium correction model (VECM), and some of the corresponding response analyses are graphically illustrated in section 4.1. Section 5 concludes.

2 Preliminaries

2.1 DGP

We assume that a statistical representation can be given to the process by which observations are made on the sectors of interest in the economy being studied. This is called the data-generation process (DGP) which for a sample period $t = 1, \ldots, T$ is denoted $\mathsf{D}_{\mathsf{W}}(\mathbf{W}_T^1|\mathbf{W}_0, \delta_0)$, when the vector of N real random variables $\mathbf{w}_t$ characterizes the economy under analysis, the history of the stochastic process $\{\mathbf{w}_t\}$ up to time $(t-1)$ is denoted by $\mathbf{W}_{t-1} = (\mathbf{W}_0, \mathbf{w}_1, \ldots, \mathbf{w}_{t-1}) = (\mathbf{W}_0, \mathbf{W}_{t-1}^1)$ (where $\mathbf{W}_0$ is the set of initial conditions), and δ_0 is a particular point in parameter space. The DGP $\mathsf{D}_{\mathsf{W}}(\mathbf{W}_T^1|\mathbf{W}_0, \delta_0)$ is sequentially factorized as:

$$\mathsf{D}_{\mathsf{W}}\left(\mathbf{W}_T^1 \mid \mathbf{W}_0, \delta_0\right) = \prod_{t=1}^{T} \mathsf{D}_{\mathsf{W}}(\mathbf{w}_t \mid \mathbf{W}_{t-1}, \delta_0) . \tag{1}$$

Since N is usually large relative to T it is not possible to analyse the interrelationships between all N variables in $\mathbf{w}_t$, and more importantly particular interest may be in a transformed sub-set $\mathbf{x}_t$ of $\mathbf{w}_t$. From the theory of reduction (see, *inter alia*, Hendry, 1995, and Mizon, 1995), there exists a local DGP for the chosen variables $\mathbf{x}_t$:

$$\mathsf{D}_{\mathsf{X}}(\mathbf{x}_t|\mathbf{X}_{t-1}, \boldsymbol{\xi}) \text{ where } \boldsymbol{\xi} \in \Xi \subseteq \mathbb{R}^s \tag{2}$$

which is derived from $\mathsf{D}_{\mathsf{W}}(\mathbf{w}_t|\cdot)$.

2.2 *Econometric Model*

Although the responses of interest are functions of the parameters of the DGP $\boldsymbol{\xi}$ these parameters are not known. Hence economic policy analysis is undertaken using an econometric model, with knowledge from economic theory and the statistical properties of the observed $\mathbf{x}_t$ guiding the specification of the model. An econometric model $\mathsf{f}_{\mathsf{X}}(\cdot)$ for $n < N$ variables $\mathbf{x}_t$ implicitly derived from $\mathbf{w}_t$ by marginalization, aggregation and transformation is denoted by:

$$\mathsf{f}_{\mathsf{X}}(\mathbf{X}_T^1 \mid \mathbf{X}_0, \boldsymbol{\theta}) = \prod_{t=1}^{T} \mathsf{f}_{\mathsf{X}}(\mathbf{x}_t \mid \mathbf{X}_{t-1}, \boldsymbol{\theta}) \text{ where } \boldsymbol{\theta} \in \Theta \subseteq \mathbb{R}^k \tag{3}$$

when $\mathsf{f}_{\mathsf{X}}(\mathbf{x}_t|\mathbf{X}_{t-1}, \boldsymbol{\theta})$ is the postulated sequential joint density at time t.

In general, $\mathsf{f}_{\mathsf{X}}(\cdot) \neq \mathsf{D}_{\mathsf{X}}(\cdot)$, and this divergence has to be taken into account when making inferences about $\boldsymbol{\theta}$ (see *inter alia* Cox, 1961, and White, 1982a). Indeed, the modeller is free to specify any form of $\mathsf{f}_{\mathsf{X}}(\cdot)$ independently of what process has actually generated the data which is almost always unknown. Precisely because the form of the econometric model is under the control of the investigator it is important that criteria are employed to assist in the specification of models, and this is why congruence and encompassing have important roles in the LSE methodology.

2.3 *Closed and Open Models*

We begin by formulating closed and open models in some generality before specializing to the VAR class of model. The specification of the econometric model given in (3) is that of the joint density for *all* n variables in $\mathbf{x}_t$ and so is a *closed* model – it is not open to the influence of any other observed variables. Let the n variables contained in the $\mathbf{x}_t$ vector be partitioned into two subsets of variables $\mathbf{x}_t' = (\mathbf{y}_t', \mathbf{z}_t')$, where $\mathbf{y}_t$

and $\mathbf{z}_t$ represent the n_1 target and n_2 policy instrument variables respectively with $n = n_1 + n_2$. Applying the conditional/marginal factorization of $\mathsf{f}_{\mathsf{X}}(\mathbf{x}_t|\mathbf{X}_{t-1}, \boldsymbol{\theta})$ then provides an *open* model of the distribution of $\mathbf{y}_t$ conditional on $\mathbf{z}_t$ given by $\mathsf{f}_{\mathsf{y}|\mathsf{z}}(\mathbf{y}_t|\mathbf{z}_t, \mathbf{X}_{t-1}, \boldsymbol{\lambda}_{y|z})$ in:

$$\mathsf{f}_{\mathsf{X}}(\mathbf{x}_t|\mathbf{X}_{t-1}, \boldsymbol{\theta}) = \mathsf{f}_{\mathsf{y}|\mathsf{z}}(\mathbf{y}_t|\mathbf{z}_t, \mathbf{X}_{t-1}, \boldsymbol{\lambda}_{y|z})\mathsf{f}_{\mathsf{z}}(\mathbf{z}_t|\mathbf{X}_{t-1}, \boldsymbol{\lambda}_z) \tag{4}$$

where $(\boldsymbol{\lambda}'_{y|z}, \boldsymbol{\lambda}'_z) = \boldsymbol{\lambda}' = g(\boldsymbol{\theta})$. In general, for there to be no loss of information on the parameters of interest when analysis is done using the conditional distribution only the conditioning variables must be weakly exogenous for the parameters of interest. Engle, Hendry and Richard (1983) define $\mathbf{z}_t$ to be weakly exogenous for parameters of interest κ if and only if these parameters are a function of $\boldsymbol{\lambda}_{y|z}$ only, and $\boldsymbol{\lambda}_{y|z}$ and $\boldsymbol{\lambda}_z$ are variation free. However, in a policy context when there may be regime shifts in the process generating the policy instruments and so changes in $\boldsymbol{\lambda}_z$, and if these changes in $\boldsymbol{\lambda}_z$ induce changes in $\boldsymbol{\lambda}_{y|z}$ policy inferences on κ using an estimate of $\boldsymbol{\lambda}_{y|z}$ that ignores these changes will be misleading. Hence it is necessary that $\mathbf{z}_t$ is *super exogenous* in order that policy responses can be reliably estimated from the conditional model. Engle *et al.* (1983) define $\mathbf{z}_t$ to be super exogenous for κ if and only if $\mathbf{z}_t$ is weakly exogenous for κ, and $\boldsymbol{\lambda}_{y|z}$ is invariant to changes in $\boldsymbol{\lambda}_z$. See Hendry and Mizon (1998) for further discussion of this concept in the policy context.

2.4 *Stationary VAR*

The class of econometric model considered in this chapter is a Gaussian vector autoregression of order p(VAR(p)) given by:

$$\mathbf{x}_t = \sum_{i=1}^{p} \boldsymbol{\Phi}_i \mathbf{x}_{t-i} + \boldsymbol{\phi} + \boldsymbol{\varepsilon}_t \tag{5}$$

with $\boldsymbol{\varepsilon}_t \sim \mathsf{IN}_n[0, \boldsymbol{\Sigma}]$, $t = 1, \ldots, T$, and $\{\boldsymbol{\Phi}_i, i = 1, 2, \ldots, p\}$ are $n \times n$ coefficient matrices. For the stationary case we make the following assumptions:

Assumption 1 $\mathsf{E}(\boldsymbol{\varepsilon}_t) = 0$, $\mathsf{E}(\boldsymbol{\varepsilon}_t\boldsymbol{\varepsilon}_t') = \boldsymbol{\Sigma}$ for all t, where $\boldsymbol{\Sigma} = \{\sigma_{ij}, i, j = 1, 2, \ldots, n\}$ is an $n \times n$ positive definite matrix, $\mathsf{E}(\boldsymbol{\varepsilon}_t\boldsymbol{\varepsilon}_s') = \mathbf{0}$ for $s \neq t$.

Assumption 2 All the roots of $det\left(I_n - \sum_{i=1}^{p} \boldsymbol{\Phi}_i \varkappa^i\right) = 0$ lie outside the unit circle.

As a consequence of the stationarity assumption we denote $\mathsf{E}(\mathbf{x}_t) = \boldsymbol{\mu}_x$ $\forall t$ and can write the infinite moving average representation of (5) as:

$$(\mathbf{x}_t - \boldsymbol{\mu}_x) = \sum_{i=0}^{\infty} \mathbf{A}_i \boldsymbol{\varepsilon}_{t-i} \tag{6}$$

when the coefficient matrices $\mathbf{A}_i$ are obtained from the recursion relations:

$$\mathbf{A}_i = \Phi_1 \mathbf{A}_{i-1} + \Phi_2 \mathbf{A}_{i-2} + \cdots + \Phi_p \mathbf{A}_{i-p}, \qquad i = 1, 2, \ldots \tag{7}$$

with $\mathbf{A}_0 = I_n$ and $\mathbf{A}_i = 0$ for $i < 0$.

Noting that $\mathsf{E}(\mathbf{x}_t) = \boldsymbol{\mu}_x = \left(I_n - \sum_{i=1}^{p} \boldsymbol{\Phi}_i\right)^{-1} \phi$ the VAR can be written in partitioned form as:

$$\begin{bmatrix} \mathbf{y}_t - \boldsymbol{\mu}_y \\ \mathbf{z}_t - \boldsymbol{\mu}_z \end{bmatrix} = \sum_{i=1}^{p} \begin{bmatrix} \Phi_{yy,i} & \Phi_{yz,i} \\ \Phi_{zy,i} & \Phi_{zz,i} \end{bmatrix} \begin{bmatrix} \mathbf{y}_{t-i} - \boldsymbol{\mu}_y \\ \mathbf{z}_{t-i} - \boldsymbol{\mu}_z \end{bmatrix} + \begin{bmatrix} \boldsymbol{\varepsilon}_{yt} \\ \boldsymbol{\varepsilon}_{zt} \end{bmatrix} \tag{8}$$

$$\begin{bmatrix} \boldsymbol{\varepsilon}_{yt} \\ \boldsymbol{\varepsilon}_{zt} \end{bmatrix} \sim \mathrm{IN}_n \left[\begin{pmatrix} 0 \\ 0 \end{pmatrix}, \begin{pmatrix} \Sigma_{yy} & \Sigma_{yz} \\ \Sigma_{zy} & \Sigma_{zz} \end{pmatrix} \right] \tag{9}$$

when $\boldsymbol{\mu}_x' = \left(\boldsymbol{\mu}_y', \boldsymbol{\mu}_z'\right)$ and

$$\Phi_i = \begin{bmatrix} \Phi_{yy,i} & \Phi_{yz,i} \\ \Phi_{zy,i} & \Phi_{zz,i} \end{bmatrix}. \tag{10}$$

The corresponding infinite moving average representation of (8) is then given by:

$$\begin{bmatrix} \mathbf{y}_{t+h} - \boldsymbol{\mu}_y \\ \mathbf{z}_{t+h} - \boldsymbol{\mu}_z \end{bmatrix} = \sum_{i=0}^{\infty} \begin{bmatrix} \mathbf{A}_{yy,i} & \mathbf{A}_{yz,i} \\ \mathbf{A}_{zy,i} & \mathbf{A}_{zz,i} \end{bmatrix} \begin{bmatrix} \boldsymbol{\varepsilon}_{y,t+h-i} \\ \boldsymbol{\varepsilon}_{z,t+h-i} \end{bmatrix} \tag{11}$$

with $\mathbf{A}_i = \begin{bmatrix} \mathbf{A}_{yy,i} & \mathbf{A}_{yz,i} \\ \mathbf{A}_{zy,i} & \mathbf{A}_{zz,i} \end{bmatrix}$ and $\boldsymbol{\varepsilon}_t = \begin{bmatrix} \boldsymbol{\varepsilon}_{y,t} \\ \boldsymbol{\varepsilon}_{z,t} \end{bmatrix}$.

Structural VAR (SVAR) and dynamic simultaneous equations models (DSEM), when they are linear, can now be represented as a linear transformation of the VAR in mean-deviation form:

$$\mathbf{B}(\mathbf{x}_t - \mu_x) = \sum_{i=1}^{p} \mathbf{B}\Phi_i(\mathbf{x}_{t-i} - \mu_x) + \mathbf{B}\boldsymbol{\varepsilon}_t$$
$$= \sum_{i=1}^{p} \mathbf{B}\Phi_i\mathbf{B}^{-1}[\mathbf{B}(\mathbf{x}_{t-i} - \mu_x)] + \mathbf{B}\boldsymbol{\varepsilon}_t \tag{12}$$

with $\mathbf{B}\boldsymbol{\varepsilon}_t \sim \mathrm{IN}_n[0, \mathbf{B}\Sigma\mathbf{B}']$, $t = 1, \ldots, T$, when $\mathbf{B}$ is a non-singular $n \times n$ matrix whose structure is chosen on the basis of economic theory or 'structural' information. The infinite moving average representation of (12) is then given by:

$$\mathbf{B}(\mathbf{x}_t - \mu_x) = \sum_{i=0}^{\infty} \mathbf{F}_i\mathbf{B}\boldsymbol{\varepsilon}_{t-i} \tag{13}$$

when the coefficient matrices $\mathbf{F}_i$ are obtained from the recursion relations:

$$\mathbf{F}_i = \mathbf{B}\boldsymbol{\Phi}_1\mathbf{B}^{-1}\mathbf{F}_{i-1} + \mathbf{B}\boldsymbol{\Phi}_2\mathbf{B}^{-1}\mathbf{F}_{i-2} + \cdots + \mathbf{B}\mathbf{F}_p\mathbf{B}^{-1}\mathbf{A}_{i-p}, \quad i = 1, 2, \ldots \tag{14}$$

with $\mathbf{F}_0 = \mathbf{B}$ and $\mathbf{F}_i = 0$ for $i < 0$.

Each of the above representations of the VAR, the SVAR, and the DSEM is for a closed model. The conditional/marginal reparameterization of (8) gives an open model for $\mathbf{y}_t$ conditional on $\mathbf{z}_t$ and the history of both, which for the DSEM is known as the reduced form:

$$\left(\mathbf{y}_t - \mu_y\right) = \pi(\mathbf{z}_t - \mu_z) + \sum_{i=1}^{p} \left(\boldsymbol{\Phi}_{yy,i} - \pi\boldsymbol{\Phi}_{zy,i}\right)\left(\mathbf{y}_{t-i} - \mu_y\right)$$
$$+ \sum_{i=1}^{p} \left(\boldsymbol{\Phi}_{yz,i} - \pi\boldsymbol{\Phi}_{zz,i}\right)(\mathbf{z}_{t-i} - \mu_z) + \mathbf{v}_t \tag{15}$$

and a closed model for $\mathbf{z}_t$:

$$(\mathbf{z}_t - \mu_z) = \sum_{i=1}^{p} \left[\boldsymbol{\Phi}_{zy,i}(\mathbf{y}_{t-i} - \mu_y) + \boldsymbol{\Phi}_{zz,i}(\mathbf{z}_{t-i} - \mu_z)\right] + \boldsymbol{\varepsilon}_{zt} \tag{16}$$

where $\mathbf{v}_t = \boldsymbol{\varepsilon}_{yt} - \pi\boldsymbol{\varepsilon}_{zt}$, $\pi = \boldsymbol{\Sigma}_{yz}\boldsymbol{\Sigma}_{zz}^{-1}$ with $\Omega = (\boldsymbol{\Sigma}_{yy} - \pi\boldsymbol{\Sigma}_{zz}\pi')$ when

$$\begin{bmatrix} \mathbf{v}_t \\ \boldsymbol{\varepsilon}_{zt} \end{bmatrix} \sim \mathsf{IN}_n\left[\begin{pmatrix} \mathbf{0} \\ \mathbf{0} \end{pmatrix}, \begin{pmatrix} \Omega & \mathbf{0} \\ \mathbf{0} & \Sigma_{zz} \end{pmatrix}\right].$$

The conditional model in (15) is an open model of the behaviour of $\mathbf{y}_t$ conditional on $\mathbf{z}_t$, whereas the marginal model in (16) is a closed model of the behaviour of the subset of $\mathbf{x}_t$ denoted by $\mathbf{z}_t$. The infinite moving average representation of (15) and (16) is given by (13) with $\mathbf{B} = \begin{bmatrix} \mathbf{I}_{n_1} & -\pi \\ \mathbf{0} & \mathbf{I}_{n_2} \end{bmatrix}$ and has the form:

$$\begin{bmatrix} \mathbf{y}_{t+h} - \boldsymbol{\mu}_y \\ \mathbf{z}_{t+h} - \boldsymbol{\mu}_z \end{bmatrix} = \begin{bmatrix} \pi(\mathbf{z}_t - \boldsymbol{\mu}_z) \\ 0 \end{bmatrix} + \sum_{i=0}^{\infty} \begin{bmatrix} \mathbf{F}_{yy,i} & \mathbf{F}_{yz,i} \\ \mathbf{F}_{zy,i} & \mathbf{F}_{zz,i} \end{bmatrix} \begin{bmatrix} \mathbf{v}_{t+h-i} \\ \boldsymbol{\varepsilon}_{z,t+h-i} \end{bmatrix}. \tag{17}$$

The infinite moving average, or transfer function, representation of the open model in (15) alone is given by:

$$(\mathbf{y}_t - \boldsymbol{\mu}_y) = \sum_{i=0}^{\infty} [\Upsilon_i(\mathbf{z}_{t-i} - \boldsymbol{\mu}_z) + \mathbf{G}_i\mathbf{v}_{t-i}] \tag{18}$$

when

$$\mathbf{G}_i = \mathbf{D}_1\mathbf{G}_{i-1} + \mathbf{D}_2\mathbf{G}_{i-2} + \cdots + \mathbf{D}_p\mathbf{G}_{i-p}, \qquad i = 1, 2, \ldots \tag{19}$$

with $\mathbf{G}_0 = \mathbf{I}$, $\mathbf{G}_i = 0$ for $i < 0$, and $\mathbf{D}_i = \left(\boldsymbol{\Phi}_{yy,i} - \pi\boldsymbol{\Phi}_{zy,i}\right)$. In addition, $\boldsymbol{\Upsilon}_i$ is determined by the recursion relations:

$$\boldsymbol{\Upsilon}_i = \mathbf{D}_1\boldsymbol{\Upsilon}_{i-1} + \mathbf{D}_2\boldsymbol{\Upsilon}_{i-2} + \cdots + \mathbf{D}_p\boldsymbol{\Upsilon}_{i-p} + \Pi_i \tag{20}$$

when $\Pi_i = \left(\boldsymbol{\Phi}_{yz,i} - \pi\Phi_{zz,i}\right)$ for $i = 1, 2, \ldots p$ with $\boldsymbol{\Upsilon}_0 = \pi$, $\boldsymbol{\Upsilon}_i = 0$ for $i < 0$, and for $i > p$:

$$\boldsymbol{\Upsilon}_i = \mathbf{D}_1\boldsymbol{\Upsilon}_{i-1} + \mathbf{D}_2\boldsymbol{\Upsilon}_{i-2} + \cdots + \mathbf{D}_p\boldsymbol{\Upsilon}_{i-p} \tag{21}$$

(see Box and Jenkins, 1976 pp. 346–7 for details).

In the following section we consider how these formulations can be used for obtaining information relevant to policy analysis.

3 Response Analysis in a Stationary VAR

A fundamental part of economic analysis is concerned with the interrelationships between economic variables, for example the price elasticity of demand for a consumer good, the interest rate elasticity of the demand for money, or the income elasticity of the demand for leisure. Though these examples involve the response of one variable to changes in another they are to be understood as partial responses within a higher dimensional system that in general is both dynamic and may involve simultaneity. Concentrating on the response of the target variables in $\mathbf{y}_t$ to changes in the instruments $\mathbf{z}_t$ we distinguish between one-off changes or impulses in $\mathbf{z}_t$ and maintained changes in $\mathbf{z}_t$. The latter are typically referred to as step changes, and the impulses are usually perceived as being unanticipated and referred to as shocks. A step change in $\mathbf{z}_t$ beginning at t and lasting for S periods is most easily thought of as a change in the mean of $\mathbf{z}_t$ such that $\mathsf{E}(\mathbf{z}_{t+s}) = \boldsymbol{\mu}_z + \nabla\boldsymbol{\mu}_z$ for $s = 1, 2, 3, \ldots S$. Whereas an impulse in $\mathbf{z}$ at time t results in $\mathbf{z}$ differing from the value it would have taken by an amount $\mathbf{Q}_{zz}\ell_{zt} \neq 0$ at time t only when $\mathbf{Q}_{zz}$ is an $n_2 \times n_2$ non-singular matrix and ℓ_{zt} is an $n_2 \times 1$ unit vector. It is also possible to distinguish between *ex ante* and *ex post* policy analysis. The former is concerned with analysing how a projected policy *would work* if it were carried out (policy simulation), and the latter evaluates how a policy that has been implemented *has worked* in the sample period.

3.1 Impulse Response Analysis

The idea of impulse response analysis is to follow the behaviour of the system when it is subjected to "typical random shocks". The proliferation of forms of impulse response analysis largely reflects different ways of interpreting the phrase "typical random shocks". A change in the definition of impulse usually means a change in the impulse response analysis. There are infinitely many observationally equivalent representations of $\mathbf{x}_t$ obtained by forming a new impulse vector $\boldsymbol{\xi}_t = \mathbf{Q}\boldsymbol{\varepsilon}_t$ when $\mathbf{Q}$ is a non-singular matrix, with the response coefficient matrix changing from $\mathbf{A}_h$ to $\boldsymbol{\Psi}_h = \mathbf{A}_h\mathbf{Q}^{-1}$ since from (6):

$$
\begin{aligned}
(\mathbf{x}_t - \boldsymbol{\mu}_x) &= \sum_{i=0}^{\infty} \mathbf{A}_i\boldsymbol{\varepsilon}_{t-i} \\
&= \sum_{i=0}^{\infty} \mathbf{A}_i\mathbf{Q}^{-1}\mathbf{Q}\boldsymbol{\varepsilon}_{t-i} = \sum_{i=0}^{\infty} \boldsymbol{\Psi}_i\boldsymbol{\xi}_{t-i}.
\end{aligned}
\qquad (22)
$$

Distinct kinds of impulse/error/shock give rise to traditional ($\mathbf{Q} = \mathbf{I}_n$), orthogonalized ($\mathbf{Q}$ such that $\mathbf{Q}'\mathbf{Q} = \boldsymbol{\Sigma}^{-1}$), and generalized. Structural VAR analysis also can be cast in this framework when the specification of $\mathbf{Q}$ is determined by "structural" considerations from economic theory. In the following sections we consider response analysis in economic policy analysis when it is the response of the target variables $\mathbf{y}_t$ to impulses in the policy instruments $\mathbf{z}_t$ that is of interest. Just as there are different types of impulse in $\mathbf{z}_t$ so there are different models within which to assess their effect on $\mathbf{y}_t$. In the next sub-sections we use the framework of the closed VAR to review a number of different types of impulse that have been used in the literature, prior to considering traditional impulse response analysis in the conditional/marginal factorization of the VAR and in the open or conditional VAR.

Closed VAR Within the closed VAR as in (8) the response of $\mathbf{y}$ through time to an impulse $\mathbf{Q}_{zz}\ell_{zt}$ in $\mathbf{z}$ at time t is given by $(\partial\mathbf{y}_{t+h}/\partial\boldsymbol{\varepsilon}'_{zt})\mathbf{Q}_{zz}\ell_{zt}$ for $h > 0$ and this is usually presented graphically as the plots of the elements of $(\partial\mathbf{y}_{t+h}/\partial\boldsymbol{\varepsilon}'_{zt})\nabla\boldsymbol{\varepsilon}_{zt}$ against h. Note that because of the dynamics in (8) this response is more easily calculated from the infinite moving average form (11) and is given by $(\partial\mathbf{y}_{t+h}/\partial\boldsymbol{\varepsilon}'_{zt})\mathbf{Q}_{zz}\ell_{zt} = \mathbf{A}_{yz,h}\mathbf{Q}_{zz}\ell_{zt}$. In order to consider the different types of impulse response analysis in this context we partition (22) to correspond to the partition of $\mathbf{x}_t$ into $\mathbf{y}_t$ and $\mathbf{z}_t$:

$$\begin{bmatrix} \mathbf{y}_{t+h} - \boldsymbol{\mu}_y \\ \mathbf{z}_{t+h} - \boldsymbol{\mu}_z \end{bmatrix} = \sum_{i=0}^{\infty} \begin{bmatrix} \boldsymbol{\Psi}_{yy,i} & \boldsymbol{\Psi}_{yz,i} \\ \boldsymbol{\Psi}_{zy,i} & \boldsymbol{\Psi}_{zz,i} \end{bmatrix} \begin{bmatrix} \boldsymbol{\xi}_{y,t+h-i} \\ \boldsymbol{\xi}_{z,t+h-i} \end{bmatrix} \tag{23}$$

where:

$$\begin{bmatrix} \boldsymbol{\Psi}_{yy,i} & \boldsymbol{\Psi}_{yz,i} \\ \boldsymbol{\Psi}_{zy,i} & \boldsymbol{\Psi}_{zz,i} \end{bmatrix} = \begin{bmatrix} \mathbf{A}_{yy,i} & \mathbf{A}_{yz,i} \\ \mathbf{A}_{zy,i} & \mathbf{A}_{zz,i} \end{bmatrix} \begin{bmatrix} \mathbf{Q}_{yy} & \mathbf{Q}_{yz} \\ \mathbf{Q}_{zy} & \mathbf{Q}_{zz} \end{bmatrix}^{-1} \tag{24}$$

and:

$$\begin{bmatrix} \boldsymbol{\xi}_{y,t+h-i} \\ \boldsymbol{\xi}_{z,t+h-i} \end{bmatrix} = \begin{bmatrix} \mathbf{Q}_{yy} & \mathbf{Q}_{yz} \\ \mathbf{Q}_{zy} & \mathbf{Q}_{zz} \end{bmatrix} \begin{bmatrix} \boldsymbol{\varepsilon}_{y,t+h-i} \\ \boldsymbol{\varepsilon}_{z,t+h-i} \end{bmatrix}. \tag{25}$$

From (23) the response of interest is now given by:

$$\frac{\partial\mathbf{y}_{t+h}}{\partial\boldsymbol{\varepsilon}'_{zt}} = \frac{\partial\mathbf{y}_{t+h}}{\partial\boldsymbol{\xi}'_{zt}}\frac{\partial\boldsymbol{\xi}_{zt}}{\partial\boldsymbol{\varepsilon}'_{zt}} = \boldsymbol{\Psi}_{yz,h}\mathbf{Q}_{zz} \tag{26}$$

which using (24) gives:

$$\frac{\partial \mathbf{y}_{t+h}}{\partial \boldsymbol{\varepsilon}'_{zt}} = \mathbf{A}_{yz,h} + [\mathbf{Q}_{zz}^{-1}\mathbf{Q}_{zy} - \mathbf{A}_{yy,h}][\mathbf{Q}_{yy} - \mathbf{Q}_{yz}\mathbf{Q}_{zz}^{-1}\mathbf{Q}_{zy}]^{-1}\mathbf{Q}_{yz}. \quad (27)$$

Traditional impulse response analysis gives the response to an impulse of unity in $\boldsymbol{\varepsilon}_t$; that is, uses $\mathbf{Q} = \mathbf{I}_n$ so that $\mathbf{Q}_{yz} = 0$ and as a result in this case $(\partial \mathbf{y}_{t+h}/\partial \boldsymbol{\varepsilon}'_{zt})\mathbf{Q}_{zz}\ell_{zt} = \mathbf{A}_{yz,h}$.Using a unit impulse for all the elements of $\boldsymbol{\varepsilon}_{zt}$ ignores information contained in its distribution, and so another choice of impulse that has often been used sets the elements of $\mathbf{Q}$ equal to the corresponding residual standard errors so that $\mathbf{Q}$ is a diagonal matrix with its ith diagonal element equal to the ith diagonal element of $\widehat{\boldsymbol{\Sigma}}^{1/2}$. In this case $(\partial \mathbf{y}_{t+h}/\partial \boldsymbol{\varepsilon}'_{zt})\mathbf{Q}_{zz}\ell_{zt} = \mathbf{A}_{yz,h} diag(\widehat{\boldsymbol{\Sigma}}_{zz})^{1/2}$ when $diag(\mathbf{M})$ here is defined as the diagonal matrix having m_{ii} as its ith diagonal element. This type of impulse response analysis is illustrated for the numerical example in section 3.3 by the solid line with triangles in Figure 14.1.

Two more widely used forms of analysis are *orthogonalized* analysis of Sims (1980) and the *generalized* analysis proposed by Koop, Pesaran and Potter (1996). The motivation for these methods is rather different. Sims (1980, p. 22) states, "In order to be able to see the distinct patterns of movement the system may display it is therefore useful to transform [the residuals which are correlated across equations] to orthogonal form." The orthogonalized impulse response analysis of Sims (1980) applies unit impulses to the transformed VAR innovations $\boldsymbol{\xi}_t = \mathbf{Q}\boldsymbol{\varepsilon}_t$ when $\mathbf{Q}$ satisfies $\boldsymbol{\Sigma} = \mathbf{Q}^{-1}(\mathbf{Q}')^{-1}$ such that $(\boldsymbol{\xi}_t) = \mathbf{I}_n$. This can be achieved by means of the Cholesky decomposition of the variance covariance matrix of errors $\boldsymbol{\Sigma}$. It is well known that the Cholesky decomposition procedure produces different impulse response functions when the ordering of the variables is changed. Indeed, there are infinitely many ways of transforming $\boldsymbol{\varepsilon}_t$ to produce orthogonal errors. The results are only invariant to the ordering of variables if there is no correlation between the errors of different equations, that is when $\boldsymbol{\Sigma}$ is diagonal. Ericsson, Hendry and Mizon (1998) emphasize that for different orderings of variables orthogonalized impulse response analysis implies different sequential weak exogeneity assumptions. The orthogonalization will only agree with a particular conditional analysis by accident. Of particular interest in the present context is the case in which the orthogonalization is only with respect to $\boldsymbol{\varepsilon}_{zt}$ and so $\mathbf{Q}_{yz} = 0, \mathbf{Q}_{zy} = 0$, and $\mathbf{Q}_{yy} = \mathbf{I}_{n_1}$ with $\mathbf{Q}_{zz}$ chosen such that $\boldsymbol{\Sigma}_{zz} = \mathbf{Q}_{zz}^{-1}(\mathbf{Q}'_{zz})^{-1}$ implying that $(\partial \mathbf{y}_{t+h}/\partial \boldsymbol{\varepsilon}'_{zt})\mathbf{Q}_{zz}\ell_{zt} = \mathbf{A}_{yz,h}$ which is the traditional impulse response. Hence orthogonalization will only produce responses different from the traditional ones when the orthogonalization extends beyond the set of variables in $\mathbf{z}_t$.

The proponents of *generalized* analysis consider that the "experiment" of shocking the system by introducing an impulse to each error in isolation is too unrealistic to be relevant, and assume instead that the contemporaneous impulses take values in accordance with the correlations implied by the covariance matrix $\mathbf{\Sigma}$. This differs from the standard deviation impulse response analysis by taking the cross correlation of the errors into account as well as their variances.

Conditional/Marginal Factorization The approaches described above have each considered impulses to the instruments in $\mathbf{z}_t$ in the VAR characterized by the joint distribution of all the variables in $\mathbf{x}_t$, but as (4) indicates the joint distribution can always be factorized into a conditional and marginal distribution. In the present context the VAR of (8) is factored into (15) and (16). The only inputs into the closed model for $\mathbf{x}_t$ in this factorization are the errors $\mathbf{v}_t$ and $\boldsymbol{\varepsilon}_{zt}$. The infinite moving average for $\mathbf{x}_t$ in terms of these errors instead of $\boldsymbol{\varepsilon}_{yt}$ and $\boldsymbol{\varepsilon}_{zt}$ is given in (17).

An impulse response experiment using this setup, analogous to the impulse response analysis experiments described above, concerns the effects of a shock affecting one of the errors $\mathbf{v}_t$ or $\boldsymbol{\varepsilon}_{zt}$. The response of $\mathbf{y}_{t+h}$ to a unit impulse in either of these errors is given by a sub-matrix of $\mathbf{F}_h$. For policy analysis, when $\mathbf{z}_t$ contains policy instruments the experiment of interest involves analysing the effects of the shock affecting one of the elements of $\boldsymbol{\varepsilon}_{zt}$ on $\mathbf{y}_t$ containing policy targets. From (17) these responses are given by $\partial\mathbf{y}_{t+h}/\partial\boldsymbol{\varepsilon}'_{zt} = \mathbf{F}_{yz,h} \neq \mathbf{A}_{yz,h}$ except when $\mathbf{B} = \mathbf{I}$. In particular, note that the traditional impulse response $\partial\mathbf{y}_t/\partial\boldsymbol{\varepsilon}'_{zt}$ when estimated from the moving average representation in (17) is given by π which in general will be non-zero, unlike $\partial\mathbf{y}_t/\partial\boldsymbol{\varepsilon}'_{zt}$ estimated from the closed VAR that is zero since $\mathbf{A}_{yz,0} = 0$. Equally the standard deviation impulse response derived from (17) is non-zero in general, and this is illustrated by the solid line in Figure 14.1.

Open VAR On the other hand, analysis of the response of $\mathbf{y}_t$ to shocks affecting $\mathbf{v}_t$ would be an investigation of the dynamic properties of the transmission mechanism. From (17) these responses are given by $\partial\mathbf{y}_{t+h}/\partial\mathbf{v}'_t = \mathbf{F}_{yy,h} \neq \mathbf{A}_{yy,h}$ except when $\mathbf{B} = \mathbf{I}$. Note that alternatively $\partial\mathbf{y}_{t+h}/\partial\mathbf{v}'_t = \mathbf{G}_h$ from (18). However, as a description of the transmission mechanism in the VAR these are not directly relevant for the analysis of a policy change in $\mathbf{z}_t$ on the future path of the targets. For completeness though the response of $\mathbf{y}_t$ to shocks in the conditional VAR errors $\mathbf{v}_t$ is illustrated by the solid line with circles in Figure 14.1. Hendry and Mizon (1998) apply the conditional analysis to a bivariate model of the log of the inverse velocity of circulation of money (*mpy*) and opportunity cost of holding money represented by an interest rate (*Rna*) in the UK. To illustrate differences between the results of the impulse response analysis experiments based on the conditional model as compared with the traditional and orthogonalized experiments they consider both possible factorizations of the joint density; that is, a conditional model for mpy_t given Rna_t and a conditional model for Rna_t given mpy_t and for both factorizations separately analyse the effects of one standard deviation shocks affecting the errors in mpy_t and Rna_t equations keeping the remaining one fixed at 0.

3.2 *Dynamic Multiplier Analysis*

For policy analysis and forecasting researchers in the Cowles Commission tradition use the open model (15) as the reduced form of a DSEM that conditions on exogenous variables and the history of endogenous and exogenous variables. The policies to be considered involve changes in the instrument variables $\mathbf{z}_t$ that are treated as exogenous variables. In this framework it is possible to analyse how $\mathbf{y}$ reacts to changes in $\boldsymbol{\mu}_z$, in $\mathbf{z}$, and in $\mathbf{v}$. In particular, *dynamic multiplier analysis* (see for example Goldberger (1964, pp. 374–8) considers the path of $\mathbf{y}_{t+h}$ when each element of $\mathbf{z}_t$ is changed by 1 unit, and is conducted in the framework of the conditional model (15). For example, the *impact multiplier* is the contemporaneous response of $\mathbf{y}_t$ to a unit change in $\mathbf{z}_t$ and from (15) is given by $\partial \mathbf{y}_t / \partial \mathbf{z}_t' = \pi$. The response of $\mathbf{y}_{t+h}$ for $h > 0$ to the unit change in $\mathbf{z}_t$ is given by $\partial \mathbf{y}_{t+h} / \partial \mathbf{z}_t' = \boldsymbol{\Upsilon}_h$ from (18) and is known as an *interim multiplier*. In this framework it is also relevant to consider the static equilibrium response of $\mathbf{y}^e$ to $\mathbf{z}^e$ when $\mathsf{E}(\mathbf{y}_t) = \mathbf{y}^e$ and $\mathsf{E}(\mathbf{z}_t) = \mathbf{z}^e \; \forall \, t$, and from (15), (19) and (20) this is given by:

$$\frac{\partial \mathbf{y}^e}{\partial \mathbf{z}^{e\prime}} = \left[\left(\mathbf{I} - \sum_{i=1}^{p} \mathbf{D}_i \right)^{-1} \left(\pi + \sum_{i=1}^{p} \Pi_i \right) \right]. \tag{28}$$

Although multiplier analysis was the form most emphasized in the DSEM literature, other responses of interest can be calculated as well. The effect of a unit change in a component of $\boldsymbol{\mu}_{y|z}$ is numerically the same as that of a unit change in the corresponding component of $\mathbf{v}_t$, a point discussed by Ericsson, Hendry and Mizon (1998). Each of the analyses just considered is appropriate for the *ex post* type of policy analysis. In *ex ante* policy analysis where a different kind of policy regime is contemplated, for example a new adaptive policy rule (different from that followed in the sample period) then the consequences of that policy rule can be investigated by coupling the conditional model with the new marginal model implied by the policy rule.

Working with just the open model has advantages since it obviates the need to model the rest of the system which may be a difficult task. Faced by the choice of working with a closed model for a subset of variables, and working with an open model that conditions on those variables that are difficult to model well (this can often be the case for policy instruments), the latter has clear advantages. On the other hand, to ensure that the super-exogeneity assumptions are on a sound footing it is necessary to model the rest of the system. Moreover, open models and dynamic multiplier analysis cannot answer certain questions of interest in the policy context. For example, to do separate analyses of the consequences of changes in the predictable part and the surprise part of $\mathbf{z}_t$ is beyond the scope of the procedure because the conditioning variable is not decomposed. Finally, note that not modelling the policy variables precludes the possibility of considering feedback. However, if $\mathbf{z}$ is strongly exogenous for the parameters of the conditional distribution, there is no need to model feedback.

3.3 Stationary Example

To illustrate the approaches described above we consider a simple bivariate model with two lags:

$$\begin{bmatrix} y_t \\ z_t \end{bmatrix} = \begin{bmatrix} 0.5 & 0.2 \\ 0.4 & 0.5 \end{bmatrix} \begin{bmatrix} y_{t-1} \\ z_{t-1} \end{bmatrix} + \begin{bmatrix} 0 & 0 \\ 0.25 & 0 \end{bmatrix} \begin{bmatrix} y_{t-2} \\ z_{t-2} \end{bmatrix}$$
$$+ \begin{bmatrix} \varepsilon_{yt} \\ \varepsilon_{zt} \end{bmatrix} \text{with} \begin{bmatrix} \varepsilon_{yt} \\ \varepsilon_{zt} \end{bmatrix} \backsim \mathsf{IN}_2 \left[\begin{pmatrix} 0 \\ 0 \end{pmatrix}, \begin{pmatrix} 0.0001 & 0.00002 \\ 0.00002 & 0.0001 \end{pmatrix} \right]. \quad (29)$$

The parameters of this model have been chosen to have a high signal/noise ratio so that the parameters could be reliably estimated. In fact, the means of the parameter estimates over 200 replications of samples of size 100 observations were:

$$\begin{bmatrix} 0.48 & 0.10 \\ 0.39 & 0.49 \end{bmatrix} \text{ and } \begin{bmatrix} 0 & 0 \\ 0.26 & 0 \end{bmatrix}$$

for the coefficients of $(y_{t-1}, z_{t-1})'$ and $(y_{t-2}, z_{t-2})'$ respectively.

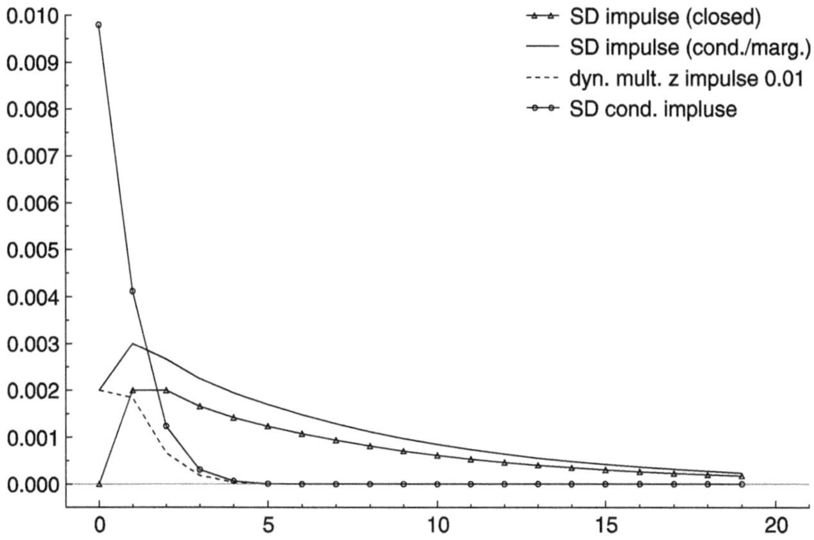

Figure 14.1 *Responses in stationary example*

The conditional model in this example is given by:

$$y_t = 0.2z_t + 0.42y_{t-1} + 0.1z_{t-1} - 0.05y_{t-2} + v_t \text{ with } v_t \backsim \text{IN}(0, 0.000096). \quad (30)$$

Using the parameter values given in the DGP (29), Figure 14.1 shows how y responds to a variety of shocks. The cases illustrated are traditional impulse response analysis and some experiments done within the marginal/conditional scheme. (In the latter framework one form of the orthogonal analysis coincides with the marginal/conditional scheme.) The response path of y to a shock of one standard deviation to ε_{zt} in the closed model is represented by the solid line with triangles. As always for closed VAR impulse response analysis this response starts at 0 and returns to 0 again as $h \to \infty$. The dashed line and the solid line with circles show respectively the dynamic multiplier analysis of the effect of setting z_t to 0.01 and the standard deviation impulse response analysis for the conditional model alone. Note the latter starts at 0.01 since the standard deviation of v_t is $0.009798 \approx 0.01$, and the former starts at $0.2 \times 0.01 = 0.002$. Finally, the solid line presents the response of y to a shock of one standard deviation (0.01) to ε_{zt} in the conditional/marginal formulation, and for $h = 0$ this takes the value of

0.2×0.01 as well. The dynamic multipliers take into account effects from contemporaneous and lagged z, unlike the impulse response experiments. Traditional impulse response analysis takes no account of contemporaneous correlation of error terms and so assumes no contemporaneous response from ε_{yt}. Because of stationarity the effects of all these one-off changes (impulses) considered above converge on zero asymptotically. However, from (30) the static equilibrium response of y to z is given by $\partial y^e/\partial z^e = (0.2 + 0.1)/(1 - 0.42 + 0.05) = 0.476$ in a static equilibrium such that $\mathsf{E}(y_t) = y^e$ and $\mathsf{E}(z_t) = z^e$ for all t giving the response in y^e to a change of 0.01 in z^e equal to 0.0048. These are the responses of y^e to step or permanent changes in z^e and noting that policy changes are usually maintained for some time rather than being one-off impulses static equilibrium responses will often be more relevant than impulse responses.

4 Response Analysis in a Non-stationary VAR

Most macroeconomic time-series variables are non-stationary and so a different framework is required for their analysis. Vector equilibrium correction (VECM) models describe more complicated systems with the response analysis based on them richer than that based on stationary VARs. As in the stationary case changes may be brought about by anticipated changes in policy or by unanticipated shocks. Responses of interest may include responses to changes in growth rates, equilibrium means, or levels of target variables with systematic application of a specific control rule as shown by Johansen and Juselius (2003).

To allow for non-stationarity of the variables we replace Assumption 2 by:

Assumption 2* The roots of $|\mathbf{I}_n - \sum_{i=1}^{p} \mathbf{\Phi}_i \varkappa^i| = 0$ satisfy $|\varkappa| \geqslant 1$, and write (5) in the VECM form:

$$\Delta \mathbf{x}_t = \sum_{i=1}^{(p-1)} \mathbf{\Gamma}_i \Delta \mathbf{x}_{t-i} + \mathbf{\Pi} x_{t-1} + \boldsymbol{\phi} + \boldsymbol{\varepsilon}_t \tag{31}$$

where $\mathbf{\Gamma}_i = -\sum_{j=i+1}^{p} \mathbf{\Phi}_j$ and $\mathbf{\Pi} = -(\mathbf{I}_n - \sum_{i=1}^{p} \mathbf{\Phi}_i)$ for $i = 2, \ldots, p-1$.

We moreover assume that the system is cointegrated, that is:

Assumption 4 The matrix $\mathbf{\Pi}$ has reduced rank r $(1 \leq r < n)$ and can be factorized into:

$$\mathbf{\Pi} = \boldsymbol{\alpha}\boldsymbol{\beta}',$$

where $\boldsymbol{\alpha}$ and $\boldsymbol{\beta}$ are $n \times r$ matrices.

To rule out the possibility of the variables in $\mathbf{x}_t$ being I(2) we make an additional assumption:

Assumption 5 The matrix $\boldsymbol{\alpha}'_{\perp}\boldsymbol{\Gamma}\boldsymbol{\beta}_{\perp}$ has full rank, where $\boldsymbol{\Gamma} = \mathbf{I}_n - \sum_{i=1}^{p-1}\boldsymbol{\Gamma}_i$, and $\boldsymbol{\alpha}_{\perp}$ and $\boldsymbol{\beta}_{\perp}$ are $n \times (n-r)$ matrices of full rank such that $\boldsymbol{\alpha}'\boldsymbol{\alpha}_{\perp} = 0$ and $\boldsymbol{\beta}'\boldsymbol{\beta}_{\perp} = 0$.

Denoting $\mathsf{E}[\boldsymbol{\Delta}\mathbf{x}_t] = \boldsymbol{\gamma}$ and $\mathsf{E}[\boldsymbol{\beta}'\mathbf{x}_t] = \eta$ we can rewrite (31) as:

$$\Delta\mathbf{x}_t = \boldsymbol{\gamma} + \sum_{i=1}^{(p-1)} \boldsymbol{\Gamma}_i(\Delta\mathbf{x}_{t-i} - \boldsymbol{\gamma}) + \boldsymbol{\alpha}(\boldsymbol{\beta}'\mathbf{x}_{t-1} - \eta) + \boldsymbol{\varepsilon}_t. \tag{32}$$

Under Assumptions 2*, 4 and 5, $\Delta\mathbf{x}_t$ can be written as (see, for example, Johansen (1995)):

$$\Delta\mathbf{x}_t = \mathbf{C}(1)(\boldsymbol{\varepsilon}_t - \boldsymbol{\Gamma}\boldsymbol{\gamma}) + \mathbf{C}^*(L)\Delta(\boldsymbol{\varepsilon}_t - \boldsymbol{\Gamma}\boldsymbol{\gamma} - \boldsymbol{\alpha}\eta)$$

where $\mathbf{C}(1) = \boldsymbol{\beta}_{\perp}(\boldsymbol{\alpha}'_{\perp}\boldsymbol{\Gamma}\boldsymbol{\beta}_{\perp})^{-1}\boldsymbol{\alpha}'_{\perp}$ and $\mathbf{C}^*(L) = \mathbf{C}_0^* + \mathbf{C}_1^*L + \mathbf{C}_2^*L^2 + \cdots$ has all roots outside the complex unit circle. Cointegration relationships can be represented as:

$$\boldsymbol{\beta}'\mathbf{x}_t = \boldsymbol{\beta}'\mathbf{C}^*(L)\boldsymbol{\varepsilon}_t - \boldsymbol{\beta}'\mathbf{C}^*(1)(\boldsymbol{\Gamma}\boldsymbol{\gamma} + \boldsymbol{\alpha}\eta).$$

To obtain the analogues of the conventional forms of impulse analysis (31) can be further represented as the infinite moving average:

$$\Delta\mathbf{x}_t = \sum_{i=0}^{\infty} \mathbf{C}_i(\boldsymbol{\varepsilon}_{t-i} - \boldsymbol{\Gamma}\boldsymbol{\gamma} - \boldsymbol{\alpha}\eta) \tag{33}$$

where $\mathbf{C}_0 = \mathbf{C}(1) + \mathbf{C}_0^* = \mathbf{I}$ and $\mathbf{C}_i = \mathbf{C}_i^* - \mathbf{C}_{i-1}^*$ for $i = 1, 2, \ldots$. The analogue of orthogonalized impulse response analysis can be obtained if the variance matrix is orthogonalized as considered above. There is also an analogue of the generalized method.

For the conditional analysis we adopt the partitioned notation for $\mathbf{y}_t$ and $\mathbf{z}_t$ so that (32) becomes:

$$\begin{bmatrix}\Delta\mathbf{y}_t\\ \Delta\mathbf{z}_t\end{bmatrix} = \begin{bmatrix}\boldsymbol{\gamma}_y\\ \boldsymbol{\gamma}_z\end{bmatrix} + \sum_{i=1}^{(p-1)} \begin{bmatrix}\boldsymbol{\Gamma}_{yy} & \boldsymbol{\Gamma}_{yz}\\ \boldsymbol{\Gamma}_{zy} & \boldsymbol{\Gamma}_{zz}\end{bmatrix} \begin{bmatrix}\Delta\mathbf{y}_{t-i} - \boldsymbol{\gamma}_y\\ \Delta\mathbf{z}_{t-i} - \boldsymbol{\gamma}_z\end{bmatrix}$$
$$+ \begin{bmatrix}\boldsymbol{\alpha}_y\\ \boldsymbol{\alpha}_z\end{bmatrix}(\boldsymbol{\beta}'_y\mathbf{y}_{t-1} + \boldsymbol{\beta}'_z\mathbf{z}_{t-1} - \eta) + \begin{bmatrix}\boldsymbol{\varepsilon}_{yt}\\ \boldsymbol{\varepsilon}_{zt}\end{bmatrix} \tag{34}$$

with the covariance matrix of $\boldsymbol{\varepsilon}_t$ given by $\boldsymbol{\Sigma} = \begin{bmatrix} \boldsymbol{\Sigma}_{yy} & \boldsymbol{\Sigma}_{yz} \\ \boldsymbol{\Sigma}_{zy} & \boldsymbol{\Sigma}_{zz} \end{bmatrix}$. Similarly (33) becomes:

$$\begin{bmatrix} \Delta\mathbf{y}_t \\ \Delta\mathbf{z}_t \end{bmatrix} = \sum_{i=0}^{\infty} \begin{bmatrix} \mathbf{C}_{yy,i} & \mathbf{C}_{yz,i} \\ \mathbf{C}_{zy,i} & \mathbf{C}_{zz,i} \end{bmatrix} \left(\begin{bmatrix} \boldsymbol{\varepsilon}_{y(t-i)} \\ \boldsymbol{\varepsilon}_{z(t-i)} \end{bmatrix} - \begin{bmatrix} \boldsymbol{\Gamma}_{yy} & \boldsymbol{\Gamma}_{yz} \\ \boldsymbol{\Gamma}_{zy} & \boldsymbol{\Gamma}_{zz} \end{bmatrix} \begin{bmatrix} \boldsymbol{\gamma}_y \\ \boldsymbol{\gamma}_z \end{bmatrix} - \begin{bmatrix} \boldsymbol{\alpha}_y \\ \boldsymbol{\alpha}_z \end{bmatrix} \eta \right). \tag{35}$$

For purposes of comparison we present here some of the response matrices that may be of interest (more are given in Hendry and Mizon, 1998). The underlying impulse responses are analogous to those of the traditional analysis discussed in section 3 above:

$$\frac{\partial\,\Delta\mathbf{y}_{t+h}}{\partial\boldsymbol{\varepsilon}'_{zt}} = \mathbf{C}^*_{yz,h} - \mathbf{C}^*_{yz,(h-1)} \quad \forall h > 0$$

$$\frac{\partial\boldsymbol{\beta}'\mathbf{x}_{t+h}}{\partial\boldsymbol{\varepsilon}'_{zt}} = \boldsymbol{\beta}'_y\mathbf{C}^*_{yz,h} + \boldsymbol{\beta}'_z\mathbf{C}^*_{zz,h}$$

when $\mathbf{C}^*(L) = \sum_{h=0}^{\infty} \mathbf{C}^*_h L^h$ with $\mathbf{C}^*_h$ partitioned as:

$$\mathbf{C}^*_h = \begin{bmatrix} \mathbf{C}^*_{yy,h} & \mathbf{C}^*_{yz,h} \\ \mathbf{C}^*_{zy,h} & \mathbf{C}^*_{zz,h} \end{bmatrix}. \tag{36}$$

The first is similar to responses seen earlier, but the second has no precedent in the analysis for stationary systems.

Proceeding to the marginal/conditional representation, we factorize (34) as:

$$\begin{aligned} \Delta\mathbf{y}_t = \boldsymbol{\gamma}_y + &\left(\pi\,\Delta\mathbf{z}_t - \boldsymbol{\gamma}_z - \sum_{i=1}^{(p-1)} \begin{bmatrix} \boldsymbol{\Gamma}_{zy} & \boldsymbol{\Gamma}_{zz} \end{bmatrix} \begin{bmatrix} \Delta\mathbf{y}_{t-i} - \boldsymbol{\gamma}_y \\ \Delta\mathbf{z}_{t-i} - \boldsymbol{\gamma}_z \end{bmatrix} \right. \\ &\left. - \boldsymbol{\alpha}_z \left(\boldsymbol{\beta}' \begin{bmatrix} \mathbf{y}_{t-1} \\ \mathbf{z}_{t-1} \end{bmatrix} - \eta \right) \right) \\ &+ \sum_{i=1}^{(p-1)} \begin{bmatrix} \boldsymbol{\Gamma}_{yy} & \boldsymbol{\Gamma}_{yz} \end{bmatrix} \begin{bmatrix} \Delta\mathbf{y}_{t-i} - \boldsymbol{\gamma}_y \\ \Delta\mathbf{z}_{t-i} - \boldsymbol{\gamma}_z \end{bmatrix} + \boldsymbol{\alpha}_y \left(\boldsymbol{\beta}' \begin{bmatrix} \mathbf{y}_{t-1} \\ \mathbf{z}_{t-1} \end{bmatrix} - \eta \right) + \mathbf{v}_t \end{aligned} \tag{37}$$

$$\Delta\mathbf{z}_t = \boldsymbol{\gamma}_z + \sum_{i=1}^{(p-1)} \begin{bmatrix} \boldsymbol{\Gamma}_{zy} & \boldsymbol{\Gamma}_{zz} \end{bmatrix} \begin{bmatrix} \Delta\mathbf{y}_{t-i} - \boldsymbol{\gamma}_y \\ \Delta\mathbf{z}_{t-i} - \boldsymbol{\gamma}_z \end{bmatrix} + \boldsymbol{\alpha}_z \left(\boldsymbol{\beta}' \begin{bmatrix} \mathbf{y}_{t-1} \\ \mathbf{z}_{t-1} \end{bmatrix} - \eta \right) + \boldsymbol{\varepsilon}_{zt} \tag{38}$$

where $\mathbf{v}_t = \boldsymbol{\varepsilon}_{yt} - \pi\,\boldsymbol{\varepsilon}_{zt}$ and $\pi = \boldsymbol{\Sigma}_{yz}\boldsymbol{\Sigma}_{zz}^{-1}$.

Special interest attaches to the case in which $\boldsymbol{\alpha}_z = 0$, that is, when $\mathbf{z}$ is weakly exogenous for the parameters in $\boldsymbol{\beta}$. As Ericsson and Irons (1995) document, this is a case that occurs with considerable regularity. (For the interpretation of weak exogeneity in cointegrated systems see Johansen, 1992, Urbain, 1992 and Ericsson, Hendry and Mizon, 1998). There is an example of such a system involving money and interest rates in Hendry and Mizon (1998). Even without weak exogeneity of $\mathbf{z}$, reliable estimates of responses can be obtained from the conditional model provided that the cointegration relations are estimated in the full system prior to formulation of the conditional model.

Equations (37) and (38) can be rewritten in the moving average form as:

$$\begin{bmatrix} \Delta \mathbf{y}_t \\ \Delta \mathbf{z}_t \end{bmatrix} = \sum_{i=0}^{\infty} \begin{bmatrix} \mathbf{C}_{yy,i} & \mathbf{C}_{yz,i} \\ \mathbf{C}_{zy,i} & \mathbf{C}_{zz,i} \end{bmatrix} \begin{bmatrix} \mathbf{I} & \pi \\ 0 & \mathbf{I} \end{bmatrix} \left(\begin{bmatrix} \mathbf{v}_{t-i} \\ \boldsymbol{\varepsilon}_{z(t-i)} \end{bmatrix} - \begin{bmatrix} \boldsymbol{\Gamma}_{yy} & \boldsymbol{\Gamma}_{yz} \\ \boldsymbol{\Gamma}_{zy} & \boldsymbol{\Gamma}_{zz} \end{bmatrix} \begin{bmatrix} \boldsymbol{\gamma}_y \\ \boldsymbol{\gamma}_z \end{bmatrix} - \begin{bmatrix} \boldsymbol{\alpha}_y \\ \boldsymbol{\alpha}_z \end{bmatrix} \eta \right) \tag{39}$$

with:

$$\boldsymbol{\beta}_y' \mathbf{y}_t + \boldsymbol{\beta}_z' \mathbf{z}_t = (\boldsymbol{\beta}_y', \boldsymbol{\beta}_z') \sum_{i=0}^{\infty} \begin{bmatrix} \mathbf{C}^*_{yy,i} & \mathbf{C}^*_{yz,i} \\ \mathbf{C}^*_{zy,i} & \mathbf{C}^*_{zz,i} \end{bmatrix} \begin{bmatrix} \mathbf{v}_{(t-i)} + \pi \boldsymbol{\varepsilon}_{z,(t-i)} \\ \boldsymbol{\varepsilon}_{z,(t-i)} \end{bmatrix}$$
$$- \boldsymbol{\beta}' \mathbf{C}^*(1)(\boldsymbol{\Gamma} \boldsymbol{\gamma} + \boldsymbol{\alpha} \eta).$$

Response analysis analogous to that developed above for the full system gives the following results applied to this conditional and marginal formulation:

$$\frac{\partial \Delta \mathbf{y}_{t+h}}{\partial \boldsymbol{\varepsilon}'_{zt}} = (\mathbf{C}^*_{yy,h} - \mathbf{C}^*_{yy,(h-1)})\pi + \mathbf{C}^*_{yz,h} - \mathbf{C}^*_{yz,(h-1)}$$

$$\frac{\partial \boldsymbol{\beta}' \mathbf{x}_{t+h}}{\partial \boldsymbol{\varepsilon}'_{zt}} = (\boldsymbol{\beta}_{\mathbf{y}}' \mathbf{C}^*_{yy,h} + \boldsymbol{\beta}_z' \mathbf{C}^*_{zy,h})\pi + (\boldsymbol{\beta}_y' \mathbf{C}^{*\prime}_{yz,h} + \boldsymbol{\beta}_z' \mathbf{C}^*_{zz,h})$$

These responses may differ considerably from those given by traditional impulse response analysis.

4.1 Non-stationary Example

To illustrate the different approaches in a system with cointegration, we present impulse response analyses analogous to those performed for the

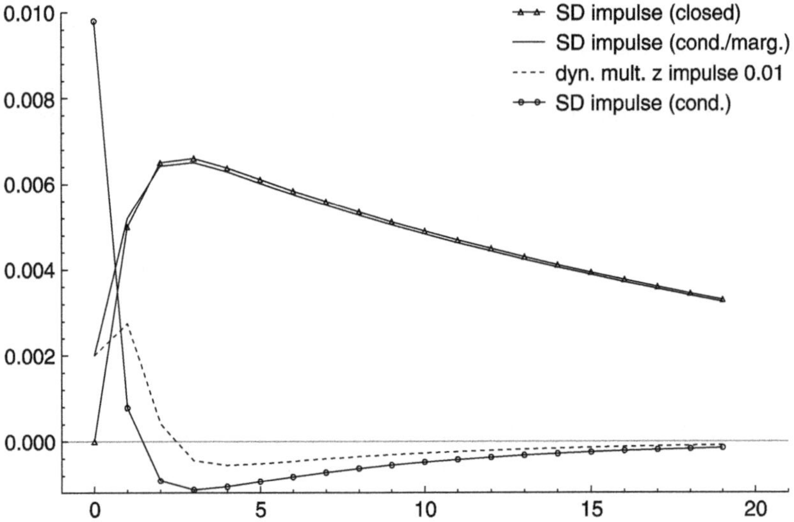

Figure 14.2 *Responses in non-stationary example*

stationary example of section 3.3. We consider a simple two-variable model:

$$\begin{bmatrix}\Delta y_t \\ \Delta z_t\end{bmatrix} = \begin{bmatrix}0.2 & 0 \\ 0.1 & 0.2\end{bmatrix}\begin{bmatrix}\Delta y_{t-1} \\ \Delta z_{t-1}\end{bmatrix} + \begin{bmatrix}-0.1 \\ 0\end{bmatrix}(y_{t-1} - 5z_{t-1})$$
$$+ \begin{bmatrix}\varepsilon_{yt} \\ \varepsilon_{zt}\end{bmatrix} \text{ with } \begin{bmatrix}\varepsilon_{yt} \\ \varepsilon_{zt}\end{bmatrix} \backsim \mathsf{IN}_n\left[\begin{pmatrix}0 \\ 0\end{pmatrix}, \begin{pmatrix}0.0001 & 0.00002 \\ 0.00002 & 0.0001\end{pmatrix}\right] \tag{40}$$

in which z is weakly exogenous for the parameters of the cointegrating vector $(y_t - 5z_t)$.

The corresponding conditional and marginal models are:

$$\begin{bmatrix}\Delta y_t \\ \Delta z_t\end{bmatrix} = \begin{bmatrix}0.2 \\ 0\end{bmatrix}\Delta z_t + \begin{bmatrix}0.18 & -0.04 \\ 0.1 & 0.2\end{bmatrix}\begin{bmatrix}\Delta y_{t-1} \\ \Delta z_{t-1}\end{bmatrix}$$
$$+ \begin{bmatrix}-0.1 \\ 0\end{bmatrix}(y_{t-1} - 5z_{t-1}) + \begin{bmatrix}v_t \\ \varepsilon_{zt}\end{bmatrix}.$$

Figure 14.2 shows results of experiments analogous to those presented for the stationary case with the difference that the depicted responses are those of Δy rather than of y. Note that for this model the static equilibrium is given by $\mathsf{E}(y^e - 5z^e) = 0$, so that when y is regarded as the target and z the policy instrument the static equilibrium response of y to z is given by $\partial y^e / \partial z^e = 5$. The response of Δy to a shock of one standard deviation to ε_{zt} in the closed model is represented by the solid line with triangles. The dashed line and the solid line with circles show respectively the multiplier analysis of the effect of setting Δz to 0.01 and the standard deviation impulse response analysis for the conditional model alone. Finally the solid line presents the response of Δy to a shock of one standard deviation to ε_{zt} in the conditional/marginal formulation. The patterns are similar to those for the stationary case with again the traditional impulse response analysis taking no account of the contemporaneous correlation of error terms.

5 Conclusion

It has been argued that for economic policy analysis using econometric models it is important that these models are relevant (describe the appropriate responses), reliable (exploit all relevant available information on these responses), and robust (are invariant to changes in the available information). This is achieved by developing congruent and encompassing models of the relationship between the policy targets and instruments, as advocated by the proponents of the "LSE methodology". Many of the models that have been used for impulse response analysis, whether of the Sims non-structural kind or of the "structural" kind, typically have not been evaluated so rigorously. Recent work by Hendry and Mizon (2000) has emphasized that the conclusions drawn from impulse response analysis may be very misleading in the presence of structural breaks despite the fact that they are endemic.

We have noted the importance of distinguishing between responses to shocks (unanticipated events), and to (known) policy changes. Throughout we have emphasized the importance of the appropriate choice of conditioning variables, and how a careful selection of the latter is preferable to arbitrary orthogonalization. Also we have shown the value of using open models that condition on the policy instruments that are themselves often difficult to model.

References

Abadir, K.M. and J.R. Magnus (2002) "Notation in Econometrics: A Proposal for a Standard", *Econometrics Journal*, **5**, 76–90.

Ahn, S.C. and P. Schmidt (1995) "Efficient Estimation of Models for Dynamic Panel Data", *Journal of Econometrics*, **68**, 5–27.

Ahn, S.C. and P. Schmidt (1997) "Efficient Estimation of Dynamic Panel Data Models: Alternative Assumptions and Simplified Estimation", *Journal of Econometrics*, **76**, 309–21.

Alonso-Borrego, C. and M. Arellano (1999) "Symmetrically Normalized Instrumental-variable Estimation using Panel Data", *Journal of Business and Economic Statistics*, **17**, 36–49.

Altonji, J. and L.M. Segal (1996) "Small Sample Bias in GMM Estimation of Covariance Structures", *Journal of Economic and Business Statistics*, **14**, 353–66.

Alvarez, J. and M. Arellano (2003) "The Time Series and Cross-section Asymptotics of Dynamic Panel Data Estimators", *Econometrica*, **71**, 1121–59.

Amemiya, T. (1977) "A Note on a Heteroscedastic Model", *Journal of Econometrics*, **6**, 365–70; and corrigenda, *Journal of Econometrics*, **8**, 275.

Anderson, T.W. and H. Rubin (1949) "Estimation of the Parameters of a Single Equation in a Complete System of Stochastic Equations", *Annals of Mathematical Statistics*, **20**, 46–63.

Anderson, T.W. (1959) "On Asymptotic Distributions of Estimates of Parameters of Stochastic Difference Equations", *Annals of Mathematical Statistics*, **30**, 676–87.

Anderson, T.W. (1971) *The Statistical Analysis of Time Series*, New York: John Wiley & Sons.

Anderson, T.W. (1984) *An Introduction to Multivariate Statistical Analysis*, 2nd ed., New York: Wiley.

Anderson, T.W. and C. Hsiao (1981) "Estimation of Dynamic Models with Error Components", *Journal of the American Statistical Association*, **76**, 598–606.

Anderson, T.W. and C. Hsiao (1982) "Formulation and Estimation of Dynamic Models using Panel Data", *Journal of Econometrics*, **18**, 47–82.

Andrews, D.W.K. and B. Lu (2001) "Consistent Model and Moment Selection Procedures for GMM Estimation with Application to Dynamic Panel Data Models", *Journal of Econometrics*, **101**, 123–64.

Angrist, J.D. and A.B. Krueger (1992) "The Effect of Age at School Entry on Educational Attainment: An Application of Instrumental Variables with

Moments from Two Samples", *Journal of the American Statistical Association*, **87**, 328–36.

Anselin, L. (2001) "Spatial Econometrics", in *A Companion to Theoretical Econometrics,* (ed.) B. Baltagi, Oxford: Blackwell.

Arellano, M. (2003) *Panel Data Econometrics*, Oxford: Oxford University Press.

Arellano, M. and S. Bond (1991) "Some Tests of Specification for Panel Data: Monte Carlo Evidence and an Application to Employment Equations", *Review of Economic Studies*, **58**, 277–97.

Arellano, M. and O. Bover (1995) "Another Look at the Instrumental-variable Estimation of Error-component Models", *Journal of Econometrics*, **68**, 29–52.

Back, K. and D. Brown (1993) "Implied Probabilities in GMM Estimators", *Econometrica*, **61**, 971–76.

Bai, J. (2003) "Inferential Theory for Factor Models of Large Dimensions", *Econometrica*, **71**, 135–73.

Bai, J. and S. Ng (2002) "Determinining the Number of Factors in Approximate Factor Models", *Econometrica*, **70**, 191–221.

Baillie, R.T. and T. Bollerslev (1989) "The Message in Daily Exchange Rates: A Conditional Variance Tale", *Journal of Business and Economic Statistics,* **7**, 297–305.

Balestra, P. and M. Nerlove (1966) "Pooling Cross Section and Time Series Data in the Estimation of a Dynamic Model: The Demand for Natural Gas", *Econometrica*, **34**, 585–612.

Baltagi, B.H. (2005) *Econometric Analysis of Panel Data*, 3rd ed., New York: John Wiley & Sons.

Barrett, A. and P.J. O'Connell (1999) "Does Training Generally Work? The Returns to In-Company Training", Institute for the Study of Labour, Discussion Paper no. 51.

Bartel, A. (1994) "Productivity Gains from the Implementation of Employee Training Programs", *Industrial Relations*, **33**, 411–25.

Basawa, I.V. and P.J. Brockwell (1984) "Asymptotic Conditional Inference for Regular Nonergodic Models with an Application to Autoregressive Processes", *Annals of Statistics*, **12**, 161–71.

Basmann, R.L. (1960) "On Finite Sample Distributions of Generalized Classical Linear Identifiability Test Statistics", *Journal of the American Statistical Association*, **55**, 650–9.

Bernanke, B.S. (1986) "Alternative Explorations of the Money–Income Correlation", in Brunner, K. and A.H. Meltzer (eds.), *Real Business Cycles, Real Exchange Rates, and Actual Policies, Vol. 25 of Carnegie-Rochester Conferences on Public Policy*, 49–99, Amsterdam: North-Holland.

Berndt, E.R., B. H. Hall, R.E. Hall and J.A. Hausman (1974) "Estimation and Inference in Non-linear Structural Models", *Annals of Economic and Social Measurement*, **4**, 653–65.

Bhargava, A. and J.D. Sargan (1983) "Estimating Dynamic Random Effects Models from Panel Data Covering Short Time Periods", *Econometrica*, **51**, 1635–59.

Bhattacharya, R.N. and J.K. Ghosh (1978) "On the Validity of the Formal Edgeworth Expansion", *Annals of Statistics*, **6**, 434–51.

Bickel, P.J. (1982) "On Adaptive Estimation", *The Annals of Statistics*, **10**, 647–71.

Blundell, R. and S. Bond (1998) "Initial Conditions and Moment Restrictions in Dynamic Panel Data Models", *Journal of Econometrics*, **87**, 115–43.

Blundell, R., S. Bond, and F. Windmeijer (2000) "Estimation in Dynamic Panel Data Models: Improving on the Performance of the Standard GMM Estimators", in Baltagi, B.H. (ed.), *Nonstationary Panels, Panel Cointegration, and Dynamic Panels. Advances in Econometrics 15*, Amsterdam: JAI Press, Elsevier Science, 53–91.

Bollerslev, T. P. (1986) "Generalized Autoregressive Conditional Heteroskedasticity", *Journal of Econometrics*, **31**, 307–27.

Bollerslev, T. P. (1987) "A Conditional Heteroskedastic Time Series Model for Speculative Prices and Rates of Returns", *Review of Economics and Statistics*, **69**, 542–47.

Bollerslev, T.P. and J.M. Wooldridge (1992) "Quasi-Maximum Likelihood Estimation and Inference in Dynamic Models with Time-varying Covariances", *Econometric Reviews*, **11**, 143–72.

Bollerslev, T. P., R.Y. Chou and K.F. Kroner (1992) "ARCH Modelling in Finance", *Journal of Econometrics*, **52**, 5–59.

Bollerslev, T. P., R.F. Engle and D.B. Nelson (1994) "ARCH Models", *Handbook of Econometrics*, Vol. **4**, 2959–3038.

Bond, S. (2002) "Dynamic Panel Data Model: A Guide to Micro Data Methods and Practice", *Portugese Economic Journal*, **1**, 141–62.

Bond, S. and F. Windmeijer (2002) "Projection Estimators for Autoregressive Panel Data Models", *The Econometrics Journal*, **5**, 457–79.

Bond, S. and F. Windmeijer (2005) "Reliable Inference for GMM Estimators?: Finite Sample Properties of Alternative Test Procedures in Linear Panel Models", *Econometric Reviews*, **24**, 1–37.

Bonnal, H. and E. Renault (2003) "On the Efficient Use of the Informational Content of Estimating Equations: Implied Probabilities and Maximum Euclidean Likelihood", Working Paper, Département de Sciences Économiques, Université de Montréal.

Bound, J., D.A. Jeager, and R.M. Baker (1995) "Problems with Instrumental Variables Estimation when the Correlation Between the Instruments and the Endogenous Explanatory Variable is Weak", *Journal of the American Statistical Association*, **90**, 443–50.

Bowden, R.J. and D.A. Turkington (1984) *Instrumental Variables*, Cambridge: Cambridge University Press.

Bowsher, C.G. (2002) "On Testing Overidentifying Restrictions in Dynamic Panel Data Models", *Economics Letters*, 77, 211–20.

Box, G. E.P. and G.M. Jenkins (1976) *Time Series Analysis, Forecasting and Control.* San Francisco: Holden-Day. First published, 1970.

Bravais, A. (1846) "Analyse mathématique sur les probabilités des erreurs de situation d'un point", *Mémoires de l'Académie Royale des Sciences de l'Institut de France* **9**, 255–332.

Breusch, T.S. (1980) "Useful Invariance Results for Generalized Regression Models", *Journal of Econometrics*, **13**, 327–40.

Brown, B.W. and W.K. Newey (1992) "Bootstrapping for GMM", Working Paper, Department of Economics, M.I.T.

Brown, B.W. and W.K. Newey (2002) "Generalized Method of Moments, Efficient Bootstrapping, and Improved Inference", *Journal of Economic and Business Statistics*, **20**, 507–17.

Brundy, J.M. and D.W. Jorgenson (1974) "Consistent and Efficient Estimation of Systems of Simultaneous Equations by Means of Instrumental Variables", ch. 8 in P. Zarembka (ed.), *Frontiers in Econometrics*, London: Academic Press.

Bultheel, A. (1987) *Laurent Series and the Fade Approximations*. Basel: Birkhauser Verlag.

Bun, M.J.G. and J.F. Kiviet (2003), "On the Diminishing Returns of Higher-order Terms in Asymptotic Expansions of Bias", *Economics Letters*, **79**, 145–52.

Bun, M.J.G. and J.F. Kiviet (2005) "The Effects of Dynamic Feedbacks on LS and MM Estimator Accuracy in Panel Data Models", *Forthcoming in Journal of Econometrics*.

Card, D. and A.B. Krueger (1992) "Does School Quality Matter? Returns to Education and the Characteristics of Public Schools in the United States", *Journal of Political Economy*, **100**, 1–40.

Cavanagh, C.L. (1983), "Hypothesis Testing in Models with Discrete Dependent Variables." Ph.D. thesis, Berkeley: University of California.

Chamberlain, G. (1987) "Asymptotic Efficiency in Estimation with Conditional Moment Restrictions", *Journal of Econometrics*, **34**, 305–34.

Chamberlain, G. and M. Rothschild (1983) "Arbitrage, Factor Structure and MeanVariance Analysis in Large Asset Markets", *Econometrica*, **51**.

Chan, N.H. and C.Z. Wei (1987) "Asymptotic Inference for Nearly Nonstationary AR(1) Processes", *Annals of Statistics*, **15**, 1050–63.

Chandra, T.K. and J.K. Ghosh (1980) "Valid Asymptotic Expansions for the Likelihood Ratio and Other Statistics Under Contiguous Alternatives", *Sankhyâ, Series A*, **42**, 170–84.

Coakley, J., A. Fuertes and R.P. Smith (2002) "A Principal Components Approach to Cross-Section Dependence in Panels", Mimeo, Birkbeck College, University of London.

Coakley, J., A. Fuertes and R.P. Smith (2006) "Unobserved Heterogeneity in Panel Time Series Models", Forthcoming in *Computational Statistics and Data Analysis*, **50**, 2361–80.

Conley, T. G. and B. Dupor (2003), "A Spatial Analysis of Sectoral Complementarity", *Journal of Political Economy*, **111**, 311–52.

Conley, T.G. and G. Topa (2002) "Socio-economic Distance and Spatial Patterns in Unemployment", *Journal of Applied Econometrics*, **17**, 303–27.

Conor, G. and R. Korajzcyk (1986) "Performance Measurement with the Arbitrage Pricing Theory: A New Framework for Analysis", *Journal of Financial Economics*, **15**, 373–94.

Conor, G. and R. Korajzcyk (1988) "Risk and Return in an Equilibrium APT: Application to a new test methodology", *Journal of Financial Economics*, **21**, 255–89.

Corcoran, S.A. (1998) "Bartlett Adjustment of Empirical Discrepancy Statistics", *Biometrika*, **85**, 967–72.

Cornish, E.A. and R.A. Fisher (1937) "Moments and Cumulants in the Specification of Distributions", *Revue del' Institute International de Statistic*, **4**, 1–14.

Cox, D.R. (1980) "Local Ancillarity", *Biometrika*, **67**, 279–86.

Cox, D.R. (1961) "Tests of Separate Families of Hypotheses", in *Proceedings of the Fourth Berkeley Symposium on Mathematical Statistics and Probability*, Vol. 1, 105–23, Berkeley: University of California Press.

Cox, D.R. (1962) "Further Results on Tests of Separate Families of Hypotheses", *Journal of the Royal Statistical Society, Series B*, **24**, 406–24.

Cressie, N. and T. Read (1984) "Multinomial Goodness-of-Fit Tests", *Journal of the Royal Statistical Society Series B*, **46**, 440–64.

Csörgõ, M. and L. Horváth (1993) *Weighted Approximations in Probability and Statistics*. New York: Wiley.

Davidson, R. and J.G. MacKinnon (1981) "Several Model Specification Tests in the Presence of Alternative Hypotheses", *Econometrica*, **49**, 781–93.

Davidson, R. and J.G. MacKinnon (1982) "Some Non-nested Hypothesis Tests and the Relations Among Them", *Review of Economic Studies*, **49**, 551–65.

Davidson, R. and J.G. MacKinnon (1993) *Estimation and Inference in Econometrics*. New York: Oxford University Press.

de Jong, R.M. and H.J. Bierens (1994) "On the Limit Behavior of a Chi-Square Type Test if the Number of Conditional Moments Tested Approaches Infinity", *Econometric Theory*, **10**, 70–90.

Delgado, M.A. and T. Stengos (1994) "Semiparametric Specification Testing of Non-nested Econometric Models", *Review of Economic Studies*, **61**, 291–303.

Dhrymes, P.J. (1969) "Alternative Asymptotic Tests of Significance and Related Aspects of 2SLS and 3SLS Estimated Parameters", *The Review of Economic Studies*, **36**, 213–26.

Dhrymes, P.J. (1971) *Distributed Lags: Problems of Estimation and Formulation*. San Francisco: Holden-Day.

Dhrymes, P.J. (1971a) "Equivalence of Iterative Aitken and Maximum Likelihood Estimators for a System of Regression Equations", *Australian Economic Papers*, **10**, 20–24.

Dhrymes, P.J. (1978) *Introductory Econometrics*, New York: Springer Verlag.

Dhrymes, P.J. (1989) *Topics in Advanced Econometrics: Probability Foundations*, New York: Springer-Verlag.

Dhrymes, P.J. (1994) *Topics in Advanced Econometrics: Vol. 2, Linear and Nonlinear Simultaneous Equations*, New York: Springer-Verlag.

Dhrymes, P.J. (2000) *Mathematics for Econometrics*, 3rd ed., New York: Springer-Verlag.

Donald, S.G., G.W. Imbens and W.K. Newey (2003) "Empirical Likelihood Estimation and Consistent Tests with Conditional Moment Restrictions," *Journal of Econometrics*, **117**, 55–93.

Doornik, J.A., M. Arellano and S. Bond (2002) Panel Data Estimation Using DPD for Ox. mimeo, University of Oxford.

Doran, H.E. and P. Schmidt (2005) "GMM Estimators with Improved Finite Sample Properties using Principal Components of the Weighting Matrix, with an Application to the Dynamic Panel Data Model," Forthcoming in *Journal of Econometrics*.

Durbin, J.M. (1954) "Errors in Variables", *Review of the Institute of International Statistics*, **22**, 23–31.

Durbin, J.M. (1970a) "Testing for Serial Correlation in Least Squares Regression When Some of the Regressors are Lagged Dependent Variables", *Econometrica*, **38**, 410–21.

Durbin, J.M. (1970b) "An Alternative to the Bounds Test for Testing for Serial Correlation in Least-Squares Regression", *Econometrica*, **38**, 422–29.

Durbin, J.M. (1973) Distribution Theory for Tests Based on the Sample Distribution Function, *Society for Industrial and Applied Mathematics*, Philadelphia, Pa, Section 2.4.

Durbin, J.M. (1980) "Approximations for Densities of Sufficient Estimators", *Biometrika*, **67**, 311–33.

Eldetron, W.P. and N.L. Johnson (1969) *Systems of Frequency Curves*. Cambridge: Cambridge University Press.

Engle, R.F. (1982) "Autoregressive Conditional Heteroskedasticity with Estimates of the Variance of the UK Inflation", *Econometrica*, **50**, 987–1008.

Engle, R.F. (2002) "New Frontiers for ARCH Models", *Journal of Applied Econometrics*, **17**, 425–46.

Engle, R.F. and G. Gonzalez-Rivera (1991) "Semiparametric ARCH Models", *Journal of Business and Economic Statistics*, **9**, 345–59.

Engle, R.E., D.E. Hendry and J.-E. Richard (1983) "Exogeneity", *Econometrica*, **51**, 277–304. Reprinted in Hendry, D.E., *Econometrics: Alchemy or Science?* Oxford: Blackwell Publishers, 1993 and Oxford University Press, 2000; and in Ericsson, N.R. and Irons, J.S. (eds.) *Testing Exogeneity*, Oxford: Oxford University Press, 1994.

Ericsson, N.R., D.E. Hendry and G.E. Mizon (1998) "Exogeneity, ointegration and Economic Policy Analysis", *Journal of Business and Economic Statistics*, **16**, 370–87.

Ericsson, N.R. and J.S. Irons (1995) Book Review of Applied Econometric Techniques, *Econometric Theory*, **14**, 121–33.

Eubank, R.L. and C.H. Spiegelman (1990) "Testing the Goodness of Fit of a Linear Model Via Non-parametric Regression Techniques", *Journal of the American Statistical Association*, **85**, 387–92.

Euler, L. (1770) De formulis integralibus duplicatis, Novi Commentarii Academiae Scientiarum Petropolitanae 14, 72–103. Reprinted in: *Opera Omnia*, Series 1, Vol. 17, 289–315.

Fan, Y. and Q. Li (1996) "Consistent Model Specification Tests: Omitted Variables and Semi-parametric Functional Forms", *Econometrica*, **64**, 865–90.

Fan, Y., Q. Li and T. Stengos (1995) "Root-N-Consistent Semi-parametric Regression with Conditionally Heteroskedastic Disturbances", *Journal of Quantitative Economics*, **11**, 229–40.

Fisher, G.R. and M. McAleer (1981) "Alternative Procedures and Associated Tests of Significance for Non-nested Hypotheses", *Journal of Econometrics*, **16**, 103–19.

Fisher, R.A. (1925) "Expansion of Student's Integral in Powers of n^{-1}", *Metron*, **5**, 109–12.

Fisher, R.A. and E.A. Cornish (1960) "The Percentile of Distributions Having Known Cumulants", *Technometrics*, **2**, 209–25.

Forchini, G. (2002) "The Exact Cumulative Distribution Function of a Ratio of Quadratic Forms in Normal Variables, with Application to the AR(1) Model", *Econometric Theory*, **18**, 823–52.

Forni, M. and L. Reichlin (1998) "Let's Get Real: A Factor Analytical Approach to Disaggregated Business Cycle Dynamics", *Review of Economic Studies*, **65**, 453–73.

Forni, M., M. Hallin, M. Lippi and L. Reichlin (2000) "The Generalised Factor Model: Identification and Estimation", *Review of Economics and Statistics*, **82**, 540–54.

Geary, R.C. (1948) "Studies in Relations Between Economic Time Series", *Journal of the Royal Statistical Society*, B, **10**, 140–58.

Geary, R.C. (1949) "Determination of Linear Relations Between Systematic Parts of Variables with Errors of Observations, the Variances of which are Unknown", *Econometrica*, **16**, 225–8.

Giraitis L. and P.C.B. Phillips (2006) "Uniform Limit Theory for Stationary Autoregression", *Journal of Time Series Analysis* (forthcoming).

Godfrey, L.G. and M.H. Pesaran (1983) "Tests of Non-nested Regression Models: Small Sample Adjustments and Monte Carlo Evidence", *Journal of Econometrics*, **21**, 133–54.

Goldberger, A.S. (1964) *Econometric Theory*, New York: John Wiley.

Goldfeld, S.M. and R.E. Quandt (1972) *Nonlinear Methods in Econometrics*, Amsterdam: North Holland.

Gonzalez-Rivera, G. and J.S. Racine (1995) "Maximum Likelihood Estimation and Testing Strategies in GARCH Models", *Proceedings of the American Statistical Association*, Business and Economics Section, pp. 47–54 (invited article).

Granger, C.W.G. and P. Newbold (1974) "Spurious Regressions in Econometrics", *Journal of Econometrics*, **2**, 111–20.

Greene, W.H. (1999) *Econometric Analysis*, 4th ed., New York: Prentice-Hall.

Grimmett, G. and D. Stirzaker (2001) *Probability and Random Processes*, 3rd edition. Oxford: Oxford University Press.

Hahn, J. and J. Hausman (2002) "Notes on Bias in Estimators for Simultaneous Models", *Economic Letters*, **75**, no.2, 237–41.

Hairer, E. and G. Wanner (1996) *Analysis by Its History*, New York: Springer-Verlag.

Hall, A.R. (1989) "Testing for a Unit Root in the Presence of Moving Average Errors", *Biometrika*, **76**, 49–56.

Hall, A.R. (1993) "Some Aspects of the Generalized Method of Moments Estimation", pp. 393–417 of G.S. Maddala, C.R. Rao and H.D. Vinod (eds.) *Handbook in Statistics, Vol. 11*, Amsterdam: Elsevier Science Publishers.

Hall, A.R., G.D. Rudebusch and D.W. Wilcox (1996) "Judging Instrument Relevance in Instrumental Variables Estimation", *International Economic Review*, **37**, 283–98.

Hall, P. and C.C. Heyde (1980) *Martingale Limit Theory and its Application*, Academic Press.

Hall, P. and J.D. Hart (1990) "Bootstrap Test for Difference Between Means in Non-parametric Regression", *Journal of the American Statistical Association*, **85**, 1039–49.

Hansen, B.E. (1993) "Autoregressive Conditional Density Estimation", unpublished manuscript.

Hansen, G. (2001) "A Bias-corrected Least Squares Estimator of Dynamic Panel Models", *Allgemeines Statistisches Archiv*, **85**, 127–40.

Hansen, L.P. (1982) "Large Sample Properties of Generalized Method of Moments Estimators", *Econometrica*, **50**, 1029–54.

Hansen, L.P. and K. Singleton (1982) "Generalized Instrumental Variable Estimation of Nonlinear Rational Expectations Models", *Econometrica*, **50**, 1269–86.

Hansen, L.P., J. Heaton and A. Yaron (1996) "Finite-sample Properties of Some Alternative GMM Estimators", *Journal of Business and Economic Statistics*, **14**, 262–80.

Härdle, W. and E. Mammen (1993) "Comparing Non-parametric Versus Parametric Regression Fits", *The Annals of Statistics*, **21**, 1926–47.

Harris, M.N. and L. Mátyás (2000) "Performance of the Operational Wansbeek-Bekker Estimator for Dynamic Panel Data Models", *Applied Economics Letters*, **7**, 149–53.

Harris, M.N. and L. Mátyás (2004) "A Comparative Analysis of Different IV and GMM Estimators of Dynamic Panel Data Models", *International Statistical Review*, **72**, 397–408.

Harvey, A.C. and G.D.A. Phillips (1980) "Testing for Serial Correlation in Simultaneous Equation Models", *Econometrica*, **48**, 747–59.

Hausman, J.A. (1975) "An Instrumental Variable Approach to Full Information Estimation for Linear and Certain Non-linear Econometric Models", *Econometrica*, **43**, 727–38.

Hausman, J.A. (1978) "Specification Tests in Econometrics", *Econometrica*, **46**, 1251–72.

Hayakawa, T. (1975) "The Likelihood Ratio Criteria for a Composite Hypothesis under a Local Alternative", *Biometrika*, **62**, 451–60.

Hayashi, F. (2000) *Econometrics*, Princeton: Princeton University Press.

Hendry, D.F. (1976) "The Structure of Simultaneous Equations Estimators", *Journal of Econometrics*, **4**, 51–88.

Hendry, D.F. (1984) Monte Carlo Experimentation in Econometrics. Chapter 16 in Griliches, Z. and M.D. Intriligator (eds.). *Handbook of Econometrics, Vol. II*, Amsterdam: Elsevier.

Hendry, D.E. (1995) *Dynamic Econometrics*, Oxford: Oxford University Press.

Hendry, D.F. and G.E. Mizon (1978) "Serial Correlation as a Convenient Simplification, not a Nuisance: A Comment on a Study of the Demand for Money by the Bank of England", *Economic Journal*, **88**, 549–63. Reprinted in Hendry, D.F., Econometrics: Alchemy or Science? Oxford: Blackwell Publishers, 1993, and Oxford University Press, 2000.

Hendry, D.F. and G.E. Mizon (1998) "Exogeneity, Causality, and Co-breaking in Economic Policy Analysis of a Small Econometric Model of Money in the UK", *Empirical Economics*, **23**, 267–94.

Hendry, D.E. and G.E. Mizon (2000) "Reformulating Empirical Macro-Econometric Modelling", *Oxford Review of Economic Policy*, **16**, 138–59.

Hildreth, C. and J.P. Houck (1968) "Some Estimators for a Linear Model with Random Coefficients", *Journal of the American Statistical Association*, **63**, 584–95.

Hill, G.W. and A.W. Davis (1968) "Generalized Asymptotic Expansions of the Cornish-Fisher Type", *Annals of Mathematical Statistics*, **39**, 1268–73.

Hillier, G.H. (2001) "The Density of a Quadratic form in a Vector Uniformly Distributed on the N-sphere", *Econometric Theory*, **17**, 1–29.

Hillier, G.H. and M. Armstrong (1999) "The Density of the Maximum Likelihood Estimator", *Econometrica*, **67**, 6, 1459–70.

Holtz-Eakin, D., W. Newey, and H.S. Rosen (1988) "Estimating Vector Autoregressions with Panel Data", *Econometrica*, **56**, 1371–95.

Hong and White (1991) "Consistent Specification Testing Via Non-Parametric Series Regressions", Working Paper, Department of Economics, University of California, San Diego.

Horowitz, J.L. and W. Härdle (1994) "Testing a Parametric Model Against a Semi-parametric Alternative", mimeo.

Hsiao, C., M.H. Pesaran, and A.K. Tahmiscioglu (2002) "Maximum Likelihood Estimation of Fixed Effects Dynamic Panel Data Models Covering Short Time Periods", *Journal of Econometrics*, **109**, 107–50.

Hsieh, D.A. (1989) "Modelling Heteroskedasticity in Daily Foreign-exchange Rates", *Journal of Business and Economic Statistics*, **7**, 307–17.

Imbens, G.W. (1997) "One-step Estimators for Over-identified Generalized Method of Moments Models", *Review of Economic Studies*, **64**, 359–83.

Imbens, G.W. and R.H. Spady (2005) "The Performance of Empirical Likelihood and Its Generalizations", Chapter 10 in *Identification and Inference in Econometric Models: Essays in Honor of Thomas J. Rothenberg*, D.W.K. Andrews and J.H. Stock (eds.), 216–44. Cambridge: Cambridge University Press.

Imbens, G.W., R.H. Spady and P. Johnson (1998) "Information Theoretic Approaches to Inference in Moment Condition Models", *Econometrica*, **66**, 333–57.

Jacobi, C.G.J. (1841) "De determinantibus functionalibus", *Crelle Journal für die Reine und Angewandte Mathemathik*, **22**, 319–52. Reprinted in: Weierstrass, K. (1884). *C.G.J. Jacobi's Gesammelte Werke*, Vol. 3, 393–438. Berlin: Georg Reimer.

Johansen, S. (1992) "Testing Weak Exogeneity and the Order of Cointegration in UK Money Demand", *Journal of Policy Modeling*, **14**, 313–34.

Johansen, S. (1995) *Likelihood-based Inference in Cointegrated Vector Autoregressive Models*, Oxford: Oxford University Press.

Johansen, S. and K. Juselius (2003) "Controlling Inflation in a Cointegrated Vector Autoregressive Model with an Application to US Data", Institute of Economics Discussion Paper no. 01-03, University of Copenhagen.

Johnson, N.L. and S. Kontz (1970) *Distributions in Statistics: Continuous Univariate Distributions-1*. New York: Willey and Sons.

Jorion, P. (1988) "On Jump Processes in the Foreign and Stock Markets", *Review of Financial Studies*, **1**, 427–45.

Judson, R.A. and A.L. Owen (1999) "Estimating Dynamic Panel Data Models: A Guide for Macroeconomists", *Economics Letters*, **65**, 9–15.

Kendall, M. and A. Stuart (1977) *The Advanced Theory of Statistics*, Vol. I. London: C. Griffin and Co.

Kinal, T.W. (1980) "The Existence of Moments of k-class Estimators", *Econometrica*, **48**, 643–52.

Kitamura, Y. (2001) "Asymptotic Optimality of Empirical Likelihood for Testing Moment Restriction", *Econometrica*, **69**, 1661–72.

Kitamura, Y. and M. Stutzer (1997) "An Information-theoretic Alternative to Generalized Method of Moments Estimation", *Econometrica*, **65**, 861–74.

Kitamura, Y., G. Tripathi, and H. Ahn (2004) "Empirical Likelihood-based Inference in Conditional Moment Restriction Models", *Econometrica*, **72**, 1667–1714.

Kiviet, J.F. (1995) "On Bias, Inconsistency, and Efficiency of Various Estimators in Dynamic Panel Data Models", *Journal of Econometrics*, **68**, 53–78.

Klein, L.R. (1969) "Estimation of Interdependent Systems in Macro-Econometrics", *Econometrica*, **37**, 171–92.

Klein, L.R., R.J. Ball, A. Hazlewood, and P. Vandome (1961) *An Econometric Model of the UK*. Oxford: Oxford University Press.

Koop, G., M.H. Pesaran and S.M. Potter (1996) "Impulse Response Analysis in Nonlinear Multivariate Models", *Journal of Econometrics*, **74**, 119–47.

Koopmans, T. (1942) "Serial Correlation and Quadratic forms in Normal Variables", *Ann. Math. Statist*, **12**, 14–33.

Kunimoto, N., K. Morimune, and Y. Tsukuda (1983) "Asymptotic Expansions of the Distribution of the Test Statistic for Overidentifying Restrictions in a System of Simultaneous Equations", *International Economic Review*, **24**, 199–215.

Lagrange, J.-L. de (1773) "Sur l'attraction des sphéroïdes elliptiques", *Nouveaux Mémoires de l'Académie Royale des Sciences et Belles-Lettres de Berlin*. Reprinted in Oeuvres, Vol. 3. Paris: Gauthier-Villars, 1869; Hildesheim/New York: Georg Olms Verlag, 1973.

Lancaster, T. (2002) "Orthogonal Parameters and Panel Data", *Review of Economic Studies*, **69**, 647–66.

Laplace, P.S. (1812) Théorie Analytique des Probabilités, in *Oeuvres Complètes, Vol. 7*, Paris: Gauthier-Villars.

Lebedev, N.N. (1972) *Special Functions and their Applications*, New York: Dover.

Lee, K.C. and M.H. Pesaran (1993) "The Role of Sectoral Jnteractions in Wage Determination in thc UK Economy", *The Economic Journal*, **103**, 21–55.

Lütkepohl, H. and H.E. Reimers (1992) "Impulse Response Analysis of Cointegrated Systems", *Journal of Economic Dynamics and Control*, **16**, 53–78.

Maasoumi, E. (1986) "Reduced form Estimation and Prediction from Uncertain Structural Models, a Generic Approach", *Journal of Econometrics*, **31**, 3–29.

Magdalinos, M.A. (1983) Applications of Refined Asymptotic Theory in Econometrics, Ph.D. thesis, University of Southampton.

Magdalinos, M.A. (1985) "Improving some Instrumental Variables Test Procedures", *Econometric Theory*, **1**, 240–61.

Magdalinos, M.A. (1988) "The Local Power of the Tests of Overidentifying Restrictions", *International Economic Review*, **29**, 509–23.

Magdalinos, M.A. (1992) "Stochastic Expansions and Asymptotic Approximations", *Econometric Theory*, **8**, 343–67.

Magdalinos, M.A. (1994) "Testing Instrument Admissibility: Some Refined Asymptotic Results", *Econometrica*, **62**, 373–403.

Magdalinos, A.M. and H. Kandilorou (2001) "Specification Analysis in Equations with Stochastic Regressors", *Journal of Business & Economic Statistics*, **19**, 226–32.

Magdalinos, M.A. and G.P. Mitsopoulos (2003) "Pearson Estimators in Regression Analysis", *Discussion Paper No 150.* Athens University of Economics and Business, Department of Economics.

Magdalinos, M.A. and S.D. Symeonides (1995) "Alternative Size Corrections for some GLS Test Statistics: The Case of the AR(1) Model", *Journal of Econometrics*, **66**, 35–59.

Magdalinos, M.A. and S.D. Symeonides (1996) "A Reinterpretation of the Tests for Overidentifying Restrictions", *Journal of Econometrics*, **73**, 325–53.

Magdalinos, T. (2004) Asymptotic Inference for General Neighbourhoods of a Unit Root. PhD thesis, University of York.

Magee, L. (1989) "An Edgeworth Test Size Correction for the Linear Model with AR(1) Errors", *Econometrica*, **57**, 661–674.

Magnus, J.R. and H. Neudecker (1979) "The Commutation Matrix: Some Properties and Applications", *Annals of Statistics*, **7**, 381–94.

Manski, C.F. (1984) "Adaptive Estimation of Non-linear Regression Models", *Econometric Reviews*, **3**, 145–94

Matyas, L. (1999) (ed.), *Generalized Method of Moments Estimation*, Cambridge: Cambridge University Press.

McDonald G.C. and D.I. Galarneau (1975) "A Monte Carlo Evaluation of Some Ridge-type Estimators", *Journal of the American Statistical Association*, **70**, 407–16.

Mikhail, W.M. (1972) "The Bias of the Two-stage Least Squares Estimators", *Journal of the American Statistical Association*, **67**, 625–27.

Mittelhammer, R.C., G.G. Judge, and R. Schoenberg (2005) "Empirical Evidence Concerning the Finite Sample Performance of EL-Type Structural Equation Estimation and Inference Methods", Chapter 12 in *Identification and Inference in Econometric Models: Essays in Honor of Thomas J. Rothenberg*, D.W.K. Andrews and J.H. Stock (eds.), 282–305. Cambridge: Cambridge University Press.

Mizon, G.E. (1995) "Progressive Modelling of Macroeconomic Time Series: the LSE Methodology", In Hoover, K.D. (ed.), *Macroeconometrics: Developments, Tensions and Prospects*, 107–69. Dordrecht: Kluwer Academic Press.

Morimune, K., and Y. Tsukuda (1984) "Testing a Subset of Coefficients in a Structural Equation", *Econometrica*, **52**, 427–48.

Mulholland, H.P. (1965), "On the Degree of Smoothness and on Singularities in Distributions of Statistical Functions", *Proc. Camb. Phil. Soc.*, **61**, 721–39.

Mulholland, H.P. (1970)"On Singularities of Sampling Distributions, in Particular for Ratios of Quadratic Forms", *Biometrika*, **57**, 155–74.

Nagar, A.L.(1959) "The Bias and Moment Matrix of the General k-class Estimator of the Parameters in Simultaneous Equations", *Econometrica*, **27**, 575–95.

Nelson, C.R. and R. Startz (1990a) "The Distribution of the Instrumental Variables Estimator and Its t-Ratio When the Instrument is a Poor One", *Journal of Business*, **63**, 125–40.

Nelson, C.R. and R. Startz (1990b) "Some Further Results on the Exact Small Sample Properties of the Instrumental Variable Estimator", *Econometrica*, **58**, 967–76.

Nerlove, M. (1967) "Experimental Evidence on the Estimation of Dynamic Economic Relations from a Time-Series of Cross Sections", *Economic Studies Quarterly*, **18**, 42–74.

Nerlove, M. (1971) "Further Evidence on the Estimation of Dynamic Economic Relations from a Time-Series of Cross Sections", *Econometrica*, **39**, 359–82.

Newey, W.K. (1985) "Generalized Method of Moments Specification Testing", *Journal of Econometrics*, **29**, 229–56.

Newey, W.K. (1990) "Efficient Instrumental Variables Estimation of Nonlinear Models", *Econometrica*, **58**, 809–37.

Newey, W.K. (1993) "Efficient Estimation of Models with Conditional Moment Restrictions", Chapter 16 in *Handbook of Statistics, Vol. 11*, G.S. Maddala, C.R. Rao and H. Vinod (eds.), 419–54. Amsterdam: North Holland.

Newey, W.K. and D.L. McFadden (1994) "Large Sample Estimation and Hypothesis Testing", Chapter 36 in *Handbook of Econometrics, Vol. 4*, R.F. Engle and D.L. McFadden (eds.), 2111–245. New York: North Holland.

Newey, W.K. and R.J. Smith (2004) "Higher Order Properties of GMM and Generalized Empirical Likelihood Estimators", *Econometrica*, **72**, 219–55.

Newey, W.K., J.J.S. Ramalho and R.J. Smith (2005) "Asymptotic Bias for GMM and GEL Estimators with Estimated Nuisance Parameters", Chapter 11 in *Identification and Inference in Econometric Models: Essays in Honor of Thomas J. Rothenberg*, D.W.K. Andrews and J.H. Stock (eds.), 245–81. Cambridge: Cambridge University Press.

Nickell, S. (1981) "Biases in Dynamic Models with Fixed Effects", *Econometrica*, **49**, 1417–26.

Ogaki, M. (1993) "Generalized Method of Moments: Econometric Applications", pp. 455–88 of G.S. Maddala, C.R. Rao and H.D. Vinod (eds.) *Handbook in Statistics, Vol. 11*, Amsterdam: Elsevier Science Publishers.

Owen, A. (1988) "Empirical Likelihood Ratio Confidence Intervals for a Single Functional", *Biometrika*, **75**, 237–49.

Owen, A. (1990) "Empirical Likelihood Ratio Confidence Regions", *Annals of Statistics*, **18**, 90–120.

Owen, A. (2001) *Empirical Likelihood*, New York: Chapman and Hall.

Pagan, A.R. and G.W. Schwert (1990) "Alternative Models for Conditional Stock Volatility", *Journal of Econometrics*, **45**, 267–90.

Pagan, A.R. (1984) "Model Evaluation by Variable Addition", ch. 5 of *Econometrics and Quantitative Economics*, Hendry, D.F. and K.F. Wallis (eds.), Oxford: Basil Blackwell.

Pagan, A.R. and Y.S. Hong (1991) "Nonparametric Estimation and the Risk Premium", in *Nonparametric Methods in Econometrics and Statistics*, W. A. Barnett, J. Powel and G. Tauchen (eds.). Cambridge: Cambridge University Press.

Parks, R.W. (1967) "Efficient Estimation of a System of Regression Equations when Disturbances are Both Serially and Contemporaneously Correlated", *Journal of the American Statistical Association*, **62**, 500–09.

Peers, H.W. (1971) "Likelihood Ratio and Associated Test Criteria", *Biometrika*, **58**, 577–87.

Peruga, R. (1988) "The Distributional Properties of the Exchange Rate Changes Under a Peso Problem", unpublished PhD dissertation. Dep. of Economics University of California, San Diego.

Pesaran, M.H. (1974) "On the General Problem of Model Selection", *Review of Economic Studies*, **41**, 153–71.

Pesaran, M.H. (2006) "Estimation and Inference in Large Heterogeneous Panels with a Multifactor Error Structure", *Econometrica*, **74**, 967–1012.

Pesaran, M.H. and R.P. Smith (1995) "Estimating Long-Run Relationships from Dynamic Heterogeneous Panels", *Journal of Econometrics*, **68**, 79–113.

Pesaran, M.H., T. Schuermann, and B.J. Treutler (2004) "The Role of Industry, Geography and Firm Heterogeneity in Credit Risk Diversification", Paper presented at NBER Conference on Risks in Financial Institutions.

Pesaran, M.H., T. Schuermann, and S.M. Weiner (2004) "Modeling Regional Interdependencies using a Global Error-Correcting Macroeconomic Model", *Journal of Business Economics and Statistics*, (with Discussions and a Rejoinder), **22**, 129–81.

Pfanzagl, J. (1980) "Asymptotic Expansions in Parametric Statistical Theory", in *Developments in Statistics, Vol. 3*, in P.R. Krishnaiah (ed.), New York: Academic Press.

Phillips, G.D.A. (1978) "The Bias and Moment Matrix of the General k-class Estimator of the Parameters in Simultaneous Equations when Disturbances are Serially Correlated: some Particular Cases", Paper presented to ESEM Geneva.

Phillips, G.D.A. (2000) "An Alternative Approach to Obtaining Nagar-type Moment Approximations in Simultaneous Equation Models", *Journal of Econometrics*, **97**, 345–64.

Phillips, P.C.B. (1980) "The Exact Finite Sample Density of Instrumental Variable Estimators in an Equation with n+1 Endogenous Variables", *Econometrica*, **48**, 861–78.

Phillips, P.C.B. (1987a) "Towards a Unified Asymptotic Theory for Autoregression", *Biometrika*, **74**, 535–47.

Phillips, P.C.B. (1987b) "Time Series Regression with a Unit Root", *Econometrica*, **55**, 277–302.

Phillips, P.C.B. (1988) "Regression Theory for Near Integrated Time Series", *Econometrica*, **56**, 1021–44.

Phillips, P.C.B. (1999) "Unit Root Log Periodogram Regression", Cowles Foundation Paper #1244, Yale University.

Phillips, P.C.B. and T. Magdalinos (2004) "Limit Theory for Moderate Deviations from a Unit Root", *Journal of Econometrics*, (forthcoming).

Phillips, P.C.B. and V. Solo (1992) "Asymptotics for Linear Processes", *Annals of Statistics*, **20**, 971–1001.

Pollard, D. (1984) *Convergence of Stochastic Processes*, Springer-Verlag.

Powell, J.L., J.H. Stock and T.M. Stocker (1989) "Semiparametric Estimation of the Index Coefficients", *Econometrica*, **57**, 1043–1430.

Priestley, M.B. (1981) *Spectral Analysis and Time Series*, Vol. II. London: Academic Press.

Qin, J. and J. Lawless (1994) "Empirical Likelihood and General Estimating Equations", *Annals of Statistics*, **22**, 300–25.

Ramalho, J.J.S. (2001) Alternative Estimation Methods and Specification Tests for Moment Condition Models, unpublished Ph.D. thesis, Department of Economics, University of Bristol.

Rao, C.R. (1973) *Linear Statistical Inference and Its Applications*, New York: John Wiley & Sons.

Reiersol, O. (1941) "Confluence Analysis by Means of Lag Moments and Other Methods of Confluence Analysis", *Econometrica*, **9**, 1–24.

Robinson, P.M. (1987) "Asymptotically Efficient Estimation in the Presence of Heteroskedasticity of Unknown Form", *Econometrica*, **55**, 875–91.

Robinson, P.M. (1988) "Root-N Consistent Semi-parametric Regression", *Econometrica*, **156**, 931–54.

Rothenberg, T.J. (1982) "Comparing Alternative Asymptotically Equivalent Tests", in Hildenbrand W. (ed.) *Advances in Econometrics*, Cambridge: University Press.

Rothenberg, T.J. (1984) "Approximating the Distributions of Econometric Estimators and Test Statistics", ch. 15 in *Handbook of Econometrics, Vol. 2*, in Z. Griliches and M. Intriligator (eds.), Amsterdam: North Holland.

Rothenberg, T.J. (1984a) "Approximate Normality of Generalized Least Squares Estimates", *Econometrica*, **52**, 811–25.

Rothenberg, T.J. (1984b) "Hypothesis Testing in Linear Models when the Error Covariance Matrix is Nonscalar", *Econometrica*, **52**, 827–42.

Rothenberg, T.J. (1988) "Approximate Power Functions for Some Robust Tests of Regression Coefficients", *Econometrica*, **56**, 997–1019.

Rudin, W. (1976) *Principles of Mathematical Analysis*, 3rd ed., New York: McGraw-Hill.

Sargan, J.D. (1958) "The Estimation of Economic Relationships using Instrumental Variables", *Econometrica*, **26**, 393–415.

Sargan, J.D. (1964) "Wages and Prices in the United Kingdom: A Study in Econometric Methodology (with discussion)", in Hart, P.E., Milis, G. and Whitaker, J.K. (eds.), *Econometric Analysis for National Economic Planning*, Vol. 16 of Colston Papers, pp. 25–63. London: Butterworth Co. Reprinted as pp. 275–314 in Hendry D.E and Wallis K.E. (eds.) (1984). *Econometrics and Quantitative Economics*, Oxford: Basil Blackwell, and as pp. 124–69 in Sargan J.D. (1988) *Contributions to Econometrics, Vol. 1*, Cambridge: Cambridge University Press.

Sargan, J.D. (1974) "On the Validity of Nagar's Expansion for the Moments of Econometric Estimators", *Econometrica*, **42**, 169–76.

Sentana, E. and S. Wadhwani (1991) "Semi-parametric Estimation and the Predictability of Stock Market Returns: Some Lessons from Japan", *Review of Economic Studies*, **58**, 5478–563.

Shapiro, M. and M.W. Watson (1988) Sources of Business Cycle Fluctuations. *NBER Macroeconomics Annual*, **3**, 11–156.

Silverman, B.W. (1986) *Density Estimation for Statistics and Data Analysis*. London: Chapman and Hall.

Sims, C.A. (1980) "Macroeconomics and Reality", *Econometrica*, **48**, 1–48. Reprinted in Granger, C.W.J. (ed.) (1990) *Modelling Economic Series*, Oxford: Clarendon Press.

Sims, C.A. (1981) "An Autoregressive Index Model for the US 1948–1975", in Kmenta, J., and Ramsay, J.B. (eds.), *Large-scale Macro-econometric Models*, pp. 283–327. Amsterdam: North-Holland.

Sims, C.A. (1986) "Are Forecasting Models Useful for Policy Analysis?", *Federal Reserve Bank of Minneapolis Quarterly Review*, Winter, 2–16.

Smith, R.J. (1997) "Alternative Semi-parametric Likelihood Approaches to Generalized Method of Moments Estimation", *Economic Journal*, **107**, 503–19.

Smith, R.J. (2001) "GEL Methods for Moment Condition Models", Working Paper, Department of Economics, University of Bristol. Revised version CWP 19/04, cemmap, I.F.S. and U.C.L. http://cemmap.ifs.org.uk/ wps/ cwp0419.pdf

Smith, R.J. (2003) "Efficient Information Theoretic Inference for Conditional Moment Restrictions", Working Paper, Department of Economics, University of Warwick. Revised version CWP 14/05, cemmap, I.F.S. and U.C.L. http://cemmap.ifs.org.uk/ wps/cwp1405.pdf

Spanos, A. (1986) *Statistical Foundations of Econometric Modelling*, Cambridge: Cambridge University Press.

Spanos, A. (1989) "On Re-Reading Haavelmo: a Retrospective View of Econometric Modeling", *Econometric Theory*, **5**, 405–29.

Spanos, A. (1990) "The Simultaneous Equations Model Revisited: Statistical Adequacy and Identification", *Journal of Econometrics*, **44**, 87–108.

Spanos, A. (1994) "On Modeling Heteroskedasticity: the Student's t and Elliptical Regression Models", *Econometric Theory*, **10**, 286–315.

Spanos, A. (1995) "On Normality and the Linear Regression Model", *Econometric Reviews*, **14**, 195–203.

Spanos, A. (1999) *Probability Theory and Statistical Inference: Econometric Modeling with Observational Data*, Cambridge: Cambridge University Press.
Spanos, A. (2000) "Revisiting Data Mining: Hunting with or without a License", *Journal of Economic Methodology*, 7, 231–64.
Spanos, A. and A. McGuirk (2001) "The Model Specification Problem from a Probabilistic Reduction Perspective", *Journal of the American Agricultural Association*, **83**, 1168–76.
Spanos, A. and A. McGuirk (2002) "The Problem of Near-multicollinearity Revisited: Statistical Parameterizations Versus Ceteris Paribus Clauses", *The Journal of Econometrics*, **108**, 365–93.
Spivak, M. (1965) *Calculus on Manifolds*, Menlo Park, California: Benjamin/Cummings.
Staiger, D. and J.H. Stock (1997) "Instrumental Variables Regression with Weak Instruments", *Econometrica*, **65**, 557–86.
Stengos, T. and B. Yan (2001) "Double Kernel Nonparametric Estimation in Semiparametric Econometric Models", *Journal of Nonparametric Statistics*, **13**, 883–906.
Stock, J.H. and M.W. Watson (2002) "Macroeconomic Forecasting Using Diffusion Indices", *Journal of Business and Economic Statistics*, **20**, 147–62.
Stone, R. (1947) "On The Interdependence of Blocks of Transactions", *Supplement of the Journal of the Royal Statistical Society*, **9**, 1–45.
Tapia, R.A. and J.R. Thompson (1978) *Non-parametric Probability Density Estimation*. Baltimore: John Hopkins University Press.
Tjur, Tue (1980) Probability based on Radon Measures, *Wiley Series in Probability and Mathematical Statistics*, New York: John Wiley & Sons.
Tzavalis, E. and M.R. Wickens (1995) "The Persistence in Volatility of the US Term Premium 1970–1986", *Economic Letters*, **49**, 381–89.
Urbain, J.-P. (1992) "On Weak Exogeneity in Error Correction Models", *Oxford Bulletin of Economics and Statistics*, **54**, 187–207.
von Neumann, John (1941) "Distribution of the Ratio of the Mean Square Successive Difference to the Variance", *Ann. Math. Statist.*, **12**, 367–95.
Wang, J. and E. Zivot (1998) "Inference on Structural Parameters in Instrumental Variables Regression with Weak Instruments", *Econometrica*, **66**, 1389–1404.
Whang, and D. Andrews (1993) "Tests of Specification for Parametric and Semi-parametric Models", *Journal of Econometrics*, 277–318.
White, H. (1982) "Instrumental Variables Regression with Independent Observations", *Econometrica*, **50**, 483–99.
White, H. (1982a) "Maximum Likelihood Estimation of Misspecified Models", *Econometrica*, **50**, 1–26.
White, H. (1984) *Asymptotic Theory for Econometricians*, New York: Academic Press.
White, J.S. (1958) "The Limiting Distribution of the Serial Correlation Coefficient in the Explosive Case", *Annals of Mathematical Statistics*, **29**, 1188–97.
Wilks, S.S. (1962) *Mathematical Statistics*, New York: John Wiley & Sons.
Windmeijer, F. (2000) Efficiency Comparisons for a System GMM Estimator in Dynamic Panel Data Models, in R.D.H. Heijmans, D.S.G. Pollock and

A. Satorra (eds.), *Innovations in Multivariate Statistical Analysis, A Festschrift for Heinz Neudecker. Advanced Studies in Theoretical and Applied Econometrics, vol. 36*, Dordrecht: Kluwer Academic Publishers (IFS Working Paper W98/1).

Windmeijer, F. (2005) "A Finite Sample Correction for the Variance of Linear Efficient Two-step GMM Estimators", *Journal of Econometrics*, **126**, 25–51.

Wooldridge, J. (1992) "A Test for Functional form Against Non-parametric Alternatives", *Econometric Theory*, **8**, 452–75.

Wu, D.M. (1973) "Alternative Tests of Independence between Stochastic Regressors and Disturbances", *Econometrica*, **40**, 733–50.

Index

For EU product safety concerns, contact us at Calle de José Abascal, 56–1°, 28003 Madrid, Spain or eugpsr@cambridge.org.

www.ingramcontent.com/pod-product-compliance
Ingram Content Group UK Ltd.
Pitfield, Milton Keynes, MK11 3LW, UK
UKHW012158180425
457623UK00018B/263

* 9 7 8 1 1 0 7 4 0 6 2 4 7 *